GENERAL
MACARTHUR
Speeches and Reports
1908-1964

Compiled by
COL Edward T. Imparato (Ret.)

TURNER PUBLISHING

TURNER PUBLISHING COMPANY

Copyright © 2000 Edward T. Imparato
Publishing Rights: Turner Publishing Company
All Rights Reserved.

Designer/Coordinator: Herbert C. Banks II

Library of Congress Catalog Number: 00-102473
ISBN: 978-1-68162-381-8

INTRODUCTION

On January 26, 1880 a child, destined for greatness was born of parents Arthur MacArthur and Pinkney Hardy MacArthur. The boy was named Douglas. His destiny was foretold by the stature of his father, an outstanding soldier of the Civil War and a very bright and spiritually oriented mother. The careful nurturing of the young boy by father and mother, began to show astonishing results early in the boy's development.

In September 1893, Arthur MacArthur was ordered to Texas and in Douglas' own words, "I hailed this move with delight. Housing the largest garrison I had ever seen, Fort Sam Houston guarded our southern borders and was one of the most important posts in the Army. It was here that a transformation began to take place in my development. I was enrolled in the West Texas Military Academy headed by the Reverend Allen Burlesoa, rector of the Army chapel. There came a desire to know, a seeking for the reason why, a search for the truth. Abstruse mathematics began to appear a challenge to analysis, dull Latin and Greek seemed a gateway to the moving words of the leaders of the past, laborious historical data led to the nerve-tingling battlefields of the great captains. Biblical lessons began to open the spiritual portals of a growing faith in literature to lay bare the souls of men. My studies enveloped me, my marks went higher, and many of the school's medals came my way. But I also learned how little such honors mean after one wins them.

"I have always loved athletics and the spirit of competition moved me to participate in as many sports as possible. I became the quarterback on the eleven, the shortstop on the nine, the tennis champion of the campus."

At the end of Douglas' four years at the West Texas Military Academy, Reverend Burlesoa showered MacArthur with silent praise stating he had graduated from the Academy with the highest honors and that he considered MacArthur the most promising student he ever had in his experience of ten years as schoolmaster both North and South.

MacArthur maintained that at an early age he established as his goal an appointment to the Military Academy at West Point, "the greatest military academy in the world." In the spring of 1898 he passed the very competitive entrance examination for a West Point vacancy. On June 13, 1899 he enrolled at the U. S. Military Academy, graduating on June 11, 1903 as a second lieutenant of Engineers recording the highest scholastic record in twenty-five years.

Everything he touched whether he was especially qualified for the mission or not, turned into a brilliant performance as evidenced by his scholastic record at West Point; his remarkable athletic ability in a number of sports not becoming great in only one but in all that he participated in; his great flexibility as with his assignment as superintendent of the military academy immediately after returning home from WWI. MacArthur at first refused the honor but was told by President Wilson and the Secretary of War that the Academy was 40 years behind the times and that he could "fix it." MacArthur's response to the Secretary was, "I am an infantry man and I want to remain with my troops." The secretary sent him to West Point anyway.

Though there were initial problems with the old guard professors he soon resolved those issues through his determination to "fix" the academy. The changes in the academy curriculum, the reorganization, the expansion of social contact with America's best universities by sending his best scholars to Harvard, Yale, Duke and many other universities for special courses were significant, sound and enlightening. Many of the programs initiated then are still in effect, eighty years later. It was his vision, courage, imagination and will, with a good measure of initiative and energy that carried MacArthur through the difficult and trying three years as superintendent of the academy. He succeeded in carrying these fine qualities all his life.

MacArthur's war time activities speak for themselves. By all the records available he never lost a battle, never lost a war and his accomplishments in World War II confirmed the reputation that he had gained as an outstanding military tactician in World War I and added to it a reputation as a superior military strategist.

Formal written comment on his professional accomplishments began with a citation on his reconnaissance in a 1914 Vera Cruz campaign and extended to messages of congratulations on the successful fighting that stabilized the United Nations in Korea position in early 1951 after the onslaught of the Chinese Communist. Included among them are statements by Presidents Hoover, Franklin D. Roosevelt, Truman and Johnson; chiefs of state and Prime Ministers Churchill, Curtin, Chiang Kai-shek, Quezon, Rhee, Yoshida; Secretary of State Byrnes, Secretaries of War Baker and Stimson, Secretaries of Defense Forrestal and Johnson; Secretary of Army Pace; Admirals Leahy, Nimitz, Halsey, and Sherman; Air Force Generals Arnold, Spaatz, Kenney and Stratemeyer; and Army Generals Pershing, Marshall and Collins. Numerous Congressmen, Lord Mountbatten, General Romulo, historian Freeman and other qualified observers also paid tribute.

Perhaps the most accurate and substantial accolade for MacArthur was announced by Britain's Field Marshal Viscount Alanbrook, Chairman of the British Chiefs of Staff during WWII. His long held secret diaries and correspondence form the basis of an explosive book, "Triumph in the West" which went on sale in 1957. Alanbrook said Eisenhower played golf instead of running the war at a crucial stage of the allied drive in Europe. Alanbrook contended Mr. Eisenhower's strong point was charm rather than military ability.

However Alanbrook had high praise for MacArthur in his Position as American Commander in the Pacific. "MacArthur was the greatest General and the best strategist that the war produced," Alanbrook wrote. He added, "MacArthur certainly outshone General George C. Marshall, United States Chief of Staff, Mr. Eisenhower and all other American and British Generals including Montgomery." Alanbrook described MacArthur after one meeting as, "a very striking personality with perhaps a tinge of the actor, but any failing in this direction was certainly not offensive."

On MacArthur's Pacific campaign Alanbrook wrote, "The masterly way in which he bad jumped from point to point leaving masses of Japs to decay behind him had filled me with admiration. He is head and shoulders bigger than Marshall and if he had been in the latter's place during the last four years I feel certain that my task in the combined Chiefs of Staff would have been easier."

Probably the most important knowledge and skill MacArthur developed over the years cannot be found in any published material about MacArthur. That skill is geopolitics; a subject foreign to American universities prior to the end of WW II. As explanation, geopolitics is the study of the influence of such factors as geography, economics and demographics on the politics and foreign policy of a country and should be the basis of our foreign policy. Such a study by our state department and especially our appointed ambassadors about the countries to which they are assigned would determine in detail the aims and aspirations of that country. Proper application of geopolitical thinking, tactics and strategy can then avoid many blunders and mistakes.

This short brief on geopolitics is presented here simply to show the master of geopolitics to be MacArthur. Through his in-depth study of world history to his exposure to the people of most of the world's emerging countries, governments and culture he held a world view of all the countries which may, in some way, effect diplomatic action by our government. MacArthur's strategic thinking always took into consideration his actions and the effect his actions may have on not only the enemy, but also the neighboring countries bordering on the particular country with which he was engaged. As an example, MacArthur while engaging Japan in war was also mindful of the aims and aspirations of the border countries - China, Korea, Russia - and also the German, English and French interests in his sphere of influence.

MacArthur was head and shoulders above our state department on the handling of the border countries. One of the greatest misjudgments of the century was made by Mr. Harry Truman and his ambassador General George C. Marshall. In an attempt to determine which China to support - Mao Tse Tung or Chiang Kai-shek - Marshall's report to Truman concluded that Mao seemed to be amenable to a gradual drift towards democracy. Truman then, without consulting MacArthur, established the new China policy.

In testimony before a congressional committee MacArthur was asked about our China Policy and he stated, "The decision to support Mao was wrong. Our country will suffer because of this decision. This is the worst mistake made by our government in a hundred years."

After MacArthur's early school days where he had the time to study the classics, especially the old classics, he rarely read fiction again. His near total reading involved non-fiction. Everything in science, technology, education, finance, politics, business, athletics; nothing seemed to escape his eye or his interest. He frequently read the Bible. One of his senior officers, Armel Dyer who served with MacArthur in the Philippines and Japan, states, "MacArthur possessed the ability to read two or even three books a night."

Of the early writers MacArthur enjoyed the renowned artist, architect, philosopher, poet and writer John Ruskin. Ruskin was noted for many things in the cultural field and it was not unusual for him to take measure of a society and attempt to describe its responsibilities. This is Ruskin's appraisal of the requirements of a civilized nation: "Five great intellectual professions have hitherto existed in every civilized nation: 1. The soldiers to defend it; 2. The merchants to provide for it; 3. The pastors to teach it; 4. The physicians to keep it in health; 5. The lawyers to enforce justice in it. And the duty of all of these is, on due occasion, to die for it.

These five professions from John Ruskin could be taken as MacArthur's five commandments.

The reader will find elements of the five threaded throughout MacArthur's speeches.

FOREWORD

The long and arduous search to find and record MacArthur's speeches and reports took a turn for the better by a chance contact with the historian at the Library of the U.S. Military Academy at West Point, New York. He revealed information concerning a doctoral dissertation written by Colonel Armel Dyer (U.S.A. Retired) while a graduate student at the University of Oregon in 1968 entitled "The Oratory of General Douglas MacArthur." Through inter-library loans we were able to obtain a copy of this outstanding work.

Although we had never met, it immediately became apparent that Colonel Dyer and I were at the same place at the same time on several instances at the close of World War II in the Pacific. Also as we had both served with MacArthur and were keenly interested in his speeches, it became my mission to locate him. I'm happy to report that after a little "detective" work and several telephone calls, Colonel Dyer and I have established a great telephone friendship. Regrettably neither of us is healthy enough to travel to meet in person.

In considering the Foreword to this work, only one name came to mind: Colonel Armel Dyer. It is with deep appreciation that comments from his work concerning MacArthur's speeches, written thirty-two years ago, are included here.

Edward T. Imparato, Colonel, U.S.A.F., Retired
Compiler

"MacArthur cannot be described as an extemporaneous speaker. His speech plan left too little room for modification or change as he proceeded in the development of the speech, and he committed too much of it to memory, whether deliberately or inadvertently.

"Delivery was one of the strongest factors in his oratory. In and of itself it constituted a form of ethical proof. He gave the impression of knowing what he was going to say. He realized the content of his words as he uttered them. His centering was artistic, and he spoke in thought units. His handsome figure, his erect posture, his serious mien, his air of sincerity, confidence, and authority, and his resonant, flexible voice generally disposed his audiences favorably toward him. Although he communicated well with his audience, he did not achieve the conversational ideal of speaking with them. But did speak to them, never at them.

"His style confirms the epigram that style is the man and man is the style. Although examples of the plain, the moderate, and the grand styles may be found in his speeches, the moderate is predominant: his style is more nearly Rhodian than Attic or Asianist. Archaic expressions and Victorian structure appear. The speeches abound in phrases and other stylistic devices that might well be labeled MacArthurisms. the presence of polysyllabic and unusual words and of abstract ideas probably precluded complete comprehension by some people.

"Most of his speeches were well organized: a short but purposeful introduction, a body, and a conclusion that usually included an emotional appeal were readily recognizable. He derived most of his speech materials from his own intellectual resources: his education, his experience, and his personal philosophy. He employed all three forms of Aristotelian proof: logical, ethical, and emotional. Ethical proof was the strongest form of persuasion in his public speeches; but he employed emotional proof with artistry, and his greatest successes at persuasion ... were dependent upon logical proof. His antecedent or non-artistic ethical proof was a major factor in almost all of his speeches.

"MacArthur was an accomplished orator. The decision whether he was a great orator must await the judgment of time. In the Aristotelian sense, his greatest strength as an orator lay first in his ethical proof based primarily upon his professional reputation and his generally recognized dedication to the ideal of Duty, Honor, Country, and second in his forthright, masculine delivery. MacArthur the orator and MacArthur the man were one and the same, for his speeches were an obvious product of the sum total of his personal and professional traits and qualities. He will probably never be so closely identified as an orator as were Charles Fox and Daniel Webster or even as were Alexander Hamilton and Winston Churchill; but his popular reputation as an orator is paramount among American military men, who as a group have only recently entered the mainstream of American public affairs and who now exercise such a voice in American foreign policy that their speeches should surely be studied. The writers of the history of American public speaking initially included the speeches of preachers, politicians, lawyers, and educator's. They subsequently added those of business men and scientists. They should now add those of military men...."

PREFACE

This work on the official and public words expressed by General Douglas MacArthur over his life time is believed to be the only complete record of his major speeches, reports to Congress and the public, his direct correspondence with men and women of note including members of Congress and correspondence - all of which have been published in a variety of sources, including books on history, biographies, newspapers, magazines, military journals and interviews with journalists and war correspondents.

The author has simply acted as "editor" in the dictionary definition of editor as one who prepares a work for publication and in this case not an editor who makes adjustments in sentences or paragraphing and wording. The individual documents of his presentation are in MacArthur's words with no attempt to change any part of his pronouncements.

The depths to which the author has gone to uncover every speech and pronouncement included a review of over 1000 books, each book containing some reference to MacArthur, numerous magazine articles, newspapers, military journals and records from appearances by MacArthur before the Congress of the United States. Some of MacArthur's congressional presentations were required by law while MacArthur was Chief of Staff of the Army and on other appearances before Congress at the request of Congressional Committees to respond to matters of military significance.

MacArthur and General Eichelberger, Commanding General of the 8th Army, before military admirers, August 30, 1945.

ACKNOWLEDGMENTS

This work was developed and assembled by the editor over a period of two years. Without the cooperation and support of individuals and organizations who felt this a necessary endeavor it would have taken ten years to assemble and edit. The individuals and organizations who made major contribution to this work are listed below:

My Research Assistant and Administrative Assistant Ellen Schaefer, who has spent hours in locating sources and many more hours verifying the accuracy of our findings. Without her dedicated effort this work could not have been completed in two years.

James W. Zobel - Archivist, General Douglas MacArthur Foundation at Norfolk, Virginia.

The Historian and History Department of the U. S. Military Academy, West Point, New York.

The Library of Congress which provided us with lists for further research on possible additional sources to contact.

The Largo Public Library Research Department, Largo, Florida.

The Clearwater Public Library Department, Clearwater, Florida, who uncovered and later secured a copy of the only known history on MacArthur Oratory by Col. Armel Dyer. The Colonel's thesis was written for a Ph.D. from the University of Oregon in 1968. This thesis we believed to be the only book of its kind ever written on any world leader.

The University of Oregon for their cooperation and for providing a copy of Col. Dyer's work on the Oratory of General MacArthur.

MacArthur arrives at Atsugi, Japan, August 30, 1945.

TABLE OF CONTENTS

EXCERPTS FROM A LECTURE PRESENTED TO THE STUDENTS MOUNTED SERVICE SCHOOL NOVEMBER 1908 FORT RILEY, KANSAS

MacArthur, at the age of 28 displayed a depth of knowledge about war from his reading of history of war from the beginning of civilization. Only 8 years out of the military academy MacArthur was speaking about the intricacies of battle maneuvers and tactics as if he had fought in a thousand wars. The great wisdom and vision expressed in this speech concerning methods on means to frustrate the enemy on a withdrawal of forces situation - "The use of explosions to destroy bridges and other avenues of approach to frustrate the enemy by retarding his progress."

The real significance of this speech was amply demonstrated by MacArthur some thirty odd years later on his strategy to slow the advancing Japanese and keep them from entering Manila as long as possible. The Japanese envisioned reaching Manila in five weeks according to their own records. MacArthur's strategy forced them to slow their pursuit. In spite of overwhelming forces it took the Japanese five months to reach Manila all the while American forces awaited reinforcements promised by President Roosevelt but never delivered.

The British High Command praised MacArthur by official documents for his bold stand and management of his retrograde action. Some have praised this episode as one of the great retrograde actions of any war.

Edward T. Imparato, Editor

This paper is intended to deal with the subject of military demolitions only in its relation to the work of tactical troops, mainly the infantry and cavalry, and omits all treatment of more systematic and extensive operations of technical troops along the same lines.

As an accessory of active operations, the value of demolitions cannot be overrated. In the Civil War such efforts were extensively employed on both sides to frustrate military movements. The most notable examples were the destruction of the Louisville & Nashville and Nashville & Chattanooga Railroads, in rear of the Army of the Cumberland, by the Confederate cavalry commanders Forrest and Morgan in 1862-63, thus interfering with the supply of the Union Army, and preventing any forward movement; the destruction of the resources of the Shenandoah Valley, Virginia, by General Sheridan in 1864, to prevent its future use as a line of operation by which the Confederate Army might invade the Northern States; the destruction of the railways in his rear by General Sherman in his "March to the Sea," thus preventing pursuit, and also cutting the connection between the Seaboard and the Gulf States; and the complete destruction of the resources of that portion of the Confederate base of operations formed by the Gulf States east of the Mississippi, by General James H. Wilson in 1865.

And it is certain that in future wars, even more than in the past, endeavors will be made by every possible means to prevent or delay the march of the enemy's troops by throwing obstacles in the way and by cutting such lines of communication as they might use.

Conversely, in order to reach an objective, it will be necessary to overcome or destroy obstructions to the movements of troops and to reestablish the continuity of highways and railroads in the most rapid and practical manner.

Troops of all arms will be actually employed in demolition during a campaign, and it is therefore desirable that every officer who may have command of a detachment should be thoroughly acquainted with the means for destroying obstacles as well as methods of using them, particularly as time is short under such circumstances and action must be quick and intelligent. In other words, all detachment commanders should be in a position to solve a problem such as the following: Given certain tools, explosives, and men, and a certain amount of time for the destruction of an obstacle, what should be done to obtain the best results?

The great advances in recent years in the sphere of high explosives have rendered more easy the execution of demolitions on a very large scale. But as yet unfortunately, the necessary steps have not been taken for the proper dissemination throughout the service of a working knowledge of this important branch of military art.

It is essential that all officers should be theoretically as fully informed as possible upon the effects of explosives, and the methods of executing demolitions, but it is still more important that they should have such practical experience in this work as will create a personnel thoroughly trained in its execution as well as in its supervision. Operations of this character should be as familiar as any other drill. They will occur almost every day during a campaign and it is necessary that they should be executed readily, and with the widest possible previous study of all of such circumstances as are apt to be found in actual service.

In time of war it is hardly possible to limit the rights of the victor or to discuss the legitimacy of the measures taken by the vanquished for the defense of the country. It is generally admitted, however, that the only permissible demolitions are those required by military necessities.

It is difficult to define accurately the scope of this phrase, of which the interested parties are themselves the sole judges. It may be laid down as a general principle, however, that all measures should be excluded that have for their object only the spreading of terror among the people or making reprisals for defeats or checks that have been suffered. As the extensive destruction of lines of communication has a considerable influence on the operations of armies from both the strategic and the tactical point of view, the only judge of the nature and the extent of such demolitions must be the military commander who alone can be held accountable for the resulting consequences. So far as concerns railroads, the rule is absolute that bridges, viaducts, tunnels and culverts are not to be destroyed or rendered unserviceable without the formal written order of the Commander-in-Chief of the army or of the generals or other officers to whom he has specifically delegated such authority.

The decision of the Commander-in-Chief depends much

on circumstances and prospective movements. Above all it is necessary to consider the extent and importance of demolitions both as to their immediate results and as to their possible future effects upon the army causing them.

The ill-timed or premature destruction of a highway, railroad, or especially of a bridge may deprive an army of a valuable means of passage and have extremely serious consequences, resulting under certain conditions in cutting off the retreat of many troops, as in the case of the destruction of the bridge of Lindenau, over the Elster, at the battle of Leipzig.

On the other hand, the Commander-in-Chief who fails to have made in time such demolitions as are necessary furnishes the enemy with an easier way of reaching him and thus deprives himself of a chance for success; as for example, the failure to destroy the bridges over the Moselle above Metz, the bridge of Donchery over the Meuse, or the Saverne tunnel, in the Franco-German War.

Demolitions may have to be carried on in the presence and under the fire of the enemy or at a distance from him, depending upon circumstances.

In the latter case, the cavalry may be charged with the most urgent work of this character, particularly during the period of mobilization, and upon lines useful to the enemy for concentrating his troops. This may also be the case in the attack of a fortified place in order to cut its lines of communication preliminary to its investment.

Infantry will, in general, be required to carry out only such hasty demolitions as the opening of breaches, the removal of obstacles, the disabling of war material, artillery and railroads and the destruction of telegraph lines and bridges of minor importance.

Whenever necessary and possible, the actual operation of destruction should be preceded by a reconnaissance made as carefully as circumstances will permit for the purpose of ascertaining exactly what provision, both of men and material, will be required.

Demolitions may be made by mechanical means, using ordinary trenching or working tools, but such work requires considerable time for accomplishing any serious damage, and cannot be done in the presence of the enemy. Under such conditions and for rapid progress, resort must be had to explosives.

Artillery may be used to demolate, but it is a well established fact that much time and an excessive expenditure of ammunition are necessary to so reduce the accessory works and other objects of the defense as to render them incapable of resisting an assault. Moreover, artillery has no appreciable effect upon many structures, such as heavy masonry bridges.

Fire may be used to destroy harvest, houses and wooden bridges but it should be resorted to only in special cases and under particular conditions... .

In conclusion it may be said that with proper care and attention there is little danger in handling high explosives. But it must always be borne in mind that dynamite and its kindred are practically instantaneous agents and allow no margin for ignorance, carelessness or neglect. In their use there will be no small accidents. One man will have but one accident.

EXCERPTS FROM A SPECIAL REPORT PREPARED FOR INCLUSION IN THE ANNUAL REPORT OF THE U.S. COMMISSIONER OF EDUCATION AUGUST 6, 1914

After his promotion to Captain in 1911, MacArthur was one of the small group of officers assigned to membership in the Army General Staff in September, 1913. The routine duties of junior members of the staff included the preparation of reports and studies on a variety of subjects. The following report is representative.

Major Vorin E. Whan, Jr., USA, Editor
A Soldier Speaks: Public Papers and Speeches of General of the Army Douglas MacArthur
© 1965, Frederick A. Praeger, Publishers, New York, NY

No country in the world has as complete a system of professional scholastic training for its officers as the United States. This is due to the inherent difference between the military establishments of foreign nations and that of our own. Their armies are at all times kept upon a war footing, as a result of which they have ample opportunity for the perfect training of the personnel in the practical duties of the military profession.

In such an army the main object is to train every man for the efficient performance of his duties in the grade which he holds when war comes. A lieutenant does not dream of becoming a captain merely as the result of war, except as a vacancy is made for him in the casualties of battle. Only in the same way does a captain expect to become a colonel; nor would the idea be tolerated that great numbers of trained line officers are to be suddenly transferred to various staff positions.

Their organizations are founded upon the theory that there is nothing mysterious in the art of war; that technical and scientific training is needed by only a small portion of military officers; that certain things which a Napoleon must know every officer must know, and can as readily acquire as he; while those things which differentiate a Napoleon from other generals cannot be acquired in any school, not even that of war.

Such a system would be thoroughly unsound if transplanted to the American Army, the organization of which is quite different from Continental armies. In fact, the most striking feature in our service is the absence of what constitutes the very essence of the foreign establishments; that is, a great standing army serving in corps, divisions and brigades, in which the average officer of any grade learns the details of his profession by practical work and with the minimum of theory.

Our system of military education must therefore differ from that of the other great nations of the world. It must be such as to educate our officers so that they will be able at a moment's notice, when the war expansion comes, to perform the duties of far-advanced grades and to render service in branches of the army, both line and staff, in which they are not commissioned in time of peace. For this reason we have established a progressive system of schools designed to teach officers and men, limited only by their indi-

MacArthur as West Point Superintendent.

vidual capacities for its assimilation, the duty of the man in arms in all grades from the lowest to highest... .

EXCERPTS FROM THE ANNUAL REPORT OF THE SUPERINTENDENT OF THE U.S. MILITARY ACADEMY JUNE 30, 1920

MacArthur returned from France at the end of World War 1, now one of the Army's youngest Brigadier Generals, to become the Superintendent of the Academy at West Point. The Academy was in a chaotic state at the beginning of his term as a result of the accelerated war-time graduation of most of the Corps of Cadets. There was, as well, some Congressional sentiment for a reduction in the course of instruction to two years. In his first annual report, MacArthur outlined the problems of the Academy and the principles on which he proposed to base their solution.

Major Vorin E. Whan, Jr., USA, Editor
A Soldier Speaks: Public Papers and Speeches of General of the Army Douglas MacArthur
© 1965, Frederick A. Praeger, Publishers, New York, NY

My assumption of the command of the United States Military Academy synchronized with the ending of an epoch in the life of this Institution. With the termination of the World War the mission of West Point at once became the preparation of officer personnel for the next possible future war. The methods of training here have always been largely influenced by the purpose of producing the type of officer which the Army at large dictated. The excellence with which the Academy's mission has been carried out in the past has been testified on the battlefields of the world for a hundred years and more. The problem which faced the authorities was, therefore, this: Have new conditions developed, have the lessons of the World War indicated that a changed type of officer was necessary in order to produce the maximum of efficiency in the handling of men at arms? West Point, existing solely as a source of supply and a feeder to the Army, if a new era faces the latter, West Point must of necessity train its personnel accordingly.

In meeting this problem those who were charged with the solution undertook the task with a full realization of its seriousness. It was well understood that it was no light affair to attempt even in moderate degree to modify a status which had proved itself so splendidly for a century and more. It was understood that change under the guise of reconstruction was destructive unless clearly and beyond question it introduced something of added benefit. It was recognized that reform to be effective must be evolutionary and not revolutionary. It was evident that many sources of help, in the nature of advice and consultation, lay outside of the Military Academy in the persons of distinguished officers of the Army at large and of professional educators throughout the country.

Careful analysis yielded the following conclusions: Until the World War, armed conflicts between nations had been fought by comparatively a small fraction of the populations involved. These professional armies were composed very largely of elements which frequently required the most rigid methods of training, the severest forms of discipline, to weld them into a flexible weapon for use on the battlefield. Officers were, therefore, developed to handle a more or less recalcitrant element along definite and simple lines, and a fixed psychology resulted. Early in the World War it was realized to the astonishment of both sides that the professional armies, upon which they had relied, were unable to bring the combat to a definite decision. It became evident, due largely to the elaborate and rapid methods of communication and transportation which had grown up in the past generation, that national communities had become so intimate, that war was a condition which involved the efforts of every man, woman, and child in the countries affected. War had become a phenomenon which truly involved the nation in arms. Personnel was of necessity improvised, both at the front and at the rear; the magnitude of the effort, both of supply and of combat, was so great that individuals were utilized with the minimum of training. In general result, this was largely offset by the high personal type of those engaged. Discipline no longer required extreme methods. Men generally needed only to be told what to do, rather than to be forced by the fear of consequence of failure. The great numbers involved made it impossible to apply the old rigid methods which had been so successful when battle lines were not so extensive. The rule of this war can but apply to that of the future. Improvisation will be the watchword. Such changed conditions will require a modification in type of the officer, a type possessing all of the cardinal military virtues as of yore, but possessing an intimate understanding of the mechanics of human feelings, a comprehensive grasp of world and national affairs, and a liberalization of conception which amounts to a change in his psychology of command. This standard became the basis of the construction of the new West Point in the spirit of old West Point.

To hold fast to those policies typified in the motto of the Academy - "Duty, Honor, Country" - to cling to thoroughness as to a lodestar, to continue to inculcate the habit of industry, to implant as of old the gospel of cleanliness - to be clean, to live clean, and to think clean - and yet to introduce a new atmosphere of liberalization in doing away with provincialism, a substitution of subjective for objective discipline, a progressive increase of cadet responsibility tending to develop initiative and force of character rather than automatic performance of stereotyped functions, to broaden the curriculum so as to be abreast of the best modern thought on education, to bring West Point into a new and closer relationship with the Army at large, has been the aim and purpose of my administration throughout the past year.

The details of the changes that have been brought about in conformity with the above policy are to be found in the report of the Academic Board on a change in the curriculum and in the reports of the various heads of bureaus, which I incorporate in the body of this report.

The results have transcended my most sanguine expectation; they will be felt throughout the Army at large with the graduation of the classes now under tuition.

The problem which I have discussed above, important as it is, dwarfs into insignificance before the real question of reconstruction that confronts this Institution. It is one of quantity rather than quality. The Reorganization Bill of June 4th practically doubled the size of the officer personnel of the Regular Army, but failed utterly to provide an increase in the supply thereof. The Military Academy was left with the same authorized strength of 1,334 cadets that it had had previously. It cannot now supply more than one-third of our officers even in times of peace. In contrast with this condition I invite attention to the fact that the Brigade of Midshipmen has now an authorization of 3,136 members to supply a commissioned personnel of the Navy of approximately 5,000. I regard a commensurate increase in the Corps of Cadets as the most necessary and constructive feature of a sound military policy that confronts the Nation today. I have recommended elsewhere legislation designed to double the strength of the Corps of Cadets, the increase to be assimilated in four annual increments, the necessary construction to be undertaken in consonance therewith. The cost of the new installations entailed thereby would amount to approximately $12 million, to be appropriated at the rate of $3 million for four years. In making this recommendation I wish to emphasize the comparatively small appropriations that have been made for construction at this Institution since its foundation in 1802. The total sum is something less than $20 million. Many of our State institutions, relying entirely on taxation within their own States, have more than doubled this amount during a much shorter life. I am informed that the yearly budget of many is more than twice that of the Military Academy. When I draw attention to the fact that the University of Chicago has from one beneficiary received more than $50 million in his lifetime, that within the last year $15 million has been left by one bequest to Princeton University, some idea will be obtained of the comparative indigence with which this school has been faced. The press has recently stated that $212 million is being sought for this year by the universities of the country for still further expansion of plant.

I bespeak a broad and mature consideration of the question lest a condition may ultimately result which will be paid for in the bitterness of American blood... .

Excerpts from the Annual Report of the Superintendent of the U.S. Military Academy June 20, 1922

By the time he had completed his three-year tour as Superintendent, MacArthur was able to see his reconstruction plan begin to reach fruition. In his final annual report, he surveyed the main features of his reforms as they were working out in actual practice. Many of the programs begun under his leadership are still in force at West Point.

Major Vorin E. Whan, Jr., USA, Editor
A Soldier Speaks: Public Papers and Speeches of General of the Army Douglas MacArthur
© 1965, Frederick A. Praeger, Publishers, New York, NY

The past year has seen four classes under instruction at the United States Military Academy for the first time since 1917. It has been possible during this year, therefore, as it has not been fully possible before, to consider and measure the success of the reconstruction plans undertaken at the conclusion of the World War. The class which has just graduated during this month is the first product of the new program.

It will be remembered how completely the old West Point was disrupted by the World War. The class of 1917 was graduated in April of that year, and the class of 1918 in August of 1917. Then the year 1918 saw the graduation of three classes, leaving on November 2nd only one class in the institution, a Fourth Class which had been admitted the previous June. An additional class was admitted later in November. When I assumed command June 12, 1919, I found these two classes in the Academy, each of them under instruction less than a year. It is no exaggeration to describe conditions with respect to the course of training at that moment as chaotic. Orders had been issued to prepare the first of the two Fourth Classes for graduation in 1920 and the second for graduation in 1921. These orders were modified in May, 1919, by changing the curriculum to a three-year basis for graduation. Hardly had the Academic Board drawn up a plan for a three-year course of study and training, than the Act making appropriations for the support of the Military Academy for the fiscal year ending June 30, 1921, was passed, containing the provision that "the course of instruction at the United States Military Academy shall be four years." Thus within a single year, preparations had to be made for three different courses of training preparatory for graduation at different periods.

This uncertainty with respect to the curriculum was not the only reason for the chaotic conditions. The morale of the cadet body was low. Following the armistice, twenty-four cadets resigned from the Fourth Class A (entered in June) and eighty-five from the Fourth Class B (entered in November). The educational qualifications for admission had been largely disregarded in the case of the cadets who entered in November, and as a consequence seventy-three of them failed in the spring tests. The traditional disciplinary system, so largely built around the prestige and influence of the upperclassmen, was impossible in a situation where there were no upperclassmen. Cadet officers had never known the example of cadet officers before them, and the body of the Corps had a most imperfect idea of the standards of bearing and conduct which have been characteristic of the cadet for over a century. The old West Point could not have been recognized in the institution as it appeared in June, 1919. It had gone: it had to be replaced.

We had the buildings and equipment for a great military educational institution; we had the traditions of the old West Point implanted in the character of its graduates; we had the experience of the World War to point our way; we had the assurance of loyal and devoted service from the fine corps of officers on duty here; and we had a point of departure in the legal establishment of a four-year course of study and training. Our problem was upon these foundations and with these guides and aids to build a new West Point which should continue the fine traditions of the old and should give the most thorough preparation of officer personnel for the next possible future war.

The Academic Board, containing the heads of all the departments of instruction and training, sat with the Superintendent as its presiding officer day by day through a great part of the summer of 1919 formulating a new program for a reconstructed West Point. This program was presented in full in my report of June 30, 1920, but it is worth while at this point to summarize briefly its main items. The Board first formulated a statement of the function of the Military Academy in the following words: The function of the Military Academy is to give, in addition to that character-building for which it has long been famous, and in addition to the necessary military and physical training, such a combination of basic general and technical education as will provide an adequate foundation for a cadet's subsequent professional career. The Board then dwelt upon the plans by which the moral fibre of the cadets would be strengthened and self-reliance and self-discipline encouraged. It emphasized the fact that in military training the purpose of West Point was to give a broad general conception of all branches of the service and of the function of each branch in the organization of the division, corps, or army; and it outlined the plans of the Tactical Department for fulfilling this purpose. It discussed the place and value of physical training in the preparation of officer personnel, and drew up a system of supervised athletics for all classes. It discussed modifications in the curriculum of studies, and adopted a course of study giving more emphasis to the liberal and cultural courses than theretofore. It stressed the necessity for, and means of, coordination between departments handling related work. It considered and outlined the methods of instruction, and made recommendations concerning the officer personnel. And it ended with a diagram of the new program of instruction and training.

The prompt approval of this Academic Board report by the War Department enabled the Academy to begin the program with the opening of academic work in September. A program, however, is in itself a lifeless thing, a mere skeleton, and it has been the constant effort of my administration to put flesh and blood upon it and to imbue it with life. The new system had to begin, of course, on a partial basis, for even at the beginning of the academic term in September, 1919, only three classes were under instruction, and the senior of these had been at the institution only since June, 1918. During the three years that have elapsed since then, the Academy has steadily progressed toward a sound and healthy body. And during this last year, as was said before, we had the opportunity for the first time to view the new course of instruction and training in its full operation with four classes. We can now consider frankly and confidently prominent features which characterize this new West Point started since the World War.

The standards of bearing and conduct in the old Corps of Cadets have been reestablished in the new Corps. Although the early classes under the new conditions lacked the precept and example set by upperclassmen, they have under the careful and tactful guidance of the officer personnel met nobly their responsibilities in carrying their share of the burden of inculcating and maintaining these standards. They have the same pride in the Corps as characterized their predecessors, and the same whole-hearted devotion to the ideals of Duty, Honor, and Country. The most precious assets of the old West Point have been conserved in the new. The graduates of today will prove to have the same character for trustworthiness as in the past.

In the matter of discipline, it is a source of great satisfaction to record a marked success in developing among the cadets a sense of their own individual responsibility for the proper performance of their duties. Self-discipline has been the ideal held before them, a discipline arising from their own conscious efforts to develop those habits of military bearing, neatness, accuracy and promptness which mark efficient officers. Demerits are still awarded, of course, but are rightly regarded as intended to be corrective rather than merely punitive. The close personal contact established between tactical officers and cadets in the discussion of reports has been an important factor in developing the new sense of discipline throughout the Corps.

It has been my policy to allow certain privileges to the upperclass cadets which would serve both as a relaxation from the rigid grind of study and training and as a means of keeping touch with the ways of ordinary life outside the walls of the institution. They have for example during the academic year been permitted to have six-hour leaves, at times when such leaves interfered with no duty. During the summer encampment period, they have been given week-end leaves interfering with no duty. All cadets have been allowed to have five dollars a month from their pay in cash to be expended at their own discretion. Although occasional abuses of these privileges will undoubtedly occur, I believe that the results as a whole have greatly benefitted the cadets. They no longer are mured up within the Academy for two years at a time. They acquire by their small business transactions and by their contact with the outside world the beginnings of an experience which will be of value to them when they graduate. Without such opportunities of business and social contact, the cadet is graduated and thrust out into the world a man in age but a high-school boy so far as his experience goes. Much of the criticism of narrowness and provincialism which has been directed at the Military Academy in the past has been due to the restricted range of interests possible for cadets during these four important formative years of their lives. They had no opportunity to familiarize themselves with the ways and methods and manner of thought of people in the world without, so that when they graduated and mingled freely with their fellows they had no common background of knowledge and feeling on current affairs. These few privileges extended to the cadets in recent years will go far to break down the walls of isolation and broaden their experience.

The most important single feature of the military training system has been the removal of the cadets from West Point to a regular army encampment for the summer period. This change from the old plan of keeping the Corps during the summer at West Point has proved a marked success. By this new system, the cadets are brought into direct contact with actual service conditions during this important period of their military training. Consciously and unconsciously during their stay in the same cantonment with enlisted men of the regular army, they absorb a vast amount of useful knowledge of the soldiers whom they will later command. They gain in those qualities of self-confidence and assurance which are so valuable to efficient leadership. They learn more of human nature; they acquire understanding, sympathy, and tact. The entire experience both broadens and deepens their character.

But the advantages of training at a cantonment away from West Point are not confined to the cadet's contact with enlisted men under actual service conditions. At such cantonments, wider opportunities are presented for extending the variety of practical military experience as a part of the training. Field Artillery practice is possible on normal ranges under conditions simulating those of actual war service - something impossible at West Point because of the topography. Observation balloons are in constant use, and cadets stationed in them are trained to observe and transmit firing data. Airplanes have a suitable field for rising and landing - there is no such field at West Point - and cadets accompany the pilots as observers. Topographical work can be planned for cadets over ground not familiar to them. Tactical problems, marches, manoeuvres can be arranged with the added interest and originality which comes from new surroundings. The great handicap to military training in modern methods which is ever present in the topography of West Point is overcome by this simple plan of removing the Corps during the summer period to a regular army cantonment. It is to be hoped that a suitable location may be found for future encampments and that a permanent policy of summer training may be formulated.

The new system of physical training, instituted with the general reorganization of the curriculum following the war, has operated this past year with four classes in attendance with the same smoothness and efficiency as in 1920 and 1921. It will be remembered that the essential feature of this new system - new not only to West Point, but to all other collegiate institutions in the country - is the instruction of each cadet in all the major branches of athletics as a part of his regular curriculum. The purpose of the system is to transmit to all the individual members of the student body the undoubted advantages which have heretofore been largely confined to those participating in inter-institutional competitions. These advantages I conceive to be the coordination of mental and physical effort, an appreciation of the principle of cooperation, the development of hardihood and courage, and the inculcation of an aggressive and determined spirit.

It is impossible not to be enthusiastic over the success of this system, now that it has been in operation with the full complement of cadets in the Academy. The former disciplinary physical training has been retained throughout the Fourth Class year as the foundation for all forms of physical activities. Parallel with this training is begun in that same year instruction in mass athletics in the sports baseball, football, basketball, soccer, lacrosse, track, tennis, golf, and hockey. By the most careful and complete organization, the cadets are divided for instruction into sections of not more than twenty-five men, and each section has one or more trained officers supervising its progress. A sufficient period, usually about six weeks, is allowed for training in each sport to enable cadets to familiarize themselves with the rules and principles of the game and to develop their latent abilities. Intramural contests, as between companies or battalions, add to the natural appeal of athletics in stimulating interest and enthusiasm.

It seems hardly necessary to emphasize the value of this system in the training of the future officer of our army. Nothing more quickly than competitive athletics brings out the qualities of leadership, quickness of decision, promptness of action, mental and muscular coordination, aggressiveness, and courage. And nothing so readily and so firmly establishes that indefinable spirit of group interest and pride which we know as morale. The cadets graduated under this system will be not only the most efficient leaders themselves, but will be equipped for supervising athletics and giving practical instruction therein to the men of their organizations.

The development of this policy of mass athletics has been the most important feature of the physical training system in the new West Point. The importance of intercollegiate athletics, has, however, not been overlooked. The policy governing Varsity sports contemplates the development of specially qualified cadets through intensive training and coaching for the purpose of putting in the field the best teams in the various games which the Academy is capable of producing. The value of the intercollegiate contests is two-fold: first, in stimulating and vitalizing corps morale; and second, in establishing interesting contacts with other institutions of the same collegiate grade as West Point. With this conception of our right policy and of the value of intercollegiate contests, we have extended the number of sports in which the Academy is represented by Varsity teams. Whereas football, baseball, and basketball, and occasionally hockey, were the only intercollegiate sports in which the Academy was formerly represented, West Point has to these added teams for lacrosse, soccer, tennis, golf, polo, track, and aquatics. And those interested in the Academy may well be proud, not only of the showing made in the competitions, but of the reputation being established in the various lines of fine, clean sportsmanship on the part of West Point teams. . .

EXCERPTS FROM A REPORT TO PRESIDENT COOLIDGE ON AMERICAN PARTICIPATION IN THE NINTH OLYMPIC GAMES, HELD IN AMSTERDAM AUGUST 22, 1928

In September, 1927, General MacArthur was elected President of the American Olympic Committee to fill the vacancy created by the sudden death of William C. Prout. His election broke a deadlock that had threatened to disrupt the organization, and he was immediately faced with the delicate task of restoring harmony before the Olympic Games of 1928. Placed on detached service, he actively supervised the preparation of the American team and its successful participation in the Games held in Amsterdam. His keen interest in athletics was evident throughout his life, but possibly his proudest moment as a non-player came with the U.S. Olympic victory of 1928.

Major Vorin E. Whan, Jr., USA, Editor
A Soldier Speaks: Public Papers and Speeches of General of the Army Douglas MacArthur
© 1965, Frederick A. Praeger, Publishers, New York, NY

Dear Mr. President:

Article X of the Constitution and Bylaws of the American Olympic Association directs the submission of a report by the American Olympic Committee on the Olympic Games. In undertaking this difficult task, I recall the passage in Plutarch wherein Themistocles, being asked whether he would rather be Achilles or Homer, replied: "Which would you rather be, a conqueror in the Olympic Games or the crier who proclaims who are conquerors?" And indeed to portray adequately the vividness and brilliance of that great spectacle would be worthy even of the pen of Homer himself. No words of mine can even remotely portray such great moments as the resistless onrush of that matchless California eight as it swirled and crashed down the placid waters of the Sloten; that indomitable will for victory which marked the deathless rush of Barbuti; that sparking combination of speed and grace by Elizabeth Robinson which might have rivaled even Artemis herself on the heights of Olympus. I can but record the bare, blunt facts, trusting that imagination will supply the magic touch to that which can never be forgotten by those who were actually present.

The standards of success of previous American Olympic teams are very high. This team proved itself a worthy successor of its brilliant predecessors. The table herewith (*not reprinted here*) shows the totals of first, second and third places and a point total, rating those places respectively as three, two and one. This gives the United States twenty-four Olympic championships, twenty-one second places and seventeen third places, or a total of 131 points. Any other system of scoring would accentuate America's margin of success... .

In achieving these victories America made seventeen new Olympic records, seven of which are world records. This represents, I believe, the greatest number of Olympic world records ever achieved at one time in any set of games, either Olympic or otherwise, by any nation, either American or foreign, in the history of athletics. This fact evidences the most noteworthy feature of the games, namely, the great advance made in the last four years throughout the world in competitive athletic excellence. This general improvement is further testified by the more general distribution of triumphs among the various nations. That this tendency will increase even more rapidly in the future is apparent.

Of equal importance with the actual competitive success which was achieved, it is a matter of pride to report that the American team worthily represented the best traditions of American sportsmanship and chivalry. Imperturbable in defeat, modest in victory, its conduct typified fair play, courtesy and courage. In this most intense competition of highly trained teams the Americans represented rivalry without bitterness, contest without antagonism and the will to win tempered and restrained by a spirit of mutual consideration and generosity. It was worthy in victory; it was supreme in defeat.

The organization of the games at Amsterdam by the Dutch Olympic Committee was excellent in every respect and could well stand as a model for the future. I cannot speak too highly of the splendid spirit of the games. It would be hard to conceive a more admirable concourse of sport, one of the most noteworthy features being the happy impartiality of the spectators of all nations.

The American team was selected in the most democratic and unprejudiced way as a result of actual competition in nation-wide contest open to all amateur athletes. Any other method would have introduced privilege and favoritism with all the attendant ills that flow therefrom. The overhead of managers, coaches and officials was materially reduced from that of previous years and it is the established policy to continue this reduction in future Olympiads. The team was of necessity transported and housed aboard the United States Lines steamship President Roosevelt. This arrangement was a most happy one and the American team was the envy in this respect of many of their less fortunate competitors. The admirable arrangement by the ship's officers and crew contributed in no small way to the splendid morale and esprit which was so noticeable throughout. In spite of the geographical hazard involved in the trip and in the severe climatic conditions, our team was at the height of its form and condition when the day of competition arrived.

Financially the trip was a great success. I am happy to say that after all accounts have been settled there is a surplus of nearly $50.000. The total cost of the enterprise was approximately $290,000, a considerable saving over preceding Olympics... .

In my opinion the time has come to put the financing of the Olympic movement upon a more solid basis than now is the case. Increasing difficulties in raising funds have been encountered every four years for the last two decades. A plan should be worked out by means of which an endowment fund of approximately $2,000,000 should be gradually raised, the interest from which would be sufficient to care for all future Olympiads. This task should be begun at once and should be spread over a series of years in the form of small contributions from all the amateur athletic contests in the country.

Detailed reports from the managers, coaches and operating heads are appended hereto and give in great detail not only the historical records of the games but recommendations for future improvement.

To the members of the Executive Committee of the American Olympic Committee and to the operations staff who have been associated with me in this great undertaking, I wish to express my profound appreciation. Their task has been a trying one. Contributing without stint of their time and effort, they had to deal with a multitude of details little understood and even less appreciated by the general public. Without the recompense of competition such as the athletes themselves enjoy, but with all the burdens of responsibility on their shoulders, they have served with a loyalty and devotion to the ideals of sport which no words of mine can adequately portray. To the press who accompanied the American team, I wish to express my gratitude for their thoroughness and fairness in portraying the various phases of the venture as they saw it. To the team I voice a real affection. It has made me proud to be an American. I reserve for my last and greatest tribute, the American Sportsman, that inarticulate public who by their contributions made this enterprise possible, who by their plaudits have inspired the team to its successes, and who by their sympathy and understanding have dignified and ennobled the entire adventure.

I cannot refrain from expressing my appreciation of the confidence that has been reposed in me by those who practically drafted me for the presidency of the American Olympic Committee. Their insistence upon my accepting the position as a national duty in spite of my reluctance has found its recompense for me in final results. Its duties have been arduous and difficult and at times have tested the limits of patience and forbearance. The complicated chancelleries of American sport - I may even say international sport as well - are even more intricate perhaps than are political chancelleries. To abstain from the conflicting interests of the various sports bodies and yet to demand of all support for the Olympic movement has been a problem which at times appeared insurmountable. It is my most earnest recommendation that within the next few months an athletic congress be called, under the auspices of the American Olympic Association, of all amateur sports associations in the United States, attended by the leading athletic figures of America, wherein the various athletic problems that have been agitating the nation during the immediate past shall be thoroughly discussed without crimination or recrimination, and policies and standards fixed so definitely as to thoroughly chart the course of American athletics for the immediate future.

"Athletic America" is a telling phrase. It is talismanic. It suggests health and happiness. It arouses national pride and kindles anew the national spirit. In its fruition it means a more sturdy, a more self-reliant, a more self-helping people. It means, therefore, a firmer foundation for our free institutions and a steadier, more determined hold on the future. Nothing has been more characteristic of the genius of the American people than is their genius for athletics. Nothing is more synonymous of our national success than is our national success in athletics. If I were required to indicate today that element of American life which is most characteristic of our nationality, my finger would unerringly point to our athletic escutcheon.

Storms have raged over questions of professionalism as opposed to amateurism; as to whether athletics are detrimental to or promote the best interest of the school and the college; as to whether they are an essential part of our educational systems; as to whether they are a valuable training for citizenship; as to whether they tend to fit one for the problems of life; as to their moral value; as to what extent women shall participate therein; as to whether they do not tend to specialization for the few rather than to recreation for the many. All of these problems have been and are being constantly met in the irresistible advance of the athletic movement throughout the nation. There is an ever-gathering constant momentum in favor of facilities for the physical development of all instead of the overtraining of a few. Athletics as an end or athletics as a means to an end are the particularly salient aspects of present-day athletics as a problem. It is the solution of these great questions that I earnestly implore the athletic leaders of America, in a spirit of flexibility, to discuss and settle at the conference I have suggested. We must build athletically not only for health but for character. In learning how to play we learn how to live.

These problems should be solved before the tenth Olympiad, which will take place in Los Angeles in 1932. The Olympic games of Greece represent one of the world's oldest traditions. Their history extends for some 1200 years. Through centuries, from the age of Tyrants to the great era

of the Free States; from the rise of Macedonia to supremacy, through the troubled years of the Achaean and Aetolian leagues; while Greece lay crushed under the rule of the Roman Senate and while it had its brief revival of prosperity under the Roman Empire; in spite of every vicissitude of fortune, year on year the Olympic games took place. The athletic code, therefore, has come down to us from even before the age of chivalry and knighthood. It embraces the highest moral laws and will stand the test of any ethics or philosophies ever promulgated for the uplift of man. Its requirements are for the things that are right and its restraints are from the things that are wrong. Its observance will uplift every one who comes under its influence. It instinctively follows a religion that has no hypocrisy in its brave and simple faith and binds man to man in links as true as steel - the religion of a gallant sportsman's loyalty and honor.

And it is under the impulse of that blameless ideal that I express the gratification of American sportsmen that we will be permitted to continue this great festival in 1932 and be host to the world in the great athletic forum of America.

To set the cause above renown,
To love the game beyond the prize,
To honor, as you strike him down,
The foe that comes with fearless eyes.
To count the life of battle good,
And dear the land that gave you birth,
And dearer yet the brotherhood
That binds the brave of all the earth.

With expressions of respect and regard, I remain, my dear Mr. President,

Very cordially yours,
Douglas MacArthur
President, American Olympic Committee

MESSAGE TO PROVIDE REINFORCEMENTS FOR THE INTERNATIONAL SETTLEMENT AT SHANGHAI JANUARY 31, 1931

The assumption by the United States of free-world leadership during World War II led to the development of our present highly centralized and complex command center in Washington, D.C. Nothing shows the magnitude of this evolution better than General MacArthur's simple, concise, and clear order for the commitment of a small precautionary force into Shanghai in 1931. This particular order was written in pencil on two small sheets of note paper.
Major Vorin E. Whan, Jr., USA, Editor
A Soldier Speaks: Public Papers and Speeches of General of the Army Douglas MacArthur
© 1965, Frederick A. Praeger, Publishers, New York, NY

Send following radio C.G. (Commanding General), Phil. Dept.. . . . On request of American Consul General, Shanghai, to furnish further protection for American lives and property in International Settlement, President directs that the 31st Infantry be dispatched to Shanghai at once. Navy will

MacArthur takes the oath of office as Chief of Staff of the Army before Major General Edward A. Kreger, Judge Advocate General of the Army (1930). At right is Secretary of War Patrick J. Hurley.

furnish transportation using Chaumont or other craft. Equip troops for indefinite stay and every emergency. Leave animals behind for present. On arrival have C.O. (Commanding Officer) report to senior American officer ashore for instructions and duty. Acknowledge. MacArthur.

RADIO ADDRESS FROM WASHINGTON, D.C.
ON THE OCCASION OF THE BEGINNING
OF THE ARMY AIR CORPS MANEUVERS
MAY 23, 1931

Although he had been a member of the court that convicted Brigadier General William B. Mitchell, the military aviation pioneer, MacArthur was a steadfast proponent of the development of air power. In May, 1931 - now a full General and Army Chief of Staff - he surprised the Army by announcing that he would personally participate in a nationwide air maneuver that featured the concentration of Army air units for use as an independent strike force. Just prior to joining the forces in the field he spoke over the radio to stir public interest in the air activities of the Army.

Major Vorin E. Whan, Jr., USA, Editor
*A Soldier Speaks: Public Papers and Speeches of General
of the Army Douglas MacArthur*
© 1965, Frederick A. Praeger, Publishers, New York, NY

Alert and poised, the Army's falcon of the sky, the First Air Division, has just been reported to me by its intrepid young commander, General Foulois, as ready and waiting. Summoned for the defense of the New England coast from a mythical enemy approaching from the North Atlantic, its flights, squadrons, wings, and brigades have been mobilized in a position of readiness.

The defense of our coasts, the maintenance of the integrity of our land from enemy air marauding, is their mission. From our far-flung air fields, spotted from the Atlantic to the Pacific, from the Great Lakes to the Rio Grande, they have winged their way to the critical area. Single-seater pursuits, diving in squadrons at 250 miles an hour; attack planes to hurl their deadly loads on ground troops; bombers with their tons of explosives 3 miles above the earth; fighters which will climb to heights of 6 miles straight up; transports which can span the nation from coast to coast between breakfast and supper; row on row, grim, waiting, they stand ready for the order of flight.

Almost unconsciously my thoughts go back to a bloody morning on the Ourcq in July, 1918. I can see the ground troops forming grimly for the attack on Fère-en-Tardenois - blue-lipped, covered with sludge and mud, chilled by the wind and rain of the fox-hole, driving home to their objective or to the judgment seat of God. And up above us that whirling, swirling mass of an air fight to belch forth a falling, sickening crash of fatality, and that gallant young eaglet Quentin Roosevelt, dying unquestioning, uncomplaining, with faith in his heart and on his lips the hope that we would go on to victory.

From twenty-two years ago and our first military plane, to this mighty air armada, what a contrast! How truly it demonstrates that the history of war is dominated by change. Wars are largely won through new ideas and inventions. The great captains of history have all been innovators. They have had background, but they have not looked backward. In addition to the valor and discipline that can be developed in the Army, they have invariably had at their disposal new methods and new ideas. The military tabulations of the world's battlefields read like an index of new weapons, new equipment, new conceptions which have in result swayed the destinies of mankind. War chariots, elephants, the Roman sword, chain-mail, gunpowder, the bayonet, the ramrod, permanent regular formations as devised by the Ottoman Turks, the regimenting of religious enthusiasm by Mohammed, the railroad, the telegraph, the airplane, the General Staff - each in its turn has brought victory.

A sure indication of health and virility in military thought is to refuse to be bound down by the limitations of equipment at present in use. We must hold our minds alert and receptive not only to the six-mile ceiling bomber and the mile-a-minute combat car which are already on the military horizon, but to the application of unglimpsed methods and weapons that the engineer, the chemist, and the physicist may provide. The next war will be won in the future, not in the past. We must go on, or we will go under.

General Fechet, our able and progressive Chief of the Air Corps, has just reported the enemy sighted in mid-Atlantic under full head of steam, accompanied by his entire force of airplane carriers. Zero hour approaches.

LETTER TO THE EDITOR OF *THE WORLD TOMORROW*
CONCERNING THE RESULTS OF A POLL
OF CLERGYMEN ON THE QUESTION OF THE
MILITARY OBLIGATIONS OF THE CITIZEN
JUNE 2, 1931

During the interwar years, a strong antipathy to all things military developed among many citizens as a result of the disillusionment following World War I. Peace societies were actively working for world disarmament as a moral and economic necessity, while many others questioned the virtues of militant patriotism. Even though he was firmly opposed to large-scale armaments for aggressive purposes, General MacArthur strongly believed in maintaining an adequate level of defense preparations. It was in this spirit that he commented on the findings of a magazine poll of American clergymen.

Major Vorin E. Whan, Jr., USA, Editor
*A Soldier Speaks: Public Papers and Speeches of General
of the Army Douglas MacArthur*
© 1965, Frederick A. Praeger, Publishers, New York, NY

I appreciate very much the courtesy of the suggestion contained in your note of April 20, and am glad, indeed, to avail myself of the privilege of commenting on the general subject of the Church in war.

My predominant feeling with reference to the majority of the replies received by your paper from 19,372 clergymen is that of surprise. Surprise at the knowledge that so many of the clergymen of our country have placed themselves on record as repudiating in advance the constitutional obligations that will fall upon them equally with all other elements of our citizenship in supporting this country in case of need.

To exercise privilege without assuming attendant responsibility and obligation is to occupy a position of license, a position apparently sought by men who do not hesitate to avail themselves of the privileges conferred by our democracy upon its citizens, but who, in effect, proclaim their willingness to see this nation perish rather than participate in its defense.

The question of war and peace is one that rests, under our form of Government, in Congress. In exercising this authority, Congress voices the will of the majority whose right to rule is the cornerstone upon which our governmental edifice is built. Under the Constitution, its pronouncement on such a question is final, and is obligatory upon every citizen of the United States.

That men who wear the cloth of the Church should openly defend repudiation of the laws of the land, with the necessary implications and ramifications arising from such a general attitude toward our statutes, seems almost unbelievable. It will certainly hearten every potential or actual criminal and malefactor who either has or contemplates breaking some other law.

Anomalous as it seems, it apparently stamps the clergyman as a leading exponent of law violation at individual pleasure.

I am mindful of the right accorded every American citizen to endeavor by lawful means to secure such changes in the Constitution or statutes as he may desire. But to concede to him the right to defy existing law is to recognize a state of anarchy and the collapse of properly constituted authority.

May I remark also that, if we acknowledge the prerogative of the individual to disregard the obligations placed upon him by American citizenship, it seems only logical to ask him to forego all rights guaranteed by such citizenship.

It also surprises me that while apparently entering a plea for freedom of conscience, these clergymen are attempting to dictate to the consciences of those who honestly differ from them over questions of national defense.

Their sentiments and implied efforts are injecting the Church into the affairs of State and endangering the very principle that they claim to uphold.

Perhaps the greatest privilege of our country, which indeed was the genius of its foundation, is religious freedom. Religious freedom, however, can exist only so long as government survives. To render our country helpless would invite destruction, not only of our political and economic freedom, but also of our religion.

Observing French Army maneuvers, accompanied by Generals Ford and Weygand. (circa 1931).

Another surprise comes in the revelation that so many seem to be unfamiliar with the struggle of mankind for the free institutions that we enjoy.

Magna Charta, the Declaration of Independence, the Emancipation, the rights of small nations and other birthrights of this generation have been bought with the high price of human suffering and human sacrifice, much of it on the fields of battle.

I am surprised that men of clear and logical minds confuse defensive warfare with the disease which it alone can cure when all other remedies have failed.

Do they not know that police systems and armed national defense are the human agencies made necessary by the deep-seated disease of individual depravity, the menace of personal greed and hatred?

Should not these clergymen turn their attention to the individual sinner and rid the country of crime rather than attack the national keepers of the peace, the most potent governmental agency yet devised for this very purpose?

It is a distinct disappointment to know that men who are called to wield the sword of the spirit are deluded into believing that the mechanical expedient of disarming men will transform hatred into love and selfishness into altruism.

May I also express surprise that some have lost sight of the fact that in none of our past wars have clergymen been required to bear arms, and that under the terms of the Geneva Convention, ratified by the United States in 1907 (Sec. 130 and 132), chaplains are non-combatants and not authorized to bear arms.

And if United States Army chaplains are ever guilty of using inflammatory propaganda, such activity is without warrant or authority by any statute or order ever promulgated in the history of the country.

Perhaps I should also remind them that, under the terms of the League of Nations, the United States would be required to maintain a standing army of at least a half-million men in order to be able to carry out its mandates.

I am curious to know how many of the clergymen who voted for the League have read the articles and understand that under them the peace of the world is to be maintained in the last analysis by armed military forces.

It is difficult to reconcile the faith of these people in the efficacy of newly organized international agencies to keep the peace and enforce respect for international covenants with their self-confessed intention to violate the existing laws of their own long-established government.

A few questions occur to me that could appropriately be asked the clergymen who replied to your questionnaire. In stating that they were in favor of the United States taking the lead in reducing armament even if compelled to make greater proportionate reductions than other countries might be willing to make, did they know that the existing total of our land forces, including regular Army, National Guard and organized reserves, is about one-third of one per cent of our population?

Did they know that in other great countries except Germany, whose army is limited by treaty, this ratio is from three to forty-five times as great?

Did they know our total forces in actual size are exceeded by those of at least fifteen other nations, although in population we are exceeded only by Russia, China and India?

Finally, did they consider the words of our Lord as given in the twenty-first verse of the eleventh chapter of St. Luke: "When a strong man armed, keepeth his palace, his goods are in peace"?

In all modesty may I not say to the opponents of national defense that our Lord, who preached the Sermon on the Mount, later in his career declared: "Think not that I am come to send peace on earth. I came not to send peace, but a sword." (St. Matthew, x, 34.)

It is my humble belief that the relation which He came to establish is based upon sacrifice, and that men and women who follow in His train are called by it to the defense of certain priceless principles, even at the cost of their own lives.

And I can think of no principles more high and holy than those for which our national sacrifices have been made in the past. History teaches us that religion and patriotism have always gone hand in hand, while atheism has invariably been accompanied by radicalism, communism, bolshevism, and other enemies of free government.

Have not those who oppose our modest and reasonable efforts for national defense miscalculated the temper and innate spirit of patriotism in the average American?

The fact that our Citizens' Military Training Camps are oversubscribed long before the opening of the camps comforts me that patriotism is still a dominant power in our land.

Any organization which opposes the defense of homeland and the principles hallowed by the blood of our ancestors, which sets up internationalism in the place of patriotism, which teaches the passive submission of right to the forces of the predatory strong, cannot prevail against the demonstrated staunchness of our position.

I confidently believe that a red-blooded and virile humanity which loves peace devotedly, but is willing to die in the defense of the right, is Christian from center to circumference, and will continue to be dominant in the future as in the past.

EXCERPTS FROM THE ANNUAL REPORT OF THE CHIEF OF STAFF, UNITED STATES ARMY FISCAL YEAR JULY 1, 1930 - JUNE 30, 1931

During this period the Army's budget allowed a total expenditure of $347 (millions); of which $214 went for maintenance, pay, forage, clothing, etc. Public works, new construction, etc., $60; miscellaneous expenditures, $16; training of troops, $7; and arms and equipment, $33.

Frank C. Waldrop, Editor
MacArthur On War
Duell, Sloan and Pearce, New York
©1942, Frank C. Waldrop

Units of the Army and the United States are found in every State of the Union and in many posts and stations in other quarters of the globe. The Chief of Staff, under the President and the Secretary of War, is responsible for the military efficiency and well-being of this far-flung organization. His is the task of assuring that the activities of each element constitute a component part of a balanced army program, designed to keep the whole in readiness to carry out the mission for which it is maintained.

Because of the varying conditions under which units operate, there are required on the part of local commanders the application of a variety of detailed methods, and the exercise of individual initiative. The supervisory influence of successively higher headquarters is applied to insure teamwork in all echelons-a coordinating process that consists mainly in prescribing the results that are to be obtained by subordinate organizations, and in inspections to insure uniformity in accomplishment.

To permit orderly progress in lower units the instructions of each next superior commander are projected progressively further into the future, until in the War Department they take on the nature of long arid continuing policies. Arbitrary and drastic changes in these are not to be expected - on the contrary, they are to be deplored and resisted. Continuous progress and improvement are mandatory, but they are to be sought through evolutionary rather than through revolutionary processes. The constant endeavor of the Chief of Staff, therefore, is to lead the Army steadily along such avenues of doctrine arid of effort as will keep abreast of pertinent developments in the political, social, economic, and military fields.

As a consequence of these considerations, it is my purpose in this report, Mr. Secretary, to discuss trends rather than isolated incidents - to point out the axial road the Army is following toward the fulfillment of its legal mission, rather than to describe the many bypaths utilized by particular elements in order finally to arrive at their common destination. I am attaching hereto such data, extracted from the detailed reports of subordinate staff officers and commanders, as will serve to amplify and illustrate particular portions of this statement.

War Planning

By far the most important duty confronting the Army, because in its broadest sense it is almost all-inclusive, is that of preparing to meet national emergencies. This duty is divided into two principal parts, namely, the development of plans applicable to the situations that might possibly confront us; and all undertakings designed to improve the Army of the United States for performing the functions that would devolve upon it in these assumed situations. Each activity in both categories has as its ultimate aim the enhancement of the Nation's ability to meet an emergency effectively and efficiently.

Our traditional policy has been to place main reliance for land defense in citizen armies, to be collected and trained after the declaration of emergency. In time of peace we have always maintained only the minimum force deemed necessary to sustain the shock of such land combat as might eventuate before the mobilization plan could become fully operative. Admirably as this system is suited in theory to our particular situation, an indispensable concomitant is the assurance that the period required for mobilization will be reduced to the practical minimum. Assuming that we have reached stabilization in the personnel and materiel strength of forces maintained in peace, and in the amount of military training to be absorbed annually by the manhood of the Nation, there is only one way in which this can be accomplished - through perfection of prearrangement. Hence the importance that attaches to planning in the War Department.

The essentials of our general mobilization plans, together with the specific legislation required in emergency to give them force, are available in appropriate documents and have been reported upon by my predecessors. These plans must be meticulously coordinated with similar ones of the Navy. They must be supported by carefully devised procurement plans, and by programs for mobilizing the industrial resources of the Nation. These two latter, in the War Department, are prepared by the Assistant Secretary of War. This whole coordinating process is one of the most important features of war planning, and I report with no small gratification that during the last half of the fiscal year 1931 unusual progress in it has been realized.

As an instance of this progress I cite an agreement reached between the War and the Navy Departments concerning the employment of aircraft. Under it the naval air forces will be based on the fleet and move with it as an important element in performing the essential missions of the forces afloat. The Army air forces will be land based and employed as an element of the Army in carrying out its missions of defending the coasts, both in the homeland and in overseas possessions. Through this arrangement the fleet is assured absolute freedom of action with no responsibility for coast defense, while the dividing line thus established enables the air component of each service to proceed with its own planning, training, and procurement activities with little danger of duplicating those of its sister service. At times in the past the difficulties blocking the path leading to a practicable agreement in this matter seemed almost insurmountable. That these were finally overcome expresses more eloquently than words the growing determination of Army and Navy officers to view and solve their common problems with the single idea of promoting the national welfare.

In another direction an accord with equally significant consequences in war planning has been reached. This involves the War Department, the Navy Department, and representative leaders in the industrial world. It deals with the peculiar or special responsibilities that devolve upon government in the efficient conduct of war, and with the nature of the machinery that should be set in motion for discharging these responsibilities. In the details of these matters there yet exist differences of opinion. But as to basic principle, there has been attained a substantial unanimity of thought that has been made of record in a document, prepared under the supervision of the Assistant Secretary of War, which could aptly be termed a "Joint Army-Navy Industry Proposal for National Organization in War."

Such agreements cannot produce maximum results until all concerned are assured that they meet the approval of the Chief Executive and the National Legislature. The War Policies Commission, created by Congress to investigate administrative policies that should be applied by the Nation in war, is, because of its membership, representative of the Executive and legislative departments of Government. On May 13 last I appeared before that commission[1] to present

---

[1] Address to the War Policies Commission is attached to this report.

to it the conclusions reached in the War Department concerning the broad problem of organizing the Nation to carry on war effectively, and to lay before it the gist of the plans we have so far developed. I am forwarding for inclusion with this report the statement I then made. What conclusions will be reached by the commission or what definite recommendations it will make are matters upon which I offer no conjecture. But I feel certain that the very fact that the results of our studies have been thus brought definitely to the attention of such a body, by which they will be subjected to searching analysis and impartial criticism, will have a healthy and lasting effect upon future efforts in war planning.

Closely allied to war planning is the subject of munition reserves. The time that must elapse subsequent to the beginning of any possible future emergency before some of the vitally essential items of equipment can come into mass production varies from a few months in some cases to more than a year in others. The necessity for maintaining reserves in these types of supplies is evident. All nations have long recognized it; the point to be determined by legislative and Executive action is the most desirable balance between considerations of current economy, which tend to decrease the reserve, and those of emergency insurance, which demand its constant aggrandizement. Under existing congressional directive our effort has been to maintain a reserve for a force of two field armies or 1,000,000 men. Through lack of sufficient appropriations we have fallen far below this level in certain essential items. This applies particularly to ammunition, which deteriorates after a number of years in storage. Savings to be made through renovation are not neglected, but they are insignificant when compared to our aggregate needs. In other items increased authorization is necessary to give us an approximate balance in supplies. The time has come when the matter of munition reserves must receive renewed attention if we are to adhere to the policy of maintaining defense measures on a balanced basis.

The development of new weapons is equally important with the maintenance of adequate supplies of existing types. Small amounts of money are appropriated annually for experimentation, and for the production of pilot models. Only through these activities can the Army keep abreast of developments that promise, in the event of war, to economize in the flesh and blood of American manhood. The latest type of the Christie[2] tank (track and wheel) was tested during the year by a specially appointed board. The results of the test were so promising that the procurement of seven of these machines for service test has been approved. Other new weapons undergoing tests are semiautomatic shoulder rifles, pack howitzers, and all-purpose field guns.

Whenever a new weapon is approved as to type, attention is turned, in the office of the Assistant Secretary of War, to insuring its prompt production in emergency. Speaking generally, no effort is made to produce these in quantity in time of peace, and consequently they do not form part of a munition reserve.

EXISTING NUCLEUS FOR EMERGENCY ARMIES

The strength and efficiency of the forces that must be ready in war to stand guard over mobilizing America, and to serve as a skeleton around which the manhood of the Nation can shape itself, are matters of direct and constant concern to the Chief of Staff. This nucleus comprises the Regular Army, the National Guard, and the Organized Reserves. The professional element - the Regular Army - is the medium through which technical information is imparted to the others, and I shall first devote my attention to some of the more important considerations affecting it.

The dispersion of the Regular Army in small detachments throughout continental United States makes it impracticable to have immediately available an adequate, balanced, and efficient force of regular troops to meet the first phases of emergency. The few Infantry troops in the United States available for immediate field service are distributed among 24 regiments located at 45 different posts with a battalion or less at 34. Artillery troops are in a similar situation. They are distributed among 7 regiments and 7 separate battalions located at 19 different posts with a battalion or less at 16. Under such conditions combined tactical training in the Regular Army alone is rendered most difficult.

A reasonable dispersion of regular forces is, of course, required in order to carry on economically citizen training in summer camps. This project is one of the most desirable features of our national defense system, and it is particularly important that nothing be done that would compel a reduction in the number of young men permitted to attend the camps annually. Too great a concentration of regulars would probably result in such a reduction, since the increase in the cost of assembling trainees would materially exceed the savings effected in overhead and upkeep expenditures. But subject to the limitations imposed by the considerations I have just discussed, regular forces should be concentrated in fewer stations.

In the past poorly devised housing programs have been largely instrumental in occasioning faulty disposition of our forces. In appreciation of this fact the whole subject of proper distribution has been intensively studied, and all recommendations for new construction now submitted to Congress are based upon the one desideratum of correcting the existing situation. Improvement will result as these programs are gradually executed. In the meantime some relief is being offered by recent War Department decisions looking to the abandonment of several border and other small posts.

The strength of the Regular Army has not fluctuated greatly in the past several years, remaining almost constant at the figures of 12,000 officers and 118,750 enlisted men (excluding Philippine Scouts). Fewer separations from the service have occurred during the last year than in the average of those just preceding, due to the unsettled economic conditions now being experienced. With subnormal industrial activity and the consequent surplus of trained civilians for every vacant position, there has been little temptation offered to Army officers and highly trained noncommis-

---

[2] J. Walter Christie, of Linden, N.J., pioneered the modern fast tank. Because the United States Army could not finance his experiments adequately, he sold Christie models to Russia, Poland and other countries. His generic designs appear in many models of today in all armies. (Frank C. Waldrop - 1942)

sioned officers to forsake military careers for the more lucrative positions of civil life.

This decrease in voluntary separations from the service is noticeable in spite of the fact that for some years the pay of professional military personnel has been disproportionately low when compared to that of civilians occupying positions of similar trust and responsibiliw. I am entirely confident that the American sense of fair dealing will ultimately accord relief in this direction, although the sworn defenders of the Nation have no desire to draw attention to the Government's pecuniary obligation to them during a period when the utmost in national economy is necessary in order properly to balance the annual budget. In this matter the Army holds true to its proud tradition that in time of need the Nation has never found military personnel backward in bearing at least its full share of the individual sacrifices demanded.

To a limited extent the decrease in cost of living has served to ameliorate the military man's financial difficulties. However, the modest reductions in retail prices experienced during the past year have not been sufficiently great to eliminate his difficulties, nor to correct the injustice that has been done him.

Stagnated promotion has been another matter of immediate concern to every officer, and therefore to the War Department. An abnormal personnel situation was created in the Army by the method of induction into the service of the World War group, which constitutes about 50 per cent of all commissioned officers. Some months ago there was forwarded to Congress a bill which if enacted into law will relieve to a great extent the unsatisfactory conditions now existing in that it will hold out to a great majority of the officers in the so-called "hump" the expectancy of eventual reasonable advancement. The purpose of the bill is simply to bring promotion back to a normal basis. The obvious norm is that established through years of accumulated experience under conditions of average inflow and outflow of personnel. The limited acceleration in promotion sought under the War Department proposal would obtain only until there should have passed through the list the great number of officers who entered the service immediately subsequent to the World War. The immediate passage of this bill should be urged upon Congress.

In spite of the effects produced by the long-standing conviction that injustice has been done through existing pay and promotion schedules, morale and discipline have been maintained at a most satisfactory level. These two intangible but most important factors are matters for my deep personal concern. Reports of the Inspector's department attest to the commendable spirit among commissioned officers, and to the excellent esprit de corps found in organizations. Statistics contained in the general appendix relating to desertions and general court-martial cases are given as illustrations of the generally satisfactory conditions in this respect among enlisted men.

I must invite your earnest attention, however, to a specific condition, which, if uncorrected, will soon be reflected in a deteriorating morale in the units affected. I refer to the quartering of Federal prisoners on military reservations. At the earnest request of the Department of Justice the War Department has made available certain posts, camps, and military penal institutions for the housing of such prisoners. Where military requirements permit the complete transfer of a post or station to the Department of Justice, this practice is believed to be sound from the standpoints of efficiency and economy. However, when Federal prisoners are maintained on Army posts which cannot, for cogent reasons, be wholly turned over to that department, the practice is vicious and damaging in its eventual effects, and should not be countenanced a moment longer than stark necessity demands. Through conferences held with officials of the Department of Justice we are assured that they recognize this, and will take the earliest practicable steps to remove Federal prisoners from military posts. I sincerely trust that by the end of the next fiscal year I may be able to report this as an accomplished fact.

The training of the Regular Army during the year has been as satisfactory as existing conditions permit. Our school system conrinues to function in a highly efficient manner, and were there available suitable positions in relatively large units for officers to apply practically the training received at the schools, we could point to a military educational system unexcelled in any nation.

An unusual feature of the year's training activities was the concentration of 663 military airplanes over Dayton, and the subsequent operation of this force along sections of the eastern seaboard. The success of the whole maneuver was illustrative of the advances made by the Air Corps in the design of equipment, in the training of its pilots, both individually and in organizations, and in the education of its staffs. Of the planes participating, 97 were from National Guard units - a circumstance that connotes the progressiveness of that component of the Army of the United States.

Minor joint Army and Navy exercises were held during the year, in every case proving of material benefit to both services in training for joint operations.

MECHANIZATION

In one aspect of training, which involves also a matter of combat organization, a change of considerable eventual import has been effected. I refer to the general field of mechanization. During the whole of the postwar period this matter has been studied, while experiments conducted in foreign armies, as well as in our own, have been carefully watched.

An explanation of the change effected in our Army requires a brief analysis of military operations and of methods for utilizing motor vehicles to facilitate the success of such operations. The employment of such vehicles purely as transportation for troops and supplies is known as "motorization" - while their application to the battlefield as actual weapons belongs to the field of "mechanization." In the following discussion I am concerned principally with mechanization.

The mission of an army in the field is to defeat the armed forces of the enemy. To do so it must conduct efficient reconnaissance and counter-reconnaissance; move swiftly in the directions indicated as desirable; concentrate its personnel and materiel at the critical point or points; strike with its full force; and exploit rapidly and fearlessly every advantage gained. Each of the several arms has been organized, maintained, and equipped for the purpose of carrying out a particular part or parts of the whole task. In the aggregate their assigned missions comprise the entire field of tactical endeavor.

There have been two theories advanced to govern the application of mechanization to these tasks. The first is that a separate mechanized force should be so organized as to contain within itself the power of carrying on a complete action, from first contact to final victory, thus duplicating the missions and to some extent the equipment of all other arms. The other theory is that each of the older arms should utilize any types of those vehicles as will enable it better and more surely to carry out the particular combat tasks it has been traditionally assigned. Under this system mechanization would permeate the whole Army, but it would be applied by each arm only as an additional means of securing victory.

In the initial enthusiasm of postwar thought the first method was considered as the ideal one. Mechanized forces were expected to supplant the established order, or at least to constitute a corps d'elite, to be supplemented where necessary by foot troops, which would hold defensively the advantages gained by the mechanized striking force. This was the controlling idea in the establishment of "mechanized forces" in our own and other armies, but continued study and experimentation have since resulted in its virtual abandonment. Inherent weaknesses and limitations in the machines themselves are such as to preclude their employment in many types of terrain. Moreover, the impossibility of having any considerable number of suitable armored vehicles immediately available upon the outbreak of war is sufficient proof that such a doctrine is not applicable in any case to the early stages of a future emergency.

Accordingly, during the last year the independent "Mechanized force" at Fort Eustis has been broken up. The Cavalry has been given the task of developing combat vehicles that will enhance its power in roles of reconnaissance, counter-reconnaissance, flank action, pursuit and similar operations. One of its regiments will be equipped exclusively with such vehicles. The Infantry will give attention to machines intended to increase the striking power of the Infantry against strongly held positions. Every arm is authorized to conduct research and experiment with a view of increasing its own power to perform promptly the missions it has been especially organized and developed to carry out. Every part of the Army will adopt mechanization - and motorization - as far as is practicable and desirable. To the greatest extent possible machines will be used to increase the mobility, security, and striking power of every ground arm, but no separate corps will be established in the vain hope that through a utilization of machines it can absorb the missions, and duplicate the capabilities, of all others.

I have reported upon this matter at some length because I feel that the continued observance of the basic doctrine now promulgated to our Army will have far-reaching and beneficial effects in future training and readiness for emergency.

CITIZEN COMPONENTS

The National Guard and Organized Reserve Corps are the two nonprofessional components of the Army of the United States. Because regular officers and men act in many instances as instructors for the other components, all advances in methods of training and of administration and changes in doctrine are communicated promptly to them. Moreover, what I have said concerning discipline and morale applies to all three components.

The strength of the National Guard approximates 190,000 officers and men. As part of the first line of defense National Guard divisions are being trained to a standard of efficiency that will permit their employment with a minimum of delay in the unhappy event of war. Not only does the Regular Army furnish commissioned and enlisted instructors to the Guard, but a large number of National Guard officers and men are detailed annually to the Regular Army service schools. Progress is steady, as is indicated by reports of inspection on training, both in armories and in summer camps. Armory facilities are often inadequate, and there are many other difficulties to be overcome by this citizen component. The continuous improvement made in efficiency speaks well for the unselfish and tireless efforts made by National Guard personnel. Moreover, this progress should be a source of intense gratification to all public-spirited citizens, for certainly it must be generally realized that the National Guard's readiness to take the field promptly would be of vital importance to the safety of the Nation in a grave emergency.

The commissioned strength of the Organized Reserve Corps has apparently stabilized near the figure of 108,000. This includes both the active and inactive lists.

On October 1, 1930, in accordance with approved policy, promotions in the Organized Reserve Corps were placed entirely upon the basis of military qualifications. This procedure requires an affirmative showing of military knowledge as determined by examination and of military ability as determined by practical tests. The reaction of the Organized Reserve Corps to this long-needed policy has been entirely favorable. In general, it may be said that reasonable opportunity exists in the Reserve Corps for the advancement of officers qualifying for such privilege. At the same time the higher grades in a few services are still blocked by the excessive number of appointments in the senior grades made during the first years immediately following the World War. This condition will be corrected by 1933 under a continued application of present policy.

In the early days of the reserve project it was necessary for the War Department to deal, to a considerable extent, with reserve officers individually. With the development of reserve organizations, however, it is becoming more and more feasible to administer them as units. A policy to this effect is being followed in the War Department, with the expectancy that it will do much to promote organizational spirit and to develop the desired teamwork among the whole corps.

One feature of the reserve problem that has given much concern to the War Department and to the higher officers in the Reserve Corps itself is that of retaining permanently therein a larger proportion of those entering from the Reserve Officers' Training Corps. Approximately 20 per cent of the officers so far commissioned from this source have been completely separated from the service. As a step toward the solution of this problem, reserve regulations were liberalized to permit promotion of these officers to the grade of first lieutenant without restriction as to vacancies, and under very reasonable requirements.

The Reserve Officers' Training Corps project, both in schools and in summer camps, continues to experience a healthy development. During the fiscal year, out of 6,770 students reporting for duty at the camps, 6,569 completed the course. I attribute this remarkable showing to the excellent discipline and morale, as well as the health of personnel that have characterized the camps. These figures are equally indicative of the splendid types of young men enrolled in the Reserve Officers' Training Corps.

The citizens military training camps are constantly gaining in popularity as their purpose and methods of operation become better understood. By June 30, 1931, about 75,000 applications for attendance at the July camps have been received, as compared with less than 60,000 in 1929. It was possible to accept for training only about 38,000. The policy of employing reserve units to administer the camps has been continued with good results, both in the training of students and in giving valuable experience to the reserve organizations so used.

ADMINSITRATIVE CONSIDERATION

The central headquarters that the Army would need in war must be in existence at all times, even if parts of it are in embryo only, and its proper functioning as an administrative machine is important alike to war planning and to current activities.

The War Department General Staff is, as you know, the foundation stone of this headquarters structure. Its activities are broad in scope and far-reaching in effect. Under the supervision of the Chief of Staff it formulates military policies; it does not carry out the many operational details required in the application of such policies. Officers detailed for duty with it, both Regular and Reserve, must distinguish clearly between their own functions and those of other established agencies, and confine their efforts to their own legitimate duties.

This military group is paralleled by a munitions staff assembled by the Assistant Secretary of War to assist him in carrying out the procurement and industrial planning duties imposed upon him by law. The objective of this staff is to assure the timely production of the supplies required under military programs, and the adequate support of military effort in emergency by the industrial resources of the Nation.

Surrounding these two staffs are the chiefs of arms and services. Each chief of arm is the principal War Department inspector for his particular branch. He is the technical advisor to the Chief of Staff concerning all matters affecting his arm, and is responsible for the efficient operation of the special service school pertaining to it. Each chief of service has similar responsibilities, and is in addition charged with carrying out the various administrative duties that devolve upon his service as an operating agency of the War Department, including that of preparing the detailed procurement plans for which he is held responsible by the Assistant Secretary of War.

Coordination among all parts of this organization is a matter of prime importance. Failure to effect it would be certain to cause duplication and conflict, with resultant maladministration and stagnation in progress.

A change in organization that has promoted cooperative effort and has had a beneficial effect in moulding unified War Department opinion on matters of moment, was the establishment of the "General Council." Its membership includes the heads of the General Staff divisions, the chiefs of arms and services, representatives of both Assistant Secretaries of War, and the commandant, Army War College. It serves as a focal point where divergent views may be digested and adjusted, and where projected activities of the several subdivisions of the department may be properly coordinated. With respect to higher authority, the body acts only in an advisory capacity, but under the chairmanship of the Deputy Chief of Staff it subjects all important questions to an impartial analysis which operates to make self-evident the answers to the great majority of those presented. For this reason its recommendations have been exceedingly helpful to the War Council. I am confident that the happy consequences so far resulting from the formation of this council are but harbingers of still greater and more far-reaching benefits yet to be realized.

To this statement could be added many paragraphs of discussion concerning subjects whose intrinsic importance would fully justify devoting space to them. My purpose has been, however, to confine my attention to those matters in which developments of the last half of the fiscal year 1931 have tended to lift them out of the routine and the ordinary. It is important to the Army and to national defense, for instance, that the troops in each of our principal foreign garrisons, favored generally by opportunity to devote their attention to their own training, and enjoying a relatively great concentration in disposition, are continuing to attain a high standard in military efficiency. But since, during the months covered by this report, no unusual changes have been made in policies affecting them, and no extraordinary incidents have arisen in connection with them, they, like many other items, are omitted as subjects for direct comment.

I do not append any formal conclusions or recommendations, for these, where I have deemed them pertinent, are included in appropriate parts of this report.

ADDRESS TO THE WAR POLICIES COMMISSION
MAY 13, 1931

My statement will bear upon the requirements of the joint resolution under which the commission is sitting. I shall propose solutions to certain of the problems before you-problems which have long been under study in the War Department.... .

PART I
MISSION OF NATION AT WAR

The history and the phraseology of the resolution are such as to lead us, unless we are watchful, into a serious error. In our attempts to equalize the burdens of and remove the profits from war, we must guard against a tendency to overemphasize administrative efficiency and underemphasize national effectiveness. The objective of any warring nation is victory, immediate and complete. It is conceivable that a war might be conducted with such great regard for individual justice and administrative efficiency as to make impossible those evils whose existence in past wars inspired the drafting of Public Resolution No.98, Seventy-first Congress. It is also conceivable that the outcome of such a war would be defeat. With defeat would come burdens beside which those we are considering would be relatively insignificant. In all we do and in all we say with reference to preparedness, and to policies to be pursued in event of war, we must never overlook for one moment the fact that while efficiency in war-making is desirable, effectiveness is mandatory... .

NECESSITY FOR ADEQUATE PLANS

Our national-defense doctrine involves the maintenance in time of peace of the minimum force necessary to hold off any aggressor until the country could prepare itself to wage war. This small standing army would also be called upon to furnish the training cadres for the national army and to supply competent staffs for field armies, corps, and hundreds of lesser units. Today our land forces are reduced to a level that requires the utmost in preparatory measures intended to facilitate the application of our vast resources to war uses, if ever this extreme action should become necessary.

In previous hearings there has been presented to this commission, by men who occupied key positions in our governmental Organization, a comprehensive review of the economic and industrial conditions that characterized our participation in the World War. Assisted by some of these same men, the War Department has studied intensively the history of that conflict in its military, economic, industrial, and social aspects. We attempt to apply the lessons so derived to conditions of the present, which naturally are not, and never can be, the same as those of 1917. As an instance of changed conditions, the present organization of our land forces is totally unlike the one prevailing prior to the World War. Today we have a skeletonized framework of a citizen army capable of absorbing rapidly the military manpower of the Nation, whereas in 1917 we had to build up practically a complete organization. Similarly, on the material side we are today in intimate touch with the industrial structure under a plan which will enable American industry promptly to absorb our war requirements. Again, as Mr. Willard and Mr. Aishton[3] pointed out to the commission, the railways are today far better prepared to meet the requirements of a sudden emergency than they were in 1917.

The problem is thus much more than one of leisurely historical research - it is an intensely alive and practical process of arranging for the best use of the Nation's assets in any emergency of the future - a process in which we are assisted by the experience of the past.

The burdens of war may be roughly classified as human and economic. To a considerable extent these burdens are occasioned by the diversion from normal activities of the manpower, material, and money required to organize, equip, and maintain essential combatant forces. Time is the vital element in the problem. The necessity for speed permits no gradual absorption of the load. If careful prearrangement has not been made, programs involving millions of men and billions of dollars must be hastily extemporized. Consequent confusion, inefficiency, waste and delays, to the point even of jeopardizing national safety, are inescapable. Profiteering and other injustices are attendant evils. These are the evils the plans and preparations of the War Department are intended to prevent.

Peace-time training of the armed forces is directed toward the same end. The Regular Army, the National Guard, and the Organized Reserves are developed so as to fit into a great war machine with the least practicable delay, and so as to impose no unnecessary burdens upon industry.

I shall discuss first those phases of our plans that deal with the human burdens of war, pointing out particularly the measures we propose for equalizing these as far as it is practicable to do so.

GENERAL MOBILIZATION PLAN[4]

As the basis for planning and training, the War Department has adopted General Washington's precept: "If we are wise, let us prepare for the worst." We have a general mobilization plan. This plan does not envisage any particular enemy. It contemplates the mobilization, by successive periods, of whatever forces would be needed... .

The speed with which effective mobilization can be carried out is dependent upon three factors:

(a) The rapidity with which personnel can be procured.

(b) The length of time required to organize units and train them for combat.

(c) The rate at which munitions can be manufactured and supplied.

For purposes of planning, the rate at which men can be procured is made the standard, and every effort is bent toward increasing the speed of the other two factors.

A mobilization plan must depend on certain basic assumptions of fact. Upon the correctness of these assumptions depends the successful application of the plan. These assumptions are so important that they deserve the careful attention of your commission. They are:

(a) That immediately upon the outbreak of war, the President will be given ample statutory powers to mobilize promptly and to use effectively the manpower and material resources of the Nation, and to make such adjustments in governmental agencies so as to mold these resources into efficient organizations.

(b) That a selective service act will be passed by the Congress on or before the first day of mobilization.

(c) That great cantonments, such as we had in the World War, will not be constructed. Full Utilization of Federal, State, county, and municipal buildings will be made as troop shelter. Where necessary, arrangements will be made to use privately owned buildings... .

PROCUREMENT OF MUNITIONS

As previously stated, the basic general mobilization plan

---

[3] Daniel Willard, president of the Baltimore & Ohio Railroad, and Richard H. Aishton, general chairman President's conference committee on federal valuation of railroads. (Frank C. Waldrop - 1942)

[4] This program, on the whole, is the very one under which we have gone to war. Changes have been only in detail, not in principle. (Frank C. Waldrop - 1942)

has set up not only requirements in men, but material requirements as well. Six field armies are composed of corps, divisions, brigades, and smaller units, and must be supported by other organizations. Each organization requires its particular unit equipment of rifles, guns, wagons, trucks, and so on almost ad infinitum. Each soldier must have shoes, coats, and a multitude of the other accessories of the fighting man. Just as the number of soldiers required during successive periods, beginning with the first day of war, has been estimated for, so has the number of all items of equipment. This information, in the requisite detail, has been furnished to the Assistant Secretary of War. It forms the basis of the industrial researches made by that official, whose aim it is to insure the procurement of all items in the quantities and at the times indicated by those responsible for conducting combat operations. The matter of procurement is one demanding constant study, revision, and compromise. If it can be shown that the demands of the military for certain items cannot be met because of too stringent specifications, then the specifications must be modified. If facilities for the manufacture of certain items are extremely limited, and probably incapable of meeting full war-time needs, then acceptable substitutes must be devised and authorized. The general need for supplying the armed forces within reason with necessaries and the subsidiary problems growing out of that need have engrossed the various divisions of the War Department for years. Those of the Assistant Secretary of War are so important, and bear so directly on that of your commission, that they deserve much consideration. I wish to emphasize particularly the importance of the various items of ammunition. Here are commodities produced in small amounts, or not at all, in peace-time, which must be furnished in almost unbelievably large quantities in a major emergency. Furthermore, the production and handling of ammunition and its explosive components by hastily trained personnel involve hazards comparable with those in the zone of combat... .

PART II
RESULTS OF FAILURE TO PREPARE

During the hearings of last March your attention was frequently invited to the lack of industrial preparation prior to our entry into the late conflict. Failure to provide for a coordinated purchasing system in the War Department has been rightly blamed for much of the difficulty that made itself felt in the early months of the war. More over, a comprehensive program for effecting the unification of American industrial effort had to be slowly and tediously developed as the war progressed. Experience in modern war has demonstrated that lack of adequate plans for industrial mobilization and for War Department procurement is the source of many evils in war, among which may be listed:

Delay in the procurement of necessary munitions, perhaps even to the point of jeopardizing national safety.

Lack of knowledge concerning the amounts of supplies needed, causing waste of resources in overproduction on the one hand, and a shortage of essential items on the other.

Lack of knowledge concerning the most logical places for munition production, resulting in improper distribution of the load and causing congestion, difficulties in transportation, inefficient use of resources, and local and finally general upsets in the price structure.

Uncoordinated purchasing by many Government agencies of tremendous amounts of supplies, encouraging competition among these agencies, and inevitably resulting in further maladjustments in the price structure.

Inequitable distribution of war's economic burdens... .

ALLOCATIONS

We plan to base war-time procurement upon allocation rather than upon the competitive bidding standard properly prescribed in peace. By allocation I mean the assignment of a definite list of facilities to each procurement agency to supply its needs. The Navy Department has given its approval to this plan, and by agreement between both departments those plants set aside to produce for one are not approached by the other. Under joint agreement certain plants will serve both. The advantages offered by this system are many.

(a) It is the only method that permits exact prearrangement for production of munitions. The aggregate of the production tasks assigned in peace make up the complete initial requirements of the War Department.

(b) Orderly distribution of initial war production can be effected in times of peace. Any other system would throw this load haphazardly upon the country in an intensive purchasing campaign when time is at a premium.

(c) Each plant is forewarned of the task it will be expected to perform, and can make some preparation to meet it. Essential production can be initiated with the least practicable delay.

(d) Competitive bidding among various agencies for the output of a single plant is prevented.

(e) Prices will be determined by negotiation, controlled by the knowledge, obtained in peace-time planning, of the items that make up costs and by all information that can be collected by the Government. A contractor refusing to take a contract at a fair price would be in a most unenviable position in war. The type of contracts designed to assure fair treatment to all will be described later.

I believe the commission should give the weight of its approval to the continuance and further development of this system.

DESCRIPTION OF MANUFACTURE

Many articles required by the Army in war are not ordinarily produced in this country, and manufacturers have no prior knowledge of the applicable production methods. Complete drawings and specifications are necessary to define any given article to a producer. Experimentation and actual production at Governmental arsenals and laboratories are conducted to develop this information, which, when properly assembled, is called a description of manufacture. The results are preserved in the form of models, drawings, and specifications, lists of operations and factory layouts, summary of machines and personnel required, and drawings of necessary jigs, dies, and fixtures.

The importance of this type of preparation was emphasized by Mr. Coffin as well as by Mr. Ferguson. This work is being done as fast as time and funds will permit. It produces, as a valuable by-product, a force of trained mechanics that may be used as Government inspectors or as instructors for others in time of war.

Another method through which these same results could be obtained would be through the placing of educational orders, a subject also discussed at length before the commission by Mr. Coffin. These have not been authorized by Congress, but are most essential for certain technical items.

An educational order is a contract placed, without advertising, for a limited quantity of a desired technical article, with any selected facility. Their use in peace would be of real advantage in hastening production in an emergency. The selected facility would gain actual experience in producing the article that it would be called upon to produce in war. There would be prepared a complete description of manufacture for the use of the United States, and there would be maintained by the plant a complete set of dies, jigs, and fixtures pertaining thereto....

Considerations Applying to the Development of Industrial Mobilization Plans

Our broad plans for industrial mobilization take cognizance of the genius of American Government and the popular concept of the responsibilities and duties devolving upon the Executive branch in time of war. They have been developed on the following basic considerations:

(a) Control of industry in war is a function of the President, acting under the authority accorded him by the Constitution, by Congress, and by public opinion.

(h) The size and the special and emergency nature of the task of coordinating American industrial effort demand a special organization, to be made available to the President promptly upon the outbreak of war.

(c) Plans must be practical rather than theoretical. In the interests of national morale they must operate justly and distribute war's burdens as equitably as practicable. They should not contemplate the imposition upon our people of unaccustomed economic processes.

(d) Emergency measures become effective primarily through the support of public opinion. Justice and fairness, supplemented by strong and intelligent leadership, will be more effective than arbitrary regulations, no matter by whom promulgated.

Necessary Administrative Machinery

There are being developed plans for setting up the administrative machinery necessary in war. In the hands of a war-time President there are invariably placed, by the Constitution, by Congress, and by public opinion, a vast responsibility and a corresponding authority. His personal leadership must make itself felt forcibly and instantaneously from the seat of government in Washington to the remotest hamlet of the country. A smooth-working organization, specially designed for the unusual and emergency tasks that will develop, is essential. Aside from the fact that in the World War every government found it necessary to set up a special administrative headquarters through which the Chief Executive could exercise his special war functions, it is evident that the existing cabinet departments are not adaptable to the performance of these duties.

(a) Their functions are specifically defined by law and custom and are not directly related to any of the activities which must be undertaken by the central industrial control in war. In general, they are overburdened by their normal peace-time functions.

(b) Several of the more important departments exist to serve particular classes, both in peace and war. It would be unfair to expect them to exercise emergency restrictive control over the people that they were created to serve.

(c) The changes required in our institutions to make use of the cabinet departments as control organizations in war would be immensely greater than those necessary if a temporary organization is created especially for the emergency.

(d) The controls and functions under discussion are not and should not be exercised in peace. The emergency organization would automatically terminate after the war. If these controls were exercised by a cabinet department, they might be continued after the end of the war to the great detriment of the country.

(e) The greatest objection to the use of cabinet departments for war control is the difficulty of collecting all the scattered agencies and authorities into a focus and directing them toward the accomplishment of a definite purpose.

The existing cabinet departments would, of course, continue to operate in war as they do in peace.

The proposed organization I am about to describe differs in some details from that of the War Industries Board of 1918, and is more comprehensive in scope. This is because of the changed conditions under which we live. However, those who have made a study of this question will see much similarity between the two.

I cheerfully acknowledge the debt that the Government owes to the pioneers who worked out the principles and theories of operation upon which our plan is based.

Director of war industry. - The director of war industry is appointed by, and is the confidential representative of, the President. The director of war industry is assisted by a small headquarters staff of experts engaged in the continuous study of such matters as price movements and their causes, substitutes for critical materials, conservation, business practices. The main body of this office is made up of two branches - one to coordinate demand or requirements; the other to coordinate supply or industry as a whole, in its efforts to meet those requirements.

Organization of demand. - Demand is organized in the requirements branch of the office of the director of war industry. This is the part of the organization that includes representatives of the using services. Otherwise the whole organization is civilian.

The organization of industry. - The industrial branch of the office of the director of war industry has a very simple organization. It consists of a coordinator of war industry assisted by an industrial advisory board composed of a few prominent industrialists, all selected by the President and assigned to duty as representatives of the Government. This organization is charged with the coordination of American industry. Each member of the board is assigned general supervision over a group of war service committees.

War service committees. - Each industry, group of industries, or component part of an industry, is invited to elect for itself an executive or war-service committee and to empower it to exercise definite control over the industry and to act for it in designated matters connected with the emergency. War service committees would represent not only manufacturers and distributors but such other interests as transportation, power, labor, and shippers. In fact, any association or organization might appoint a war service committee.

The war service committee is thus not a governmental organization. It is elected by and exercises only the powers delegated to it by the industry it represents.

PLANS FOR SETTING UP WAR INDUSTRIAL ORGANIZATION

It could be objected that since this Organization is not to be set up until after the beginning of an emergency, time will be consumed in perfecting its details, and the whole machine will have no information or operational plan on which to start. This has been provided for in the following manner.

First of all the director and his principal assistants will be selected by the President, because of their suitability, and called promptly to Washington. This will be facilitated by the preparation and keeping up to date in time of peace of a list of names of men with the special qualifications necessary. A program of this description is now being initiated by the department, and in which the cooperation of national industrial associations and other Government agencies will be sought. To provide promptly for each of these assistants the necessary nucleus of office personnel there will be detailed to each section upon the outbreak of the emergency one of the officers engaged in the peace-time study of the particular matter involved. This officer will secure the necessary clerical help, and transfer immediately to appropriate office space all statistics, studies, and plans that have been accumulated on the subject during the planning period. The Navy has agreed in principle to assist in this matter.

To help establish the body of officers from which this nucleus could be secured, there is, in addition to the planning work itself in both services, the Army Industrial College. In this school eminent industrialists annually deliver lectures on appropriate subjects and discuss present trends in the relationships of government to business. The course gives the student an elementary understanding of the industrial processes in this country.

The nucleus provided in this way will permit the new officials to begin functioning promptly. Expansion will be relatively easy, and it is expected that the. Army officers loaned to the Organization, except those who must necessarily remain in the requirement section, will be returned to us at an early date.

PRICE CONTROL

Practically every government in recorded history, in peace and war, has attempted to control prices of commodities and services. But the factors of supply and demand and price do not respond readily to Government fiat. Hence, almost unbroken failure has followed each attempt. Autocracy compels subterfuge and evasion and dries up the sources of supply. A weak government finds its orders widely ignored.

Yet, a first concern of Government is to assure the well-being of its citizens. Hence, it must ever seek, so far as possible, a fair distribution of the advantages and burdens of national existence.

War conditions make peculiar demands for Government control. Also, then, if popular morale is high, many restrictive measures are feasible which would not be accepted in normal times. Nevertheless, even then governmental effort has never accomplished all that was sought.

Certain conditions in war, particularly in the early stages of war, disturb the price structure or are increased in their disturbing intensity as the price structure itself is upset. They are-

(a) Unusual governmental demands, requiring us to call into production many high-price producers who cannot profitably operate in peace.

(b) Reckless governmental buying. The Government's practice in the end is contagious and leads to, and almost compels, reckless private buying.

(c) High-cost production due to the necessity of employing unskilled workers as industry expands.

(d) Increased insurance, interest, and tax rates as hazards of trade and demands for money increase.

(e) Restriction or threatened restriction of essential imports.

(f) Inflation of the currency as the Government seeks to finance its augmented purchases and is increasingly responsive to the opposition to increasing tax burdens.

Our economic experts differ as to the causes and effects which enter the problems involved in these abnormal conditions. They differ also as to the desirable and effective remedies. They agree that a major factor of disturbance is purely psychological, and that this factor is susceptible to governmental alleviation. Thus, if the Government adopts a firm and reasonable attitude - if, in the stress of war, it maintains an air of confidence and calm - then that confidence and calm are usually reflected in the minds and activities and business of the people. The War Department has studied widely the story of price-control efforts. It has sought the expert knowledge of men of authority. Its conclusions are-

(a) Some measures for price control are inevitable and must be taken early in any major war.

(b) Moderate control undoubtedly can be instituted initially, particularly with respect to basic raw materials. Added control should be undertaken as it becomes necessary, and might finally cover the whole range of commodities.

(c) Coordination of Army purchasing, as contemplated in the plan presented to you, and the elimination of all competitive buying between branches of the Army will be strictly enforced. A like cooperation and a like freedom from competitive buying among all governmental agencies should be assured through the activities of the director of war industries. Thus the Government itself would avoid a major cause of price disturbance and would prevent its own agencies from themselves increasing its final costs.

(d) Governmental departments must have dependable agencies for determination of fair prices. The price offered in any one locality for any commodity must be uniform.

(e) Prices determined by the War Department for special supplies, and by a control agency for general purchasing, must be set for definite areas and for short periods of time.

(f) The prices promulgated as fair and reasonable should be determined by agreement between Government and the representatives of industry. To facilitate this, the plan contemplates a maximum use of fact-finding Federal and State agencies and the war-service committees. The latter particularly should have detailed data as to price factors and trade conditions in each industrial area.

(g) Tax laws should be so framed as to require the minimum of inflation, and to recapture all unusual profits. A registration of wealth at or soon after the beginning of any war would facilitate fair treatment and have a salutary effect upon the national morale.

Freezing of prices would appear to be a doubtful expedient because so many factors are involved that injustice must follow. Evasion and court appeals are inevitable. In the end the Government's effort would probably be largely gesture. Attempts at enforcement would likely create antagonism, and the Government would lose the essential elements of good will. Without complete and unstinting popular support no nation can hope to fight to victory.

Since the Supreme Court has definitely determined that no price-fixing agency of Government may set a price on a citizen's property and compel him to give that property to the Government at that price, any fixed price is effective in Government buying only when it is enforced by public opinion. Beyond this the Government is compelled to commandeer - and this as a general method of war-time procurement is not desirable from any standpoint. Forcible taking should be reserved, then, to occasions of real necessity and the citizen's road to judicial appeal should not be made long or difficult.

The principles followed by the Food Administration in the World War must be kept in mind. These were -

(a) To take into account the interests of both producers and consumers and so enlist the support of each.

(b) To depend for enforcement upon the popular morale and collective patriotism.

(c) To move commodities in as direct a line as possible from producers to consumers.

(d) To prevent hoarding and waste.

(e) To minimize the evils of dealing in futures.

(f) To permit reasonable profit based on costs and to disregard replacement values.

The War Department plan for procurement provides fully for a proper and considered distribution of the war load. It provides facilities for the determination of reasonable prices to be paid for special equipment. Our proposals include the setting up of an agency to determine prices for general governmental buying. The plan places no handicap before the citizen who wishes judicial determination of the fairness of the price given. It assures intelligent and conservative buying; thus it avoids needless burden on the industrial structure; thus, too, it prevents the creation within business of fantastic notions of the extent of the Government's needs. It provides for a reduction of the contractual hazards of war production, thus eliminating the necessity for consideration by contractors of excessive factors of safety in bidding. It provides for prompt and final settlement of contractual claims, thus making unnecessary an estimate in the contractor's bid of an amount which will compensate him for the delay in receipt of money due.

The industrial plan assures that the Government itself will not unnecessarily upset economic and industrial conditions.

Price-control efforts, in consequence, will be directed gradually and in general recognition of their necessity and reasonableness. Good will and cordial acquiescence will assure their success. Injustice and harshness will be avoided because in the determination of prices industry will have voice. The spontaneous cooperation born of patriotism and enthusiasm will not degenerate into an enforced and begrudging compliance. Production will proceed quickly and efficiently and economically. Finally, the citizens will feel that the restrictions to which they submit are restrictions they themselves have imposed in the interests of the common welfare.

PRIORITY CONTROL

Priority is a method of control that was widely developed in the World War, particularly by the War Industries Board. It was used mainly:

(a) To direct the flow of materials and services into the channels of supply of the war- making agencies.

(b) To divert the use of resources from nonessential needs into channels of essential production.

(c) To assure the equitable distribution of materials and services to the civilian population.

In war the primary national interest is a speedy and successful termination of military effort. Every citizen recognizes the paramount right of Government to the use of anything which assures early success in war. Our laws are fashioned in the knowledge of the popular recognition of the fact that in war the individual must give way to the Nation and must forego some of the personal liberty and security he demands in peace.

Since the demand for essential commodities becomes imperious in war, some agency must distribute equitably available supply to recognized need. Thus the greater need takes precedence over the lesser need, the immediate need over that which may safely wait. Also, those things essential to national life and effort are preferred to those which are not so insistently important.

Priority does just that. Wisely and sympathetically administered, it facilitates maximum military effort at minimum burden to all, and assures to each individual need a reasonable share in the common supply.

The plan presented to you provides definitely for the exercise of priority determinations as between the respective needs of Government agencies and as between Government and civilians through the director of war industries.... .

OTHER WAR AGENCIES

We do not propose the initial organization of an independent fuel administration or a food administration because we believe that ordinarily the director of war industry would be able to furnish all the control necessary in these matters. It is not proposed to take over the railroads in time of war unless such action is unavoidable. There exists a definite plan for the operation of railways in war, already described to the commission by Mr. Willard and Mr. Aishton. The railways and the War Department cooperated in its formulation and it is believed to be practical in every respect.

We have made provisions for a war trade board and for a director of public relations. The functions of both will be of great importance, but are sufficiently described by the tides given for the purposes of this discussion. There will also be set up such governmentally owned corporations as may prove to be necessary.

PROPOSED LEGISLATION

Congressional authorizations would be necessary before certain parts of the plan I have sketched for you could go into operation. We have assumed that these authorizations would be promptly given, provided appropriate congressional committees, during years of peace, approve of the details of plans and proposed bills. Tentative drafts of proposed legislation are attached to the plan already furnished the commission. It is felt that the enactment of detailed laws at a time when war is not imminent is not desirable, because such action would probably result in enactment into law of measures so rigid in their provisions as to be a hindrance rather than an assistance in the changed conditions of any future emergency. Certain laws, general in their provision, would unquestionably serve a splendid educational purpose and would clarify some doubtful points that impede progress in planning. However, the passage of such laws might be held by some to be an indication of lack of good faith in our professions of desire for peace.

SUMMARY

In the foregoing discussion I have sought to describe briefly War Department planning activity that is intimately related to the problems for which this commission is seeking solutions. It is obvious that some *of* this activity lies outside the scope of War Department fixed responsibility. The reasons for this apparent inconsistency are easily explainable.

In the actual conduct of war armies and navies and their supporting air fleets are but important elements in the whole war-making team. In time of peace, however, only the War and Navy Departments have direct legal responsibilities affecting the national security, and only in these services do we find specific planning against the possibility of aggression. These departments take the lead in order to secure, and translate into concrete plans, opinions and data from many sources affecting the functioning of some of the other governmental agencies in the conduct of war. Otherwise such plans would probably be neglected, and consequently unavailable when needed. Speaking generally, therefore, the plans of the War and Navy Departments must cover the whole range of essential war-time activity.

It must be apparent that the theories and principles on which our plans are based do not differ essentially from those expressed by the majority of the witnesses who have previously appeared before you. The goal we seek is that sought by the men responsible for the drafting of Public Resolution No.98. Our plans simply set forth the methods whereby it is believed these principles and theories could be applied in the event of another great emergency.

We would be bold indeed to maintain that the methods so proposed are in every case the best. It may perhaps be charged that our plan is too conservative. But it is to be remembered that in case of need the War and Navy Departments must be ready to place these plans before the President and before Congress with the recommendation that they be adopted to govern the conduct of the war. Our responsibility in this matter is too great to permit the inclusion in our plans of any proposed policy of whose successful operation in war we do not feel we can give assurance. Certainly, our plans are the result of honest effort. They are developing along lines that we believe experience has pointed out and present conditions dictate.

Progress in this work demands but insignificant amounts from the public revenue. Study, thought, and research are required, and these, to the best of our ability, we are giving.

I think it pertinent also to say here that the voluntary assistance we constantly receive from other departments, from associations, and from patriotic industrialists is of the utmost value and fully appreciated by the Government. We are studying ways and means through which this assistance may be more efficiently organized and so facilitate crystallization of information and opinion and promote mutual understanding of these important subjects.

CONCLUSIONS

The department's conclusions concerning the problems facing this commission are as follows:

Educational programs concerning the true meaning of modern war and its certain results in human and economic wastage are conducive to promotion of peace.

Reasonable measures for defense are indispensable to a peace-minded nation as a deterrent to any possible aggressor and as a nucleus upon which to expand in case of need.

Modern war demands the prompt utilization of all the national resources. Measures for transforming potential strength into actual strength must work in emergency with the utmost speed and effectiveness.

The greatest need of a nation at war is immediate and decisive victory.

Public opinion is the most potent force in war. The United States will never enter a war except in response to insistent popular demand, incited by foreign aggression, and consequently the Government will have initially the complete support of a high national morale. Maintenance of this morale will depend upon the effectiveness of national efforts against the external enemy and upon the justice and fairness of governmental programs as applied to our own population.

The human burdens of war must be equalized in so far as possible. To this end liability for combat service must be determined under a selective-service system developed along the general lines of that used in the World War.

The economic burdens must be equalized through:

(a) Systematic registration of wealth and all accretions thereto during the period of the emergency; and tax legislation framed to place an equitable burden thereon.

(b) Orderly and economic procurement by the Government itself.

(c) Strong and intelligent leadership based on exact information and exercised through an organization adapted to the purpose.

(d) Application of governmental controls to meet requirements of the specific situation and to prevent any profiteering at the national expense.

(e) Prompt resumption of normal peace conditions upon the termination of the war. During the progress of any war the President should appoint a committee to study and prepare plans for demobilization. These plans must facilitate the reemployment of men returning to civil life from the Army and Navy, and the freeing of industry of the accumulations of stocks produced to meet war requirements.

All of the above demand an intensive and intelligent planning program carried out continuously in time of peace. This planning is the responsibility of the whole Federal Government, which should seek the advice and assistance of civilians in all walks of life. Because of their peculiar responsibilities, the War and Navy Departments must be definitely required to carry on this work as the agents of the whole Government.

Congress should satisfy itself at frequent intervals as to the progress of plans under development by requiring their presentation to appropriate committees of Congress. This should include the presentation of all proposed emergency legislation.

RECOMMENDATIONS

The War Department recommends that, in answer to Public Resolution No.98, Seventy-first Congress, a like joint resolution be adopted by Congress which will make public announcement to the Nation of the policies set forth in the foregoing conclusions. It is recommended also that these policies be grouped in the following three categories:

Group A. - Those policies which will assure practical and efficient peace-time preparation for the emergency of war, promulgated and published in such a way as to have a serious, sobering effect upon every man, woman, and child when he or she contemplates the possibility of war.

Group B. - Those policies which will facilitate the successful conduct of war and effect a just and equitable distribution of war's human and economic burdens when once it has been deliberately undertaken.

Group C. - Those policies which will enable the Nation to demobilize after a war in a rational and orderly fashion.

THE GENERAL COUNCIL[5]

In organizing the General Staff in 1903, the primary purpose was to establish a selected body of specially qualified officers who, freed from all administrative responsibilities, would devote their entire time to major problems of national defense.

At the outset the General Staff was small, and while officers at times worked individually on problems, it was clearly intended by Mr. Root[6] that on the completed solutions there would be a real meeting of the minds, effected when the principal General Staff officers were assembled from time to time for that purpose. In his testimony before Congress prior to the passage of the act, and referring particularly to the section organizing the General Staff, Mr. Root said, "That [section] purposes to create by detail from the officers of the Army a body of officers who shall, in the first place, be charged with the duty of doing the military thinking, of doing what the Navy has a board engaged in now, and what we ought to have in the Army and have not today."

After the World War the reorganization of the General Staff followed very generally the system we used in France. Our General Staff problems fall into four or five natural divisions. The organization of the War Department General Staff into five divisions results in a very convenient system and, if operated properly, it will give good results. Already it has accomplished a tremendous amount of fine work, notwithstanding the attacks that have been made upon it.

Unfortunately, however, these General Staff divisions, or some of them, have grown into small bureaus, entirely too self-contained. The chief of each such division has generally presented his cases to the Chief of Staff either directly or through the Secretary of the General Staff. The result has been that there has been little or no proper meeting of the minds on important subjects. Uncoordinated action has too often resulted. Here and there administrative work has been taken over by these divisions in violation of the law and to the embarrassment of work of first importance. These conditions are slowly being corrected and today informal conferences are held periodically, attended by the Deputy Chief of Staff, presiding, the assistant chiefs of staff, with proper representation of the other departments in order to give balanced discussion on important matters.

In order that such a procedure may be put in definite form and its importance be understood throughout the department, I recommend that the conference proposed be officially recognized and announced in an order signed by the Secretary of War himself.

Such an organization will have a far-reaching effect. Many problems of first importance are awaiting solution or proper coordination by such a body. Much excellent work has been done throughout the War Department. It is now necessary to study it all and fit each part together into the whole picture.

The membership proposed gives a balanced representation. All interested parties are assured of a hearing. Better work and better feeling throughout the War Department will result.

EXCERPTS FROM THE ANNUAL REPORT OF THE CHIEF OF STAFF, UNITED STATES ARMY FISCAL YEAR JULY 1, 1931 - JUNE 30, 1932

Fiscal year just ended will be recorded as a most significant one in the long history of the American Army. Although military activities comprehended little more than normal

---

[5] This was the first attempt to improve the General Staff system and relieve the Chief of Staff of the complexities of dealing separately with each chief of branch. The solution of this problem was finally reached in March, 1942, when President Roosevelt, acting under authority of a law providing for reorganization of the executive departments of the Federal Government, abolished the various branches of the Army which had previously been fixed by statute, and regrouped the Army into three commands of (1) air force, (2) land force, (3) supply service, each commanded by a lieutenant-general and these then reporting to the Chief of Staff on their problems and progress. (Frank C. Waldrop - 1942)

[6] Elihu Root, Secretary of War, August 1, 1899, to February 1, 1904.

training and administration, the Army has nevertheless been the focus during the year of a widespread public interest and attention. During no other period since the conclusion of the World War have such questions as the mission, size, composition, and cost of the Army of the United States been accorded so much space in the public press and so occupied the time of Members of Congress as has been the case during the past twelve months. Conflicting opinions and measures advocated in Congress and through the publicity media of the Nation have kept insistently before the public eye many of the fundamental issues involved in the maintenance of an adequate national defense.

The reasons for this unusual manifestation of official and unofficial interest in our military organization are found in a series of conditions and circumstances of world-wide import.

The tense situation in the Far East, which, for some weeks during the past winter flamed into open hostilities, emphasized again the untrustworthiness of treaties as complete safeguards of international peace. This, supported by a general appreciation of the potentialities in the Sino-Japanese difficulty for a widespread disaster, gave rise to a feeling of apprehension among portions of our population and was reflected in expressions of anxious concern as to the adequacy of our defensive structure. Domestic interest in the Far Eastern situation was heightened by the dispatch, on February 2, 1932, of the Thirty-first United States Infantry[7] to the troubled Shanghai area to assist in preserving the integrity of the International Settlement. The regiment's five months' service there was happily accompanied by no untoward incident and was performed in entire keeping with the best traditions of the American Army.

An international conference at Geneva, still in session at the end of the fiscal year, has for some months been studying formulae for effecting universal reductions in the armies of the world. During the past decade preceding disarmament conferences have dealt principally with the naval phases of this general problem. Concerted efforts toward scaling down armaments invariably evoke a sympathetic interest in this country, and popular approval has always been given to any diminution in our own strength agreed upon by our official representatives. In this instance the predominant opinion, as reflected in the public press, has been that, measured both by absolute and relative standards, the United States has already accomplished a degree of reduction in its land forces that stands as a unique example among world powers. Unquestionably there has crystallized among important elements of our citizenry a strong sentiment in opposition to further weakening of American military strength unless accompanied by sweeping and drastic cuts in the armies of other nations.

But by far the most notable feature of the year, both in its direct and indirect effects upon the Army, as well as in its universal and inescapable influence upon every phase of contemporaneous existence, has been the increased severity of the prolonged economic depression. In the face of a constantly growing Treasury deficit the need has grown acute for drastic reduction in governmental expenditures. The necessity for retrenchment has become so great as to constitute a dominant factor in the shaping of national policy.

The War Department has fully appreciated the seriousness of the financial stringency. In submitting its budgetary estimates for the current year there was rigidly excluded from the list of projected activities every item, no matter how worthy in itself, that was not clearly necessary for bare maintenance of existing strength. These estimates took into account the increased purchasing power of the dollar, and their total was reduced accordingly. The savings so effected were considerable ones, the aggregate of $295,250,000 carried in the estimates being approximately $38,000,000 less than the sums appropriated for the preceding year. But it is important to remember that in this country appropriations for military purposes have always been scrutinized with the most zealous care. Each year, even in times of relative prosperity, pressure to diminish them is applied by both the executive and legislative branches of the Government. As a result the reduced estimates submitted by the War Department for the fiscal year 1933 represent only the amounts on which the present Military Establishment can be temporarily maintained, rather than the continuing annual requirements of national defense.

Notwithstanding these facts, there were proposed during the past year many additional reductions in Army appropriations and revisions in laws applying to military activities, the supporters of which were apparently not fully aware of the resulting effects upon national security. These proposals involved such vital things as the retirement of large numbers of Regular Army officers; curtailment of military training for civilians; abolition of essential water-transport organizations; revision of basic organization in the Army; establishment of a separate subdepartment of Air, and even the amalgamation of the diverse activities and functions of the War and Navy Departments.

Although brought forward principally as economy measures, the inevitable effect of some of these proposals would be increased immediate and future expense for the United States. Many of them crystallized into bills submitted to the National Legislature, and in some instances determined efforts were made to secure their enactment into law. During this process, committees and individual Members of Congress presented a series of important questions to the War Department for study and recommendation. The conclusions reached as a result of exhaustive investigation in the General Staff will be reviewed in the ensuing pages of this annual report. I am keenly aware of the fact that some of the able and patriotic men who have taken a deep interest in our national defense problems have, in particular instances, given their support to solutions differing I from those developed in the War Department. The opinions of these men are entitled to the utmost consideration, and it is not my intent or desire to appear unappreciative of their motives and abilities. Moreover, many of the questions concerned are recurring ones, and in a world of progress and change it cannot safely be assumed that present answers, even if completely satisfactory for the moment, will remain permanently au-

---

[7] This is the famous regiment that was later the backbone of MacArthur's little army in the Philippine struggle of 1942. The Thirty-first has always served outside the United States and has never been home. (Frank C. Waldrop - 1942)

thoritative. Their constant study by governmental officials and private citizens alike is necessary if adequate provision for the national security is to be maintained but without incurring the burdensome expense of needlessly large military establishments. These facts serve only to emphasize the necessity for frank and impartial discussion in public records of our basic requirements in national defense and of the measures we have adopted for their satisfaction.

AMERICAN POLICY
AND CHARACTER OF MILITARY ESTABLISHMENT

At no time in our peace-time history has American policy been so shaped as to develop a military force for aggressive purposes. Preservation of internal order and defense of our territory and rights have marked the extreme limits of our intentions. At times our immediately available military strength and our peace-time preparation have fallen far below the requirements of this sane and moderate purpose, with results in emergencies that have been less than cataclysmic only because of fortuitous circumstances.

In 1920, with the lessons of the World War fresh in mind, the Congress devised a practical program that constituted the first real attempt in the United States to adjust military preparation accurately to defensive needs, and so framed that program as to assure other nations of its nonaggressive purpose.

Before that time only two general systems existed in the world as the basis of military organization. One was the conscript system; the other, the employment of the professionalized soldier. The former provided the maximum of defense with the minimum of cost by prescribing service with the colors as a civic duty. The latter entailed abnormal costs due to the necessity of reimbursing along professional lines the personnel involved. For this reason all the great military machines maintained in modern times in some of the larger foreign powers have been built up under the conscript system.

In our own case, tradition and public sentiment have always precluded Conscription as the basis of a peace-time defense policy. Maintenance of a professional force sufficiently strong for adequate protection would have entailed prohibitive expense, even for a country as rich as the United States. Consequently, the plan developed by Congress at the end of the World War, and written into the national defense act, represents a new departure in military preparedness.

This system places ultimate reliance for the Nation's defense upon a citizen army, the great proportion of which must be organized, trained, and equipped after the beginning of any emergency. Thus it deliberately contemplates a delay of several months between any declaration of war and the time large-scale operations could be initiated, a circumstance that gives convincing proof of its nonaggressive intent. To make possible an orderly mobilization and effective employment of a citizen army in emergency, and to protect the country until mobilization could be accomplished, Congress recognized the need for organizing some permanent military forces, and of authorizing certain continuing preparations, particularly along organizational, training, and material procurement lines.

Specifically, the 1920 law provided for a small professional force and for a limited training of civilians, on a voluntary basis, through the National Guard, the Organized Reserves, the Reserve Officers' Training Corps, the citizens' military training camps, and the National Rifle Association.

The establishment of this conservative system for land defense was unquestionably one of the most constructive measures evolved by any government in recent years. In it are combined efficiency, economy, and respect for American ideals and traditions. It is the product of a long evolutionary process during which the Congress was guided by our military experiences under a variety of conditions and circumstances. Improvement in it should be sought by the same method, and any drastic change should be adopted only after mature consideration of all factors involved, and having in view the continuing welfare of the whole body politic.

THE REGULAR ARMY - SIZE, DUTIES, AND DISTRIBUTION[8]

The foundation of our defensive structure is the professionalized element thereof. The Regular Army should be ready at all times to furnish any troops required by internal emergencies and initial defense against surprise attack. The civilian components depend upon it for instruction, leadership, and technical progress, while in case of general mobilization it is the model and directing head for all. The national defense act provided that it should comprise approximately 18,000 officers and 280,000 men. During the decade just past this strength has, in the interests of immediate economy, been progressively reduced until appropriations are now made on the basis of 12,000 officers and 125,250 men, including the Philippine Scout contingent. On June 30, 1932, the actual figures were 12,180 officers and 119,888 enlisted men. This is below the point of safety.

The continuing tendency to cut further into this already weakened backbone of our military skeleton has been viewed with great concern by the War Department. As early as 1925 the General Staff undertook an exhaustive analysis of our particular situation in an attempt to determine as accurately as possible the minimum strength requirements of the Regular Army in order to carry out the missions imposed upon it by the national defense act. The detailed conclusions then reached are contained in Part 3 of the Hearings before the Committee on Military Affairs, House of Representatives, Sixty-ninth Congress, second session. While minor revisions in that document would be necessary to bring it completely up to date, in its essentials I regard it as sound today as when it was written. I quote a short extract from it.

"The Regular Army, as prescribed in the national defense act, strength 17,728 officers and 280,000 enlisted men, is the minimum trained and disciplined force that should be immediately available to meet the requirements of the United States...

"The Regular Army, of the strength and organization herein provided (14,063 officers, 165,000 men), is the least force that will furnish in time of peace the necessary garrisons for the overseas possessions; for the Regular Army harbor defenses of the United States; will provide a small fairly well-balanced mobile force, with the requisite com-

---

[8] At the time this was written, Germany as a modern military power did not exist, but note how MacArthur included its potentialities in his comparative study of armies of the world. (Frank C. Waldrop - 1942)

bat units of sufficient strength to conduct effective training; will furnish the necessary Regular Army personnel for the civil components and will provide the general overhead necessary for all of the above.

"It will not permit effective preparation in time of peace of a timely and adequate mobilization in the event of a national emergency, as contemplated by the national defense act."

In view of the vital missions devolving upon the Regular Army this modified program represents the minimum scale upon which we may prudently maintain it, yet its existing strength is approximately 2,000 officers and 40,000 enlisted men short of the recommended figures. The expedients to which the War Department must constantly resort in order that the missions assigned the Regular Army by the national defense act may be even approached can be appreciated only by those who have to carry this grave responsibility.

Since, within limits, the problem of armaments is a relative one, it is pertinent to make some comparisons between our Army and those of other great powers. In the following tables the aggregate strength shown in the last two columns for the American Army and Reserves is inclusive of the Regular Army, the National Guard, and the Organized Reserves.

The first comparison is on the basis of population:

(See Table 1, page 40)

Organized military strength in proportion to national wealth is illustrated in the succeeding table. The figures given in the first column as to national wealth are the best estimates available for 1930. While to bring the table up to date these should probably be considerably reduced, it may be safely assumed that each should be reduced by approximately the same proportion. The comparison therefore remains fairly accurate.

(See Table 2, page 40)

Among the nations of the world the United States ranks first in wealth and fourth in population, yet each of 16 others maintains a military establishment exceeding in strength the aggregate of our Regular Army, National Guard, and Organized Reserves. The largest is the French Army, with its total of almost 7,000,000, followed by those of Italy and Russia in that order. The list includes even such small countries as Yugoslavia, Belgium, and Portugal.

To organize and maintain such establishments practically all major foreign powers, except Great Britain, have resorted to conscription. Pay for the individual conscript is insignificant and per capita costs are greatly reduced. Even so, in most foreign countries a much larger proportion of the annual budget is devoted to Army maintenance than is the case in the United States. Our expenditures for current military activities of the Army have amounted for a number of years to between 6 and 7 per cent of total Federal disbursements. The best available figures for expenditures by some foreign countries for similar purposes are:

	Per cent
France	17.4
Great Britain	7.9
Italy	25.4
Japan	13.1

Accurate comparisons between the military needs of any two countries are almost impossible to make because of the great number of indeterminate factors in their respective defense problems. It is interesting to note, however, that the treaty of Versailles, under which Germany was disarmed, permitted that nation of 65,000,000 people to retain a professional force of 100,000 for internal police and the guarding of frontiers. By applying the same ratio to the United States, the "police component" of our professional force, exclusive of the quotas stationed in foreign possessions, would total about 190,000 officers and men.

Brief consideration of the distribution of our existing Regular Army and of the responsibilities devolving upon it gives even a clearer impression of its inadequate strength. Garrisons of important foreign possessions should be sufficiently strong to sustain themselves, without large reinforcement, for a reasonable length of time in any emergency. The reasons for this are obvious, since the exigencies of war may force them to depend for a considerable period upon their own resources, at the same time that their safety may be of the most profound importance to the United States. Yet in no case have we been able to assign to them the numbers that repeated studies show to be demanded by prudence. Essential data concerning these garrisons appear in the following table (strength as of June 30, 1932):

(See Table 3, page 40)

Deducting these figures from the total numbers appropriated for in recent years, there is left for continental United States approximately 10,085 officers and 89,170 enlisted men. The numbers actually present in continental United States on June 30, 1932, were about 9,750 officers, 820 warrant officers, and 83,600 enlisted men.

From this force there is taken personnel for all War Department and corps area overhead, and for technical services, civilian training, school faculties, and student bodies. It supplies personnel for river and harbor development. This particular activity, administered with great success for many years by the Army engineers, furnishes the officers of that corps the finest possible peace-time training for the manifold construction, engineering, and procurement tasks that devolve upon them in time of war. A variety of other important military and civil duties make additional demands upon the available strength of the Regular Army.

After all these essential needs have been satisfied there is left in the United States for organization into tactical units approximately 3,000 officers and 55,000 men. Due to the requirements of civilian training, and because of the distribution of existing housing facilities, these units are scattered in small posts and detachments throughout the length and breadth of continental United States. This reduces transportation expenses for civilian trainees attending summer camps and keeps a small number of professionally trained soldiers available in every section. But in this situation combined training by the various arms and services of the Regular Army is limited to small concentrations. Many garrisons are at such reduced strength as to constitute little more than service detachments for local maintenance and for civilian training camps. As a result of the heavy special demands made upon the troops it has become extremely difficult, and

SOLDIERS PER 1,000 POPULATION, 1930
(MOTHER COUNTRIES ONLY)

Country	Population	Active army, including active air force		Active army and reserves, including active air force	
		Strength	Per 1,000 population	Strength	Per 1,000 population
United States	124,746,573	132,399[a]	1.06	421,317[a]	3.38
United Kingdom	45,625,000	232,623	5.10	607,573	13.32
France	40,922,408	388,946	9.50	6,720,958	164.24
Italy	42,000,000	397,863	9.47	5,992,619	142.68
Japan	64,448,000	230,000[a]	3.57	2,130,000[a]	33.05
Russia (U.S.S.R.)	158,000,000	624,000	3.95	5,152,000	32.61

[a] Navy Air Force not included.

Table 1.

SOLDIERS PER BILLION DOLLARS' NATIONAL WEALTH, 1930
(MOTHER COUNTRIES ONLY)

Country	Active army, including active air force		Reserves, including active air force		Total, including active air force	
	Strength	Soldiers per billion dollars	Strength	Soldiers per billion dollars	Strength	Soldiers per billion dollars
United States ($400,000,000,000)	132,399[a]	331	288,818	722	421,317[a]	1,053
United Kingdom ($121,663,000,000)	232,623	1,912	374,950	2,082	607,573	4,994
France ($58,200,000,000)	388,946	6,683	6,322,012	108,797	6,720,958	115,480
Italy ($25,000,000,000)	397,863	15,915	5,594,756	223,790	5,992,619	239,705
Japan ($51,017,000,000)	230,000[a]	4,508	1,900,000	37,242	2,130,000[a]	41,751
Russia (U.S.S.R.) ($73,740,000,000)	624,000	8,462	4,528,000	61,405	5,152,000	69,867

[a] Navy Air Force not included.

Table 2.

STATION	STRENGTH		REMARKS
	Officers	Enlisted Men	
Hawaii	757	13,466	Principal naval base in Pacific. No great fleet, either ours or foreign, could operate across that ocean without possesing three islands. Thus, they constitue our great defensive outpost in that ocean.
Panama	418	9,537	Necessary to permit concentration of United States Fleet in either ocean. Channle of sea communication between eastern United States and west coast of South America, with Asia, America. Importance to United States in emergency incalculable and might be almost vital.
Puerto Rico	52	938	Most important United States possession in Caribbean. Still partly undevelope. Enlisted personnel native to island.
Philippines	633	11,111	Outpost of American civilizatin in the western Pacific. Strength given includes 65 officers, 6,472 enlisted men, Philippine scouts. Important to United States as advanced defense base in event of any trouble in Far East.
China	45	719	Under present conditions some force necessary for insuring observation of international treaties.
Alaska	10	309	Small contingent for use in minor emergencies.
Total	1,915	36,080	

Table 3.

in some cases almost impossible, for even the smallest units to follow a progressive training program.

As a further consequence of its extreme dispersion and its paucity of numbers, the Regular Army's ability to furnish a small, well-balanced field force for prompt employment in emergency has been badly impaired. This is a matter for real concern, and in itself would constitute sufficient support for the conclusion of the War Department that the regular forces should be increased by at least 40,000, or approximately two war-strength divisions.

Proposed reduction in commissioned officers. - Our unfavorable situation with respect to relative strength in professional forces emphasizes the need for the utmost efficiency in the development of mobilization plans, in maintaining adequate administrative, procurement, and supply services and in preparation of civilian components to perform their functions promptly in emergency. These are difficult tasks, and they fall principally upon the shoulders of commissioned officers.

It is necessary also to visualize the existing force as the framework of a much larger war establishment rather than as a balanced fighting unit in itself. Of primary importance in a skeletonized army are those elements not easily extemporized or quickly developed when emergency arises. Aside from a large proportion of technical services, technical experts, and military instructors, such an army should be strong in that element most difficult to develop and most essential to an army in the field-military leadership. From every standpoint there is indicated the importance of an adequate professional officer corps. It energizes the whole framework in peace and directs the assembly and employment of the expanded organization in case of war. It was with these considerations in mind that the General Staff, in 1925, recommended a minimum strength for the professional officer corps of about 14,000. Repeated analyzes of the subject have served to confirm the accuracy of the conclusions then reached.

There was nevertheless seriously proposed in Congress during the past year, and actually adopted by the House of Representatives, a provision for retiring from active service 2,000 of the 12,000 Regular officers now on the active list. Fortunately, the proposal was rejected by the Senate, and shortly after the close of the fiscal year the House receded from its original position. During the time the project was before the Congress, the War Department many times expressed its unalterable opposition thereto for reasons which I shall briefly discuss. No other attack aimed exclusively at the Army during the year was so surely calculated to accomplish the disastrous emasculation of our defensive system as was this one. More than any other also it was made the object of popular interest and discussion. The great preponderance of editorial opinion was definitely opposed to the cut, though there was a small section of the press which came to its support. This latter element invariably misstated the General Staff's motives in combating the project, constantly assuming that the department was actuated solely by a desire to protect individual officers from a diminution of income. The truth is that this phase of the question was never raised by the War Department in communications to the President, to the Congress, or to the public. Departmental opposition was based upon principle, upon the studied

conclusion that under existing conditions, and in view of the character of our defensive structure, the number of officers is already below the minimum requirements of national security.

Proponents of the retirement bill urged in its support that of the 12,000 officers now on the active list, only some 5,000 are actually serving at home and abroad with troops of the Regular Establishment. This is a cogent reason for increasing the strength of the officer corps but not for reducing it. The normal requirements of troops are approximately 6,300 officers, but with the reduced number now on the list the department has never been able to assign this number. In an effort to provide some relief I initiated during the past year an intensive study of the duties and functions of all officers in the District of Columbia with a view of reducing the total to the absolute minimum. That study had not been completed at the end of the fiscal year, but it is obvious that the number of officers made available for troop duty by such methods will be insignificant when compared to the aggregate needs.

Moreover, if the total strength in officers were further reduced, the quotas assigned to duty with troops and to civilian training would have to suffer far more than their proportionate share of the loss. This is because the overhead and functional requirements of the whole Army are largely independent of the size and number of the tactical units maintained. Unless we are to abandon all pretense of carrying out the essential provisions of the national defense act, and of providing a reasonably effective defensive skeleton for this country, these requirements must be satisfactorily met. Under existing conditions minimum numbers only are assigned to the development of mobilization and other preparatory plans in the War Department and in the corps areas; to administrative duties throughout the Army; to the designing, developing, and supplying of needed equipment; to duty on staffs and faculties of schools; and to the performance of a great variety of miscellaneous military and civil duties. Reductions in the size of the Army cannot affect the importance of these activities, nor to any appreciable extent their volume. As a consequence, any further losses would necessarily be largely absorbed by reducing the contingents on troop duty, serving with civilian components, and undergoing instruction at educational institutions. That is to say, peace-time training of man power, the very basis of all preparation designed to produce fighting organizations in emergency, would be sharply curtailed. An already serious situation would be aggravated, and steady progress toward a realization of the minimum objectives of the national defense act would become well-nigh impossible.

In some of the discussions concerning the proposal £or retiring 2,000 officers it was inaccurately stated that the Regular Army's commissioned strength is greatly in excess of that of the British Army, the only other military force in any of the great powers maintained by voluntary recruitment. The fact is that there are 12,120 active officers in the British Army, not counting any commissioned personnel of the Air Corps, nor any of the professional officers in the Dominions. Approximately 2,000 officers of the air force are considered constantly available for operation with the Army, making a total of about 14,120 professional officers for duty with the British Army, compared to our aggregate of approximately 12,000. In addition there are in the British Empire 6,650 more professional officers on the active lists of the Dominions and India. I cite these figures as evidence of the lack of precision that in general characterized the arguments advanced by supporters of the reduction scheme.

As a summary of War Department opinion concerning the vital need for a strong officer corps, I quote below from a letter written in May, 1932, in answer to an inquiry from a Member of Congress:

"Skilled officers, like all other professional men, are products of continuous and laborious study, training, and experience. There is no short cut to the peculiar type of knowledge and ability they must possess. Trained officers constitute the most vitally essential element in modern war, and the only one that under no circumstances can be improvised or extemporized.

"An army can live on short rations, it can be insufficiently clothed and housed, it can even be poorly armed and equipped, but in action it is doomed to destruction without the trained and adequate leadership of its officers. An efficient and sufficient corps of officers means the difference between victory and defeat. Our small Regular Army would be impotent, through its own unaided efforts, to defend this Nation against powerful and sustained attack. Likewise, an unorganized and untrained population would be tragically helpless in the face of organized and trained units. The two parts of the system thus articulate with and complement each other to insure that America's enormous latent strength would not be dissipated through hostile action before it could be harnessed into a powerful military machine.

The only continuing body in which reside the professional knowledge and technical skill capable of accumulating, organizing, training, and leading to victory a national army of citizen soldiers is the professional officer corps. Constantly they concern themselves with the mobilization plans for personnel and material necessary in a great emergency, and make every practicable prearrangement for the successful operation of these plans should need arise.

Commissioned personnel of the citizen components supplement the corps of Regulars, they give generously and patriotically of their time and effort in peace so that, as the numerically preponderant mass of the officers in an emergency army, they may function promptly and effectively. But their devotion and their efforts in this preparation would be wasted without the efficient guidance of their mentor - the Regular officer. Through schools, study, research, and practical training, the Regulars devote their lives to keep abreast of the times in complicated and rapidly changing arts and sciences, and within the limits imposed by available opportunity impart the results to the officers of the citizen components.

So I repeat that in the last analysis our whole defensive system rests upon the efficient performance of a corps of Regular officers, sufficient in strength to carry out the vitally essential duties imposed upon it by the act of 1920.

Proposed method for effecting reductions. - An integral part of the original bill for effecting a 16 per cent reduction in the officer corps was the method provided for its accomplishment. The purpose was to retire the older officers in each of the several grades. It was urged that this would pro-

mote efficiency by eliminating "deadwood" and by giving younger officers the incentive of more rapid promotion.

The claim to increased efficiency was based, in both instances, on mistaken premises. This action would not accelerate promotion, and it would not eliminate the least efficient of our officers.

The bill proposed that the reductions be absorbed by all grades proportionately to their existing strengths. Thus retirements under the act, except for a small additional reduction prescribed for the spring of 1933, would not create vacancies, but the net result would be that almost every officer remaining on the list would have a considerable number of years to serve prior to retirement. How, then, could there be any promotion? Only through deaths and miscellaneous separations from the service. An already stagnated situation would have become vastly worse, and for some years practically every officer of the Army would have remained in his present grade.

The second premise presupposes that efficiency necessarily varies inversely according to age. This erroneous assumption was probably founded upon the fact that in war commanders of combatant units should be comparatively young men. But both in peace and war there is a multitude of important tasks not only performed as well by older men as by the younger ones, but in many instances far better. The officer corps is composed of men between the ages of 21 and 64. In the normal case any officer showing the least signs of mental or serious physical deterioration is separated from the active list long before he reaches the age for statutory retirement. As a result most of the men remaining in the Army until retired by law are highly efficient in the performance of their duties. With mental vigor unimpaired and physical attributes still in satisfactory condition, their peculiar value to the Government lies in their fruitful experience and ripened judgment - indispensable elements in the key positions of every organized activity.

Complete files of efficiency ratings are maintained on commissioned personnel. These are made out yearly by each officer's immediate superior and then forwarded to the War Department, where they are carefully analyzed and evaluated. On the basis of accumulated reports each officer is classified as "superior," "excellent," or "satisfactory," depending upon the degree of success he has attained in varied types of duty and upon the character and ability he has displayed as a military leader. In the two higher classifications are included only those officers whose records, even in a corps of which the standards are exceedingly high, have been outstanding... .

PROMOTION AND PAY OF OFFICERS

Almost inevitably there must enter into any consideration of our professional officer corps the subjects of promotion and pay. Proper policies with respect to them are exceedingly difficult to evolve - particularly in view of the extraordinary conditions resulting from the sudden increase in officer strength just after the World War... .

In 1929 analyzes were made of the increases in compensation received by various groups in the service of the United States during the 20-year period 1908 - 1928.

The following table presents that information in summarized form:

Services	Pay Range 1908	Pay Range 1928
Cabinet	$12,000	$15,000
Assistant Secretaries	4,500	9,000-10,000
Congress	7,500	10,000
Judiciary	6,000-13,000	10,000-20,000
Foreign Service	1,000-3,000	2,500-9,000
Civil Service (clerical)	720-3,000	1,260-6,000
Post-office Inspector	1,200-3,000	2,800-4,500
Civil Service (mechanical)	601-1,878	1,327-5,333
Public Schools, D.C.	500-2,100	1,400-4,000
Army and Navy	1,870-9,538	1,719-9,700[a]

[a] Maximum permanent salary.

It is pertinent here to remark that in spite of the condition illustrated in the above table the Army and Navy and other services involved in the joint pay act of 1922 suffered, in the temporary pay reductions of the current year, a greater proportionate loss than other classes of governmental officials in the same pay ranges. This arose from the fact that the salaries shown above for officers of these services consist partly in so-called allowances, and in each of these the cut made was in excess of the 8.3 per cent reduction in actual pay.

Moreover, the economy act automatically suspends those provisions of the 1922 pay law that provide for increases based on length of service, and thus further discriminates against military and naval officers as compared to civil officials whose salaries are permanently fixed by law. In certain cases it seems apparent that the provisions of the economy act are operating to the disadvantage of officers to an extent not contemplated by Congress when that legislation was enacted. As an extreme example: A second lieutenant, with dependents, who, on July 1, 1932, completed five years' service, and who, were it not for the economy act, would have automatically passed into the next higher pay period, loses, because of that act, total annual pay and resultant additional allowances aggregating $1,062.05. Thus, under the conditions cited, a second lieutenant suffers a loss of pay and allowances equal to more than 48 per cent of his present annual pay and allowances - a loss almost six times greater than the 8 1/3 per cent loss of pay imposed upon civil officers of the United States receiving annual salaries up to $10,000.

Compared to the pay of positions of comparable authority and responsibility in civil life, Army and Navy compensation is disproportionately low. Even in the teaching profession, long known as relatively low paid, in New York City the superintendent of schools normally receives $25,000; the assistant superintendent, $12,500; examiners, $11,000; district superintendents and principals of high schools, $8,500 to $10,000; elementary-school principals, $5,000 to $7,500; high-school teachers, $2,148 to $4,844; and grade-school teachers, $1,608 to $3,654.

For many years the aim of our pay laws has been to remunerate officers on such a scale that, while permitting no substantial savings from income, would nevertheless relieve the individual of worry concerning problems of mere existence and encourage application to his military duties. In justice to the officer a retired pay had to be provided, both to take care of those permanently incapacitated in their

country's service and those who had spent substantially their entire active lives in that service. Everything considered, this is a sound policy, and one whose application is becoming more and more general in the great industrial organizations of this country. The method is correct, the only requirement is the placing of present schedules on a basis that will insure a reasonable and appropriate living standard.

An exhaustive study, made in 1929 by an interdepartmental pay board, representing the six services involved in the joint pay act of 1922, is contained in Senate Document No. 259, Seventy-first Congress, third session. That board recommended that pay be based primarily on grade held and secondarily on length of service in grade. This recommendation, however, was based upon the assumption that promotion laws would be simultaneously revised so as to relieve the present stagnated conditions. To bring existing pay schedules into closer coordination with costs and standards of living it urged substantial increases for all grades. The board recommended that the present practice of dividing compensation into pay and allowance components be discontinued, but that in all cases pay should be decreased by approximately 15 per cent when Government quarters were occupied. Recommendations were also submitted to effect revisions in the pay schedules for enlisted men.

The board submitted its findings about a year after the beginning of the present depression. Price indices had not then fallen to the levels of the past year, and temporary pay reductions in all professions had still been largely avoided. But it is to be remembered that the data used by the board pertained to a relatively long period of years, including at least one major depression. The recommended schedule was brought forward as a reasonable rate of pay for officers under average conditions in this particular epoch of our national history. It was not visualized as applying exclusively to periods of extreme financial stringency any more than to those of extreme inflation, such as prevailed for some years prior to 1930. Whether or not the board's detailed recommendations eventually receive favorable action in Congress it cannot be gainsaid that officers' pay has been far too low.

Having in mind the vital need for ruthless reductions in current expenditures, I submit no recommendation looking toward immediate correction of existing pay schedules. During the present economic stringency officers of the services affected by the joint pay act of 1922 must look upon the sacrifices imposed by inadequate compensation as important personal contributions to the Government's program of retrenchment. But the moment the condition of the Federal Treasury permits, it will become one of the most important duties of the War Department to urge this matter strongly upon the attention of Congress.

OFFICER EFFICIENCY

Since the success of our system of defense is peculiarly dependent upon the proper functioning of professional officers, the inevitable effects upon their morale of stagnated promotion and inadequate pay are of the utmost concern to the War Department. But in discussing these subjects I have not intended to imply that officers, whether serving with troops or in any of the many important positions where supervision by higher authority is almost impossible, are performing their duties inefficiently. The exact opposite is the truth. Speaking from a lifetime's direct and intimate association with the Army, I give it as my opinion that the professional efficiency of the officer corps is at the highest peak it has ever attained. Two contributory causes to this gratifying condition have been the operation of our class B law and the~excellence of our school system.

Under the class B law there are constantly weeded out of the Army those officers classed as unsatisfactory. Before receiving his initial commission in the Army every officer undergoes a searching examination of his mental, moral, and physical qualifications. Thereafter his assignments to duty and the training he receives are intended to increase progressively his value to the Military Establishment. As a consequence it could not be expected that any great number of officers would be affected by the purging process of class B procedure.

Nevertheless, the War Department, in its determination to maintain the standard of performance on the highest plane, has separated more than 300 officers from the service under the provisions of this act. As the intent of the law and the results attained under it are becoming more clearly understood throughout the service, the War Department is striving to make a greater rather than a lessening use of the authority it accords. This applies particularly to the higher grades, in which the minimum standards of acceptable performance can logically be established on a much higher plane than in the lower ones.

The American Army's school system is unsurpassed in excellence anywhere in the world. Foreign ministers of war and chiefs of staff have remarked to me that they would cheerfully sacrifice whole regiments from their military strength if they could duplicate our system in their respective countries.

Our educational process is progressive, practical, and comprehensive. It is so arranged as to impart first the specialized and technical training appropriate to the particular arm to which an officer belongs. It next provides thorough General Staff and command training in the General Service School at Fort Leavenworth and culminates in the postgraduate course at the Army War College. The system is protected from the dangers of inbreeding and of provincialism by detailing annually about 125 selected officers as students at foreign schools, at the Naval War College, and at prominent civil institutions of learning. As a consequence we not only have the best military educational system existing in the world, but that system is constantly developing and improving in excellence and in the results it is attaining.

Our annual exchange of students with the Navy has proven particularly beneficial. At the Army War College, the Naval War College, the Army Industrial College, and the Chemical Warfare School the officers of each service are afforded opportunity to learn something of the problems, methods, and personnel of the other. This has contributed in no small measure to the fine spirit of cooperation and understanding that characterizes the relationships of the two services.

When we consider the care with which our officers are initially selected, the splendid educational and training process through which they progress, and the thoroughness with which the unfit are sought out and eliminated, it is perhaps not so strange that average efficiency is remarkably high. While naturally we have officers of varying degrees of ability, the excellence with which most of them perform their assigned duties is a constant source of gratification and almost of astonishment to me. I do not hesitate to say that in my opinion there is no other large group in the world today, in any line of endeavor, of which the standards of ability, devotion to duty, loyalty, and character are maintained on a higher plane than is the case in our officer corps.

Under every possible contingency and eventuality the loyalty and professional efficiency of the officer corps can be counted upon with certainty. But in addition to these indispensable qualities there is demanded in a successful military establishment, both in peace and war, a fine esprit and morale which inspires initiative, and which is principally engendered by the feeling that outstanding service is appreciated and rewarded in appropriate recognition by the Government. Revision of pay and promotion policies is therefore necessary, not only as a matter of justice to the individual but as a sound proceeding in the interests of the Government itself... .

CIVILIAN COMPONENTS OF THE ARMY[9]

As heretofore pointed out, military preparation under the American system involves two general categories of activity - one professional, the other civilian. I have outlined in preceding sections some of the principal duties of the professional or Regular Army element. One of the most important of those duties is to serve in an instructional capacity toward the civilian components, bringing to each the latest developments in organization, equipment, tactics, and other branches of the military art.

It is apparent, of course, that no matter how efficient may be our small professional force, the requirements of a general mobilization are so vast that there must be provided, in time of peace, some means of assisting the Regular Army in emergency in the intricate business of assembling, caring for, organizing, and training and leading a great citizen army.

This is the purpose of our civilian training program.

Provisions of the Army appropriation bill, as it emerged from the military subcommittee in the past session of Congress, would have suspended or seriously curtailed important features of this training. To such a procedure the War Department was unalterably opposed.

Civilians are trained in the National Guard, the Organized Reserves, the Reserve Officers' Training Corps, the citizens' military training camps, and the National Rifle Association, although only the first two of these are available, as organizations, for use in the event of emergency. The others are in no sense part of our organized Military Establishment, but all are supported or assisted by the Federal Government.

National Guard. - The National Guard is the only one of the civilian components comprising relatively complete military organizations. It thus is the only one that could be

---

[9] This is where the untutored citizen finds his place in the mass army trained and led by career professionals. (Frank C. Waldrop - 1942)

ready with reasonable promptitude to take the field in support of the Regular Army for the protection of the country during the process of mobilization. While essentially a State force, the National Guard is available under the law to the Federal Government in emergency and in peace receives Federal aid and assistance through appropriations, Regular Army instructors, and in other ways.

The aggregate strength of the guard is approximately 190,000, as compared to a total of about 490,000 authorized in the national defense act of 1920. Its training is accomplished through 48 periods of armory drills and a 2-week tour of active training annually. Its higher staffs, as well as those of the Officers' Reserve Corps, participate periodically in command post exercises conducted by corps area commanders. The War Department considers this to be the minimum continuing schedule under which the guard can keep reasonably prepared for emergency duty.

Today the efficiency of the guard is probably at the highest point it has yet attained in time of peace. This is attributable to the character of the officers and men composing it, to the skill with which its Regular Army instructors have performed their duties, and to a faithful adherence to the modest training program just outlined. Of the organized forces available to the United States in emergency the guard is numerically the strongest component, counting both officers and enlisted men. In view of the relative weakness of the aggregate organized forces available to the United States, a subject discussed in earlier sections of this report, the welfare and efficiency of the National Guard have an important bearing upon the readiness of this country to defend itself.

In the opinion of the War Department this component should be maintained at its existing strength; all types of aid it now receives from the Federal Government should be continued on the present basis; and, above all, nothing should be done that curtails its program of training or reduces the number of Regular officers habitually assigned to it.

Officers' Reserve Corps. - The Officers' Reserve Corps is composed of approximately 84,000 civilians holding reserve commissions in the Army of the United States. This number is exclusive of some thousands commissioned in the National Guard and others carried on an inactive status.

Reserve officers voluntarily devote a portion of their time throughout the year to the study of military subjects and to keeping abreast of developments in the military art. In addition, under existing authorizations, we have been able to give them, on the average, about two weeks of active training every third or fourth year. While in camp they are reimbursed at the rates of pay provided for Regular officers of similar grade and are transported to and from the training camp at the expense of the Government.

With an essentially sound background in elementary military training, periodic tours of active service are necessary in order that Reserve officers may remain familiar with practical problems of troop leading, and with the administration and supply of military organizations in the field. This is a vital factor in Reserve training, and for certain classes of officers, at least, the active duty tour should be more frequent than at present.

Numerically, Reserve officers will constitute the preponderant portion of our commissioned personnel in any great emergency. The combined strength of the Regular Army and the National Guard in officers is approximately 25,500, whereas any mobilization involving as many as 2,000,000 men would require the services of at least 150,000 officers. In any operation of considerable size, therefore, American manhood would necessarily march to war largely under the leadership of Reserve officers.

The War Department has devoted much time and attention to establishing the Officers' Reserve Corps on a satisfactory and stable basis. Sound appointment and promotion policies have been evolved and promulgated. These meet the approval of the mass of Reserve officers. Correspondence courses of all types are functioning satisfactorily, and there exists a commendable spirit of service and cooperation among all elements of the Reserve. The results being attained more than justify expenditures in this activity.

In view of the responsibilities that will fall upon these men in the event of war, and even considering the aid and assistance that will then be given them by the professional officer corps, it must be quite obvious that the present program of training is far from an excessive one.

The Army appropriation bill, as it originally emerged from sub-committee, proposed specifically to eliminate pay for Reserve officers on tours of active training, according them only transportation and subsistence during the period involved. This was manifestly unjust and unfair to citizens who are striving loyally and faithfully to prepare themselves for the exigencies of military emergencies. The War Department's progressive program for Reserve training would have been partially disrupted and badly disarranged, since a large portion of Reserve officers would have found themselves unable to attend camp because of the financial sacrifices entailed. The morale of the whole Reserve Corps would have suffered a serious blow had its members gained the impression that the Government did not greatly appreciate and did not particularly desire the continuation of their efforts.

Such a prospect was viewed by the War Department with real concern. If this proposal had been adopted there would have been largely vitiated the continuous efforts made in the past 12 years to develop a satisfactory Reserve, and its effects could not have been overcome in many years, if at all.

Reserve Officers' Training Corps camps and citizen' military training camps. - Replacements for the Officers' Reserve Corps are obtained principally from the Reserve Officers' Training Corps. It comprises a group of young men who undergo elementary military training, either on a voluntary basis or as a required course, in certain of our schools and colleges. Four years of theoretical and practical training in the technique and tactics of small units are supplemented by a short period of active training in the field - an essential procedure in a reasonable preparation for commission as a Reserve lieutenant. Graduates of these institutions now form the largest element of the Officers' Reserve Corps, exceeding in number those with World War experience.

This method of maintaining the strength of the Reserve officer contingent is economical and effective, and, from the standpoint of the great majority of the trainees, is most satisfactory. During the past year the Office of Education, Department of the Interior, conducted an extensive survey among Reserve Officers' Training Corps graduates to determine their opinions regarding this phase of their college education. The complete report, which is available in Pamphlet No. 28 of the Interior Department, indicates the high regard in which this training is held by the men who have been through it. Almost unanimously they recommended its continuance. The results of this survey are highly gratifying, since they furnish convincing evidence that military training in colleges, considered vitally important by the War Department in the maintenance of an adequate defensive establishment, has likewise proved of material value to the individuals involved.

The citizens' military training camps are composed of young men between specified age limits who apply for a period of summer training and who meet the standards set as to physical, mental, and moral qualifications. Training in them is progressive, so that any individual attending more than one of the camps passes successively through more advanced stages of military training. To a certain extent they serve as a feeder for the Organized Reserves, but the principal aim is to impart to a selected portion of American youth a sufficient military training to qualify them, with a short additional training after the beginning of any emergency, as leaders of small units in a citizen army. Through these camps there is gradually being built up a sprinkling of young men familiar with the elementary phases of military organization and training. In any future emergency these men will be of great assistance to the Regular Army, the National Guard, and more especially to the Reserve regiments whose enlisted strength will consist almost wholly of recruits.

Much has been said of the value of these camps because of the physical, moral, and citizenship training received in them. These are beneficial by-products, and the War Department is highly gratified that their worth in this regard has been generally recognized by the public.

But from the standpoint of the War Department, and in view of the manifold and intricate training and organizational problems that would accompany any serious emergency, the great value of the camps is the military training they impart to a small cross section of American youth. In this capacity they are a real military asset to the country and worth far more than the additional expenditure they necessitate.

A proviso in the original Army appropriation bill would have suspended these camps for the fiscal year 1933. Such actions would have interrupted the sequence of the camps and have interfered with the progressive training being given to the young men in them. The bill also would have denied to the members of the Reserve Officers' Training Corps an opportunity to complete their course by practical field training, and would have largely nullified the theoretical military work they had done during their years in college.

A more permanent damage would have resulted from the inescapable impression created that these camps are valueless in our program of preparedness and can be safely discontinued whenever, for financial or other reasons, their maintenance presents difficulties to the Federal Government.

In this report I have presented evidence to show that the preparatory activities in this country are insignificant compared to those carried on in other countries of considerable size. Our theory involves the organization and training of a skeletonized army, constituting a well-trained nucleus capable of promptly and efficiently absorbing great levies of recruits in the event of war. The Regular Army, the National Guard, and the Organized Reserves are the principal members of the nucleus, but the sprinkling of partially trained men of military age throughout all classes of our citizenry is an asset which we should constantly endeavor to maintain and develop. Annual increments to it are necessary; the program must not be interrupted with every vicissitude of national existence.

I believe the necessity for and the value of these camps are generally understood by the public. Their popularity constantly increases, as is evidenced by the fact that in the year just past some 90,000 boys applied for admittance to the citizens' military training camps when only about 37,000 could be accommodated.

Press reaction to the various proposals for curtailing civilian training was generally adverse, and the only one of them finally adopted by the Congress was for the temporary suspension of the national rifle matches. With the exception of this one activity, therefore, the civilian training program will be carried forward in the current fiscal year on about the same scale as heretofore.

MECHANIZATION AND GENERAL MUNITIONS DEVELOPMENT[10]

In recent years probably no other subject has so engaged the attention of military students as has that of adapting the peculiar capabilities of the motor-propelled vehicle to the requirements of battle. In this country and in all foreign armies the possibilities of increasing fighting strength and conserving manpower through a maximum utilization of machines continue to be assiduously explored.

The inclusion in military units of motor-driven vehicles purely as transportation for troops and supplies is known as "motorization," while their employment on the battlefield as actual weapons is termed "mechanization."

During the past fiscal year visible progress in the Army toward mechanization consisted in the procurement of seven combat vehicles of the Christie combination wheel and track type at a cost of $262,000 and 12 armored cars of the most modern design at an approximate cost of $190,000. In addition, the Tank School and Tank Board, previously located at Fort George. G. Meade, Md., were transferred to and combined with the Infantry School at Fort Benning, Ga. Because of the unusual facilities for experimentation, test, and study offered at the Infantry School, it is confidently expected that progress in the development of tactics and equipment suitable for infantry missions will be facilitated. A Cavalry center for similar purposes was established at Fort Knox, Ky.

Viewed solely from the standpoint of acquisition of mechanized equipment, these accomplishments appear inconsequential when compared to our probable total requirements in a major mobilization. By way of contrast it is interesting to note that when the armistice was signed the

---

[10] This section clearly foreshadows the Army of 1942, with all its ground arms under one command, its supply system under another, and its air power under a third - all three under the General Staff's direction. (Frank C. Waldrop - 1942)

United States Government had made arrangements for the production of 19,000 tanks to be used in the 1919 campaign.

Because of the peculiar and far-reaching nature of the general problem involved, however, progress in its solution cannot be measured by any such simple process. In explanation of the present War Department policies governing this important matter and of our present state of preparedness with respect to it, I shall review briefly the conditions that gave birth to the tank idea and the progress we have made in adapting that idea to our own needs.

The fire power of modern weapons is so great that when they are properly located in strongly held defensive positions exposed men cannot live in the zones lying within their effective ranges. This organized fire, based principally upon interlacing fires of machine guns and supported by artillery, is the principal obstacle to movement on the battlefield; and until disrupted or smothered is capable of stopping all direct and unarmored assaults upon the defensive position.

Up to and including the first years of the World War almost the only method applied to the disorganization of defensive fires was the concentration by the attacker of superior artillery strength. So long as the ranges and capabilities of small arms were such as to compel the defense to adopt a substantially linear formation, this method met with a sufficient degree of success to induce attacking forces to seek superiority through the perfection of its detail. But with every increase in the efficiency of firearms, defending forces were enabled to distribute their formations in greater depth and still bring the fire of all units to bear upon the vital zone in front of the main position. The artillery bombardment thus had increasingly larger areas to cover, while the defender could make a maximum use of accidents of terrain and of artificial cover to protect himself. Moreover, the movement into position by the attacker of the great amount of material necessary to produce the effect desired generally apprized the enemy of the imminence of decisive action. With the element of surprise removed, the defense was enabled to concentrate whatever reserves he had available so as to limit any initial advantage gained by the attacking army. Assaults, even when locally successful, became almost prohibitively expensive in men, material, and time.

Finally, the problem became of such difficult proportions that when the absence of flanks on the western fronts had limited all offensive movement in that theater to frontal attack and the bombardment method had failed to produce real results, military men were forced to recognize the existence of a practical stalemate under the conditions and methods then prevailing.

In the desperate search for some weapon that could help restore a superiority of power in favor of the attack, the central powers resorted to the use of chemicals, a method that was substantially countered by protective equipment and by retaliation. The Allies brought forward the motor-propelled armored vehicle, capable of cross-country travel. Mobile armor, after a lapse of centuries, had made its reappearance on the battlefield because a means had finally been found of transporting over varied terrain a protective shield capable of stopping the bullets then in use. This development, however, was a slow and laborious one because of the intricate technical nature of the necessary equipment.

From the day the tank made its appearance on the western front as a clumsy, awkward, mechanically unreliable, and painfully slow armored vehicle, the attention of technical experts in all armies has been devoted to the development of a completely suitable combat machine.

As a measurable degree of success attended these efforts, there was inevitably suggested the possibility of employing such weapons in other kinds of tactical enterprise. The attainment of victory imposes upon an army the necessity for undertaking a variety of activities which may be grouped into several rather well-defined categories. It must conduct efficient reconnaissance and counter reconnaissance from the outset of the campaign; move swiftly in the directions indicated as desirable; concentrate its personnel and materiel at the critical point or points; hold firmly all areas vital to its own success; strike with the maximum power of fire and shock; and exploit rapidly and fearlessly every advantage gained. Each of the several arms has been organized, equipped, and trained for the purpose of carrying out a particular part or parts of the whole task. In all categories of activity the two principal material characteristics contributing to the success of military units are speed in movement and power in action. To enhance these is the constant effort of responsible authorities in every arm of the service.

In the field of reconnaissance the airplane has entered the battle team with an unquestioned ability to perform many of the missions that before the World War fell exclusively upon the Cavalry, and many additional ones that previously could not be performed at all. In supplying long-range information regarding the general dispositions of the enemy, its services are now indispensable. Moreover, under reasonably favorable conditions, it can continue its reconnaissance over all portions of the hostile areas throughout the duration of the campaign, even during battles, and furnish the ground arms with a variety of important information obtainable in no other way.

While the air force, in addition to its many other tactical and strategical uses, has thus relieved the Cavalry of some of its former responsibilities, it cannot give to ground forces undisputed possession of the area lying toward the enemy in which the maneuvering of the Army must take place. A highly mobile ground force of some fighting power is still necessary for this purpose and to cover the slower moving main army. This has always been a responsibility of the Cavalry, utilizing the horse as a means of rapid transportation and often as a shock weapon in actual assaults. In the latter role the modern bullet has driven the horse from the battlefield, and in the former his relative degree of usefulness is gradually diminishing. But the traditional Cavalry missions of covering the advance or retreat of the main army, of conducting terrestrial reconnaissance, and of exploiting victory by pursuing a disorganized army remain unchanged. Cavalry interest in mechanization has therefore been centered principally in armored cars and cross-country vehicles possessing a high degree of strategic mobility, with fighting power and tactical mobility an important though secondary consideration.

To date we have been able to set aside only one unit of Cavalry for exclusive use as a laboratory in which to develop applicable tactics and methods and test the machines made available. To attempt more in the present state of development would entail useless expense without compensating advantage. The evolution of the mounted trooper into the mechanized cavalryman will necessarily take place over a considerable period of time, and will become practically complete only when machines have been developed capable of performing every function heretofore devolving upon the horse, and these machines will have been made available in adequate quantities. This, for reasons I will explain later, cannot be accomplished suddenly In the meantime the Cavalry must still depend upon mounted units in carrying out certain of its missions, particularly during the early stages of any war, or in terrain unsuited to the operation of existing motor vehicles. Thus, while we may safely predict that the horse will more and more be eliminated from armies, it is equally certain that under present conditions some mounted units must be kept available for use in emergency.

The activities of the Infantry in this development have naturally followed more closely the original conception under which the tank made its appearance on the western front in 1915. Upon this arm has always fallen the brunt of the task of dislodging the enemy from defensive positions. The ideal machine for assistance in this mission must of necessity have a high degree of tactical mobility, even at the expense of reducing, if necessary, road or strategic mobility. Remembering that the greatest obstacle to tactical mobility is the band of fire laid down by the defense, an essential requisite in the assaulting tank is sufficient armor to protect against the preponderant mass of this fire, namely, that from all types of small arms. More than this is impractical, at least at present, because every increase in armor means a corresponding loss in speed and cross-country ability. Sufficiently heavy armor to protect from field guns would completely immobilize any machine of usable size. For protection of this kind the tank must rely upon rapid movement, surprise, proper use of ground, and the supporting guns of its own army.

The Artillery also has made much progress in substituting machines for animals as motive power, and the early motorization of practically all field artillery can be predicted. Because of the nature of the artillery mission and equipment, however, this arm has not been so concerned in the development of protective armor for its personnel. Its problem in this matter is principally one of mobility, whereas the search for satisfactory combat vehicles has had in every case to steer its way between the requirements of armored security on the one hand and speed and cross-country ability on the other.

In considering the extent to which the theory of mechanization can be practically applied, it is necessary to recall some of the obvious limitations of the motor-driven armored vehicle. One of these is its inability to negotiate certain types of terrain. Swamps, mountains, thick woods, streams, and extremely rough ground are in general effective obstacles to its use. In such areas, if important from a military viewpoint, the Infantry, Cavalry, and Artillery must operate without the assistance of mechanized units.

Another important factor is the lack of sustained defensive power in a machine, whether armored or not. When stationary in exposed positions, they are easy prey to artillery fire, and their usefulness in battle is limited to situations demanding their continuous movement. For the defense of a position, units capable of making a maximum use of the ground for shelter, and of delivering an overpowering concentration of fire against assaulting elements, are essential. In other words, as long as there is necessity in warfare of taking, occupying, and defending positions or areas, troops having capabilities similar to those of Infantry and Artillery are indispensable elements in an army. Even here nothing static in training, equipment, and organization is implied. If the attack is to be supported by strong mechanized units, inevitably development in infantry equipment must be toward inclusion of greater numbers of weapons capable of disabling the tank. This will entail parallel changes in organization, training, and transportation methods.

As would naturally be expected in a development of such recent origin, all models of combat vehicles so far produced tend to become obsolete as a result of continued progress in this branch of the mechanical sciences. The best tank of the World War is now hopelessly antiquated, and it is safe to predict that the best of today will be considered of small relative value a few years hence. Eventually a greater degree of stabilization will probably apply, and the effective life of each model will be substantially greater. Under present conditions, however, any attempt to maintain large units equipped with the latest and most efficient models of combat vehicles would entail the replacement of great amounts of equipment every few years. Manifestly the expense of such a procedure would be enormous.

Another factor complicating the problem of tank design is the continuous progress in producing bullets of extraordinary armor-piercing qualities. There has recently been developed a very high-velocity bullet (5,800 foot-seconds) which gives promise of ability to pierce at will any armor now carried on tanks and other fighting vehicles. If this development should prove capable of general application in all types of small arms, tank design and possibly even the whole theory of mechanization will necessarily undergo revolutionary changes.

In view of these considerations present progress toward mechanization must consist principally in the production of the best in pilot models; making precise prearrangements for speeding up their production in emergency; procuring annually sufficient numbers for thorough tactical test and for developing tactical doctrine of mechanized units; and indoctrinating the whole Army in methods of cooperation so as to capitalize fully the inherent capabilities of these machines and make allowances for their inherent weaknesses.

Our actual experience in the development of pilot models has been on the whole encouraging, though not without its bitter disappointments.

Immediately following the close of the World War the using services, then principally the Infantry, had much difficulty in settling upon the performance characteristics desired in a suitable Infantry tank. The influence of World War experience was still strong, and there was visualized a necessity for a group of machines of great size and power, as well as for numbers of smaller ones. Much study and discussion finally resulted in the production of two so-called medium tanks (22 tons) produced by the Ordnance Department. The hope was that this type would constitute an all-purpose Infantry tank, combining the essential characteristics of both the "heavy" and "light" tanks employed during the World War. There was also procured the first model of the Christie tank, a type featuring a convertible track and wheel chassis.

Until 1927 these were the only tanks of postwar design actually procured by the War Department, and their cost was extremely high because of the experimental nature of the project. During this period, however, the ideas of the using service reached a more definite focus, and attention was turned to the production of speedier vehicles of lesser tonnage.

Each experiment furnished valuable lessons, and succeeding models have gradually approached more nearly the type of vehicle considered necessary.

The first machine that gave sufficient promise to warrant more extended test than was possible in a pilot model was known as the T1E1. In 1928, 6 of these were procured, 4 of which were fighting vehicles and 2 cargo carriers. While infinitely better than the wartime models, they still fell short of what appeared to be minimum requirements, particularly in speed.

On the other hand, the Christie models, although invariably speedy, were generally most unreliable mechanically. Because of its speed this particular tank, probably more than any other, was responsible for awakening the Cavalry to the possibility of supplanting the horse in some of its units with fighting machines. Mechanical defects were partially overcome, and eventually it was determined to procure a reasonable quantity for thorough test. As I have already stated, seven of these were acquired during the past fiscal year and are being tested by both the Infantry and the Cavalry. Preliminary reports indicate that mechanical defects are still such as to bar the adoption of these machines as standard equipment, but hope exists that improved models may yet prove satisfactory. Current appropriations provide for the procurement of five additional machines of the convertible wheel and track type.

In armored cars our development has been more satisfactory, the engineering problems involved being generally less difficult of solution. Since 1928, 23 of these have been procured, the latest model, of which we now have 12, giving every indication of its suitability. Eight others are in process of procurement, and a greatly improved 4-wheel-drive type is being secured from commercial sources.

The total cost since 1920 of our experiments and procurements in fighting vehicles has been approximately $2,000,000. The results attained are not to be measured in the small number of modern machines now on hand, but principally in the tremendous progress we have made toward the production of a satisfactory pilot model.

It is obvious that for some years to come, at least, there cannot possibly be available in the initial stages of any great emergency large units completely equipped with the most modern types of fighting vehicles. But the Army's mission requires its readiness for defense under conditions of the moment. It must be prepared to utilize existing means at the same time that it strives to develop more efficient means to accomplish the defeat of the enemy. Far-reaching changes, such as that implied in mechanization, are subject to many delays, errors, setbacks, and discouragements. Commanders and staffs must, therefore, visualize early operations in which only a very few mechanized units will be on hand, and develop methods that will be effective in spite of this shortage, at the same time that tactics are evolved for the employment of machines when they have become available in quantity.

This brings up the important question of providing for the speediest possible production by commercial concerns of tanks and other types of armored vehicles in emergency. The prearrangements involved are intricate in nature. They cannot be pushed to ultimate completion until such time as various experimental types have reached a stage justifying their adoption as standard by the Army, and exact manufacturing specifications are prepared. Thereafter plans will necessarily be revised continuously to conform to changing conditions in industry and to further improvements in approved types. In spite of difficulties definite progress in this direction has been realized. The supply branches, working under the supervision of the Assistant Secretary of War, are making every practicable preparation. As a result it is now possible to predict that, in any emergency involving a major mobilization, tanks will reach quantity production in approximately 12 months. While this estimate may eventually be somewhat reduced, it is certain that an appreciable length of time will always be required for the conversion of manufacturing plants from peacetime activity to production of this character.

Exactly what effect progress in mechanization will have upon the number of men necessarily mobilized in a major emergency no person can possibly yet foretell. We know that the airplane and the tank of the World War necessitated the establishment of large supply, maintenance and repair organizations in their rear, and the ratio of required personnel to operating machines was extremely large. Complicated weapons and machinery, when applied to the battlefield, have tended to require a more highly trained personnel and the employment of more rather than fewer men.

General munitions development. - Allied to the subject of mechanization is that of general munitions development and improvement. In this work the same broad policies are observed as those I have heretofore described as applying to the training and organizational phases of military preparation. Under our system no effort is made to be prepared instantaneously for a major war. Rather, the aim is to accomplish in peace, and as economically as possible, all those preliminary tasks and investigations which will facilitate in emergency the efficient mobilization, training, and equipping of a citizen soldiery. In weapons and equipment we strive to foresee probable war needs, both as to type and quantity, and make necessary arrangements for prompt satisfaction of those needs. Experimentation, test, approval as to type, procurement of moderate quantities for training of personnel, and arrangements for emergency production are the sequential steps in every such program.

One of the most extraordinary recent advances in new equipment has been the production of a heavy bombing airplane of vastly increased efficiency. It represents the greatest single development of the past decade in performance characteristics of this type of plane. Capable of carrying 2,000 pounds of bombs and a crew of four men, it has a maximum speed of about 165 miles per hour and a cruising radius of some 500 miles. The significance of this achievement can be well appreciated when it is recalled that only two or three years ago a 100-mile cruising speed and a radius of action of 250 miles were considered satisfactory in heavy bombing planes. A few of these remarkable ships were secured during the year for exhaustive service tests, and more are now on order.

Improvements in antiaircraft fire-control instruments and guns have continued. The speed and accuracy with which antiaircraft fire can now be delivered are little short of amazing, and our pilot models in this type of equipment are at least the equal of any others now existing. There is real need, however, for funds to purchase reasonable quantities with which to arm existing units. While in certain types of weapons we are justified in postponing quantity production until after the beginning of any emergency, in airplanes and antiaircraft materiel we should, for obvious reasons, always have on hand moderate amounts for immediate defense, in the event of war, of vital industrial and population centers.

During the past year much effort has been centered on the semiautomatic shoulder arm. Tests have demonstrated the efficiency of the latest model produced, known as the Garand.[11] Attention is now being directed toward a redesign of the gun to permit the employment of the standard caliber of ammunition used in our Army. There is every reason to believe that this effort will be attended with complete success, and a number of these guns have been ordered for exhaustive service test.

In the aggregate there are hundreds of items in which our technical experts are developing models, the most efficient of their kind. These items vary in character from the delicate radio instruments for communication between fast-moving combat vehicles to heavy seacoast guns for harbor defense.

The Army's intense interest in these projects is not occasioned by a belief that any machine or weapon in itself is or can be the dominant factor in war. That factor is man himself. It is men who declare war, and it is men who must uphold on the battlefield the decision the nation has made. Armed conflict, which occurs when all other means of adjusting vital international differences have failed, continues until the determination of one contestant to carry on the struggle has been overcome.

The power that men exert in battle may be represented as the algebraic sum of a variety of elements, among which are leadership, numerical strength, morale, organization, mobility, logistic arrangements, individual skill and training, and the quality and quantity of weapons and equipment. Before engaging in decisive action each side makes every effort to be stronger in all these elements than is the other. If either opponent enjoys overwhelming superiority in any one of them and approximate equality in all the others, it will almost certainly be successful. Thus a tremendous and even decisive superiority may accrue to an army if its enemy has failed to recognize and to exploit the advantages offered by scientific achievements. It is, therefore, one of the fundamental responsibilities of peace-time military establishments to develop the utmost efficiency in weapons and equipment as well as in all other elements that go to make up combat power. While the most effective equipment does not necessarily make the most effective army, properly employed it enhances the power of an army to serve the State by which it is maintained....

AMALGAMATION OF THE WAR AND NAVY DEPARTMENTS[12]

Brought forward during the past session of Congress as a proposal for effecting great economies in governmental expenditures were bills to consolidate the War and Navy Departments into a single department of national defense. These bills, with one exception, specifically provided also for setting up a separate subdepartment of air, coordinate with and independent of the new subdepartments of War and Navy. Proponents of the scheme urged that the suggested arrangement would improve the efficiency of the national defense, and there were described in glowing terms the alleged advantages that would accrue to the United States. Disregarding alike the lessons of history and the advice and counsel of contemporaneous military and naval authorities, the authors of these assertions employed the most extravagant language in support of their personal Opinions. However, it was noticeable that no specific program nor any well-considered analysis of our situation was submitted in support of the claims advanced.

This particular proposal is a constantly recurring one and has been intensively studied, both in the War and Navy Departments of this country, as well as by soldiers and statesmen throughout the civilized world. Certain countries, because of peculiar factors in their defense problems, have organized separate air ministries, but in at least two of the principal world powers the arrangement has given rise to great dissatisfaction, and is still being made the subject of experimentation. Moreover, not a single power having a navy of major proportions has today a unified department of national defense. Invariably this particular project, attractive though it is in theory, has been rejected as inefficient, uneconomical, and uselessly cumbersome.

Effect of amalgamation on efficiency. - I invite your attention first to the effects of the proposed amalgamation upon efficiency, which means upon the fighting power of our defense establishments.

Administrative and organizational systems in the military and naval services can improve efficiency only as they facilitate preparatory activity for fighting, and make pos-

---

[11] Designed by John C. Garand, a civilian employee of the Army's arsenal at Springfield, Mass. In 1942, on the Bataan Peninsula, in the Philippine Islands, the Garand got its battle test. Douglas MacArthur sent the War Department a radiogram in its praise. The Garand is now in general issue to the service. (Frank C. Waldrop - 1942)

[12] Some day, when men are found who can grasp all the technical details of war in air, on land and on sea, this amalgam will occur. When will that be? Curiously enough, it was Douglas MacArthur who commanded the first really large amalgam of forces in our history. In 1942, after breaking through the Japanese siege of the Philippines to Australia, he was made commander of the "United Nations' Forces" in the "Southwest Pacific." It was a shadowy command and there were numerous signs that MacArthur was not overly impressed by the honor. But he undertook it with his usual vigor and strong will. It comprised land, sea and air areas not only of the United States but of our Australian, Dutch, and other Allies. It was, as this was written, still in process of organization. (Frank C. Waldrop - 1942)

sible a better control, maintenance, and employment of units actually engaged in operations. Proponents of the department of national defense make the claim that under it better coordination would obtain among the fighting services, and as a consequence thereof, that the efficiency of the whole would be greatly enhanced. Pointing out that the Army and Navy have, in war, the common basic mission of fighting, the argument is advanced that they should logically be combined into a single organization.

The superficiality of these generalizations is clearly revealed when investigation delves into the basic factors controlling organization and methods in the fighting services. The need or desirability for greater coordination and the possibilities of securing it, wherever required, by amalgamating higher organizations should be examined in the fields of tactics, strategy, and administration.

Necessity for greater tactical coordination. - The ultimate mission of the two services is, in a very true sense, the only element in common between fighting on the land and on the sea. The line between the Army and Navy fields of activity, namely, the coastline, is an insurmountable geographical obstacle for each. The Army never goes to sea except for transportation to a land objective, and then only under the adequate protection of the Navy. The possibilities of employing land armaments against naval forces are limited to repelling naval attacks against the shore line. On the other hand, naval equipment is manifestly useless in land operations except in those isolated instances where a battle takes place immediately upon the coast. It has no power of taking a defended land area or of holding an area against land attack. While the advent of aircraft has served to broaden the zone of possible contact between land and naval organizations, it has not affected the essential differences in their media of normal action.

Combined tactical operations between armies and navies have been exceedingly rare in military history. Usually they have involved a forced landing on hostile shores or cooperative action in the conduct of a siege. In the normal case the activities of the two services are widely separated. The Navy is concerned with the preservation of our sea communications and the destruction of those of the enemy. The Army's efforts are directed toward the defeat of the hostile land forces and the gaining of the national objectives laid down by the President and by the Congress.

So the line of demarcation between the Army and Navy is clear-cut and permanent in character. Existing organization has been developed through the years to enhance the power of each service to perform its fundamental mission in its own particular sphere of activity. Under any system of administration, separate commanders, specialized staffs, particularized training and individual supply arrangements must remain as essentials for each. Certainly, the necessity for tactical cooperation in isolated instances of combined action cannot be considered as a sufficient reason for revolutionary changes in higher organization. But in this connection I wish to point out that training in each service foresees and provides for these unusual situations, and through cooperative action everything possible is being done to assure the success of our arms in any such contingencies of the future.

Necessity for close tactical coordination between air units and land or sea forces. - Tactical operations by air are not separated from those on land and sea by any such definite line of demarcation as exists between those of the Army and the Navy. Superficial argument has been advanced that if it is in accordance with principles of sound organization to establish separate forces for fighting on land and sea respectively, it is equally in accordance with such principles to set up a separate organization for fighting in the air. While anyone would be bold indeed who would predict that conditions of the remote future will not be such as to make this contention substantially correct, the fact remains that at present the implied analogy is inapplicable.

It seems almost unnecessary to point out that modern armies and navies are just as dependent upon their air components as they are upon any of the other arms heretofore organized, trained and equipped for the performance of special and vital functions. The continuing tendency is for air units to assume a constantly increasing importance in the conduct of military operations. These supporting air units must be continuously trained, respectively, with the Army and Navy, and must constitute integral parts of the command with which they are operating. An army's need for aviation is not confined to any particular type of unit. Observation planes for the ground arms and for the high command; attack planes to operate against selected targets in the hostile position; bombardment planes to destroy or damage the enemy's services and installations; and pursuit planes to combat the hostile air force are all necessary to any army engaged in a major battle.

The necessity for this intimate association is as apparent from the viewpoint of the air units as from those operating on the surface of the earth. With its existing limitations the full value of the air force striking power is realized in the normal case only when its peculiar capabilities are employed in furtherance of the missions of other arms having the power of sustained and relatively permanent effort in action. In this way only can full advantage be taken of the temporary demoralization and material damage inflicted upon the enemy by our own air contingent.

Even when acting semi-independently the air force must look to the Army or Navy for assistance. The bases of air units operating at sea are component parts of the high seas fleet and are dependent upon that fleet for protection. On land, for the most effective employment of aircraft, operating fields must be established reasonably close to the objective to be attacked - a result that must be accomplished by and under the protection of land forces. When fields are situated too far back, even if the objective still lies within the radius of action of modern fast bombers, the planes are forced to spend too much time in the air in the performance of a single mission. Spectacular nonstop flights of the past few years covering distances of great length have undoubtedly created a false impression in the popular mind as to the vulnerability of remote objectives to air attack. In each of these ventures everything possible was discarded from the plane in favor of fuel capacity, whereas a military plane must carry a full complement of fighting equipment and must return to its base.

There will unquestionably arise in war, of course, special

situations in which it will be desirable to launch air attacks on objectives out of immediate reach of land or sea forces. When such need arises any available air unit, from either the Army or Navy, or both, would be fully capable of performing such a mission. The converse is not true. Air units trained entirely independently of the Army and Navy, and acting under an independent commander, would be of little if any use to the land or sea forces engaged in a particular battle. Teamwork is essential to tactical success. This comes only through combined training of all arms engaged in any tactical operation and through unity of command.

It must be quite obvious that amalgamation of higher organization and the setting up of an independent air force could not contribute to actual fighting efficiency but would in fact diminish it.

Necessity for greater strategical coordination. - The alleged necessity for increased coordination through amalgamation, then, must be visualized either in the realm of strategy and broad policy, or in the field of administration and logistics. The latter of these properly applies to the economies to be realized through consolidation, which I shall discuss under a subsequent heading.

The national strategy of any war - that is, the selection of national objectives and the determination of the general means and methods to be applied in attaining them, as well as the development of the broad policies applicable to the prosecution of war - are decisions that must be made by the head of the State, acting in conformity with the expressed will of the Congress. No single departmental head, no matter what his particular function or title, could or should be responsible for the formulation of such decisions. For example, in every war the United States has waged, the national objective to be attained has involved the Army in land attacks against areas held by the enemy. In every instance missions have been prescribed for the Navy that had in view the assisting and facilitating of the Army's efforts. Yet in no case could these missions and objectives have been properly prescribed by the Secretaries of War and Navy acting in unison or by a single supersecretary acting for both. The issues involved were so far-reaching in their effects, and so vital to the life of the Nation, that this phase of coordinating Army and Navy effort could not be delegated by the Commander in Chief to any subordinate authority. Any such attempt would not constitute delegation, but rather abdication.

It is important also to remember that a major war now constitutes a struggle between whole peoples; it is no longer simply a clash between professional armies and navies. The fighting forces are but the cutting edge of a great machine that is built up, maintained, and energized by the combined resources of an entire country. Thus there can be no true department of national defense except that combination of governmental activity that embraces the whole field of human endeavor. This we now have in an organization that places one man - the President - at the top of all executive departments and makes him at the same time the Commander in Chief of the fighting forces.

For the purpose of developing and making available to the Commander in Chief and the Federal Government a unified opinion from the fighting services concerning these questions of national import, the Joint Army and Navy Board was organized some years ago. It is not an executive or operating staff, but since it comprises the responsible military and naval authorities of the Government, it serves at one and the same time as an advisory staff to the President and as a coordinating body on those questions where concerted or cooperative action of the Army and Navy is indicated as advisable. The record shows that its efforts have been efficient and productive of good results, no small part of which is attributable to the fact that the board has constantly appreciated the unwisdom of interfering in any matter exclusively the concern of either service. Were it organized as a superstaff of a superdepartmental head, no such discrimination would be possible, and nothing but confusion, resentment, and inefficiency could result.

To sum up: Governmentally we have today, from the standpoint of national strategy and policy, the strongest possible organization for war. It seems almost incomprehensible that this organization, which incidentally has been the envy of soldiers, sailors, and statesmen abroad, should be tampered with in its major elements in favor of a highly speculative experiment.

Economy in consolidation. - The sponsors of amalgamation give as one of the principal advantages to be gained thereby economy in governmental expenditures. Broad and unjustified assumptions as to the savings to be effected through the proposed reorganization have been freely made. On the floor of the House it was asserted that $100,000,000, and even more, would be automatically cut from the annual defense budget, and this with a positive increase in combat effectiveness. Yet no one has been able to point out a single major line of operation or administration along which important economies could be effected without dangerously impairing efficiency. No definite schedule of activities in which savings could be accomplished has been brought forward. Small and trivial concrete instances of overlapping functions between the Army and Navy have been cited, and from these trivialities a general conclusion has been drawn that their elimination would result in great economies. On such a basis as this have rested the extravagant claims to which I have alluded.

Economy in separate air establishment. - I invite your attention first to some of the inevitable effects upon economy of setting up a separate air establishment.

In considering this project, one outstanding fact must be constantly borne in mind. Neither the Army nor the Navy can operate without strong aviation contingents. Therefore, were all military and naval aviation incorporated into a separate air establishment, it would still be necessary to attach permanently to the Army and Navy at least the quantities in aviation necessary to carry out essential supporting operations. This would mean that having unified an air service, it would immediately be physically redivided, substantially along the same lines as at present. Under similar conditions this has been largely the experience in France and in Great Britain, in each case giving rise to a great amount of inefficiency and dissatisfaction. The only alternative would be to set up, in effect, three air organizations instead of two as at present.

The existing aggregate strength in air facilities of the Army and Navy are not excessive, and the advocates of this bill do not so contend. We do not have too many aviators, airplanes, hangars, aircraft carriers, and flying fields. Economy claims, as far as the air force is concerned, are based upon the allegation that consolidation of the air components would eliminate any existing duplications in administrative and technical control. Analysis of the facts leads to the conclusion that whatever economies were effected would be more than overbalanced by increased expenditures.

It must be realized that neither of the air components now requires nor has elaborate overhead organizations. This economy arises from the fact that under existing conditions the aviation arms of the Army and Navy are not required to perform the overhead functions which they would be bound to incur as a separate organization. All the Army Air Corps purchases of nontechnical equipment, all its medical service, construction work, pay, supply, and commissary requirements are handled through the Regular Army establishments which exist for the purpose of specializing in this work and satisfying these particular needs of the combatant arms. But with the air force established as a single branch, independent of the Army and Navy, it would still have need for all these types of services. It would then necessarily acquire its own quartermaster corps, medical corps, construction corps, and so on, the result being a heavy increase in overhead expense. If an amalgamated air force continued to depend upon the Army and Navy for all these services, there would be little difference, except in increased complications as to administration, between the new organization and the one now existing.

To balance against all these increased expenses would be only the savings that could be accomplished through the elimination of some of the local maintenance facilities at those Army and Navy air stations located close to each other along the coast line, and possibly by combining into a single office some of the functions with respect to personnel, engineering, and research. Possibilities along these lines are not great because naval and military aviation are each highly specialized activities and complete consolidation of these specialized functions could not possibly be effected. Furthermore, the two services now work together in these matters as efficiently as they possibly could under a unified organization.

The extravagance of a separate air ministry has been well illustrated by the experience of Great Britain, in which country the dissatisfaction with their existing arrangement is constantly voiced. Admiral Lord Beatry, a prominent British naval commander of the war, and one of the eminent public men of that country today, in 1930 wrote as follows:

"I view with dismay the grim prospect of superimposing expenditure for the air service on the already heavy expenditures of the Army and the Navy. We are the highest-taxed country in the world and yet we commit ourselves to the extravagance of having three fighting services. Reduce them to two and we should save millions of public money, with greater efficiency, as in the United States."

Here we see the American method held up as the ideal one by a man whose ability and experience compel a serious consideration for his opinions. Thus experience and reason alike demonstrate that establishment of a separate Air Corps would not result in economy, but would actually have the contrary effect.

Economies in general administration and supply. - It remains then to examine the possibilities of effecting real administrative economies through the amalgamation into a single organization of the existing War and Navy Departments.

Under any kind of consolidation the Army and Navy would each require, in administrative organization and personnel, the establishments now maintained for this purpose. This statement is modified only by the observation that there might be effected some minor economies, which I will touch upon later, through a consolidation of certain small facilities and services. In an amalgamated organization there would be superimposed over existing staffs, and directly under the secretary of national defense, the large supergeneral staff of personal and technical assistants which that official would require in order to do any real coordinating and administering of the branches of his department. Anything less than this would in no sense be a "consolidation" of administrative functions and organizations; it would mean only the insertion of an additional echelon of command between the President and the Army and Navy. The uselessness and futility of such a procedure are obvious.

I need not dwell again on the need in both the Army and Navy for specialized services and systems in supply, training, administration, and maintenance. But I invite attention to the findings of two boards that have studied seriously, from the standpoint of economy as well as efficiency, the proposition of amalgamating War and Navy Departments into a single department of national defense. One of these met in the United States; the other in Great Britain.

In 1925 President Coolidge appointed a board to study the best means of developing and applying aircraft in national defense. This board was headed by the late Senator Dwight Morrow. Civilians predominated in the membership, the military members including only one retired major general and one retired admiral.

After a thorough and painstaking investigation the Morrow board reported adversely upon the proposition of forming a department of national defense. The following are extracts from the Morrow board report:

"…If the two present service organizations were consolidated under a single secretary, it would at once become necessary to create a supergeneral staff. No secretary of national defense could operate the two organizations without subsecretaries and technical advisers. This supergeneral staff, which would be in addition to the present service staffs, would necessarily comprise Army and Navy advisers who had been educated not only in their own particular schools but who would be required to have taken courses in the schools of the services to which they did not belong. It is difficult to see how any such superorganization would make for economy in time of peace or efficiency in time of war.

"…We do not recommend a Department of National Defense, either as comprising the Army and the Navy or as comprising three coordinate departments of Army, Navy, and Air. The disadvantages outweigh the advantages."

In 1922 the British Cabinet appointed a technical committee with a civilian as chairman, Sir Alfred Mond and later Lord Weir, to study the question of combining certain services common to the Army, the Navy, and the air force. The principal services were supply, transport, intelligence, education, medical, and chaplains. The end sought was to reduce the cost of the existing triplicate organization. The following quotation from the report of that board is pertinent:

"...After a preliminary discussion we were disposed to think that by the complete amalgamation of some of the common services, if practicable, substantial economies could be effected. After careful consideration we came to the conclusion that the amalgamation of the common services of the three departments is not advisable, and we doubt if any substantial economies would therein be effected."

Thus an American board and a British board have independently arrived at the same answer: "... We doubt if any substantial economies would therein be effected."

It cannot be too often repeated that procurement, supply, and similar services are maintained in military and naval establishments only as a means to an end - effectiveness in combat. Their organization, methods of procedure, training, and their physical location in each case conform to the special needs of the forces they serve and to the special functions they themselves perform. Wholesale consolidation of such organizations is entirely impracticable.

Procurement of supplies and equipment for the Army is under the supervision of the Assistant Secretary of War, and the effects of consolidation upon this activity are discussed in some detail in the annual report of that official.

The principal producing establishments of the Army and Navy are the arsenals and navy yards. In general these have no counterpart in commercial industry and each one has been established for experimentation in and the production of a particular class of technical equipment. To eliminate any of these necessary establishments will reduce by that amount the ability of the Army and Navy to develop modern weapons and equipment and to supply defense forces in the early stages of a war pending the conversion of necessary civilian plants. Even in the unthinkable event that Congress should determine that from the standpoint of materiel we are too well prepared for war, then it has the power to direct the discontinuance of those establishments deemed superfluous without trying an experimental and expensive consolidation of organization.

The savings to be made through consolidated purchasing of ordinary supplies are in many cases more apparent than real. Nevertheless, wherever such action is productive of real results it is invariably employed by cooperative action between the Army and Navy, either by purchasing one from the other or under combined contracts. During the past three years the money value of the items involved in these cooperative agreements has been approximately $18,500,000. I cite this fact only to demonstrate that there is nothing in the present organization which prevents a full realization of all possibilities for economy in consolidated procurement.

Admittedly there are some details of activities in which, viewed solely from a statistical standpoint, economies might be effected by consolidation. Where permanent hospitals are located in close proximity to each other, savings could be made in overhead by amalgamation. The same applies to recruiting and to a less extent to storage facilities. Even here the need for the particular service or thing affected would not be lessened. The only saving possible would be in local overhead. Moreover, these are all minor considerations and should not be taken as controlling factors in a problem as comprehensive and significant to the welfare of the United States as is this one.

Proponents of the amalgamation scheme constantly cite as an additional argument the undoubted trend toward consolidation noticeable in the modern business world. Such comparisons are apt to be misleading. Yet even here it may be remarked that the practice in many of these great industrial mergers has been to operate each subsidiary corporation as a unit. Separate purchasing, sales, advertising, production, technical, engineering, and administrative organizations have been frequently maintained. Business has recognized that there are limits to the saving to be realized through amalgamation and mergers. The following quotation from Charles Dawes' book, *The First Year of the Budget*, is apropos.

"Coordination of activities does not of necessity follow by grouping them in one building. There is a limit to the effectiveness of coordination by amalgamation into one organization. The United States Steel Co., for example, is well coordinated, and yet it could not so effectively function if its plants were physically consolidated. The reform of our Government business system must properly be through the coordination of existing and functioning agencies rather than by the substitution through legislation of new and central organizations to take their place."

Examples of consolidation. - The French nation has had a very recent practical experience in consolidation of the fighting services. In March of this year, when a new cabinet came into power, the Ministries of War, Navy, and Air were combined into a Ministry of National Defense. The plan was to accomplish the work of the consolidated ministry under three heads: Command, administration, and armament. Thus control of active operations, of administration and of supply were to be carefully coordinated throughout the three fighting services. General Weygand, who, during the war, was the brilliant chief of staff to Marshal Foch, and who now is a very popular figure in France, was named chief coordinator of defense in the hope that this would help rally public sentiment to the support of the project. In defending the proposed measure before the Chamber of Deputies, the Prime Minister advanced many of the same arguments that have been voiced in this country.

In spite of the propaganda and publicity that heralded the birth of the new ministry, and the care taken to place able and popular men in key positions, its existence was very brief. In June of this year the French Government returned to the old system, abandoning the amalgamation experiment. As the best means of effecting coordination in those administrative functions where such action is desirable, the French have now established a committee similar in form and function to our Joint Army and Navy Board.

In the organization of our Government under the Constitution, Congress, on August 7, 1789, established the Department of War, whose Secretary was charged with duties relative to land and naval forces, ships, and warlike stores of the United States, or such other matters respecting military or naval affairs as the President should assign to him. Here we have the exact counterpart of the department of defense now proposed. But in 1798 naval operations against France assumed such importance that Congress provided for a Navy Department, specifically severing it from all connection with the War Department, which separation has been maintained ever since. If the department of national defense were to be successful at all, it should surely have been so at the very beginning when there was no weight of tradition, habit, and experience against it to be overcome. Economy and efficiency were certainly no less sought after in those early troubled years than they are today. When Congress abandoned the unsuccessful attempt to administer the two great fighting services through a single department, it was but conforming to the lessons of history, to the accumulated experience of civilized peoples, and to the dictates of logic.

CONCLUSION

National security, by its very nature, is a matter that touches intimately the welfare of every element of our population. The public pays the premiums for this type of insurance, and has a right to know in unmistakable terms just what protection it is receiving in return.

In this report I have touched, upon American basic policy with respect to land defense, and have discussed various organizational, training, and administrative features of our Military Establishment. I have endeavored to indicate those directions in which our preparatory program does not appear entirely adequate to our defensive needs, and to point out the ultimate effects upon national security of further curtailment or radical changes in the essentials of that program.

Not all existing deficiencies pertain to numerical strength, but in each case correction involves, in varying degree, the element of cost. Appropriate remedies for some of them would require a considerable financial outlay. In these cases it is unquestionably the consensus of popular and official opinion that the country should continue to assume, during the period of the present economic stringency, whatever additional risk to national security is inherent in these shortages. Regardless of any person's individual convictions concerning the wisdom of such a policy, it must be loyally and whole-heartedly accepted by every public servant.

But there is nothing of jingoism in the assertion that this country cannot afford to entrust its ultimate security to anything other than its own readiness to protect itself. Such a readiness requires adequate organized strength; a leaven of partially trained citizens; carefully developed mobilization plans, both as to manpower and materiel; and real efficiency and splendid morale in existing military units. The program briefly summarized below represents, in my opinion and in that of the General Staff, the minimum scale on which our military preparation should be authorized.

For the present:

There should be no diminution in the scope of activity, the scale of training, or the strength of any civilian component or of the Regular Army.

The laws governing promotion in the Regular Army should be revised so as to provide a reasonable rate of advancement. Such a rate should insure that every man entering the service as a lieutenant at an average age will, provided he meets all requirements established for retention of his commission, reach the grade of colonel between the ages of 50 and 52.

All types of preparation to meet the Army's munition requirements in emergency should continue on their present basis.

The following should be accomplished the moment Congress considers the state of the Federal finances will permit:

Pay laws of the Military Establishment should be revised so as to bring the schedule into line with the cost of maintaining a reasonable and appropriate living standard.

The strength of the Regular Army should be increased to 14,000 officers and 165,000 enlisted men.

Additional funds should be provided for the accumulation of reasonable amounts of specialized equipment, particularly for antiaircraft units, both in the Regular Army and the National Guard.

Moderate increases in the amounts provided for the training of the Officers' Reserve Corps should be authorized.

In closing I repeat that the defensive system established by the national defense act is, in its broad essentials, almost ideally suited to the needs of this country. The aim of that law is national security, and it authorizes no type of preparation that exceeds the reasonable requirements of this purpose. But under the reduced appropriations of recent years the degree of preparedness that we have been able to attain does not approach in any particular that prescribed as necessary by Congress in 1920. It even falls far short of that visualized in the modified program repeatedly recommended to Congress by the War Department since 1925.

The Army's numerical weakness has in no wise lessened the weight of the responsibilities it is forced to carry. The soldier's duty is to produce the maximum of national security with the means made available by his Government, and when he considers the means to be inadequate he must redouble his efforts to enhance their quality and effectiveness. This spirit I believe to be implicit in our Military Establishment, and within the limitations imposed by existing legal authorization, all components of the American Army have striven, and will continue to strive, faithfully and efficiently to perform the missions assigned them by the Congress of the United States.

EXCERPTS FROM THE ANNUAL REPORT OF THE CHIEF OF STAFF, UNITED STATES ARMY FISCAL YEAR JULY 1, 1932 - JUNE 30, 1933[13]

Review of the Army's accomplishments during the fiscal year just ended and analysis of the major problems now confronting it reveal the marked degree in which they have been influenced by the extraordinary social and economic conditions prevailing throughout the period. For the Military Establishment the year has been a notable one, but the reasons for its unusual significance involve events and conditions of universal import rather than any particular circumstance of military activity or of purely technical interest.

---

[13] It was in this period, one hardly need point out, that Germany emerged as a power bent on conquest, peaceful or otherwise - but bent on conquest. (Frank C. Waldrop - 1942)

The history of American development during the past 3 years will concern itself principally with the origin, progress, and effects of acute economic disorders that have included all nations in their grip. It will comprise a story of growing stagnation in business, alarming increases in privation and hardship, dwindling public revenue mounting tax rates, and sharp contractions in customary governmental activities and expenditures. But probably as the most significant development of the period there will be recorded the initiation, in the spring of 1933, of a powerful governmental offensive against the forces of depression, as an incident of which we have witnessed the entry of Federal agencies and public funds into entirely new fields of activity.

Time and again national leaders have likened existing conditions to those of war. This comparison has been employed to illustrate the extent to which every phase of our national life has been affected by the economic depression, and to indicate the solidarity of national effort that must be attained in order to bring about revival of business activity. In this way also public attention has been focused upon the necessity for unprecedented measures in attacking the Nation's critical and pressing problems.

In this difficult struggle the Army of the United States has been affected in many ways. Sharp reductions have been made in the sums normally appropriated for its maintenance, while the Commander in Chief has assigned to it unique responsibilities in his coordinated campaign for economic rehabilitation. As a consequence, the Army, in its efforts to meet the requirements of basic defense missions, has faced the double difficulty of reducing costs on the one hand and at the same time executing unusual and exacting duties on the other.

CIVILIAN CONSERVATION CORPS

As an important feature of his recovery program, the President approved, on March 31, 1933, an act of Congress authorizing the establishment of a Civilian Conservation Corps and its utilization on reforestation and other needful work throughout the country. The law aimed at an immediate reduction of unemployment and privation throughout the country, making its objectives humanitarian as well as utilitarian in character. The strength of the conservation army was initially fixed at 250,000, but was later increased to 300,000.

Under the plan first outlined by the President, the Department of Labor was made responsible for selecting and certifying recruits, and the War Department was charged with receiving certified applicants and organizing them into units. The Departments of Interior and Agriculture were placed in control of all other functions, including those of establishing and maintaining work camps and supervising forestry operations. A Director of Emergency Conservation Work was installed as the supervisory authority over the whole project.

Under this directive the War Department's mission was definitely limited, both as to scope and duration. After receiving and enrolling the men and giving them the usual immunizing treatments against disease, the Army was to initiate records, issue necessary clothing and equipment, and organize companies of approximately 200 men each. Thereafter, the Army's duty was to transport each unit to the railhead nearest its particular forest project and there turn it over to the proper Agriculture or Interior officials. The plan of the Director thus contemplated the earliest possible termination of military contact with the project.[14] This purpose met with the full approval of the War Department since it promised a minimum of interference with activities vital to proper discharge of the continuing responsibilities placed upon the Army by the National Defense Act.

Because of its experience in organizational work, the Army encountered no unusual difficulty in complying with every requirement of the restricted mission assigned it. But in some other phases of the project difficulties began to appear almost immediately and on April 10 the President made radical changes in the original plan. By that time it had become apparent to him that the establishment and administration of hundreds of camps and cantonments in our national parks and forests represented a task of greater magnitude than could be handled effectively by agencies not specifically trained and equipped for such work. Thereupon the Army was called upon to assume, under the general supervision of the Director, complete and permanent control of the Civilian Conservation Corps project, excepting only the functions of selecting recruits and of supervising technical work in the forests. The immediate objective of the War Department became the assembly of approximately 300,000 men - more than were enlisted during the Spanish-American War - establishing them in a series of small camps in various and often isolated regions throughout the United States, and making therein adequate provision for health, welfare, and maintenance.

An obvious need under this enlarged mission was for a considerable number of officers to administer the 1,450 camps eventually authorized, and to supervise the territorial districts into which the camps were grouped. To supplement available Regular personnel, the President authorized the use of a limited number of officers from the junior grades of the Reserve Corps. Small contingents were also provided by the Navy and the Marine Corps.

The plan of the War Department for assignment of personnel, assembly of supplies and equipment, and establishment of maintenance systems was worked out to conform to the rate at which the Department of Labor certified applicants for enrollment. For the first month of the undertaking this rate, due to a variety of causes, was only about 1,530 per day. During that period progress was impeded many factors over which the War Department had no control. Comparatively few work projects had yet been approved in the eastern and central portions of the country, in which regions enrollments were particularly heavy; money was allotted for short periods only; and the War Department's authority in the conduct of detailed operations was too narrowly circumscribed to permit of speed in their execution.

Early in May the War Department submitted to the Director of Emergency Conservation Work a chart forecasting results

---

[14] One of the prime blunders of the New Deal was stubborn refusal to give the CCC military training. If it had done so we could have gone into this war with an extraordinary corps of noncommissioned officers skilled in weapons and command. (Frank C. Waldrop - 1942)

under the conditions then prevailing. It showed that only about 115,000 men would be located in some 375 camps by July 1. Each succeeding day made more evident the accuracy of this estimate and the certainty that final accomplishment would fall far short of the President's announced objective.

Consequently, on May 10 the Director asked the War Department to submit a plan under which the entire Conservation Corps could be established in forest camps by July 1. Since organizational work and immunizing treatments at reconditioning camps and the transportation of units to final destination involved a minimum of 3 weeks, such a schedule meant that the last recruit would have to enter a reconditioning camp by June 7.

Beginning on May 12, an average of about 8,500 had to be enrolled daily. As a corollary to this, reconditioning camps had to be rapidly evacuated to provide space for incoming recruits. This, in turn, required speedy selection and preparation of all forest camps for reception of units. Clearly, the attainment of these objectives required the immediate application of emergency methods.

The General Staff, having anticipated the possibility of an Executive decision speeding up the tempo of the mobilization, was ready with a practicable program. This plan called for the prompt approval by the Director of about 300 additional work projects, the immediate transfer of necessary funds to the War Department, the removal of certain restrictions applying to purchase of supplies, and the issue to the Department of Labor of appropriate instructions concerning selection of applicants. Provided these things were done, the War Department stood ready to guarantee success. Recommendations to this effect were submitted on May 12 and were promptly approved by the President. From that moment the Army started moving ahead at full speed. Defense functions were temporarily relegated to second place and in every line of activity priority was given to the execution of this emergency task.

To make available the maximum number of Regular officers there was ordered an early graduation at practically all service schools and a considerable withdrawal of commissioned personnel from all kinds of normal duty. Revised instructions were communicated to field commanders, to each of whom was accorded the requisite authority to carry out successfully his portion of the whole mission.

On July 1, the War Department reported that the mobilization had been completed on schedule. This accomplishment was widely heralded in the public press. Within 7 weeks after approval of the Army's operational plan, the assembly of the Conservation Corps had been completed and its units had been transported, often over great distances, to 1,315 camps, distributed throughout the country. With few exceptions each camp comprised 2 Regular officers, 1 Reserve officer, 4 enlisted men of the Regular Army, and about 200 men of the Civilian Conservation Corps. A total of 3,109 officers of the Regular Army, 532 officers of the Regular Navy and the Marine Corps, and 1,774 Reserve officers were on duty in the camps.

While the work camps were being established, the Inspector General of the Army was directed to make a thorough inspection of every feature of the Civilian Conservation Corps operating under the jurisdiction of the War Department. Reports covering almost every detail of administration, sanitation, morale, and general conditions of the camps are now on file and are available for official use by any agency of the Government.

These and other reports indicate that the Conservation Corps men are, on the whole, satisfied with their living conditions and appreciate the opportunity for self-support given them by the Government. In most places the men are sheltered in tents, which are floored. Medical and hospital facilities are satisfactory. Athletic equipment, costing less than $1 a man, is available. Traveling libraries and daily periodicals are furnished each camp and the men are enabled to attend religious services conducted by ministers of their respective faiths. Appropriate educational and vocational training programs have been established and are functioning with good effect.

Although administered by military men, the Conservation Corps constitutes a purely civil organization. Officers have no definite authority to compel individual obedience to regulations promulgated for the collective good. Nevertheless, disciplinary troubles have been insignificant, largely due to the high order of leadership displayed by the officers in immediate charge and to the cooperative attitude of the men themselves.

Every phase of the Army's responsibility in the Civilian Conservation Corps program has been discharged expeditiously, economically, and efficiently. Not a single man certified for enrollment by the Department of Labor or the Veterans' Administration has been delayed, through failure of any agency of the War Department, in reaching his final destination. In spite of the need for haste, no measure has been adopted that has exposed individuals of the Civilian Conservation Corps to unnecessary hardship or avoidable discomfort. The enormous quantities of supplies required have been procured at minimum cost and the needs of the corps in all types of equipment have been foreseen and promptly satisfied. Cooperation among the several departments of the Government concerned and with the transportation systems of the country has been exemplary.

COMPARISON OF CONSERVATION CORPS WITH MOBILIZATION AND RECRUITING IN 1917

These results are in striking contrast to those attending the recruiting campaign carried on during the early months of America's participation in the World War. Upon the declaration of war by Congress on April 6, 1917, voluntary recruiting was initiated throughout the United States. By June 7 of that year the number of volunteers accepted by the Army approximated the strength of the Civilian Conservation Corps attained during the same period in 1933. These figures represent almost the only similarity between the two projects.

In 1917, our organization effort was characterized by excessive cost, confusion, delay, and inefficiency. Recruits accepted were often compelled to undergo considerable periods of comparative hardship, without adequate food and shelter. Reserve stocks of supplies were almost nonexistent. Such equipment as was available could not be promptly distributed and organizational and training work was consequently delayed. Commands were lacking in qualified leaders, both commissioned and noncommissioned, and disciplinary troubles were far too prevalent. There existed no carefully devised plan for the procurement of supplies, with the result that most purchases had to be made on an emergency basis and at excessive cost.

The causes for the contrasting results in these two mobilization efforts are readily discernible. The first and most important is our more favorable position now with regard to the number and efficiency of Regular officers. Experienced leadership and executive ability in all echelons are vital to efficient administration of extensive projects. In this respect the assets of the Regular Army for this latest mobilization were more than double those of 1917, and the War Department was able to throw almost instantly a force of about 3,000 well-trained leaders into this emergency task. As previously indicated, this number of officers was made available by ordering early graduation at schools, by stripping Regular units, and by withdrawing large numbers of Regular instructors from the Reserve Officers' Training Corps, the Officers' Reserve Corps, and the National Guard.

The Officers' Reserve Corps is another great asset that was almost wholly lacking in 1917. Training for this component habitually includes instruction in duties pertaining to mobilization and organization, with the result that Reserve officers were well equipped to supply necessary reinforcements to the Regular establishment. While only some 1,800 of them were on Civilian Conservation Corps duty at the close of the fiscal year, the fine service they have rendered gives conclusive evidence of the advantages accruing to the United States through possession of a sizable pool of trained Reserve officers.

Reserve supplies and equipment played an important part in the success of the mobilization. Although existing stocks are not properly balanced and lack certain items that would be vitally essential in a military emergency, they contain much greater quantities of clothing and ordinary equipage than was the case in 1917. As a result it was possible to issue to the Civilian Conservation Corps necessary items of individual and organizational equipment without going through the time-consuming processes of manufacture and purchase.

Sound methods and policies applying to every phase of mobilization, which have been developed since the World War and inculcated in the officers of all components of the Army, were likewise of inestimable value in organizing the Civilian Conservation Corps. Plans prepared for the emergency of war were applicable, after rapid revision in some of their details, to most of the problems that arose. This was particularly true in the assembly and enrolling of personnel and in the procurement and issue of supplies. These plans, executed by officers thoroughly familiar with their contents and objectives, operated with maximum efficiency and minimum cost to the Government.

But any comparison between the Civilian Conservation Corps project and a mobilization incident to an emergency of war must recognize one vital and far-reaching difference in the requirements of the two situations. In war, the Regular Army would, coincidentally with the execution of mobilization plans, be compelled to concentrate many of its skeletonized units and fill them up with officers and men for prompt employment in battle. In the current mobilization,

this dual demand upon its personnel and facilities has not existed, and far from filling up vacancies in Regular units, many organizations have been almost dismantled by the detail of their officers, noncommissioned officers and specialists to the Civilian Conservation Corps camps.

To epitomize the military lessons of the 1933 mobilization, it has given renewed evidence of the value of systematic preparation for emergency, including the maintenance of trained personnel and suitable supplies and the development of plans and policies applicable to a mobilization. Particularly has it served to emphasize again the vital need for a strong corps of professional officers and for an efficient body of commissioned Reserves.

EFFECT OF THE CIVILIAN CONSERVATION CORPS PROJECT UPON ARMY ACTIVITY AND READINESS FOR EMERGENCY

Employment of the Army on tasks incident to the emergencies of peace, no matter how great their importance to the general welfare, cannot justify continued neglect of fundamental defense missions. As an executive agency the primary duty of the War Department is to provide the maximum possible degree of national security under the general policies of and with the means made available by Congress.

It is true that certain benefits have accrued to the Army through its administration of the Civilian Conservation Corps project. Junior officers in particular have obtained valuable training in mobilization processes and in leadership. Staffs have been enabled to test in a practical way certain phases of theoretical plans. The procurement services have been afforded opportunity to meet and solve many problems incident to emergency expansion. But, far outweighing these specific advantages, there have resulted disadvantages which, if long continued, will have most damaging effects upon the efficiency of the Army and its readiness for emergency. Some of these are even now apparent.

Manifestly the detail of some 3,000 Regular officers to the Civilian Conservation Corps project could not be accomplished without sharp curtailment in normal activities. Among those most seriously affected are education of Regular officers, instruction of the National Guard, the Organized Reserve, and the Reserve Officers' Training Corps, and training and general efficiency of Regular Army units. Each of these activities is essential to a reasonable readiness to meet the requirements of military emergencies.

Our military school system is unsurpassed in excellence anywhere in the world. It has demonstrated its value in peace and on the battlefields of the World War. It is a laboratory in which the effects of new developments upon accepted doctrine are analyzed and interpreted and is the principal channel through which the results of this process flow to the Army of the United States. The military fitness of our officer corps, and therefore of the whole Army of the United States, depends in marked degree upon the successful and continuous functioning of the school system. For the great majority of officers there is no substitute in peace for the training and professional education received therein.

For years the Regular Army has experienced difficulty, occasioned by shortage of officers, in discharging satisfactorily some of its basic responsibilities. Because of this shortage a reduction in the percentage authorized for school detail finally became mandatory, and Chiefs of Arms and Services are now permitted to allot as students at special service schools only 4 per cent of their commissioned personnel as compared to 8 per cent heretofore obtaining. Further curtailment in this direction would have the most serious and lasting effects upon the efficiency of all components of the Army. Nothing short of a major emergency could justify even a single year's suspension of the school system's operation.

About 1,600 officers of the Regular Army are normally assigned to instructional work with the civilian components and with the Reserve Officers' Training Corps. It is scarcely necessary to dwell upon the importance of this work. An untrained National Guard and Officers' Reserve Corps would be entirely incapable of carrying out their emergency mobilization tasks. Continuous professional instruction of these elements is vital to the success of the system prescribed in the National Defense Act. Without such professional instruction their support by Federal appropriations descends to the level of a wasteful and futile subsidy.

Of the 1,600 Regular officers on civilian instruction duty, about 460 are normally assigned to the Officers' Reserve Corps, in which some 85,000 men carry active commissions. Another 460 are on duty as inspector-instructors of the National Guard, which comprises roughly some 14,000 officers and 175,000 enlisted men; 680 are allotted to the Reserve Officers' Training Corps for a student strength of 114,000.

Withdrawals to meet the requirements of the Civilian Conservation Corps reduced these assignments to an approximate total of 700 officers. This number is entirely inadequate to provide necessary instruction for civilian components and to insure their readiness for employment in a major mobilization. Normal allotments of instructors will be urgently required with the opening of the 1933-34 indoor training season.

An equally if not more serious aspect of the current shortage in officers for military assignments involves the combat elements of the Regular Army. Even in normal times we are unable, under the 12,000 officer set-up, to meet the full peace-time requirements of these units. During the past few years this shortage has averaged about 1,500. This already unfavorable situation became particularly acute with the detail of hundreds of officers to the Civilian Conservation Corps.

In many cases there is but one officer on duty with an entire battalion, and organizations are further crippled by the detail of some of their most experienced noncommissioned officers to Civilian Conservation Corps duty. Illustrative of the general condition is that of the First Division, located principally in the Second Corps Area. In the eastern portion of the United States this unit constitutes the only one of reasonable size that is fairly well concentrated for prompt employment in emergency. Its peace-time authorization in captains and lieutenants is 403, but today only 127, including all those serving in staff capacities, are actually on duty with it. In the 26th Infantry of that division only 7 company officers have been present for duty since the mobilization of the Civilian Conservation Corps.

This lack of officers has brought Regular Army training in the continental United States to a virtual standstill, and has almost destroyed the readiness of units for immediate and effective employment on emergency duty. Such a condition is the very antithesis of that which should prevail and constitutes a matter of the most serious import to national defense. Its prompt correction is mandatory if Regular Army units are to regain their ability to respond effectively, in any crisis to orders of the President.

The urgent need for Regular officers in these various categories of military activities led the War Department to recommend the assignment of additional Reserves to duty with the Conservation Corps, provided that project is maintained on the present scale through the coming winter. This recommendation was approved shortly after the close of the fiscal year, and subject to the proviso just stated, will be carried out so far as is necessary to meet the more acute aspects of the existing situation.

Beneficial results of other kinds will accompany the application of such a policy. Thousands of Reserve officers have been without employment and have volunteered for duty in the work camps. A moderate increase in the numbers utilized will involve a relatively insignificant addition to the total cost of the project. It will tend to relieve distress among the dependents of a body of men of proved patriotism and of demonstrated ability for this type of work. Moreover, since there is normally little opportunity for Reserve officers to obtain training in practical leadership, experience in Civilian Conservation Corps camps will materially increase their value to the Government. But of transcendent importance - every one of them so employed will release a Regular officer for reassignment to activities that are vital to military effectiveness.

As indicated in a prior paragraph there have been certain directions in which the Army has benefitted through its administration of the Civilian Conservation Corps. But there is one other item, aside from the vital matter of officers, in which Army efficiency and readiness have been materially impaired. This concerns the detail of some thousands of enlisted men to work camps. While the effects of their temporary loss are in no wise comparable to those resulting from the absence of commissioned personnel, yet combat units are habitually so sadly depleted in strength that not a single man can be spared without further impairing efficiency and readiness for emergency service. It is appreciated that their employment in this great project of the President's is essential, and will continue to be so to the date of its completion. But no effort should be spared to insure their prompt return to their respective organizations as rapidly as they can be relieved from current tasks.

The success of the Civilian Conservation Corps mobilization has attracted attention to the American Army's readiness to perform important tasks incident to emergencies of peace. Our people have always counted with complete confidence upon the loyalty, devotion to duty, and professional ability of the Army, and upon its efficiency in coping with problems incident to war, to earthquake, fire, flood, and drought. Its latest accomplishment has demonstrated its value as an agency splendidly trained and organized to meet and solve, upon a moment's notice, administrative and organizational problems of nation-wide scope and magnitude.

The Four-Army Organization[15]

The four-army organization, initiated during the early months of the year just past, seeks to insure the prompt and unified employment in emergency of existing elements of the Army of the United States, as well as the rapid integration and preparation of additional forces.

Under the systems employed in many foreign countries military training is so nearly universal, and prearrangement for mobilization is so perfected that their full military power may be brought to bear at the decisive point within a matter of days or weeks. In our own case geographical isolation has served to lessen the necessity for such a degree of preparedness. The American defense system definitely recognizes that a period of some months must intervene between any declaration of war and the time when fully developed citizen armies could be ready for employment.

If attacked, we would necessarily commit our forces to action by increments, the better-prepared elements carrying the full burden of initial operations. Consequently, peacetime preparation must assure readiness for the tactical employment of existing forces as well as for efficient conduct of a mobilization. The amended National Defense Act of 1920 was devised with this end in view.

As that act marked a new departure in military preparation, the War Department at once encountered a number of new and difficult problems. Among them were the initiation of a sound organization for the National Guard, the formation of an adequate Officers' Reserve Corps, the establishment of the Reserve Officers' Training Corps and the Citizens' Military Training Camps, and the development and execution of training and administrative programs for all components. A substantial degree of progress in all these and the development of basic methods applicable to general mobilization were necessary before there could be undertaken practical preparation in the field of higher tactical organization.

The principal agencies of the War Department for executing the details of mobilization plans, and for supervising normal peace-time activities of all components, are the nine corps area commands, which were constituted soon after the approval of the National Defense Act.

The Four-Army Plan

For strategical military purposes the United States is divided into four Army areas, and for military administrative purposes into nine corps areas:

First Army

First Corps Area: Headquarters at Boston, Mass. - Maine, New Hampshire, Vermont, Massachusetts, Rhode Island, Connecticut

Second Corps Area: Headquarters at Governors Island, N. Y. - New Jersey, Delaware, New York

Third Corps Area: Headquarters at Baltimore, Md. - Pennsylvania, Maryland, Virginia, District of Columbia

Second Army

Fifth Corps Area: Headquarters at Fort Hayes, Columbus, Ohio - Ohio, West Virginia, Indiana, Kentucky

Sixth Corps Area: Headquarters at Chicago, Ill. - Illinois, Michigan, Wisconsin

Third Army

Fourth Corps Area: Headquarters at Atlanta, Ga. - North Carolina, South Carolina, Georgia, Florida, Alabama, Tennessee, Mississippi, Louisiana

Eighth Corps Area: Headquarters at Fort Sam Houston, San Antonio, Tex. - Texas, Oklahoma, Colorado, New Mexico, Arizona (in part)

Fourth Army

Seventh Corps Area: Headquarters at Omaha, Nebr. - Missouri, Kansas, Arkansas, Iowa, Nebraska, Minnesota, North Dakota, South Dakota

Ninth Corps Area: Headquarters at Presidio of San Francisco, Calif. - Washington, Oregon, Idaho, Montana, Wyoming, Utah, Nevada, Arizona (in part), California; Alaska (attached)

They are territorial and administrative rather than tactical commands and until this year there had been established no organizational framework through which troops mobilized in emergency could be assembled, maneuvered, and operated as a unit against an aggressor. Without such a network of command and staff, properly echeloned between the War Department and fighting units, we were little better prepared, except in the matter of stronger and more efficient civilian components and greater prearrangement in the field of mobilization, than we were in 1917. Writing some years after the World War of our situation at the time of our entry into that conflict, General Pershing said:

"It was evident that considerable time must elapse before we could actually have more than a nominal force in the battle lines. Our very small Regular Army was scattered in weak detachments over the country and in our outlying possessions. There were no complete and permanent units larger than regiments, and even these were not suitably organized and equipped for major operations."

It was to effect as great an improvement as practicable in this phase of our military preparation that the four-army plan was formulated and its execution initiated.

Briefly, in this organization every existing unit is assigned to a definite place in a larger tactical organization, and each is provided with a commander and the principal elements of his staff. This process applies to all echelons from the lowest to the highest, and to all components of the Army of the United States, with the result that it establishes a direct chain of tactical control from the smallest unit to the Commander in Chief himself. The purely military organization heads up in the commander of the group of armies thus constituted, who is necessarily the Chief of Staff. The num-

---

[15] The reorganization of our old army system into this four-army plan can best be compared to re-wiring the telephone exchange of a city the size of Chicago. Today, the United States is guarded by four armies according to that plan. Our expeditionary forces are over and above these. (Frank C. Waldrop - 1942)

ber of armies was fixed by the desirability of assigning one to each of the natural defensive regions in continental United States, of which there are four.

To initiate organization and planning activity in the several Army commands instructions were communicated to corps area commanders on August 9, 1932, which contained the following:

"The purposes of armies are:

(a.) To provide appropriate agencies to complete the development of war plans prepared by the War Department General Staff.

(b.) To provide commanders and staffs for higher units, prepared to take the field and execute the plans prepared by them.

(c.) To provide agencies for the conduct of command post and other suitable peace-time training exercises.

(d.) To provide as a preliminary step to any general mobilization an adequate force, within the minimum of time with the maximum of training, sufficient to protect any general mobilization that may be necessary.

(e.) To provide a force sufficient to handle all emergencies short of a general mobilization.

2. The three field Army areas as flow constituted are hereby abolished, and in lieu thereof, under the provisions of section 3, National Defense Act, as amended by act of June 4, 1920, and by direction of the President, four armies are hereby established. In addition to his other duties, the Chief of Staff is hereby placed in command of this Army group, composed of four armies.

3. *Composition of field headquarters and of armies.* - The composition of field headquarters and of armies will be *as* follows:

(1) General headquarters.
   Commanding General, General Headquarters, The Chief of Staff.
   Staff: War Plans Division, General Staff, and such other personnel from the War Department General Staff as may be designated.

(2) Army headquarters:
   Army Commanders: The senior corps area commander assigned to each army.
   Staff: The Army Commander's Corps Area Chief of Staff and such other members of his corps area as he may designate.

First Army. - First, Second, and Third Corps Areas. Its mission deals with the North Atlantic and the northeastern frontier.

Second Army. - Fifth and Sixth Corps Areas. Its mission deals with the strategical area of the Great Lakes and the central northern frontier.

Third Army. - Fourth and Eighth Corps Areas. Its mission deals with the region of the Gulf of Mexico and the southern frontier.

Fourth Army. - Seventh and Ninth Corps Areas. Its mission deals with the Pacific coast.

On October 22, 1932, these instructions were supplemented by a letter to Army commanders, from which the following is quoted:

"The primary objective underlying the formation and development of the Army group is the welding of existing military units into an integrated tactical machine capable of instantaneous response to the orders of the President. The importance of this project as a step toward increasing military readiness for emergency can scarcely be overestimated.

"Heretofore the War Department has never been linked to fighting elements by that network of command and staff necessary to permit the unified tactical functioning of the American Army. As a consequence the availability of the military establishment for combat service has always been measured in fractions of its numerical strength.

"In emergencies of the past, the War Department has invariably been compelled to relinquish to one or more virtually independent field commanders its functions in the control of operations, while the Department itself has been overwhelmed with matters relating to organization, administration, supply and other features of mobilization. This fundamental error has always required improvisation and extemporization in filling the organizational void lying between the War Department and fighting units. It has compelled needless delay in the development of sizable military formations. It has resulted in an essentially dual control of the Army, from which have sprung inefficiency and lack of coordination.

"The establishment of the skeletonized Army group on a satisfactory basis, and the decentralization to each Army commander of responsibility for local organization and planning tasks in emergency, will promote practicality in peacetime preparation. The existence of an adequate system of command and staff will insure that immediately available strength is equal to numerical strength. The Chief of Staff, in war, will be enabled to center his attention upon the vital functions of operating and commanding field forces. Moreover, successful accomplishment of this project will link, in the most effective manner, military activities in the zone of the interior to those in the theater of operations.

"The organizational, planning, training, and preparatory tasks inherent in a project such as herein contemplated devolve mainly upon the several Army commanders. The whole success of the plan depends in the final analysis upon their vision, energy and resourcefulness. They will necessarily depend upon the means now available within their respective commands. On the other hand, the greatest latitude and initiative possible will be accorded, and interference by the War Department will be held to the practical minimum." ...

APPROPRIATIONS FOR ARMY MAINTENANCE

The annual appropriation act for the fiscal year 1934, approved March 4, 1933, carried a total of about $270,000,000 for military activities of the Army. This sum was approximately $65,000,000 less than that made available for similar purposes for the fiscal year 1932, and, aside from all savings effected by reason of lowered commodity prices and officers' pay cuts, provided for sharp contractions in activities essential to permanent efficiency of the Army. Among the curtailments required were almost complete cessation in procurement of motor vehicles, practical suspension of mechanization and similar programs, reduction in airplane replacement, and marked contraction in target practice and other phases of practical training, particularly for the Regular Army.

As finally passed, the bill unquestionably represented in the opinion of Congress, the minimum amounts necessary for a single year's maintenance, on a depression basis, of the country's Military Establishment. The inescapable dangers in permitting deterioration in essential materiel and in suspending prosecution of necessary development programs were pointed out by the Department and were clearly understood by the committees of Congress. But the crying need for reduction in Federal expenditures impelled that body to make the most extensive cuts it believed prudent under its constitutional duty of providing for the national defense and of raising and maintaining armies.

The adjustments demanded as a result of this shrunken appropriation were serious ones, but the War Department was preparing a plan to put them into effect with the least possible damage to national defense when, on March 28, information was received from the Bureau of the Budget that an additional cut of about $80,000,000 would have to be made.

This was a stunning blow to national defense.[16]

The whole matter of progressive reductions in the sums made available for the Military Establishment has become so serious as to warrant here a statistical review of the successive steps taken in this direction during the past several years.

The last fiscal year in which appropriations for the support of the Military Establishment were comparatively free from the destructive influence of the existing economic situation was 1932. For that period military appropriations aggregated $334,764,748. This total was distributed as follows:

Regular Army and overhead for all components of the Army of the:

United States	$285,627,022
National Guard	35,109,142
Organized Reserves	6,537,785
Reserve Officers' Training Corps	3,978,900
Citizens' Military Training Camps	2,779,129
National Board for the Promotion of Rifle Practice	732,770
Total	$334,764,748

The following fiscal year (1933) Congress decreased the appropriation by a total of $48,771,771. This decrease was distributed to activities as follows:

Regular Army and overhead for all components of the Army of the:

United States	$46,283,116
National Guard	1,645,577
Organized Reserves	183,437
Reserve Officers' Training Corps	(a) 109,484
Citizens' Military Training Camps	175,505
National Board for the Promotion of Rifle Practice	593,620
Total	$48,771,771

(a) Increase

For the fiscal year 1934 Congress further decreased the amount available for military activities to $269,673,353. This reduction of $16,319,624 was distributed in the following amounts to the various components and activities:

Regular Army and overhead for all components of the Army of the:

United States	$15,444,661
National Guard	178,701
Organized Reserves	....
Reserve Officers' Training Corps	612,953
Citizens' Military Training Camps	103,624
National Board for the Promotion of Rifle Practice (a)	20,315

(a) Increase

The sum of the cuts absorbed under appropriation acts during these 2 fiscal years were, in terms of the 1932 appropriations:

	Percent
Regular Army and overhead for all components of the Army of the:	
United States	38
National Guard	10
Organized Reserves	6
Reserve Officers' Training Corps	10
Citizens' Military Training Camps	16
National Board for the Promotion of Rifle Practice	159

Hardly had the legislation appropriating the above sums for the fiscal year 1934 been enacted by Congress and approved by the President, when there was received from the Director of the Bureau of the Budget the instructions of March 28 previously referred to. His communication tentatively limited expenditures for the departmental and military activities of the War Department during the fiscal year 1934 to $196,000,000.

The data accompanying the memorandum of the Director of the Bureau of the Budget indicated that the proposed authorizations were allocated to activities as follows (omitting funds for departmental expenses):

Regular Army and overhead for all components of the Army of the:

United States	$182,351,959
National Guard	6,400,312
Organized Reserves	1,134,458
Reserve Officers' Training Corps	1,685,005
Citizens' Military Training Camps	45,000
National Board for the Promotion of Rifle Practice	2,700
Total	$191,619,434

In comparison with the appropriation for 1934 the Budget Bureau figures required the following reductions:
(See Table 4, page 63).

---

[16] Do not forget the annual report for 1932 you have just read. It was in this period that training of artillery with live ammunition was abandoned for economy's sake and the U.S. Regular Army was reduced to firing .22 calibre charges in toy cannon, to simulate artillery fire on miniature ranges. Only sighting equipment remained really standard military issue. Frank C. Waldrop (1942)

Translated into terms of its effect upon the Military Establishment this proposal contemplated -

The retirement of some 3,000 to 4,000 Regular officers.

The discharge of about 12,000 to 15,000 enlisted men of the Regular Army.

The elimination of field and armory drill training for the National Guard.

The elimination of all active duty training for the Officers' Reserve Corps.

The elimination of the Citizens' Military Training Camps.

The elimination of field training for the Reserve Officers' Training Corps.

The elimination of field training for the Regular Army.

The almost complete dismantling of the technical services of the Army, including the discharge of civilian technicians engaged in research, design, development, and experiment.

The cessation of procurement of necessary equipment and nearly all supplies except clothing and food.

From these many indirect effects would have been experienced, particularly by reason of losses in Regular officers.

Because of lack of instructors, inactive training for civilian components would have almost ceased, and the military school system would have been practically paralyzed. Manifestly such results would have meant the scrapping of the system prescribed in the National Defense Act, and the reduction of the American Military Establishment to the status of a Federal constabulary.

The War Department therefore vigorously contested these figures as being entirely inadequate for each of the components of the Army of the United States. The adjustment of the requirements of the Military Establishment to the Government's retrenchment program was the subject of continuous and intensive study by the War Department, and of written and oral presentations to the Director of the Bureau of the Budget. As a result that official, under date of June 9, 1933, communicated a decision increasing the total authorized expenditures for departmental and military activities to $224,964,758. In forwarding this decision to the Secretary of War, the Director of the Bureau of the Budget stated:

"The allocation of this amount is entirely within your dis-

	Amount of reduction	Percentage of reduction
Regular Army and overhead for all components of the Army of the United States	$41,547,286	19
National Guard	26,884,552	81
Organized Reserves	5,219,890	82
Reserve Officers' Training Corps	1,790,426	52
Citizens' Military Training Camps	2,455,000	98
National Board for the Promotion of Rifle Practice	156,765	99
Total	$78,053,919	29

Table 4.

	ORIGINAL TENTATIVE ALLOCATION BY BUDGET BUREAU	WAR DEPARTMENT ALLOCATION	INCREASE BY WAR DEPT. OVER BUDGET BUREAU'S ORIGINAL ALLOCATION
Regular Army and overhead for all components of the Army of the United States	$182,351,959	$197,143,143	8%
National Guard	6,400,312	18,040,344	182%
Organized Reserves	1,124,458	1,989,966[a]	76%
Reserve Officers' Training Corps	1,685,005	2,629,900	56%
Citizens' Military Training Camps	45,000	100,000	2,122%
National Board for the Promotion of Rifle Practice	2,700	50,000	1,752%
Total	$191,619,4334	$220,853,353	15%

[a]In addition to $2,340,198 from Civilian Conservation funds.

Table 5.

cretion and you are authorized by the President to take such steps as may be necessary in order that your expenditures may be within the $224,964,758 herein specified."

The allocation of this amount (again omitting funds for departmental expenses) as made by the War Department is indicated in the following table of comparison with the original tentative allocation of the Bureau of the Budget:

(See Table 5, page 63).

Just after the close of the fiscal year, the Director of the Bureau of the Budget increased the allotment for the National Guard by approximately $6,000,000. Half of the sum was provided by the Budget Bureau as an increase in total authorized expenditures. The remainder had to be secured by reducing the amounts for other military activities. Subsequently the President, upon the earnest recommendation of the executive committee of the Reserve Officers' Association, approved a $1,000,000 increase in the total authorizations and directed it be used for training of the Organized Reserves.

The expenditure program for the fiscal year 1934, in accordance with the final instructions received from the Director of the Bureau of the Budget, represents the following percentages of reduction from the corresponding amounts available for the fiscal year 1932:

	Percent
Regular Army and overhead for all components of the Army of the:	
United States	32
National Guard	31
Organized Reserves	(a) 48
Reserve Officers' Training Corps	35
Citizens' Military Training Camps	66
National Board for the Promotion of Rifle Practice	93
Total	33

(a) This percentage disregards funds provided from Civilian Conservation Corps money amounting to $2,340,598.

Effect of Reduced Appropriations upon Materiel

In distributing the successive reductions in military appropriations since 1931, the War Department has striven determinedly to maintain the structural framework of trained personnel indispensable to orderly mobilization in emergency. So far as possible every reduction has been absorbed by continuing in service obsolete and inefficient equipment, and where absolutely necessary, by suspending technical research and development work. There has resulted also a serious shortage in ammunition both for target practice and for reserve stocks. The hope was and is that no grave emergency might arise to demand prompt and effective employment of the Army of the United States before these deficiencies could be made good under conditions of greater national prosperity.

The risks involved in such a policy are clearly recognized, yet in view of the necessities of the situation, it has been followed as a lesser evil than that of permitting deterioration either in strength or efficiency of the human organization maintained as the backbone of our land defense establishment.

The extent to which the Army has suffered in the matter of materiel, even under the appropriations of 1932 and immediately preceding years, is clearly indicated in the results of an analysis made by the War Department in June of this year. This study was prepared in response to instructions, received through the Secretary of War, that the War Department submit for consideration in connection with the public-works program, a list of its essential needs in various types of materiel. In conformity with those instructions, only items deemed essential to modern efficiency and necessary under a well-balanced program of preparedness were included in the estimates. Sums for needed ammunition reserves were deliberately excluded, principally because of their great size.

I give here a summary of the major items recommended for immediate procurement, together with the approximate amounts involved:

Army housing, including Hawaii, Panama, and National Guard construction	$135,000,000
Mechanization	23,000,000
Motorization, general	39,000,000
Antiaircraft equipment, including motorization	33,000,000
Modernization and motorization of the:	
Field Artillery	35,000,000
Aircraft	39,000,000
Total	$304,000,000

These figures, excepting the amounts shown for construction, represent the extent to which the Army is deficient in modern weapons and equipment. This deficit has not occurred suddenly but rather is the cumulative result of years of failure to provide adequately for procurement and replacement.

The situation in motorization is typical. The term "motorization" as used in the Army pertains to the utilization of motor vehicles by military units for transportation purposes; mechanization on the other hand pertains more particularly to the use of motor vehicles as weapons on the battlefield.

Practically all units are inadequately supplied with transportation equipment, while extensive studies and experiments have demonstrated that in many organizations efficiency would be greatly enhanced by substitution of motor trucks for animal-drawn vehicles. Such a substitution would be accompanied, moreover, by an actual saving in money in the units affected.

The great proportion of the motor equipment now in possession of the Army was built during the World War and is obsolete as well as largely worn out. The total needs of the Regular Army for general motorization purposes are 9,385 trucks and 279 tractors. For the National Guard, aggregate requirements are about 19,500. Ever since the World War the American Army has not only failed to keep pace with world trends toward increasing mobility in military forces but has actually retrogressed in this respect. Under the 1934 authorizations this deterioration will be accentuated.

The situation with respect to fighting vehicles is similar. This subject, which was discussed at some length in my report last year, commands an increasingly intense interest throughout the Army.

Except for about a dozen machines produced during the

past few years, every tank in the Army today is of World-War manufacture. Their number is entirely inadequate. Even more serious than this is the fact that they are so obsolete in design as to be completely useless for employment against any modern unit on the battlefield. Their maximum cross-country speed is not over 4 or 5 miles an hour, whereas an ability to go 18 to 20 is mandatory, and a greater one is highly desirable.

In recent disarmament discussions there have been advanced proposals looking toward the elimination, by international agreement, of so-called "heavy tanks" (classed as those over 16 tons). But such proposals, at least to my knowledge, have not affected the types in which our Army is most interested; that is, those of about 12 tons and under.

The recommendations of the War Department for a greater degree of mechanization do not contemplate accumulation of vast quantities of expensive and, in a certain sense, experimental tanks and armored cars. On the contrary, all that is sought is opportunity to equip 2 infantry regiments and 1 cavalry brigade with the types of modern vehicles that have given the greatest promise of their suitability. Such a program is necessary first, to provide for thorough tactical tests and for the development of applicable training methods and doctrines and, second, to have available a limited number of organizations suitably trained and equipped to carry on this type of action in sudden emergency. This matter is of the utmost importance to the efficiency of the Army and to its ability to fulfill its missions in any crisis.

A policy permitting limited procurement of these special fighting machines in time of peace would enable industrial establishments of the country to study and solve the difficult problems incident to their production. With such an opportunity for self-education they could render the Government much more efficient, economical, and expeditious service in the event of war. This last reason is a weighty one, for even under favorable conditions as to availability of facilities, materials, and labor, it would require at least 12 months for commercial concerns to remodel their factories and attain quantity production in this type of weapon.

Our aggregate expenditures since 1920 for experimental and development work in mechanization have been about $2,000,000, only a fraction of the amounts spent for similar purposes by some of the foreign nations. For example, within the space of 4 years England appropriated $20,000,000 for mechanization projects in its army. The item of $23,000,000 needed to prosecute the proposed program would go a long way toward correcting our existing weakness in this particular respect.

Just as is the case in motorization and mechanization, each of the other items in the above list represents a serious deficiency in needed equipment. It is obvious that as long as these conditions persist the military effectiveness of the Army is below acceptable standards, and additional risks to the Nation's safety are incurred. The War Department strongly recommended that remedial action be instituted under the general authority and purposes of the public-works program. Priorities were indicated so that any lesser amounts provided might be applied to the most essential needs.

Final announcement as to the amounts that would be made available for these purposes by the Public Works Administration had not been made by the end of the fiscal year. But it seems pertinent to point out that much of the equipment desired is of such a nature as to require expenditure of public funds in industries and localities suffering particularly from the depression. Its manufacture would contribute effectively and immediately to the relief of unemployment. Moreover, the money would be applied to a critical governmental need, and would yield clear returns to the continuing welfare of our country. For national defense still remains the first duty of a sovereign power.

EFFECT OF REDUCED APPROPRIATIONS OF TRAINING EFFICIENCY AND PERSONNEL

In no other profession are the penalties for employing untrained personnel so appalling and so irrevocable as in the military.

Suspension of military training or further slashing into the Army's existing organization would produce a tragic situation - a situation even more serious in its eventual results than that discussed in the preceding section. Efficiency would fall off rapidly. Future correction would involve years of intensive work to make good months of current neglect. In the event of an emergency human and material costs and risk of defeat would be multiplied.

Mutual confidence, morale, and teamwork in a military force are the products of unremitting and intelligent effort. Continuity of training along lines determined by incessant study and research is the price of professional skill. That these things are essential to military success is a fundamental truth established by the experience of centuries. Today they are of greater moment than ever before, since modern weapons are so varied in type and some of them so complex in construction that exploitation of their full possibilities in combat requires the utmost In technical and professional ability.

The first essential of an efficient training system is a strong corps of highly qualified Regular officers. Such a body must attain the professional ability to analyze and interpret the lessons of history and evaluate them in the light of present and constantly changing conditions. From these it must develop correct principles, methods, and technique applying to every phase of the military art. Its size should be sufficient to insure efficient performances of all duties devolving upon it under the American system of national defense. Among other things it must provide the officers required in foreign garrisons and in the permanently manned harbor defenses of the country. It must furnish commissioned personnel for all types of technical duty in the procurement and development services and for all portions of the general overhead required by the Army of the United States. A part of its strength must be set aside for the maintenance of professional efficiency through school operation, and another for carrying on the many activities involved in peace-time preparation for mobilization.

In addition to these varied duties the Regular officer corps must provide military instruction for all elements of the Army of the United States. The first objective of this instructional work is to bring to a satisfactory level of proficiency the technical qualifications of every man in every component who will act as a unit commander in a war.

These leaders bear unmeasurable responsibilities. Lack

of skill in the individual soldier inevitably results in exposure of his own life to unnecessary risk. But lack of skill in the officer directly endangers the lives of his followers and comrades, as well as his own. Unless he is a man of practiced judgment and technical ability it is certain that his unit will, in battle, suffer futile and needless losses. Without officers, and I mean trained officers, armies are nothing but mobs, and successive disaster must almost certainly bring final defeat before commanders can absorb the lessons they should have learned in peace. An army without trained leaders is a contradiction in terms.

The fitness of officers therefore is a matter of serious concern to the War Department, a concern that would be intimately shared by the whole American people if there were universal appreciation of these basic truths. But because war is of infrequent occurrence, and because its dramatic rather than its technical side is emphasized in popular histories of military campaigns, the shibboleth persists that a commander's duty comprises nothing more than urging his men forward to the charge. Men who would tremble at the thought of plunging a surgeon's knife into the abdomen of a suffering appendicitis patient seem to have, although equally ignorant of applicable technique, a bland confidence in their ability to maneuver thousands through the dangers of a shell-torn field to the never-changing end of glorious victory. Though they might stand in helpless wonder before the intricacies of a machinist's lathe they apparently assume that the complicated and dangerous weapons of modern war miraculously operate themselves, to the consternation of the enemy and our own benefit.

No man, whatever his calling, can have greater need for the ultimate in professional knowledge and skill than he to whom falls, for example, the responsibility of leading a single infantry battalion in battle. The mere bringing up of his battalion to the front, adequately prepared for battle, represents the fruition of weeks or months of intensive effort based upon years of self-preparation. Every man in the unit must have been diligently and properly practiced in the use of rifle, bayonet, and gas mask. Specialists must be expert in the use of machine guns, automatic rifles, 1-pounder cannon, and 3-inch mortars. The commanding officer must know that his supply and communication units are well trained and that his medical detachment is ready to render efficient service. He must be assured that each man knows how to conduct himself under shellfire, under air, tank, and gas attacks, and through every vicissitude of modern battle. He must train every element of the command to work smoothly and efficiently with every other. And finally the leader must have developed to the highest degree his own understanding of human nature and his capacity for personal leadership, for in battle men will follow only those whose demonstrated efficiency inspires confidence and respect.

Once the commander has brought his unit into position for attack, he must decide correctly upon the best formations and methods to be employed against the particular opposition he has encountered. He must give appropriate orders to every unit in his battalion and to elements attached to it; he must make sure that his communications will keep him in touch, throughout the progress of the engagement, with each portion of his whole command and with cooperating units. Every factor applying to supply, reserves, wounded personnel, entanglements, entrenchments, transportation, and, above all, to the morale of his men must be studied and provided for. He must be able to follow with a discerning eye the progress of the battle so that at its crisis he may make the most effective use of all his remaining assets. And he himself must be so accustomed by peacetime maneuvers to efficient performance of his control functions that the stress and nervous strain of battle will not paralyze his brain and nullify the efforts of his whole command.

Hundreds of other officers throughout the Army are held responsible for duties which, though frequently different in character, require an equal degree of professional training and are, in some cases, even more important to the success of the whole. All these individuals must work as a team - every man and every action must be so integrated as to produce the maximum in combat effectiveness. Such possibilities may be realized only through continuous and intelligent study, development, experimentation, and practical training.

Four times during the nineteenth century the United States went to war under conditions that forced us to incur needless sacrifices by committing units to action under the leadership of hastily and imperfectly trained commanders. In spite of these repeated lessons, the same error was committed in 1917. In seeking evidence on this point we are not confined to testimony from the leaders of our own Army. The writings of our Allies and of our opponents in the late war are particularly revealing in their comments upon American battle operations. Foch, Hindenburg, Ludendorff, and many others have praised without stint the courage and dash of American units on the Western Front. But even while those veterans of many battles were lost in admiration for the bravery of troops that could sustain appalling numbers of casualties and still keep on attacking, they were aghast at the useless and costly sacrifices we made because of unskilled leadership in the smaller units. Training - professional training - and the skill and knowledge and morale resulting therefrom are the first indispensables to efficiency in combat.

With this general background it is not difficult to understand why the War Department has opposed, as wholly illogical and dangerous to national defense, every attempt to diminish our already inadequate corps of Regular officers or to reduce its opportunities for training. The Department has insisted upon maintaining the proficiency and sufficiency of the Regular officer corps, no matter what other reductions policy may compel in the Military Establishment.

These considerations account also for the determined effort the Department has made to preserve the integrity of civilian component training. The value to national defense of the civilian forces is measured by the extent to which they are equipped to perform the specific tasks allotted to them as emergency responsibilities. Because of the limited opportunities for military training that, even under the best of conditions, are available to these components, their instruction necessarily differs from that of the Regular Army in its greater degree of specialization. As far as possible every officer of the National Guard and of the Reserves is now assigned to the position he would be expected to fill in an emergency of the immediate future, and to the greatest practicable extent his training is directed toward qualifying him for the particular duties applying thereto. In this way each can be expected to acquire reasonable proficiency in his particular military function, providing only that he is offered and avails himself of training opportunities and that his morale and interest are maintained at high levels.

For similar reasons the department has also resisted any further diminution in the enlisted strength of our professional force. The experienced noncommissioned officers and other enlisted men of the Regular Army would have important organizational and training missions in the event of any major mobilization. In this work they supplement and extend the effort of officers, particularly in teaching technique applying to weapons and to small units. The existence of a strong and experienced nucleus would enable the whole to attain a satisfactory battle efficiency in a minimum of time.

This point was discussed at a hearing held on April 26 of this year by the Military Affairs Committee of the House of Representatives. I quote here a short extract from my answer to a question as to the possibility of employing in battle enlisted men with little or no training.

"Of course, you can put an untrained person on the battle line just as you could put a novice in front of a typewriter in your office. In the latter case you would pay for inefficiency in multiplied costs. Although the salary you pay a good typist includes a factor that reimburses the worker for months of training spent in a secretarial school, increased efficiency nevertheless results in economy. Put a recruit in baffle and the Nation pays in blood of its manhood and in multiplied risk of defeat. This country has time and again paid fearful prices for adhering to the doctrine that 'a million men would spring to arms overnight.' Men experienced in the actual business of fighting have learned this lesson, even if some of the theorists sitting far in the rear have failed to do so.

"With fine officers and noncommissioned officers in an established organization a recruit can take his place rather effectively in ranks after a few short weeks of intensive training. But even under these ideal conditions a certain amount of time is necessary. It varies according to the age, physical condition, and previous experience of the recruit. Time must be allowed for necessary inoculations against disease, for hardening the men who come from cities and towns, for teaching them to shoot, march, and, above all, to obey without question when under the stress of battle. These things take time no matter how intensive the training program. But the important thing is that the training of the officers and noncommissioned officers capable of absorbing these recruits takes a much longer period. Let us remember that we are preparing in time of peace the nucleus, the backbone, of an emergency army. We are getting the experts ready to handle the intensive training of large bodies in emergency.

"To my lot in the World War fell many unusual opportunities for observing at first hand the value of training in baffle. It is my professional opinion that far from overtraining any element of the Army of the United States we are not able under existing conditions to reach the standards that should prevail in the skeletonized nucleus that we maintain."

One of the fundamental purposes in maintaining a professional force is to make constantly available to the Federal Government a reasonable amount of military strength capable of immediate and effective action in emergency. In many situations promptitude in the employment of relatively small forces might obviate the necessity for later operations on a large scale. In our Military Establishment only Regular personnel is obligated exclusively and continuously to the service of the Government and is instantaneously responsive to the orders of the President. Full advantage in emergency may be taken of this degree of availability only where it is accompanied by an equal readiness from a professional viewpoint. It is therefore one of the principal duties of the War Department to see that Regular Army units are well organized, highly trained, adequately equipped, and so located as to be capable of rapid concentration toward any threatened point.

In the continental United States there is today a total of some 87,000 enlisted men of the Regular Army. Normally, about 55,000 of these, widely scattered in military stations throughout the whole country, are available for assignment to combat units. In emergency, many of these would have to turn immediately to the performance of important training, organization, and mobilization tasks. But others would necessarily move without delay to insure the safety of vital industrial and population centers and to protect against sudden raids and attacks. Their readiness for such missions should be well-nigh perfect. For some years the Regular Army has been so small as to endanger its ability to discharge this dual responsibility. Yet unless both missions are satisfactorily accomplished in emergency the results might easily become disastrous.

Under the programs supported by the appropriations of 1933 and immediately preceding years, theoretical training of the Army of the United States has been maintained on a satisfactory basis. The general and special service schools have been functioning efficiently, inactive training for the National Guard and Reserves has been developing along sound lines, and garrison instruction for Regular units has been handicapped only by a shortage in officers and by the extremely small numbers of men available for duty in each organization.

In field training the situation has not been so encouraging. The maneuver field offers the only possible peace-time approach to battle conditions, and tactical exercises should not only be of frequent occurrence, but for them there should be assembled combat units, auxiliary services, and staffs sufficiently large to simulate battlefield situations and to present fairly accurate pictures of war's characteristic problems. Because of the greatly reduced strength of Regular units, field exercises on this scale have not been possible and the instruction of Regular and Reserve officers and of enlisted men, in these extremely skeletonized maneuvers, has left much to be desired.

In spite of difficulties, slow progress has been realized. But under the situation now facing us not only will progress be practically suspended, but many of the results so far attained will be lost. No funds will be available for the modest expenses incurred in field exercises for the Regular Army. Fewer Reserve officers can be called to active duty for 2 weeks' training. Lack of money will prohibit nearly all target practice and in other ways limit the opportunity of the soldier to learn and remain familiar with the practical phases of his profession. While at the end of the fiscal year it appeared probable that theoretical instruction could be carried forward in 1934 on about the same scale as in 1933, this, without appropriate practical work, cannot sustain efficiency.

Our minimum requirements in the fields of personnel and training include theoretical instruction for all components of the Army and for the Reserve Officers' Training Corps and the Citizens' Military Training Camps on the scale of the 1932 program; an Officers' Reserve Corps of about 120,000 with 2 weeks' active duty training for 30,000 annually; maintenance of the National Guard at least at existing strength with 48 armory drills yearly and 2 weeks' field training in as large formations as practicable; target practice and field exercises, to include maneuvers by large commands, for all tactical units of the Regular Army, and an enlisted strength of 165,000. This number of enlisted men will provide training cadres of satisfactory strength and an efficient tactical force of reasonable size constantly available for emergency use.

FUTURE TRENDS IN ORGANIZATION, TRAINING, AND EQUIPMENT OF THE ARMY

...The American Army is convinced that the Air Corps, in any war of the future, will be ca;;ed upon to carry a burden demanding efficiency, morale, and numbers. To build up and have ready for immediate use a satisfactory air contingent the War Department has sacrificed much else that is required in a well-balanced defense program, with the result that no other arm or service of our Army is relatively so well prepared as is the Air Corps. The purpose has been to insure adequate air support for the Army against any attack that might be launched against this country during the early months of any war. Manifestly it would be nothing less than folly to accentuate too far the disparity in the state of readiness between air and ground arms for - as has been so often demonstrated - it is not one weapon, one arm, or one component that assures victory; it is the skillful, coordinated, and effective employment of all in proper balance.

To sum up: The inevitable trend in warfare is toward greater speed of strategic maneuver through maximum utilization of relatively fast machines for transportation; increased fire-power on the battlefield through employment of weapons of much greater efficiency, with a resultant wider dispersion in tactical formations; more power in the attack through utilization of combat vehicles invulnerable to small-arms fire and capable of cross-country travel; growing dependency upon air forces for information, for assistance in defense of the coast line, for attacks against hostile ground troops, and for bombardment of sensitive points in the enemy's supply organization. All these things point to the probability that any major war of the reasonably proximate future will see a swing away from the tremendous and ponderous combat forces that have characterized campaigns of the past 75 years and that in their place will appear relatively mobile, highly trained, and very powerful, though somewhat smaller, formations. Control of such units in combat would be difficult, if not impossible, with old methods, but fortunately, alongside other technical developments, there have been comparable ones in signal communications to facilitate teamwork and coordinated action.

Tactical units such as those described must be supported by stronger maintenance, supply, and other auxiliary services than have heretofore been required. The conception of the "nation in arms" will not be abandoned, but in its application a smaller proportion of populations will probably be included in the actual fighting elements of armies than was the case during the World War, and a greater one will be engaged in producing the airplanes, tanks, guns, trucks, ammunition, and other intricate weapons that will be rapidly used up on the battlefield.

As heretofore pointed out, the physical aspects of such changes will occur very slowly and gradually, unless the world should find itself again confronted with the catastrophe of a major war. But trends of this description must be recognized and evaluated by a military establishment, so that in emergency its efforts to protect the nation will be effective under conditions then prevailing. In a major crisis defeat would certainly follow slavish devotion to outmoded method and obsolete ideas.

To the greatest extent practicable our own Army is striving to adjust its organization, training, doctrine, and tactical methods to insure maximum readiness in this respect. The four-army plan envisions a prompt mobilization of a few hundred thousand of the best-trained combat troops available rather than the immediate assembly of millions of men total unacquainted with the requirements and technique of modern warfare. Experimental and development work in weapons, transportation, fighting vehicles, and related items is carried on as intensively as practicable under current appropriations, so as to attain a moderate degree of preparedness to meet the conditions that may reasonably be expected to develop. But years of insufficient appropriations for these purposes have left us deficient in personnel and training and in modern equipment.

To attain a reasonable degree of preparedness in the munitions field the funds heretofore recommended for this purpose should be immediately provided. Likewise, annual appropriations should support the strength in personnel and the programs of training for all components outlined in a preceding section of this report... .

SPECIAL CONSIDERATIONS APPLYING TO CIVILIAN COMPONENTS

The missions, requirements, and general conditions of the civilian components have already been generally discussed in those sections of this report that pertain to the Army as a whole. But efficient development and preparation of these elements for their vitally important place in our system of land defense involve some special measures and some considerations applying to them exclusively.

The civilian components constitute a volunteer reserve for the professional force, and the greater portion of the time they devote to military purposes, particularly in the Officers' Reserve Corps, is gratuitously given. Consequently, among them a high morale is essential, not only to efficiency but to their very existence.

Since, with negligible exceptions, no member of the civilian components gains a livelihood from military activity, the matter of emoluments has not for them the vital importance that it has for professional soldiers. Their principal incentive for pursuing military training as an avocation is a patriotic desire to fit themselves for efficient service in a national emergency. Their greatest reward is definite assurance that the value of their efforts is recognized and appreciated by the Government. They are entitled to, and it is essential that they be accorded, proper opportunity to prepare themselves for emergency duty. It is important also that policies controlling appointments, promotions, and administration clearly evidence the Government's interest in their welfare and efficiency.

Selection and promotion of personnel in the National Guard are accomplished under State authority. For the Officers' Reserve Corps appropriate policies, crystallized some 2 years ago after continuous study throughout the period since the World War, have received practically unanimous support from the members of that organization. Favoritism and special influence have no weight in initial appointments, and promotion is accomplished under methods that recognize efficiency and experience. These policies have been faithfully adhered to by the Department, with splendid effect throughout the Corps.

With organization and administration of the civilian components established on a satisfactory basis, the chief concern of the War Department is to insure their steady development as an efficiently trained portion of the Military Establishment. Their theoretical training usually involves but slight direct expense, and can be largely controlled by administrative regulations and policy. Winter classes under Regular Army instructors, closely supervised and progressive correspondence courses, and individual contacts are all utilized to promote the military efficiency of these elements. During recent years it has been possible also, under congressional authorization, to detail annually a few selected officers for short terms at the Army's general and special service schools.

But opportunity for active-duty training is rigidly limited by the sums provided for the specific purpose, since existing law very properly provides that during such tours each member of the civilian components will receive the normal pay of his grade. In the National Guard the number of armory drills with pay in any year is also fixed by appropriations. As pointed out in a prior section of this report, there is no substitute for field and other practical work, and a reasonable amount of it is essential to efficiency. This fact is fully realized by the civilian components, and failure to provide such opportunity would be interpreted by them as a complete lack of governmental appreciation of their personal sacrifice and would result finally in a distinct loss of interest and morale and definite deterioration in their dependability for defense purposes.

In the sense that the training of the average officer of the civilian components is specifically directed toward qualifying him for a particular position in emergency, he must be considered a specialist. The purpose is to insure that he will be entirely competent for his particular war assignment. On the other hand, Regular officers, professionally equipped by lifelong devotion to military careers, must bring to an expanded emergency army that broad background of general experience and varied training that will enable them to coordinate and unify the activities of all arms and services. The professional and civilian contingents have each their specific places to fill in an amalgamated whole, and the training

and development of each must conform to the duties and responsibilities that will devolve upon it in a national crisis.

Under the practically stabilized and consistently followed training programs of recent years the civilian components have made steady and commendable progress in attaining a proficiency essential to their respective missions. They now represent a considerable investment in time, effort, and money, and an asset for emergency use that should be jealously guarded. Future policies should countenance no curtailment of programs that have attained these results, and in the case of Reserve officers should provide for some expansion of field training. Junior combat officers of that corps should be called to active duty annually for 2 weeks' practical training and others in accordance with their somewhat lesser needs. The total yearly quota should not be less than 30,000.

The Reserve Officers' Training Corps and the Citizens' Military Training Camps should be continued on the basis prevailing for the past several years. The value of these as feeders for the Officers' Reserve Corps and as agencies for imparting a degree of military training to a typical cross-section of young Americans has been clearly established. Their cost to the Government is insignificant compared to the resulting benefits.

Activities of all these organizations were scheduled for drastic curtailment under the expenditure program proposed by the Bureau of the Budget in March of this year. The details of the reductions ordered in that directive as well as the compromise obtained through the War Department's persistent efforts have been discussed in a prior section of this report. But even under the program now authorized some deterioration must be anticipated. National Guard drills have been cut from 48 to 36, and while that body is undertaking to conduct the remaining 12 without remuneration such an arrangement cannot be expected to have a permanent basis. The 20,000 Reserve officers normally trained for 2 weeks each year will be cut to 10,000, even including those on duty with the Civilian Conservation Corps. The Reserve Officers' Training Corps camps will be of shorter duration, and drastic limitations will be placed on the numbers permitted in Citizens' Military Training Camps.

The schedule necessary for retention of efficiency in all these has already been indicated. But it is desired here to emphasize that unless these organizations are professionally equipped to carry out their specific functions in an emergency, then every cent spent upon them in the past and in the future will be wasted, and the dependence now placed upon them under the American system of national defense will be completely unjustified.

GENERAL ORGANIZATION AND ADMINISTRATION

The search for greater economy and efficiency in Government has very naturally included inquiries into the suitability of departmental organization, and various proposals for general reorganization have been laid before committees of Congress and other appropriate agencies. The higher administrative organization of the Army of the United States has, from time to time, been subjected to certain criticisms. Schemes for its revision have been advanced with the assertion that great benefits would result from their adoption. While some of these statements, by their very extravagance, have attracted considerable attention, it is noticeable that none of them has ever been accompanied by a definite schedule of possible economies nor by any convincing argument as to the manner in which efficiency could be enhanced.

Manifestly, there is nothing sacrosanct in particular details of organization. Efficiency requires that in broad outline well-defined, logical, and easily understood groupments be set up, but within the limits so established there can be many variations as to detail with no adverse effects upon desired results. This is in direct opposition to the theory often advanced that through adoption of some particular organizational plan there is guaranteed perfect results and that any variation therefrom is certain to lead to inefficiency and extravagance. Such a conception is, of course, absurd. The human element always dominates details of organization.

The heart of the military section of the War Department organization is the General Staff, organized in 1903, and drastically reorganized in 1920 as a result of World War experience. It comprises 92 specially selected Regular officers, drawn from all branches of the Army to serve 4-year terms in this capacity. They have been trained to look beyond the special interests of branch, grade, or component, to the efficiency of the Army of the United States as a whole. The General Staff also includes in its membership selected officers from the National Guard and the Officers' Reserve Corps, who serve as the representatives of their components to insure proper consideration of their needs and viewpoint in the development of general policy.

The value of the General Staff as a coordinating, planning, and advisory body has been clearly demonstrated, and, to my knowledge, no one even remotely acquainted with military procedure and requirements has, in recent years, suggested its abolition. In carrying out its functions it considers all problems under the four general heads of personnel, intelligence, operations and training, and supply. Staff organization follows this division of functions and is as satisfactory a grouping as can be devised.

Each of the several technical and supply services is an operating agency set up to meet the requirements of the Army of the United States in a particular class of supplies, equipment, or services. Their responsibilities in research, experimentation, development, procurement, storage, and issue are so well known as to need little discussion. The only revision that has been proposed with respect to them is to effect some consolidation so as to maintain fewer bureaus. This suggestion is born of the prevalent but mistaken idea that in consolidation lies the sure road to economy and efficiency. The Army's long experience is full of lessons to the contrary. Moreover, we do not now maintain, as separate organizations, all the operating services that were found to be necessary during the World War. For example, in that conflict a separate Transportation Corps was established, as was also a Construction Corps, both of which were originally included, as they are now, in the set-up of the Quartermaster Corps.

Each of the combat arms also has a chief in Washington. These chiefs supervise the schools of their respective arms, and, on appropriate subjects, act as technical advisers to the General Staff and the Chief of Staff. Each is the special representative in the War Department of the personnel of his arm. They analyze and classify officers' efficiency reports,

survey the professional and personal needs of individuals, and make recommendations for assignments. Their offices are the focal points in which are digested matters pertaining to the morale and efficiency of the several fighting branches. Their headquarters establishments are not large and their abolition could save only very small sums. Any saving so effected would be many times outweighed by resulting inefficiencies and by loss of morale in the combat branches.

The field organization in the continental United States heads up into nine corps area headquarters. In peace they coordinate and control the various activities of all components within their respective areas, and in war would constitute the principal agencies through which the War Department would carry out a mobilization. In each corps area is maintained a small staff that studies the local problems involved in a mobilization and prepares in every possible way to meet them.

The efficacy of our administrative system, with its directing headquarters in Washington and operational responsibility centered in the nine corps areas, was abundantly tested in the Civilian Conservation Corps mobilization. That intricate and delicate task was accomplished so quietly, so effectively, and so speedily that, except for publicity accorded it in the press, the mass of our people would have been unaware of its operation. Perusal of the narrative account I have given of that mobilization will demonstrate the magnitude of the operation and the thoroughness of the test to which War Department administration was subjected.

Revision should not be undertaken solely for the sake of change. We have 12,000 Regular officers. They understand our organization. For the most part they have been through at least some of the various echelons of our school system and have been educated in the functions and organization of the War Department and subordinate headquarters. To a considerable extent the same holds true of commissioned personnel in the civilian components. Drastic revision would create confusion and therefore, far from increasing efficiency, would, in its general effect, operate in the opposite direction.

Much could be written on comparative organization in other armies. But I think it enough to say that our organization is founded upon experience, is well understood throughout our Army, has proven satisfactory to date, and is well adapted to the needs of emergency.

Any claim that reorganization of the military section of the War Department would save millions is absurd. The actual numbers of men on duty in it could be but little reduced without going back to the wholly inadequate organization of the pre-war period. Moreover, the total cost of the War Department, which constitutes the great administrative overhead for the whole Army of the United States, does not even equal the amounts that it has been asserted could be saved from it by reorganization.

This is not to say, of course, that improvement is impossible. The reverse is true. But since the basic outlines of existing organization and procedure have proven satisfactory, and personnel is thoroughly familiar with them, progress should be sought by evolutionary rather than revolutionary methods.

For example, considerable results have been achieved during the past year through determined efforts to simplify procedure and reduce the volume of routine correspondence and reports incident to peace-time administration. Many periodic reports, involving more than 500,000 separate documents that heretofore flowed annually into the War Department and corps area and department headquarters, have been eliminated. Many of these reports represented a duplication of effort, and some of them required months of preparation. The time and labor saved by their discontinuance are now being devoted to more useful military purposes, while a worth-while saving in expense has been effected.

Two other accomplishments incident to this effort have been the discontinuance of post and regimental personnel sections and the adoption of an abridged edition of Army Regulations for small units. The abridged regulations will serve as a practical administrative guide for all officers in any emergency mobilization, and real economies will result through elimination of nonessential documents from a volume that will necessarily have a tremendous distribution. In the general task of simplifying procedure and reducing paper work corps area commanders have cooperated effectively, since the need for progress in this direction is quite as evident in the field as it is in Washington.

The reduced funds available for 1934 will compel additional discharging or furloughing of civilian personnel and the attempt to achieve greater simplification of procedure and to cut down paper work must be continued. There are limits, however, to the possibilities of effecting savings in this direction, since the great majority of statistical records and most of our routine correspondence are required either by laws governing purchasing, supply, and administration or by sound methods of organization and operation.

Every phase of organization, training, procurement, administration and supply is constantly subject to study by the Inspector General's Department and other agencies in the effort to reduce administrative costs and increase efficiency. Some of these investigations are conducted jointly with the Navy, and where efficiency, particularly in procurement, can be increased by joint action it is invariably carried out.

It is to be expected that possibilities for improvement in various lines will continue to be uncovered. But it would be a backward and a costly step to wreck the basic outline of organization. To do so would be to lose, at one stroke, all the improvements so far made in the existing set-up, and render valueless the great store of experience accumulated by personnel of all components in particular methods of procedure. Such a move would be justifiable only on a definite showing of material and clear-cut increases in efficiency and economy, and such a showing, I state with confidence, has not and cannot be made so long as our basic system of national defense is to remain substantially as at present.

DISARMAMENT

The international conference at Geneva for the reduction and limitation of armaments, after 17 months of more or less continued deliberation, has, at the date of this report, arrived at no solution. A measure of accord has been reached on principles, but successful adjustment of the widely divergent attitudes of the several nations on practical essentials has so far been unattainable. This lack of substantial accomplishment is apparently due not only to the complexity of technical aspects of the problem but also to varying requirements in defense establishments.

In numerical strength our Army is so small that in this respect it does not constitute even a minor factor in the difficult problem facing the delegates at Geneva. The organized land forces of the United States still rank seventeenth in size among the world's armies, whereas if organized on the basis of population, total wealth, and length of frontier our Army would be second to none. No land-disarmament program yet seriously proposed has contemplated such a sweeping and universal reduction of armies that world levels in military strength would descend to that already existing in this country. Even under the theory of maintaining only "police components" the United States would be entitled to increase, rather than be compelled to decrease, its permanent forces.

Certain aspects of the disarmament effort involve problems completely separated from the subject of relative numerical strength. For example, proposals at Geneva have stressed the desirability of adopting certain rules of warfare and of eliminating so-called "aggressive" weapons. To any rule of warfare designed to protect noncombatants from aerial bombardment or poison-gas dissemination, there can be none other than full and unanimous concurrence. The matter of abolition of certain types of weapons has not, however, been found so readily acceptable, since resultant effects on the defense situations of the several nations are variable.

Two weapons that have been much discussed are the bombing airplane and the heavy mobile gun. Nations whose boundaries are coterminous with those of powerful potential enemies naturally regard the bombing plane, with its threat to vitally important industrial centers, as a particularly aggressive or offensive type of weapon. They place the heavy mobile gun in the same classification, because of its ability to demolish land fortifications. Such nations have urged the abolition of these weapons in order that the power of an attacking army might be reduced. On the other hand, in countries relatively isolated from potential enemy States, the bombing plane and the heavy mobile gun are considered especially effective as a defense against attack from overseas, and, on the theory that the defense should be strengthened over the offense, their retention rather than their abolition is indicated.

It can readily be appreciated, therefore, that willingness of the United States to agree to abolition of bombardment aviation and mobile artillery above 155 millimeters in caliber, whenever unanimous agreement on this point should be obtained, constitutes a tremendous contribution to the success of the disarmament conference, and one that entails a distinct sacrifice in our own readiness for defense.

Aside from some readjustments that would become necessary in our forces through universal agreement for abolition of these two, and possibly one or two other types of weapons, it is difficult to single out any item in which our existing Military Establishment could be affected by any program of disarmament acceptable to other great powers. More than this, with the exception of those recommendations that involve certain types of airplanes, every proposal made to the Public Works Board by the General Staff for modernization of our Army lies well within the limitations that would be imposed upon us by any probable disarmament agreement.

The American system of land defense is obviously designed strictly and exclusively for defense. It is incapable of delivering sudden and powerful blows in a crisis, and therefore cannot be adapted speedily to the requirements of offensive warfare on a major scale. This fact is universally appreciated by military men throughout the world. But the smallness of our organized forces places an extraordinary premium upon efficiency. The whole purpose of the War Department is to maintain a strength and to attain an efficiency that will permit satisfactory functioning of the land-defense system established by Congress in 1920.

CONCLUSION

In concluding this report I invite attention again to the recommendations included in its several sections. As has often been explained, the United States does not need a military establishment comparable to the great armies existing in certain of the foreign nations. The professional-civilian military system prescribed in the National Defense Act is almost ideally suited to our requirements, provided only the strength and efficiency of the several elements are maintained at reasonable levels. The aim of the recommendations I have made herein is simply to provide and maintain the requisite efficiency and strength. Immediate adoption of every measure advocated would still leave us with an organized army of approximately half the size that Congress, after exhaustive study of World War experiences, deemed essential to the country's continued safety and authorized in the 1920 amendments to the National Defense Act.

In the obvious state of unrest now prevailing throughout the world, evidences of which are plainly visible even in our own country, an efficient and dependable military establishment, constantly responsive to the will of its Government, constitutes a rock of stability and one of a nation's priceless possessions. As much as at any other time in our history, the Army's efficiency should engage the earnest attention of every loyal citizen. It is my conviction that at this moment the Army's strength in personnel and materiel and its readiness for employment are below the danger line. I consider it of the most urgent importance to the United States that this condition be rectified without delay.

U.S. HOUSE OF REPRESENTATIVES
MILITARY AFFAIRS COMMITTEE EXECUTIVE SESSION
JANUARY 21, 1934

Development of the G.H.Q. Air Force plan by the General Staff, the inadequateness of the (then) present air equipment of the Army, and the need for a planned development such as that out lined by the War Department was explained to the House Military Affairs Committee by General Douglas MacArthur, Chief of Staff, during its executive sessions concluded in February 1934.

General MacArthur's statement contains a detailed description of the separation of air power from the ground forces and foreshadows our modern army organizations. As you read this account of haggling and struggling, compare the figures MacArthur was seeking to have Congress accept with the production of military aircraft the President ordered for 1942 - 60,000 planes, an order expanded again before May 1.

Representative John J. McSwain (Chairman) presided at the hearing and introduced General MacArthur as follows:

Frank C. Waldrop, Editor
MacArthur On War
Duell, Sloan and Pearce, New York
©1942, Frank C. Waldrop

Gentlemen of the Committee, we are very glad indeed to have the Chief of Staff of the United States Army present this morning, Gen. Douglas MacArthur, with his Deputy Chief of Staff and some of his personal aides.

I was very much pleased to notice, General MacArthur, in the press of last Saturday and Sunday, I think it was, a statement concerning a suggestion from the War Department to increase the air power of the Army of the United States; and the Committee, I am quite sure, will agree with me that the air power of the United States is a very vital and important factor in the event of future conflict. We assume, of course, General MacArthur, that that statement was, at least, quasi-official, or, at least, that the War Department knew something about it; that it was not mere newspaper talk; or, at least, we hope it is not mere newspaper talk. We want to have you state this morning, if you will, your own views and the War Department views, if you can, regarding the proposed increase in the air power of the Army. You may direct your remarks as you think best to this general subject which is now before us, and which is engaging the attention of the entire public. It is surprising how many resolutions I receive on my desk every day from Chambers of Commerce, civic bodies, as well as associations of Reserve officers, and others, urging the expansion and increase in the air power, which is, as they say, a first line of defense - the primary fighting force in the event of war. Now, will you please proceed in such a way as suits your convenience and as may be dictated by your good judgment.

The testimony of General MacArthur proceeded as follows:

Gen. MacArthur - The release, Mr. Chairman, which was carried in the press was a formal and written release from the War Department, prepared by my direction; so that -

Mr. May (interposing) - Pardon me, but it was official?

Gen. MacArthur - An absolutely official release. As you will notice, it dealt only with subjects falling within the scope of the authority legally delegated to the War Department, and projected itself no further. In other words, it did not touch upon any phase of air development dealing with joint Army-Navy policy. It was strictly a War Department document. It was the general statement of a policy of the War Department, which it was hoped that the Congress would eventually put into active operation.

You have stated something of the importance of air combat with reference to national defense in future wars. This is a subject, which perhaps, above all others, has engaged the attention of the American War Department since the close of the World War, due not only to the potentialities of the air as a medium of war, but also partially due to the newness and undeveloped characteristics of the arm. There are no well-defined trends in this comparatively new branch of warfare which enable the charting of future possibilities with certainty. There must be large elements of conjecture and of imagination. The War Department and the Navy Department, in visualizing, after the World War, their own individual development, foresaw also the possibility that only a limited total of appropriations would be available for the development of all air components.

After a protracted series of conferences between professional soldiers and sailors, and with the advice and cooperation of the Congress, there were finally set forth definite standards for the development of the air components of both of the services.

These were put into effect by two laws passed, as I recall, in 1926. This legislation embodied the "Five-Year Plans" as they are colloquially designated. General ratios for the development of the two services were established, and limitations upon that development, covering the span of five years, were outlined.

Eight years have passed since that time, and due to the insufficiency of appropriations, the Army has not reached the fruition of the program. The Navy, I am glad to be able to say, has been more successful, and has completed its program. For further development, the Navy has just proposed another program, which I understand has already received the sanction of the House of Representatives.

The Army feels that due to the interrelation of programs joint consideration is necessary to the needs of the two services. The development of Army aviation, of course, should proceed entirely in step with that of the Navy. We have for years been working along very definite lines. As long as ten years ago, in the so-called "Lassiter Board" - of which the present very brilliant Deputy Chief of Staff was a member - the employment of air forces in military operations was projected into the future along broad lines.

In broader perspective, this employment divides itself into two parts: that which inherently pertains to ground troops of the Army, and that which involves the use of an Air Force by the Commander in Chief as a general reserve, to be thrown in at any definite point where he believes it advisable. The general conception of the G.H.Q. striking force was set forth by that Board.

I may say, in describing the general functions of the two broad groupments, that those elements of air defense which are inherently part and parcel of other forces, are the observation groupments which function directly with ground troops in tactical operations. By that I mean the observation squadrons which furnish the reconnaissance information, spot the targets and assists in controlling the fire of artillery. That type of air unit is equipped principally with observation planes.

Back of these echelons, we have the main striking element of the air - the G.H.Q. force, which is equipped with three types of planes - attack, pursuit and bombardment. They are to be used just as you would use a slingshot. They are thrown at the point where they will be the most damaging. For cohesion, coordination, and to prevent their dissipation on minor missions, they are held together as a great general reserve under the commanding general in the field.

Their uses would be varied. They could be used as a great deciding factor in a mass combat. They could be used for rapid reinforcement at distant threatened points, such as our outposts in Panama or in Hawaii. They could be used in independent missions of destruction, aimed at the vital arteries of a nation, or they might of necessity be divided up and used in detail.

There has been a tremendous development in the airplane itself. I refer not only to the normal development of commercial aviation, but also to the special and individualized types with their peculiarly military missions. The development has been so rapid that it has been of doubtful wisdom to purchase, at any particular moment, great numbers of even the best types then existing.

The types that we now have are changing, perhaps, more rapidly in performance characteristics than at any other time since the World War.

The three types that, in major quantities, would compose the G.H.Q. air forces are attack, pursuit and bombardment. With reference to the bombardment - the name of this group practically describes Its purposes and functions.

The pursuit type is peculiarly to destroy an air enemy - in protection of the bombers or in general combat.

The attack type not only has protective functions somewhat similar to the pursuit type, but also is equipped to lay down smoke screens in the accomplishment of such a purpose. They have the definite mission of attacking ground troops. This type is peculiar to the United States Army.

These three types have been rapidly stepped up in speed. Speed is the essence of the protective potentialities of the air man. And by speed I do not mean entirely straightway speed: I refer to the maneuvering possibilities of the ship.

As these wonderful inventors and developers of aircraft proceed some remarkable results are being achieved. The three types are beginning to blend; and I personally believe that within the next ten years, you will probably see such a marked improvement that one type will do the work that is now divided among the three types. Our latest bombers attain a speed of about 210 miles per hour. That is many miles faster than our present pursuits make. I believe the speeds will increase. I believe the sizes of ships will probably increase, and that you will have the same general development which occurred with the other type of ship, the seagoing ship, which started in as a small man-of-war, expanded and grew and grew, until it finally embodies certain definite characteristics, which are now found in all of the main sea fighters.

The development of the five-year plan in the Army -

Mr. Goss (interposing) - You mean the first five-year plan?

Gen. MacArthur - Yes - was placed under an Assistant Secretary of War for Air, and the General Staff had practically nothing to do with the air program, except the normal routine of handling personnel, and as an advisory group on some subjects which pertain not only to the air, but to other branches.

That office is now vacant and in July it became necessary to have its functions carried on by other agencies in the War Department. The Secretary of War turned the military features over to the General Staff, and the procurement features over to the Assistant Secretary of War, just as is the case with the other branches of the service.

That brought the Chief of Staff for the first time into direct supervision of the problems of the development of the air.

I at once took the necessary steps, through boards and other means, to study development, to perfect plans for employment, and to analyze all other elements of our air defense problem-a process which has been going on since that time.

The program which was released the other day represents the General Staff's crystallized opinion on this one phase of the subject, as developed by months of study.

A disturbing feature of our existing situation, as uncovered by the Staff study, is the relatively low proportion of planes that can fairly be classed as fighting ships, as compared to the total numbers accumulated during the past five years. As a first effort to correct this situation the War Department attempted to secure an item of $39,000,000 from the Public Works Administration with which to purchase fighting airplanes.

I wish to emphasize that up to the present the General Staff has had nothing whatsoever to do with the planes that have been purchased. This is a matter that has been entirely in the hands of the Assistant Secretary of War for Aviation, acting with the immediate advice of the Chief of Air Corps. Under the arrangement as now set up the General Staff still has nothing to do with the actual purchase of the planes, this being a function of the Air Corps under the supervision of the Assistant Secretary of War.

The function of the General Staff, acting with the advice of the Chief of Air Corps, is to determine whether the planes to be purchased shall be fighting types or non-fighting types. That is, it surveys our whole situation and determines whether our most pressing need is for bombing, pursuit and attack planes, or whether our most urgent requirement is for training, observation, transport or other non-fighting classes.

Under the present set-up, after this preliminary determination has been made, it becomes the duty of the Assistant Secretary of War, acting with the advice of the Chief of Air Corps, to determine the actual specifications of the planes to be purchased.

If, up until the time this new arrangement went into effect, any errors and mistakes have been made in the procurement of Army aircraft, they can be attributed only to the air elements themselves, since the General Staff has had nothing to do with such questions. Responsibility for these functions rested entirely with the Chief of Air Corps and with the Assistant Secretary of War for Aviation.

Statements have recently appeared in the press or been made over the radio that the General Staff has forced the purchase of slower types than those desired. Such statements are fallacious and without foundation in fact. They constitute sheer propaganda of the most vicious sort, and are inspired by those who seek to obtain a control over the incidents of Army Air comparable to that now being exposed so brilliantly by Senator Black's investigating committee with reference to civil aviation.

The Chairman - General, may I ask you at this point, what is the minimum strength of that G.H.Q. air force that you would suggest? What is the minimum of the studies that the General Staff estimates to be feasible?

Gen. MacArthur - I would like to speak, Mr. Chairman, in terms of tactical units, rather than numbers. I think a great

mistake was made in trying to delimit the air force by speaking of numbers. But to answer your question - later if you desire it I will try to give some estimate in terms of numbers - I would rather give you a general conception:

The G.H.Q. air force contemplates five wings. Perhaps I should sketch very briefly the organization of the Air Corps. They have tactical units, just as have the other branches. The smallest is called the flight, usually of five planes. It corresponds, in general, to the platoon or fraction of a company or troop. The next larger element is the squadron, which corresponds roughly with the company. Then comes the group, which corresponds with the battalion. Then comes the wing, which corresponds roughly to the regiment. The G.H.Q. air force -

Mr. Hill (interposing) - Excuse me one moment, General. But it would give us a better conception, I believe, if we knew just how many planes there are in a flight or a squadron. I have some idea. I have a flight in my own home town, but -

Gen. MacArthur (interposing) - The figures are flexible.

Mr. Hill - They are not definitely fixed?

Gen. MacArthur - They should not be. Expansional possibilities should be allowed, which will make them more or less elastic. A wing, however, would have at least 200 planes, and generally more. Under conditions now current I believe that the G.H.Q. air force should have five wings. There should be two pursuit wings. There should be one attack wing. There should be two bombardment wings - that is, two pursuits, two bombardments, and one attack; we should have at least five wings.

We have now, as a nucleus of such a force, for use in an emergency, two wings: we have the West Coast wing and the East Coast wing.

To answer your question categorically, I should say that the G.H.Q. air force should certainly have at least 1,000 planes.

The Chairman - As a minimum?

Gen. MacArthur - Yes.

The Chairman - And strengthening each of these organizations as occasion may require?

Gen. MacArthur - Yes. The size of the tactical unit of the air should be just as flexible as the size of the tactical unit of any other branch. It depends somewhat on circumstances. At certain points and under specialized conditions you need different-sized tactical units from those at others. So that efficiency requires flexibility in the air, just as it does in the other branches. But, in order to be effective, that force should represent a thousand planes at least.

As time goes on - as I say, we are treading untried paths - you might require a force very much larger. But you might find, if the types coalesce, that such a force might be unwieldy. You might feel You would obtain better results in subdividing it. That is conjectural. But as a general rule, I would figure that force at about one thousand planes.

Mr. Edmiston - General, from the study that the War College, or whatever branch it is -

Gen. MacArthur (interposing) - The General Staff.

Mr. Edmiston - From the study that the General Staff has made since the War, have you not pretty well agreed that the air service will have an increasing function in any future wars?

Gen. MacArthur - I think that the whole trend throughout the world has been along that line. All air forces, in spite of the incessant talk of disarmament and the efforts made at Geneva to curtail them, are increasing. Of course, weapons of war not only have a certain inherent need and necessity, but they are very sensitive to "relativity," that is to say, what the other fellow has, and the air trend has been up.

The Chairman - General, I wish that you would finish your general statement, and then some of the other Members of the Committee may desire to ask you questions. When you have concluded your statement, the Members of the Committee will ask you whatever questions occur to them.

Gen. MacArthur - Yes. It was in accordance with this very sketchy general outline I have given you that the War Department set forth its plan.

The Chairman - General, as I understand the defensive strategy of America, it is purely one of defense; and if I understand it correctly, the war plans that the War Department may have, and that the joint planning board of the Army and the Navy may have, all are based and predicated upon the assumption of defense only.

Gen. MacArthur - Absolutely. The whole organization of the American Army would be different were it designed for offensive action.

The Chairman - Yes. Now, General, having been a member of the Committee when the acts of July 2 and July 26 were enacted in 1926, which created the five-year program for the Navy and the Army, respectively, I remember that that legislation was predicated upon the conclusions of the Morrow Board.

Gen. MacArthur - Yes.

The Chairman - Upon which were eminent representatives of both the Army and the Navy, as well as distinguished civilians?

Gen. MacArthur - correct.

The Chairman - And the ratio of 1,000 to the Navy, and 1,800 to the Army was then determined as the result of those studies?

Gen. MacArthur - That is correct.

The Chairman - Exactly?

Gen. MacArthur - It was so written into the law.

The Chairman - That was written into the law. Now, General, as I view the situation, the Navy, upon a defensive mission, would have to guard, so far as the continental United States is concerned, only ten or twelve, possibly, of entry ports towards which any enemy fleet might advance in order to invade the integrity of the United States; whereas the Army, through its air force, through its coast guard, and through its land forces, is expected to defend the entire frontier, whether by land or by water; and that entire frontier totals between 9,000 and 10,000 miles.

Now, if as a result of recent action by the House of Representatives, at least - if there should be approved by the Senate and the President and enacted into law, the air force of the Navy is to be increased to a total of 2,184 planes, in order to defend the continental United States at about ten or twelve vulnerable points, by the old-time "Rule of Three," to what extent should the air forces of the United States Army be increased in order to enable it to accomplish its mission of defending our entire frontier, to the North and the South and~to the East and the West?

Gen. MacArthur - Certainly, answering very generally, proportionately. But I would like to give my own conception along the general lines that you have suggested.

The mission of the Navy is to protect the United States, just as the mission of the Army is to protect the United States. They do it in different media. The first line of defense, the far-flung line, is the Navy; the final and main line of defense, the Army. Both of them have definitely to protect not only the mainland of the United States, but its borders, its possessions and its vital interests as well. Only they do it in two entirely different ways. The Navy goes out on the waters, and endeavors to interpose itself as a screen to prevent any element of attack from breaking through and reaching the United States. They protect the United States, just as we do. But they do it on the sea, rather than on the land. If an enemy breaks through or eludes the Navy, or the Navy is necessarily engaged elsewhere, the next element, and the only element that is left to destroy him, is the Army.

So that there is no such thing really as a complete geographical line of demarcation between the services which those two groups will perform. It is quite possible that they may be both needed in the endeavor to crush an attacking enemy.

A great misconception has grown up with reference to the subject of coast defense. The term "coast defense" in itself is something of a misnomer. No nation that has ever lived could stand the cost of a cordon defense applied to such borders as has the United States. The system of cordon defense is a discarded theory. Rather you should have a rapidly concentrating force which can be ahead of the enemy at any place where he is going to strike; and you hold such a force in an interior position to throw to any exterior point

We do have, on our coasts, harbor defenses at certain specified points, which are primarily for the protection of Navy bases, so that the Navy will have a refuge. The Navy is not a completely independent unit. It must have the Army to support its bases and to protect it when it comes into port. We, of course, hold those particularly important points, too, to ward off the depredations of marauding attacks. But the primary purpose is to maintain bases for the fleet to occupy. But they are merely strong points, they are merely fortified strong points on a potential battle front.

The main defense is not the fixed fortifications that we put there, but it is the mobile navy and the mobile troops that we would throw there immediately if the enemy started to attack at that point - the same mobile forces that we would throw to another threatened point. Such is the very essence of the G.H.Q. air force. It can be thrown to any point on the coast for its protection. The proper conception, in my opinion, of the line of demarcation between the Navy air and Army air is that the Navy air, like everything else that attaches to the Navy, should be for the purpose of increasing the fighting powers of the fleet. Anything that improves the power and strength of the fleet is money well spent.

So that any development of the air, which increases the air potentialities of the cruising fleets, certainly must be regarded as logical and proper. Any developments of the air which would not be present with the fleet, should properly be a function of a land-based force and belong to the Army. I do not care by what nomenclature you may call it, it is in reality a land function, and in basic terms, therefore, an Army function.

There is no real conflict, therefore - although the press and a great section of the country, and even many professional men on both sides have fought very bitterly over this nebulous question of coast defense - it presents no real basis of discussion and disagreement at all. The air forces that properly belong to the Navy are the air forces that go with the fleet. And the air forces that are to be used and launched as attack units from the land belong to the Army. That does not mean, of course, that the Navy should be limited in its general training and control or prevented from having land bases, where their air training is done, where their reequipping is done, and where they may even have special missions. But it does mean that the statute which was enacted by Congress, many years ago and which settled this question after the most thorough discussion by all the most competent professional elements in the Nation at the time, stated, in effect, that the aviation for the Navy should be based upon the fleet, and that the aviation for the Army should be based upon the land.

It has been one of the most unfortunate circumstances of air development that the various groups have not had the conception I have just outlined; because it has resulted in friction and in contention, and the growth of an idea in civilian circles that neither the Army nor the Navy knew exactly what they were driving at.

Congress, after elaborate study, fixed the general ratio of airplane strength in the Army and Navy at 18 to 10. And with the air problem in such a continuous state of flux, with the lack of crystallization that you can expect at any definite moment in the near future, I would say that that was about as good a rule of thumb as any I know.

The Chairman - I think it will be well at this point, for the information of the Committee, if I refer to the statutes with regard to that.

A proviso contained in the Act of June 5, 1920 (41 Stat.954) reads as follows:

"That hereafter the Army Air Service shall control all aerial operations from land bases, and Naval Aviation shall have control of all aerial operations attached to a fleet, including shore stations whose maintenance is necessary for operation connected with the fleet, for construction and experimentation and for the training of personnel."

Gen. MacArthur - There is a practicable system of cooperation between the War and Navy Departments, as well as between the Army and Navy field forces. Through the medium of the Joint Board and its auxiliary boards, there has been established the policy of what is known as "paramount interest": when the two services reach an area where they are operating in conjunction with each other, and one or the other has a predominant interest, the senior of that service which has a predominant interest takes command of all the forces. For instance, in an area in which the Navy fleet was operating, and in which their interests were predominant, the Navy admiral would have control of all elements, not only of his own service, but also those of the Army. He would have not only control of such Army elements of the air as may be present, but of all other elements of the Army. As an illustration, when troops were sent from Manila to Shanghai a year and a half ago for the protection of the International Settlement the predominant interest in that situation was a Navy interest. The Asiatic fleet was there, and the Admiral commanding the fleet took command of the Army elements. The 31st Infantry passed to his command. Similarly, there would be instances where the Navy elements in the sphere of operations would pass under the Army command. So that, at any point, any area of battle where the two services act in conjunction, the coordination is secured through that one which has predominant interest taking control completely of both branches.

The Chairman - General, it has always confused me, however, in discussing that problem, as to which commander on the ground, the Naval commander or the land troop commander, should determine whose interest is predominant.

Gen. MacArthur - That question is, of course, determined in the final analysis by joint action of the controlling heads here in Washington or by the Commander in Chief, the President of the United States.

The Chairman - General, will you give your attention to this consideration with air power proper: if the minimum strength, as a striking force, of 1,000 planes, in five wings, is essential; and if the maximum strength be 1,500 planes, as such striking force immediately available to strike as a unit in any direction, it is manifest that there would have to be a reservoir, a reserve, to supply fatalities in this striking force. And in view of the Army Air Corps as a whole, would it not be necessary to increase not only the number of planes and personnel necessary to constitute this G.H.Q. striking force, but also to increase the air component as a whole, in order to have an ample reservoir in order to enable it as a whole to accomplish its other missions?

Gen. MacArthur - The very fabric of our system of National Defense is based upon a reserve drawn from the civil population. It is just as essential for the air as it would be for any other branch.

The Chairman - Thank you.

Mr. Hill - What would you do with this G.H.Q. fleet in time of peace? Would they be more or less concentrated, or would they be scattered around during certain seasons of the year? What would you do with them?

Gen. MacArthur - For the purposes of administration, training, and control, it would be handled along the same general lines that we now practice. It would be commanded by an Air officer responsible to the commanding general, but would not be concentrated in any one place. It could be concentrated, however, for training at any time.

Mr. Hill - But they might be housed, so to speak, throughout the United States?

Gen. MacArthur - The subdivisions would be.

Mr. Hill - They would be. Your thought would be that they would be added to what we have in the air force?

Gen. MacArthur - Yes. We have, of course, the nucleus now of what amounts to a G.H.Q. air force. You will remember, for example, the maneuvers held around Boston two years ago?

Mr. Hill - Yes.

Gen. MacArthur - Air units were concentrated suddenly from the entire Army. We now have the nucleus of a G.H.Q. air force, two wings, the Eastern Wing and the Western Wing. The Eastern Wing is based on Langley Field, Va., and the Western Wing on March Field, Calif. But it is inadequate.

Mr. Hill - You feel that this increase is the very minimum that we should have to have the proper air force?

Gen. MacArthur - Yes, I feel that we should -

Mr. Hill (interposing) - Have you gone into the question of cost at all, General? That is, what this increase would cost in the way of materiel and personnel? Have you gone into what this increase would cost?

Gen. MacArthur - Only in a general way. I can give you rough estimates.

Mr. Hill - You know that question always arises.

Gen. MacArthur - That question naturally arises. Money, unfortunately, seems to be the basis of everything in this world.

Mr. Hill - That is right.

Gen. MacArthur - But I do not think it is especially pertinent to this authorization. This is not an appropriation bill. It is merely an authorization. The bill that you are considering, as I understand it, envisions a general authorization and does not involve the immediate expenditure of any money.

Mr. Hill - Yes: but you realize this - that even though it is only an authorization, the House always wants to know what this thing will cost. You understand that?

Gen. MacArthur - Yes. But, of course, that would depend upon what you write into the bill.

Mr. Hill - Did the recommendation of the General Staff contain any additional authorization, so far as the personnel of the officers and the enlisted personnel are concerned?

Gen. MacArthur - We believe the minimum immediate increase should be the 403 officers previously authorized to augment the Air Corps, and the number of 6,240 enlisted men who were taken from the other branches of the service - I believe not in accordance with the correct interpretation of the previous statute enacted by you - for transfer from the other branches to the Air Corps. That would be the minimum.

Mr. Hill - Well, of course, those 403 officers would be in addition to the Army personnel; and that number of enlisted personnel would be in addition to the Army enlisted personnel.

Gen. MacArthur - Absolutely. I know of nothing more destructive than to try to pass a constructive piece of legislation, which will be based upon the destruction of some other elements of national defense.

Mr. Hill - Well, these other elements are pretty well skeletonized anyhow, are they not?

Gen. MacArthur - They are starved and skeletonized. As I have said to this Committee a number of times, they are below the danger point. The National Defense Act was one of the greatest acts that was ever written, but it has never been supported financially by its creators.

Mr. Hill - I do not want to get off the subject of the air; but of course, you feel, General, that what we ought to do is not only to increase the air and establish these General Headquarters forces, as suggested by you and the Staff, but we ought also to increase the other branches?

Gen. MacArthur - That is my opinion, but I would not wish to prejudice this special feature by involving other general subjects which would probably succeed in killing this.

I believe, to answer that I think is in your mind - this authorization should carry specific increases of the officers and men that I have stated.

Mr. Hill - It ought to be so written into the law?

Gen. MacArthur - It ought to be written into the law.

Mr. Hill - So that there can be no question but what these increases are additions to the existing strength, both in officers and enlisted men?

Gen. MacArthur - That is correct. You know without my explaining the difficulties we have in getting the added personnel of which I have spoken.

Mr. Hill - Yes, I appreciate that; and I agree thoroughly with what you have said, to wit, that the intent and purpose of the Committee and of Congress, as expressed in the Act of 1926, has not been carried out.

Gen. MacArthur - I do not think there is any question about it.

Mr. James - General, what was the name of this last board?

Gen. MacArthur - The last board had no name, but if I named it I would call it "The Drum Board." Gen. Drum was the senior member on the board. The membership, in addition to the Deputy Chief of Staff (who is Gen. Drum), included the Chief of the Air Corps, the Chief of the War Plans Division, the Chief of Coast Artillery, and the President of the War College.

Mr. James - What are their names, and was there anybody else?

Gen. MacArthur - The members of that board were Gen. Drum, Gen. Foulois, Gen. Kilbourne, Gen. Gulick, and Gen. Simonds.

Mr. James - What was the date of their report?

Gen. MacArthur - I could not tell you, but I think their report was made in the month of August. I can verify that if you desire. Do you remember, Gen. Drum?

Gen. Drum - You approved it the 11th of October.

Gen. MacArthur - The 11th of October, the final report that they put in was approved on that date.

Mr. James - Now, you are talking about 403 officers. You mean, the 403 officers that were in the authorization of 1926?

Gen. MacArthur - I do.

Mr. James - How many additional officers did they recommend?

Gen. MacArthur - The board did not go into that subject.

Mr. James - And the 6,250 enlisted men?

Gen. MacArthur - I do not think the general increases that will be necessary would have to be covered by special legislation. The present National Defense Act carries an authorization for 6,000 officers more than have been appropriated for; and an authorization of nearly 160,000 men more than have been appropriated for. So that it would be merely a question of getting the necessary appropriations; you would not need the authorization.

But our purpose in especially delimiting these officers and men was to prevent by "appropriation law," if I can coin such a phrase, the choking down of the intent of the 1926 act, and to have this number in addition to what we now get under the appropriations. And I believe if it is not written into law, it will be practically impossible of accomplishment.

Mr. James - The Air Corps got practically all of the 6,250 men, did they not?

Gen. MacArthur - Yes, sir. We built the Air Corps up to what it was authorized. We were faced with the situation of a young and new branch which, if it did not have its troops, would possibly decline. And so we sacrificed the older branches of the service and took the men from them. That was when we furled the flags of many of the old regiments, and in the regiments that were left we cut out battalions, and in the battalions that were left we cut out companies.

At that time the Chief of Air Corps advised against it; but the opinion of the General Staff at that time was that it should be done, even if the sacrifice fell heavily on other branches.

The same policy would have applied to the officers; but statutory requirements made it impracticable. So we supplied that requirement as far as practicable through the use of Reserve officers, as they graduated from Kelly School.

Mr. James - Of course, Congress did authorize the increase of 6,250 men, at that time, but those 6,250 men were not appropriated for. Mr. Buchanan, of the Appropriations Committee, in response to a request of me, said that for many years the appropriation bill could only be increased a certain amount to take care of that increase?

Gen. MacArthur - That is my understanding.

Mr. James - And it was the Commander in Chief of the Army who insisted upon these men being taken from other branches of the service and put in the Air Corps rather than the Congress, or the Army, or anybody else. Is that true?

Gen. MacArthur - The decision of the Commander in Chief was that the total strength should not be increased.

The decision to make the transfers of the enlisted personnel from the other branches was the decision of the War Department. But the limitation that there should be no increase in the total strength was made by the then President of the United States.

Mr. James - When was the Lassiter Board appointed?

Gen. MacArthur - The Lassiter Board, as I recall, was appointed about ten years ago.

Mr. James - Gen. Drum was a member of that board?

Gen. MacArthur - Gen. Drum was a member, yes.

Mr. James - And Maj. Gen. Wells and Gen. Lassiter. Who were the other members?

Gen. MacArthur - I do not know.

Gen. Drum - General Heintaelman, Colonel Hunt and Lieutenant Colonels Gulick and Lahm.

Mr. James - That report did not reach Congress until 1926, did it?

Gen. MacArthur - I could not tell you.

Mr. James - It did not reach Congress until 1926, and we took no action, because the Secretary of the Navy would not allow that bill to come to Congress until such time as there was an agreement as to how many planes there should be for the Navy. When it was decided that there should be 1,000 and the Army 1,800, I then introduced a bill, and that was the first time that the Lassiter Board report reached Congress. Was the Army consulted at that time, about the Lassiter Board increase?

Gen. MacArthur - At that time? I do not know. I was not in the Department.

Mr. James - Were you consulted as to the 1,000 planes now pending?

Gen. MacArthur - Were we consulted on the Navy program now under consideration?

Mr. James - Yes.

Gen. MacArthur - I knew nothing about it until I saw it in the press. Had it been submitted to me I would have been heartily in accord with its provisions.

Mr. James - How many planes did the Lassiter Board provide for?

Gen. MacArthur - I could not tell you.

Mr. James - Can you tell how many, Gen. Drum?

Gen. Drum - My recollection is around 2,500. I am not sure of the figure, but I think it was 2,500 on a 10-year program.

Mr. James - How many officers?

Gen. Drum - I am not sure. My recollection would be rather vague, but I would say that the officers must have been somewhere around 4,000; but I am not sure. I could check that up very easily.

Mr. James - Well, that was ten years ago. You were a member of both boards. Are you now advocating in 1934 less planes, less men and less officers than you recommended to Congress up to 1924?

Gen. MacArthur - I do not think we are - not if you accept our recommendation. What I am anxious to do is to get an authorization which will not limit us by the strait-jacket of numbers such as was written into the 1926 bill. It is quite possible that the future development of the air will demand much higher figures than any that have been considered. It is quite possible, on the other hand, that anticipated totals may not be reached. I believe that there should be a degree of flexibility in the matter.

And as I said, Mr. Chairman, I do not believe that you should attempt to fix numbers, any more than you fix the number of guns you give the artillery, and so on. I think the language should be general enough to permit sufficient latitude to care for changing conditions.

Mr. James - Well, you are asking for 1,000 planes, and that would only give us a total of 3,300; and my recollection is that we recommended 4,000 or more in 1924?

Gen. MacArthur - I am perfectly agreeable to have you write in any added figure that you desire.

Mr. James - These 1,000 planes, or 1,500, are all to be concentrated in the United States?

Gen. MacArthur - They are all to be primarily concentrated in the United States. I contemplate the use of those planes, however, in any emergency wherever it might be necessary. I contemplate, in case of necessity, throwing the entire outfit into Panama, or over to Hawaii, as the practicability of getting them over there becomes more and more apparent, and their need more definite. I am not even sure you could not get them over to the Philippines. You might have to do it in jumps - to Hawaii, Guam and Luzon. But I would throw them to any place where necessity arose. But they will primarily be concentrated for training in the United States.[17]

(There was an informal discussion which the reporter was directed not to report.)

Mr. Thomason - I have been listening with interest to General MacArthur, and I am in agreement with his pro-

---

[17] This is air power as we know it today. (Frank C. Waldrop - 1942)

gram. But I also agree with Mr. Goss that, in view of what happened yesterday, it embarrasses me all the more, and that we certainly need to have a co-related program of some sort in connection with national defense; and if we go along, as we did yesterday, without making a fight - until a proper investigation can be made, why, I think it would be very easy to make me a strong advocate of a Board of National Defense, because, due to the cleverness of the Naval Affairs Committee, they will come in and steal the entire aviation program for the United States.

Hearings on the War Department Appropriation Bill Regarding Pay and Promotion Situation
1934

During the hearings on the War Department appropriation bill there was intermittent discussion of the pay and promotion situation in the Army. Representative Ross Collins, of Meridian, Miss., chairman of the subcommittee and proponent of Army reductions, attempted to bring out points favorable to his ideas. Collins, who fancied himself as an authority on all Army matters, including pay, promotion, motorization and mechanization, was MacArthur's No. 1 heckler in or out of Congress. He ridiculed MacArthur as a strutter and frequently implied the General neither understood nor desired conversion of the Army to motors in the air and on the ground. This following passage is an interesting example of the conflicts between the two men - Collins asking questions that flicked at the dignity and efficiency of the officer corps - MacArthur declining to answer them directly but always keeping his poise. Excerpts from the portions of the testimony which Mr. Collins permitted to be printed follow:

Frank C. Waldrop, Editor
MacArthur On War
Duell, Sloan and Pearce, New York
©1942 by Frank C. Waldrop

Pay of Officers

Mr. Collins - General, you spoke about the pay of officers being less than that of other employees of the Government. Was that your statement?

Gen. MacArthur - Not quite, Mr. Chairman. I said in the relative increases from time to time, as the living conditions in this country have improved, the relative increases of pay of Government employees have been less rapid in the six uniformed services than in any others.

Mr. Collins - I appreciate the fact all of us feel that we are not making quite as much money as our talents entitle us to make.

Gen. MacArthur - I did not put it quite that way.

Mr. Collins - It is true that an Army officer has more ways of increasing his salary than the ordinary employee of the Government, is that not true?

Gen. MacArthur - I do not think the average Army officer is able to increase his salary at all.

Mr. Collins - That is, by means of his percentage increase per year.

Gen. MacArthur - In addition to his base pay he gets certain emoluments from the Government.

Mr. Collins - The average civilian has not those methods of increasing his salary from time to time.

Gen. MacArthur - He has not those methods, but he has other methods which are probably much greater.

Mr. Collins - Which are, as a matter of fact, probably less.

Gen. MacArthur - That, of course, is a matter of opinion.

Mr. Collins - Then his retirement allowance is very much less, is it not?

Gen. MacArthur - The normal civilian does not retire at all. To be forced to retire is a disobligation of an Army officer.

Mr. Collins - I am talking about a civilian employee of the Government.

Gen. MacArthur - They have certain bases of retired pay.

Mr. Collins (interposing) - Their retired pay is about $100 a month?

Gen. MacArthur - A maximum of $100 a month.

"Overage" Officers

Mr. Collins - Do you think it is in the interest of efficiency to have all these old officers in the grades, say, of lieutenant colonel and below?

Gen. MacArthur - The ideal Army list, of course, is one in which officers reach the higher grades at the earliest possible time. That is, where they can combine with experience, the physical vigor that comes with approximate youth.

However, you must understand that the actual list is due to the absorption after the World War of a large group of officers who had demonstrated on the battlefield their peculiar efficiency for military service.

The Army was expanded immediately after the World War by several thousand officers, and the natural men to take those positions were the men who had served during the war with distinguished records. The same condition follows every war.

Mr. Collins - It was an easy matter to get into the Army as an officer after the war, was it not, immediately after the war?

Gen. MacArthur - Boards were appointed of general officers who passed upon the qualifications of the applicants.

Mr. Collins - And it was an easy matter to get in, comparatively speaking?

Gen. MacArthur - I could not tell you; I did not serve on those boards. I do not know.

Mr. Collins - Anyway, a large number came in at that time?

Gen. MacArthur - That was required by law.

Mr. Collins - General, is not the correct way to advance officers, to start a young officer in the Army and let him remain in the position of second lieutenant - how many years?

Gen. MacArthur - My own personal opinion would be that he should serve in that grade three years.

Mr. Collins - And then go to -

Gen. MacArthur (interposing) - The grade of first lieutenant.

Mr. Collins - Then serve how long?

Gen. MacArthur - I should say he should serve in that grade about three more years, or perhaps four.

Mr. Collins - And then go to the grade of captain and serve how long?

Gen. MacArthur - I should say an officer should be a captain within seven years of entering the service.

Mr. Collins - And a major within what time?

Gen. MacArthur - The ideal condition would probably be that he would be a major within 15 years' service.

Mr. Collins - And then a lieutenant colonel?

Gen. MacArthur - Shortly afterwards.

Mr. Collins - Two or three years?

Gen. MacArthur - Three or four years.

Mr. Collins - And then be a colonel within what time?

Gen. MacArthur - I should say a man should be a colonel, if it is possible, after about 25 years' service under peace conditions.

Mr. Collins - And those lengths of service would be required so as to familiarize a man with all of the different phases of the several grades?

Gen. MacArthur - Yes, and to familiarize him with the increasing responsibility; to develop his wisdom with experience.

OFFICERS' PROMOTION BILL

Mr. Collins - I have examined your promotion bill, and the promotion bill you have, as I view it, merely carries these older officers as just deadweight. You star certain of the officers that you think ought to be promoted, and then these starred officers carry up the other officers.

Gen. MacArthur - Yes.

Mr. Collins - That is the bill that is generally known as the MacArthur bill?

Gen. MacArthur - The starred officers are based upon actuarial tables. The whole basis of my promotion bill is to take the normal flow, over many years, of casualties, and apply it so that you bring a normal man who enters the service, say, at 22, to the grade of colonel at about 52.

I applied this actuary's curve with that limiting condition; and that curve hit certain men, and those men became what we called starred men; they became the loci that were to determine the flow of promotions for the Army; the men who were not starred went up with those who were.

It was an endeavor to provide a uniform system and give a flow of promotion to everybody in the service.

Mr. Collins - And the starred officer would carry up every man between him and the next starred officer?

Gen. MacArthur - Yes; not because there was any starring of men because of selection based on ability. It was merely as the curve happened to hit those individuals, due to their age and service. The term "starred" is perhaps an unfortunate one.

Mr. Collins - The starred officers are exactly the right age officers?

Gen. MacArthur- -Exactly; that is it.

Mr. Collins - And the unstarred officers were the overaged officers?

Gen. MacArthur - Exactly.

Mr. Collins - The present set-up makes the pay cost of our Army just about as high as it is possible to make it, does it not?

Gen. MacArthur - High, due to stagnation of promotion in grades.

Mr. Collins - That is what I say; with the same number of officers, the present set-up makes it about as high as it is possible to make it.

Gen. MacArthur - It is high due to the slowness of promotion.

EXCERPTS FROM THE ANNUAL REPORT OF THE CHIEF OF STAFF, UNITED STATES ARMY FISCAL YEAR JULY 1, 1933 - JUNE 30, 1934

Determination of the level at which military strength is to be supported in the United States and establishment of the system under which it is to be attained are responsibilities of the American people, expressing their will through Congress. The soldier's task is a professional one, involving the technical phases of military preparation in all its ramifications. His mission is to produce the maximum of national security with the means made available by the approved acts of Congress.

From a broad national viewpoint, therefore, the Army is an operating agency, having little voice in the formation of governmental policy, either foreign or domestic. But since the Army is composed of men who, throughout a lifetime of public duty, devote their talents and energies to mastery of the military profession, there is developed in it a specialized knowledge of facts and conditions that bear directly upon the vital subject of national security. This information, in its fundamental features and implications, is indispensable to the public and its elected representatives if they are to arrive at correct decisions concerning the country's essential defense needs. Wisdom in all such decisions is necessary, since to support a needlessly elaborate national defense is to dissipate uselessly a portion of the Nation's resources; to maintain too little is to court disaster.

It is, then, clearly the duty of the military head of the Army to place periodically before the Secretary of War, and through him to make available to interested sections of the public, accurate analyzes of the principal factors in our land-defense problem, including specific reports on the current strength and efficiency of the military forces, and professional conclusions as to their ability and readiness to discharge the missions for which they are maintained.

The amended National Defense Act is the legal charter of the American system of land defense. It establishes in broad outline the composition of the Army of the United States and prescribes the limiting numerical strength of two of its principal components, the Regular Army and the National Guard. It makes provision for civilian training, arranged in several categories so as to suit the convenience of volunteers in every walk of life. It provides also for the performance of preparatory work demonstrated by experience to be necessary, particularly as applied to the emergency mobilization of men and materiel.

This military system was evolved by Congress in the light of startling World War lessons. From our own experiences in that conflict we learned that a world power, no matter how pacific its purposes, may not always be able to avoid the commitment of war. We found once again that military weakness may inspire in others such contemptuous disregard for our national rights that violations thereof become frequent, flagrant, and finally unbearable. We found also that hasty improvisation of an efficient fighting force is wholly impossible, even when the treasure of the Nation is spent without stint.

The plan developed in 1920 was, therefore, so designed as to give the Nation a justified confidence in its own security, but without constituting, in any particular, a menace to the peace of the world.

That law is in fact a clear exposition of pacific intent. Even if accorded the full financial support intended when written, our Military Establishment would be incapable of sudden aggressive employment against any first-class power. It would still constitute nothing more than a sound skeleton upon which to build the forces that would be necessary to attain victory against any but the weakest of enemies. The plan conforms to the traditions of our people in permitting no type of compulsory military service in time of peace, nor the maintenance of an unnecessarily large professional compo nent. It was intended to provide for the United States nothing more than that reasonable defensive posture which our first President earnestly exhorted us to maintain as the best assurance of remaining at peace.

In spite of its moderate purposes, the National Defense Act has been given but limited and decreasing support. Our military framework has become so attenuated that the ideal of reasonable security sought by the Congress which enacted it is far from attainment. Our Regular Army and National Guard are at considerably less than half the strength contemplated in the law. The Officers' Reserve Corps is inadequately supported in the essentials of training. We have no enlisted Reserve. Stocks of materiel are in vital respects inadequate even for limited forces, and, such as they are, comprise principally World War equipment, manifestly obsolescent. The preparatory missions devolving upon the Military Establishment in time of peace cannot in some respects be efficiently performed; while the grave responsibilities that would fall to it in emergency would require frantic improvisations and wasteful and possibly ineffective sacrifice of the Nation's manhood and material resources. These are facts - demonstrable both in the light of history's lessons and through logical analysis of existing conditions.

This blunt expression of War Department conviction divulges the secrets of our weakness, which if known only to professional soldiers had probably best remain concealed. Unfortunately, they are secrets only to our own people in whom resides exclusively, in the last analysis, the power for correction. They are fully known to qualified military observers abroad and to all those governments that give more credence to the conclusions of the trained soldier than we do.

The purpose of this report is to present a comprehensive and undistorted picture of the Military Establishment, to point out specifically wherein defects now exist and to outline the efforts being made within the Department to correct or minimize these, and finally to submit a coordinated program of military preparation scaled to the minimum level consistent with our country's reasonable security.

EARLY POST-WAR DEVELOPMENT

An efficient army cannot be a static organism. Its evolution must keep pace with and is in large part dependent upon constantly evolving changes in the industrial, scientific, so-cial, and political fields. Adherence to out-moded tools, methods, and organization spells obsolescence, one of the most insidious and at the same time one of the most disabling diseases that can attack an army. Yet time and again during the past century and a half the American Army has been forced by circumstances to endure extended periods of practically complete stagnation in technical development, largely because of public failure to understand that the consequences are always an increased danger to the Nation's peace and safety, and certain to be reflected, should war occur, in multiplied cost and sacrifice. The decade beginning in 1921 very definitely constituted such a period. For this there were several contributory causes.

In the early post-war years the Army had to devote its attention almost exclusively to important problems of liquidation remaining as the aftermath of a gigantic mobilization, and to those arising out of the drastic changes in the Military Establishment required by the amended National Defense Act of 1920. These and related tasks were unduly prolonged and made more burdensome by repeated readjustments in organization and administration entailed by constantly dwindling financial support. So completely did these tasks occupy the attention of the War Department and the Army that more than 10 years ago the Secretary of War was constrained to report:

"Nothing is more important than to afford this force (Regular Army) a few years of uninterrupted opportunity to accomplish its own reconstruction, and to fulfill its functions concerning the other components of the Army of the United States."

An even more serious result of inadequate appropriations was the virtual abandonment of every activity in excess of bare maintenance of the insufficient forces allowed.

Under these conditions responsible military officials fully realized that as the Army experienced progressive diminution in actual strength, it was likewise falling further behind the requirements of modern efficiency in equipment, training, and readiness for emergency. As early as 1922 the Secretary of War made a full report of the deplorable consequences of extreme skeletonization, and stated that, without an immediate increase in the Regular Army, efficiency could not be sustained. This and subsequent protests were ignored; indeed, further reduction was imposed, greatly intensifying the difficulties of the War Department and further imperiling the efficiency of the Army.

Yet with the passage of time, earnest and effective work in the Army and the War Department gradually succeeded in accomplishing many of the tasks that were essential preliminaries to the introduction of modern equipment and attendant revisions in organization and methods. By the close of the calendar year 1930 the elementary organizational work arising out of the National Defense Act and the several major readjustments required by subsequent appropriation laws had been largely completed; the military school system was functioning on a satisfactory basis; instruction and administration of the civilian components had crystallized under sound and continuing policies, while appropriate sections of the General Staff had made satisfactory progress in the development of basic methods applicable to a modern mobilization. With these accomplishments representing a relatively high degree of administrative readiness for emergency, the Army was ready to turn its attention more distinctly toward tactical efficiency.

In the field of materiel a somewhat comparable situation prevailed. Technicians had made great progress in the preliminary work of developing and testing new or improved models of military equipment, the potential value of which could not be doubted. But lack of money had, except in one or two items, prohibited the procurement of these in usable quantities, compelling the Army to adhere to training methods, unit organization, and a tactical doctrine applicable to weapons of definitely inferior characteristics. But by 1930 important classes of equipment left to the Army as a legacy from the World War were either almost completely used up or were approaching mechanical exhaustion. In others obsolescence had become so pronounced as to preclude their employment in any major emergency. Partial replacement could not long be deferred, and it was essential that every dollar spent should contribute in maximum degree to military efficiency.

From every standpoint therefore the time appeared propitious for initiating an intensive program of modernization, even though the handicap of insufficient funds was as serious as ever before. As a consequence of these considerations, when I assumed, almost 4 years ago, the duties of Chief of Staff, I did so with the definitely formed determination of concentrating the energies of the Military Establishment toward this end. My purpose was not only to evolve, in the light of modern developments, a broad program of logical and coordinated objectives in every essential phase of military preparation, but to insure, so far as funds would permit, the Army's maximum progress toward each of the specific objectives so established. This undertaking marked the beginning of a new phase in the Army's post-war development.

The task thus set up was and is a most comprehensive one. All factors contributing toward military efficiency are involved. These include weapons and equipment in their constantly changing forms and applications; general and detailed organization; tactical doctrine; mobilization planning; and the strength, leadership, training, and morale of personnel. Among all these there exists such an intimate interrelationship that none can be completely isolated from the others in estimating its probable effect, or the Army's requirements in each. But since it is necessary to proceed from the simple to the complex in reaching an accurate answer to a problem so involved as that of determining the size, form, and character of the required Military Establishment, each of these factors must be examined separately and somewhat in detail in attempting to constitute therefrom a composite objective.

HIGHER TACTICAL ORGANIZATION OF THE ARMY OF THE UNITED STATES

Effective tactical employment of an army is wholly impossible in the absence of a complete and properly devised network of command and staff which, beginning with the lowest unit and extending through successively higher echelons to culminate in the Commander in Chief, assures the responsiveness of every element to the decisions of a single authority.

In approaching the problem of modernization, the forging of missing links in the chain of tactical command was established as the first objective, not only because of its great importance, but for the further reason that substantial progress in it could be accomplished by administrative action alone.

This matter, which very properly remained somewhat in the background as long as the Army was principally engaged in problems of reconstruction and readjustment and of administrative stabilization, assumed a high priority the moment attention was turned to increasing the Army's effectiveness as an integrated fighting ma-chine. Efficient agencies through which to exercise the necessary control cannot be hastily improvised; adequate preparation in this field is indispensable to success in any sudden emergency of major proportions.

To appreciate fully the significance of the policies adopted within the past 3 years to assure tactical unification, it is necessary to note briefly wherein the organizational set-up prevailing prior to 1932 was inapplicable to the requirements of field operations.

The principal War Department agencies for executing the details of mobilization plans and for supervising normal peace-time activities of all components are the nine corps area commands, which were constituted soon after the approval of the National Defense Act. They are territorial and administrative rather than tactical organizations and as such must remain in place and in operation throughout the progress of an emergency. Until 1932 there was no complete chain of tactical control paralleling the administrative system represented in the corps area commands. Consequently the American Army, if mobilized for field service, would have comprised, under these conditions, simply a collection of skeletonized divisions, each reporting directly to the War Department. Immediate and unified employment of all units available would have been impossible. Our situation was very similar to the one that existed in 1917, concerning which General Pershing has since written as follows:

"It was evident that considerable time must elapse before we could actually have more than a nominal force in the battle lines. Our very small Regular Army was scattered in weak detachments over the country and in our outlying possessions. There were no complete and permanent units larger than regiments, and even these were not suitably organized and equipped for major operations."

A plan for permanently welding existing units into a tactical whole was, after months of study, put into effect more than 2 years ago. Under its provisions all Regular Army and National Guard units in each of the areas bordering our four strategic frontiers have been organized into a unified army and subdivided into appropriate tactical groupments by the Army commander. Headquarters for each of the armies and corps commands have been established, although on a skeletonized basis. At the head of this tactical framework stands a G.H.Q., with the Chief of Staff as the military commander of the whole. This development is known as the "four-army organization."

Responsibilities devolving upon the army commanders include the development of appropriate war plans for the defense of their respective strategic regions; maintenance of a complete network of tactical command and staff throughout their armies; the conduct of appropriate training exercises including those for headquarters of higher units; and perfection of all necessary prearrangements to insure prompt and effective employment of troops in any crisis.

The four-army organization is more far-reaching in its implications than mere establishment and training of needed tactical groupments. It implies a fundamental change in the technique of preparation for land defense.

Until the adoption of this organization, War Department doctrine and planning emphasized as the first emergency need the initiation of a general mobilization program intended to produce a great civilian army. All other anticipated emergency missions became in effect secondary to this, based on the assumption that effective tactical action would be practically impossible until very large armies should become available. Such a conception was a direct outgrowth of experiences on the Western Front, where unusual conditions, as represented in flankless and heavily fortified lines, demanded great superiority in manpower as the price of victory, and where extraordinarily fine networks of roads and railways made possible the supply and maintenance of almost unlimited forces. Upon the conclusion of the World War the natural impulse, even of professional soldiers, was to look upon the huge armies of that conflict as the exemplification of another step in the evolution of warfare rather than as a product of special and unique circumstances.

But continued study and reflection and many significant scientific developments of the past decade combined to expose fundamental flaws in this theory, particularly as applied to our own national situation. There can be no doubt that thoroughly efficient and completely modernized forces, though of only moderate size, will be capable of striking telling blows. An attack by such units might be delivered against our sensitive areas with devastating suddenness, and the only sure defense would be prompt intervention of defensive forces featuring an equal degree of speed and power.

The four-army organization therefore places emphasis upon instant availability of a maximum proportion of existing forces, and is based upon the assumption that these can and will be raised to a high state of modern efficiency. The plan is a definite and direct outgrowth of the theory of modernization.

Decentralization to each army commander of responsibility for local organization and planning tasks promotes practicality in peace-time preparation because of its specific application to the defensive needs of a particular strategic region. The most effective and speediest use will be made of every unit in the Military Establishment. The Chief of Staff, in the event of war, will be able to center his attention upon the vital functions of operating and commanding field forces as a unified whole.

The progress made in the War Department and in subordinate commands under this concept of tactical unification and readiness to act received its first practical test in the field maneuver held in New Jersey in September of this year. This exercise featured the operation of a G.H.Q. and of headquarters of two armies and of their subordinate corps and divisions. The value of maintaining and training skeletonized headquarters for higher tactical units was reflected in the smooth and effective functioning of those establishments under conditions approximating the early stages of an actual campaign.

Briefly, an emergency of the gravest character was assumed to exist in New Jersey, resulting from a surprise invasion by modern forces while the attention of our own Army and Navy, with their air contingents, was engaged in a totally different direction. Orders initiating necessary defensive action were promptly issued to the commanders of the first and second armies, under whose direction the movements of covering troops (assumed) toward the affected area were begun. An account of the technical and tactical incidents of the succeeding situations would be of little interest except to professional men. But of specific concern to every citizen should be the conclusive proof furnished by the test that whatever troops might be available at the beginning of any emergency could be promptly employed, under the four-army organization, as an integrated machine rather than compelled to operate in the confusion of uncoordinated and ineffective action until the necessary staffs and headquarters could be improvised.

Practically every higher official and military student who analyzed the results of this exercise was convinced that perpetuation and perfection of the four-army organization are essential to our scheme of defense.

Materiel

Almost every important cause for change in tactics, training methods, and detailed organization of military units has its origin in scientific accomplishments in the fields of transportation and communication, weapons, and other technical equipment useful to an army operating in the field. Modernization implies the *development and acquisition, in all necessary types, of equipment of maximum efficiency, and the adoption of methods calculated to produce the most effective results from their coordinated use.*

Ten years of relative stagnation in this respect cannot, under any circumstances, be overcome instantaneously. To illustrate: Even after technicians have successfully completed the laborious work of developing a satisfactory model of a particular weapon, a sound doctrine affecting its use cannot be perfected solely upon a knowledge of its performance characteristics. The Staff is justified in formulating general policies with respect to employment, organization, training methods, and supply and maintenance only after new weapons have been procured in sufficient numbers to undergo thorough tactical experimentation. But the production of even small quantities of such new and special mechanisms requires time - often many months. Moreover, results obtained in this step-by-step procedure must constantly be checked against these attending similar efforts in related fields; for instance, progress toward mechanization must be influenced by developments in ammunition, antitank weapons, transportation facilities, and the like. Finally, there remains the task of training and indoctrinating the whole Army in the technic and tactical uses of the new equipment as it becomes available. All this manifestly is a time-consuming process, and clearly indicates the need for promptitude in initiating corrective programs whenever glaring deficiencies are found to exist.

The inadequacy of the American Army's present equipment is best demonstrated by specifically comparing some of its principal types with models which have been developed since the World War.

The Army's cross-country combat vehicles - commonly known as "tanks" - are hopelessly out of date. This class of weapon was brought out during the World War to provide protection for infantry in the open against the mass of small-arms fire which swept the battlefield. Its purpose was to restore to the attack a measure of the power it had lost to the great defensive strength of organized small-arms fire, particularly that of machine guns.

The earliest models of these weapons used on the Western Front were almost complete failures due principally to mechanical weaknesses. Intensive effort between 1915 and 1918 improved them materially, but even so, the best types appearing before the armistice were so susceptible to mechanical failure that many able combat soldiers were extremely doubtful that they could ever attain any important tactical value except in a special situation such as existed on the Western Front. The so-called "light tank" with which the American Army emerged from the war weighed about 7 tons, was capable of a maximum speed under favorable conditions of about 4 miles per hour, was armed with either a machine gun or a 1-pounder cannon, and carried sufficient armor to protect against small-arms ammunition then in use. It was mechanically unreliable.

The rapid advances being made in antitank defenses toward the close of the war proved so effective that a successful future for tanks was clearly dependent upon marked improvement in their performance characteristics. Every major power initiated construction programs to this end, our own efforts being handicapped, as in all other directions, by the paucity of funds provided for the purpose. But, by devoting every available dollar toward the development of a satisfactory experimental model, there were finally produced single units of real promise. The latest types are capable of a sustained speed of some 40 miles an hour on roads and of some 20 miles an hour across country, except in difficult terrain. These advances have been accompanied by equally significant ones in the reliability of the machine and in the effectiveness and power of its armament.

We find ourselves at present in this situation: We have on hand some hundreds of the World War tanks, totally unsuited to the conditions of modern war and of little value against an organized enemy in the field. Of tanks that can be classed as modern we have a total of 12, only 1 of which is of the type determined by tests to be the most efficient. Funds provided in the 1935 appropriations will secure for us in the near future a total of 64 tanks and combat cars with which a real beginning can be made toward the development of modern tactical doctrine as applied to them. This encouraging advance still leaves us, except in the efficiency of the model now available, relatively far behind in this phase of military preparation.

The most effective field gun of the World War was known as the "French 75 mm." The American Army had about 3,500 of these in its possession upon the signing of the Armistice and today it is the weapon with which our Field Artillery units are equipped. Compared to models which have been produced since that time, it is a markedly inferior piece. Its maximum traverse without shifting the trail is 6°, while it cannot be fired at the longer ranges except by digging a hole in which to drop the spade. It is incapable of rapid transportation on its own wheels since these are of the traditional wood and steel construction, and fast movement invariably results in damage to the mechanism of the gun. The latest model field gun developed in our service has, from a single position of the trail, a traverse of almost 90° and an elevation of 45°, giving it an enormously increased flexibility of fire. Wheels have been developed which permit towing of the gun at high speeds with no resulting damage. Manifestly a unit armed with the new weapon would enjoy a tremendous advantage over any equipped with the older type. Only through major alterations can the large number of guns now on hand be given the approximate characteristics of the new weapon. The project should be promptly initiated, since increased mobility in the other arms will be largely wasted unless accompanied by a comparable increase in flexibility of artillery fire and the speed with which artillery units can be brought into supporting positions.

In Infantry equipment technical advances have also been important. The magazine rifle, caliber .30, model 1903, was undoubtedly the most efficient military rifle of its time. Equipped with a bayonet, it has been the basic weapon of the American Infantry for 30 years, during which time improvements have applied solely to types of ammunition used. As a replacement for this weapon there has been developed a semiautomatic rifle of extraordinary efficiency. Its weight is no greater than that of the older model while its rate of accurately directed fire is three times as high, and fatigue incident to firing is much less. So far we have only 80 of the new rifles, with 1,500 provided for in the current appropriation bill.

Important improvements have been made also in all types of small-arms ammunition. The range of the normal bullet has been almost doubled, and armor-piercing ammunition has been greatly increased in efficiency. In machine guns the most important improvements relate to the .50 caliber. At present we have a serious deficiency in this type which, of all weapons so far produced, offers the greatest possibilities for defense against fast-moving tanks and is, in addition, particularly effective against hostile aircraft.

Another development of great significance involves antiaircraft materiel. Weapons used for this purpose during the World War were largely of an improvised character and consequently of low efficiency. Ever since, technicians have been developing machine guns and rapid-fire cannon so designed as to be particularly suitable for fire against air targets. Great improvements have been made also in instruments for the rapid and accurate adjustment of fire and in intelligence systems for the detection of the approach of hostile aircraft. Without appending any technical description of this materiel, it is sufficient to say that its efficiency is such as to constitute, when employed in quantity, a distinct threat to many types of air attack. Its value is unquestioned, in spite of which fact we have been able to procure only an insignificant amount. As in other activities, we have been forced to resort to expedients for the utilization of obsolete equipment, with the result that in this important matter we are likewise woefully behind the times. This equipment, in general, is intricate in design. Its production therefore requires time, as does also the attainment of the necessary skill in its operation. The importance of acquiring reasonable amounts of this equipment is further emphasized by the possibility that its employment may become vitally necessary in the very first phases of any future emergency.

Improvements in transportation, particularly motor vehicles, have been largely a product of commercial activity, as distinguished from those made in strictly military equipment. These improvements have opened up great possibilities for increasing mobility through substitution of motor vehicles for horse and mule transportation. Until last year almost the only equipment available for use consisted of war stocks, which are outmoded, inefficient, and expensive to maintain.

During the fiscal year 1934 an allotment of $10,000,000 was made to the War Department by the Public Works Administration to be applied to this glaring deficiency. Equipment is now being procured under this authorization, but we are still far from attaining the necessary progress, and additional sums are urgently needed for the purpose.

In aircraft the situation has been somewhat different. Following the enactment of the Air Corps law of 1926, the procurement of 1,800 planes was begun in five yearly increments. Although this schedule has not been fully maintained because of insufficiency of funds, all planes procured, either as original or replacement equipment, have been of the most efficient types available at the particular time. Thus, while no other class of military equipment shows, over an equal span of years, a greater increase in power, efficiency, and effectiveness, in this one arm we have not fallen behind in quality. Indeed, investigation reveals that in some types of fighting airplanes our latest models are appreciably better than any others known to exist. The most crying need is for equipment necessary to build up a completely organized G.H.Q. Air Force, and thereafter for a maintenance program which will keep the whole Air Force reasonably well modernized in types and numbers.

In numerous other classes of equipment significant improvements have been realized. Obviously any army supplied with all these modern weapons and mechanisms would be immeasurably stronger in mobility and fire power than an opponent equipped with the types our Army is forced to use. Assuming approximate equality otherwise, the badly equipped force would be hopelessly outclassed from the moment it came in contact with its enemy. It could not escape defeat and destruction. It is useless to expect satisfactory modernization of the Army until this situation has been substantially corrected; and in our own case efficiency is of paramount importance because of the smallness of our total forces.

The matter of keeping available an adequate war reserve of munitions and equipment presents many perplexing difficulties, chief of which is attainment of the required end without occasioning useless expense to the Government. Technical improvement is a continuing process. At irregular intervals engineers produce models in every type of weapon that represent distinct advances over older ones. Manifestly, to attempt the constant maintenance in the latest types of the great stocks of weapons and equipment needed to satisfy the full initial requirements of an emer-

gency army is outside the realm of reason. Any such attempt would require the complete and periodic replacement of each item. The cost would be prohibitive.

Moreover, such an ambitious program would be based upon a conception of instantaneous readiness to strike with our full national power in an emergency. This is the very antithesis of the spirit of our defense system and the National Defense Act. The American policy, it must be repeated, seeks nothing further than our own national security through the permanent maintenance and training of an efficient skeleton upon which to build an emergency army, and to insure adequate protection during the process of mobilization. This applies to weapons and to equipment as well as to personnel, and the plan advocated by the War Department for maintaining a satisfactory degree of modernization in materiel conforms in every detail to this objective.

The plan is summarized as follows:

"Continuous experimentation and development to insure possession of models which in efficiency are equal, and if possible superior, to any other in their respective classes.

"The procurement of each type in moderate quantities so as to develop applicable changes in doctrine, training methods, and organization, and to maintain a combat force of reasonable size in a state of readiness for efficient emergency action.

"All necessary replacements to be made in the latest models available.

"Determination of probable war needs in each essential class of munitions.

"Every possible prearrangement in peace for prompt quantity production in emergency."

Adherence to this program represents, in the field of materiel, the minimum preparation consistent with safety.

It is easy, of course, to overemphasize the influence of machinery in war. It is man that makes war, not machines, and the human element must always remain the dominant one. Weapons are nothing but tools and each has its distinctive limitations as well as its particular capabilities. Effective results can be obtained only when an army is skillfully organized and trained so as to supplement inherent weaknesses in one type of weapon by peculiar powers in others.

The combat vehicle, for instance, was designed to make possible the carrying out of an attack in the face of intensive small-arms fire. But it has no defensive power and, even assuming its complete success in attacking a position, troops organized and equipped to seize and hold the position must arrive there practically simultaneously with the tank attack. Thus even in the attacking role the mechanized units must be supplemented by other classes of troops.

That tanks and combat cars alone are incapable of furnishing a complete answer to the problems of the battlefield is even more noticeable when considering their dependence upon adequate bases. To escape certain destruction on the battlefield, combat vehicles must either keep moving rapidly or under adequate cover. Movement and firing exhaust fuel and ammunition, rendering it necessary that mechanized units be in intimate contact with supply and repair facilities and that these facilities and the areas in which situated be adequately protected from hostile attack. For the defense of such areas and positions, units capable of making a maximum use of the ground for shelter and of delivering an overpowering concentration of fire against assaulting elements are essential. Defense of this kind can be conducted only by troops having capabilities similar to those of Infantry and Artillery.

Another limitation of the tank is its inability to operate in swamps, mountains, thick woods, streams, and extremely rough ground. In such areas, if important from a military viewpoint, the Infantry, Cavalry, and Artillery must be prepared to carry out missions both of attack and defense without mechanized assistance.

Every other class of weapon possesses certain inherent limitations on its use, and none is capable of universal application to all situations. The idea that some particular machine will completely dominate battlefields of the future is a figment of the imagination. Such contentions not only ignore mechanical limitations, but do not take into account the ingenuity of man in developing neutralizing agencies for the engines of destruction he himself has created.

Nevertheless, in the absence of modern equipment in all essential classes, we are compelled to train and prepare the Army too distinctly in the 1918 pattern, whereas our effort should be to look ahead and mold it to the requirements of future emergencies. Although the exact and detailed nature of any conflict of the future cannot be foreseen, it is not difficult to distinguish those changes in general outline which must result from the increased mobility and firepower assured by weapons and equipment already existing.

Future warfare will witness a maximum utilization of relatively fast machines for transportation, with consequent greater frontages in strategic deployments; increased unit firepower through employment of weapons of great efficiency, with a resultant wider dispersion in tactical formations; increasing efforts by all commanders to utilize the strategic and tactical mobility of machines so as to attack by surprise, particularly from the flanks; avoidance, so far as possible, of frontal assaults against strongly held positions, even where the attack is supported by combat vehicles and other types of modern weapons; and growing utilization of air forces for information and for bombardment of sensitive points in the enemy's supply organization. To enhance speed, armies will seek to limit the physical size of combatant elements and will strive to attain perfection in supply and maintenance arrangements. Unified and effective control throughout such fast-moving elements will demand a like perfection in signal communications.

A schedule of our immediate requirements in munitions has been prepared in the War Department. It comprehends the minimum quantities needed to permit attainment of a reasonable degree of readiness for warfare of the future. Acquisition of this new equipment would enable the professional forces to develop appropriate tactical methods and organization and to indoctrinate all components; it would permit personnel to become practiced in the operation of new weapons, a requirement that has constantly grown more exacting as equipment has become more intricate in nature; and finally it would insure maximum combat efficiency in the units which must first meet any invader.

This last consideration is of vital importance since the American defense system envisions gradual rather than simultaneous commitment of forces to action whenever an emergency may arise. Upon these initial covering forces may well depend the eventual success of the whole war effort. To fail to make certain that they have the advantage of the best in weapons and equipment would be an inexcusable folly.

THE ARMY AIR CORPS

The possession of a strong and highly efficient Air Corps is indispensable to an army's success in war. In every inquiry into such questions as Air Corps organization, strength, training, and employment this fact must always be borne in mind.

For two reasons the ratio of the peace strength of the Air Corps as compared to its required mobilization strength should be higher than the admissible minimum in certain other portions of the Military Establishment. The first of these involves the possibility that, simultaneously with the beginning of an emergency, air elements may be called upon to engage in heavy fighting. The second is that, like the Navy, the power of an air force is expressed in terms of equipment which, because of its intricacy, requires a considerable time for its production, and which under no conditions can be efficiently improvised. These considerations explain the extraordinary concern of the War Department as to the peacetime strength, efficiency, and readiness for emergency of the Army Air Corps.

Efforts toward its further development and thorough modernization have been continuous ever since there was confided to the Chief of Staff, in July 1933, responsibility for supervision over the military phases of Air Corps development. Prior to that time this responsibility was centered exclusively in a civilian Assistant Secretary of War. Immediately following this change in higher control, a War Department board, of which one of the members was the Chief of the Air Corps, was convened to study the Army's needs in aviation. Exhaustive analysis resulted in certain definite recommendations for building up this arm to a satisfactory level. Of these recommendations the most important proposed an immediate increase in strength, primarily to establish a G.H.Q. Air Force. Under the plan this unit would, both in organization and mission, occupy an independent status under its own Air Corps commander, subject only to the authority of the military head of the Army.

The Secretary of War later convened a board of six civilians and five general officers to study the subject of Air Corps organization and requirements. The chairman was the Hon. Newton D. Baker, Secretary of War during the administration of President Wilson. This group of extraordinarily able men began hearings in April 1934, and for 3 months subjected this whole question to earnest analysis and investigation. At the end of that time it submitted a program for the organization and development of American military aviation. That report should be studied in detail by every official who bears specific responsibilities in connection with the Nation's defenses. It should be the basis for a definite national policy in the development of the Army Air Corps. Because of space limitations, I give below only a few excerpts from the board's final conclusions and recommendations.

Our national defense policy contemplates aggressive action against no nation; it is based entirely upon the defense of our homeland and overseas possessions, including protection of our sea- and air-borne commerce. We do not advocate any increase in our armaments beyond the minimum deemed essential for this purpose...

Aviation has increased the power of the offense where countries at war border upon or are very close to each other, and has enhanced the power of the defense where contestants are widely separated; consequently, it is advantageous to our national policy. However, it has vital limitations and inherent weaknesses. It cannot invest or capture and hold territory; operating bases, land or floating, are absolutely essential to its operations and they have to be protected from land, air, and sea attacks; operations of large air forces are dependent on at least fairly good weather; under present developments, in distant overseas flights, all available load capacity has to be devoted to fuel, leaving little space for military munitions.... Aircraft in sufficient numbers to threaten serious damage can be brought against us only in conjunction with sea forces or with land forces which must be met by forces identical in nature and equally capable of prolonged effort

General Organization

The committee has studied the various considerations and arguments advanced during the last 16 years in behalf of the proposal to concentrate all national defense aviation under one executive department - i.e., a Department of Air, or a Department of National Defense with three separate subdivisions - Army, Navy, and Air. Thorough study and analysis of the various European organizations indicate clearly that they accord with conditions and circumstances peculiar to Europe but have no general application to the United States or Japan, which maintain their air components as integral parts of their Army and Navy The possibilities of economy in such a consolidation were explored with conclusions that the existing organization would be less expensive. Joining the foregoing considerations with vital and far-reaching military objections, the committee is convinced that the adoption of any plan along the lines indicated above would be a serious error, jeopardize the security of the Nation in an emergency, and be an unnecessary burden on the taxpayer.

Cooperation with Civil Aviation

In the opinion of the committee, a major measure to insure the existence of a satisfactory nucleus of an aircraft industry in the United States is the establishment, with the President's approval, of an annual program of procurement for the Army and the Navy. If these programs are based on a normal annual replacement of the Army's airplane strength, as recommended herein, plus that of the Navy, the committee believes that the airplane industry of the United States can be maintained on a sound basis and adequate from a national defense viewpoint.

In view of the importance of the aviation industry to national defense, the committee believes the Government should not enter into competition with private industry by the manufacture of airplanes in Government factories.

Military Responsibility of the Chief of Staff

The application of the principle, "Unity of Command," is as essential in the War Department as in an Army in the field. The military adviser to the President, as Commander in Chief, and to the Secretary of War as head of the War Department, is the Chief of Staff. The duties placed on this office by law, as well as by sound organization, require the Chief of Staff to command and control, from a purely military viewpoint, the Army and all its various parts.

G.H.Q. Air Force

The War Department policy to organize the tactical combat units of the Air Corps located in the continental United States into a General Headquarters Air Force is advocated by the committee. It believes this force, when adequately equipped and organized, will be able to carry out all the missions contemplated for a separate or independent air force, cooperate efficiently with the ground forces and make for greater economy. It should be organized without delay and commanded by a leader with suitable general officers' rank who has had broad experience as an airplane pilot-his headquarters should be with his troops, away from Washington, and his jurisdiction should include all questions of organization, training and maneuvers, and maintenance and operation of technical equipment and inspection thereof, relative to the General Headquarters Air Force....

With a view to facilitating the combat operations of the General Headquarters Air Force, provisions should be made for adequate landing fields in all strategic areas.

Strength of the Air Corps in Personnel and Airplanes

The existing strength in personnel and airplanes is inadequate to meet the Army requirements of the national defense. There is faulty distribution and utilization of existing airplanes in that an undue proportion are rendered unavailable for combat training and fighting purposes....

The strength in airplanes recommended by the latest (1933) War Department study - viz., 2,320 airplanes - is the minimum considered necessary to meet our peace-time Army requirements. The committee believes some increase may be necessary from time to time to provide for larger reserves and as may be justified by War Department studies.

Training

Training of the individual at the primary and advanced flying school at the Air Corps training center is thorough and efficient except that too little attention has been paid to cross-country, instrument, night, and radio-beam flying, to mastery of navigation and communication instruments, and to the study of meteorology.

Frequent scheduled training of Air Corps tactical units in conjunction with ground troops should be provided.

In order that Air Corps pilots be thoroughly trained in all essentials, an average of 300 flying hours per pilot per year should be provided.

The committee recommends that more adequate provision be made for ammunition and live bombs for training....

The committee recommends that every available opportunity be utilized to concentrate Air Corps tactical units by wings in the minimum possible number of posts and stations.

....In general aviation the United States leads the world; it is superior in commercial aviation, its naval aviation is stronger than that of any other power, and with more financial support its Army aviation can be raised to a world position equal to that held by our Navy.

Many of these conclusions generally parallel those arrived at by the Morrow Board and by some 14 other committees and commissions that have, since the World War, made exhaustive investigations of the subject. It is significant that dispassionate study, uncolored by prejudice or personal interest, has invariably found a necessity for strong and efficient air components as integral parts of the Army and Navy; has been convinced of the soundness, in view of the specific Situation of the United States, of the existing plan of general organization; and has definitely repudiated the contention that consolidation of military and naval air forces into a separate department of government offers an acceptable solution to the country's defense problem.

In spite of the unanimity with which nonpartisan and disinterested governmental bodies charged with study of this question have supported our existing general organization as opposed to any possible alternative, this remains the most argumentative point involved in all popular discussion concerning the American air establishment. Extremists and partisans have professed to see a panacea in an "Independent air ministry." In general, the burden of their argument consists in a citation of Western European practice. Such argument wholly fails to recognize the essential differences between the American and the European situations. Moreover, it ignores the difficulties that certain of those nations are experiencing in preparing armies and navies, from which the air contingents have been removed, for effective action in emergency. Finally, such reasoning does not take into account the fears freely expressed in those countries that effective coordination between the air ministry and either or both of the others will be most difficult to obtain in any serious emergency. Debates in the French Senate in 1933 and 1934 clearly indicate that these major problems are still unsolved after 15 years of experience with the separate air-ministry organization.

Technically, the concept of consolidation involves an illogical combination and to some extent is regarded, even by those countries that have adopted it, as an expedient rather than as a fully acceptable solution to the problems involved. Air force must be based either on the surface of the earth or on the sea, and its offensive targets are found on those surfaces. This basic law clearly differentiates two categories of air force - one based on the fleet, the other based on land. These two types of aviation are differentiated not only by dissimilarities in objectives and equipment, but also by fundamental and unsurmountable differences between the types of forces with which they must cooperate. Consequently, even if higher organization should theoretically unify all air forces, practically there must be two different categories, with different organization, training, equipment, and doctrines of operation.

Organization of ground, sea, and air forces is influenced vitally by national situations, particularly as concerns time and space factors. A country immediately surrounded by potential major opponents must have an initial organization and plan permitting immediate functional operation. Contiguous countries of small area, such as the Western European powers, have created unified air forces to meet the probable situations of the earlier stages of war, even though thereafter their air forces will necessarily be differentiated more and more into the two categories of Army and Navy aviation.

Because of this country's relatively high degree of isolation, our own surest defense against powerful and sustained air attack is to deny to an enemy the use of adequate bases, either land or sea, within practicable striking distance of our vital areas. To prevent acquisition of such bases our Army and Navy must be ready to act promptly and efficiently, and each must be properly supported by its own air forces. Thus it is not only our privilege but our wisest course to differentiate our air forces clearly in peace-time, and to insure in each category the special organization, training, and operative doctrine which will make it of maximum efficiency.

For us, therefore, the technical advantages of an independent air force are totally negative. The disadvantages are, on the other hand, numerous and great. Every gain in scientific development has increased organizational and other differences between the Army and the Navy, and rendered it more unlikely that any group of men could become expert in understanding of both. Operative skill demands specialization. The group of aviators who are to cooperate with land forces, to be truly efficient, must be qualified soldiers, in all that the term implies.

The existing organization is likewise advantageous from the standpoint of economy. In the Military Establishment, the Air Corps is furnished quartermaster, medical, signal, ordnance, and other ground services by the same agencies that provide them for the remainder of the Army. But an independent air ministry, to satisfy its requirements in supply, maintenance, and administration, would necessarily establish new organizations of these types, with consequent duplication and additional expense. The only alternative would be to make the personnel of existing supply and maintenance services responsible to two separate commanders, Army and air. Resulting confusion and inefficiency would soon render such an expedient intolerable.

Armies have always found it necessary to combat the concept of vertical organization. Each new arm and technical service has in its early phases of development sought and sometimes obtained a status of relative independence, which in the long run has been found to defeat its true purpose. Artillery, once separately constituted, was later brought into the Army and planted firmly into the Infantry-Artillery team by the principle of unity of command. The new arm, aviation, must be given the special consideration afforded to young growing agencies, but to an increasing extent it should become an integral and vital element of the organization through which teamwork is insured.

There will undoubtedly be occasions in war when air operations beyond the immediate theaters of land or sea forces will be desirable. Such operations are provided for in the organization of the General Headquarters Air Force. When the program of the War Department is completed, this force will insure air superiority in any operations within practical striking distance of our borders. It will provide units suitable to reinforce our fleet aviation in coastal sea lanes or to operate therein under Army command in the absence of the fleet. It will fulfill all the missions of land campaign that could be performed by aviation of a separate department, with insurance that there will be coordination of all elements in a common plan.

From the viewpoint of higher coordination the soundness of the existing organization has been demonstrated by experience. The President is the Commander in Chief, and as such decides upon the objectives and broad strategy of any war. The War and Navy Departments employ all forces that they respectively control to execute his decisions, each in its own sphere.

Since arguments advanced in favor of revision in higher organization are frequently based upon the fallacious charge that Army and Navy coordination and cooperation are impossible under the existing set-up, I give here a brief explanation of the procedure under which this important end is achieved.

Before doing so, however, it is pertinent to point out that the necessity for such coordination does not involve the mass of the administrative or tactical operations with which the two departments are ordinarily concerned. Their respective fields of action, specific missions, organizations, weapons, and training are so widely differentiated that prearrangements for cooperative action are required only in matters touching upon certain phases of broad policy or upon specific administrative or tactical situations. An effective machinery has been established for insuring teamwork in these special instances.

The Joint Board is the foremost of several cooperatively organized agencies that exist for this purpose. It invariably takes cognizance of those instances where there is indicated a necessity for combined action, either in current activities or in planning for emergency action. Immediately subsidiary to the board is a joint planning committee, which is charged with the detailed development of joint plans and agreements to carry out board decisions.

The Joint Aeronautical Board, which includes in its membership the respective chiefs of the Army and the Navy Air Corps, promotes cooperation in all technical phases of aircraft development and employment. The Joint Economy Board studies and reports upon all instances where, through the cooperative action of the two services, a saving to the Government may be realized. Finally, the Army and Navy Munitions Board operates in the field of munitions procurement, with its principal mission that of insuring the speedy and economical satisfaction of the Army and Navy's material requirements in war.

Agreements reached by the Joint Board become binding upon the two services when signed by both secretaries. In a strict sense, the board is advisory rather than administrative in function; yet since its membership includes the highest military and naval officials, assurance that its agreements will be faithfully carried out is almost automatic.

Theoretical criticism has been made to the effect that equal Army and Navy representation precludes the possibility of the board reaching a definite decision in any case where an unsurmountable difference of opinion between the two services might exist. The premise is correct, but forms no basis for adverse criticism. The opposite is true. In any plan, project, or program involving joint or cooperative action on the part of the two defense services and in which opposing professional viewpoints cannot be composed by their designated representatives, there is only one authority that can or should be permitted to intervene; namely, the President. The issues involved are far too serious in their possible effects upon national security to permit any lesser authority,

either professional or civil, to take the responsibility of decision. Equal representation assures that in cases of this kind, which so far in the long history of the board have been completely nonexistent, full and complete analyzes of the opposing considerations and opinions will be presented to the Commander in Chief. In other words, the board constitutes in theory and in practice an ideally organized defense staff of professional men for the President of the United States.

The composition of the board presents another advantage in preventing consideration by it of questions exclusively the concern of either service. If constituted, along with its subsidiary agencies, as a legalized superstaff, no such necessary discrimination could be exercised, and only confusion and inefficiency would result.

The board facilitates the exchange of professional ideas on many subjects and the promotion of friendly official intercourse. It is not out of place for me to pay tribute here to the spirit of helpfulness and cooperation that I have invariably encountered among its naval membership during by 4 years' tour as Chief of Staff... .

TRAINING

Training distinguishes an army from an armed mob. Its purpose is the production of efficiency in the use of weapons, individually and collectively; skill in the multitudinous processes of marching, living, and fighting under conditions imposed by war; and cohesiveness and unification among the individual members of an army so as to make possible a purposeful employment of their mass effort.

From the beginning of warfare, professional skill and discipline have invariably been most important, and frequently the decisive factors in battle. To quote instances would imply a necessity to argue the obvious. Yet strangely enough this outstanding lesson of each of our own as well as of all other wars has invariably been the one most speedily forgotten by our people during years of peace. It has been the history of the American Army that adequate opportunity for its proper training has habitually been, except in war, injudiciously curtailed.

Every increase in the complexity of armaments places a correspondingly higher premium on excellence in training. To use modern equipment effectively, the individual soldier must become proficient in the operation of intricate mechanisms. Moreover, since trends in warfare are toward greater speed in movement and increased dispersion on the battlefield, close and continuous supervision over the individual members of a command is becoming more difficult, if not impossible. Training and indoctrination in all ranks are consequently more than ever before indispensable to effective fighting. Only the thoroughly trained army can possibly exploit to the maximum degree the advantages offered by modernized equipment.

Broadly speaking, training activity may be classified into the three general categories of high command and staff training, officer training, and troop training.

In the first of these classifications the lack of funds for concentrating sizable bodies of troops has largely limited practical training possibilities to command post exercises - that is, the establishment and operation in the field of higher unit headquarters. This condition will, it is hoped, be corrected in the near future, so that annually the troops of 1 of the 4 armies will actually be concentrated for maneuvering.

Officer training is accomplished in service schools, in daily performance of appropriate duties in staff or command positions, and in special field exercises. Our school system is unexcelled in quality anywhere in the world, and its value has been thoroughly tested, both in war and peace. Of all training activities of the Army, it alone is supported on a basis comparable to our needs.

Troop training - that is, the instruction of individuals and combat units themselves - suffers from extreme skeletonization of organizations. For this there can be no real correction until Congress authorizes a needed increase in the Regular Army so that sizable combat units may be established and maintained without occasioning a complete collapse in the necessary administrative, technical, and mobilization overhead of the Army.

The training of the private soldier involves the technique of his weapons, methods of individual conduct in battle, physical condition, and discipline. The training of the corporal must extend beyond this so as to assure his ability to lead his unit successfully through every vicissitude of campaign. Particularly must he be skillful in methods of combining their individual efforts so as to produce maximum effect. In like manner each next higher commander must shoulder heavier responsibilities in the employment and care of increasing numbers of men and weapons, and consequently must be more efficiently trained in the whole profession of arms.

Obviously, less time is required for the training of a private than for any other member of a combat unit. Upon this axiom is based the American practice of maintaining, for the bulk of the forces required in war, only a framework of military formations. The soundness of this plan is, however, directly dependent upon proper strength and professional skill in the framework, as well as upon the existence of a small force constantly ready to take the field. From these considerations it is simple to deduce one of the primary missions of the peacetime army; namely, the production of such a degree of efficiency in every unit of the existing establishment that its expansion to an emergency status may be accomplished without confusion or loss of time.

Attainment of this objective is not possible through adherence to and constant practice in a prescribed ritual. Frederick was the foremost tactician and drill master of his day, and his skill was reflected in the brilliant victories of his army, almost invariably gained over superior numbers. But application of his training methods to a modern army would produce farcical results. Basic human qualities are the only elements in an army that remain unchanged from year to year and from age to age. Consequently, the only features of training methods that can be considered as relatively stable are those practices which have proved effective in adapting man's physical and spiritual characteristics to the requirements of mass conflict. All other phases of training are subject to the same evolutionary influences that apply to the military profession as a whole. Moreover, knowledge of immutable principles, though necessary, is not in itself sufficient. There must be continuously developed the most effective methods for the application of these principles to conditions and circumstances which are never exactly repeated, but on the contrary regroup and reform themselves in ever new patterns, under the influence of new ideas and new weapons, and new industrial developments.

A second training mission of the Regular Army is therefore the development of modernized training methods suited to conditions of the moment.

In fulfilling its function as the military laboratory the Regular Army's training methods as well as its detailed organization and tactical doctrine must respond instantly, on an experimental basis, to the requirements of every new and pertinent influence. When, but not until when, results crystallize along general lines, they should be promptly communicated to all civilian components. Thus these latter will enjoy periods of relative stability in the detailed processes of preparation, which, in view of their limited training opportunities, are necessary to the production of basically sound military formations.

The professional knowledge developed in the Regular Army flows to the civilian components through service schools, instructional literature, and individual officers assigned to duty with those components. This instructional task is a vitally important one. The genius of the National Defense Act lies in its provision for maintaining a trained civilian framework through which emergency formations can be produced before the protective capacity of existing units is exhausted. Without efficient training, this civilian nucleus can have little if any value, and efficiency demands that principles and methods taught conform accurately to the requirements of modern warfare.

Concurrently with its tasks of experimentation and instruction, the professional element must carry out another important training duty. This is the preparation and maintenance of a strong Regular Army contingent for immediate action in any serious emergency. Requirements of civilian training and of preparation for mobilization compel a considerable dispersion in the Regular Army. But any real regard for the country's security demands constant availability of reasonably well-concentrated bodies of professional troops to serve as the spear head of forces needed to protect the general processes of mobilization. This contingent must be ready for instantaneous use - which means that it must not only be ready for action without any extraordinary expansion but that it be thoroughly modernized in training as well as equipment.

To assure that present methods are free of obsolescence there was organized during the past summer a board of officers to which was assigned the task of making a comprehensive survey of individual and unit training in the Army. Each chief of combatant arm, or one of his principal assistants, was named as a member of the board. The directive under which the board is conducting its studies is as follows:

More than 3 years ago I made definite decision to undertake an orderly program for progressive modernization of the Army of the United States.

For some years it had been realized that circumstances of the first post war decade had compelled the Army to lag behind in adapting its organization, equipment, and tactical doctrine to modern requirements, and for a variety of reasons the opening of the calendar year 1931 was a propitious moment for initiating a broad plan for correcting these conditions. To a large extent the elementary organizational work imposed upon the military establishment by the act of 1920 had been accomplished; the military school system was functioning on a satisfactory basis; instruction and administration of the civilian components had crystallized under sound and continuing policies; and, most important of all, many improvements in weapons and other military equipment had reached a stage of development where their profound influences upon future military operations was clearly indicated. Added to all this was the further consideration that great quantities of equipment left to the Army as a legacy from the World War were either almost completely exhausted or were approaching uselessness in value. Replacement could not long be deferred, and it was essential that every dollar spent for new items should contribute in maximum degree to military efficiency.

Prosecution of the general purpose of modernizing the Army required the formulation of definite, though interrelated, projects applying to organization, materiel, and tactical doctrine.

Exhaustive study of higher organizational needs resulted in the development of the four-army plan, through the adoption of which there have been established more logical mobilization objectives than formerly existed, while the Army has been more effectively integrated as a tactical machine.

In the field of materiel, essential requirements in new or improved classes of ground and air equipment have been broadly determined, and some progress has been made in the procurement of modern types. Development of new equipment has in turn indicated a need for partial revision in tac tical organization, which need has formed the basis for such important projects as the G.H.Q. Air Force, and the mechanization of selected Infantry and Cavalry units. Personnel requirements have been once again completely restudied, and the War Department's conclusions and recommendations repeatedly presented to the Military Committees of the Senate and the House.

While none of these projects has yet reached a satisfactory state of development, due either to insufficient time or, in some instances, to the absence of legislative authority, there has been established for each a concrete objective which, added together, constitute a partial representation of the War Department's goal in modernization.

The next essential step in this program is to begin the revision of training doctrine and methods so as to conform to all other developments. This is to be undertaken immediately. A board of officers … is appointed for the purpose of making a critical and comprehensive analysis of existing methods of individual and unit training, with particular reference to the basic phases thereof, and proposing such revisions in methods and in governing regulations as may be considered desirable. Necessary clerical and technical assistance for the board will be obtained, by cooperative action among themselves, from personnel under their respective jurisdictions.

The board's membership has been specially selected so as to reflect the views of all the combat arms, as represented either by its chief or one of his principal assistants. These officials are the technical advisers of the War Department on this type of subject and are in close touch with their re-spective school faculties and special boards. This assures full consideration of the training requirements of each arm and a report in which clear distinction will be made between the phases of training common to all and those having a more limited application.

In carrying out its mission the board will necessarily record its conclusions concerning the objectives of peace and war training respectively, together with the relationships that should exist between them; the desirable priority in types of training for the attainment of these objectives; and the time necessary to complete each essential step, whether technical or disciplinary, under conditions now existing and under those that will probably prevail in an emergency mobilization.

In emergency, time is an essential factor, frequently a vital one. Since it is impossible to predict the length of the preparatory period that may be permitted us after the actual declaration of a war, it is necessary that the sequence of emergency training be such as to produce, at any given moment, the most efficient units attainable in the time elapsed. It is because of this necessity for utilizing every minute to the greatest advantage that the subject derives its extraordinary importance, as well as its controversial character. In formulating its conclusions on this point the board will encounter extremes of argument.

On the one hand there is a school of thought which proposes to limit training objectives, particularly in war, so as to include only an ability to use the particular weapon with which the individual is armed, and some familiarity with the practical duties devolving upon troops in the field. The purpose of the members of this school is to exclude from training programs all activity which they believe to be nonessential, and by intensive and undivided effort to produce, within a matter of days, a unit in which soldiers can march and shoot. Among the activities they class as relatively nonessential are drills primarily designed to develop individual alertness and obedience, and mass cohesiveness - in short, discipline.

On the other hand are many officers who, while recognizing the obvious value of this kind of technique, insist that a thoroughly instilled discipline is equally important. They consider it a fundamental error to look upon a combat unit as nothing more than a collection of artisans, and believe that the teamwork and morale resulting from so-called disciplinary training are not only worth their cost in time, but are prerequisites to success in any kind of difficult fighting. They believe that training systems, both of peace and war, must be designed accordingly.

It is of course important that training methods of peace be readily adjustable to the conditions of war, since the Army's basic mission is protection of the Nation in emergency. But though this adaptability must be assured, it is necessary also that the somewhat dissimilar objectives of peace and war training be thoroughly considered. One of the purposes of peacetime training is to produce and constantly maintain a corps of highly efficient instructors, and an organized framework of enlisted cadres that can absorb numbers of hastily trained recruits in emergency without dangerously lowering combat effectiveness. This purpose represents an additional requirement upon peace methods over and above the objectives of the war system, and must be provided for in the plan developed by the board.

Modern developments in weapons and other materiel useful to military units, as well as the trends in tactics that may be logically anticipated from these developments, of course, exert a marked influence on training requirements. Speaking generally, it has been the history of warfare that only heavily massed formations are applicable to hastily and imperfectly trained units. Tactical employment of organizations featuring thin lines with large intervals and distances has been possible only with troops highly trained in technique and imbued with splendid discipline. The growing power of firearms and the advent of airplanes, tanks, gas, and other modern weapons point to a necessity for increased dispersion both in frontage and depth. Training doctrine must anticipate the implications of such changes and conform thereto.

All these, as well as many related questions, must be thoroughly analyzed. The board is expected to make an exhaustive survey of professional opinion, and to explore thoroughly every source of pertinent information. This project constitutes an essential phase in the general program to modernize the Army of the United States, and successful accomplishment of the board's mission will permit orderly, balanced, and essential progress in that direction... .

CONCLUSION

Measures for assuring national safety are worthy of the thoughtful and continuing consideration of every citizen.

Crises that result finally in the employment of defense forces give little warning of their approach, and it is futile to hope that there might be accomplished a reasonable preparation after growing tension once indicates immediate danger. Armies and navies, in being and known to be efficient, give weight to the peaceful words of statesmen, but feverish effort to create them when once a crisis is imminent simply provokes immediate attack. Moreover, individual proficiency in the profession of arms and development of efficient fighting organizations both require time, no matter what the intensity of effort or the lavishness of expenditure. Reasonable preparation constantly carried forward as a feature of national policy is not only necessary to assure avoidance of the bitterest consequences of war but is a wise investment in the maintenance of peace.

Under the separate headings of this report I have discussed the essentials of a land defense which the General Staff believes to be the minimum consistent with any reasonable regard for the continued security of the United States.

Measured by any possible standard, full accomplishment of this program would still leave us far behind all other major powers in strength of organized land forces. Our relative standing would be no higher than sixteenth. Preparation on the scale proposed would, however, offer to our Country a justified assurance in freedom from attack or, at the worst, from extreme consequences in the event of attack.

In some of its essentials this program is not greatly different from similar ones proposed annually by the War Department for many years. Since none of these programs has ever been adopted in its entirety, it might possibly, though mistakenly, be inferred that the American people and their representatives have, after mature deliberation, declined to undertake any military preparation in excess of that now obtaining. The fact is that the problem of land defense has not been critically analyzed outside of the War Department since 1920, and has received very little attention except as an included item in appropriation programs. But its importance justifies and demands independent and objective study-with appropriations adjusted to the necessities discovered thereby, rather than the reverse.

The proposals of the General Staff have been formulated with full regard for current governmental economy as well as in full realization of the fact that retrenchment that cripples national defense is extravagance past the point of folly. They are conservative to a degree, and for that reason difficult to popularize. They have not the emotional appeal, either of the ill-advised and deplorably provocative statements of the jingoist, or of the stupid utterances and specious arguments of the extreme pacifist. They are addressed to reason alone and must depend for their support upon the slow processes of education rather than upon the driving methods of propaganda.

But though the War Department, as an agency of government, cannot and does not resort to exaggeration, it has the plain duty of employing reiteration. Inherent in the War Department's governmental responsibility is an advisory and educational function, and no discouragement, no delay, no failure, should deter responsible officials from bringing these fundamental truths again and again to public notice.

In closing my tour of duty as Chief of Staff, I express to you, sir, my sincere appreciation for the uniform support you have accorded my plans and administration. To the officers and enlisted men of the Army, to their wives and families, I say good-bye with admiration and affection. They need no eulogy from me. They are writing their own history in the annals of our Nation's successes; but when I think of their patience under adversity, of their modesty in accomplishment, and of their loyal and unquestioning devotion, I am filled with an emotion I cannot express. I want them to know that I have done my best, that I have kept the soldier faith.[18]

STATEMENT BEFORE THE SUBCOMMITTEE OF THE HOUSE MILITARY AFFAIRS COMMITTEE ON ITS CONSIDERATION OF A BILL TO INCREASE THE NUMBER OF APPOINTMENTS TO THE U.S. MILITARY ACADEMY MAY 1, 1935

As a former Superintendent of the Academy, MacArthur was convinced of the need to increase tile size of the Corps of Cadets. The expansion of the postwar Regular Army over

---

[18] This farewell was premature. The work of reorganizing the Army was incomplete as MacArthur's formal tour of duty as Chief of Staff closed, so the President required him to stay on. The annual report for 1935 rounds out this extraordinary tour, and it also rounds out the making of the modern American Army. (Frank C. Waldrop - 1942)

that maintained prior to 1914 had necessitated the commissioning of large numbers of officers who were not West Point graduates. General MacArthur's view was that, if the size of the graduating classes of the Academy were increased, at least half of the new second lieutenants entering the Army each year could have the benefit of West Point training. His affection for and sincere belief in the value of the U.S. Military Academy are evident in his brief statement to the House Subcommittee.

Major Vorin E. Whan, Jr., USA, Editor
A Soldier Speaks: Public Papers and Speeches of General of the Army Douglas MacArthur
© 1965, Frederick A. Praeger, Publishers, New York, NY

Mr Chairman and Gentlemen of the Subcommittee,

I had prepared a voluminous memorandum for presentation to you today, but after hearing the comprehensive and, to my mind, completely convincing testimony of the witnesses who have preceded me, I feel it would be unnecessary to cover again ground which has already been so thoroughly assayed.

There is an old saying that "the proof of the pudding is in the eating thereof." The United States of America has been eating of the West Point pudding for 133 years and has found it not only solidly substantial but exceedingly nutritious and palatable. It has met the test of a double standard - military and educational. Along military lines its graduates have been the dominating and controlling factor in all of the wars in which our nation has engaged during the last century, and in each and every one of these wars they have given us victory. Never has our beloved country suffered defeat. What more do you ask? With astonishment, with almost incredible amazement, I ask you in all humility, but with all earnestness, in God's name, what more *could* you ask? As a military standard, this institution is the envy of the General Staffs of the Armies of the world, and in making this statement I speak with the high authority of an intimate, and in many cases, a personal knowledge of these staffs. The keystone of the arch which marks the entrance to the Gymnasium at West Point bears the unforgettable words: "On these fields of friendly strife are sown the seeds that on other days and other fields bring forth victory." Words merely scrolled in stone at West Point, but stamped blood-red into immortal history on the victorious battlefields of the nation. Victory, and still victory, and always victory.

And along purely educational lines the graduates of the Military Academy have been equally successful. In every walk of life they have been characterized by painstaking thoroughness, by loyal devotion, by basic soundness of character. And again, I ask you, what more do you demand from any education? To build character, to make men, what more *could* any institution of learning do? The public school system of this country is famous in the land. It is the envy of foreign educators throughout the world - and in making this statement I again speak with the authority of an intimate, and in many cases, a personal knowledge of those concerned. At the apex of this system, indeed as its very apotheosis, stand the two service schools. It would be fatuous to hold them faultless, but no school has yet been founded, nor probably ever will be that ca make a fool into a wise man. But West Point with its merciless competitive tests does eliminate the fools and does train and develop the wise. You are its trustees. Five days ago you voted to expand the Naval Academy. I ask only your similar support for the Military Academy. It is a proven product through the ages. "The proof of the pudding is in the eating thereof." Mr. Chairman, I rest our cause with thanks to you and the Subcommittee for your patience.

Excerpts from the Annual Report of the Chief of Staff, United States Army Fiscal Year July 1, 1934 - June 30, 1935

As he prepared to step down as Army Chief of Staff, General MacArthur in his last annual Report set forth a blueprint for preparing the Army to fight a modern war. It is a remarkable prediction of the manner in which World War II was to be fought, and its broad principles still apply to the nuclear battlefield of today. Although the Army in 1935 was hardly a match for the forces of the other major powers, his leadership had laid the foundation for the amazing expansion of our armed forces that began scarcely five years later.

Major Vorin E. Whan, Jr., USA, Editor
A Soldier Speaks: Public Papers and Speeches of General of the Army Douglas MacArthur
© 1965, Frederick A. Praeger, Publishers, New York, NY

For the first time since 1922, the Army enters a new fiscal year with a reasonable prospect of developing itself into a defense establishment commensurate in size and efficiency to the country's minimum needs. Obstacles, which for 13 years have impeded, if not inhibited, progress toward this goal, have only recently been either swept aside by Congress or materially reduced in importance. The present year definitely marks the beginning of a long-deferred resumption of military preparation on a scale demanded by the most casual regard for the Nation's safety and security.

The general form and composition of the Army of the United States are prescribed in the National Defense Act, as amended shortly after the close of the World War. Implicit in that law is the clear intent of Congress to develop and maintain the Army solely for the promotion of domestic tranquillity and for assuring freedom from attack. The purpose was to provide a protective shield in the lee of which citizens might pursue their normal habits and occupations, undisturbed by threat of organized violence regardless of its origin. This conception of the Army's function is the very cornerstone of our whole military structure.

In its broad organizational features, the system established by the 1920 law is unique. Before that time only two general methods existed in the world as the basis of military organization. One was the conscript system; the other, the employment of the professional soldier. The former affords maximum strength at minimum cost, by prescribing service with the colors as a civic duty; the latter is productive of the highest possible unit efficiency but entails abnormal expense due to the necessity of reimbursing along professional lines all personnel involved. For this reason, all the larger military machines of modern times are based primarily upon conscription, although to mold annual levies of conscripts into usable military machines there is required also the maintenance of professional cadres.

In this country, tradition and sentiment preclude conscription as the basis of a peace-time Army. Maintenance of a professional force sufficiently strong for every requirement of emergency would entail prohibitive costs, even for the United States. Consequently, the plan written into the National Defense Act, while based exclusively upon voluntary enlistment, is so devised as to present a workable compromise between the frequently conflicting considerations of desired efficiency and immediate economy.

The system places ultimate reliance for the Nation's defense upon a citizen Army, the great proportion of which must be organized, trained, and equipped after the beginning of any emergency. To insure efficiency in such a mobilization, Congress established a permanent military nucleus or framework around which, in war, a complete Army could be built up. This nucleus has the responsibility of carrying on essential peace-time preparation in organization, training, and materiel procurement, and of providing emergency protection until mobilization could be completed. Specifically, the 1920 act provides for a relatively small Regular Army and for the organization and partial development of a National Guard and Organized Reserves. Training of other volunteers is authorized through the Reserve Officers' Training Corps, the Citizens' Military Training Camps, and the National Board for the Promotion of Rifle Practice, although these three organizations are in no sense parts of the Army of the United States.

Manifestly, this system would entail a delay of several months between any declaration of war by Congress and the time that large-scale operations could be initiated. The plan thus carries its own proof of nonaggressive intent, since instant readiness to strike overwhelming blows is the first requisite of an army deliberately seeking to act aggressively. Our Army is concerned only with national safety. But the minimum acceptable level of security envisioned by the framers of the 1920 law cannot be achieved unless the fundamental features of the defensive system therein prescribed are supported on a reasonable basis.

For 13 years, the curve representing the Army's ability to perform its vital emergency missions has been trending continuously and dangerously downward. The principal causes have been insufficient strength in the Regular Force, growing obsolescence in important items of equipment for all components, injudicious curtailment of training, progressive consumption of reserve supplies, and inadequacy of funds for many essential activities. Confronted by these obstacles, the Army, though it has intensified effort and resorted to every possible expedient, has been powerless to preserve effectiveness at a satisfactory level.

Elimination of difficulties involving the broad questions of size and general financial support of the Army does not fall within the scope of military authority. Concerning such matters, the War Department function is advisory only and in this capacity it frequently, between 1922 and 1935, expressed its conviction that in conditions then prevailing resided grave potentialities for disaster. During the past 5 years,

the Department has insistently urged upon appropriate congressional committees the stark seriousness of this situation.

In persisting in this effort, the War Department has never been concerned with establishing the validity of its own excuses for any possible failure of the future, but only in attempting to assure that no such failure, with its disastrous consequences to the country, should occur.

So long as the necessary means were withheld, Congress assumed responsibility for every defect traceable to insufficient support. But within recent months funds have been provided to meet many of the most critical of the Army's accumulated deficiencies. To the extent delimited by these authorizations, Congress has placed directly upon the shoulders of the Army itself full responsibility for the efficiency of the country's military defenses. To discharge that responsibility faithfully and skillfully has become the immediate mission and paramount duty of the War Department and of all military personnel.

IMPROVEMENTS RECENTLY AUTHORIZED IN THE ARMY

Enlisted strength of the Regular Army. - The duties of the Regular Army are many and upon their successful performance depends the effectiveness of the entire Military Establishment. Without the leadership and unifying influence of an efficient Regular Army, the American system could, at the best, produce nothing more than a collection of unintegrated and isolated units of doubtful efficiency and of little value to the Federal Government.

The Regular Army is the professional instructor and leader of the whole establishment and is responsible for keeping all elements abreast of modern developments in doctrine, technique, and weapons. It provides essential administrative overhead for the entire force, including supply and service organizations to meet the needs of a mobilization. It must furnish permanent garrisons for oversea possessions and for important harbor defenses of the United States. Because it is the only portion of the Army of the United States composed of personnel continuously and instantly subject to orders of the President, it has the responsibility of initial protection in emergency. A considerable proportion of its strength must be so organized as to provide this protection promptly and effectively. Finally, the Regular Army is charged with the development of all plans for emergency action and must assume leadership in execution of those plans when necessary.

Every defect in the Regular Army is thus inevitably reflected in deficiencies throughout the entire Military Establishment. Consequently, when Congress turned its attention to rehabilitation of our land defenses, its first concern was to assure the ability of the professional element to carry out its missions. The greatest and most obvious weakness was in enlisted strength.

The National Defense Act prescribes an enlisted strength of 280,000 for the Regular Army. During the process of attrition following the year 1922, this number was reduced to 118,750, exclusive of the Philippine Scouts. Difficulties resulting from extreme skeletonization quickly became more than serious. Every emergency mission of the Regular Army was jeopardized and important peace-time duties could not be properly performed. An excessive proportion of its strength was used up in overhead which, regardless of other considerations, had to be maintained. This disproportionate employment extended all the way down to the basic units - the companies, troops, and batteries of the combat arms. These were so weak in actual fighting strength that their sudden commitment to action would have entailed a costly wastage of trained officers, noncommissioned officers, and specialists, without commensurate results. Under these conditions the assembly of even a small combat force would have stripped the country of trained professional personnel and left a mobilization woefully lacking in efficient leadership. Foreign garrisons were too weak; the Air Corps was undermanned; modernization projects were severely handicapped, and in every essential activity were inefficiencies resulting from lack of enlisted men.

Recurrent studies in the War Department approached the problem from the standpoint of bare requirements for the performance of essential missions. Invariably the conclusion was reached that a strength of 165,000 enlisted men for the Regular Army represents the absolute minimum consistent with safety. Recommendations to the Congress have, ever since 1930, made this item the principal feature of the War Department program for rehabilitation.

Finally, in the appropriation bill for 1936, the necessary congressional approval was accorded. Recruiting of 46,250 additional men began on July 1st of this year. The beneficial influence of this act of Congress upon the future efficiency of our military defenses and the security of the country is beyond calculation.

Its first result will be the filling out of the attenuated skeletons now attempting to function as tactical units in the Regular Army. The Air Corps will be raised to its authorized strength. Mechanized elements in the Infantry, Cavalry, and Artillery will be given a sufficient strength to push development in this important phase of modern warfare. Companies, troops, and batteries will be able to conduct efficient training and their readiness for efficient field service will be markedly increased. The combat effectiveness of the whole Army will be doubled and its ability to carry out a prompt and orderly mobilization will be reasonably assured.

In the interests of immediate economy, practically the entire increase is to be initially absorbed in the lowest enlisted grade; that is, as unrated privates at $21 per month. This arrangement prevents reconstitution of units rendered inactive during the long process of attrition, some of which are badly needed in order to balance the larger combat organizations to which they pertain. It prevents also the appointment in existing organizations of the necessary percentage of specialists and noncommissioned officers to insure efficiency in technical activities and leadership positions. These are serious handicaps, but they must be accepted as of far less importance than insufficiency in aggregate strength. Leadership of a high order must be applied to the problem and, until the situation can be corrected, imagination and energy must overcome difficulties incident to faulty organization in this regard.

There exists a very real necessity, however, for restudying and revising our present system of grades and ratings. The purpose of noncommissioned grades is to clothe se-

lected enlisted men with the formal military authority essential to the command and control of small units. The primary purpose of ratings is to provide a graduated scale of increased pay for duties requiring an unusual degree of individual skill. Without a suitable method for rewarding ability of this kind, the necessary number of men basically qualified physically and mentally for service in these important positions cannot be secured. More over, experience shows that even those obtained will too often, as soon as they have been carefully trained in some craft or trade, forsake the Army for the far more remunerative opportunities of civil life.

Existing law establishes seven grades in the Army from master sergeant to private, inclusive. It sets up also a series of specialists' ratings to which increased pay is attached in varying amounts; the numbers that may be assigned to each being fixed by percentages definitely prescribed in the law. These percentages are far too low to meet present needs, to say nothing of the additional requirements incident to the mechanization and motorization of the Army. Another defect is that upon retirement the specialist is reduced to the same scale of pay as the unrated private, a manifestly unfair and unjust practice. The net result is that the Army labors under marked disadvantages in its effort to organize units according to modern needs and to maintain in key positions the type of men required by the importance of the duties pertaining thereto.

In this regard, the situation of the Army is most unfavorable as compared to the Navy. For example, the average pay per man in naval aviation is $180 greater per year than in the Army Air Corps, although individual duties and functions are identical. For the bulk of the enlisted men in the military and naval services the discrepancy is even greater, averaging about $250.

The first need of the Army is that the schedule of fixed percentages controlling the numbers of grades and ratings be materially raised so as to provide a more satisfactory rate of pay among highly qualified enlisted personnel. In addition, the retired pay of the specialist should be based upon his active duty remuneration, just as in the case of a noncommissioned officer.

For some time this matter has been under advisement in the War Department, and exhaustive studies have been made to determine the detailed requirements of the several arms and services. The subject assumes a constantly increasing importance because every step toward modernization creates a corresponding need for a higher level of training and a greater proportion of skilled specialists. A complete and coordinated plan for revision of the existing system should be developed and submitted to Congress at the earliest opportunity.

Revision of Regular Army promotion system. - A second important accomplishment of Congress with respect to professional personnel was the revision of the promotion system for officers. This matter has engaged the earnest attention of the War Department for years and has evoked a sympathetic interest in Congress. Prior failure to enact corrective legislation must be laid more to difficulties in evolving a fully acceptable plan than to any lack of interest.

A reasonable flow of promotion is essential to progressive and thorough training of military leaders. It is in addition a powerful stimulant to morale, since steady advancement to positions of increased responsibility, authority, and rank is the only practicable way in which outstanding military service can, in time of peace, be rewarded by the Government. Unless there is a proper flow of promotion, there is no incentive which appeals to ambition and the natural self-respect of men and impels them to follow their profession enthusiastically rather than merely as a means of livelihood. The Army requires men imbued by the highest professional instincts. There is no monetary recompense for the soldier that is sufficient to attract the type of man that is needed. Unless there is the professional reward of advancement, carrying with it opportunity for leadership and increased responsibility, which is irrespective of actual livelihood, the whole tone of the establishment begins to fail and go down. Stagnation destroys initiative, saps ambition, and encourages routine and perfunctory performance of duty.

For some years the promotion situation for officers has been deplorable. Some of these difficulties were caused by commissioning in a single group a large number of officers immediately after the World War. Though most of them fell within the same age brackets and had substantially equal amounts of commissioned service, the senior officers in this group were assured of reaching the colonel grade while the juniors in the same group would still be captains. Officers just below the World War contingent, although they entered the service as second lieutenants at normal ages, were facing the prospect of remaining in company grades up to and beyond the age of 50.

But without regard for the existence of this special problem, the promotion rate has been far from satisfactory and has grown progressively worse. Finally, through experience, there became available sufficient data to show that without some revision in the system young men entering the service could not attain successive grades except at the following approximate ages: Captain at 39, major at 47, lieutenant colonel at 54, and colonel at 58 or 59. This meant that in the average case an officer would have only 5 or 6 years remaining to serve after reaching the grade of colonel. Even if thereafter he should, through selection, be stepped up with reasonable rapidity to brigadier general and then to major general, the normal individual could have served as a corps area commander for only about 1 year, while the Chief of Staff would necessarily have changed every 5 to 6 months. Moreover, before the average officer could have attained through service in the field grades the broad experience necessary to qualify him as a brigade or division commander in war, he would have been too old to meet the physical requirements of those commands. Such a prospect was a serious one for the Government.

To produce an officer corps of maximum value and efficiency, individuals commissioned at an average age of 24 should advance steadily through the lower grades at a rate that will bring them to a colonel's command at 50. Such a promotion rate permits progressive development and training, which is mandatory if we are to have ready for emergency a sizable pool of relatively young officers of wide experience and broad professional attainments.

Up to and including the grade of colonel, Army promotion, except in the Medical and Chaplains' Corps, has for some years been based exclusively upon seniority in length of commissioned service. Fixed numbers are maintained in each grade, vacancies being filled by the promotion of the senior officer from the grade next below. While this system does not permit any differentiation in promotion based on estimated ability, it does avoid the evil of favoritism which is exceedingly difficult to eradicate in any method purporting to base promotion solely on relative fitness. Regardless of any inherent disadvantages in the seniority system, its principles have long commanded the support of the majority of Army officers as the basis for a general plan of advancement. But for some years it has been clear that its continued application during periods of peace required the adoption of some method for moderate acceleration of the promotion rate.

The plan sponsored for the past 5 years by the War Department and finally enacted into law during the past session of Congress accomplishes such an acceleration. It retains the advantages of seniority promotion but in varying degree provides somewhat faster promotion for every officer below the grade of colonel. Specifically it directs promotion to first lieutenant at the end of 3 years' commissioned service and to captain at the end of 10. It makes moderate increases in the number of colonels, lieutenant colonels, and majors, but applies also certain checks and balances which will prevent undue rapidity of promotion in the event circumstances should suddenly change. Under its provisions no officer can reach the grade of colonel with less than 26 years' service nor the grade of lieutenant colonel with less than 20.

I consider the enactment of this law to be a constructive achievement on the part of Congress, the result of which will be an officer corps increased in efficiency and stimulated in morale. These results will be accomplished at a minimum of cost and without injustice to any individual.

Pay. - Incidental to this important matter of morale, another act of the recent congressional session is having a most gratifying effect. Pay in the Army is based almost exclusively upon length of service. With the repeal of the Economy Act it was naturally assumed that the pay status of each officer and enlisted man automatically became that which would have obtained if no restrictive laws had ever been passed. Subsequently, however, administrative rulings held that no credit could be given for any service performed during the period the Economy Act was in force. The unfortunate result was that every junior, that is, all persons having less than 30 years' service, would permanently lose longevity credits for more than 2 years' service. Congress not only corrected this misunderstanding but likewise established a fixed level of allowances for quarters and subsistence, thus removing a particularly irritating cause of hardship among junior officers on city and other types of duty involving relatively high expense. By another provision of law, proper allowances have been authorized for officers during travel to their homes upon retirement.

West Point increase. - In June of this year Congress passed a law increasing the authorized number of cadets at West Point from 1,374 to 1,960. This bill had the support of the War Department because its future effect upon the composition of the professional officer corps and upon the efficiency of defense measures will be most salutary.

Officers are commissioned from many sources, of which the Military Academy is only one. Yet our whole Army has been developed spiritually in the image of West Point. Since the beginning of the nineteenth century its graduates in uninterrupted stream have entered the military service as a life's career. All of them have been nurtured in West Point's teachings of discipline, courage, and loyalty - the cardinal virtues of the soldier. All of them have been imbued with the conceptions of duty, integrity, and patriotism which constitute the very basis of West Point training and which these graduates have in turn transplanted into the Army. In a very real sense that institution has thus become the heritage, not merely of those who happen to be its graduates, but of every officer in the service. Between the two groups there is no distinction in their jealous concern for their own and the Army's reputation for unimpeachable integrity and readiness for self-sacrifice in the country's service. Should this high regard for the soldier's creed be banished from the Army, if it should even be noticeably lowered, our whole system of military administration would collapse like a house of cards. Moreover, the American Army, as an instrument of democratic government, would no longer be the rock of stability and protection that it is but would sooner or later degenerate into a positive menace. Assurance that it will be forever maintained in full conformity with these high standards will not be lacking so long as the officer corps includes a fair proportion of West Point graduates. Over a period of years this proportion should be not less than 50 per cent.

This is not to say that the product of any other institution is not the equal of that from West Point in intelligence, ability, and basic worth. The Army's long list of brilliant leaders that have risen from the ranks or have been commissioned from other universities is proof sufficient of the quality of leadership obtained through those channels. But it is, nevertheless, an accepted fact that West Point imparts to the young man during his formative years an enduring respect for ideals of service and standards of conduct that are not so continuously and insistently stressed elsewhere. And, in urging the Army's need for absorbing annually a strong increment of the West Point product, no group has been more earnest or sincere than our distinguished body of nongraduate leaders. Among those who have so expressed themselves I name only Winfield Scott, Andrew Jackson, Theodore Roosevelt, and Leonard Wood.

Since experience shows that during and following every war we have a tremendous influx of officers from other sources, it is necessary, in order to sustain a 50 per cent average of West Point graduates, to secure from that institution during years of peace somewhat more than half of the annual increment. Very soon, we will begin to have an increased number of yearly separations from the Army due to the passing from the active list of many men commissioned in a body during and after the Spanish-American War. This abnormal outflow will continue intermittently until the last of the World War officers have disappeared from the active rolls of the service. A graduating class of approximately 400 will be necessary to sustain the proper proportion of West Point graduates, and a cadet corps as established by the new law will produce this average number of graduates.

An added motive for increasing the size of West Point is the existing need for a moderate expansion in the professional officer corps. Efficient performance of Regular Army missions requires a minimum number of approximately 14,000 officers in active service, or about 2,000 more than we now have. The reenforcement should not be accomplished suddenly but should be absorbed by increments over a period of years, so that unmanageable humps will not be created in the list. No better way suggests itself to begin this necessary enlargement than through the assignment of more cadets at West Point. The enactment of this law assures, beginning 4 years from now, a gradual expansion of the officer corps on an orderly and efficient basis, assuming that the necessary congressional authorizations will be forthcoming.

Strength of the National Guard. - This component is a military force pertaining to the several States, maintained primarily to insure domestic tranquillity. As a more or less organized militia, it has been in existence since colonial days. But as a national defense force of continuous and general value, it dates from the passage of the National Defense Act in 1916. The 1920 amendments to that act directed a general reorganization of the Guard and provided for a development which has immeasurably raised its efficiency. Except for the Regular Army, it is the only component organized into relatively complete tactical units.

From a national viewpoint, the mission of the National Guard is the early and effective reenforcement of the Regular Army in an emergency. Since it is obligated to service whenever Congress may declare a national emergency to exist, it is supported with Federal funds. It is organized into 18 infantry divisions, 4 cavalry divisions, and certain elements of corps, army, and auxiliary troops. All these must be trained sufficiently in time of peace to be instantly effective in domestic disturbances and to be capable, with a short period of additional preparation, to engage efficiently in battle.

During the period of its development since 1920, the National Guard reached and finally became stabilized at a strength of approximately 190,000, at which level it has been supported by Congress for several years. After much study of the problem, the War Department concluded that its effective training in time of peace and the importance of its emergency mission required a minimum strength of approximately 210,000. In the past session of Congress an addition of 5,000 men to its present strength was authorized as a first step toward building up to this desirable minimum. The War Department has always held also that to maintain the guard in the requisite state of efficiency a training schedule of 48 armory drills and 2 weeks of field service annually was necessary. While this program was reduced somewhat during the fiscal years coinciding with the most serious phases of the economic depression, it has since been fully restored and will obtain during the fiscal year 1936.

To provide for the professional instruction of the guard and to insure that it is kept abreast of modern developments in technique, the Regular Army details to it a corps of instructors. Of these, some 460 are officers. In addition, selected National Guard officers are given special courses at the several service schools and wherever possible field maneuvers of the guard are held in conjunction with Regular units.

Since the National Guard is numerically the strongest of

the Army's components and its emergency mission is a vitally important one, all these measures for insuring the strength and efficiency of its personnel are fully justified and should be constantly carried forward.

Training of the Organized Reserves. - The National Defense Act provided for a Reserve, to consist of enlisted and commissioned elements. However, since neither pay nor training was authorized for enlisted men, this section of the Reserve has never been developed except for a few thousand specialists of various classifications. In practice, therefore, the Reserve consists almost entirely of the Officers' Reserve Corps.

The Officers' Reserve Corps was established to provide the bulk of the commissioned officers required in the units that would be raised in war to support the Regular Army and the National Guard. This corps is expected also to fill emergency vacancies in Regular Army tactical units and in the great number of overhead establishments required during a mobilization.

The aggregate strength of the Officers' Reserve Corps is not limited by legislation. But its value is measured by the extent of its training, and this in turn is determined by availability of funds.

Training of Reserves is accomplished under two general methods. The first of these involves theoretical instruction through conferences, lectures, and correspondence courses; the second, practical work during annual exercises in the field. Theoretical instruction involves only nominal cost to the Government except for the pay of Regular personnel, including some 460 officers, habitually assigned to this duty. When undergoing training in the field, however, a Reserve officer receives the pay of his grade, and it is the availability of funds for this type of training that, in the end, determines the efficiency of the Reserve. For some years the War Department has advocated the active-duty training of 30,000 Reserve officers annually. Since the aggregate requirements in Reserve officers total 120,000, the proposed schedule would enable the War Department, on the average, to give each Reserve officer 2 weeks' active duty 1 year out of each 4. Up to the fiscal year 1934, approximately 20,000 Reserve officers annually received this practical training. In the 2 succeeding years, this figure was reduced to 12,000 and 16,000, respectively, but in the new bill has been raised again to 20,000. Likewise, the number of Reserve officers authorized to attend the general and special service schools has been considerably raised over that allowed in 1934.

Reserve Officers' Training Corps. - The Reserve Officers' Training Corps was established as a logical feeder for the Officers' Reserve Corps. In the land-grant schools and colleges the law requires the institution to give military training in return for Federal aid received. In other institutions this type of training is on a completely voluntary basis. Six hundred and eighty Regular officers, as well as a considerable number of enlisted men, are detailed to instructional work in these institutions.

The results obtained fully justify the cost of this movement, and the War Department has been most anxious to accomplish some expansion of the Reserve Officers' Training Corps. The 1936 appropriations provide $1,000,000 additional for the establishment of new units in qualified educational institutions. The bill again authorizes a 6-weeks' period of active duty training to supplement the theoretical work of college courses. During the year 1934, this period was reduced to 30 days, but the results obtained were unsatisfactory from a training viewpoint.

Citizens' Military Training Camps. - Citizens' Military Training Camps were established to afford military training to those volunteers among American youth who were denied the privilege of attending college. The training is progressive through four annual camps and a graduate of the complete course becomes eligible for a commission in the Officers' Reserve Corps. However, this training is not lost upon those who do not pursue it to the end, since their value as prospective noncommissioned officers in a mobilization is greatly increased.

The War Department has held for some years that a minimum of 37,500 young men should be trained in these camps annually and has urged the desirability of training as many as 50,000. In 1934 and 1935, the number that could be trained fell to about 14,000 or 15,000, but the new bill will permit 30,000 to attend the camps during the coming year.

Weapons and equipment. - It is impossible to establish an order of priority, based upon relative value or indispensability, among the several factors that represent an army's combat power. Strength, discipline, patriotism, courage, and morale are essential, as are professional skill, leadership, and mobility. None of these may be neglected without incurring risk of defeat whenever battle is joined. But even where an army has attained proficiency in all these, it has still another vital need. This involves the quality and quantity of its weapons and equipment.

The tools of the soldier's trade are diversified in type and many of them complicated in design. Their characteristics markedly influence an army's organization, mobility, tactical doctrine, and technique of training. For example, it is manifestly impossible to organize and train an army in methods applicable to machine guns if the only weapons available for use are antiquated muskets. In the same way, an army cannot be properly prepared to use and to cooperate with modern fast-moving tanks if it has nothing except the cumbersome types left over from the World War. Without modern weapons in adequate amounts, an army cannot train itself in peace for their effective use in war. An even more compelling reason for assuring the excellence and adequacy of munitions is the vital need for them in emergency. Destruction is certain to be the portion of an army, no matter how excellently it may be prepared in all other respects, at any moment it opposes on the battlefield an enemy its own equal in all other essential factors and markedly superior to it in munitions.

The problem of sustaining efficiency in munitions and in keeping them available in the necessary quantity is a most difficult one. This difficulty is due both to the tendency of such materiel to grow obsolete and relatively useless, and to the continuous need for replacing items worn out or consumed in peace-time activities. In evolving a munitions program designed to meet the requirements of this problem, the War Department has applied the same principles that control other phases of military preparation under the American system. That is, no attempt is made in time of peace to maintain, constantly and immediately available for emergency use, the vast quantities of supplies that would be needed in active operations. Instead, the plan comprehends the barest requirements of peace-time preparation and depends for war supply upon the production of material after the beginning of an emergency. The time lag thus visualized between any declaration of war by Congress and the time that large-scale operations could begin corresponds to the delay that our defensive system entails in the raising and training of armies.

Specifically, the program requires a continuous experimentation and development by technicians so as to assure that the pilot models of the American Army will be at least the equal in efficiency of those possessed by any other army. It requires also that these advanced models be procured in adequate amounts to permit the development of appropriate organization and tactics and to supply the covering forces required in the very early stages of an emergency. In addition, there is carried on a continuous preparation in the field of munitions procurement so as to reduce the time for attaining quantity production after an emergency has been declared by Congress. This process, which by law is placed under the supervision of the Assistant Secretary of War, involves detailed surveys of America's industrial capacity and every practicable prearrangement that will insure the availability of munitions by the time they are needed.

To fall behind the schedule fixed by this modest program involves danger to the United Stares. Yet in the past 13 years ve have failed to make the necessary progress in that portion of the plan requiring peace-time procurement.

In almost every category of munitions, the types with which the American Army is supplied were produced during or prior to the World War. Since that time experimentation has produced models of greatly increased efficiency, but with one or two exceptions none of these have been procured in usable quantities during the past 13 years.

We emerged from the World War with some 4,000 pieces of light field artillery. These were of the model known as the "French 75 mm." This was a splendid gun but it is not to be compared with pilot models since developed in our Army. The newer weapon has greatly increased flexibility of fire, longer range, and is not subject to damage when traveling at high speeds, whereas the older gun could not be towed at a greater speed than 7 or 8 miles per hour. In other classes of artillery, equally striking improvements have been made in experimental equipment.

Our Infantry is still armed with the Springfield rifle of the model of 1903. This weapon, which was undoubtedly the foremost infantry weapon of its time, is now definitely outmoded by the invention of a semiautomatic rifle which has a greatly increased rate of fire and whose operation involves less fatigue to the soldier. The infantry mortar has been so greatly improved that by comparison the one of the World War period is almost useless.

Ammunition has likewise been steadily improved in quality since 1918. Latest types of small-arms ammunition have almost doubled the range of similar World War calibers and tremendous advances have been made in the production of armor-piercing bullets. While in this class of supply yearly procurement has been in the most improved types available,

the amounts authorized have been so inadequate that the result has been a constant diminution of stocks held in war reserve. The inadequacy of our available ammunition, in all essential calibers, is at this moment a matter for serious concern.

Until the end of 1934, the Army's motor equipment was largely that left over from the World War. In general, the trucks and motors employed by the Army are commercial types and the unsuitability of the 1918 models as compared to those of the present day is a matter of common knowledge. Moreover, the development of good roads and the increased efficiency of the motor have unmistakably indicated the wisdom of a major substitution of motors for animal-drawn transportation. Such a substitution has been very greatly handicapped in our Army due to the lack of funds to make the change.

The story with respect to tanks, combat cars, and other types of armored vehicles is a similar one. We have developed models in this type of weapon which are beyond doubt the equal and in some respects probably superior to any others in the world. Opportunity to obtain them in quantity was for many years almost completely denied and the end of 1934 still found us equipped with the unreliable, underpowered, and inefficient models of World War design.

The same observations apply to nearly every other type of equipment such as engineering materiel, radios, and other communication equipment and gas appliances.

With respect to airplanes, deterioration in quality has not been so noticeable due to the relatively short life of this class of materiel. Frequent replacement having been necessary, the Air Corps has spared no effort to see that each new increment of airplane equipment has been of the highest efficiency then obtainable.

The seriousness of this general situation has been repeatedly emphasized in official reports and in annual recommendations to Congress. Until 1934, little relief was obtained and while experimentation was continued to assure the development of efficient pilot models the quantities made available for current training and for initial emergency use were, in most instances, negligible.

Within the past 2 years this situation has been markedly improved. With $10,000,000 made available by the Public Works Administration' there have been purchased numbers of motor vehicles for accomplishing a partial motorization in both the Regular Army and the National Guard. From the same source $6,000,000 was obtained to apply to our needs in ammunition and $7,500,000 for the procurement of airplanes.

All funds allocated to the War Department by the Public Works Administration were primarily for the purpose of providing work relief, and the projects for which they could be spent were deter-mined in detail by officials of that Administration. While in every case they have been applied to existing deficiencies, they have not always been allotted in strict accord with the Army's most critical needs. In all some $100,000,000, of which about $32,000,000 was allowed for strictly military purposes as distinguished from construction, has been received from the Public Works Administration. Could the expenditure of the entire sum have been controlled exclusively by the importance of the Army's requirements an even greater degree of improvement would have been realized.

With funds provided in appropriations since 1934, we have initiated a procurement program in modern tanks and combat cars, of which 78 are now in production and 69 are provided in the current bill. A total of 3,340 of the new semi-automatic rifle has been authorized. Somewhat increased sums have been devoted also to the procurement of new artillery, both field and antiaircraft, as well as for Infantry mortars and other miscellaneous equipment. For Air Corps purposes, exclusive of pay and other major items financed out of other funds, the 1936 bill allotted over $45,000,000, an increase of almost 66 per cent over the previous year's authorization.

Obviously, the sum total of the increments so far authorized does not make good the deterioration of the past 13 years. These authorizations are important, however, and insure some immediate improvement in our munitions situation. Moreover, it is quite evident that Congress has become alive to the necessity of pursuing a reasonable program of munitions rehabilitation.

Miscellaneous improvements. - In many other directions, advances of varying importance have been recently authorized in the Army. The national rifle and pistol matches, for which no funds have been appropriated during the past several years, have been restored. There is now going on a considerable construction of barracks and quarters and of storage and other facilities out of funds provided by the Public Works Administration. Much of this work has already been completed. The amount allotted for this purpose was about $68,000,000 and application of this sum to the Army's construction needs has resulted in vast improvements both in efficiency and in morale and in a reduction of upkeep costs. While there must still remain in use many of the dilapidated structures that the Army has been occupying ever since the World War, a large portion of them has been replaced by modern buildings.

More than $2,200,000, also secured from the Public Works Administration, has been devoted to the construction, improvement, and repair of National Guard camps. With some $6,000,000 obtained from Public Works, a partial rehabilitation of essential coast defenses is being accomplished. Finally, and of great importance, Congress has set up funds for the specific purpose of conducting combined field maneuvers on a moderate scale. The need for this kind of training has been acute and has existed ever since the World War. Its initiation is further evidence that the purpose of Congress is to insure satisfactory efficiency throughout the Army of the United States.

It is thus evident that in many essential phases of military preparation Congress has recently authorized advances along lines urged by the War Department. In certain instances these authorizations follow in detail the recommendations submitted. The Army's task is to make the best possible use of the additional assets that have thus become available. This responsibility is a heavy one and it involves more than mere reenforcement of old formations or expansion of old conceptions.

For five years the central theme of War Department recommendations to Congress has been the necessity for modernization of the Military Establishment. This purpose must influence the solution of every problem now facing us. Instant advantage must be taken of the present opportunity to mold our Army more distinctly into a unified, mobile, efficient, and strictly modern machine. Clear vision must be supplemented by tireless energy, and no effort must be spared to derive the utmost in combat power from every dollar available for the Army.

In a report such as this, it is manifestly impossible even to indicate all of the detailed activities in which this improvement must obtain or to describe the methods whereby it is to be accomplished. It is possible, however, and highly desirable that there should be announced the fundamental considerations which have formed the basis of the War Department recommendations and which must serve as guideposts in the Army's future progress.

Intensive training. - Foremost among the considerations governing the War Department's purposes is the insistent need for maximum technical proficiency among a reasonably strong corps of professional soldiers. Modern warfare constantly increases in complexity. Weapons have grown more complicated in design and require the utmost in technical skill for their effective use. These multiply the potential combat power of the individual and this circumstance automatically permits and even dictates greater dispersion on the battlefield. Compact masses are a battle characteristic of the past, and close control obtained by personal contact, is no longer possible. Effective results will obtain only where each soldier is a master of technique and so thoroughly indoctrinated in correct tactical methods as to function satisfactorily under conditions of relative isolation and independence.

Since more than ever before professional skill is a prerequisite to battle success, those elements upon which fall the vital responsibility of initial emergency defense must be developed in time of peace to the highest possible level of proficiency. This objective cannot be fully attained on any part-time basis. Only the professional soldier and the professional unit can be instantly ready to act effectively against a modern enemy. Even they can attain this degree of readiness only when intelligently instructed and sufficiently supplied with modern munitions.

The Army's first responsibility then is to insure that every available man is employed continuously in profitable training activity. Military housekeeping is necessary - but Congress did not authorize an expansion of the Army for the maintenance of posts or the elaboration of necessary overhead organizations. There exists no justification for increasing the numbers necessarily used for these purposes heretofore. To do so would not only be an inexcusable blunder, it would constitute little less than a breach of good faith. We need trained fighting soldiers. We have the opportunity to produce them. If we fail to do so, Congress can with justice accuse us of failing to appreciate our own responsibilities and to visualize the real necessities of the moment.

In my report for 1934, I alluded to the activities of a War Department board then engaged in exhaustive study of the Army's training needs. Aside from many other direct benefits resulting from the board's work, it attracted renewed attention to this problem.

Through the facilities of their respective service schools, the chiefs of the combat arms and services have made great strides in developing training plans for use in emergency.

One of the aims has been to determine through actual test the minimum length of time required to prepare organizations to take their places, as regiments, in brigade and divisional training. To reach this stage of development in the infantry, it has been determined that intensive training for 16 weeks will suffice. But it is not to be understood that within a period of 16 weeks a whole army can be produced capable of exploiting to the full the advantages offered by the many types of weapons now available to the soldier. To combine, in battle, the possibilities of swift-moving and powerful elements of infantry, artillery, cavalry, Signal Corps, anti-aircraft artillery, and the air force will require the utmost in efficient leadership as well as perfect cohesion and constant practice throughout all ranks of the command.

The standards of training applicable to armies that may be rapidly raised and rushed into service in an emergency furnish no measure of the efficiency to be demanded from those enjoying opportunities for uninterrupted training in time of peace. These latter elements, upon which will fall the full burden of defense during the first stages of a crisis and which will be required to establish and operate the machinery for mobilization as well as to furnish professional instructors for emergency levies, must make up in skill and proficiency what they are certain to lack in numbers. Their officers must be imbued with a spirit of progress and thoroughly indoctrinated in the potentialities of modern weapons employed in conformity with modern conceptions.

The battle responsibilities of officers have multiplied even more swiftly than those of the individual soldier. In particular, the difficulties of retaining control of fighting lines constantly increase. But this control is the basic function of all commanders, and they must not give way to the tendency to establish themselves as mere message centers in a complicated system of signal communication. Theirs is a task of leadership - continuous, energetic, and courageous leadership - and if they become immersed in the staff problems of battle, they will abandon the Army to leaderless effort and almost certain defeat. Constant insistence on these essentials and constant training in applicable method and doctrine are necessary to insure efficiency.

Increased mobility. - The next consideration underlying the War Department recommenda tions is the need for greater mobility. The protective power of modern weapons is so great that where these are strongly and deliberately organized for defense they practically assure invulnerability. Only through surprise action can collision with the enemy's prepared positions be avoided, and to gain surprise nothing is more important than superiority in mobility. The constant trend in the modern world is toward greater and greater speed. Any army that fails to keep in step with this trend is, far from making necessary progress toward modernization, going steadily and irrevocably backward.

The airplane, the physical embodiment of the spirit of speed, has become an indispensable member of the military team. The rest of the Army must develop itself so as to work efficiently with this new and speedy member. This generalization assumes definite meaning when it is understood to imply a necessity on the part of the Army to strive for a mobility permitting it to take advantage of the military opportunities created by an air force exploiting its own cooperative powers to the full, rather than compelling the air force to waste itself away in hovering around an inert and cumbersome ground contingent as a mere protective and locally assisting agency.

The means whereby the increased mobility is to be obtained are almost unlimited. Starting with the foot soldier, the load he has habitually carried must be reduced. Already great advances have been made in this direction and more must be accomplished. Thus the infantryman will be able to approach the battlefield more rapidly and in better condition and will be able to move about it more freely once he has arrived. Suitable transportation must be provided for all articles essential to the foot soldier but which he need not habitually carry into battle. Beyond this, staff work must be so perfected as to provide, wherever possible, highway transportation for complete infantry units, and to do this without smothering the Army under a mass of mechanical equipment whose use would be only intermittent.

Within all combat units up to and including the division, material heretofore carried for unforeseen contingencies must be thrown aside. Trust must be reposed in improved supply systems to bring these emergency equipments to the battlefield at the time and place they may be needed. Rolling reserves in ammunition, food, and other articles of daily consumption must be reduced to the safe minimum.

This process of stripping from combat units every useless impediment must go further than the mere removal of contingent supplies and equipment. It will likewise affect organization. Difficulty in movement mounts rapidly with the size of the command, and the effort must be to reduce every echelon to the smallest possible size consistent with requisite power in shock and fire action. Homogeneity promotes mobility. The small units of the front lines - certainly to include the battalion of infantry - must abandon the attempt to include within themselves every type of tactical power of which they may have occasional need. Emergency and special fires must be furnished by supporting troops separately organized so that the front line unit and its commander may concentrate upon one objective and one type of problem and carry their own tasks swiftly to completion. Each portion of the whole command must trust every other portion to perform its own missions properly and promptly. Our whole tactical organization must be developed in this concept.

As there constantly appear upon the military horizon new weapons, with their new tactical possibilities and their new threats to our own safety, the instant reaction of every commander is to include them, as well as neutralizing agencies against them, within his own command and under his own direct control. Manifestly every organization should be so armed as to facilitate performance of its particular missions, both in offense and in defense. But in the interests of mobility, to say nothing of efficiency and economy, smaller units should so far as practicable be organized homogeneously. Reliance for special types of support and special classes of protection should be confidently placed in other members of the team suitably equipped for the purpose, and likewise homogeneously organized.

For transportation purposes in the field we have already made considerable progress in the substitution of motors for horses and mules. This trend is due not only to the steady development of good roads but more markedly to the continuous improvement in the quality and availability of cross-country vehicles. Admittedly there exist certain minor functions within every unit where the presence of animals, either riding or draft, would be a convenience, sometimes almost a necessity. But in every case where motorization promises substantial net gains the substitution should be made, and ingenuity and improvisation must find a way to overcome any incidental disadvantages.

The existing motorization program calls for a more sweeping substitution in the National Guard than in the Regular Army. This is largely because the professional force must be prepared for any kind of action, even guerrilla in character. The Regular Army must, under present conditions, Continue to include a sufficient strength in animal transportation to insure mobility and adequacy of supply in terrain where the motor cannot efficiently operate. On the other hand, any set of conditions requiring mobilization of the National Guard would almost surely imply the establishment of a rather formal theater of operations - and reasonable road nets will be available for use. Motorization will also facilitate mobilization of the Guard, since motor vehicles can be assembled and put in use with less delay than would be involved in the expansion and training of animal-drawn transport units.

Another splendid opportunity for increasing mobility lies in mechanization. By this term is meant the employment of motor-propelled vehicles as weapons on the battlefield. The first of the vehicles so employed was the tank, invented during the World War. Its purpose was to break through and to disrupt the fixed bands of machine-gun fire that swept the battlefield and imposed a practical paralysis on tactical movements in areas exposed to such fire.

Because of the special conditions that prevailed on the western front, possibilities for tank employment were limited to frontal assaults. Due also to the mechanical unreliability of the machines then in use, no more extended operations could probably have been successfully undertaken. The result was that tanks came to be generally regarded as weapons useful only for close support of heavy infantry attacks, with their required speed indicated by the rate of marching troops and with their capabilities limited to the disruption of organized small-arms fire along strongly fortified fronts.

This function of combat vehicles is a most important one. But this constricted conception of mechanization fails utterly to conform to the principles which must guide the American Army in its further development. The great strides made since the World War in the mechanical efficiency of combat vehicles have opened to them an extensive field of usefulness.

The attainment of victory imposes upon an army the necessity for undertaking a variety of activities which may be grouped into several rather well-defined categories. It must conduct efficient reconnaissance and counterreconnaissance from the outset of the campaign; move swiftly in the directions indicated as desirable; concentrate its personnel and materiel at the critical point or points; immobilize its enemy and hold firmly all areas vital to its own success; strike with the maximum power of fire and shock; and exploit rapidly and fearlessly every advantage gained. Each of the several arms has been organized, equipped, and trained for the purpose of carrying out a particular part or parts of the whole task.

In our Army each of the combat arms has been charged with the responsibility of so adapting the characteristics of combat vehicles to its own uses as to produce maximum efficiency in the performance of its own particular missions. Consequently the principal interest of the infantry in this matter involves vehicles capable of participating in heavy attack. The cavalry, responsible for those missions which demand maximum ground mobility, is concentrating upon the development of mechanized units characterized by great strategical as well as tactical mobility.

A properly equipped mechanized cavalry will not only be most useful in facilitating the safe and uninterrupted movement of other forces but, because of its combined fighting power and great road speed, will concentrate within itself a tremendous capacity for distant surprise action. It offers to the commander-in-chief a logical connecting link between the destructive attacks of air units and the more slowly delivered but more powerful and sustained blows of the bulk of his army.

In this latter capacity the combat vehicle should prove to be of extraordinary effectiveness. A modern army is a highly organized and in some respects a delicately adjusted mechanism. Its most sensitive points are found on its flanks and in its rear areas where, generally speaking, they are safe from attack except by extremely mobile units. Foremost among these units in point of speed and flexibility of movement is the air force. The blows that can be delivered by a strong air unit are sudden and, depending upon the vulnerability of the target, peculiarly devastating. Obviously, however, except where the attacker's preponderance of air force is so overwhelming as to be completely free to pursue an unimpeded course of action, the bombardments of these sensitive points must be intermittent and infrequent in occurrence. Consequently, unless other elements of the attacking army can take advantage of the opportunities created by the air force, the damage caused by it is likely to be promptly repaired and important tactical opportunities will he lost. On the other hand, if the commander has available special units which can speedily support air operations and sustain the opportunities created by it until additional forces can come into action, the operation may well lead to decisive results. This vitally important sustaining role must be played by an efficient mechanized force - and other elements of the army must in turn, arrive at the scene of action with a minimum of delay.

The definite objectives in mechanization toward which the Army is now working involve a specific number of infantry, cavalry, and artillery units. These objectives do not indicate the ultimate possibilities in the use of combat vehicles and certainly they should not, in the slightest degree, limit the development of theory and doctrine pertaining to this class of weapon. Indeed the present program represents no more than immediate peacetime requirements based on facts and principles already fully demonstrated.

For example, our Army has not exhausted the possibility of transporting into and even through the vicissitudes of battle itself the infantry of entire divisions. Could there be developed a light, inexpensive vehicle with a reasonable degree of mechanical efficiency in cross-country travel, and capable of transporting and partially protecting two or three well-armed infantrymen, a great opportunity for increasing battle mobility would be presented. An organization so equipped would, in effect, bridge the gap now existing between the fields of mechanization and motorization. For distant support of fast-moving units of tanks and combat cars it would be invaluable. Possibilities for its use, when properly ccordinated with the artillery and other arms, would be innumerable. Whether or not such a development can come about depends almost exclusively upon the practicability of developing small, inexpensive, and reliable vehicles that could in emergelcy be produced rapidly and in great numbers. The inventive genius of our technicians has here a glowing opportunity for service.

In insisting upon the development of the combat elements of the Army into an efficient, speedy, unencumbered fighting machine, the War Department is well aware that modern weapons have introduced new and difficult problems of maintenance, which require the establishment of strong and highly efficient facilities for supply, repair, and replacement. Indeed, it is partially because of the increasing need in military establishments for these comprehensive services and facilities that it is so important now to adhere rigidly to the purpose of forbidding their unnecessary inclusion in combat units. A natural concern for the perfect mechanical functioning of each machine gun, automatic rifle, pistol, and cannon, and for the operation of supply and communication services, is responsible for the desire in each commander to gather to himself the necessary means for repair, supply, and maintenance. When carried to the extreme, the result of this practice is so to load down the combat elements with impedimenta that the Army is buried under its own weight and incapable of rapid movement. With the increasing need for technical support, this tendency is certain to be emphasized. But the combat leader trained in the necessities of modern battle must rigidly set his face against it. All these necessary services must function mainly in the rear, in areas so well protected by location and by auxiliary troops that considerations involving their safety do not paralyze the troops operating in the front. Commanders must keep before their eyes the need for celerity in movement. They must insist that the maintenance services adopt methods and practices which will automatically and without request speedily evacuate wounded, replace useless equipment, furnish adequate communication, and keep the Army supplied with ammunition and other items of habitual consumption. Specialists and technicians must be held to this standard of performance even under conditions where the forward units are moving rapidly and over considerable distances.

To sum up, nothing is more important to the future efficiency of the Army than to multiply its rate of movement. A law of physics that applies with equal force to warfare is that while striking force increases directly with the mass applied, it increases according to the square of the speed of the application. Through proper organization in all echelons, through the development and perfection of reliable combat machines capable of speedy maneuver, and through the improvement of transportation, maintenance, communication, and supply arrangements, the objective of greater and still greater speed must be pursued.

Command system. - There must be a complete restudy and analysis of existing networks of command. Every moment consumed in initiating a movement is equally valuable with those required for the movement itself. Through a thorough overhaul of current methods, possibly even to the extent of eliminating one or more of the echelons of command that have heretofore obtained in our Army, further possibilities may be discovered for saving time and promoting control and efficiency.

The concept underlying the Four Army Organization, a development initiated more than 2 years ago, is maximum speed in the coordinated and effective use of all forces existing at any given moment. The plan establishes over all combat units of all components a skeletonized but permanent network of tactical command extending all the way from the commander in the field down to the last private in the ranks. It assures a logical grouping of larger tactical units under professional leaders and staffs and, in each strategic region, permits perfection of prearrangement for bringing National Guard units promptly to the support of the professional elements holding the forward lines of defense. It emphasizes the importance of speed, skill, training, and leadership as opposed to mere numbers and, in this conception, seeks to improve the readiness of the whole Army to engage successfully in active operations. Its mobilization objective is the rapid preparation for effective action of only those forces that may be required - it negatives any purpose of calling to the colors vast hordes of men whose services in the Army may not prove necessary to victory. Not only must there be constant effort toward the perfection of the broader phases of this organization, but improvement along the same lines must be sought all the way down to the smallest unit and to the last man.

Air Corps development. - The Army Air Corps is embarked upon a process of reorganization and rehabilitation, which if carried forward consistently will produce an establishment commensurate to the country's needs in this important respect. Within the past year a General Headquarters Air Force comprising all elements of the Air Corps, except those engaged in technical development, procurement, administration, and formal schooling, has been established. These latter functions remain under the jurisdiction of the Chief of the Air Corps. The mission of the General Headquarters Air Force is to develop and maintain a unit of maximum quality and efficiency and adequate in strength to meet the probable initial requirements in emergency. It is subject only to the orders of the military head of the Army.

Under existing conditions this organization of the Air Corps is ideally suited in type to the country's needs. The matter of its higher organization has been much discussed and debated for many years - one result of which has been a lack of stability and continuity in policy. This in turn has impeded progress, diverted attention from primary objects, and created dissensions in a team in which perfect harmony should prevail.

Our General Headquarters Air Force is fully capable, so far as organization is concerned, of performing every mission that could be carried out by an air force organized separately from the Army. At the same time it is much more economical. It has no need for setting up a complete supply and maintenance system, and is made the recipient of many essential services which, if independently organized, it would have to provide for itself.

Not only are the basic features of the present organization supported by the experienced leadership of the Air Corps itself, but they have received the approval of the President, the Secretary of War, the General Staff, and of innumerable students of government and of warfare. Prominent among these latter are the members of the Baker Board.

To assure for a reasonable period continuity of policy in this regard, it would be most helpful if a determination could be attained unequivocaly to refuse consideration, for at least 5 years, of any scheme pertaining to reorganization, regrouping, or revision that would tend to disturb the existing set-up or distract attention from basic objectives. With this definite assurance there would remain no excuse for the introduction of false or irritating issues that not only impede progress but for the moment at least are inconsequential. Within 5 years it is hoped that approximate stabilization in strength will have been reached and if conditions then indicate the wisdom of analyzing once again such matters as basic organization and control, their thorough consideration will be in order. With such temporary stability guaranteed, the whole attention of the Air Corps can be devoted to the perfection of its training and the developinent of adequate strength.

So far as tactical and strategical doctrine is concerned, there exist two great fields for Air Force employment; one fully demonstrated and proved, the other largely conjectural. The first of these fields includes military missions, the performance of which will facilitate success of the whole Army. These involve attacks against bases, depots, bridges, defiles, transportation nets, and communications that are often out of reach of other arms. In more closely ooordinated action thev involve also reconnaissance, observation, attacks against opposing ground troops, and high~speed communication and transportation. In addition to all these is the responsibility of protection against hostile air contingents.

The more conjectural use of the Air Force involves its employment against unarmed centers of population and of industry. Deliberately to plan for such a use involves an aggressive intent, for by no stretch of the imagination could such attacks be initiated by any nation seeking nothing except its own defense.

However, there exists the possibility that a defending nation might have to resort to this use in retaliation - so as to induce discontinuance of such attacks already launched against its own cities. In considering these repugnant possibilities, there are two pertinent facts applying to our own situation.

The first of these facts is that in any struggle of the ghastly type just outlined nations occupying a more constricted area than the United States would be at a marked disadvantage. Concentrated objectives are much more vulnerable to air attack than are dispersed ones.

The second pertinent fact is that the United States enjoys industrial advantages which would enable it, in war, to produce more planes than any other nation in the world. These two considerations should certainly give pause to any as-sailant contemplating indiscriminate bombardment of our people. On the other hand the sentiment of this country it is confidently believed, will always repudiate and forbid the unprovoked initiation of this kind of war by our own forces.

Certainly our attitude in this much-discussed question would be, in any emergency, a waiting one - but if this kind of action is finally forced upon us, we have the assurance that the General Headquarters Air Force will he suitably organized to perform its missions efficiently. The only requirement will be the necessary equipment, which requirement is equally important when considering the definitely foreseen missions of the Air Corps. As a consequence of these considerations the attention of our own Air Corps should be concentrated upon increasing its readiness to carry out military missions. Once it attains the necessary strength in personnel and planes and the requisite degree of training to carry out all these, we need have no fear as to its ability to meet any eventuality of war.

No effort must be spared to attain the minimum objectives in strength and training announced by the Baker Board. So far as possible, without further legislative action, progress toward these objectives has already begun. The specific legislative needs of the whole program are listed in a later section of this report.

Training of civilian components. - Instruction in the National Guard and the Officers' Reserve Corps must of course reflect the necessity for producing fighting units of greater fire power, greater mobility, and of the highest possible excellence in training.

The National Guard is permanently organized, at reduced strength, into tactical units comprising both officers and enlisted men. It is especially important that these be maintained as properly administered organizations characterized by dependable discipline and sound basic training, since they are intended for early support of the Regular Army in emergency. Moreover, the Guard should be furnished as rapidly as possible, with weapons and equipment of the latest types and thoroughly practiced in their use.

But the special conditions under which the Guard is maintained sharply differentiates the character of its training from that of the Regular Army. The brief periods available to the Guard for training must be employed toward attainment of its principal objective - production of basically sound units. It is in no sense responsible for the development of doctrine, organization, and methods applicable to new weapons and to changing conditions. The law requires simply that the Guard be organized and trained in the model of the Regular Army.

This important duty of mililtary exploration falls squarely upon the Regular Army. Every logical idea must be tested and every new weapon so fitted into the whole machine as to produce maximum tactical effects. Constant adaptation of organization and methods to new possibilities must, in the Regular Army, be the rule rather than the exception. The accuracy of the conclusions drawn will be determined by the intelligence and zeal of profession personnel and by the availability of modern equipment with which to work.

From the Regular Army the Guard has the right to expect progressive instruction based upon this process of test and experimentation. Thus the Guard may concentrate its attention upon its own tasks, secure in the knowledge that it is protected against the insidious evils of obsolescence.

We cannot too often recall to mind the importance of the missions that will devolve upon the civilian components in the event of war. The Regular Army's responsibilities with respect to their preparation for war are equally as important as those applying to its own readiness. No one part of our military establishment can insure the country's integrity under attack. All are needed and the Regular Army as the professional leader and instructor must see to it that all are fit to do their duty.

Combined maneuvers. - Until last year lack of funds prevented the holding of field exercise except on a limited basis and in close proximity to home stations of the participating troops. Normally they involved only small units - exceptionally a division.

In September of 1934, a General Headquarters command post exercise was held in New Jersey, with gratifying results. Unfortunately money was not available for the concentration of troops, so only commanders and staffs participated. The 1936 appropriation bill carries funds for the concentration and training of troops of one army. The exercise next fall will mark the beginning, in our Army, of combined field training by units larger than the division. This opportunity must be exploited to the full. In addition to all other beneficial purposes to be served, these maneuvers represent to the War Department and to the troops involved a vast laboratory for developing the practices whereby the utmost in mobility, fire power, and unification is to be attained. Regular Army units, in particular, attending these exercises should arrive at concentration points prepared through prior garrison training to test out every promising innovation in systems of supply, in attack and defense formations, in organization and administration, and in methods for utilizing every new type of weapon available.

A particular value of such exercises is that they present opportunity for analyzing the probable effect of air attacks upon sizable formations and service installations of ground troops. While we know that efficient air units will practically inhibit route marches in proximity to the enemy, we have not worked out satisfactorily in large units the formations, methods, and special arrangements that will minimize vulnerability of the ground forces and increase their powers of defense. This matter is of extreme importance and must he earnestly investigated.

Combined exercises of this kind should annually form the culminating feature of training programs. Their expense is small compared to their value. They are carried out under the supervision of our most experienced commanders and our most carefully trained staffs, which assures that from them will be derived the last ounce of progress and of perfection in training.

Miscellaneous missions. - In many fields of activity the Army must reexamine its methods and practices to determine their present and future applicability.

Money has been made available by Congress for establishing additional units of the Reserve Officers' Training Corps. This movement is one of the most important of our preparatory activities and its full possibilities can be realized only if the best thought of the War Department and the persistent effort of all instructors are devoted to that end. Stereotyped instruction should not be countenanced. Formal disciplinary drills should be limited to barest requirements and concentrated effort should be directed toward indoctrinating embryo Reserve officers in modern conceptions of warfare.

The shortage of Regular officers will preclude assignment of instructors to new units in the ratio heretofore prevailing, and every officer on this duty will be called upon to carry additional burdens. But the full responsibility for efficiency in the Reserve Officers' Training Corps should not rest upon the instructors. Every effort should be made to awaken college authorities to their own opportunities in this regard, particularly by holding out to students the promise of some immediate reward for efficient service in this organization. To this end, nothing would be more effective than an agreement among school authorities to accord regular college credits on a uniform basis for work in the Reserve Officers' Training Corps. Adoption of such a practice would constitute recognition of the value to the State of this kind of training and would be according to the whole movement the credit due it in developing character and cooperative instincts among its participants. In the broadest sense, the Reserve Officers' Training Corps is an educational movement and it should be so recognized by the Government and colleges alike.

The general and special service schools of the Army continue to function efficiently. Nothing should be allowed to interfere with their operation and, wherever conditions permit, student quotas should be increased. This applies particularly to officers from the National Guard and the Officers' Reserve Corps. Our schools are the foci of professional research and the springs from which flow to all components the refreshing stream of advanced, but carefully considered, theory. They, like all other elements of the Army, must guard against the human tendency to adhere too closely to established custom and procedure. New things should not, merely because of their newness, be condemned as fanatical. Equally important, impractical doctrine should not be advocated simply because of glittering surface promise. A study of the past furnishes a guide for the future, but blind and slavish adherence to outmoded doctrine is the sure mark of decadence.

The Army must continue to carry its assigned duties with respect to the Civilian Conservation Corps and other activities related to the President's program for economic rehabilitation. In all these, its past record is assurance of its continued efficiency and faithful performance of duty.

It is repeated that in every line of military endeavor the Army has just fallen heir to new responsibilities and duties in the production of an adequate military establishment. For many years we have rightly traced the blame for glaring inefficiencies to the inadequacy of the Army's support. Now, however, the sincerity of our past protestations can be proved only by accomplishments that will promptly turn every recruit into an efficient soldier and every dollar into an equal measure of national defense. The reforms recommended by the War Department and authorized by Congress can, in the last analysis, come about only through the intelligent and concerted action of the Army itself.

PRINCIPAL LEGISLATIVE NEEDS

The Army's principal needs for additional legislative authorization involve air development, the establishment of an enlisted reserve, definite programs in the procurement of modern weapons and equipment, and some expansion in the present scale of reserve training.

Air Corps. - The first need of our Air Corps is for fighting planes. The difficulties of sustaining strength and efficiency in air equipment for the Army can scarcely be appreciated by the layman. The principal obstacles are the rapidity with which this materiel grows obsolete, its appalling rate of wastage, and its high unit cost.

Under present conditions it is accepted as an axiom that a military plane more than 5 years old has almost no combat usefulness. While it is logical to suppose, judging from past experience in similar developments, that the useful life of these machines will increase somewhat as the industry grows older and periodic innovations are less startling, yet the fact remains that at present a complete turnover every 5 years is almost inescapable in the combat elements of the Air Corps. Having regard for this factor alone, procurement of 500 planes annually would fully sustain an efficient force of approximately 2,500, even if the useful life of a plane for training and like purposes were no greater than in the fighting units. This was the approximate objective established by the Baker Board. But there is to be considered also the casualty rate, currently estimated at about 20 per cent yearly. In this regard, also, distinct improvement should soon be realized. But under present conditions, in order to develop within a reasonable time an effective and balanced force of 2,500 planes with a small complement of operating reserves, an annual procurement of 800 completely equipped planes is necessary.

Legislative authorization to this effect should form the basis of a continuing air program until the required strength in the Army Air Corps has been attained. Thereafter a schedule of procurement calculated to sustain both strength and efficiency should be adopted. With this expansion assured, Air Corps progress toward efficiency, discussed in a preceding section, would go forward swiftly and surely.

Another need of the Air Force involves the development of adequate operating bases. During a period of some months Congress has been considering a bill for this purpose. It should be passed and necessary development should be initiated without delay.

Enlisted Reserve. - We have an obvious and very important need for an efficient and reasonably strong Enlisted Reserve.

In the same law in which Congress fixed the strength of the Regular Army at 18,000 officers and 280,000 men, and the National Guard at 430,000, it authorized the formation of an Enlisted Reserve. At that time there were in the United States 4,000,000 well-trained veterans of the World War, all of suitable age for military service. It was hoped that not only would many thousands of these trained veterans enlist in the Reserve but that also a considerable proportion of future graduates of the Citizens' Military Training Camps and men discharged from the Regular Army would enroll for Reserve service. Since, however, neither pay nor training of any kind was offered as an inducement, these expectations were not realized.

This failure was not of serious moment so long as a considerable number of the World War veterans were in ages suited to military service. The Enlisted Reserve, under the conditions stated, would have constituted little more than a roster of trained men, and such a roster was already available in the War Department records of the World War personnel.

With the passage of time this situation has changed materially for the worse. The average age of veterans of the World War is now beyond that suited to the enlisted grades of an emergency army. Moreover, the strength of the Regular Army and of the National Guard is far below that authorized in the 1920 law. These conditions compel the reopening of the question of providing a suitable Enlisted Reserve, a project that has been several times proposed by the War Department within recent years.

The reason for maintaining an Enlisted Reserve is to insure instant availability in emergency of men capable of functioning efficiently in a tactical organization. Consequently it must be composed of thoroughly trained men of good physical condition, whose domestic relationships are such that their sudden call to active duty would not occasion undue hardship upon dependents. Unless both these conditions are satisfied a reserve of this particular kind is relatively useless.

The minimum required strength of such a reserve is that necessary to raise the Regular Army to full peace strength immediately upon mobilization. To meet this requirement approximately 120,000 are necessary and since some allowance must be made for wastage, an average strength of about 150,000 should be sought. With such a reserve available there would be far less likelihood of a critical situation arising.

There exist several possible methods for building up a reserve, the most efficient of which is represented in a method whereby all enlistments in the Regular Army are divided into two periods, the first with the colors, the second with the reserve. This system assures the professional efficiency of every individual in the reserve without undertaking a program of annual training with its attendant expense. This system likewise promotes simplicity in administration and control and a desirable homogeneity among the whole command whenever the reserve is called out for emergency use. Finally it makes a maximum and economical use of the active force in building up its own reserve contingent.

The ability of a professional force to develop such a reserve depends upon two factors: its own size, and the average length of reserve service as compared to active service. For example, assume an enlisted force of 100,000 men with a 5-year enlistment period divided into 3 years' active and 2 years' reserve. Making no allowances for attrition or for reenlistments, the maximum attainable size of the reserve would be 67,000 men. But merely by reversing the length of the active and inactive periods the size of the reserve would jump to 150,000 men. In practice many modifying factors would influence these theoretical results but the example given clearly illustrates the principle involved. In the British Army, the only other one organized along lines remotely comparable to our own, the normal enlistment is for 12 years, much of which is ordinarily spent in the reserve.

Experience has shown that an efficient reserve cannot be developed in the total absence of remunerative reward. Pay, however, need be no more than nominal, sufficient only to induce the individual to keep proper authority informed of his whereabouts and to present himself annually at a convenient place for physical examination. It is to be emphasized that membership in such a reserve involves no hardship or sacrifice in time of peace. This component could be called to active duty only in emergency, and since its members would be men of military age, in good health, and with little or no obligations to dependents, they would in any event be liable for service in the armed forces. But membership in such a body does involve instant availability for military service, and it is for this availability that the trained individual should be paid.

With an active army of 165,000 the total enlistment period need be no more than 5 years with authority residing in the Secretary of War to prescribe either 2 or 3 years with the colors and, in each case, the remainder with the reserve. This flexibility in administering the system would be effective in maintaining it at the desired size. I believe that pay of $12 per year, paid quarterly, coupled with a governmental promise of a bonus of $100 to be paid each member whenever the reserve is called out for war service, would insure the development, within 5 years, of a satisfactory organization. Annual expense under this scale would be small. Details of administration would present no great difficulty. The mobilization centers of the Army are located at corps area headquarters and the bulk of administrative details would be largely decentralized to them.

The military program next presented to Congress should include a complete plan for developing a reserve of the kind indicated - and once the necessary legal authority is received it should be rapidly organized and so maintained as to insure its efficiency in emergency.

Munitions. - To attempt to supply within a single year all of the Army's immediate requirements in modern weapons and equipment would involve a needlessly costly method of attaining satisfactory efficiency in this important item. Greater efficiency and economy would be secured by spreading procurement over a reasonable number of years. By adopting this method each annual increment comprehends all technical improvements previously developed and automatically maintains a constantly increasing trend in quality. In this way, also, manufacturing costs are minimized since producers may anticipate steady rather than rush orders, while extensive factory modifications, always required when large amounts of specialized equipment must be produced rapidly, are unnecessary. Congress should prescribe a 5-year program of procurement with the understanding that thereafter a reduced schedule of development and replacement would be permitted so as to sustain efficiency. Governed by this mandatory program, the War Department would submit yearly to Congress detailed analyses of the items recommended for immediate procurement... .

CONCLUSION

To maintain in peace a needlessly elaborate military establishment entails economic waste. But there can be no compromise with minimum requirements. In war there is no intermediate measure of success. Second best is to be defeated, and military defeat carries with it national disaster - political, economic, social, and spiritual disaster. Under the several headings of this report there is sketched in rough outline a military establishment reasonably capable of assuring successful defense of the United States. I have this confidence in its ability, although in size the proposed army is not remotely comparable to many now existing and even falls far below the legal limits prescribed in the National Defense Act.

There are, of course, certain favorable factors which minimize the need in our country for maintenance in peace of a huge military machine such as exists in almost every other major power. Chief among these factors are geographical isolation and the existence of cordial relationships across our land frontiers.

Additionally influencing the determination of the War Department to emphasize quality rather than quantity in further development of the Army is the conviction that relatively small forces exploiting the possibilities of modern weapons and mechanisms will afford in future emergencies a more dependable assurance of defense than will huge, unwieldy, poorly equipped, and hastily trained masses. Adherence to such a policy likewise serves the interests of economy, since of all costs of war, both direct and indirect, none is so irreparable and so devastating as that measured in the blood of its youth. The United States should not hold to the "nation in arms" as a principal tenet in its doctrine of defense if by that term is indicated an unreasoned purpose of cramming into the armed forces every citizen of military age and capable of carrying a gun. Beyond all doubt any major war of the future will see every belligerent nation highly organized for the single purpose of victory, the attainment of which will require integration and intensification of individual and collective effort. But it will be a nation at war, rather than a nation in arms. Of this vast machine the fighting forces will be only the cutting edge; their mandatory characteristics will be speed in movement, power in fire and shock action, and the utmost in professional skill and leadership. Their armaments will necessarily be of the most efficient types obtainable and the transportation, supply, and maintenance systems supporting them will be required to function perfectly and continuously. Economic and industrial resources will have to assure the adequacy of munition supply and the sustenance of the whole civil population. In these latter fields the great proportion of the employable population will find its war duty.

More than most professions the military is forced to depend upon intelligent interpretation of the past for signposts charting the future. Devoid of opportunity, in peace, for self-instruction through actual practice of his profession, the soldier makes maximum use of historical record in assuring the readiness of himself and his command to function efficiently in emergency. The facts derived from historical analysis he applies to conditions of the present and the proximate future, thus developing a synthesis of appropriate method, organization, and doctrine.

But the military student does not seek to learn from history the minutia of method and technic. In every age these are decisively influenced by the characteristics of weapons currently available and by the means at hand for maneuvering, supplying, and controlling combat forces. But research does bring to light those fundamental principles, and their combinations and applications, which, in the past, have been productive of success. These principles know no limitation of time. Consequently, the army extends its analytical interest to the dust-buried accounts of wars long past as well as to those still reeking with the scent of battle. It is the object of the search that dictates the field for its pursuit. Those callow critics who hold that only in the most recent battles are there to be found truths applicable to our present problems have failed utterly to see this. They apparently cling to a fatuous hope that in historical study is to be found a complete digest of the science of war rather than simply the basic and inviolable laws of the art of war.

Were the accounts of all battles, save only those of Genghis Khan, effaced from the pages of history, and were the facts of his campaigns preserved in descriptive detail, the soldier would still possess a mine of untold wealth from which to extract nuggets of knowledge useful in molding an array for future use. The successes of that amazing leader, beside which the triumphs of most other commanders in history pale into insignificance, are proof sufficient of his unerring instinct for the fundamental qualifications of an army.

He devised an organization appropriate to conditions then existing; he raised the discipline and the morale of his troops to a level never known in any other army, unless possibly that of Cromwell; he spent every available period of peace to develop subordinate leaders and to produce perfection of training throughout the army, and, finally, he insisted upon speed in action, a speed which by comparison with other forces of his day was almost unbelievable. Though he armed his men with the best equipment of offense and of defense that the skill of Asia could produce, he refused to encumber them with loads that would immobilize his army. Over great distances his legions moved so rapidly and secretly as to astound his enemies and practically to paralyze their powers of resistance. He crossed great rivers and mountain ranges, he reduced walled cities in his path and swept onward to destroy nations and pulverize whole civilizations. On the battlefield his troops maneuvered so swiftly and skillfully and struck with such devastating speed that times without number they defeated armies overwhelmingly superior to themselves in numbers.

Regardless of his destructiveness, his cruelty, his savagery, he clearly understood the unvarying necessities of war. It is these conceptions that the modern soldier seeks to separate from the details of the Khan's technique, tactics, and organization, as well as from the ghastly practices of his butcheries, his barbarism, and his ruthlessness. So winnowed from the chaff of medieval custom and of all other inconsequentials, they stand revealed as kernels of eternal truth, as applicable today in our effort to produce an efficient army as they were when, seven centuries ago, the great Mongol applied them to the discomfiture and amazement of a terrified world. We cannot violate these laws and still produce and sustain the kind of army that alone can insure the integrity of our country and the permanency of our institutions if ever again we face the grim realities of war.

All these and many other equally important considerations have been fully weighed by the General Staff in determining the minimum level of military strength and preparation representing reasonable security for the United States. If the War Department program is accorded the additional but relatively inexpensive legislative support herein recommended there exists no reason why this objective should remain beyond attainment. With such support assured:

The Regular Army will, within 5 years, become the model of professional and technical ability that it must be as the heart and core of the security forces. It will be in sufficient strength to discharge its important peacetime duties and, with its small reserve of instantly available and seasoned soldiers, will be ready at a moments notice to move against any threatened attack. Its air contingent will be strong, efficient, and capable of teaming with the ground forces to deliver decisive blows against an enemy or to perform any less closely coordinated type of mission that may be required by circumstances.

The National Guard will continue its steady progress in efficiency and will be sufficiently strong and ready to assure support of the professional element in a major crisis.

The Officers' Reserve Corps will be trained individually and organizationally to furnish a valuable and indispensable reinforcement to our commissioned leadership.

The ability of the Reserve Officers' Training Corps and the Citizens' Military Training Camps to fulfill their functions as sources of trained personnel will be enhanced.

Finally there will be assurance that minimum required quantities of modern weapons, including airplanes, tanks, rifles, cannon, and all other articles and items essential to an army will either be available when needed or will be produced with the least possible delay.

In epitome this is the goal the War Department has set. Through long stretches the road toward it is now open and unobstructed. With the professional force acting as the pacemaker the whole Army of the United States must now push steadily and rapidly forward, confident that when major obstacles are again encountered their timely removal will be authorized, or some practicable way be found around them.

At the time of preparing my last report I had thought that its submission would coincide with the termination of my tour as Chief of Staff. But I am happy to have had the opportunity through an additional year to continue the struggle to free the Army of shackles tending to chain it to obsolescence and stagnation. In many particulars this task remains uncompleted. My successor in this office will inherit responsibility for them as well as for consolidating and making maximum use of gains already realized. Speaking from my own experience I know that in his every effort he will have the unswerving support of the whole Army - the most able, loyal, devoted, and unselfish body of public servants that this Nation or any other has produced.

VETERANS OF THE RAINBOW (42ND) INFANTRY DIVISION OF WORLD WAR I
JULY 14, 1935
WASHINGTON, D.C.

Mr. President and gentlemen of the Rainbow division, I thank you for the warmth of your greeting. It moves me deeply. It was with you I lived my greatest moments. It is of you that I have my greatest memories.

It was 17 years ago - those days of old have vanished, tone and tint; they have gone glimmering through the dreams of things that were. Their memory is a land where flowers of wondrous beauty and varied colors spring, watered by tears and coaxed and caressed into fuller bloom by the smiles of yesterday. Refrains no longer rise and fall from that land of used to be. We listen vainly, but with thirsty ear, for the witching melodies of days that are gone. Ghosts in olive drab and sky blue and German gray pass before our eyes; voices that have stolen away in the echoes from the battlefields no more ring out. The faint, far whisper of forgotten songs no longer floats through the air. Youth, strength, aspirations, struggles, triumphs, despairs, wide winds sweeping, beacons flashing across uncharted depths, movements, vividness, radiance, shadows, faint bugles sounding reveille, far drums beating the long roll, the crash of guns, the rattle of musketry - the still white crosses.

And tonight we are met to remember.

The shadows are lengthening. The division's birthdays are multiplying; we are growing old together. But the story which we commemorate helps us to grow old gracefully. That story is known to all of you. It needs no profuse panegyrics. It is the story of the American soldier of the World War. My estimate of him was formed on the battlefield many years ago and has never changed. I regarded him then, as I regard him now, as one of the world's greatest figures - not only in the era which witnessed his achievements but for all eyes and for all time. I regarded him as not only one of the greatest military figures but also as one of the most stainless; his name and fame are the birthright of every American citizen.

The world's estimate of him will be founded not upon any one battle or even series of battles; indeed, it is not upon the greatest fields of combat or the bloodiest that the recollections of future ages are riveted. The vast theaters of Asiatic conflict are already forgotten today. The slaughtered myriads of Genghis Khan lie in undistinguished graves. Hardly a pilgrim visits the scenes where on the fields of Chalons and Tours the destinies of civilization and Christendom were fixed by the skill of Aetius and the valor of Charles Martel.

The time indeed may come when the memory of the fields of Champagne and Picardy, of Verdun and the Argonne shall be dimmed by the obscurity of revolving years and recollected only as a shadow of ancient days.

But even then the enduring fortitude, the patriotic self-abnegation, and the unsurpassed military genius of the American soldier of the World War will stand forth in undimmed luster; in his youth and strength, his love and loyalty, he gave all that mortality can give. He needs no eulogy from me or from any other man; he has written his own history, and written it in red on his enemy's breast. But when I think of his patience under adversity, of his courage under fire, and of his modesty in victory I am filled with an emotion I cannot express. He belongs to history as furnishing one of the greatest examples of successful and disinterested patriotism. He belongs to posterity as the instructor of future generations in the principles of liberty and right. He belongs to the present - to us - by his glory, by his virtues, and by his achievements.

The memorials of character wrought by him can never by dimmed. He needs no statues or monuments; he has stamped himself in blazing flames upon the souls of his countrymen; he has carved his own statue in the hearts of his people; he has built his own monument in the memory of his compatriots.

The military code which he perpetuates has come down to us from even before the age of knighthood and chivalry. It embraces the highest moral laws and will stand the test of any ethics or philosophies ever promulgated for the uplift of mankind. Its requirements are for the things that are right, and its restraints are from the things that are wrong. Its observance will uplift everyone who comes under its influence. The soldier, above all other men, is required to perform the highest act of religious teaching - sacrifice. In battle and in the face of danger and death he discloses those divine attributes which his Maker gave when He created man in his own image. No physical courage and no brute instincts can take the place of the divine annunciation and spiritual uplift which will alone sustain him. However horrible the incidents of war may be, the soldier who is called upon to offer and to give his life for his country is the noblest development of mankind.

On such an occasion as this my thoughts go back to those men who went with us to their last charge. In memory's eye I can see them now - forming grimly for the attack, blue lipped, covered with sludge and mud, chilled by the wind and rain of the foxhole, driving home to their objective, and to the judgment seat of God. I do not know the dignity of their birth, but I do know the glory of their death. They died unquestioning, uncomplaining, with faith in their hearts and on their lips the hope that we would go on to victory.

Never again for them staggering columns, bending under soggy packs, on many a weary march from dripping dusk to drizzling dawn. Never again will they trudge ankle deep through the mud on shell shocked roads. Never again will they stop cursing their luck long enough to whistle through chapped lips a few bars as some clear voice raised the lilt of "Madelon." Never again ghostly trenches, with their maze of tunnels, drifts, pits, dugouts-never again, gentlemen unafraid.

They have gone beyond the mists that blind us here and become part of that beautiful thing we call the Spirit of the Unknown Soldier. In chambered temples of silence the dust of their dauntless valor sleeps, waiting. Waiting in the chancery of Heaven the final reckoning of Judgment Day: "Only those are fit to live who are not afraid to die."

Our country is rich and resourceful, populous and progressive, courageous to the full extent of propriety. It insists upon respect for its rights, and likewise gives full recognition to the rights of all others. It stands for peace, honesty, fairness, and friendship in its intercourse with foreign nations.

It has become a strong, influential, and leading factor in world affairs. It is destined to be even greater if our people are sufficiently wise to improve their manifold opportunities. If we are industrious, economical, absolutely fair in our treatment of each other, strictly loyal to our Government, we, the people, may expect to be prosperous and to remain secure in the enjoyment of all those benefits which this privileged land affords.

But so long as humanity is more or less governed by

motives not in accord with the spirit of Christianity, our country may be involved by those who believe they are more powerful. Whatever the ostensible reason advanced may be - envy, cupidity, fancied wrong, or other unworthy impulse may direct them.

Every nation that has what is valuable is obligated to be prepared to defend against brutal attack or unjust effort to seize and appropriate. Even though a man be not inclined to guard his own interests, common decency requires him to furnish reasonable oversight and care to others who are weak and helpless. As a rule, they who preach by word or deed "Peace at any price," are not possessed of anything worth having, and are oblivious to the interest of others including their own dependents.

The Lord Almighty, merciful and all-wise, does not absolutely protect those who unreasonably fail to contribute to their own safety, but He does help those who, to the limit of their understanding and ability, help themselves. This, my friends, is fundamental theology.

On looking back through the history of English-speaking people, it will be found in every instance that the most sacred principles of free government have been acquired, protected, and perpetuated through the embodied, armed strength of the peoples concerned. From Magna Carta to the present day there is little in our institutions worth having or worth perpetuating that has not been achieved for us by armed men. Trade, wealth, literature, and refinement cannot defend a state - pacific habits do not insure peace nor immunity from national insult and national aggression.

Every nation that would preserve its tranquility, its riches, its independence, and its self-respect must keep alive its martial ardor and be at all times prepared to defend itself.

The United States is a preeminently Christian and conservative nation. It is far less militaristic than most nations. It is not especially open to the charge of imperialism. Yet one would fancy that Americans were the most brutally bloodthirsty people in the world to judge by the frantic efforts that are being made to disarm them both physically and morally. The public opinion of the United States is being submerged by a deluge of organizations whose activities to prevent war would be understandable were they dis-

Officers of the 84th Brigade, Rainbow Division, near Fresnes, France, August, 1918. Left to Right: Lieutenant Reginald Weller, Captain Walter Wolf, Brigadier General Douglas MacArthur, Lieutenant William Wright, Lieutenant Wilfred Bazinet.

tributed in some degree among the armed nations of Europe and Asia. The effect of all this unabashed and unsound propaganda is not so much to convert America to a holy horror of war as it is to confuse the public mind and lead to muddled thinking in international affairs.

A few intelligent groups who are vainly trying to present the true facts to the world are overwhelmed by the sentimentalist, the emotionalist, the alarmist, who merely befog the real issue which is not the biological necessity of war but the biological character of war.

The springs of human conflict cannot be eradicated through institutions but only through the reform of the individual human being. And that is a task which has baffled the highest theologians for 2,000 years and more.

I often wonder how the future historian in the calmness of his study will analyze the civilization of the century recently closed. It was ushered in by the end of the Napoleonic Wars which devastated half of Europe. Then followed the Mexican War, and the American Civil War, the Crimean War, the Austro-Prussian War, the Franco-Prussian War, the Boer War, the opium wars of England and China, the Spanish-American War, the Russo-Japanese War, and finally, the World War - which for ferocity and magnitude of losses, is unequaled in the history of humanity.

If he compares this record of human slaughter with the 13th century when civilization was just emerging from the Dark Ages, when literature had its Dante; art its Michelangelo and Gothic architecture; education, the establishment of the famous colleges and technical schools of Europe; medicine, the organization of hospital systems; politics and the foundation of Anglo-Saxon liberty, the Magna Carta - the verdict cannot be that wars have been on the wane.

In the last 3,400 years only 268 - less than 1 in 13 - have been free from wars. No wonder that Plato, the wisest of all men, once exclaimed, "Only the dead have seen the end of war." Every reasonable man knows that war is cruel and destructive. Yet, our civilization is such that a very little of the fever of war is sufficient to melt its veneer of kindliness. We all dream of the day when human conduct will be governed by the Decalogue and the Sermon on the Mount. But as yet it is only a dream. No one desires peace as much as the soldier, for he must pay the greatest penalty in war. Our Army is maintained solely for the preservation of peace - or, for the restoration of peace after it has been lost by statesmen or by others.

Dionysius, the ancient thinker, 20 centuries ago uttered these words: "It is a law of nature, common to all mankind, which time shall neither annul nor destroy, that those that have greater strength and power shall bear rule over those who have less." Unpleasant as they may be to hear, disagreeable as they may be to contemplate, the history of the world bears ample testimony to their truth and wisdom. When looking over the past, or when looking over the world in its present form there is but one trend of events to be discerned - a constant change of tribes, clans, nations; the stronger ones replacing the others, the more vigorous ones pushing aside, absorbing, covering with oblivion the weak and the worn out.

From the dawn of history to the present day it has always been the militant aggressor taking the place of the unprepared. Where are the empires of old? Where is Egypt, once a state on a high plane of civilization, where a form of socialism prevailed and where the distribution of wealth was regulated? Her high organization did not protect her. Where are the empires of the East and the empires of the West which once were the shrines of wealth, wisdom, aud culture? Where are Babylon, Persia, Carthage, Rome, Byzantium? They all fell, never to rise again, annihilated at the hands of a more warlike and aggressive people; their cultures memories, their cities ruins.

Where are Peru and Old Mexico? A handful of bold and crafty invaders destroyed them, and with them their institutions, their independence, their nationality, and their civilization.

And, saddest of all, the downfall of Christian Byzantium. When Constantinople fell, that center of learning, pleasure, and wealth - and all the weakness and corruption that goes with it - a pall fell over Asia and southeastern Europe which has never been lifted. Wars have been fought these nearly 5 centuries that have had for at least one of their goals the bringing back under the Cross of that part of the world lost to a wild horde of a few thousand adventurers on horseback whom hunger and the unkind climate of their steppes forced to seek more fertile regions.

The thousand years of existence of the Byzantine Empire, its size, its religion, the wealth of its capital city were but added incentives and inducements to an impecunious conqueror. For wealth is no protection against aggression. It is no more an augury of military and defensive strength in a nation than it is an indication of health in an individual. Success in war depends upon men, not money. No nation has ever been subdued for lack of it. Indeed, nothing is more insolent or provocative or more apt to lead to a breach of the peace than undefended riches among armed men.

And each nation swept away was submerged by force of arms. Once each was strong and militant. Each rose by military prowess. Each fell through degeneracy of military capacity because of unpreparedness. The battlefield was the bed upon which they were born into this world, and the battlefield became the couch on which their worn out bodies finally expired. Let us be prepared, lest we, too, perish.

They will tell of the peace eternal,
And we would wish them well.
They will scorn the path of war's red wrath
And brand it the road to hell.
They will set aside their warrior pride
And their love for the soldier sons.
But at the last they will turn again
To horse and foot and guns.

They will tell of the peace eternal,
The Assyrian dreamers did.
But the Tigris and Euphrates
Ran through ruined lands,
And amid the hopeless chaos
Loud they wept and called their chosen ones
To save their lives at the bitter last,
With horse and foot and guns.

They will tell of the peace eternal,
And may that peace succeed.
But what of a foe that lurks to spring?
And what of a nation's need?
The letters blaze on history's page,
And ever the writing runs,
God, and honor, and native land,
And horse and foot and guns.

Excerpts from a Report on National Defense in the Philippines to the President of the Philippines
April 27, 1936

When he had completed his tour as Army Chief of Staff, MacArthur was still only fifty-five years old. There was literally no place to go except to a position of lesser responsibility. He was host happy, therefore, to accept the offer of President-elect Manuel Quezon to assist the new Commonwealth of the Philippines to develop a defense establishment. Officially appointed as the Military Advisor to the President of the Commonwealth, he drew up a ten-year development plan for the Philippine defense forces. This plan was intended to provide the Philippines with a viable defense capability by 1046, when the islands were to receive their complete independence from the United States. Although aware of the difficulties in building an effective fighting force in a nonindustrial Asiatic country with no modern military tradition, he was still confident that the job could be done. His program was not destined to run its entire course, but it remains a highly interesting blueprint for the defense of a newly emerging nation.

Major Vorin E. Whan, Jr., USA, Editor
A Soldier Speaks: Public Papers and Speeches of General of the Army Douglas MacArthur
© 1965, Frederick A. Praeger, Publishers, New York, NY

The development of a defensively strong Philippine nation is necessary to international peace. It is essential to the continued growth and spread of democratic practices in the Orient. It is vital to the prosperity and to the collective and individual liberty of the millions of Filipinos who, as a new nation, are, under existing conventions, to acquire within ten years a sovereign status. In short, the character and adequacy of Philippine defenses will be the common source of important forces and influences that are certain, during years to come, to act and react with far-reaching results throughout the world. To establish the accuracy of these statements it is necessary only to glance for a moment at the local situation as an articulated part rather than as a detached phenomenon of civilization's development.

The Philippine Islands, stretching their length through sixteen degrees of latitude off the southeastern coast of the Asiatic Continent, lie athwart all principal trade routes extending to the westward from the countries bordering on the Pacific Ocean. They comprise an important, in some respects the most important, section of the great and vaguely defined region known as the Far East. In that area develop-

ments of the next century and more are destined to engage the concerned attention of thoughtful statesmen and businessmen throughout the world. Such extensive changes will occur there in economic orders, industrial methods, and social cultures that they will inevitably attain a universal influence upon the prosperity and welfare of all civilized peoples.

Possibly these changes will come about so quietly and naturally that, in spire of their profound importance, little popular attention will be focused upon them. Spectacular achievements of individuals, crimes and catastrophes, and wars, either actual or threatened, will undoubtedly continue their practical monopoly of the world's headlines, and some of these events may, of course, attain the proportions of revolutionary advances or of cataclysmic disasters. But even so, in Europe and the Americas, they will still be nothing more than colorful incidents in the history of a civilization that has definitely entered the stages of refinement and adjustment. They may evidence faulty operation in a machine that, admittedly is still imperfect in design, but they will not indicate that an entirely new type of mechanism is being substituted. But in Eastern Asia such a substitution is certain to occur, featured by great migrations, lasting changes in national customs, vast turnovers in regional industries, and extraordinary advances in the standards of living of hundreds of millions of people. To the world these will be portentous events.

The Chinese is the oldest of present-day civilizations. Though it attained its golden age many hundred years after the Egyptians had established a powerful and highly organized state in the fertile valley of the Nile, little now remains of that earlier development except desolate monuments in a bleak and forbidding desert, and buried tombs and cities, of slight modern interest except for the archaeologist.

Beginning with China's rise to ancient pre-eminence, the full force of progressing civilization has been exerted principally in a westerly direction. Chronologically, the early Chinese development was followed by the Persian rise to power in Asia Minor where, about 500 years before the Christian Era, a collection of tribes and small nations were finally united into an extensive Empire, for a while to endure as the chief country of the world. But Persian dominance ceased abruptly when it challenged, on the borders of the Aegean Sea, a newer and hardier civilization in the Grecian city-states, against which the Asiatic armies dashed to the own destruction. Protected by the fighting qualities of the sturdy Greek, the center of the world's culture remained in Athens until Greece, in turn, encountered and fell before the rising power of Rome, still further to the west. But just as Persian culture noticeably influenced the development of its conqueror, so was much of the Grecian civilization preserved in the customs and practices of the Roman people.

For centuries the new Empire dominated the history and progress of Europe. Roman law and roman customs followed the Roman legions into every region and province of the Mediterranean basin, surged northward to the shores of the North Sea and the Channel, and across them through Britain and Ireland. The definite imprint of these ancient Mediterranean civilizations has never been obliterated, even though innumerable wars, adjustments, inventions, cultural advances, and political changes have intervened to evolve the Europe that we know today.

In the fifteenth century Columbus pushed westward across the Atlantic in the first of the great explorations that marked the beginning of America's known history. Within a space of three hundred years there was firmly established in the northern half of the Western Hemisphere a collection of colonies that proved themselves equal of challenging, on their own ground, the power of the mightiest European nation then existing. Favored by geography, climate, and an untold wealth of natural resources, the United States and, to a somewhat lesser extent, the other countries of the Americas have advanced unbelievably in power, wealth, and influence, and have established within their boundaries a civilization in the familiar European pattern.

The next step to be taken in Europeanizing the world's economic and industrial practices - a step already definitely begun - is still inexorably toward the west.

Already European civilization embraces an area of magnificent extent and governs the lives of countless millions of people. In all that great area and among all those populations sudden and universal changes in economies, industries, and social customs are not soon to be expected. Further advances, adjustments and improvements will continue to occur, just as they continued to occur in Europe throughout the period of American development. But inevitably the avaricious forces of progressing civilization seek opportunity for revolutionary rather than merely evolutionary effect - and such opportunity now exists in Eastern Asia. Through great stretches of that area transportation, communication, sanitation, and all the other indices by which we measure cultural and living standards are scarcely less advanced than they were even before Genghis Khan swept down from the Gobi to prove that the ancient Chinese power had faded, and that the Chinese people were no longer capable of self-protection.

In limitless extent of undeveloped resources Africa, of course, should present an attractive field to the ever advancing forces of civilization. But forbidding climate, impenetrable jungles, and diseases that attack with peculiar ferocity every invasion, still protect to some extent the native element in its exclusive possession of that continent, except in its more accessible and temperate sections. In Eastern Asia conditions are profoundly different. There exists a culture that centuries ago built great cities and the most elaborate defensive work, of that day, known to man. But nurtured in its ancient isolation, that culture fell victim to inbreeding and resulting paralysis that have endured for two thousand years. This is the significant difference between this type of Oriental and the European developments. The latter still demonstrated the virility of continuous improvement, while the former is cursed with the weakness and ineptitude of suspended growth.

The adaptability of Oriental people, climate, and resources to the practices of Western culture, particularly Western industrial methods, has already been proven by at least one Asiatic nation. In less than one hundred years it has progressed with remarkable speed from a state of complete isolation and stagnation to one of feverish industrialization and militant activity, resulting in a dominant position in the Far East. This renaissance is beginning to spread over all Eastern Asia. The processes by which all such great changes have historically been accomplished are now in motion. Weak and backward regions, especially those accessible to invading forces, are both politically and economically, successively falling under foreign domination. Within these areas the lives and occupations of the inhabitants are undergoing profound changes.

Not only is every person and every mile of territory along the whole western border of the Pacific certain to be affected, the influence of this development will reach back into the industrial centers and capitals of the Occident. The industrial machine of Europe and America has been for many years geared up to the requirements of development and exploitation in the Western Hemisphere, so that now that domestic demand is sinking closer to the level of mere maintenance, production far exceeds consumption. Every existing market has been feverishly competed for and exploited, but those so far developed are too small to absorb the overages that world industry constantly produces.

Extensive markets must be found, or production must be curtailed and standards of living must recede - consequences that would result in great upheavals and would be fatal to governments and industry alike.

So the industrial and economic revolution in East Asia, with its growing demand for credits and manufactured goods has begun just in time, if intelligently handled, to cushion the shock of compulsory readjustment in Europe and America, if not to postpone indefinitely the necessity for such readjustment. For many years the new market will sustain a capacity to absorb vast quantities of manufactured products, paying for these in equivalent quantities of the raw materials that Occidental countries grow increasingly to need.

The particular Western nations that will be most favored in this stupendous opportunity are those that take the most enlightened, active, and prompt interest in Far Eastern problems; those that establish their contacts with the East on the basis of mutual desire to cooperate and assist rather than merely to exploit; and those that have, by their statesmanlike and sympathetic treatment of native peoples, won and held the respect, confidence, and friendship of the Orient.

Of all Western nations none is more fortunate in the location and character of its contact with the Far East than is the United States in its position in the Philippine Islands.

The Philippines comprise island areas of more than 114,000 square miles, occupied by a population probably 20 per cent greater than the 14,000,000 normally attributed to them. They support a varied type of agriculture and industry, the principal products being sugar, hemp, copra, and minerals. They came under the domination of Spain in the early part of the sixteenth century and remained a possession of that country until they were ceded to the United States under the terms of the Treaty of Paris in 1898.

From the moment that the United States acquired legal title to the Philippines, its policy with respect to them has been dictated by a purpose of preparing them for, and finally to confer upon them, complete independence. Evidence of the existence of this policy is found in the public utterances of Presidents from McKinley to the present, and was definitely expressed in the form of legislative intention in the Jones Act of 1916.

Administration of foreign possessions with such an objective does not conform to international custom. Historically, European nations have looked upon the possession of outlying territories largely as an opportunity for their own economic betterment. Since maximum commercial exploitation of colonies is usually dependent upon rigid political control, every concession to local autonomy has always been granted slowly and reluctantly. American expressions of an opposite purpose have frequently been viewed, therefore, as political duplicity, designed only to deceive the inhabitants of the Philippines, and minimize the possibility of rebellion. Nevertheless, the policy was pursued steadily to its logical conclusion. Parenthetically, it may be here remarked that by voluntarily relinquishing political domination over the Islands the United States may have, wittingly or unwittingly, actually strengthened between the two nations all those ties and bonds that are forged from mutual respect, friendship, and consideration, and which in the long run are the only ones that can have a lasting effect in furthering America's interest in this corner of the globe.

The American effort in the Philippines was naturally influenced by the political concepts underlying the progress of civilization in the United States. Three controlling precepts in the American doctrine have been personal liberty, religious freedom, and the maintenance of democratic institutions that insure to every citizen a voice in his own government. These principles are often epitomized in the expression "Government only by the consent of the governed." to inculcate in Filipinos an appreciation of and respect for these concepts, the United States established a system of public education in the Islands, encouraged the development of agriculture and industry, and accorded a constantly increasing degree of autonomous government. As a result of thirty-five years' progress under these liberal policies, the Philippines gradually became an outpost of democratic civilization in the Far East. Their standards of living were raised to higher levels than those enjoyed by any other Malayan people. The degree of individual liberty and religious freedom enjoyed by Filipinos came to equal those of any other country of the world. Illiteracy was gradually diminished. Finally, there was established within the Islands a government that, except for the control represented in the power of an American Governor-General, was almost exclusively Filipino. All those things occurred prior to the enactment of the Tydings-McDuffie Act in 1934.

During this development period the United States retained full responsibility for the defense of the Islands. For various reasons it had not been considered desirable to compel or to authorize the Filipinos themselves to maintain strong military forces. Aside from police units, such native regiments as were organized were officered principally by Americans and were incorporated bodily as part of the United States Army. The number of troops so maintained usually represented practical equality with the number of American troops stationed in the Islands.

As a general result of their progress under American tutelage, the Islands, by 1935, could be considered as well prepared politically to assume responsibility for their own government. Economically they had prospered to an unusual degree, even though in this respect they had a glaring weakness in their extreme dependence upon free access to the American markets. But in the fundamental obligation of sovereign government, namely, that of providing for the common defense, the Philippines were woefully unprepared for independence.

A common recognition of this vital fact was one compelling reason for establishing temporarily, the in Tydings-McDuffie Act, a Commonwealth or transitional form of government which, in its ten years' duration, would afford Filipinos an opportunity to correct this situation. It was realized that development of a reasonably adequate defense system in the Islands was important to the United States as well as to the Filipinos themselves. Very naturally the United States cannot ignore or forget its thirty-five years of liberal instruction, patient training, and material as well as sentimental investment in the Philippines. Not only would the growth of democracy and democratic institutions in the Western Pacific be completely destroyed should the Philippines ever fall under the domination of a despotic foreign power, but American pride and prestige would receive a severe, if not unendurable blow. Local unrest and strained international relationships would almost certainly create an embarrassing situation for the United States and might conceivably draw us into a major war.

To be noted, too, is the importance the Philippines are assuming in the Western Pacific due to commercial airways expansion. They are at the western end of the succession of islands that mark a natural air route connecting North America and Eastern Asia. Lying within one day's airplane flight of the Philippines are areas in which lives one-quarter of the earth's population. Much of the future air business supported by all these people will flow to the eastward, with consequent commercial benefit to the United States, provided only that it can be assured of ample facilities, services, and cooperation along the route. Every station on the trans-Pacific air system now being established (1936) belongs to the United States and it requires no gift of prophecy to assert that our country will make every reasonable effort to encourage maximum use of the route described. As this trade develops and expands, Luzon airfields will be the focus where eastbound traffic will be concentrated and westbound traffic will be distributed to destination. Realization of this project will require a stable government here, as well as ample and efficient air facilities. It will require also on the part of the local government the liberal and sympathetic attitude of democracy rather than the selfish and arbitrary attitude of autocracy.

To epitomize the foregoing in a single paragraph, it is obvious that the best interests of both the United States and the Philippines will be served by taking the necessary steps to guarantee the safety of these Islands. Thus will be assured the uninterrupted development of the Filipino-American culture and economy, founded here through the cooperative effort of the two peoples. With adequate protection this country will flourish as a brilliant product of democracy, contribute to stability and peace in the Far East, and advance the living standards of its people to the full extent attainable under efficient use of its own resources. Without protection it will inevitably disintegrate and be desolated by destructive force.

When it became evident in 1934 that the installation of a

Commonwealth Government would take place during 1935, preliminary steps were taken by Filipino leaders to provide for establishing an applicable National Defense System....

Thereafter, upon mutual agreement between President Roosevelt and President-elect Quezon, I was detailed to the post of Military Advisor to the Commonwealth, the appointment to become effective upon the inauguration of the new government and upon my relief as Chief of Staff of the American Army. I immediately selected several officers of the American Army to serve as my assistants and with them began the development of a defense plan applicable to Philippine requirements....

The National Assembly promptly incorporated into legislation the essential provisions of the plan as submitted to the President and by him to the Legislative body. The law was designated the National Defense Act, and was approved by the President on December 21, 1935.

The Act places upon the military establishment the responsibility, under the President as Commander-in-Chief, not only of organizing, training, and maintaining an Army to insure protection against foreign aggression, but also of performing all those functions of internal police that were formerly carried out by the Philippine Constabulary.

The law outlines a National Defense policy, a territorial and administrative organization, the methods to be followed in giving essential military training to citizens and for selecting them for service, and, within the limits so prescribed, charges the President with the responsibility for such details of training, organization, and maintenance as are necessary to attain the objective of national security.

In direct control of the whole military establishment, under the immediate supervision of the President, is the Chief of Staff. He is assisted by a General Staff and by the Chiefs of the several Services and Bureaus. Among these assistants is the Provost Marshal General, who is in direct charge of all national police work heretofore performed by the Constabulary, and of the processes of registering and inducting individuals into the military service in accordance with law.

For administrative and training purposes the Islands are divided into military districts, which are subdivided into provinces.

The Army itself is to consist of a Regular Force and a Reserve Force, which will be predominantly land units, but which will be supported, so far as practicable, by an Air Force and a Marine Division, known as the Off-Shore Patrol. Essential Harbor defense units, when finally evacuated by the American Army, will be maintained.

The Philippine Defense System guarantees, if efficiently administered, a maximum of protection at a minimum of expense. It reposes responsibility for ultimate defense, not in a costly professional force that could conceivably be made the instrument of autocracy, but in the people themselves, the final repository of power in a democracy. Fundamentally the plan does nothing more than to prescribe the methods and provide the means whereby the Filipino citizenry, normally engaged in pursuits of peace, can prepare itself to exert its full defensive power whenever necessary.

The plan completely negatives any possibility of employing the Army in aggressive action and makes no attempt to attain a more militaristic objective than the development of each island in the Archipelago as a citadel of defensive strength. While, in modern times, no government will admit an intent to use military force offensively, the Philippine Government is one of the few whose word in this respect is not susceptible to a suspicion of doubt. No method exists, and none is projected, for utilizing the new Army beyond the limits of its own territory. In a nation that is the sole occupant of an isolated island group, with no mercantile marine to convert into troop carriers, and with no fleet to protect a troop ship against even the weakest of naval attacks, the impossibility of employing an army in an overseas campaign must be obvious, even to the professional alarmist who can discover dastardly intent in innocence itself.

The Army, to be composed principally of a Reserve Force of citizen soldiers, contains also a small Regular Element made up of individuals who follow the profession of arms as a career, and who are constantly in the service of the Government. The Reserve Force is to consist of those able-bodied male citizens between the ages of 21 and 50 who have been duly trained for military service, and thereafter assigned to the Reserve Force.

To attain a high level of efficiency at little cost in the Reserve Force, the plan requires the individual to undergo military training as a duty to the State. Under this type of system, generally known as Universal Military Service, training is normally accomplished by the annual conscription of young men of a given age, and their intensive training under professional soldiers. The average length of the training period must be sufficient to attain required training standards, but in the interests of governmental economy must be no greater than this. Moreover, the shorter the period the less the sacrifice required from the individual, particularly in the demands made upon his time during productive years. To satisfy these somewhat conflicting considerations, the Philippine system resorts to various expedients. It provides for elementary military training as a by-product of public school education and affords military instruction on Sundays and holidays to young men not attending school. Later, during the years that the individual remains subject to military service after completion of his principal tour of instruction, the plan provides for short refresher courses, mainly on week-ends. By liberal use of these and similar methods the length of the principal training period is limited, for the average trainee, to five and one-half months, whereas none of the larger European countries has felt justified in reducing this period below twelve months, while some have fixed it at twenty-four.

The Regular Force, because of its higher unit cost, is to be maintained at the lowest level consistent with performance of its missions. It will have four principal duties, of which the first is to operate the training system for civilians; the second is to provide in peace and in war the technical and administrative overhead required by the entire military establishment; the third is to insure continuous availability of a reasonably strong and highly trained military force for whatever use the government may choose to make of it; and the fourth is to perform the policy work throughout the Islands that has heretofore been carried out by the Philippine Constabulary. Ultimate strength of the professional element will be 930 officers and approximately 10,000 enlisted men.

An army developed under the principle of universal service is necessarily a progressive growth that can attain its maximum results only after there has elapsed a period of years equal to the length of time the trained citizen remains attached to the Reserve Force. Under the Philippine law, this total length of obligation is to be 30 years, of which the first ten comprise the individual's assignment to the First Reserve, and the two succeeding decades his service in the Second and Third Reserves, respectively.

The first objective of the Philippine Plan is the training, organizing, and equipping of the First Reserve. Forty thousand will be trained each year, to be organized into Reserve divisions, supported by auxiliary arms and services. Each Division will be located in and responsible for the defense of the particular geographical area in which its individual members ordinarily reside. During the succeeding ten-year period the Second Reserve will be similarly organized, equipped, supported, and finally, the Third Reserve will accumulate for employment as replacement, maintenance, and auxiliary troops.

The controlling principle in the tactical organization for land forces is the development of military units for the performance of specific missions, the tactical formations prescribed for the new Army differ in essential details from those found in any other, and in particular cases even show variations among themselves, so as to conform to the particular defense problems in the different regions of the Philippines.

Tactical organization must, of course, be such as to produce the essential qualities of mobility and fire power. Nothing is more important to the effectiveness of an army than an ability to more rapidly. A law of physics that applies equally to warfare is that while striking force increases directly with the mass applied, it increases according to the square of the speed of the application. Through proper organization in all echelons, through the development and perfection of reliable combat units capable of speedy maneuver, and through the improvement of transportation, maintenance, communication, and supply arrangements, the objective of maximum speed must be pursued. These truisms apply to all armies but, in application, they differ widely. Mobility in a jungle does not imply an equal mobility in a developed region, and the means by which it is attained differ as completely as do the characteristics of terrain in which armies operate.

From the moment that the forces of any potential enemy should appear upon the horizon, the task of the Philippine Army becomes that of foiling the purpose of the attacker and inflicting upon him the utmost in casualties during every hour of the day and night. To hold the enemy under destructive fires, to concentrate upon him the maximum volume of fire at every point where he is operating at a disadvantage, particularly at the moment he attempts to effect a lodgement on shore, is the mission of every unit of the defending force. A war of relentless attrition, of resistance from the water's edge to the furthermost retreat left available to the defending army, is the doctrine and purpose of any military unit that finds itself in the inescapable situation that faces the Philippine military establishment. Consequently, the mobility sought is that applying particularly to small units which, while giving ground stubbornly and skillfully where forced to do so, can be quick local concentration strike back in speedy counter-strokes and with overwhelming fire at every opportunity presented. Tactical mobility and fire power secured through individual and collective training of soldiers, intimate knowledge of the country in which the operation takes place, and proper armament represent the basic needs of the new Army. Obviously, units should be relatively small, free of all impedimenta that cannot be easily transported over difficult country, and trained to a minimum of dependence upon elaborate supply establishments and a maximum utilization of local resources for transportation and subsistence. Conservation of ammunition, simplicity in supply, messing and camping arrangements, and development of the utmost endurance and hardihood among the soldiery of the command are all important tenets in the doctrine of the land elements of the new Army.

As emphasized in the President's message to the National Assembly, the acquisition by the Philippine Government of a battle fleet lies completely outside the realm of practicability. The item of cost alone precludes serious contemplation of such a project. To a lesser extent the same considerations apply to the development of an air fleet.

However, the defense plan recognizes the vital need for some marine and air equipment, the war purpose of which will be to deny the use of Philippine territorial waters to a hostile fleet and to preserve communications between the islands of the Archipelago. A secondary function of these elements will be to provide a valuable adjunct in law enforcement.

These limited missions have a bearing upon the particular types of equipment with which the Army should be supplies. Particularly it will be the task of these Units to prevent huge expeditionary forces of any enemy from approaching these coasts with impunity, and constantly to threaten the safety of any hostile surface craft attempting to operate in Philippine waters.

Because of lack of funds, multiplicity of types is to be avoided, and, whenever practicable, simple, relatively inexpensive items are to be preferred over the more elaborate and expensive varieties. For example, a fast, small torpedo boat is a more appropriate vessel for the Off-Shore Patrol than is a submarine, in spite of the grater effectiveness of the latter weapon under many condition. A relatively small fleet of such vessels, manned by crews thoroughly familiar with every detail of the coastline and surrounding waters, and carrying, in the torpedo, a definite threat against large ships, will have distinct effect in compelling any hostile force to approach cautiously and by small detachments.

In the fighting element of the Air Corps, fast bombers with a reasonable radius of action will be the principal item of equipment. Other tactical types will be limited to the numbers needed for tactical support of the bombers maintained, while training planes will be procured in the amounts necessary. Three of these have been procured and are being used at Camp Murphy to give preliminary pilot instruction to individuals selected for complete training courses in the American Army at Randolph Field, Texas. A command plane has been purchased and will son arrive in Manila. Under the plan every centavo that can be spared from other equally essential purposes will eventually be invested in the development and maintenance of a bombing fleet of reasonable size so as to assure the ability of marine and air units, working in complete cooperation, to deny use of territorial waters to hostile surface craft.

With respect to the internal police functions heretofore carried out by the Philippine Constabulary, the National Defense Act makes no fundamental change other than the incorporation of Constabulary personnel in the Army and the consequent transfer of responsibility for law enforcement from the Chief of Constabulary to the Chief of Staff.

Practically, the principal result of this change is a considerable financial saving to the Philippine Government through the combination of police and defense duties. The distribution of Regular Army garrisons through the Islands automatically provides reserves, that, in case of need, will be promptly available for emergency use as police forces. Consequently, the number of men habitually assigned to this single duty may, with entire safety, be greatly reduced. From the personnel so saved are to be organized the training cadres and skeleton units necessarily maintained throughout the Islands as the framework for organizing, training, and maintaining the citizen Army.

One phase of law enforcement that, in the past, has occasioned considerable embarrassment to local authorities involves the protection of outlying islands and isolated sections of the coastline against spoilation by armed robbers and brigands using small boats to make sudden forays against virtually helpless inhabitants. The self-respect of the Commonwealth and the rights and security of its citizens demand that positive and resolute means be promptly instituted to insure cessation of this brigandage. Heretofore, adequate garrisons and mobile reserves for performance of this necessary mission could scarcely be provided from available personnel, but with consolidation of police and defense functions and the development of trained civilian units, the assignment of sufficient regular personnel for the protection of outlying regions can be undertaken without incurring unjustified risk at other points.

Because of the nature of Philippine geography, successful performance of this particular duty requires the use of suitable types of small boats. Pending the development of the Off-Shore Patrol, this kind of equipment is not available to the Army. As a temporary expedient the President has directed the Secretary of Agriculture and Commerce to cooperate with Army authorities by making Coast Guard cutters available for Army use as required. With this assistance the Army is proceeding promptly to the elimination of this particular menace to the peace and prosperity of Filipino citizens.

The defense plan provides for courses in military training which will be preliminary to the induction of trainees into the Army for their principal period of instruction. These courses are provided in the public school system and, for those not attending school, through the Junior Reserve.

Some of the purposes of this training have already been mentioned, the principal one being to shorten the period that trainees will require with the Colors in order to attain a minimum acceptable proficiency as soldiers. Trainee instruction removes the individual entirely, for the period of its duration, from civil pursuits and to this extent interrupts the normal current of his existence. Moreover, the longer the period of trainee instruction the greater the expense to the government for such items as subsistence, uniforms, and general maintenance. Preliminary courses, therefore, are to insure that, with minimum demands upon the individual and with little cost to the government, the trainee may enter upon his principal period of instruction reasonably proficient in elementary military practices, thus permitting rapid progress in higher training.

Another reason for instituting preliminary military training is its educational value, particularly as to the privileges and obligations of citizenship and the functions of defense establishments in a democratic and peacefully intentioned State. Because of the long history of the Philippines as a dependency, its citizenry has not been faced with the problem of providing continuously and effectively for the nation's defense, and consequently has not been impressed with the penalties that inevitably follow a lack of readiness to protect national territory and rights. The military courses in the schools are intended to promote clear thinking on these subjects and to develop that sense of responsibility and determination that are necessary if the integrity of the Philippines is to be permanently preserved.

A third reason for instituting military instruction in the public school system is it value in promoting an appreciation of health, sanitation, cooperative methods and organizational discipline, as well as to improve the physical vigor and well-being of individuals. The value of military instruction for these purposes is so obvious as to require no argument. As a by-product of this type of training, it is intended to extend eventually to all individuals undergoing it, the privilege of taking all approved types of vaccinations and inoculations with a view of promoting the general health of the community and of minimizing danger of epidemics.

A final reason for instituting courses of preliminary training in schools, and in the Junior Reserve as explained below, is to insure partial training of those who will be denied opportunity for undergoing a normal period of trainee instruction during their twenty-first year. For various reasons, one of which is lack of sufficient funds, it will never be possible to induct into the service for trainee instruction all able-bodied male citizens annually attaining the age of twenty-one. By establishing preliminary training on the broadest possible base, all those omitted from annual trainee classes will nevertheless have acquired some knowledge of military practices and methods, and will be partially prepared for service in the event of a major emergency.

Training in the Junior Reserve is intended to reach those young men whose attendance at school is terminated at a relatively early age. Between the years of 18 and 21, such young men are required, at certain seasons of the year, to report for weekend training at military stations established in the immediate vicinity of their homes. Fundamentally, the purposes of this training are identical with those listed for that conducted in the public school system.

None of this preliminary instruction will interfere in any way with the productive activity of the individual receiving it, or with his ability to carry on all responsibilities devolving upon him in civil life.

The school courses are progressive in character. Training of the younger students will involve only such subjects as citizenship, sanitation, hygiene, and physical culture. As the individual enters successively higher grades on the school system, his military instruction becomes more and more technical or professional in nature, and by the time he has graduated from high school, it is expected that he will have attained a considerable proficiency in all its phases of training applying to the individual soldier and to small units.

The inescapable price of liberty is an ability to preserve it from destruction. Supineless sovereignty cannot long exist; defenseless independence is an anomalous combination of terms. In devoting the resources of government to the execution of the functions for which established, the first concern must be to insure the protection of the governed - to provide the means for enforcing their right to live under codes, laws, and institutions of their own making. The amount of resources, both tangible and intangible, so devoted and so used is the premium a nation pays to insure its existence.

The need for minimizing this expense, always important, was a paramount consideration in the development of the Philippine defense plan. The Commonwealth Government has at its immediate disposal no such tremendous financial reserves and pools of credit as are available to some of the older and larger nations. Continuing governmental deficits would almost certainly result in the defeat of the very purpose for which a military establishment is to be developed, which is the preservation of the status that the Philippines are to acquire ten years hence.

To produce economy the first essential is that statesmanship and accepted lessons of world experience be applied to basic design; that is, that the form and size of the defense organism be dictated by probable needs, which may be determined only when there is brought into proper perspective every significant factor of geography, international politics, and commercial relationships as well as national psychology and objectives. General methods of organization, training, and administration must be so devised that, while producing the required professional fitness throughout the Army, they will entail the least possible expense to the government.

In devising a plan appropriate to the Philippines, the need for economy not only dictated an application of the principle of universal military service, but it had also a definite influence in moulding details of plans involving organization, training, administration, and armament. As a result, judged either by absolute or relative standards, efficiency with maximum economy is the outstanding characteristic of the system prescribed in the National Defense Act.

In carrying out a national undertaking of this character, there is only one substitute for money, which is the patriotism and spirit of sacrifice of individual citizens. These elements, with proper direction and skillful employment, will combine into a tremendous surge of energy of far greater effectiveness than can be developed by money alone, no matter what the lavishness of expenditure. Success, under the Philippine system, is peculiarly dependent upon the determination of the Filipino people to organize and train themselves as a citizen soldiery, and upon their enthusiastic cooperation in making whatever individual effort may be necessary to accomplish this purpose. The whole plan is based upon the fundamental conviction that the Filipino people ardently desire to attain and sustain a status of self-respecting security. This accounts for its extraordinary economy....

AN ADDRESS TO THE FACULTY AND STUDENT BODY OF THE COMMAND AND GENERAL STAFF SCHOOL
AUGUST 3, 1936
BAGUIO, PHILLIPINE ISLANDS

The publication of the new defense plan for the Philippines aroused a storm of controversy. Elements of the American community were opposed to independence for the Filipinos and ridiculed the idea that they could defend their homeland. Japan's' propaganda, for reasons that later became obvious, attacked General MacArthur and President Quezon on the defense issue. His visit to the Command and General Staff School at Baguio gave the General an opportunity to defend his proposals.

Major Vorin E. Whan, Jr., USA, Editor
*A Soldier Speaks: Public Papers and Speeches of General
of the Army Douglas MacArthur*
© 1965, Frederick A. Praeger, Publishers, New York, NY

The basic military problem facing the Philippine Government is whether with its present resources of population and wealth it can develop a defensive force capable of withstanding a more powerfully armed opponent. Does the old boxing adage, so often quoted in athletic circles, "A good big man will always defeat a good little man," unfailingly apply in war? The answer is that the axiom would apply only if the two opponents should meet the issue of combat under practically identical conditions. If each could concentrate its entire army in the vital battle area, and if each were compelled to solve substantially similar problems of supply, transportation, reinforcement, and tactical operation, the larger army would always win. But this equality of conditions never exists in warfare, and war has therefore shown many startling reversals in which the apparently weaker opponent achieved victory. From the classic Biblical example of David and Goliath through the successful Revolutionary War which established American independence, the history of the world is replete with illustrative examples.

In the case of the Philippines, it would be an impossibility for any potential enemy to bring to the Philippine area anything like a preponderant portion of his army. He would indeed have difficulty in concentrating into the vital area as large a force as the Philippine Army which would oppose him. Any conceivable expeditionary force might actually find itself out-numbered.

This country has the enormous defensive advantage of being an island group. Hundreds of miles of water separate it from any other land. The protective value of isolation has time and time again been demonstrated in military history. No other operation in warfare is so difficult as that of transporting, supplying, and protecting an army committed to an overseas expedition. The English Channel has been the predominant factor in the freedom from invasion enjoyed by the British Islands throughout their modern history of many wars. Although Europe has, time and again, seethed with supposedly invincible armies, of which at least two have made elaborate and definite preparations for the invasion of the Island Kingdom, never since modern armies have come into being with their enormous size and huge amounts of impedimenta has Great Britain been compelled to drive off a land attack from its shores. The British Navy has, of course, been a powerful factor in sustaining this security. But in this dual combination of defenses, the ocean obstacle has been the first and more important, and the Navy has been the one to increase the effectiveness of the first.

The United States undoubtedly owes its existence as an independent nation to the friendly Atlantic. The War of the Revolution would have most certainly resulted in ignominious defeat for the Colonies had geography separated them from the mother country by a mere land frontier rather than by 3,000 miles of ocean. In the War of 1812 this factor again permitted the Colonies to withstand the forces of the mightiest empire then existing and preserved the American nation from re-submission to British control.

In the case of the Philippine Islands, we have then as its first favorable factor in solving its defensive problem a geographical separation from every possible land enemy. It is true that there is no thought of attempting to develop here a powerful battle fleet. But it is pertinent to point out that the major duty of a great fleet is to preserve overseas communication. Inshore defense is only a subsidiary function. This function for the Philippines will be performed by flotillas of fast torpedo boats, supported by an air force. Due to the exclusively defensive posture of the Philippine nation, great battle fleets are not necessary to insure its preservation. The islands themselves are to be developed as a citadel of defensive strength and the essential function of air and naval forces will be that of denying transports the opportunity of anchoring close to Philippine shores for the debarkation of troops and supplies.

The threat to large surface ships residing in small fast torpedo boats supported by air detachments was recently indicated in the Mediterranean. It is significant that following the lesson there demonstrated, Great Britain, Germany, and other powers are following the Italian example in adding this particular weapon as an important category in defensive equipment.

But geography did not cease its defensive favors to the Philippines when it made them an isolated group. Nature has studded these islands with mountainous formations, making practicable landing places for large forces extremely few in number and difficult in character. The vital area of Luzon, in which dwell approximately 7 million Filipinos, presents in all its long shore line only two coastal regions in which a hostile army of any size could land. Each of these is broken by strong defensive positions, which if properly manned and prepared would present to any attacking force a practically impossible problem of penetration.

But nature has still further endowed the Philippines with defensive possibilities: 60 per cent of the national terrain consists of great forest areas, impenetrable by powerful military units. The mountainous terrain, the primeval forests, and the lack of communications, combine to create a theater of operations in which a defensive force of only moderate efficiency and strength could test the capabilities

of the most powerful and splendidly equipped army that could be assembled here.

Other islands of the Archipelago possess similar defensive possibilities. In some instances no practicable landing places for large forces exist. In every case determined troops at the shore line could deny landing to an attacker of many times their own number.

It is a human trait to magnify the potentialities of an enemy and to underestimate one's own strength. Too often we are apt to take counsel of our own fears. In contemplating the defense of the Philippines we should visualize the enormous effort necessary to launch and prosecute a huge overseas campaign. The difficulties to be overcome by the aggressor in such a situation are not even dimly understood by the layman. Only those who have participated in or witnessed the extraordinary expenditure of energy and money required in such operations can appreciate the obstacles that invariably stand in the way of success. In the World War the United States had practically to change the entire course of its industrial activity in order to send to France the forces required there. Billions upon billions of dollars were poured into the venture and over 100,000,000 people devoted their full energy to its success. Yet, in spite of the fact that its expeditionary forces were dispatched to permanent ports and bases that were in the firm possession of American allies, and no tactical operations of any kind were required in order to establish it ashore, more than a year elapsed before the American Army could place a single complete division on the battlefront.

The amount of shipping that must be withdrawn from commercial activity and transformed into vessels suitable for troop transportation is so great as to present, in itself, a major problem, even to a power rich in maritime resources. To transport 300,000 men with essential equipment and supplies for only 30 days requires approximately 1,500,000 tons of shipping. The greatest total maritime tonnage of any nation operating in the Pacific Ocean is but 4,700,000 tons. These figures give only a faint indication of the serious logistical problems that must be solved whenever an overseas expedition is proposed.

Of all military operations, the one which the soldier dreads the most is a forced landing on a hostile shore. It is at that time he is at his weakest, the enemy at his strongest. His transport frequently arrives at the end of an unpleasant voyage. Crowded accommodations and generally unpleasant conditions have not tended to improve his morale. At the critical moment his ships are forced to come to a standstill in order to undertake the debarkation of the attackers in small boats. At this time motionless targets, they are subjected to an intensive attack from fast-moving torpedo boats and even faster-whirring bombers of the air. Each small boat, with only a fraction of men has to make its way in through a pitiless fire of artillery, machine guns and musketry - a fire of deadly accuracy because delivered from prepared and protected positions. Yet through this veritable holocaust his small unprotected boat with no means of effective response to the enemy fire must reach the shore, perhaps through a dangerous surf, to discharge its occupants in an attempt to build up a firing line to over-come an emplaced enemy. Subject to desperate counterattack on the beach, perhaps engulfed in poisonous waves of gas, deprived of the inspirational presence of great masses of his comrades, he has always the feeling that goes with a forlorn hope. Lucky indeed the command that can achieve success on such a day and in such a way.

The outstanding World War example of an overseas operation accompanied by landing against a defended shore was the Allied operation at Gallipoli. In the initial stages of that abortive campaign the Gallipoli Peninsula was very inadequately defended and the early naval bombardments encountered only antiquated forts. While it is true that the land attacks were poorly coordinaled and failed to achieve the element of surprise because of the warning given the defenders through naval bombardments, still errors of omission and commission of this type are invariably characteristic of attempted landings against defended beaches. The complete failure of the Allied attack is a matter of history. The only point in mentioning it here is to remark that it emphasized again for all students of warfare the tremendous difficuLties attendant upon overseas operations and to indicate the degree of reluctance with which any General Staff would commit a major portion of its army to a venture of this character.

In contemplating such an attack any government would have an additional cause for hesitation. This is the tendency of wars to spread and draw into the maelstrom of battle nations that originally had no apparent cause for participating in the quarrel. The World War illustrated this tendency with particular emphasis. Any government that should prepare and send overseas a force of sufficient strength to attack the Philippines would have to consider carefully the possibility of any other potential enemy taking advantage of the situation and entering the contest at a time when the aggressor was seriously committed and possibly even embarrassed in the Phillppines.

The layman might attempt to deprecate the force of the considerations I have just enumerated by quoting the experience of Italy in its conquest of Ethiopia. In doing so, he would be guilty of a fundamental error in reasoning, because the implied analogy is almost completely false. The conditions under which Italy invaded and conquered Ethiopia were fundamentally different from those that will exist here after the Defense Plan has reached its full development. Let me amplify:

Ethiopia had no army worthy of the name. Ethiopian troops were sketchily equipped with weapons largely medieval in their characteristics. Ethiopian forces were torn by internal strife; they dad no effective leadership; they were loosely organized, and were in fact totally lacking in every phase of modern organization, equipment, and training. Italy was not required to make a landing against a defended shore line. She had two principai land bases from which to begin the campaign, namely, Italian Somaliland and Eritrea. Even so, press reports indicated that the initial mobilization for the canspaign began months and months befor~ the first troops were actually shipped, and were so ~tensive as to test the capacity of Italian resources.

I have no hesitancy in stating, and I believe that my professional opinion in this matter would be substantiated by every General Staff in the world today, that had Ethiopia adopted an adequate system of military development ten years ago and thereafter continued faithfully to organize, train, and equip its military forces in that concept, the Italian armies would not be in Addis Ababa today. More than this, I do not believe that under such conditions the military conquest of Ethiopia would have been attempted.

In the face of this wealth of facts and lessons favoring the defensive potentialities of an island empire, the query naturally arises as to why there should be any serious question as to the ability of the Filipinos to defend themselves with reasonable effectiveness. The answer again is a very simple one. It is be-cause the United States has never stationed in this American possession a sufficient force to defend the Islands against land attack. Since the end of insurrection days the American Army, including its Filipino contingent, has averaged about 10,000 men. With defending forces represented by this pitifully small garrison and with the broad Pacific lying between them and their nearest supporting troops, it was appreciated by all that the Philippines could not be held against strong surprise land attack. This fact was thoroughly understood by the professional soldier and sailor who repeatedly protested and complained, "The Philippines cannot be successfully defended with its present garrisons." By the layman, however, the modifying phrase was ignored and it was translated into the slogan "The Philippines cannot be successfuuy defended," and this shibboleth finally attained the dignity of an expression of popular opinion. No conclusion could be more false. An adequate garrison can defend the Philippines for as long as available sup-plies and provisions will sustain the Army and its supporting population. Considering the productivity of these islands in the matter of food, this period of feasible defense will undoubtedly extend, once the necessary training has been accomplished and the necessary equipment accumulated, far beyond the capacity of any attacker to maintain a large expeditionary force in these territorial waters.

The defensive possibility in the Islands is not entirely an academic question. The Philippine insurrection of almost forty years ago gave us a valuable lesson along this line. In that campaign a poorly equipped and loosely organized force of irregulars, which probably never exceeded 20,000 in its total strength, compelled the American Government, with its bases thoroughly established here and with complete command of the ocean, to support large forces here engaged in bitter field campaign for a period of several years - forces which at one time numbered almost 100,000 men. Had the Filipino Army been properly organized and adequately equipped, the resources in men and money expended by the American Government would have been multiplied many-fold.

Another great advantage accrues to an army when it serves a government whose military policy is purely and passively defensive such as it is here. Under such conditions the Army as a whole and in each of its parts is not diverted by extraneous objectives and missions, but rather is permitted to concentrate its full attention on one specific problem in one specific area. Each unit of the defending army may then, in any future war, operate on a battlefield thoroughly known to its officers and men - on a battlefield in which every part has been thoroughly prepared with the single purpose of preventing penetration by the enemy. The relative advantage enjoyed by a force occupying ground deliberately selected and organized for defense was proven by World War experience to be repreeented in a numerical advantage of some four or five to one.

The respect accorded to any army organized for a definite and specific defensive task, as in the present instance, is well illustrated in the case of Switzerland. The military system applying in that country more closely parallels the Philippine plan than does any other now in existence. The Swiss Army has no objective except to defend the homeland, within its own antional boundaries. It has taken advanlage of every geographical feature to increase its tactical power and to make more difficult the problem of any potential invader. So clearly have the general staffs of Europe appreciated the strength of a nation organized and prepared to defend itself with the full power of its citizenship, that for decade after decade, Switzerland, although its population numbers little more than one-fourth that of the Philippines, has maintained its territory inviolate and has successfully avoided entry into any of the conflicts that have engulfed other nations of Europe.

If there are those who scoff at the thought that Filipinos can successfully defend themselves, when once their citizenry has been trained in the profession of arms and equipment in reasonable amounts has been accumulated, let us not forget that the idea of Philippine self-sufficiency in this respect is essentially a new idea. Scoffers will never be lacking when any new concept is advanced. Usually, however, they are found among those who know little or nothing of the facts, but who arrogate to themselves the dogmatic wisdom of popular slogan and glib generality. Those who lightly regard the difficulties of conquering the Philippines know nothing of war themselves and next to nothing about the actual potentialties of the Filipino people, Philippine assets, and Philippine terrain. They forget that this country is numerically stronger than such nations as Turkey, Switzerland, Yugoslavia, Sweden, Siam, Portugal, Persia, Norway, Hungary, Greece, Finland, Czechoslovakia, Denmark, Chile, Argentina. Austria, Bugaria, and many others now armed to the teeth. Canada has about two-thirds of the population strength of the Philippines. Mexico about the same population as the Philippines. Brazil is the only nation besides the United States in the American continents, including North, South, and Central America, that has a greater population. Indeed, only fourteen nations in the world, I have been informed. have a greater population than the Philippines. In the general staffs of the world, I assure you, you would find no dissenting voice to the assertion that, when the Philippine Defense Plan has reached fruition, it will represent a defensive strength that will give hesitation to the strongest and most ruthless nation in the world. Let me remind you that there were a multitude of skeptics who maintained that Fulton's steamboat would not float, that the Arnacal flight would not reach Madrid, that the Wright brothers would not get their airplane off the ground, that Ericsson's *Monitor* would be a dismal failure, and that Marconi was a visionary at best, and possibly a lunatic at the worst. Defeatists have always been present to greet every new thought, every new idea, and every new attempt at constructive progress. Defeatists laughed at America's attempt to free herself from British control, but today the United States is possibly the most powerful nation in the world.

Defeatists ask how, within the ten years' military budget of $80 million, can a sufficient force be equipped including an air component and an offshore patrol of torpedo boats. Planes cost $30,000 each, boats $35,000. The tea-year budget provides $10 million for the air components, $5 million for the Off-Shore Patrol. To complete the fiscal analysis in broad outline, $30 million go to the Regular force and $35 million to the Reserves. With this latter personnel serving as a civic duty, practically without professional remuneration, a large and adequate part of this latter sum is available for military supply and equipment. Parenthetically, the yearly defense budget amounts to about 22 per cent of the estimated annual governmental income, much less than in most countries.

Only recently I saw two moving pictures that reminded me of this type of defeatist opposition. One portrayed the story of Louis Pasteur and the world's continued and incessant skepticism which so jeopardized his efforts. The other was the film showing the knock-out of Joe Louis by the German Schmeling. Ninety-nine per cent of the sporting world vociferously proclaimed the impossibility of such an outcome. Why? They did not know the facts; they refused to listen to such an unbiased and clear-thinking expert as Damon Runyon when he intimated the possibility that the German would reach his goal. He based his conclusion solely upon fact not upon blind hysteria and imitative ballyhoo and thereby arrived at a correct estimate.

I wish to reiterate my fixed opinion that when the Philippine Defense Plan reaches fruition the people of these Islands will be in a favorable posture of defensive security. The question, of course, is one that no sane man would care to see resolved in the only way that it can ever be answered finally and conclusively - namely, by the test of conflict. But so far as the study of history and some considerable experience with armies and with warfare can lend a color of value to my opinion I am certain that no chancellery in the world, if it accepts the opinions of its military and naval staffs, will ever willingly make an attempt to willfully attack the Philippiacs after the present development has been completed.

Finally, this one impelling question naturally presents itself as lying at the heart of the issue here involved. "If the Fhillppines does not prepare for its own defense, to maintain its own security and to preserve its own independence, how are these functions to be performed?" Surely, no other race or nation will expend its youth and its treasure for the defense of this Archipelago. Yet, we know that defenselessness invites aggression and that when unprotected, economic and political independence cannot continue to exist. Pacific habits do not insure peace. Trade, wealth, literature, and refinement cannot defend a state. If others are not to perform these functions for the Filipinos, certainly they must gird themselves for the task. Without security there can eventually be only slavery. With slavery will come national death.

ACCEPTING THE BATON OF FIELD MARSHALL
FROM PRESIDENT QUEZON
AUGUST 24, 1936
MALACANAN PALACE, MANILA, PHILIPPINES

MacArthur accomplished this (Filipinos accepting conscription for military training) mostly through his unique ability to evoke in Filipino hearts the nobility of the soldier's mission. They remembered best his eloquence on this subject when he accepted the baton of Field Marshall from President Quezon at Malacanan Palace.

Major General Courtney Whitney
MacArthur: His Rendezvous with History
Alfred A. Knopf, New York, 1956

The military code, has come down to us from even before the age of knighthood and chivalry ... The Soldier, above all men, is required to perform the highest act of religious teaching - sacrifice. In battle and in the face of danger and death he discloses those divine attributes which his maker gave when He created man in his own image. However horrible the incidents of War may be, the soldier who is called upon to offer and give his life for his country, is the noblest development of mankind.

PHILIPPINE ASSEMBLY
CIRCA 1936

...the Philippine Assembly delayed on appropriations; some politicians tried to cut down the amounts MacArthur needed and even tried to postpone the defense effort entirely. Here again MacArthur had no weapon but the earnest persuasion of his own oratory. In a speech to the Assembly he outlined the philosophy on which he was building the defense establishment.

Major General Courtney Whitney
MacArthur: His Rendezvous with History
Alfred A. Knopf, New York, 1956

...the lessons of history, the conclusions of acknowledged masters of warfare and of statesmanship and sentiments and aspirations of the Filipino people. It is founded on enduring principles that are fundamental to any plan applicable to our needs.

The first of these principles is that every citizen is obligated to the nations defense ... No man has the inalienable right to enjoy the privileges and opportunities conferred upon him by free institutions unless he simultaneously acknowledges his duty to defend with his life and with his property the government through which he acquired these opportunities and these privileges. To deny this individual responsibility is to reject the whole theory of democratic government. This principal knows of no limitation of time or condition. It is effective in war, in peace and for as long as the nation shall endure.

The second great principle is that our national defense system must provide actual security. Indeed, an insufficient defense is almost a contradiction in terms. A dam that crumbles under the rising flood is nothing more than a desolate monument to the wasted effort and lack of vision of its builders....

The next principle to which I hold is the insistent need for current and future economy. Although there are no costs of peace comparable to those that would surely follow defeat in war, it is nevertheless incumbent upon the government to avoid unnecessary expenditure...

STATEMENT ON AID TO GREAT BRITAIN IN RESPONSE
TO A REQUEST FROM WILLIAM ALLEN WHITE,
CHAIRMAN OF THE COMMITTEE TO DEFEND AMERICA
BY AIDING THE ALLIES
SEPTEMBER 16, 1940

To open the way for promotion of younger officers, MacArthur retired from the Army in December, 1937, and settled down in Manila to enjoy family life with his wife and infant son. Maintaining his interest in defense affairs and disturbed by the success of the aggressive totalitarian states in Europe and Asia, he became an early supporter of aid to the Allies.

Major Vorin E. Whan, Jr., USA, Editor
A Soldier Speaks: Public Papers and Speeches of General of the Army Douglas MacArthur
©1965 Frederick A. Praeger, Publishers, New York, NY

You have asked my military opinion as to whether the time has come for America to give continued and further aid to England in the fight for civilization. The history of failure in war can almost be summed up in two words: too late. Too late in comprehending the deadly purpose of a potential enemy; too late in realizing the mortal danger; too late in preparedness; too late in uniting all possible forces for resistance; too late in standing with one's friends. Victory in war results from no mysterious alchemy of wizardry but entirely upon the concentration of superior force at the critical points of combat. To face an adversary in detail has been the prayer of every conqueror in history. It is the secret of the past successes of the Axis powers in this war. It is their main hope for continued and ultimate victory. The greatest strategical mistake in all history will be made if America fails to recognize the vital moment, if she permits again the writing of that fatal epitaph: too late. Such coordinated help as may be regarded as proper by our leaders should be synchronized with the British effort so that the English-speaking peoples of the world will not be broken in detail. The vulnerability of singleness will disappear before unity of effort. Not too late, not tomorrow, but today.

SECOND INAUGURATION OF PRESIDENT QUEZON
DECEMBER 30, 1941
CORREGIDOR

Never before in all history has there been a more solemn and significant inauguration. An act, symbolical of democratic processes, is placed against the background of a sudden merciless war.

The thunder of death and destruction, dropped from the skies, can be heard in the distance. Our ears almost catch

MacArthur with Lord Gowie, Governor of Australia; Brigadier General Marshall and Major General Sutherland.

the roar of battle as our soldiers close on the firing line. The horizon is blackened by the smoke of destructive fire. The air reverberates to the dull roar of exploding bombs.

Such is the bed of birth of this new government, of this new nation. For four hundred years the Philippines have struggled upward toward self-government. Just at the end of its tuitionary period, just on the threshold of independence, came the great hour of decision. There was no hesitation, no vacillation, no moment of doubt. The whole country followed its great leader in choosing the side of freedom against the side of slavery. We have just inaugurated him, we have just thereby confirmed his momentous decision. Hand in hand with the United States and the other free nations of the world, this basic and fundamental issue will be fought through to victory. Come what may, ultimate triumph will be its reward.

Through this its gasping agony of travail, through what Winston Churchill calls 'blood and sweat and tears,' from the grim shadow of the Valley of Death, Oh Merciful God, preserve this noble race.

"I Shall Return" Statement
March 17, 1942
Batchelor Field (or Alice Springs) Australia

The well-known words "I shall return," while not made in a public address by General MacArthur, deserve mention here among some of the General's better and lesser known remarks. After leaving the Philippines March 12, 1942, MacArthur made his way to Australia where he was pressed by reporters for a statement. He issued the following statement: "The President of the United States ordered me to break through the Japanese lines and proceed from Corregidor to Australia for the purpose, as I understand it, of organizing the American offensive against Japan, a primary object of which is the relief of the Philippines. I came through and I shall return."

MacArthur mentioned later that he made the famous remark casually enough, but the words became a psychological rallying point for the Filipinos, and for many Americans. When American forces and MacArthur returned to the Philippines in October 1944, the General's first words, spoken into a microphone, were: "People of the Philippines: I have returned. By the grace of Almighty God, our forces stand again on Philippine soil… ." *It would be difficult to exaggerate the importance of the words "I shall return" and MacArthur's prestige with the Philippine people during the years 1942-44.*

From "Representative Speeches of General of the Army Douglas MacArthur" compiled by the Legislative Reference Service, Library of Congress, ordered to be printed April 29, 1964.

Remarks to the Australian Broadcasting
Company upon Arrival
March 21, 1942
Melbourne, Australia

I am glad indeed to be in immediate cooperation with the Australian soldier. I know him well from World War days and admire him greatly. I have every confidence in the ultimate success of our joint cause; but success in modern war requires something more than courage and a willingness to die: it requires careful preparation. This means the furnishing of sufficient troops and sufficient material to meet the known strength of the potential enemy. No general can make something out of nothing. My success or failure will depend primarily upon the resources which the respective Governments place at my disposal. My faith in them is complete. In any event I shall do my best. I shall keep the soldier's faith.

Remarks Made at a Reception
for General MacArthur Held by the
Prime Minister of Australia
March 25, 1942

Only those in Australia at the time of MacArthur's arrival there on March 17, 1942, could feel the depth of honor and respect they had for MacArthur. From paralyzing fear and despair, doom and gloom the Australian and Americans felt the new era of the War had begun. It was as if a Spiritual rebirth had come and a real feeling of "now we can win this war" effected all of us there. The attitude turned from one of withdrawal and defense to one of optimism and attack.

Edward T. Imparato, Editor

I am deeply moved by the warmth of greeting extended to me by all of Australia. The hospitality of your country is proverbial throughout the world but your reception has far exceeded anything that I could have anticipated. Although this is my first trip to Australia, I already feel at home. There is a link that binds our countries together which does not depend upon written protocol, upon treaties of alliance, or upon diplomatic doctrine. It goes deeper than that. It is that indescribable consanguinity of race which causes us to have the same aspirations, the same hopes and desires, the same ideals and the same dreams of future destiny.

My presence here is tangible evidence of our unity. I have come as a soldier in a great crusade of personal liberty as opposed to perpetual slavery. My faith in our ultimate victory is invincible and i bring to you tonight the unbreakable spirit of the free man's military code in support of our just cause. That code has come down to us from even before the days of knighthood and chivalry. It will stand the test of any ethics or philosophies the world has ever known. It embraces the things that are right and condemns the things that are wrong. Under its banner the free men of the world are united today. There can be no compromise. We shall win or we shall die, and to this end I pledge you the full resources of all the mighty power of my country and all the blood of my countrymen.

Mr. Prime Minister, tonight will be an unforgettable memory for me. Your inspiring words and those of your compatriots will be emblazoned always in my memory as though they had been carved on stone or bronze. Under their inspiration I am taking the liberty of assuming the high honor of raising my glass in salute to your great country and its great leaders.

The MacArthurs - Arthur, Jean Faircloth and Douglas.

125

Statement Issued on the Fall of Bataan on April 10, 1942 and of Corregidor on May 7, 1942
May 1942

Soon after his arrival in Australia, it became evident to General MacArthur that he would not be able to relieve the Philippine garrison before starvation forced their surrender. Despite the realities of the military situation, news of the final surrender nevertheless came as a shock to him. He felt a personal obligation to the fallen defenders of Bataan and Corregidor that only the liberation of the Philippines could discharge.

Major Vorin E. Whan, Jr., USA, Editor
A Soldier Speaks: Public Papers and Speeches of General of the Army Douglas MacArthur
©1965 Frederick A. Praeger, Publishers, New York, NY

The Bataan Force went out as it would have wished, fighting to the end its flickering forlorn hope. No army has ever done so much with so little and nothing became it more than its last hour of trial and agony. To the weeping Mothers of its dead, I can only say that the sacrifice and halo of Jesus of Nazareth has descended upon their sons, and that God will take them unto himself.

Corregidor needs no comment from me. It has sounded its own story at the mouth of its guns. It has scrolled its own epitaph on enemy tablets. But through the bloody haze of its last reverberating shot, I shall always seem to see a vision of grim, gaunt, ghastly men, still unafraid.

MacArthur's Opinion Regarding a Japanese Attack on India
May 8, 1942

Churchill presented Roosevelt with the thought that the Japanese intended to half their advance on Australia and, instead, launch an attack on India. He wished the American buildup in the Pacific to be transferred to the British command in Southeast Asia. Roosevelt was apparently impressed enough to send me a personal message asking my opinion. On May 8th I sent my outline of the situation to the President.

General of the Army Douglas MacArthur Reminiscences
McGraw-Hill Book Company, New York, 1964

The fall of Corregidor and the collapse of resistance in the Philippines, with the defeat of Burma, brings about a new situation. At least two enemy divisions and all the air force in the Philippines will be released for other missions. Japanese troops in Malaya and the Netherlands East Indies are susceptible of being regrouped for an offensive effort elsewhere since large garrisons will not be required because of the complacency of the native population. The Japanese Navy is as yet unchallenged and is disposed for further of-

MacArthur speaks to 32nd Division troops at Camp Cable, Queensland, Australia.

fensive effort. A preliminary move is now under way probably initially against New Guinea and the line of communications between the United States and Australia. The series of events releases an enormously dangerous enemy potential in the Western Pacific. That the situation will remain static ismost improbable.

I am of the opinion that the Japanese will not undertake large operations against India at this time. That area is undoubtedly within the scope of their military ambitions, but it would be strategically advisable for them to defer it until a later date. On the other hand, the enemy advance toward the south has been supported by the establishment of a series of bases while his left is covered from the Mandated Islands. He is thus prepared to continue in that direction. Moreover, operations in these waters will permit the regrouping of his naval and air forces from the East. Such is not the case in a movement towards India. He must thrust into the Indian Ocean without adequate supporting bases, relinquishing the possibilities of concentrating his naval strength in either ocean.

The military requirements for a decisive Indian campaign are so heavy that it can not be undertaken under those conditions. On the other hand, a continuation of his southern movement at this time will give added safety for his eventual move to the west.

In view of this situation I deem it of the utmost importance to provide adequate security for Australia and the Pacific area, thus maintaining a constant frontal defense and a flank threat against further movement to the southward. This should be followed at the earliest possible moment by offensive action.

STATEMENT ON HIS ACCEPTANCE OF AN HONORARY DEGREE FROM THE UNIVERSITY OF WISCONSIN
JUNE 1, 1942

General MacArthur received sixteen honorary degrees from universities and college, both in the United States and aborad, during his long public career. The degree tendered by the University of Wisconsin was particularly meaningful since he had been appointed to the U.S. military Academy from the Fourth Congressional District of that state. His famous father, Lieutenant General Arthur MacArthur, was a native of Wisconsin, and his son always considered the state a second home. The degree was accepted in his behalf by Major General George Grunert, Commanding General of the Sixth Corps area.
Major Vorin E. Whan, Jr., USA, Editor
A Soldier Speaks: Public Papers and Speeches of General of the Army Douglas MacArthur
©1965 Frederick A. Praeger, Publishers, New York, NY

No honor could move me to deeper emotion than to enter into the University community to which you today admit me. In the environs of this great Commonwealth I first ventured upon those academic paths which a lifetime of study has developed in me.

I feel the warmth of a wanderer returning in the twilight of his days from scenes of struggle and agony and death to the still cloistered halls of youth and peace. You have for one thrilling moment transplanted me from the arbitrament of the destructive mechanics of force to the constructive ennoblement of a seat of learning, of a school in search for the right way of life.

And in the end, through the long ages of our quest for light, it will be found that truth is still mightier than the sword.

For out of the welter of human carnage and human sorrow and human weal the indestructible thing that will always live is a sound idea, and none is more immutable than the university idea. You have honored me today, but you have done for me much more than that. You have rededicated me to an imperishable ideal, and you have refreshed the battle worn spirit of an old soldier with the fragrance that clusters around the sacred memories of the magic word "home."

STATEMENT MADE ON SELECTION BY THE NATIONAL FATHER'S DAY COMMITTEE AS "FATHER OF THE YEAR"
JUNE 18, 1942

MacArthur's pride in his four-year-old son, who had come through the events of the Philippine defense without losing his boyish enthusiasm, was reflected in his public acknowledgment on being named "Father of the Year," for 1942.
Major Vorin E. Whan, Jr., USA, Editor
A Soldier Speaks: Public Papers and Speeches of General of the Army Douglas MacArthur
©1965 Frederick A. Praeger, Publishers, New York, NY

Nothing has touched me more deeply than the action of the National Father's Day Committee. By profession I am a soldier and take pride in that fact, but I am prouder, infinitely prouder, to be a father. A soldier destroys in order to build; the father only builds, never destroys. The one has the potentialities of death; the other embodies creation and life. And while the hordes of death are mighty, the battalions of life are mightier still. It is my hope that my son when I am gone will remember me not from the battle but in the home repeating with him our simple daily prayer; "Our Father who are in heaven...."

STATEMENT ON THE AMERICAN "DOUGHBOY" FOR THE DOUGHBOY COMMITTEE
OCTOBER 19, 1942
NEW YORK, NEW YORK

MacArthur's firm support of the foot soldier as a key element in military success dated back to his transfer to the infantry in World War I. his affection for the least glamorous branch of the service is evident in the following tribute.
Major Vorin E. Whan, Jr., USA, Editor
A Soldier Speaks: Public Papers and Speeches of General of the Army Douglas MacArthur
© 1965, Frederick A. Praeger, Publishers, New York, NY

The sound of marching feet always echoes the rise or fall of Empire. From time immemorial the victor in war has been symbolized by the foot solder, he who with a steel weapon in his hand, challenges his enemy to have and to hold a square yard of mud-covered ground. He is affectionately called in our Army the "Doughboy." he plods and groans, sweats and toils, he growls and curses, and at the end dies, unknown, uncomplaining, with faith in his hear, and on his lips a prayer for victory. He passes on in anonymity except for his loved ones, but for those of us who know, we revere and bless the name of "Doughboy."

STATEMENT ON THE AMERICAN RED CROSS AND ITS SERVICES TO THE SOLDIER NOVEMBER 11, 1942

The American Red Cross is an expression of humanitarianism. When tragedy interrupts, as sooner or later it must, succor for the injured, the helpless, the destitute, speeds by land, sea and air. No call however great or small passes unheeded. The Red Cross never fails the solder. It brings to him a hint of home, a touch of cheer, whether he be in teeming jungle or Arctic waste. It bears a gift to him from no one and yet from all. It warms him with the comfort that some-

one thinks of him and someone prays for him. It truly follows in the train of the Prince of Peace.

STATEMENT MADE ON THE FIRST ANNIVERSARY OF THE FALL OF BATAAN APRIL 9, 1943

A full year after the fall of the Philippines, the Allies had shifted to the offensive in the Pacific. Japanese naval power had been fatally weakened at the Battle of Midway, in June, 1942, while their ground advance had been rolled back at Guadalcanal and Papua. General MacArthur's unchanging goal, to return to the scene of his first defeat, was plainly evident in these anniversary messages.

Major Vorin E. Whan, Jr., USA, Editor
A Soldier Speaks: Public Papers and Speeches of General of the Army Douglas MacArthur
© 1965, Frederick A. Praeger, Publishers, New York, NY

A year ago today, the dimming light of Bataan's forlorn hope fluttered and died. Its prays by that time, and it prayed as well as fought, were reduced to a simple formula, rendered by hungry men through cracked and parching lips,

MacArthur, President Franklin D. Rosevelt and Admiral Nimitz in Hawaii, July 1944.

"Give us this day our daily bread." the light failed. Bataan starved into collapse. Our flag lies crumpled, its proud pinions spat upon in the gutter; the wrecks of what were once our men and women groan and sweat in prison toil; our faithful Filipino wards, sixteen million souls, gasp in the slavery of a conquering soldiery devoid of those ideals of chivalry which have so dignified many armies. I was the leader of that Lost Cause, and from the bottom of a seared and stricken heart, I pray that a merciful God may not delay too long their redemption, that the day of salvation be not so far removed that they perish, that it be not again too late.

STATEMENT MADE ON THE FIRST ANNIVERSARY OF THE FALL OF CORREGIDOR MAY 6, 1943

Corregidor surrendered a full year ago today. Intrinsically it is but a barren, war-worn rock, hallowed, as so many other places, by death and disaster. Yet it symbolizes within itself that priceless, deathless thing, the honor of a Nation. Until we lift our flag from its dust, we stand unredeemed before mankind. Until we claim again the ghastly remnants of its last gaunt garrison, we can but stand humble supplicants before Almighty God. There lies our Holy Grail.

STATEMENT TO THE PRESS CLUB OF MILWAUKEE JUNE 24, 1943

In years to come, during the occupation of Japan, General MacArthur was to have his problems with some members of the press. Charges of censorship were made by correspondents and angrily denied by the occupation authorities. Anyone interested in his views on the freedom of the press could well find their answer in this mid-war declaration.

Major Vorin E. Whan, Jr., USA, Editor
A Soldier Speaks: Public Papers and Speeches of General of the Army Douglas MacArthur
© 1965, Frederick A. Praeger, Publishers, New York, NY

It is with warmth of heart that I greet the Press Club of my old home, and salute its fine tradition. In the long struggle of humanity up the road of progress nothing temporal so certainly marks the civilization of a society as the extent to which it has achieved freedom of the press and freedom of speech. Long experience has taught that only by "continual winnowing and sifting" can the truth be found. In that vital process, so basic to American freedom, of finding and spreading the truth, the American newspaperman has no superior and few equals. In the months and years immediately ahead our decisions will be right if based on truth. Laying that sound foundation for the judgments of our people is one of the greatest challenges that ever confronted American journalism. I have complete faith in American newspapers and in the men and women who make them. I am confident they will be more than equal to the task that is theirs.

STATEMENT ON THE PACIFIC STRATEGIC SITUATION AUGUST 9, 1943

In late summer, 1943, the initiative in the Pacific war passed to the Allies. At this turning point in the war, MacArthur's evaluation of the situation was quietly confident.

Major Vorin E. Whan, Jr., USA, Editor
A Soldier Speaks: Public Papers and Speeches of General of the Army Douglas MacArthur
© 1965, Frederick A. Praeger, Publishers, New York, NY

We are doing what we can with what we have. Our resources are still very limited, but the results of our modest but continuous successes in campaign have been cumulative to the point of being vital. A measure of their potentiality can be obtained by imagining the picture to have been reversed, with the enemy capturing Guadalcanal and besieging Port Moresby rather than we in possession of Munda and at the gates of Salamaua. Such a contrast would have meant defeat for us in the war for the Pacific.

The margin was close, but it was conclusive.

Although for many reasons our victories may have lacked in glamorous focus, they have been decisive of the final result in the Pacific. I make no predictions as to time or detail, but Japan on the Pacific fronts has exhausted the fullest resource of concentrated attack of which she was capable, has failed, and is now on a defensive which will yield just in proportion as we gather force and definition. When that will be I do not know, but it is certain.

REMARKS AT A DINNER IN MACARTHUR'S HONOR GIVEN BY THE PRIME MINISTER AND MEMBERS OF THE AUSTRALIAN PARLIAMENT MARCH 17, 1944

The liberation of Manila was still a year in the future when MacArthur reviewed the first two years of the effort to turn back the Japanese thrust toward Australia. Just before initiating the campaign to regain the Philippines, MacArthur paid tribute to those men whose sacrifices had made this beginning possible.

Major Vorin E. Whan, Jr., USA, Editor
A Soldier Speaks: Public Papers and Speeches of General of the Army Douglas MacArthur
© 1965, Frederick A. Praeger, Publishers, New York, NY

Mr. Prime Minister:

I cannot tell you the sense of distinction I feel in being Australia's guest tonight. It adds another link to the long chain of friendship which binds together our peoples and our countries. It is a symbol of that unity of effort that recognizes but one indomitable purpose - victory.

The last two years have been momentous ones for Australia. You have faced the gravest peril in your history. With your very life at stake, you have met and overcome the challenge. It was here the tide of war turned in the Pacific and the mighty wave of invasion broke and rolled back. Two years ago, when I landed on your soil, I said to the people of the Philippines whence I came, "I shall return." Tonight I repeat those words: "I *shall* return." Nothing is more certain than our ultimate re conquest and liberation from the enemy of those and adjacent lands. One of the great offensives of the war will at the appropriate time be launched for that purpose. With God's help it should be decisive not only of redemption but of Japanese isolation from southern conquests and of Chinese restoration of Pacific Ocean communication.

On such an occasion as this my thoughts go back to those men who went on their last crusade in the jungle thicknesses to the north where they made the fight that saved this continent. With faith in their hearts and hope on their lips they passed beyond the mists that blind us here. Their yesterdays make possible our tomorrow. They come from the four quarters of the world, but whatever the land that gave them birth, under their stark white crosses they belong now to Australia forever. I thank you, sir, for the high honor and hospitality of tonight in their and their comrades' names. I shall always recall it as joined with their immortal memory.

STATEMENT TO THE LAYMEN'S NATIONAL COMMITTEE FOR BIBLE WEEK, FOR PRESENTATION ON A NATIONAL RADIO PROGRAM OCTOBER 3, 1944

A dedicated Christian, General MacArthur maintained a keen interest in the spiritual welfare of his men and repeatedly stated his belief that much of America's success on the field of battle came from the strength of our religious heritage. When asked for one of his favorite prayers two weeks before the invasion of Leyte, he chose a prayer for strength.

Major Vorin E. Whan, Jr., USA, Editor
A Soldier Speaks: Public Papers and Speeches of General of the Army Douglas MacArthur
© 1965, Frederick A. Praeger, Publishers, New York, NY

In reply to the request for a message by the Laymen's National Committee I send a prayer taken from an old Bible which has fortified me in these bitter days of strife and struggle: "Give me, O Lord, that quietness of heart, that makes the most of labor and of rest. Save me from passionate excitement, petulant fretfulness and idle fear. Teach me

Shorlty after landing on the beach, General MacArthur was handed the microphone of the Voice of Freedom radio transmitter to deliver his first message to the Filipino people. The general ignored the rain that had begun to fall, and started his famous speech with the words, "People of the Philippines, I have returned."

to be alert and wise in all responsibilities, without hurry and without neglect. When others censure, may I seek thy image in each fellow man, judging with charity as one who shall be judged. Banish envy from my thoughts and hatred from my lips. Help me to be content, amid the strife of tongue, with my unspoken thought. When anxious cares threaten my peace, help me to see thee, that I may find my rest and be made strong for calm endurance and valiant service."

"I HAVE RETURNED" RADIO ADDRESS
OCTOBER 20, 1944
LEYTE, PHILIPPINES

People of the Philippines; I have returned. By the grace of Almighty God, our forces stand again on Philippine soil, soil consecrated in the blood of our two people. We have come, dedicated and committed to the task of destroying every vestige of enemy control over your daily lives and of restoring upon a foundation of indestructible strength the liberties of your people.

At my side is your President Sergio Osmena, worthy successor of that great patriot Manuel Quezon, with members of his cabinet. The seat of your government is now therefore firmly reestablished on Philippine soil.

The hour of your redemption is here. Your patriots have demonstrated an unswerving and resolute devotion to the principles of freedom that challenges the best that is written on the pages of human history. I now call upon your supreme effort, that the enemy may know, from the temper of an aroused and outraged people within, that he has a force there to content with no less violent than is the force committed from without.

Rally to me. Let the indomitable spirit of Bataan and Corregidor lead on. As the lines of battle roll forward to bring you within the zone of operations, rise and strike. Strike at every favorable opportunity. For your homes and hearths, strike! For future generations of your sons and daughters, strike! In the name of your sacred dead, strike! Let no heart be faint. Let every arm be steeled, the guidance of Divine God points the way. Follow His name to the Holy Grail of righteous victory.

RESTORATION OF THE CIVILIAN COMMONWEALTH GOVERNMENT OF THE REPUBLIC OF THE PHILIPPINES
FEBRUARY 27, 1945
MANILA, PHILIPPINE ISLANDS

More than 3 years have elapsed - years of bitterness, struggle, and sacrifice - since I withdrew our forces and installations from this beautiful city that over and under fire, its churches, monuments, and cultural centers might, in ac-

Restoration of the Civilian Commonwealth Government of the Republic of the Philippines with President Osmena, February 27, 1945.

cordance with the rules of warfare, be spared the violence of military ravage. The enemy would not have it so. And much that I sought to preserve has been unnecessarily destroyed by his desperate action at bay. By these actions he has wantonly fixed the future pattern of his own doom. Then we were but a small force struggling to stem the advance of overwhelming hordes treacherously hurled against us behind the masks of professed friendship and international good will. That struggle was not in vain. God has indeed blessed our arms.

The girded and unleashed power of America supported by our allies turned the tide of battle in the Pacific and resulted in an unbroken series of crushing defeats upon the enemy, culminating in the redemption of your soil and the liberation of your people.

My country has kept the faith. Its soldiers come here as an army of freemen dedicated with your people to the cause of human liberty, and committed to the task of destroying those evil forces that have fought to suppress it by brutality of the sword.

An army of freemen has brought your people once again under democracy's banner to rededicate their churches, long desecrated, to the glory of God and public worship; to reopen their schools to liberal education; to till the soil and reap its harvest without fear of confiscation; to reestablish their industries that they may again enjoy the profit from their sweat and enjoy their homes unafraid of violent intrusion.

Thus to millions of your now liberated people comes the opportunity to pledge themselves, their hearts, their minds, and their hands to the task of building a new and stronger nation, a nation consecrated in the blood nobly shed that this might be a nation dedicated to make imperishable those sacred liberties for which we have fought and for which many have died.

On behalf of my Government, I now solemnly declare, Mr. President, the full powers and responsibilities under the Constitution restored to the Commonwealth, whose seat is here reestablished as provided by law. Your country is once again at liberty to pursue its destiny to an honored position in the family of free nations. Your capital city, severely punished though it be, has regained its rightful place as a symbol of democracy.

FLAG RAISING CEREMONIES
MARCH 2, 1945
CORREGIDOR

Of all the places liberated during the reconquest of the Philippines, probably none held more poignant memories for MacArthur than Corregidor. Here he had directed the long defense of Bataan in those early difficult days of 1941. It was from its South Dock that he had boarded the PT boat that took him to his new assignment in Australia. In a hard-

Flag raising ceremony at Corregidor, March 2, 1945.

fought engagement, the 503rd Airborne Regimental Combat Team, assisted by elements of the 34th Regimental Combat Team, retook the island by parachute and amphibious assault. MacArthur's promise to the Philippine Garrison to return with help had now been accomplished.

Major Vorin E. Whan, Jr., USA, Editor
A Soldier Speaks: Public Papers and Speeches of General of the Army Douglas MacArthur
© 1965, Frederick A. Praeger, Publishers, New York, NY

Colonel Jones:

The capture of Corregidor is one of the most brilliant operations in military history. Outnumbered two to one, your command by its unfaltering courage, its invincible determination, and its professional skill overcame all obstacles and annihilated the enemy. I have cited to the order of the day all units involved and I take great pride in awarding you as their commander the Distinguished Service Cross as a symbol of the fortitude, the devotion, and the bravery with which you have fought. I see the old flagpole still stands. Have your troops hoist the colors to its peak, and let no enemy ever haul them down.

MESSAGE BROADCAST TO THE AMERICAN PEOPLE ON V-E DAY MAY 8, 1945

MacArthur was plagued in the conduct of his Pacific Campaign by the shortage of resources resulting from the early decision of the U.S. Government to concentrate on the European theater. Although our massive industrial output permitted assumption of the offensive against Japan before the Germans were defeated, the Pacific forces were chronically short of many resources they needed. MacArthur pointed out in his message on V-E Day that the full weight of Allied power could now be brought to bear on the Japanese Empire.

Major Vorin E. Whan, Jr., USA, Editor
A Soldier Speaks: Public Papers and Speeches of General of the Army Douglas MacArthur
© 1965, Frederick A. Praeger, Publishers, New York, NY

I rejoice with you in the triumph of Allied arms which has restored human liberty to the enslaved peoples of Europe - rejoice that this phase of the titanic struggle in which our country has long been engaged has now been brought to a victorious conclusion, and rejoice that this Command, presently engaging our remaining enemy on many fronts, will now be reinforced by those vast and powerful resources of war heretofore employed on the battlefields of Europe. Through this additional strength the Japanese Empire will be the more speedily vanquished with greater economy of American and Allied life than otherwise would be possible.

We rejoice over these things and in deep gratitude pay tribute to the gallant fighting men and service women who with our Allies have made them possible. In the historic pattern of our race they who in their hearts abhor war have by necessity risen to magnificent and masterful heights in the prosecution of war and taught our enemies, who for generations have practiced and sought to live by war an irrefutable lesson in its utter futility as an instrument of national progress.

At the same time we pay tribute to those other great forces constituting our national strength which are equally essential to the attainment of victory. I refer to those who by their toil and technical skill have forged the weapons without which the stoutest heart and strongest arm is lost in the crucible of modern war - and to the mothers, wives, and other loved ones of our fighting men who by their courage and fortitude and patience have steeled the soldier hearts to an unyielding will for victory. In war, the balance of power being otherwise equal, the spiritual strength of his home dominates the soldier at the front and ofttimes controls the tide of battle itself. In this spiritual strength those brave and noble American mothers, of whom I speak in all humility and admiration, have never been found wanting - to them, the unsung heroines of war, is due more than to all others the accolade of victory.

Yet, while we rejoice over the great successes which now permit us to gird our full national strength the better to meet the tests of battle in the East, it is well that we pause to reflect in realistic appreciation of the effect of war upon the victorious as well as upon the vanquished. War's cost, regardless of motive or result, is heavy. The lessons of its destructive effect are no less compelling upon us in victory than upon our enemies in defeat. The survival and progress of humanity under the burdens this war has imposed is only possible if thereby the consciousness of mankind is aroused to the realization that war is inimical to human progress and a more constructive means is sought and found to preserve order and settle disputes among the peoples of the earth. The trend of current thought offers promise that this will be done, and as the representatives of the Allied nations now convene in search for the way it is incumbent upon all to give of their full support and pray for Divine guidance of their deliberations in the achievement of this lofty purpose.

The members of this Command salute their comrades-in-arms, victors of the war in the West, as we rededicate ourselves to the task which yet lies ahead in the East. However monumental such task, with the help of Almighty God we shall not fail.

SPEECH BEFORE THE PHILIPPINE CONGRESS AT THE TERMINATION OF THE PHILIPPINE CAMPAIGN JULY 9, 1945

The end of the major operations on Luzon came in the early summer of 1945. As the country was liberated from the Japanese, General MacArthur reestablished civil government. With the long-awaited independence near, the Commonwealth Government convened the Philippine Congress in Manila. MacArthur, always a strong supporter of freedom for the Islands, spoke to the legislators of the problems still to be overcome in preparation for the full sovereignty they were to achieve in the coming year.

Major Vorin E. Whan, Jr., USA, Editor
A Soldier Speaks: Public Papers and Speeches of General of the Army Douglas MacArthur
© 1965, Frederick A. Praeger, Publishers, New York, NY

Mr. President and Gentlemen of the Congress of the Philippines:

It is cause for profound satisfaction to see this legislative body, instrument of democratic expression, restored to the people.

You convene at a time when we are still locked in mortal combat with an enemy who vigorously seeks to exploit racial prejudice and to suppress human freedom as the ideology of mankind. Since the beginning of time men have crusaded for freedom and for equality. It was this passion for liberty which inspired the architects of my own government to proclaim so immutably and so beautifully that "All men are created equal" and "that they are endowed by their Creator with certain inalienable rights - that among these are Life, Liberty, and the pursuit of Happiness." On such rights rests our basic concept of human freedom, in defense of which we have fought and still continue to fight on the battlefields of the world. These rights are the very antithesis to the totalitarian doctrine which seeks to regiment the people and control the human will as the price for presumed efficiency in government. The recent collapse of one people after another dedicated to this totalitarian theory of government offers complete and eloquent proof that the enduring strength of a body politic arises from the degree of freedom accorded its individual members, and not from any seeming efficiency gained at the sacrifice of that freedom. It behooves you therefore to safeguard these sacred rights no less zealously in peace than you have defended them in war.

You convene at a time when you are soon to realize your long-sought political independence. Prior to the start of hostilities in the present war those who opposed your independence did so on the ground that you yet lacked the stature as a race essential to self-government; that you lacked the economic stability to sustain self-government; and that you lacked the resources essential to defend self-government. All these contentions are untenable.

Yours is a culture which for 400 years has progressively become a blend between the culture of the East and the culture of the West - with resulting racial character influenced by the best of each. Your combat record on Bataan and the magnificent spiritual and physical resistance of the great masses of your people to the enemy efforts at pacification have given to the world the true measure of the strength of your character and established your undisputed spiritual capacity for self-government under any standards.

That strength of character has been manifested time and again when your people were brought under the extreme test of enemy brutality and otherwise subjected to the horrors of war. During the battle for Manila I have seen mothers anguished of soul for their dead children, I have seen fathers bereft of all whom they held dear and with all mate-rial possessions gone, I have seen a continuous line of refugees from south Manila slowly trudging north over the pontoon bridge on the Pasig - without food, water, or shelter, and knowing not whither to go in search of sanctuary - but through the stark terror and tragedy of it all there is one thing I have never heard, one thing I have never seen. I have never heard a whimper; I have never seen a tear. It is just that courage and fortitude and resiliency of your people that has permitted this city of Manila to rise above the destruction of February last, without starvation, without food riots or other disorder, and without epidemic. There was exemplified the strength of the Filipino character - the height of your stature as a race - adequate answer to those who would question your spiritual capacity for self-government.

Those who would say that the economy of the country will not sustain a free and independent nation would appear to anticipate arbitrary tariff barriers to drastically restrict or eliminate your trade with the United States. I am fully confident that the American people will extend to you the full measure of trade advocated by your late great President Manuel Quezon and do everything else within their power to assist you along the road to your national destiny.

Prior to this great war the question of national defense offered the most serious obstacle to the reality of your political independence. Altered world conditions resulting from the war have removed this obstacle. Defense is no longer national, it has become international. No nation however powerful may in future with safety rely exclusively upon its own defense potentiality - but must resort to international defense in concert with other nations. This does not mean that you may with impunity fail to take such defensive dispositions as are reasonably within your power, but rather that in addition to such dispositions you must bring yourself into such international alignment that offers best hope for the preservation of future peace in the Pacific basin.

You convene at a time when not only must your people rededicate themselves and all that is within them to the task of waging total war against our yet unconquered enemy, but at a time when many of your cities and towns lie ravished in the wake of that brutal enemy's retreat, with many thousands of your countrymen prostrate and in want. Thus the burdens upon you are heavy. It is absolutely essential that you operate without undue friction. Petty jealousy, selfish ambition, and unnecessary misunderstanding must not be permitted to impede progress and rend your country. The success of your joint venture with America offers the one great hope for solution to the conflicting problems of the East and West. Now more than at any other time in your history you must realize the vision of the magnificent goal toward which you strive. Only by united action can you attain fruition. In every other major step in which you have succeeded you have done so through the strength of unity. Do not fail now.

To assist you, the Army will progressively give you all the aid in reconstruction which the military situation will permit, and the appropriate civil agencies of the United States will do all that lies within their power - but such assistance is not enough if it be without the full support and willing toil of your own people. It is therefore of utmost importance both in the successful prosecution of the war and the reconstruction of your country that this legislative body in constructive collaboration with the coordinate branches of government - executive and judicial - provide the people with a vigorous, inspiring, impartial, and discerning leadership on a course realistically charted to serve those great national purposes.

In the forty-six years of my military service, large parts of which have been dedicated to the interests of the Filipino people, no honors that I have received have moved me more deeply than those this Congress has recently bestowed upon me. I accept them with a full heart as a tribute to the historic part my Country has played in the progress of your people. I accept them and throughout life shall treasure them in token of the mutual understanding, faith, and affection which binds us, the one to the other.

The relations between the American and Filipino people are sanctified by the blood of both, nobly and selflessly shed upon Philippine soil. From north to south, from east to west, the stark white crosses dot your landscape where we laid our mutual dead to sleep forever. Their sacrifice lives as a flaming torch to fire the will and steel the hearts of free men to resist likewise if need be unto death all efforts, however devious the means, to compromise that freedom for which they died.

God grant that your people may with the same fortitude and determination that has permitted them with unyielding spirits to rise above the stern realities of the past, face the future with faith and hope - erect and unafraid. God grant that under your leadership they may march proudly forward to high destiny of honor and dignity among all of the peoples of the earth. That will be my prayer always.

Accepting the Degree of Doctor of Laws, Honoris Causa, Santo Thomas University, Philippine Islands
August 24, 1945

Your Excellency, the Apostolic Delegate, Rector, and members of the faculty of Santo Tomas University, for over 400 years - years of war and peace, of happiness and sorrow, of life and death - this university has stood - bulwark of Christianity in the East.

For 400 years it has thus had the opportunity to inculcate into the minds and hearts of generation upon generation of the Filipino people the teachings of Christ and the enlightened knowledge of Western culture - and Western ideals.

For 400 years, while its physical appurtenances have crumbled in the dust of antiquity, necessitating restorations to meet the ravages of time and changing concepts of modern requirements, the soul of the university has maintained its great and noble influence upon the generations who have lived and died.

When my country assumed the mantle of sovereignty over these islands at the turn of the century, it found here a people in whom was already deeply implanted a veneration for and devotion to the principles of Christianity, with minds already enlightened to the knowledge that in the culture of the Western World lay progressive ideas designed to advance the cause of the human race.

Thus, when it sought to fashion here its own political philosophy - or any modification thereof which might better serve the capacity, temperament, and welfare of the people - a philosophy designed to give higher dignity to man as an individual and to bestow upon him the blessings of greater freedom of thought and action, a social order indeed predicated upon increased tolerance and understanding, the depth of the Christian faith, already firmly implanted in the soul of the Filipino race, offered a solid foundation upon which such concept of human relations might be erected.

So when this great struggle, which we are just now bringing to a victorious conclusion, swept the earth - a struggle between those things that are wrong and those things that are right - a struggle which placed in the very balance survival of the teachings of Christ and the civilization of mankind whose course had been charted from those teachings - the spiritual strength of the Filipino people faced its vital test.

The world now knows how steadfastly they kept the faith even unto death - that faith born of Christianity and of democracy.

The struggle is now over - the cause of right and justice has prevailed. Christianity, democracy, and the essence of Western culture have survived - and the East is about to be opened to an enlightened age wherein its peoples progressively may attain that higher degree of human dignity which the war has been fought to preserve. They will find a blend between the culture of the East and the culture of the West which best suits their character and divergent philosophies of life. Thus to mankind someday will come a realization that the same sun with which the Creator, in his infinite wisdom, has endowed all peoples on earth, gives light and warmth to the entire universe - both to the East and to the West - and that the distinction between the two is basically geographical in character - and all hesitancy against the assimilation of the cultural strength of the one by the other will eventually disappear. Then will come hope for lasting peace between the peoples of the earth - peace based upon the mutual faith and under-standing of all mankind - upon an admixture of ideas and ideals that will best serve the advancement of the human race - and finally upon the realization that only through peace may mankind find progress, happiness, and his very survival.

As I reflect upon this great test of strength for Christianity in its isolated entrenchment here in the East, I realize the great honor which is due the university of Santo Tomas for the historic role it has played through the ages in erecting the indestructible foundation upon which the faith of the Filipino people during this critical period has rested. In that realization - and in the humility of a soldier who knows that all men and all things are dependent upon the will of Almighty God - I accept the honor which you have here elected to confer upon me - an honor which I shall treasure in reverent appreciation all of the days of my life.

REMARKS AT THE SURRENDER CEREMONIES
SEPTEMBER 2, 1945
USS *MISSOURI*, TOKYO BAY

The formal surrender ceremonies in Tokyo Bay ending the war with Japan were conducted for the Allies by General MacArthur as the newly appointed Supreme Allied Commander. The Japanese delegation acknowledged the end of their ancient empire in ceremonies whose stark simplicity underscored the enormity of the tragedy finally brought to a close.

Major Vorin E. Whan, Jr., USA, Editor
A Soldier Speaks: Public Papers and Speeches of General of the Army Douglas MacArthur
© 1965, Frederick A. Praeger, Publishers, New York, NY

We are gathered here, representatives of the major warring powers, to conclude a solemn agreement whereby peace may be restored. The issues, involving divergent ideals and ideologies, have been determined on the battlefields of the world and hence are not for our discussion or debate. Nor is it for us here to meet, representing as we do a majority of the peoples of the earth, in a spirit of distrust, malice, or hatred. But rather it is for us, both victors and vanquished, to rise to that higher dignity which alone befits the sacred purposes we are about to serve, committing all of our peoples unreservedly to faithful compliance with the undertakings they are here formally to assume.

It is my earnest hope and indeed the hope of all mankind that from this solemn occasion a better world shall emerge out of the blood and carnage of the past - a world founded upon faith and understanding - a world dedicated to the dignity of man and the fulfillment of his most cherished wish - for freedom, tolerance, and justice.

The terms and conditions upon which surrender of the Japanese Imperial forces is here to be given and accepted are contained in the instrument of surrender now before you.

As Supreme Commander for the Allied Powers I announce it my firm purpose, in the tradition of the countries I represent, to proceed in the discharge of my responsibilities with justice and tolerance, while taking all necessary dispositions to insure that the terms of surrender are fully, promptly, and faithfully complied with.

I now invite the representatives of the Emperor of Japan and the Japanese Government, and the Japanese Imperial General Headquarters, to sign the instrument of surrender at the places indicated.

The Supreme Commander for the Allied Powers will now sign on behalf of all the nations at war with Japan.

The representative of the United States of America will now sign.

The representative of the Republic of China will now sign.

The representative of the United Kingdom will now sign.

The representative of the Union of Soviet Socialist Republics will now sign.

The representative of Australia will now sign.

The representative of Canada will now sign.

The representative of France will now sign.

The representative of Netherlands will now sign.

The representative of New Zealand will now sign.

Let us pray that peace be now restored to the world, and that God will preserve it always.

These proceedings are closed.

VJ DAY BROADCAST
SEPTEMBER 2, 1945
USS *MISSOURI*, TOKYO BAY

My fellow countrymen, today the guns are silent. A great tragedy has ended. A great victory has been won. The skies no longer rain death - the seas bear only commerce - men everywhere walk upright in the sunlight. The entire world is quietly at peace. The holy mission has been completed, and in reporting this to you, the people, I speak for the thousands of silent lips, forever stilled among the jungles and the beaches and in the deep waters of the Pacific which marked the way. I speak for the unnamed brave millions homeward bound to take up the challenge of that future which they did so much to salvage from the brink of disaster.

As I look back on the long tortuous trail from those grim days of Bataan and Corregidor, when an entire world lived

MacArtrhur's speech made September 2, 1945 at the surrender ceremony on the USS Missouri *after the document was signed.*

in fear, when democracy was on the defensive every-where, when modern civilization trembled in the balance, I thank a merciful God that He has given us the faith, the courage, and the power from which to mold victory.

We have known the bitterness of defeat and the exultation of triumph, and from both we have learned there can be no turning back. We must go forward to preserve in peace what we won in war.

A new era is upon us. Even the lesson of victory itself brings with it profound concern, both for our future security and the survival of civilization. The destructiveness of the war potential, through progressive advances in scientific discovery, has in fact now reached a point which revises the traditional concept of war.

Men since the beginning of time have sought peace. Various methods through the ages have attempted to devise an international process to prevent or settle disputes between nations. From the very start workable methods were found insofar as individual citizens were concerned, but the mechanics of an instrumentality of larger international scope have never been successful. Military alliance, balances of power, League of Nations all in turn failed, leaving the only path to be by way of the crucible of war.

The utter destructiveness of war now blots out this alternative. We have had our last chance. If we do not devise some greater and more equitable system Armageddon will be at our door. The problem basically is theological and involves a spiritual recrudescence and improvement of human character that will synchronize with our almost matchless advance in science, art, literature, and all material and cultural developments of the past 2,000 years. It must be of the spirit if we are to save the flesh.

We stand in Tokyo today reminiscent of our countryman, Commodore Perry, 92 years ago. His purpose was to bring to Japan an era of enlightenment and progress by lifting the veil of isolation to the friendship, trade, and commerce of the world. But, alas, the knowledge thereby gained of Western science was forged into an instrument of oppression and human enslavement. Freedom of expression, freedom of action, even freedom of thought were denied through suppression of liberal education, through appeal to superstition, and through the application of force.

We are committed by the Potsdam Declaration of Principles to see that the Japanese people are liberated from this condition of slavery. It is my purpose to implement this commitment just as rapidly as the armed forces are demobilized and other essential steps taken to neutralize

MacArthur signs the Japanese surrender document aboard the USS Missouri, *September 2, 1945.*

the war potential. The energy of the Japanese race, if properly directed, will enable expansion vertically rather than horizontally. If the talents of the race are turned into constructive channels, the country can lift itself from its present deplorable state into a position of dignity.

To the Pacific Basin has come the vista of a new emancipated world. Today, freedom is on the offensive, democracy is on the march. Today, in Asia as well as in Europe, unshackled peoples are tasting the full sweetness of liberty, the relief from fear.

In the Philippines, America has evolved a model for this new free world of Asia. In the Philippines, America has demonstrated that peoples of the East and peoples of the West may walk side by side in mutual respect and with mutual benefit. The history of our sovereignty there has now the full confidence of the East.

And so, my fellow countrymen, today I report to you that your sons and daughters have served you well and faithfully with the calm, deliberate, determined fighting spirit of the American soldier and sailor based upon a tradition of historical trait, as against the fanaticisin of any enemy supported only by mythological fiction. Their spiritual strength and power has brought us through to victory. They are homeward bound - take care of them.

STATEMENT UPON THE COMPLETION OF THE DEMOBILIZATION OF THE JAPANESE ARMED FORCES IN COMPLIANCE WITH THE TERMS OF THE SURRENDER AGREEMENT OCTOBER 16, 1945

Unlike Germany, whose armed forces had been shattered and largely overrun by V-E Day, the Japanese capitulated while large ground forces were still undefeated in China and on the home islands. The fanatical resistance that had made necessary the virtual extinction of the Japanese garrisons in the South Pacific led many to expect similar problems in placing the occupation forces in control of Japan. Surprisingly, there was no trouble at all, and the demobilization was completed without incident. The occupation thus got of to a positive start that it never lost.

Major Vorin E. Whan, Jr., USA, Editor
A Soldier Speaks: Public Papers and Speeches of General of the Army Douglas MacArthur
© 1965, Frederick A. Praeger, Publishers, New York, NY

Today the Japanese Armed Forces throughout Japan completed their demobilization and ceased to exist as such. These forces are now completely abolished. I know of no demobi-

MacArthur receives Emperor Hirohito at the U.S. embassy in Tokyo (1945).

lization in history either in war or peace, by our own or by any other country, that has been accomplished so rapidly or so frictionlessly. Everything military, naval or air is forbidden to Japan. This ends its military might and its military influence in international affairs. It no longer reckons as a world power either large or small. Its path in the future, if it is to survive, must be confined to the ways of peace.

Approximately seven million armed men, including those in the outlying theaters, have laid down their weapons. In the accomplishment of the extraordinarily difficult and dangerous surrender in Japan, unique in the anals of history, not a shot was necessary, not a drop of Allied blood was shed. The vindication of the great decision of Potsdam is complete.

Nothing could exceed the abjectness, the humiliation and the finality of this surrender. It is not only physically thorough but has been equally destructive on Japanese spirit. From swagger and arrogance the former Japanese military have passed to servility and fear. They are thoroughly beaten and cowed and tremble before the terrible retribution the surrender terms impose upon their country in punishment for its great sins.

Again I wish to pay tribute to the magnificent conduct of our troops. With few exceptions they could well be taken as a model for all time as a conquering army. No historian in later years, when passions cool, can arraign their conduct. They could so easily - and understandably - have emulated the ruthlessness which their enemy freely practiced when conditions were reversed; but their perfect balance, between implacable firmness of duty on the one hand and resolute restraint from cruelness and brutalities on the other, has taught a lesson to the Japanese civil population that is startling in its impact. Nothing has so tended to impress Japanese thought - not even the catastrophic fact of military defeat itself. The revolution, or more properly speaking the evolution, which will restore the dignity and freedom of the common man, has begun. It will take much time and require great patience but if public opinion will permit of these two essential factor - the world will be repaid. Herein lies the way to true and final peace.

The Japanese Army, contrary to some concepts that have been advanced, was thoroughly defeated before the surrender. The strategic maneuvering of the Allies had so scattered and divided it, their thrusts had so immobilized, disintegrated and split its units, its supply and transportation lines were so utterly destroyed, its equipment was so exhausted, its morale so shattered, that its early surrender became inevitable. Bastion after bastion, considered by it as impregnable and barring our way, had been by-passed and rendered impotent and useless, while our tactical penetrations and envelopments resulted in piecemeal destruction of many isolated fragments. It was weak everywhere, forced to fight where it stood, unable to render mutual support between its parts and presented a picture of collapse that was complete and absolute. The basic cause of the surrender is not to be attributed to an arbitrary decision of authority. It was inevitable because of the strategic and tactical circumstances forced upon it. The situation had become hopeless. It was merely a question of "when" with our troops poised for final invasion. This invasion would have been annihilating but might well have cost hundreds of thousands of American lives.

The victory was a triumph for the concept of the complete integration of the three dimensions of war - ground, sea, and air. By a thorough use of each arm in conjunction with the corresponding utilization of the other two, the enemy was reduced to a condition of helplessness. By largely avoiding methods involving a separate use of the services and by avoiding methods of frontal assault as far as possible, our combined power forced collapse with relative light loss probably unparalleled in any campaigns in history. This latter fact indeed was the most inspiring and significant feature, the unprecedented saving in American life. It is for this we have to say truly - thank God. Never was there a more intensive application of the principle of the strategic-tactical employment of limited forces as compared with the concept of overwhelming forces.

Illustrating this concept, General Yamashita recently stated in an interview in Manila, explaining reasons for his defeat, that "Diversity of Japanese command resulted in complete lack of cooperation and coordination between the services." He complained: that he was "not in supreme command, that the air forces were run by Field Marshal Terauchi at Saigon and the fleet run directly from Tokyo," that he "only knew of the intended naval strike at Leyte Gulf 5 days before it got underway" and professed "ignorance of its details."

The great lesson for the future is that success in the art of war depends upon a complete integration of the services. In unity will lie military strength. We cannot win with only backs and ends, and no line however strong can go alone. Victory will rest with the team.

DECISION IN THE WAR-CRIMES TRIAL OF GENERAL HOMMA, FORMER JAPANESE COMMANDER IN THE PHILIPPINE ISLANDS
MARCH 21, 1946

Among the most distasteful tasks General MacArthur faced after the war was the review of the verdicts in the Japanese war-crimes trials. The case of Lieutenant General Masaharu Homma was a typical example of the problems he was called on to consider. General Homma commanded the forces opposed to General MacArthur in the defense of the Philippines. He was tried after the war in Manila for his complicity in the infamous Bataan "Death March," was found guilty and sentenced to death. After receiving a personal plea for clemency from General Homma's wife, General MacArthur confirmed the sentence and in his review clearly reiterated the inescapable able responsibility of command.

Major Vorin E. Whan, Jr., USA, Editor
A Soldier Speaks: Public Papers and Speeches of General of the Army Douglas MacArthur
© 1965, Frederick A. Praeger, Publishers, New York, NY

I am again confronted with the repugnant duty of passing final judgment on a former adversary in a major military campaign. The proceedings show the defendant lacked the basic firmness of character and moral fortitude essential to officers charged with the high command of military forces in the field. No nation can safely trust its martial honor to leaders who do not maintain the universal code which distinguishes between those things that are right and those things that are wrong. The testimony shows a complete failure to comply with this simple but vital standard. The savageries which resulted have shocked the world. They have become synonyms of horror and mark the lowest ebb of depravity of modern times. There are few parallels in infamy and tragedy with the brutalization of troops who in good faith had laid down their arms. It is of peculiar aversion that the victims were a garrison whose heroism and valor has never been surpassed. Of all fighting men of all time none deserved more the honors of war in their hour of final agony. The callousness of denial has never been exceeded. This violation of a fundamental code of chivalry, which has ruled all honorable military men throughout the ages in treatment of defeated opponents will forever shame the memory of the victorious troops. I can find no circumstances of extenuation although I have searched for some instance upon which to base palliation.

In reviewing this case I have carefully considered the minority views presented by distinguished Justices of the United States Supreme Court in negation not only as to jurisdiction but as to method and merit. My action as well as the record in this case would be incomplete were I to fail the obligation as the final reviewing authority of frank expression on issues of so basic a nature. I do so from the standpoint of a member of the executive branch of the government in process of its responsibility in the administration of military justice.

No trial could have been fairer than this one, no accused was ever given a more complete opportunity of defense, no judicial process was ever freer from prejudice. In so far as was humanly possible the actual facts were fully presented to the commission. There were no artifices of technicality which might have precluded the introduction of full truth in favor of half-truth, or caused the slanting of half-truth to produce the effect of nontruth, thereby warping and confusing the tribunal into an insecure verdict. On the contrary, the trial was conducted in the unshaded light of truth, the whole truth and nothing but the truth. Those who would oppose such honest method can only be a minority, who either advocate arbitrariness of process above factual realism, or who inherently shrink from the stern rigidity of capital punishment Strange jurisprudence it would be, which for whatever reason defeated the fundamental purpose of justice - to rectify wrong, to protect right and to produce order, safety and well-being. No sophistry can confine justice to a form. It is a quality. Its purity lies in its purpose, not in its detail. The rules of war and the military law resulting as an essential corollary therefrom have always proven sufficiently flexible to accomplish justice within the strict limitations of morality.

If this defendant does not deserve his judicial fate, none in jurisdictional history ever did. There can be no greater, more heinous or more dangerous crime than the mass destruction, under guise of military authority or military necessity, of helpless men incapable of further contribution to war effort. A failure of law process to punish such acts of criminal enormity would threaten the very fabric of world society. Human liberties, the fundamental dignities of man, the basic freedoms upon which depend the very future of civilization, all would be in peril and hazard. Soldiers of an army invariably reflect the attitude of their General. The leader is the essence. Isolated cases of rapine may well be exceptional, but widespread and continuing abuse can only be a fixed responsibility of highest field authority. Resultant liability is commensurate with resultant crime. To hold otherwise would be to prevaricate the fundamental nature of the command function. This imposes no new hazard on a commander, no new limitation on his power. He has always, and properly, been subject to due process of law. Powerful as he may become in time of war, he still is not autocratic or absolute, he still remains responsible before the bar of universal justice. From time immemorial the record of high commanders, of whatever side, has been generally temperate and just. The lapses during this latest war are contrary to past trend. By universal practice such military transgressions are tried by military tribunals. No escutcheon is more unsullied of revenge and passion than that of the United States. Firmly rooted in long and noble tradition, American military justice may safely be predicted to remain so.

I approve the finding of built and direct the Commanding General, United States Army Forces in the Western Pacific, to execute the sentence.

ALLIED CONTROL COUNCIL FOR JAPAN
APRIL 5, 1946
TOKYO, JAPAN

There was a strong and concerted effort on the part of the Soviet representative and the British government to partition Japan in the manner done in Germany. MacArthur would have none of that and his strong word to the Russian representative on the Allied Council caused the Soviets to back away from the issue and no further attempts on incursion on the council's action was taken.

Edward T. Imparato, Editor

I welcome you with utmost cordiality in the earnest anticipation that, in keeping with the friendship which has long existed among the several peoples represented here, your deliberations throughout shall be governed by good will, mutual understanding, and broad tolerance. As the functions of the Council will be advisory and consultative, it will not divide the heavy administrative responsibility of the supreme commander as the sole executive authority for the Allied Powers in Japan, but it will make available to him the several viewpoints of its members on questions of policy and action. I hope it will prove to be a valuable factor in the future solution of many problems.

To assist the Council in the fulfillment of its objectives, instructions have been given that copies of all directives issued to the Japanese Government shall promptly be furnished it, together with such background information as may be appropriate to permit a full understanding thereof, or as the Council may specifically desire. Matters of substance will normally be laid before it prior to action. Any advice the Council as a whole or any of its individual members may believe should be helpful to the supreme commander will at all times be most welcome, and given the most thorough consideration. As my manifold other duties will not normally permit me to sit with the Council, I have designated a deputy to act as Chairman thereof. To promote full public confidence in its aims and purposes, it is advisable that all formal sessions be open to such of the public and press as existing facilities will accommodate. There is nothing in its deliberations to conceal even from the eyes and ears of our alien adversary. Through such a practice of pure democracy in the discharge of its responsibilities, the world will know that the Council deliberations lead to no secret devices, undertakings, or commitments. The suspicion, the distrust, the hatred so often engendered by the veil of secrecy will thus be avoided and in the undimmed light of public scrutiny we will therefore invite full confidence in the sincerity of our purposes and the rectitude of our aims. As supreme commander I can assure you that I entertain no fear that such an opportunity for public discussion will have the slightest adverse effect upon the discharge of my executive responsibilities.

The purposes of the occupation are now well advanced. Japanese forces on the home islands have been disarmed, demobilized, and returned to their homes, and in other respects the Japanese war machine has been neutralized. Dispositions have been taken to eliminate for all time the authority and influence of those who misled the people of Japan into embarking on world conquest, and to establish in Japan a new order of peace, security, and justice; to secure for the Japanese freedom of speech, religion, and thought, and respect for the fundamental human rights; to remove all obstacles to the strengthening of democratic tendencies among the Japanese people; and to readjust the Japanese industrial economy to produce for the Japanese people, after reparations, an equitable standard of life. All of these dispositions in implementation of principles outlined in the Potsdam Declaration have already been taken.

My policy in the administration of Japan for the Allied Powers has been to act as far as possible through existing instrumentalities of the Japanese Government. The soundness of this policy has been unmistakably reflected in the progress of the occupation. I have sought, while destroying Japan's war potential and exacting just penalties for past wrongs, to build a future for the people of Japan based upon considerations of realism and justice. Without yielding firmness, it has been my purpose to avoid oppressive or arbitrary action, and to infuse into the hearts and minds of the Japanese people principles of liberty and right heretofore unknown to them. As success of the Allied occupational purposes is dependent upon leadership as well as upon direction - only to urge the firm application of those very principles which we ourselves defended on the battlefield may we, as victors, become architects of a new Japan, a Japan reorientated to peace, security, and justice. This policy shall continue to be the aim of my administration and should serve to guide the Council through its deliberations.

Were it otherwise - were we but to insure the thoroughness of Japan's defeat, then leave her prostrate in the ashes of total collapse, history would point to a task poorly done, but partially complete. It is equally for us now to guide her

people to rededicate themselves to higher principles, ideals, an purposes; to help them rise to the full measure of new and loftier standards of social and political morality - that they firmly may meet the challenge of future utility in the service of mankind. In the consummation of this high purpose, we, as victors in the administration of the vanquished, stand charged to proceed in that full unity of purpose which characterized our common effort in the war just won.

It is no small hindrance that in reaching this goal there are those throughout the Allied world who lift their voices in sharp and ill-conceived criticism of our occupational policies; some, honestly inspired but with no knowledge of conditions existing in this far distant land, who would see applied here wholly unadaptable principles and methods; some who, lacking both vision and patience, see but the end desired, being blind to the means without which that end is impossible of achievement; some who opposed the guiding principles adopted at Potsdam and who, unwilling now to join in full unity of purpose, seek to foment dissatisfaction in others to the end that such principles be reshaped to their will, or other implementation be impeded; some who, from selfish motives, will exploit as slaves a thoroughly defeated nation and people, thus serving the identical policy of evil which Allied soldiers opposed unto death on the battlefields of the world; and some who, for various reasons, are out of sympathy with Allied policies and aims, and seek to sabotage success of the occupation.

To the people of the Allied world I would say, in answer to such criticism, that history has given us no precedent of success in a similar military occupation of a defeated nation - anywhere, at any time - to serve as a guide to assist in reshaping and to meet the aims to which we are here solemnly committed. It thus has become necessary for us, in meeting that challenge of the past, to devise new guiding principles and new methods by which to solve the problems of the future. To serve this purpose, a wise and farseeing policy was formulated at Potsdam, fully attuned to the noble ideals, principles, and standards in defense of which the Allied nations firmly and in complete unity took their stand. Through our implementation of that policy lies best hope that the errors responsible for the failures of past occupations may be avoided in the task to which we are here no less inseparably dedicated. The road ahead is not an easy one, but it is my firm purpose that, within the underlying precepts governing occupational policy, the objective be reached. I fervently hope that each member of the Council will exert his best effort to support of that purpose, eliminating insofar as possible misconceptions which but sow the seeds of disunity and serve the cause of failure.

A new Constitution has been evolved, patterned along liberal and democratic lines, which the Japanese Government intends to submit for consideration to the next incoming National Diet. This proposed new Constitution is being well and freely discussed by the Japanese people, who show a healthy disposition to subject all provisions thereof to critical public examination through the media of press and radio. Regardless of changes in form and detail which may well result from this open form of public debate and the ultimate consideration of the National Diet and the Allied

Powers, if the underlying principles remain substantially the same when finally adopted, the instrument will provide the structure that will permit development in Japan of a democratic state, fully conforming to existing Allied policy. If we are firmly to implement that policy, it is incumbent upon us to encourage and assist the Japanese people in re-shaping their lives and institutions thereunder - scrupulously avoiding superficial and cynical criticism of motive or purpose and destructive influence upon their will to do just that which it is our firm purpose they shall do. While the drafting of an acceptable constitution does not of its~f establish democracy, which is a thing largely of the spirit, it does provide the design for both structural and spiritual changes in the national life, without which so fundamental a reform would be utterly impossible. With it there is hope for accomplishing that reshaping of national and individual character essential to form the strong foundation of popular spirit upon which a democratic state must rest. It is yet too early to predict to what degree changes embodied in such reform will become fixed in the social and political life of Japan. It is inescapably true, however, that the course thus charted to the fulfillment of Allied policy in the democratization of Japan is the only course that points to success - that the degree of that success will depend in a large measure upon the patience and encouragement with which we ourselves are willing to endow the test.

While all provisions of this proposed new Constitution are of importance, and lead individually and collectively to the desired end as expressed at Potsdam, I desire especially to mention that provision dealing with the renunciation of war. Such renunciation, while in some respects a logical sequence to the destruction of Japan's war-making potential, goes yet further in its surrender of the sovereign right of resort to arms in the international sphere. Japan thereby proclaims her faith in a society of nations governed by just, tolerant, and effective rules of universal social and political morality and entrusts its national integrity thereto. The cynic may view such action as demonstrating but a childlike faith in a visionary ideal, but the realist will see in it far deeper significance. He will understand that in the evolution of society it became necessary for man to surrender certain rights theretofore inherent in himself in order that states might be created vested with sovereign power over the individuals who collectively formed them - that foremost of these inherent rights thus surrendered to the body politic was man's right to resort to force in the settlement of disputes with his neighbor. With the advance of society, groups or states federated together through identical process of surrendering inherent rights and submitting to a sovereign power representing the collective will. In such manner was formed the United States of America, through the renunciation of rights inherent in individual States in order to compose the national sovereignty; the State first recognized and stood guarantor for the integrity of the individual and thereafter the Nation recognized and stood guarantor for the integrity of the State.

The proposal of the Japanese Government - a Government over people who now have reason to know the complete failure of war as an instrument of national policy - in effect but recognizes one further step in the evolution of mankind, under which nations would develop, for mutual protection against war, yet higher law of international, social, and political morality. Whether the world is yet ready for so forward a step in the relations between nations, or whether another and totally destructive war - a war involving almost mass extermination - must first be waged, is the great issue which now confronts all peoples.

There can be no doubt that both the progress and survival of civilization is dependent upon the timely recognition of the imperative need for some such forward step - is dependent upon the realization by all nations of the utter futility of force as an arbiter of international issues - is dependent upon elimination from international relations of the suspicion, distrust, and hatred which inevitably result from power threats, boundary violation, secret maneuvering, and violence to public morality - is dependent upon a world leadership which does not lack the moral courage to implement the will of the masses who abhor war and upon whom falls the main weight of war's frightful carnage - and finally is dependent upon the development of a world order which will permit a nation such as Japan safely to entrust its national integrity to just such a higher law to which all peoples on earth shall render themselves subservient. Therein lies the road to lasting peace.

I therefore commend Japan's proposal for the renunciation of war to the thoughtful consideration of all of the peoples of the world. It points the way and the only way. The United Nations Organization, admirable as is its purpose, great and noble as are its aims, can only survive to achieve that purpose and those aims if it accomplishes as to all nations just what Japan proposes unilaterally to accomplish through this Constitution - abolish war as a sovereign right. Such a renunciation must be simultaneous and universal. It must be all or none. It must be effected by action - not words alone - and open, undisguised action which invites the confidence of all men who would serve the cause of peace. The present instrumentality to enforce its will - the pooled armed might of its component nations - can at best be but temporary expedient so long as nations still recognize as coexistent the sovereign right of belligerency. No thoughtful man will fail to recognize that with the development of modern science another war may blast mankind to perdition - but still we hesitate - still we cannot, despite the yawning abyss at our very feet, unshackle ourselves from the past. Therein lies the childlike faith in the future - a faith that, as in the past, the world can somehow manage to survive yet another universal conflict. In that irresponsible faith lies civilization's gravest peril.

We sit here in Council, representatives of the military might and moral strength of the modern world. It is our responsibility and our purpose to consolidate and strengthen the peace won at the staggering cost of war. As we thus deal in the international sphere with some of the decisive problems I have but briefly outlined, it is incumbent upon us to proceed on the high level of universal service that we may do our full part toward restoring the rule of reason to international thought and action. Thereby may we further universal adherence to that higher law in the preservation of peace which finds full and unqualified approval in the enlightened conscience of all the peoples of the earth.

Addressing the first meeting of the Allied Council for Japan, Tokyo, April 5, 1946.

PHILIPPINE INDEPENDENCE DAY
JULY 4, 1946
MANILA, THE PHILIPPINES

Mr. High Commissioner, Mr. President, Ladies and Gentlemen:

With this ceremony a new nation is born - a nation conceived in the centuries old struggle of a people to attain the political liberty to embark upon its own national destiny - a nation dedicated to the furtherance of those rights and those principles which serve to compose and advance man's dignity upon the earth - a nation upon whom the eyes of all oppressed peoples are today cast with the burning light of a new faith.

Forty-eight years ago, the mantle of American sovereignty fell over this land and this people. It was the beneficent sovereignty of a liberator pledged to be withdrawn as soon as the well-being of the people would safely permit. America never wavered in that purpose - America today redeems that pledge.

For forty-eight years our Army has stood on these shores. An Army of free men dedicated to humanity's higher service, its role has never been to rule, never been to subjugate, never been to oppress. These years have seen many men come and go - men truly representing a cross section of that land beyond the seas who brought with them a better understanding of the West and carried back with them a better understanding of the East - and through it all helped develop a relationship of mutual understanding, mutual respect and mutual affection. The qualities which now bind our two peoples together, founded upon a community of interest and dedication to common purposes and common ideals, will not diminish with the sovereign change this day has wrought. For forty-eight years, as our two peoples have marched forward, shoulder to shoulder toward a common destiny, through the bitterness of war and the oft times onerous adversities of peace, a purposeful relationship has welded which will not yield to sovereignty, nor to any man-made convention, nor to any artificial political distinction - a relationship which will last forever.

For forty-eight years since my father first led our army down Singalong Road to liberate this great city of Manila, close identification with you has been my personal privilege. Through these years I have witnessed with admiration your magnificent progress in self-sufficiency and your long, earnest and unyielding aspiration for independence. Through these years of steady and advancing preparation, by your resolute perseverance in holding firmly to the course long charted by the architects of your political future despite seem-

Independence Day Ceremony, Manila, The Philippines, July 4, 1946.

ing unsurmountable obstacles which barred the way, the world must bear witness that you have earned the right that this day of destiny might be.

Let history record this event in flaming letters as depicting a new height of nobility in the relationship between two separate and distinct peoples of the earth - peoples of the East and peoples of the West. Despite racial, cultural and language differences and great distances of geographical separation, they forged an affinity of understanding which survived both the vagaries of peace and the shock of war. They shattered for all time the deceptive philosophy that "East is East and West is West, and never the twain shall meet," by demonstrating, through complete and effective cohesion, that peoples of the East and peoples of the West had common cause in human progress - and can live together and work together and strive together toward a common destiny.

Let history record this event in the sweep of democracy through the earth as foretelling the end of mastery over peoples by power of force alone - the end of empire as the political chain which binds the unwilling weak to the unyielding strong. Let it be recorded as one of the great turning points in the advance of civilization in the age-long struggle of man for liberty, for dignity, and for human betterment.

As this infant republic stands at the threshold of an adventure in the society of other nations upon an identical sovereign plane, its political destiny depends upon the courage and wisdom of its leadership and the unity of its people.

Never in history have more vital and complex issues stirred mankind than today. Never have issues weighed more heavily upon the destiny of the human race. In their solution, this new republic will be called upon to take its stand. God grant that it may raise its voice firmly and fearlessly in alignment with those great forces of right which seek to avoid the destructive influences which, despite our past victories, still harass the world.

I rejoice with you that your great political goal has this day been reached, and shall watch your forward march under the banner of your own sovereignty with deep pride in the achievements of your past and with abiding confidence in those of your future. In behalf of the great Army which I here represent, I stand at salute to the Republic and the people who proudly compose it - this land, this people that I have known so long and loved so well.

EULOGY FOR PRESIDENT MANUEL QUEZON
ON THE REINTERMENT OF HIS BODY IN MANILA
AUGUST 1, 1946

The personal friendship of General MacArthur and President Manuel Quezon was a close and long-standing one, going back to MacArthur's first tour of duty in the Philippines, in 1903. It was Quezon who gave the General the opportunity to build the Philippine Army in 1936. Their collaboration in the dark days of 1941-42 deepened the regard of each for the other. It was a source of great regret to MacArthur that President Quezon did not live to see his homeland liberated from the Japanese. His old friend had died of tuberculosis in the United States less than three months before the Leyte landings. The eulogy that follows was prepared for the occasion of the return of President Quezon's body for burial in the Republic he had done so much to bring into existence.

Major Vorin E. Whan, Jr., USA, Editor
A Soldier Speaks: Public Papers and Speeches of General of the Army Douglas MacArthur
© 1965, Frederick A. Praeger, Publishers, New York, NY

It is a source of deepest regret that my duties in the occupation of Japan at this critical moment have not permitted me personally to be present reverently to pay homage at the final rites over the bier which contains the mortal remains of President Quezon. He was my dear friend of long years, and it was my privilege to share with him many of the varying conditions which have beset human life during our age. And in this tragic moment, as we close the scrolls of his life and works and hearken to their profound and controlling influence upon the destiny of his people, I attest to and join in the applauding judgment of history of the path of duty he strode upon this earth.

Of all men of all time, none more truly merited the appellation of patriot-statesman. Few could, as did he, replace the uniform of the soldier with the mantle of statescraft, yet maintain with voice and pen in undiminished vigor the crusading fight in the self-same cause for which he had fought by the violence of arms.

Throughout his long years of public service, never did he compromise the principle which he thus espoused - never did he divert his gaze from the goal which he thus resolutely sought. That he lived to bring its realization in full sight be-speaks the unconquerable determination with which he endowed his lofty purpose. That his native land now stands as one of the free and independent nations of the world is responsive, more than to all else, to the indomitable will by which he developed in the conscience of his people a firm belief in their destiny as a race, and an unshakable conviction that they lacked not the capacity fully to support independent sovereignty once attained.

Two years ago, while preparing to join in the final blow for his people's liberation, death forever closed his lips and stayed his pen, but the immortal spirit which sustains his soul remains forever a dominant influence upon the destiny of the Republic for which he gave so much.

His hours of life were full - hours of peace and hours of war - of anguish and of joy - of defeat and of victory - and, as with all men, of failure and of success - the rattle of musketry as he fought through the uncharted mountain wilderness to seek by war what he later won by peace - the bitter gall of defeat and surrender - the University cloisters where he learned of Christianity, of Western culture, of tradition, and of the law - the shifting fortunes of political struggle as he rose steadily to the fame of position and power - those great crusades he conducted beyond the seas - his advocacy and his success in the cause of Philippine independence - the clouds of war spreading over the Orient - the swirl of enemy bombers - the crash of death and blood and disaster - again the bitterness of defeat - then the exultation, with the rising tide of victory, as he saw our armies standing on the road back six hundred miles from Philippine soil - followed by still waters and silence.

His soul being before the seat of Almighty God, judge of all men and of all things, Manuel Quezon's mortal remains are now committed to the tender care of the people he loved so deeply and served so well - his cherished own. Father of this infant Republic, which he planned but never saw, he has returned - he has come home forever.

STATEMENT ON THE FIRST ANNIVERSARY OF THE SIGNING OF THE JAPANESE SURRENDER AGREEMENT SEPTEMBER 2, 1946

During the Japanese occupation, General MacArthur issued statements on various occasions summarizing the progress in the rebuilding of Japan. At the end of the first year of occupation, the job of demilitarizing the Japanese was well advanced, but the form of the reconstruction had not yet been clearly established.
Major Vorin E. Whan, Jr., USA, Editor
A Soldier Speaks: Public Papers and Speeches of General of the Army Douglas MacArthur
© 1965, Frederick A. Praeger, Publishers, New York, NY

A year has now passed since the surrender terms were signed on the battleship *Missouri*. Much has been accomplished since then - much still remains to be done. But over all things and all men in this sphere of the universe hangs the dread uncertainty arising from impinging ideologies which now stir mankind. For our homeland there is no question, and for the homelands of others, free as are we to shape their own political order, there is no question. But which concept will prevail over these lands now being redesigned in the aftermath of war? This is the great issue which confronts our task in the problem of Japan - a problem which profoundly affects the destiny of all men and the future course of all civilization.

The philosophy underlying the first year of occupation was written at Potsdam and reaffirmed on the *Missouri*. It is a simple philosophy embodying principles of right and justice and decency - those social qualities in human relationship which through the ages have animated free men and those who longed to be free. Its impact and its lasting imprint upon the Japanese character and conscience and mind can only properly be visualized and assayed by an understanding of the Japanese philosophy evolved through generations of feudalistic life.

For centuries the Japanese people, unlike their neighbors in the Pacific basin - the Chinese, the Malayans, the Indians and the whites - have been students and idolaters of the art of war and the warrior caste. They were the natural warriors of the Pacific. Unbroken victory for Japanese arms convinced them of their invincibility, and the keystone of the entire arch of their civilization became an almost mythological belief in the strength and wisdom of the warrior caste. It permeated and controlled not only all branches of government but all branches of life - physical, mental and spiritual. It was interwoven not only into all government pro-

cess but into all phases of daily routine. It was not only the essence but the actual warp and woof of Japanese existence. Control was exercised by a feudalistic overlordship of a mere fraction of the population, while the remaining seventy million, with a few enlightened exceptions, were abject slaves to tradition, legend, mythology and regimentation. During the progress of the war, these seventy million heard of nothing but Japanese victories and the bestial qualities of Japan's opponents. Then they suddenly felt the concentrated shock of total defeat. Their whole world crumbled. It was not merely an overthrow of their military might - not merely a great defeat for their nation - it was the collapse of a faith, it was the disintegration of everything they had believed in and lived by and thought for. It left a complete vacuum morally, mentally and physically. And into this vacuum flowed the democratic way of life. The American combat soldier came with his fine sense of self-respect, self-confidence and self-control. They saw and felt his spiritual quality - a spiritual quality which truly reflected the highest training of the American home. The falseness of their former teachings, the failure of their former leadership, and the tragedy of their past faith were infallibly demonstrated in actuality and realism. A spiritual revolution ensued which almost overnight tore asunder a theory and practice of life built upon two thousand years of history and tradition and legend. Idolatry for their feudalistic masters and the warrior caste was transformed into hatred and contempt, and the hatred and contempt once felt for their foe gave way to honor and respect. This revolution of the spirit among the Japanese people represents no thin veneer to serve the purposes of the present. It represents an unparalleled convulsion in the social history of the world. The measure of its strength and durability lies in the fact that it represents a sound idea. Given encouragement and the opportunity to develop, it can become more deep-seated and lasting than the foundations upon which their false faith was built.

It represents, above all else, the most significant gain during the past year of occupation - a gain for the forces of democracy in furtherance of a durable peace, which must be consolidated and extended if we would discharge our responsibility as victory has given us that responsibility. Its underlying concept, new to Japan but fashioned from the enlightened knowledge and experience of the free of the world, will remain the cornerstone to Japanese freedom unless uprooted and suppressed by the inroads of some conflicting ideology which might negate individual freedom, destroy individual initiative and mock individual dignity. Ideologies of extreme too often gain converts and support from true liberals, misguided by slanted propaganda and catch phrases which hold as "reactionary" all things which spring from the underlying concept of the past. Such propaganda seeks too often to exploit the knowledge common to all men that sociological and political changes from time to time are mandatory if we would keep our social system abreast of the advance of civilization.

Should such a clash of ideologies impinge more directly upon the reorientation of Japanese life and thought, it would be no slight disadvantage to those who seek, as intended at Potsdam, the great middle course of moderate democracy, that a people so long regimented under the philosophy of an extreme conservative right might prove easy prey to those seeking to impose a doctrine leading again to regimentation, under the philosophy of an extreme radical left.

If we would in the furtherance of this task guide the Japanese people the more firmly to reshape their lives and institutions in conformity with those social precepts and political standards best calculated to raise the well-being of the individual and to foster and preserve a peaceful society, we must adhere unerringly to the course now charted - destroying here what yet should be destroyed, preserving here what should be preserved, and erecting here what should be erected. This will require all of the patience, all of the determination, and all of the statemanship of democratic peoples. The goal is great - for the strategic position of these Japanese Islands renders them either a powerful bulwark for peace or a dangerous springboard for war.

MESSAGE TO THE WAR DEPARTMENT IN SUPPORT OF CONGRESSIONAL APPROPRIATIONS FOR THE OCCUPATION OF JAPAN FEBRUARY 20, 1947

Part of the Allied control over Japan after the war included a continued economic blockade, which led to severe food shortages in the autumn of 1946. General MacArthur diverted for the use of the Japanese people large quantities of Army food which had been stockpiled in the Pacific. Some members of the Congress questioned utilization of Army appropriations to feed former enemies. When he was asked for an explanation by the War Department, General MacArthur sent the following reply.

Major Vorin E. Whan, Jr., USA, Editor
A Soldier Speaks: Public Papers and Speeches of General of the Army Douglas MacArthur
© 1965, Frederick A. Praeger, Publishers, New York, NY

There is a popular misconception that the achievement of victory in modern war, wherein a clash of ideologies is involved, is solely dependent upon victory in the field. History itself clearly refutes this concept. It offers unmistakable proof that the human impulses which generated the will to war, no less than the material sinews of war, must be destroyed. Nor is it sufficient that such human impulses merely yield to the temporary shock of military defeat. There must be a complete spiritual reformation, such as will not only control the defeated generation but will exert a dominant influence upon the generations to follow as well. Unless this is done, victory is but partially complete and offers hope for little more than an armistice between one campaign and the next - as the great lesson and warning of experience is that victorious leaders of the past have too often contented themselves with the infliction of military defeat upon the enemy power, without extending that victory by dealing with the root causes which led to war as an inevitable consequence.

Thus in the occupation of Japan, while we have destroyed Japan's war-making power and neutralized from a material standpoint its war-making potential, we are yet in the process of finalizing the victory that the ensuing peace at war's great cost may be vital and real. This will require a complete reformation of the Japanese people - reformation from feudalistic slavery to human freedom, from the immaturity that comes of mythical teachings and legendary ritualism to the maturity of enlightened knowledge and truth, from the blind fatalism of war to the considered realism of peace.

In the accomplishment of this purpose, all policy in the ad-ministration of the occupation is attuned to those very ideals for which we fought - that by example we may point the way. This in turn is infusing in the Japanese mind both an understanding of and an enthusiasm for our own concept in human relationship - a concept which embodies within itself a spiritual repugnance to war.

If we are successful in the accomplishment of this purpose, we shall not only have finalized the victory by bringing under control basic causes of war, but we shall have erected here in the Western Pacific a strong bulwark against the reappearance and spread of those same causes which are calculated to plunge the world into future war - for history has shown the futility of dependence upon the violence of war alone to preserve the peace. This is the stake for which we strive.

It is yet too early to measure the degree of final success, but Japan is now already governed by the form of democratic rule and the people are absorbing its substance. They have learned by the hard way the futility of resort to arms for individual and national advancement, and appear to have completely assimilated this bitter lesson. Having repudiated war and renounced all rights of belligerency, they have placed their full reliance for future protection on the good faith and justice of mankind, and are proceeding through legislated reform to develop here a state dedicated, in full reality, to the welfare of the people. Given encouragement, this can prove the exemplification of the superiority, in the advancement of the human race, of moral force, generated by spiritual strength, over physical force, with all resources employed for constructive rather than destructive purposes. A spontaneous development which offers both encouragement and inspiration as a measure of the progress of this concept lies in the increasing number of the Japanese people - already estimated at over two million - who, under the stimulus of religious tolerance and freedom, have moved to embrace the Christian faith as a means to fill the spiritual vacuum left in Japanese life by collapse of their past faith. This is partially responsive to the opportunity for comparison between the qualities of the old and the new - to an understanding of those principles of tolerance, justice and human decency which govern our action in the tragedy of their defeat - and, more particularly, from close-hand observation of the American soldier, standing in their midst, reflecting, as he does, those fine traits of character, outgrowth of the American home. Through the firm encouragement and strengthening of this yet frail spearhead of Christianity in the Far East lies hope that to hundreds of millions of backward peoples, now easy prey to the ignorant fatalism of war, may come a heretofore unknown spiritual strength based upon an entirely new concept of human dignity and human purpose and human relationship - the very antithesis to those evil attributes which throughout history have led to war.

The American forces committed to occupational duty in Japan, now cut to only a fraction of their former strength, are at the lowest numerical level consistent with either reasonable security or the accomplishment of the regeneration of an entire race from its traditional threat to peace to a powerful bulwark against the recurrence of war - with its orderly emergence from the chaos of destructive defeat to economic, political and social stability. And highlighting all else, of course, lies the grave responsibility of protecting our national security against future threat to our Pacific Coast. In short, the consolidation of the gains which victory has brought, that we may have peace. Our task is thus but a final phase of war, and it is inescapable that its avoidance may only be at the expense of victory itself.

In war the complete blockade of a force dependent for food and other supply from outside sources is the most effective weapon known to military science. It was through the use of this weapon that our starving men on Bataan and Corregidor were finally forced to yield to the enemy hordes who surrounded them. It was through the use of this same weapon, more than any other, that the Japanese armed forces were finally brought to the futility of further resistance, as segment after segment of their extended positions, by envelopment, were cut off from needed supplies on the grim road back. Thereafter, when reconquest of the Philippines completely severed the Japanese war-gained Empire and permitted a blockade of the Japanese home islands themselves, traditionally dependent for sustenance from sources without, total collapse became imminent.

Since the surrender this blockade of the Japanese home islands has been continued, extended, and intensified. Not only have Manchuria, Korea and Formosa, long contributors to Japanese sustenance, been taken away but many millions of Japanese citizens have been repatriated from the outside back into these four home islands. Trade and financial intercourse with the rest of the world is by our decree so prohibited as to constitute economic strangulation.

Cut off from our own projected relief supplies in these circumstances, countless Japanese would face starvation - and starvation breeds mass unrest, disorder and violence. Worse still, it renders a people easy prey to any ideology, however evil, which bears with it life-sustaining food. To permit such a condition to arise would be to repudiate those very ideals and principles on which our country has always stood and for which many of our countrymen selflessly have died. For under the responsibilities of victory the Japanese people are now our prisoners, no less than did the surviving men on Bataan become their prisoners when that peninsula fell. As a consequence of the ill treatment, including starvation, of Allied prisoners in Japanese hands, we have tried and executed many Japanese officers upon proof of responsibility. Yet can we justify such punitive action if we ourselves in reversed circumstances, but with hostilities at end, fail to provide the food to sustain life among those Japanese people over whom we now stand guard within the narrow confines of their home islands?

Nor must sight be lost of the circumstances under which such food and other emergency relief supplies are provided. There is involved an appropriation of public funds only for the purpose of their acquisition, the corresponding cost becoming thereafter a charge against Japan, which should be protected by a first lien on every asset within Japan. It is not charity, nor have I found that the Japanese want charity. It is but a means to secure needed life-preserving sustenance until such time as we ourselves relax the restrictions which now prevent Japan from securing the same by the normal methods of trade and commerce with the other nations of the world. Nor, if reasonable precautions are taken, will the American taxpayer ultimately be out of pocket a single dollar as a result.

At most it is but a temporary measure in discharge of a clear responsibility which victory has imposed. It must be and remain our firm purpose to restore peace and normalcy at the very earliest time practicable, and it is my full intention to recommend removal of the existing military controls over Japan just as soon as civilian controls safely may be substituted. History points out the unmistakable lesson that military occupations serve their purpose at best only for a limited time, after which a deterioration rapidly sets in - deterioration of the populace in an occupied country which becomes increasingly restive under the deprivation of personal freedom, inherent in such a situation - and deterioration of the occupying forces which in time assume a dominant power complex pointing to the illusion of a master race.

While I have herein discussed our national responsibilities of occupation largely from the viewpoint of Japan, much that I have said applies with even more poignant force to Korea, wherein our public commitment to assist in the establishment of a stable free government, for a friendly people liberated by Allied arms, imposes upon us an even more solemn obligation.

I am in fullest accord with the desire of the American Congress to practice the most rigid economy in the administration of government which our national interests reasonably may permit. Economy in both blood and supply was a rule which guided every strategic plan in the prosecution of our phase of the Pacific war - and economy has since been the rule here in the extension and consolidation of victory. A rationalization of the cost involved in this great task shows it to be, in the aggregate, infinitesimal compared with that which might have been incurred in a comparable period of extended combat.

I have observed the workings of the American Congress for many years, and have never seen it hesitate vigorously to preserve and advance our American interests. When provided with full knowledge of the situation, I do not believe, therefore, that it will take any action which would prejudice fulfillment of occupation objectives, to which we are already committed and in honor bound, as a prerequisite to finalizing the victory and insuring the peace.

STATEMENT ON THE POST-SURRENDER POLICY FOR JAPAN ADOPTED BY THE FAR EASTERN COMMISSION JULY 13, 1947

The primary objective of American occupation policy was to insure that Japan did not become a military threat to the free nations of the world. To some people, this meant simply the disarmament of the former enemy. General MacArthur, from the start of the occupation, realized that reorientation of the whole Japanese society was more important to long-term chances for peace in the Pacific than a punitive disarmament. He was, therefore, very pleased when the Far Eastern Commission, composed of representatives of the eleven nations that fought against Japan, adopted a liberal policy for Japanese reconstruction. With this sign of Allied support, he could predict confidently that the peace would be won in the Pacific.

Major Vorin E. Whan, Jr., USA, Editor
A Soldier Speaks: Public Papers and Speeches of General of the Army Douglas MacArthur
© 1965, Frederick A. Praeger, Publishers, New York, NY

The policy decision just adopted by the Far Eastern Commission dealing with the post-surrender treatment of the Japanese problem is one of the greater state papers of modern history. It establishes definitely the type, the extent, and the scope of Japan's future, and the position the Japanese nation shall occupy in relation to the world at large. It not only ratifies the course which thus far has been taken, but signifies a complete unity of future purpose among the eleven nations and peoples concerned. It at once sweeps aside fears currently felt that the great nations of the world are unable to reconcile divergent views on such vital issues in the international sphere and demonstrates with decisive clarity that from an atmosphere of conflicting interests and opposing predilections may emerge common agreement founded upon experience and shaped to a realistic appreciation of world conditions and the basic requirements of a progressive civilization. For in this agreement have been firmly resisted two insidious concepts, poles apart but equally sinister - the one which would seek harsh and unjust treatment of our fallen foe, and the other which would seek partially to preserve and perpetuate institutions and leadership which bear responsibility of war guilt. The first would have produced a mendicant country dependent upon charity to live, while the second would have encouraged the regrowth of anti-democratic forces with the consequent revival of international distrust and suspicion. It confirms by the considered action of the representatives of the Allied nations a sound moderate course based upon a concept embodying firmness but justice, disarmament but rehabilitation, lower standards but the opportunity for life - a concept shunning both the extreme right and the extreme left and providing for the great middle way of the ordinary man.

The basic and easily the most essential requirement of the policy - disarmament and demilitarization - has already been fully accomplished. Even were there no external controls, Japan could not rearm for modern war within a century. This primary objective has led all aims in the occupation of Japan. Japanese military forces have been disarmed, demobilized, and absorbed in peaceful pursuits, and Japan's remaining war potential has either been destroyed or completely neutralized. The political and economic phases of the disarmament program have been effected through the dissolution of the alliance long existing between government and industry, the breaking up of monopolistic combines and practices which have suppressed private enterprise, and the raising of the individual to a position of dignity and hope, with provision made for a new leadership untainted by war responsibility and both mentally and spiritually equipped to further democratic growth. The transition stage of destroying those evil influences which misguided Japan's past has been virtually completed and the course has been set upon which Japan is now embarked toward a peaceful and constructive future. We thus see here the transformation of a state which once proclaimed its mastery of war into one which from material improverishment and spiritual dedication now seeks its destiny as a servant of peace.

This action representing the agreement of the Allied nations engaged in the Pacific war not only confirms the post-surrender policies previously evolved and largely implemented, but it establishes at the same time a norm for the restoration of peace. Resting squarely upon those same principles and ideals written at Potsdam, reaffirmed on the *Missouri,* and subsequently translated into action in the occupation of Japan, this accord provides the entire framework for a treaty of peace - a treaty which, if it is to be faithfully honored, should constitute within itself a charter of human liberty to which the Japanese citizen will look for guidance and protection, rather than shun with the revulsion of shame - a treaty which, without yielding firmness in its essential mandates, should avoid punitive, arbitrary and unrealistic provisions, and by its terms set the pattern for future peace throughout the world. It should in full reality mark the restoration of a peace based upon justice, goodwill and human advancement. Such a treaty may now be approached with the assurance of complete understanding in principle and full unity of purpose in evolving its detail.

Viewing this international accord in the light of the great strides made by the Japanese themselves toward the achievement of those very objectives which it prescribes, without confusion, without disorder, and with steady progress toward economic recovery despite the destruction of war and defeat, it becomes unmistakably clear that here in Japan we shall win the peace.

MESSAGE FROM MACARTHUR
READ BY THE MAYOR OF HIROSHIMA
AT THE PEACE FESTIVAL
MARKING THE SECOND ANNIVERSARY
OF THE DROPPING OF THE FIRST ATOMIC BOMB
AUGUST 6, 1947

The Japanese people, more than any other, have reason to know the full impact of the nuclear era. To MacArthur, Hiroshima's experience was a plain warning to mankind that war's destructiveness had reached the ultimate.

Major Vorin E. Whan, Jr., USA, Editor
A Soldier Speaks: Public Papers and Speeches of General of the Army Douglas MacArthur
© 1965, Frederick A. Praeger, Publishers, New York, NY

Two years ago the shadow of mounting violence overhung the earth, and men and races and continents desperately struggled to resolve the issues of war. Then, over Hiroshima was launched a yet mightier weapon, and warfare assumed a new meaning in deadliness and destruction, and the agonies of that fateful day serve as warning to all men of all races that the harnessing of nature's forces in furtherance of war's destructiveness will progress until the means are at hand to exterminate the human race and destroy the material structure of the modern world. This is the lesson of Hiroshima. God grant that it be not ignored.

STATEMENT ON THE SECOND ANNIVERSARY OF V-J DAY SEPTEMBER 2, 1947

After two years of occupation, the guidelines being followed in the reorientation of Japan were well established. The chief architect of this plan stressed the moral issues involved in the Japanese renaissance in his anniversary report on the progress of the occupation.

Major Vorin E. Whan, Jr., USA, Editor
A Soldier Speaks: Public Papers and Speeches of General of the Army Douglas MacArthur
© 1965, Frederick A. Praeger, Publishers, New York, NY

Two years have now passed since that fateful September 2nd on the *Missouri,* when the Allies on the one hand and the Japanese on the other entered into the solemn commitments underlying surrender conditions. It is unnecessary to restate the results of the ensuing occupation as they are now largely of historical record, but it is appropriate today to reflect upon the lesson learned, not alone in terms of the present and the immediate future, but more particularly its long-range influence upon the progress of civilization. For the opportunity here afforded to bring to a race, long stunted by ancient concepts of mythological teaching, the refreshing uplift of enlightenment and truth and reality, with practical demonstrations of Christian ideals, is of deep and universal significance.

During those two years, both sides - Allies and Japanese - have by adherence to the letter and spirit of their respective undertakings acquitted themselves honorably and well - and both have benefitted from the relationship. History records no other instance wherein the military occupation of a conquered people has been conducted with the emphasis placed, as it has been here, upon the moral values involved between victor and vanquished. Right rather than might has been the criterion. The fruits of this policy are now self-evident. Japan today stands out as one of the few places in a distraught world where, despite an economy of critically short supply, there is a minimum of fear, of confusion, and of unrest - where the people are diligently endeavoring to expiate the breach of the peace for which their nation stands universally condemned, to overcome the poverty left by war and defeat, and to elevate themselves to trusted and useful membership in the family of nations. Avoiding vengeance, intolerance, and injustice, Allied policy, apart from its rigidly destructive phase designed to eliminate from Japanese life both the will and the capacity to wage war, has rested squarely upon the fundamental concept which finds immortal exposition in the Sermon on the Mount. And by bringing into clear focus the commanding influence moral values thus have played in this relationship between nations and men, the results here attained invoke standards which might well be recognized and carried forward if the grave international issues which perplex mankind are to be resolved dispassionately in harmony and peace. There is no novelty in this simple concept, but too often it is ignored in the international sphere - betrayed through the misuse of power over the lives and destinies of others, with war the price the world inevitably has paid for this, man's greatest folly.

A peace treaty is shortly to be discussed. It is essential that it be approached in that same tolerant and just atmosphere to insure that this defeated country has the opportunity to become self-sustaining, rather than reduced to a condition of mendicancy. A post-treaty Japan should not become a burden upon the economy of any other country. For it is a well-tested historical truism that a people given a fair chance will reach the niche in human society to which their own industry, their own skill, and their own perseverance entitle them, without largess from others - that largess stultifies rather than quickens private initiative and individual energy, so essential to human progress. It is furthermore a false concept which contends that democracy can only thrive if maintained in plenty. On the contrary, history shows that it springs from hardship and struggle and toil, to flourish naturally in the hearts of men who cherish individual freedom and dignity - or not at all. A spiritual commodity, it is neither for purchase nor for sale.

There need be no concern over fears recently expressed of imminent economic collapse. It must be understood that the actual collapse of the Japanese economy, which was a major Allied war aim, occurred prior to the surrender as a result of attrition caused by the crushing force of Allied arms, the severance of Japan's lifelines abroad, the wresting from Japan of Manchuria, Korea, Formosa and the island groups mandated to her following the First World War, and the destruction of Japan's shipping afloat and her centers of industry and commerce at home. The economic prostration of the country was complete at the beginning of the occupation, industry then being at a practical standstill. In reality, since the surrender, under the guidance of the occupation and with American help, Japan has been gradually restoring her shattered economy and the curve is up not down. The industrial output has now risen to over 45 per cent of pre-war normal, and the improvement can be expected to continue. This relative stability, especially by comparison with more fortunately favored countries, and even under the blighting effects of practical blockade, has been one of the most amazing and encouraging features of the occupation period. To become self-supporting, however, it is essential that the economic isolation imposed by the Allies be modified so that trade with the outside world can be resumed.

If Japan in the post-treaty era is given a just opportunity to live in freedom and peace with her neighbors in the community of nations, there will be no threat to the survival and strengthening of the democratic processes here inaugurated under the occupation. For democracy, once firmly rooted in the human heart, has never voluntarily yielded before any other conflicting ideology known to man. If liberty and public morality do not bring national stability, nothing can.

MESSAGE TO THE PEOPLE OF JAPAN ON THE FIRST ANNIVERSARY OF THE NEW JAPANESE CONSTITUTION MAY 3, 1948

In 1947, after long deliberation by the Japanese Government, a new Constitusion was adopted to replace the old Meiji Constitution, which had virtually excluded the people of Japan from control of their own destiny. General MacArthur chose the first anniversary of the new Constitution as the opportunity to impress again upon the Japanese the importance of the individual's responsibility in a representative democracy. Although his message was directed at Japan's inexperienced democrats, it has relevance for the citizens of any democratic state.

Major Vorin E. Whan, Jr., USA, Editor
A Soldier Speaks: Public Papers and Speeches of General of the Army Douglas MacArthur
© 1965, Frederick A. Praeger, Publishers, New York, NY

One year ago your new Constitution became the supreme law of the land, and the cause of human freedom advanced as a mantle of personal dignity thereby fell upon every Japanese citizen. The people turned their eyes toward the dawn of a higher concept of life, heralded by a charter which provides the design for a political and social edifice resting upon the pillars of liberty and justice.

Adapted from the experience of the ages, this charter embodies the most enlightened advances in the concept of human relationship which civilization thus far has been able to evolve, and as it now stands it lags behind none in form, in substance, or in progressive thought. But the written word alone gives only indirect protection to the rights and privileges which it ordains. Such protection resides actually in the resolute will of the people in whom the sovereign power dwells. And no man is entitled to the blessings of freedom unless he be vigilant in its preservation and vigorous in its defense.

It is for the people, therefore, as empowered by its terms, to translate this charter into living and resourceful actuality, that the new Japanese way of life may be fashioned according to its general design, a workable and beneficent way of life which while fundamentally in complete harmony with Japanese character and culture and basic needs, yet overlooks no gain elsewhere made toward advancing human welfare. For the course of civililation is not static, and it is therefore for the Japanese people in shaping their own free destiny carefully to scrutinize the lessons history has taught in other lands and search for weak practices as well as strong, failure as well as success, in order that the way may be oriented to the best that experience provides. The concept of human freedom is immutable, but its translation into living actuality is subject to progressive advance as the minds of men find reorientation with enlightened knowledge and changing conditions with which society must cope.

Today great ideological issues are stirring mankind. These issues are clearly defined as between democracy and despotism - freedom and slavery. While the great majority of the peopies of the earth seek freedom, the forces of despotism, composed of willful minorities, are on the march in every land. Whether they be of the extreme left or of the extreme right makes little difference, for their purpose is to destroy freedom, and the two often exert pressure in common accord in the effort to achieve this purpose. While only minorities compose these pressure groups, they garner support from the ignorant, the gullible, and the weakminded. Their fundamental aim is to destroy the highly developed moral concepts of the modern world and to superimpose upon the ashes thereof a social system which experience has shown to be barren of truth and light, without hope or promise and bereft of faith, a system under which the masses of men are denied the fruits of their toil and the benefits of their skill to enrich a ruling few, neither responsive to the popular will nor dedicated to the public good. Defense against such minority pressure lies more than all else in the spiritual strength of the people and the unyielding firmness of their chosen leaders. For the lessons of contemporary history make it unmistakably clear that when peoples or their leaders shrink or yield before such pressure or permit invisible controls to be superimposed upon representative government by any minority groups whatsoever, governments fall and freedom perishes.

The past year has witnessed notable progress in the reshaping of Japanese life to confirm to Japan's constitutional mandates. The entire body of Japanese law has now been modified and the structure of government redesigned to render it a thoroughly democratic instrument, truly representative of the popular will. The highly centralized controls previously existing have been severed, with each community within the broad outline of the charter left the untrammelled right and fixed responsibility to manage its own affairs, exercise its own police power, and resolve its own peculiar social problems.

The very essence of democracy lies in the reservation of the maximum of political power in the people for exercise up through the smallest political subdivisions of government. Its antithesis lies in the concentration of the political power in the hands of a few for exercise down to the smallest political subdivisions of government. Japan, traditionally govrned under the latter, is now fully oriented toward the former as all segments of Japanese life, freed from arbitrary and oppressive centralized control, are becoming welded into strong and purposeful communities, which in common cause and for the common benefit will give vitality to a free nation. Ceaseless vigilance must be maintained to insure that the maximum of local autonomy is preserved if democracy, now firmly planted, is to survive.

The Japanese people are coming to understand, apply and cherish the rights and privileges conferred by the new Constitution. It is encouraging to note that care is being exercised to avoid the perversion of grants of liberty into seeming grants of license, and that there is a growing understanding that with every right and privilege conferred there is a corresponding obligation imposed - an obligation to exercise that right and privilege in such manner as to avoid violence to the rights and privileges of others. Every segment of Japanese society will find its authority for advance within the provisions of this great charter, and yet unrelaxed vigilance is necessary to insure that by operation of government no one segment advances at the expense of any other. Thus you will find that if you avoid conferring special privilege upon any one segment you will confer equal privilege uon all and the Constitution will thereby serve its avowed purpose of providing that equal protection shall be extended to every citizen of the land.

You have reoriented your economy toward a system based upon the principles of free competitive enterprise, and with it are reorganizing the concentration of economic power which long has suppressed any possibility for equality of opportunity, one of the great pillars to democratic life. And by wise and advanced laws you have safeguarded against any reversion to monopolistic control. If this course be firmly held and unceasing vigilance be maintained to hold to a minimum the burden of the expense of government uon the individual, you will leave unimpaired the incentive to maximized initiative and energy and the assumption of reasonable risks inherent in economic adventure, all essential to progress in a free economy.

It is heartening to observe a growing consciousness of public responsibility on the part of the people, as increasingly is heard the expression of public opinion. For the most effective curb upon excesses or corruption in government or any segment of Japanese life lies in an informed public opinion and its vigorous and fearless defense against threat to the public interest. An informed public opinion is dependent in turn upon a free, responsible and courageous press, and it is gratifying that the Japanese press during the past year has shown great progress in the development of those qualities. It appears increasingly to understand that in the constitutional guarantee of a free press, a responsible press is intended - a press which will play a vital role in the orientation of public opinion by propagating the truth in order that the people wherein sovereignty rests may make sound political decisions with minds uncorrupted by slanted, distorted or false propaganda.

The past year has witnessed impressive gains in the enhanced dignity and improved working conditions of labor. And both labor and management in the social struggles inherent in a society which is free are displaying a growing awareness of the fact that labor-management disputes involve triangular rather than bilateral interests, with the public interest by far the predominant one. In Japan with its economy of scarcity resulting from war and destruction no segment of society is without want and consequently many demands are understandably motivated by the wish for more of the fundamentals of life, but if a sound course is to be charted, each segment must realistically assess the resources available and measure its demands to correspond to its fair share. This necessitates more than all else responsible leadership and, on the part of the rank and file, ceaseless vigilance to insure that Japan's already meager resources be not imperiled by irresponsible action.

Japan today is a land of relative calm and purposeful effort in a turbulent and confused surrounding. That it is so reflects great credit upan the stamina, resiliency and deter-

mination of its people. So it must remain. For such a Japan with all effort dedicated to building a new and impregnable citadel of democracy in the East will provide its people with the blessings of a truly free way of life and thereby prove a factor for stability in a world torn by the uncertainties of confusion and fear.

ADDRESS AT THE CEREMONIES INAUGURATING THE REPUBLIC OF KOREA
AUGUST 15, 1948

The postwar development of the split between the Communist bloc and the free world led to the practical partition of Korea. This unfortunate nation had only recently been liberated from a Japanese occupation of almost forty-five years. The Communist-occupied north was unwilling to permit a free nationwide election, and in 1948, when it became obvious that the impasse might last indefinitely, South Korea was established as an Independent Republic. As he participated in the inaugural exercises, General MacArthur could not know that his pledge of American friendship would so soon be followed by the commitment of our military forces in a new Asiatic war.

Major Vorin E. Whan, Jr., USA, Editor
*A Soldier Speaks: Public Papers and Speeches of General
of the Army Douglas MacArthur*
© 1965, Frederick A. Praeger, Publishers, New York, NY

I am profoundly moved to stand on the soil of Korea in this historic hour, to see liberty reborn, the cause of right and justice prevail. For forty years I have observed with admiration the efforts of your patriots to cast off the oppressive bonds of foreign power. Their unyielding firmness in refusing to compromise with destiny the freedom of the Korean people has exemplified before the world the immutable truism that the spirit of liberty once infused in the human heart never dies.

Yet in this hour, as the forces of righteousness advance, the triumph is dulled by one of the great tragedies of contemporary history - an artificial barrier has divided your land. This barrier must and will be torn down. Nothing shall prevent the ultimate unity of your people as freemen of a free nation. Koreans come from too proud a stock to sacrifice their sacred cause by yielding to any alien philosophies of disruption.

As on this soil of the Asiatic mainland you face to the West where fear and threat and tragedy now fill men's minds, as peoples are locked in mortal combat and ideological pressures are exerted in search of weaknesses in freedom's armor, you must realize that events in the making here and beyond that Western horizon may well determine the issue of a world at peace or a world at war. For three years my country's guns have been silent as we have sought in concert with all other peoples to fashion from the moral resources of the modern world a norm of human relationship which effectively would preserve the peace. Our efforts have been retarded by an evil spirit of greed and avarice and lust for power, but your national rebirth today is living proof that the concept of human freedom is far too deeply rooted in human society to ever perish.

As you embark upon your destiny as a free and independent Republic, the measure of the wisdom of your chosen leaders will do much to provide the measure of your strength as a nation. If they secure the well-being of the individual and establish his position upon a plane of personal dignity with the opportunity of progress limited only by the nature and degree of his industry, you will evolve here a strong nation of happy and industrious citizens which will prove an impregnable bulwark against the assaults of all dissident elements. For the defense of the democratic way of life rests more than all else in the human spirit. He alone is fit to enjoy the blessings of personal liberty who is ready at all times resolutely to defend it.

The people of my country have long entertained a close friendship for the people of yours. As early as the year of 1882 in a treaty of amity and commerce between our two peoples, it was proclaimed that there should be "perpetual peace and friendship" between the United States and Korea. The American people have never deviated from this pledge and you may rely upon the invincible continuance of that friendship.

President Rhee, you and the distinguished group which has been chosen to assist you in the leadership of this infant Republic will face issues of the most complex nature known to political experience. The manner in which these issues are resolved will determine in large measure not only the unity and well-being of your own people but also the future stability of the continent of Asia. I have faith in you and your countrymen and pray that Almighty God may sustain you in your hallowed task.

MESSAGE TO THE UNITED NATIONS ASSOCIATION OF JAPAN, MEETING IN TOKYO
OCTOBER 24, 1949

Like most people, General MacArthur was convinced that general nuclear war would be a disaster for mankind. He was hopeful, despite increasing tensions between East and West that the United Nations might prove the way to continue peace. The following message was intended to assist the local organization in its effort to build Japanese support for the United Nations.

Major Vorin E. Whan, Jr., USA, Editor
A Soldier Speaks: Public Papers and Speeches of General of the Army Douglas MacArthur
© 1965, Frederick A. Praeger, Publishers, New York, NY

I express to you the deep conviction that the United Na-

Ceremonies inaugurating the Republic of Korea, August 15, 1948.

tions, the world's highest hope, is not the creation and the responsibility of a few talented men, but that it is, and rightfully should be, the fervent concern and active interest of all men of good will in every area of the earth. I could seek no greater reward and satisfaction from the burden of my office as Supreme Commander for the Allied Powers than that the United Nations become the fervent concern and active interest of every Japanese in the land.

The often weary and always difficult forward progress of the human race in government, has been a progress now slow, now more rapid, here slight, there considerable; but in its varied manifestations, certain uniformities are clear enough. The gains have come with the spread to more and more of the people of the enjoyment of their rights. The rights of the people have been best respected when the people themselves have been most vigilantly alert to acts of government.

The United Nations is no mirage. As a realistic organization its manifold activities already reach into wide fields, as the program sponsored here today will make abundantly clear. I commend to you a close scrutiny of what those activities are. I commend to you the declaration of human rights proclaimed by the General Assembly of December 10, 1948, for all the people of the world. Above all I commend to you the sobering thought, for your most intimate pondering and constant reflection, that the success of the United Nations, as of all great political organs, will depend upon the alertness of the common people of the world to its activities, the insistence of the common people of the world that its tasks be accomplished, and the readiness of the common people of the world to stand to its defense.

Statement on the Third Anniversary of the Japanese Constitution
May 3, 1950

As the Japanese people gained experience with democratic processes under their new Constitution, it soon became evident that the new system was taking root more rapidly than anyone had hoped. The Communist Party of Japan, tolerated as a legal political party, desperately tried to destroy the new democracy by subversive agitation. By 1950, its excesses had led the occupation authorities to consider what steps should be taken to keep the Communists from perverting the freedoms of democracy in order to destroy freedom itself. General MacArthur stressed this age-old problem of a democratic order in his anniversary message on the third birthday of the Constitution.

Major Vorin E. Whan, Jr., USA, Editor
A Soldier Speaks: Public Papers and Speeches of General of the Army Douglas MacArthur
© 1965, Frederick A. Praeger, Publishers, New York, NY

Today marks another anniversary of the birth of New Japan. On this day three years ago, groping for the way to regeneration through the human and material wreckage of war's after-math, the Japanese people firinly turned their backs upon a tradition founded upon myth and legend which had brought them to national disaster, and set a course instead along the enlightened road of truth and realism. In so doing they dedicated themselves to those immutable concepts of ethics and morality evolved through the ages by men who have sought the spiritual and material fruits of human freedom.

During the years which have since passed they have demonstrated a marked ability to live and advance within the frame-work of these great constitutional precepts. Their political progress under the established norms of representative democracy, their economic progress under the broad pattern of free private competitive enterprise, and their social progress through the ruin and despair of war's end, to the peace, serenity and hope which now prevails throughout the land, have provided a bright overtone to an otherwise distraught and confused post-war world.

The checks and balances established to safeguard against abuse of the powers conferred by the Constitution have firmly served their purpose during this period of political reorientation and democratic growth, and issues of interpretation and application have found their peaceful solution in the forum of public debate or under the established judicial process, rather than in the crucible of social violence. Above all, there has been an increasingly healthy awareness and acceptance of that individual political responsibility which exists where sovereignty rests with the people. In this, indeed, lies best assurance for Japan's continued advance as an exponent and practitioner of representative democracy. And as Japan goes, so in due time may go all of Asia. For men will come to see in Japan's bill of rights and resulting social progress the antidote to many of Asia's basic ills. If Japan proceeds firmly and wisely upon the course now set, its way may well become the Asian way, leading to the ultimate goal of all men - individual liberty and personal dignity - and history may finally point to the Japanese Constitution as the Magna Charta of free Asia.

While the checks and balances against abuse of the powers of government are thus demonstratively adequate, in Japan as elsewhere there exist only broad and undefinitive constitutional safeguards against abuse of those personal liberties conferred by the bill of rights. And in Japan as elsewhere this vulnerable point in freedom's armor is under constant pressure by a small minority which through the perversive use of liberty and privilege seeks to encompass freedom's destruction. This type of minority pressure is not unknown to Japan, and its people are therefore forewarned of the dreadful consequences possible therefrom. For in Japan's very recent past an even smaller minority - then the militarists and their collaborators - coerced the Japanese people into a war leading to inevitable and, indeed, foreseeable disaster. Now as they still grope to regain their equilibrium following that disastrous experience, this other minority, taking advantage of still unreplenished war-born impoverishment, seeks to lull their intuitive sense of caution into an even greater disaster - this time without even the pretense of service to legitimate national ends, but under foreign dictation to establish a domestic basis favorable to the ultimate subjugation of Japan to the political control of others.

Established in the immediate postwar era as a political partner under constitutional protection and dedicated to the advance of certain political, economic and social theories, the Japanese Communist Party proceeded initially in moderation and thereby enlisted some public support. In its endeavor to press this advantage, however, it went the way of all Communist movements, becoming increasingly intemperate in political and social activity, and in due course aroused a popular revulsion which in turn relegated the party into virtual political eclipse. More latterly its shattered remnant, in frustration born of this failure, has cast off the mantle of pretended legitimacy and assumed instead the role of an avowed satellite of an international predatory force and a Japanese pawn of alien power policy, imperialistic purpose and subversive propaganda. That it has done so at once brings into question its right to the further benefits and protection of the country and laws it would subvert and raises doubt as to whether it should longer be regarded as a constitutionally recognized political movement. Such doubt should, of course, be resolved calmly, justly and dispassionately with the same consideration and safeguards extended to any anti-social force in a peaceful and law-abiding community. The saying that to be forewarned is to be forearmed is particularly appropriate to this issue. For in the development of its counterparts abroad there is provided the opportunity clearly to observe the underlying objectives of this movement and the end to which it inevitably has led where it successfully has gained control over the sovereign power. Thus while here, as in the other democracies of the world, it professes championship of the workers' rights in order to enlist support within labor's ranks, events abroad demonstrate that the worker loses all rights under Communist political rule; where here as elsewhere it poses as an ardent advocate of freedom of speech and peaceful assembly, of freedom to worship in accordance with conscience, and of the other freedoms which flow from the universally recognized fundamental human rights, events irrefutably disclose the complete suppression of all freedom with the ascendancy of Communist political power. Indeed, history offers no slightest evidence of increase in social stability, preservation of social justice or continuation of social progress in the spiritual vacuum which lies in the wake of Communism's advance. Any thought that Japanese Communism might preserve a more moderate domestic course than characterizes the movement abroad was thoroughly disabused by its open submission to external control, its embarkation upon the spread of false, malicious and inflammatory propaganda intended to mislead and coerce the public mind, and its public adoption of objectives both anti-Japanese and inimical to Japan's public interest. Experience, the great teacher, indeed points to no greater hypocrisy than the perorations of those who thus align themselves with this form of international political perfidy, social deception, and territorial fraud and seek an alliance of expediency with the fundamental human rights, giving lip service to their preservation solely to provide a screen of respectable plausibility to mask a sinister subversive design to destroy liberty as the obstacle to personal power. The tragedy is that in every community it gains some converts among those citizens inherently law-abiding but mentally abnormal, frustrated, gullible or uninformed; and becomes because of this facade of respectability a seemingly responsible movement to which lawless elements may rally in order to fully exploit the vulnerable points inherent in democratic freedom.

There is involved no question of the privilege extended to all free people constitutionally to advocate evolutionary change, for Communism now makes but a shallow pretense of seeking such an objective. Its tactics are almost entirely confined to such as are conducive to arousing social unrest and public hysteria as the means toward establishing a more favorable base for ascendancy to political power. Its pressure is by no means localized to within national or regional borders, as through a high degree of centrally controlled direction and coordination of policy and tactic at the international level, it is able at will, from the principal capitals within the Communist orbit, to bring to bear upon individual areas of freedom the full power of its subversive attack. It employs this coordinated force with ruthlessness and cunning and seeks to reduce the spirituality which bulwarks modern civilization by exploiting weaknesses in detail as they appear. The problem thus rapidly confronting Japan, as other countries throughout the world, is how locally to deal with this anti-social force in order to prevent, without impairment of the legitimate exercise of personal liberty, such an abuse of freedom as to imperil the national welfare. Thus far, here as elsewhere, reliance has been placed in the counter-pressure of an aroused public opinion finding its expression at the ballot box where people of right have the opportunity to pass upon the responsibility of all aspirants for elective leadership. While this safeguard serves to arrest the danger of the emergence through constitutional means of a lawless and irresponsible leadership, it less adequately protects against the danger that the abusive use of freedom may create conditions of unrest and lawlessness favorable to the emergence of just such a leadership through intimidation and force.

The issue is therefore clear and unequivocal - how far may the fundamental human rights be exercised unabridged without becoming the instrument of their own destruction? It is an issue which confronts all free peoples, forewarned that others have lost their liberties because, blindly following an ideal, they have failed to see the dangers inherent in reality. While it is the universal desire of all free men to preserve unabridged the exercise of their personal liberties, there is thus an issue projected into every law-abiding society which may not be ignored without hazarding the survival of liberty itself. I have the utmost faith that should coming events presage the need for definitive action here to preserve the public welfare against the destructive potential of this form of insidious attack, the Japanese people will proceed with wisdom, serenity and justice, without failing the integrity of their Constitution.

MEMORANDUM FOR THE SOVIET MEMBER, ALLIED COUNCIL FOR JAPAN
JUNE 25, 1950

In dealing with the Soviet attempts to interfere in the occupation of Japan, MacArthur was more apt to speak bluntly than was the practice of some of the other U.S. representatives. In June, 1950, after a long series of provocations, the Communist Party and its newspaper were temporarily suppressed by General MacArthur. Their relief from suspen-

sion was made dependent on their future responsible behavior. *This action drew a violent protest from General Kusma Derevyanko, the Soviet member of the Allied Council, which MacArthur answered with a firm rejection of the Russian representative's complaints.*

Major Vorin E. Whan, Jr., USA, Editor
A Soldier Speaks: Public Papers and Speeches of General of the Army Douglas MacArthur
© 1965, Frederick A. Praeger, Publishers, New York, NY

I have received your note of June 24th and have carefully considered its context in vain search for some semblance of merit and validity. Rarely indeed have I perused such a conglomeration of misstatement, misrepresentation and prevarication of fact. Without new or constructive thought, it is but a labored repetition of the line of fantastic propaganda which for some time has been emanating from centers within the orbit of Communist totalitarian imperialism. So complete is the unrealism of its premise that it offers no basis for rational discussion. Its plain purpose to support and encourage those few irresponsible Japanese bent upon creating mass confusion and social unrest leading to violence and disorder is a shameful misuse of diplomatic privilege which ill-becomes the representative of a nation charged with a measure of responsibility in the democratic reorientation of Japan. I am accordingly left no other alternative than to disapprove its intemperate proposals, and indeed to reject the complete context of the document itself.

MACARTHUR'S REPORT ON THE CURRENT ESTIMATE OF KOREAN OPERATIONS
JULY 20, 1950

On June 25, 1950, the Communist government of North Korea launched a full-scale invasion of South Korea with the avowed intention of settling the unification problem by force. The United Nations took up the challenge and, largely with U.S. military assistance, went to the support of the Republic of Korea. Caught completely by surprise, the ill-prepared South Korean Army was smashed trying to hold Seoul. The remnants retreated south of the Han River with the Communists in close pursuit. General MacArthur, designated Commanding General of the United Nations Command, moved the few U.S. divisions in Japan to Korea to halt the North Korean advance. By late July, the situation had been stabilized.

Major Vorin E. Whan, Jr., USA, Editor
A Soldier Speaks: Public Papers and Speeches of General of the Army Douglas MacArthur
© 1965, Frederick A. Praeger, Publishers, New York, NY

With the deployment in Korea of major elements of the Eighth Army now accomplished, the first phase of the campaign has ended and with it the chance for victory by the North Korean forces. The enemy's plan and great opportunity depended upon the speed with which he could overrun South

MacArthur receiving the UN Flag from U.S. Army Chief of Staff, General J. Lawton Collins. MacArthur had been made UN commader on 8 July. The ceremony was held on top of the Dai Ichi building, the HQ of SCAP. July 14, 1950.

Korea once he had breached the Han River line and with overwhelming numbers and superior weapons temporarily shattered South Korean resistance. This chance he has now lost through the extraordinary speed with which the Eighth Army has been deployed from Japan to stem his rush. When he crushed the Han line the way seemed entirely open and victory was within his grasp. The desperate decision to throw in piecemeal American elements as they arrived by every available means of transport from Japan was the only hope to save the situation. The skill and valor thereafter displayed in successive holding actions by the ground forces in accordance with this concept, brilliantly supported in complete coordination by air and naval elements, forced the enemy into continued deployments, costly frontal attacks and confused logistics which so slowed his advance and blunted his drive that we have bought the precious time necessary to build a secure base.

I do not believe that history records a comparable operation which excelled the speed and precision with which the Eighth Army, the Far East Air Force and the Seventh Fleet have been deployed to a distant land for immediate commitment to major operations. It merits highest commendation for the commanders, staffs and units concerned and attests to their superior training and high state of readiness to meet any eventuality. This finds added emphasis in the fact that the Far East Command, until the President's great pronouncement to support the epochal action of the United Nations, had no slightest responsibility for the defense of the free Republic of Korea. With the President's decision it assumed a completely new and added mission.

It is, of course, impossible to predict with any degree of accuracy future incidents of a military campaign. Over a broad front involving continuous local struggles, there are bound to be ups and downs, losses as well as successes. Our final stabilization line will unquestionably be rectified and tactical improvement will involve planned withdrawals as well as local advances. But the issue of battle is now fully joined and will proceed along lines of action in which we will not be without choice. Our hold upon the southern part of Korea represents a secure base. Our casualties despite overwhelming odds have been relatively light. Our strength will continually increase while that of the enemy will relatively decrease. His supply line is insecure. He has had his great chance but failed to exploit it. We are now in Korea in force, and with God's help we are there to stay until the constitutional authority of the Republic is fully restored.

STATEMENT ON THE IMPORTANCE OF FORMOSA TO U.S. SECRUITY, SENT BY MACARTHUR TO THE COMMANDER-IN-CHIEF, VETERANS OF FOREIGN WARS, FOR USE AT THE VFW'S 51ST ANNUAL NATIONAL ENCAMPMENT AUGUST 27, 1950 CHICAGO, ILLINOIS

The presence of the Chinese Nationalist Government on the island of Formosa was a distracting factor at the start of the Korean War. In addition to sending U.S. aid to Korea,

President Truman ordered the U.S. Navy to protect Formosa from attack by the Red Chinese. The Formosan area was added to General MacArthur's zone of responsibility. In late July, he visited the island briefly on an inspection trip. A controversy in the United States over the propriety of his visit followed his return to Japan. He then took the occasion of a message to the Veterans of Foreign Wars to explain the vital position Formosa played in our Pacific defense.

Major Vorin E. Whan, Jr., USA, Editor
A Soldier Speaks: Public Papers and Speeches of General of the Army Douglas MacArthur
© 1965, Frederick A. Praeger, Publishers, New York, NY

In view of misconceptions currently being voiced concerning the relationship of Formosa to our strategic potential in the Pacific, I believe it in the public interest to avail myself of this opportunity to state my views thereon to you, all of whom having fought overseas understand broad strategic concepts. To begin with, any appraisal of that strategic potential requires an appreciation of the changes wrought in the course of the past war. Prior thereto the Western strategic frontier of the United States lay on the littoral line of the Americas with an exposed island salient extending out through Hawaii, Midway and Guam to the Philippines. That salient was not an outpost of strength but an avenue of weakness along which the enemy could and did attack us. The Pacific was a potential area of advance for any predatory force intent upon striking at the bordering land areas.

All of this was changed by our Pacific victory. Our strategic frontier then shifted to embrace the entire Pacific Ocean, which has become a vast moat to protect us as long as we hold it. Indeed, it acts as a protective shield for all of the Americas and all free lands of the Pacific Ocean area. We control it to the shores of Asia by a chain of islands extending in an arc from the Aleutians to the Mariannas held by us and our free allies. From this island chain we can dominate with air power every Asiatic port from Vladivostok to Singapore and prevent any hostile movement into the Pacific. Any predatory attack from Asia must be an amphibious effort. No amphibious force can be successful without control of the sea lanes and the air over these lanes in its avenue of advance. With naval and air supremacy and modest ground elements to defend bases, any major attack from continental Asia toward us or our friends of the Pacific would be doomed to failure. Under such conditions the Pacific no longer represents menacing avenues of approach for a prospective invader - it assumes instead the friendly aspect of a peaceful lake. Our line of defense is a natural one and can be maintained with a minimum of military effort and expense. It envisions no attack against anyone nor does it provide the bastions essential for offensive operations, but properly maintained would be an invincible defense against aggression. If we hold this line we may have peace - lose it and war is inevitable.

The geographic location of Formosa is such that in the hands of a power unfriendly to the United States it constitutes an enemy salient in the very center of this defensive perimeter, 100-150 miles closer to the adjacent friendly segments - Okinawa and the Philippines - than any point in continental Asia. At the present time there is on Formosa a concentration of operational air and naval bases which is potentially greater than any similar concentration on the Asiatic mainland between the Yellow Sea and the Strait of Malacca. Additional bases can be developed in a relatively short time by an aggressive exploitation of all World War II Japanese facilities. An enemy force utilizing those installations currently available could increase by 100 per cent the air effort which could be directed against Okinawa as compared to operations based on the mainland and at the same time could direct damaging air attacks with fighter-type aircraft against friendly installations in the Philippines which are currently beyond the range of fighters based on the mainland. Our air supremacy at once would become doubtful.

As a result of its geographic location and base potential, utilization of Formosa by a military power hostile to the United States may either counterbalance or overshadow the strategic importance of the central and southern flank of the United States front-line position. Formosa in the hands of such a hostile power could be compared to an unsinkable aircraft carrier and submarine tender ideally located to accomplish offensive strategy and at the same time checkmate defensive or counter-offensive operations by friendly forces based on Okinawa and the Philippines. This unsinkable carrier-tender has the capacity to operate from ten to twenty air groups of types ranging from jet fighters to B-29-type bombers, as well as to provide forward operating facilities for short-range coastal submarines. In acquiring this forward submarine base, the efficacy of the short-range submarine would be so enormously increased by the additional radius

of activity as to threaten completely sea traffic from the south and interdict all sea lanes in the Western Pacific. Submarine blockade by the enemy with all its destructive ramifications would thereby become a virtual certainty.

Should Formosa fall and bases thereafter come into the hands of a potential enemy of the United States, the latter will have acquired an additional "fleet" which will have been obtained and can be maintained at an incomparably lower cost than could its equivalent in aircraft carriers and submarine tenders. Current estimates of air and submarine resources in the Far East indicate the capability of such a potential enemy to extend his forces southward and still maintain an imposing degree of military strength for employment elsewhere in the Pacific area.

Historically, Formosa has been used as a springboard for just such military aggression directed against areas to the south. The most notable and recent example was the utilization of it by the Japanese in World War II. At the outbreak of the Pacific War in 1941, it played an important part as a staging area and supporting base for the various Japanese invasion convoys. The supporting air forces of Japan's army and navy were based on fields situated along southern Formosa. From 1942 through 1944, Formosa was a vital link in the transportation and communications chain which stretched from Japan through Okinawa and the Philippines to Southeast Asia. As the United States carrier forces advanced into the Western Pacific, the bases on Formosa assumed an increasingly greater role in the Japanese defense

Ceremony returning Seoul to the South Korean government, September 29, 1950.

scheme. Should Formosa fall in the hands of a hostile power, history would repeat itself. Its military potential would again be fully exploited as the means to breach and neutralize our Western Pacific defense system and mount a war of conquest against the free nations of the Pacific Basin.

Nothing could be more fallacious than the threadbare argument by those who advocate appeasement and defeatism in the Pacific that if we defend Formosa we alienate continental Asia. Those who speak thus do not understand the Orient. They do not grasp that it is in the pattern of Oriental psychology to respect and follow aggressive, resolute and dynamic leadership - to quickly turn from a leadership characterized by timidity or vacillation - and they underestimate the Oriental mentality. Nothing in the last five years has so inspired the Far East as the American determination to preserve the bulwarks of our Pacific Ocean strategic position from future encroachment, for few of its peoples fail accurately to appraise the safe-guard such determination brings to their free institutions. To pursue any other course would be to turn over the fruits of our Pacific victory to a potential enemy. It would shift any future battle area 5,000 miles eastward to the coasts of the American continents, our own home coasts; it would completely expose our friends in the Philippines, our friends in Australia and New Zealand, our friends in Indonesia, our friends in Japan, and other areas to the lustful thrusts of those who stand for slavery as against liberty, for atheism as against God.

The decision of President Truman on June 27th lighted into flame a lamp of hope throughout Asia that was burning dimly towards extinction. It marked for the Far East the focal and turning point in this area's struggle for freedom. It swept aside in one great monumental stroke all of the hypocrisy and the sophistry which has confused and deluded so many people distant from the actual scene.

CEREMONY RETURNING SEOUL
TO THE SOUTH KOREAN GOVERNMENT
SEPTEMBER 29, 1950

Mr President:

By the grace of a merciful providence our forces fighting under the standard of that greatest hope and inspiration of mankind, the United Nations, have liberated this ancient capital city of Korea. It has been freed from the despotism of Communist rule and its citizens once more have the opportunity to live under that immutable concept of life which holds invincibly to the primacy of individual liberty and personal dignity.

The ravage of war which has been visited upon your land, Mr President, by those forces of evil which seek to subvert the spiritual qualities of modern civilization, has been viewed with universal concern and distress. And fifty-three nations of the earth rose up in righteous wrath and indignation and pledged their full effort toward your relief. Such was the spiritual revulsion against the march of imperialistic communism seeking the conquest, exploitation, and enslavement of others. It reflects an invincible union of men and ideals against which no material weapons could long prevail and while inevitably force must meet force it offers hope for the

ultimate peaceful triumph of that spiritual quality without which the human mind cannot produce sound and enduring ideas. It is through the spirit that we must save the flesh.

In behalf of the United Nations Command, I am happy to restore to you, Mr. President, the seat of your government that from it you may the better fulfill your Constitutional responsibilities. It is my fervent hope that a beneficent providence will give you and all of your public officials the wisdom and strength to meet your perplexing problems in a spirit of benevolence and justice, that from the travail of the past there may emerge a new and hopeful dawn for the people of Korea.

In humble and devout manifestation of gratitude to Almighty God for bringing this decisive victory to our arms, I ask that all present rise and join me in reciting the Lord's prayer:

"Our father which art in heaven, hallowed be thy name. Thy kingdom come, thy will be done on earth as it is in heaven. Give us this day our daily bread, and forgive us our trespasses as we forgive those who trespass against us. And lead us not into temptation, but deliver us from evil, for thine is the kingdom, and the power, and the glory, forever and ever. Amen."

(I introduce the chairman of the United Nations Commission of Korea)

(I introduce the dean of the diplomatic corps, the American Ambassador)

(the President of the Republic of Korea)

Mr. President, my officers and I will now resume our military duties and leave you and your government to the discharge of the civil responsibility.

These proceedings are closed.

MESSAGE TO THE COMMANDER-IN-CHIEF,
NORTH KOREAN FORCES
OCTOBER 1, 1950

The remarkable change in fortunes in the Korean fighting after the Inchon landing raised the question of whether U.N. forces should cross the 38th Parallel, the boundary between North and South Korea. After some initial confusion, the victorious U.N. formations moved north to complete the destruction of the North Korean armed forces and the implementation of U.N. directives concerning the unification of Korea. While preparing a continuation of the offensive, MacArthur called on the opposing commander to stop hostilities in the hope that further useless sacrifice might be spared the Korean people.

Major Vorin E. Whan, Jr., USA, Editor
A Soldier Speaks: Public Papers and Speeches of General of the Army Douglas MacArthur
© 1965, Frederick A. Praeger, Publishers, New York, NY

The early and total defeat and complete destruction of your armed forces and war-making potential is now inevitable. In order that the decisions of the United Nations may be carried out with a minimum of further loss of life and destruction of property, I, as the United Nations Commander-in-Chief, call upon you and the forces under your command, in whatever part of Korea situated, forthwith to lay down your arms and cease hostilities under such military supervision as I direct - and I call upon you at once to liberate all United Nations prisoners of war and civilian internees under your control and to make adequate provision for their protection, care, maintenance and immediate transportation to such places as I indicate. North Korean forces, including prisoners of war in the hands of the United Nations Command, will continue to be given the care dictated by civilized custom and practice and permitted to return to their homes as soon as practicable. I shall anticipate your early decision upon this opportunity to avoid the further useless shedding of blood and destruction of property.

COMMUNIQUE NO. 12
NOVEMBER 24, 1950

As winter steadily deepened in North Korea and rumors of Communist Chinese troop movements multiplied, the U.N. forces continued to advance toward the Yalu River boundary. Moving north on the east and west coasts against light resistance, General MacArthur's forces hoped to finish the campaign by the end of the year. In his daily communique, the General described the situation just before the second major turning point of the war.

Major Vorin E. Whan, Jr., USA, Editor
A Soldier Speaks: Public Papers and Speeches of General of the Army Douglas MacArthur
© 1965, Frederick A. Praeger, Publishers, New York, NY

The United Nations' massive compression envelopment in North Korea against the new Red armies operating there is now approaching its decisive effort. The isolating component of the pincer, our air forces of all types, have for the past three weeks, in a sustained attack of model coordination and effectiveness, successfully interdicted enemy lines of support from the north so that further reinforcement therefrom has been sharply curtailed and essential supplies markedly limited. The eastern sector of the pincer, with noteworthy and effective naval support, has steadily advanced in a brilliant tactical movement and has now reached a commanding enveloping position, cutting in two the northern reaches of the enemy's geographical potential. This morning the western sector of the pincer moves forward in general assault in an effort to complete the compression and close the vise. If successful this should for all practical purposes end the war, restore peace and unity to Korea, enable the prompt withdrawal of United Nations military forces, and permit the complete assumption by the Korean people and nation of full sovereignty and international equality. It is that for which we fight.

COMMUNIQUE NO. 14
NOVEMBER 28, 1950

The final U.N. drive toward the Yalu met a massive Red Chinese counteroffensive, splitting the wings of MacArthur's army and forcing a rapid withdrawal. The intervention of Red China presented the United Nations Command with an entirely new situation. In only two days, the prospects for a quick peace in Korea had disappeared. General MacArthur later commented that the U.N. offensive, even though it failed to reach its objectives, did serve the purpose of forcing the Red Chinese to begin their offensive prematurely.

Major Vorin E. Whan, Jr., USA, Editor
A Soldier Speaks: Public Papers and Speeches of General of the Army Douglas MacArthur
© 1965, Frederick A. Praeger, Publishers, New York, NY

Enemy reactions developed in the course of our assault operations of the past four days disclose that a major segment of the Chinese continental armed forces in army, corps and divisional organization of an aggregate strength of over 200,000 men is now arrayed against the United Nations forces in North Korea. There exists the obvious intent and preparation for support of these forces by heavy reinforcements now concentrated within the privileged sanctuary north of the international boundary and constantly moving forward. Consequently we face an entirely new war. This has shattered the high hopes we entertained that the intervention of the Chinese was only of a token nature on a volunteer and individual basis as publicly announced and that therefore the war in Korea could be brought to a rapid close by our movement to the international boundary and the prompt withdrawal thereafter of United Nations forces, leaving Korean problems for settlement by the Koreans themselves.

It now appears to have been the enemy's intent in breaking off contact with our forces some two weeks ago to secure the time necessary surreptitiously to build up for a later surprise assault upon our lines in overwhelming force, taking advantage of the freezing of all rivers and roadbeds which would have materially reduced the effectiveness of our air interdiction and permitted a greatly accelerated forward movement of enemy reinforcements and supplies. This plan has been disrupted by our own offensive action which forced upon the enemy a premature engagement.

This situation, repugnant as it may be, poses issues beyond the authority of the United Nations Military Command - issues which must find their solution within the councils of the United Nations and chancelleries of the world.

STATEMENT READ AT THE DEDICATION CEREMONY
OF THE UNIVERSITY OF THE RYUKYUS
FEBRUARY 12, 1951
SHURI, OKINAWA

General MacArthur's United Nations Command responsibilities in Korea did not relieve him from the continuing task of preparing for the end of the occupation of Japan. He additionally was busy with other tasks of the Far East Command, including supervision of the island of Okinawa. Despite the still critical operations being conducted in Korea, he found time to send a message to the new University of the Ryukyus.

Major Vorin E. Whan, Jr., USA, Editor
A Soldier Speaks: Public Papers and Speeches of General of the Army Douglas MacArthur
© 1965, Frederick A. Praeger, Publishers, New York, NY

Establishment of the University of the Ryukyus is an event of outstanding importance in the cultural and intellectual history of these islands. It is, moreover, particularly appropriate that the University, founded upon the ancient site of the throne of Ryukyuan kings, should be dedicated on the birthday of one who though personally humble was himself kingly among the great of the world - Abraham Lincoln. As in youth he made such purposeful use of his meager yet fine resources - chiefly the Bible, Shakespeare, and Euclid - so too the eventual greatness of this institution will depend not on the multiplicity but the quality of its resources and its wisdom in using them.

The first and forever primary task of this University must be to educate Ryukyuan youth that they may develop to the fullest their own capacities for service. They must he inspired with the desire to increase and enrich opportunities for those who come after them to develop similarly, that the potentialities which have so long lain fallow in their homeland may be brought to fruition. This new institution should be so grounded in the traditions of the people whose intellectual aspirations it embodies as to conserve and pass on their rich cultural legacy, and yet provide for its students knowledge of the best in all civilizations of the past and those of our own time. And may its students, as the result of the opportunity the University offers, make their own contribution to the sum of human knowledge.

Conceived in the aftermath of war and intended to flourish in the ways of peace, the University is born as the champions of freedom rally once more to defend their heritage against those forces that would enslave the mind of man. This concern for freedom of learning, for things of the spirit, which brought this University into being has never been dimmed by the obscurantism and oppression designed to extinguish it. This dedication is, therefore, another expression of faith and an unshakable resolve that the ideals for which our universities have stood throughout the centuries, in the great tradition of which this institution now takes its place, will continue to foster and perpetuate, forever eager in their quest for truth - and forever free!

COMMENTS MADE ON THE COMPLETION OF A TOUR OF THE KOREAN BATTLE FRONT
FEBRUARY 13, 1951

The Chinese Red Army, after its intervention in late November, 1950, managed to drive below the capital of South Korea before its forward movement was decisively stopped. The Tenth Corps, which had been evacuated from the east-coast port of Hungnam, joined the main body of the Eighth Army, permitting the resumption of the offensive by the United Nations Command in late January. Early in February, 1951, this new advance by MacArthur's forces was again approaching the capital city of Seoul. With winter still gripping the Korean countryside, the seventy-one-year-old commander made a battlefront tour during which he issued a number of statements to the press. The two statements that follow indicate the general strategy being followed in dealing with the large Red Chinese forces. Seven weeks later, General MacArthur was relieved of all his commands by President Harry S. Truman.

Major Vorin E. Whan, Jr., USA, Editor
A Soldier Speaks: Public Papers and Speeches of General of the Army Douglas MacArthur
© 1965, Frederick A. Praeger, Publishers, New York, NY

What the future has in store in Korea continues to be largely dependent upon international considerations, and decisions not yet known here. Meanwhile, the Command is doing everything that could reasonably be expected of it. Our field strategy, initiated upon Communist China's entry into the war, involving a rapid withdrawal to lengthen the enemy's supply lines with resultant pyramiding of his logistical difficulties and an almost astronomical increase in the destructiveness of our air power has worked well. In the development of this strategy the Eighth Army has achieved local tactical successes through maximum exploitation of the air's massive blows on extended enemy concentrations and supplies but in the evaluation of these successes sight must not be lost of the enemy's remaining potential for reinforcement and re-supply. We must not fall into the error of evaluating such tactical successes as decisively leading to the enemy's defeat just as many erred in assessing our strategic withdrawals in the face of Communist China's commitment to war as a decisive defeat inflicted upon us.

We are still engaged in a war of maneuver with the object of inflicting as heavy a punishment upon the enemy as possible, striving constantly to keep him off balance to prevent his obtaining and holding the tactical initiative while at the same time avoiding the hazards inherent in his numerical superiority. The concept advanced by some that we should establish a line across Korea and enter into positional warfare is wholly unrealistic and illusory. It fails completely to take into account the length of such a line at the narrowest lateral, the rugged terrain which is involved and the relatively small force which could be committed to the purpose. The attempt to engage in such strategy would insure destruction of our forces piecemeal. Talk of crossing the 38th Parallel at the present stage of the campaign except by scattered patrol action incidental to the tactical situation is purely academic. From a military standpoint we must materially reduce the existing superiority of our Chinese Communist enemy engaging with impunity in undeclared war against us, with the unprecedented military advantage of sanctuary protection for his military potential against our counterattack upon Chinese soil, before we can seriously consider conducting major operations north of that geographic line.

Meanwhile, however, the complete coordination of our land, sea and air forces and the consequent smooth synchronization of their combined operations, with each arm contributing its full part, continues to inflict terrific losses upon the enemy. General Ridgway is proving himself a brilliant and worthy successor to General Walker in command of the Eighth Army and with Admiral Struble in command of the Fleet and General Partridge in command of the Air comprise an ideal trio of field commanders.

161

STATEMENT ON KOREAN OPERATIONS GIVEN AT A PRESS CONFERENCE IN WONJU, KOREA FEBRUARY 20, 1951

I am entirely satisfied with the situation at the front where the enemy has suffered a tactical reverse of measurable proportion. His losses have been among the bloodiest of modern times. As these are from Communist China's best troops, it will be difficult to adequately replace them. The enemy is finding it an entirely different problem fighting 350 miles from his base than when he had this "sanctuary" in his immediate rear, with our air and naval forces practically zeroed out. He is paying now for the illusion so falsely but effectively propagandized when Communist China initiated undeclared war that he had decisively defeated these same forces. Our strategic plan notwithstanding the enemy's great numerical superiority is indeed working well and I have just directed a resumption of the initiative by our forces. All ranks of this international force are covering themselves with distinction and I again wish to especially commend the outstanding teamwork of the three services under the skillful direction of their able field commanders, General Ridgway, Admiral Struble and General Partridge. Our successes are in great part due to the smooth synchronization of the power of the three arms. This, indeed, is the most vital factor in modern war. The question of the recrossing of the 38th Parallel continues to arouse public discussion. While President Truman has indicated that the crossing of that parallel is a military matter to he resolved in accordance with my best judgment as theater commander, I want to make it quite clear that if and when the issue actually arises I shall not arbitrarily exercise that authority if cogent political reasons against crossing are then advanced and there is any reasonable possibility that a limitation is to be placed thereon. Meanwhile I repeat that at this time the question is academic. I note that Marshal Stalin has just predicted the annihilation of our forces in Korea, but his comrades will have to do lots better than they have yet done to prove him a prophet.

CITY HALL
APRIL 18, 1951
SAN FRANCISCO, CALIFORNIA

After MacArthur's return from Japan and his retirement from active military service, his great delight from his fellow countrymen's reception was beyond his expectations. MacArthur decided on a national tour of major U.S. cities to spread the word on his views of the path the United States should follow to insure protection of our country, insure the rights of all our people are not abridged and that politics and spending for unessentials be reined in for the good of the nation and to ensure the freedom and liberty for all. His following speeches on his major U.S. tour points the way to great success while touching on character, faith, politics and its shortcoming - faulty foreign policy.

Edward T. Imparato, Editor

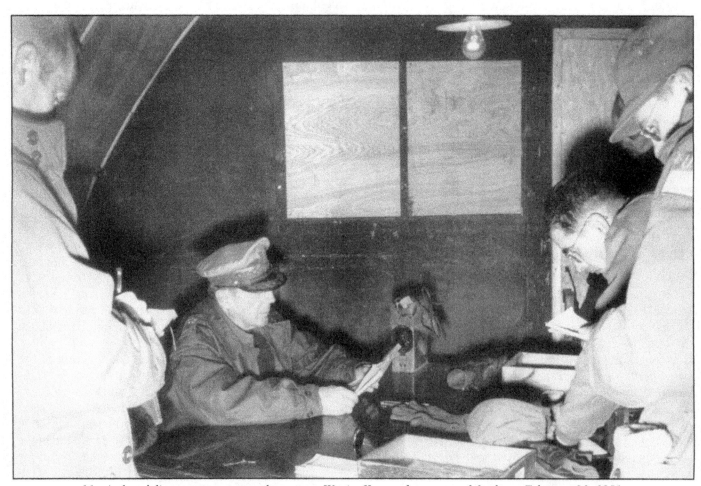

MacArthur delivers a statement to the press at Wonju, Korea after a tour of the front, February 20, 1951.

I cannot tell you what it means to be home - how I have longed for it, dreamed of it, through the dreary years of absence abroad. My emotions almost defy description as I find myself once more among my own people - once more under the spell of the great American home which breeds such magnificent men as I have just left fighting the battle in Korea. Theirs is a cause and a limitation which requires both courage and determination, and I can report to you they have met the test in every way. They are splendid. In Japan it has just been my privilege to welcome California's own division - the 40th - sent there, not for commitment to Korea, but to serve a no less vital purpose in defense, by arms if need be, of the bastion we have helped erect there in the pattern of American democracy. The arrival of your fine sons on Japanese soil signalizes to the Japanese people the firm intention of our country to assist them in repelling any predatory attack which might eventuate. It is my fervent hope that events will render their stay a short one and permit their return without commitment to the hazard of actual war. They are adding to the magnificent record of past national service of California's citizenry. Speaking for both Mrs. MacArthur and myself, I cannot tell you how deep is our appreciation for the wonderful hospitality with which this great city has welcomed us. The memory of it will live in our hearts always.

I was just asked if I intended to enter politics - my reply was "no" - I have no political aspirations whatsoever. I do not intend to run for any political office and I hope that my name will never be used in a political way. The only politics I have is contained in a simple phrase - known well by all of you - "God Bless America."

Again our sincerest thanks.

JOINT MEETING OF THE TWO HOUSES
OF THE U.S. CONGRESS
APRIL 19, 1951
WASHINGTON, D.C.

MacArthur uses this moment to honor the servicemen in Japan and Korea and to assure the mothers and fathers they are in good hands. His vision of the world military situation and the economics of world-wide trade is a classic.

Edward T. Imparato, Editor

Mr. President, Mr. Speaker, and distinguished Members of the Congress, I stand on this rostrum with a sense of deep humility and great pride-humility in the wake of those great American architects of our history who have stood here before me, pride in the reflection that this forum of legislative

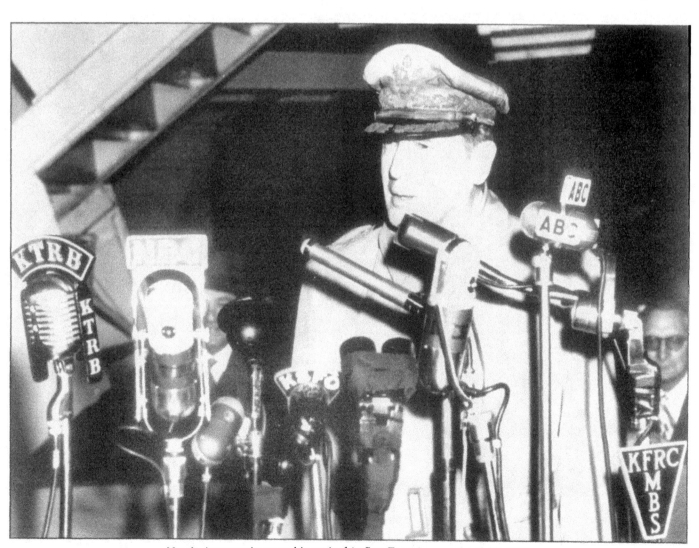

MacArthur speaks upon his arrival in San Francisco on April 18, 1951.

debate represents human liberty in the purest form yet devised. Here are centered the hopes and aspirations and faith of the entire human race.

I do not stand here as advocate for any partisan cause, for the issues are fundamental and reach quite beyond the realm of partisan consideration. They must be resolved on the highest plane of national interest if our course is to prove sound and our future protected. I trust, therefore, that you will do me the justice of receiving that which I have to say as solely expressing the considered viewpoint of a fellow American. I address you with neither rancor nor bitterness in the fading twilight of life with but one purpose in mind - to serve my country.

The issues are global and so interlocked that to consider the problems of one sector, oblivious to those of another, is but to court disaster for the whole.

While Asia is commonly referred to as the gateway to Europe, it is no less true that Europe is the gateway to Asia, and the broad influence of the one cannot fail to have its impact upon the other.

There are those who claim our strength is inadequate to protect on both fronts - that we cannot divide our effort. I can think of no greater expression of defeatism. If a potential enemy can divide his strength on two fronts, it is for us to counter his effort.

The Communist threat is a global one. Its successful advance in one sector threatens the destruction of every other sector. You cannot appease or otherwise surrender to communism in Asia without simultaneously undermining our efforts to halt its advance in Europe.

Beyond pointing out these simple truisms, I shall confine my discussion to the general areas of Asia. Before one may objectively assess the situation now existing there, he must comprehend something of Asia's past and the revolutionary changes which have marked her course up to the present. Long exploited by the so-called colonial powers, with little opportunity to achieve any degree of social justice, individual dignity, or a higher standard of life such as guided our own noble administration of the Philippines, the peoples of Asia found their opportunity in the war just past to throw off the shackles of colonialism, and now see the dawn of new opportunity, a heretofore unfelt dignity, and the self respect of political freedom.

Mustering half of the earth's population and 60 percent of its natural resources, these peoples are rapidly consolidating a new force, both moral and material, with which to raise the living standard and erect adaptations of the design of modern progress to their own distinct cultural environments. Whether one adheres to the concept of colonization or not, this is the direction of Asian progress and it may not

Address, joint meeting of the two Houses of the U.S. Congress, April 19, 1951, Washington, D.C.

be stopped. It is a corollary to the shift of the world economic frontiers, as the whole epicenter of world affairs rotates back toward the area whence it started. In this situation it becomes vital that our own country orient its policies in consonance with this basic evolutionary condition rather than pursue a course blind to the reality that the colonial era is now past and the Asian peoples covet the right to shape their own free destiny. What they seek now is friendly guidance, understanding, and support, not imperious direction; the dignity of equality, not the shame of subjugation. Their prewar standard of life, pitifully low, is infinitely lower now in the devastation left in war's wake. World ideologies play little part in Asian thinking and are little understood. What the peoples strive for is the opportunity for a little more food in their stomachs, a little better clothing on their backs, a little firmer roof over their heads, and the realization of the normal nationalist urge for political freedom. These political-social conditions have but an indirect bearing upon our own national security, but form a backdrop to contemporary planning which must be thoughtfully considered if we are to avoid the pitfalls of unrealism.

Of more direct and immediate bearing upon our national security are the changes wrought in the strategic potential of the Pacific Ocean in the course of the past war. Prior thereto, the western strategic frontier of the United States lay on the littoral line of the Americas with an exposed island salient extending out through Hawaii, Midway, and Guam to the Philippines. That salient proved not an outpost of strength but an avenue of weakness along which the enemy could and did attack. The Pacific was a potential area of advance for any predatory force intent upon striking at the bordering land areas.

All this was changed by our Pacific victory. Our strategic frontier then shifted to embrace the entire Pacific Ocean which became a vast moat to protect us as long as we hold it. Indeed, it acts as a protective shield for all of the Americas and all free lands of the Pacific Ocean area. We control it to the shores of Asia by a chain of islands extending in an arc from the Aleutians to the Marianas held by us and our free allies. From this island chain we can dominate with sea and air power every Asiatic port from Vladivostok to Singapore and prevent any hostile movement into the Pacific. Any predatory attack from Asia must be an amphibious effort. No amphibious force can be successful without control of the sea lanes and the air over those lanes in its avenue of advance. With naval and air supremacy and modest ground elements to defend bases, any major attack from continental Asia toward us or our friends of the Pacific would be doomed to failure. Under such conditions the Pacific no longer represents menacing avenues of approach for a prospective invader - it assumes instead the friendly aspect of a peaceful lake. Our line of defense is a natural one and can be maintained with a minimum of military effort and expense. It envisions no attack against anyone nor does it provide the bastions essential for offensive operations, but properly maintained would be an invincible defense against aggression.

The holding of this littoral defense line in the western Pacific is entirely dependent upon holding all segments thereof, for any major breach of that line by an unfriendly power would render vulnerable to determined attack every other major segment. This is a military estimate as to which I have yet to find a military leader who will take exception. For that reason I have strongly recommended in the past as a matter of military urgency that under no circumstances must Formosa fall under Communist control. Such an eventuality would at once threaten the freedom of the Philippines and the loss of Japan, and might well force our western frontier back to the coasts of California, Oregon, and Washington.

To understand the changes which now appear upon the Chinese mainland, one must understand the changes in Chinese character and culture over the past 50 years. China up to 50 years ago was completely nonhomogeneous, being compartmented into groups divided against each other. The warmaking tendency was almost nonexistent, as they still followed the tenets of the Confucian ideal of pacifist culture. At the turn of the century, under the regime of Chan So Lin, efforts toward greater homogeneity produced the start of a nationalist urge. This was further and more successfully developed under the leadership of Chiang Kai-shek, but has been brought to its greatest fruition under the present regime, to the point that it has now taken on the character of a united nationalism of increasingly dominant aggressive tendencies. Through these past 50 years, the Chinese people have thus become militarized in their concepts and in their ideals. They now constitute excellent soldiers with competent staffs and commanders. This has produced a new and dominant power in Asia which for its own purposes is allied with Soviet Russia, but which in its own concepts and methods has become aggressively imperialistic with a lust for expansion and increased power normal to this type of imperialism. There is little of the ideological concept either one way or another in the Chinese makeup. The standard of living is so low and the capital accumulation has been so thoroughly dissipated by war that the masses are desperate and avid to follow any leadership which seems to promise the alleviation of local stringencies. I have from the beginning believed that the Chinese Communists' support of the North Koreans was the dominant one. Their interests are at present parallel to those of the Soviet, but I believe that the aggressiveness recently displayed not only in Korea, but also in Indochina and Tibet, and pointing potentially toward the south, reflects predominantly the same lust for the expansion of power which has animated every would-be conqueror since the beginning of time.

The Japanese people since the war have undergone the greatest reformation recorded in modern history. With a commendable will, eagerness to learn, and marked capacity to understand, they have, from the ashes left in war's wake, erected in Japan an edifice dedicated to the primacy of individual liberty and personal dignity, and in the ensuing process there has been created a truly representative government committed to the advance of political morality, freedom of economic enterprise, and social justice. Politically, economically, and socially Japan is now abreast of many free nations of the earth and will not again fail the universal trust. That it may be counted upon to wield a profoundly beneficial influence over the course of events in Asia is attested by the magnificent manner in which the Japanese people have met the recent challenge of war, unrest, and confusion surrounding them from the outside, and checked communism within their own frontiers without the slightest slackening in their forward progress. I sent all four of our occupation divisions to the Korean battlefront without the slightest qualms as to the effect of the resulting power vacuum upon Japan. The results fully justified my faith. I know of no nation more serene, orderly, and industrious - nor in which higher hopes can be entertained for future constructive service in the advance of the human race.

Of our former ward, the Philippines, we can look forward in confidence that the existing unrest will be corrected and a strong and healthy nation will grow in the longer aftermath of war's terrible destructiveness. We must be patient and understanding and never fail them, as in our hour of need they did not fail us. A Christian nation, the Philippines stand as a mighty bulwark of Christianity in the Far Fast, and its capacity for high moral leadership in Asia is unlimited.

On Formosa the Government of the Republic of China has had the opportunity to refute by action much of the malicious gossip which so undermined the strength of its leadership on the Chinese mainland. The Formosan people are receiving a just and enlightened administration with majority representation on the organs of government, and politically, economically, and socially they appear to be advancing along sound and constructive lines.

With this brief insight into the surrounding areas I now turn to the Korean conflict. While I was not consulted prior to the President's decision to intervene in support of the Republic of Korea, that decision, from a military standpoint, proved a sound one, as we hurled back the invader and decimated his forces. Our victory was complete and our objectives within reach when Red China intervened with numerically superior ground forces. This created a new war and an entirely new situation - a situation not contemplated when our forces were committed against the North Korean invaders - a situation which called for new decisions in the diplomatic sphere to permit the realistic adjustment of military strategy. Such decisions have not been forthcoming.

While no man in his right mind would advocate sending our ground forces into continental China and such was never given a thought, the new situation did urgently demand a drastic revision of strategic planning if our political aim was to defeat this new enemy as we had defeated the old.

Apart from the military need as I saw it to neutralize the sanctuary protection given the enemy north of the Yalu, I felt that military necessity in the conduct of the war made mandatory:

1. The intensification of our economic blockade against China;

2. The imposition of a naval blockade against the China coast;

3. Removal of restrictions on air reconnaissance of China's coastal areas and of Manchuria;

4. Removal of restrictions on the forces the Republic of China on Formosa with logistical support to contribute to their effective operations against the common enemy.

For entertaining these views, all professionally designed to support our forces committed to Korea and bring hostilities to an end with the least possible delay and at a saving of countless American and Allied lives, I have been severely criticized in lay circles, principally abroad, despite my understanding that from a military standpoint the above views have been fully shared in past by practically every military leader concerned with the Korean campaign, including our own Joint Chiefs of Staff.

I called for reinforcements, but was informed that reinforcements were not available. I made clear that if not permitted to destroy the enemy buildup bases north of the Yalu; if not permitted to utilize the friendly Chinese force of some 600,000 men on Formosa; if not permitted to blockade the China coast to prevent the Chinese Reds from getting succor from without; and if there were to be no hope of major reinforcements, the position of the command from the military standpoint forbade victory. We could hold in Korea by constant maneuver and at an approximate area where our supply line advantages were in balance with the supply line disadvantages of the enemy, but we could hope at best for only an indecisive campaign, with its terrible and constant attrition upon our forces if the enemy utilized his full military potential. I have constantly called for the new political decisions essential to a solution. Efforts have been made to distort my position. It has been said that I was in effect a warmonger. Nothing could be further from the truth. I know war as few other men now living know it, and nothing to me is more revolting. I have long advocated its complete abolition as its very destructiveness on both friend and foe has rendered it useless as a means of settling international disputes. Indeed, on the 2nd of September 1945, just following the surrender of the Japanese nation on the battleship *Missouri*, I formally cautioned as follows:

"Men since the beginning of time have sought peace. Various methods through the ages have been attempted to devise an international process to prevent or settle disputes between nations. From the very start, workable methods were found insofar as individual citizens were concerned, but the mechanics of an instrumentality of larger international scope have never been successful. Military alliances, balances of power, leagues of nations, all in turn failed, leaving the only path to be by way of the crucible of war. The utter destructiveness of war now blots out this alternative. We have had our last chance. If we will not devise some greater and more equitable system, Armageddon will be at our door. The problem basically is theological and involves a spiritual recrudescence and improvement of human character that will synchronize with our almost matchless advances in science, art, literature, and all material and cultural developments of the past 2,000 years. It must be of the spirit if we are to save the flesh."

But once war is forced upon us, there is no other alternative than to apply every available means to bring it to a swift end. War's very object is victory - not prolonged indecision. In war, indeed, there can be no substitute for victory.

There are some who for varying reasons would appease Red China. They are blind to history's dear lesson. For history teaches with unmistakable emphasis that appeasement but begets new and bloodier war. It points to no single instance where the end has justified that means - where appeasement has led to more than a sham peace. Like blackmail, it lays the basis for new and successively greater demands, until, as in blackmail, violence becomes the only other alternative. "Why," my soldiers asked of me, "surrender military advantages to an enemy in the field?" I could not answer. Some may say to avoid spread of the conflict into an all-out war with China; others, to avoid Soviet intervention. Neither explanation seems valid. For China is already engaging with the maximum power it can commit and the Soviet will not necessarily mesh its actions with our moves. Like a cobra, any new enemy will more likely strike whenever it feels that the relativity in military or other potential is in its favor on a worldwide basis.

The tragedy of Korea is further heightened by the fact that as military action is confined to its territorial limits, it condemns that nation, which it is our purpose to save, to suffer the devastating impact of full naval and air bombardment, while the enemy's sanctuaries are fully protected from such attack and devastation. Of the nations of the world, Korea alone, up to now, is the sole one which has risked its all against communism. The magnificence of the courage and fortitude of the Korean people defies description. They have chosen to risk death rather than slavery. Their last words to me were, "Don't scuttle the Pacific."

I have just left your fighting sons in Korea. They have met all tests there and I can report to you without reservation they are splendid in every way. It was my constant effort to preserve them and end this savage conflict honorably and with the least loss of time and a minimum sacrifice of life. Its growing bloodshed has caused me the deepest anguish and anxiety. Those gallant men will remain often in my thoughts and in my prayers always.

I am closing my 52 years of military service. When I joined the Army even before the turn of the century, it was the fulfillment of all my boyish hopes and dreams. The world has turned over many times since I took the oath on the plain at West Point, and the hopes and dreams have long since vanished. But I still remember the refrain of one of the most popular barrack ballads of that day which proclaimed most proudly that - "Old soldiers never die; they just fade away."

And like the old soldier of that ballad, I now close my military career and just fade away - an old soldier who tried to do his duty as God gave him the light to see that duty.

Goodbye.

60TH CONTINENTAL CONGRESS
OF THE DAUGHTERS OF THE AMERICAN REVOLUTION
APRIL 19, 1951
WASHINGTON, D.C.

In this speech to the D.A.R., MacArthur ties his respect for the D.A.R. to his mother's prior association with them. He therefore solicits their assistance in checking the political drift back to the heights it once felt to the low point in the political crisis. He thanks them for their endless diligence in maintaining the standards of conduct for the Ameri-can people and for their goal of reminding America of our glorious heritage. They are the guardians of our American heritage.

Edward T. Imparato, Editor

When I heard from your President-General, Mrs. Patton, that this distinguished group would be in session today, I determined to stop by to avail myself of an opportunity I have long sought, personally to pay you the tribute that is in my heart. Of all of the great societies of the country during the past century, I know of none which has fought more diligently for the preservation of those great ideals which bulwarked our forefathers in their efforts to secure and preserve freedom. The complexities and confusion largely resulting from internal subversion and corruption and detailed regimentation over our daily life now threaten the country no less than it was threatened in Washington's day. Under these harmful influences we have drifted far away and to a dangerous degree from the simple but immutable pattern etched by our forefathers. It behooves this distinguished society to assert a dynamic leadership in checking this drift and regaining the ground which has been lost. In this hour of crisis all patriots look to you.

WASHINGTON CIVIC CEREMONY
APRIL 19, 1951
WASHINGTON, D.C.

The honor you do Mrs. MacArthur and myself by the warmth your generous welcome today has moved me deeply. Our thanks and appreciation are very real and very sincere.

I am glad, indeed, to visit once again this great capital city. It brings back poignant memories of former military service here when life was gentler and happier. Washington is a magic name. In Asia it looms over the horizon as the focal point for all eyes - the beacon for those who are seeking the way and truth and the light. In Asia too I have seen your sons serving the cause of human freedom. Indomitable in battle and restrained in occupation, their conduct throughout has reflected the high moral standards of the American home. Your pride in them can be limitless. None could be better. It is my fervent hope that they may soon return in the wake of an honorable and enduring peace. Such was my constant prayer and single purpose in the Asia campaigns.

Again my thanks and appreciation for your heartwarming welcome. We shall remember and treasure it always.

CITY HALL
APRIL 20, 1951
NEW YORK, NEW YORK

MacArthur honors New York City as the greatest city in the world and recognizes the complex admixture of its diverse society.

Edward T. Imparato, Editor

This is the greatest city in the world. What an inspiration to see it again with its admixture of citizens drawn from all parts of the universe. It is the living example of the ability of men of every race and clime to live and progress together. I have just come from another striking example of unification where men of differing races and different languages are fighting shoulder to shoulder in a common cause. Many are your own sons, ready and fit, and writing a brilliant battle record

The tremendous reception you have given me recalls a somewhat similar homecoming in which I participated as a Cadet from West Point long, long ago. It was Admiral Dewey's return from the war in the Pacific. The years have passed, indeed, since then but the hospitality of New York seems only to have grown with time. And today as I watched your throngs, a great pride and a great confidence came upon me for here I saw in this great city, this melting pot of the men of all races, an indomitable force which cannot fail to maintain our freedom and our way of life. This, I said to myself, is America - and this with God's help we shall keep American.

Again my thanks and deepest appreciation from both Mrs. MacArthur and myself for your heart-warming reception. We shall never forget it. You have made us feel we are indeed home.

STATEMENT ON WEST POINT'S SESQUICENTENNIAL (1802-1952)
AS PUBLISHED IN *THE ASSEMBLY*, VOL. X, NO. 1
APRIL 1951

General MacArthur remained closely identified with the U.S. Military Academy throughout his life. As a distinguished graduate of the institution and former Superintendent, he was frequently called on to provide statements for use by the Academy. The year of his return from Japan was the beginning of West Point's Sesquicentennial celebration. In honor of this important anniversary, General MacArthur sent a message for use in the Association of Graduates monthly publication, The Assembly.

Edward T. Imparato, Editor

Fifty years have passed since I participated in West Point's Centennial exercises. These fifty years of war and peace have seen emerge from West Point's classes a succession of graduates who have given the country an indomitable leadership which has never failed the Academy's great traditions. As I look beyond those fifty years to the day I joined the long grey line, I recall I then felt that as an Army "brat" the occasion was the fulfillment of all my boyish dreams. The world has turned over many times since then and the drams have long vanished with the passing of the years, but through the grim murk of it all, the pride and thrill of being a West Pointer has never dimmed. And as I near the end of the road, what I felt when I was sworn in on the plain so long ago, I can still feel and say - that is my greatest honor. I have no doubt but that those who now compose the Corps will find the same satisfaction I do now in reflecting upon this day of their fifty more years hence.

SOLDIER FIELD
APRIL 26, 1951
CHICAGO, ILLINOIS

MacArthur reaffirms his faith in the American people to find and resolve its problems.

Edward T. Imparato, Editor

I cannot find the words adequately to express my sense of gratitude for the cordiality of your welcome. The memory of it will long live in my heart and prove a source of added strength to help me meet my responsibilities of citizenship in the great issues which now stir mankind.

I have been encouraged in many ways by the events which have followed my return from long absence abroad. Foremost of the encouraging signs has been the demonstration that the American people are keenly alive to their own responsibilities and unhesitatingly voice their views on the direction of the policy of government. It is for future events to ascertain whether they still retain the ultimate authority over government as intended by the Constitution or whether such authority has been lost in the drift from the pattern ordained by the architects of our political institutions.

I have only recently left many of your sons on the battle line in Korea and I can report to you that they are splendid in every way. Despite the inhibitions under which they fight, they are writing a proud record of valor and indomitable determination unsurpassed in our military annals. I have believed a realistic policy should fill the long existing vacuum left in the wake of Red China's commitment to war against us - a policy designed to affect the early restoration of peace, through victory, with a consequent saving of countless American lives. It is difficult to ask men to fight and die unless we give them a realistic mission and means to accomplish it. What is our policy in Korea? Some will tell you that the pacification and unification of all Korea is the objective - an objective which indeed still stands as the formal mandate of the United Nations. Others tend to overlook such a formally stated policy and will tell you that our objective is achieved upon clearing South Korea of invading forces. Still others ignore both explanations and frankly say that our objective now is to continue to engage the enemy forces in Korea in a prolonged and indecisive campaign of attrition notwithstanding the constantly increasing cost in American blood. Who will tell you in the traditionally ringing tones of the American patriot that our objective is victory over the nation and men who, without provocation or justification, have warred again us and that our forces will be furnished all the sinews and other means essential to achieve that victory with a minimum of cost in human life? The tragedy is that since the advent of the war with Red China there has been no definition of the political policy which would provide a solution for the new problems thereby created. This has resulted in a policy vacuum heretofore unknown to war. However great the effort to distract attention from the main issues by introducing into public discussion extraneous and irrelevant matters, the fundamental question still remains the same - what is the policy for Korea? Our losses there in ratio to the men committed have already

MacArthur rides in a New York City parade. April 20, 1951.

reached staggering proportions. These losses are progressively mounting by thousands each month. It is this steady increase that arouses in the mothers and fathers of America's sons such understandable anguish and uncertainty. Nor is it difficult for those nations with but token forces in ratio to our own calmly to advocate no deviation from this course.

It is in this situation of complete unrealism that, while meticulously implementing the directives given me, I have strongly urged the need for a positive policy attuned to the military realities and designed to stop, through strength, this slaughter of America's sons.

I have endeavored since my return home to keep the issue on a higher level than partisan politics. The lives of your sons call for this measure of consideration. For the enemy bullets have no respect for political affiliation and strike down the son of a Democrat just as surely as the son of a Republican. Although my public life is now closed and I no longer carry any responsibilities of the National Administration, I feel my responsibility of National Citizenship no less deeply. I shall continue to advocate a positive and realistic policy for Korea - one designed to bring the war to an early and honorable end with maximum protection for your sons now engaged. I shall continue to fight against that greatest scourge of mankind, Communism, as long as God gives me the power to fight. I shall work with you in the discharge of our common responsibilities of citizenship to the end that American policy be based upon the thoughts and needs and aspirations of the American people, unyielding to undue political pressures from abroad. I shall stand with you for an America rededicated to those sacred and immutable ideals and concepts which guided our forefathers when drawing the design of American freedom. For although without command authority or responsibility, I still proudly possess that to me the greatest of all honors and distinctions - I am an American!

DEDICATION OF MACARTHUR SQUARE
APRIL 27, 1951
MILWAUKEE, WISCONSIN

MacArthur recalls his entry into military service from Milwaukee 52 years ago.

Edward T. Imparato, Editor

I cannot tell you with what emotion I come once again to my ancestral home. The warmth of your welcome has moved me more deeply than words can express. It has etched on my heart a memory I can never forget.

It was 52 years ago that Milwaukee sent me forth into the military service, and I now report to you that service is ended. I want you to know that I have done my best and always have I kept the soldier faith.

These 52 years have wrought monumental changes in this great city. It has risen majestically to tower among the great civic centers of the world - a mighty monument to the vision, ingenuity and determination, not only of its metropolitan leaders, but of each of the thousands of citizenry who have given of their life and time so fully to the task. It fills

me with an indelible sense of supreme confidence in the future of our beloved land.

Again my thanks and deepest appreciation.

I am profoundly grateful for the opportunity to participate in the dedication of this magnificent monument. It will be a fitting tribute to the valor and sacrifice of the American soldier. Its full glory will be an imperishable reminder to all mankind of those deeds which preserved our liberties on the battlefields of the world. It stands as solemn warning to those who would destroy freedom, either externally or internally. America will not now nor in future yield that for which so many of these men died. I do not know the dignity of their birth, but I do know the glory of their death. They died that mortal ideals might not perish. This monument will do even more than commemorate them. It will serve to rally all Americans to the task of maintaining the moral strength which has built our past. It will constantly remind of those sacred and immutable concepts - liberty, justice and truth - upon which long has rested the Republic's fate. It will be for all eyes and for all time a symbol of an ever stronger nation whose history still is the future.

EXTRACTS OF STATEMENTS BEFORE THE
U.S. SENATE COMMITTEES ON FOREIGN RELATIONS
AND ON ARMED SERVICES,
82ND CONGRESS, 1ST SESSION
MAY 3-5, 1951

One of the outgrowths of MacArthur's address to the Congress in April, 1951, was a joint hearing conducted by the Senate Committees on Foreign Relations and Armed Services. The subject of the Senate inquiry was the military situation in the Far East, including the facts surrounding the relief of General MacArthur. For a period Of three days, the General answered the questions of the Senators over a great range of subjects. His testimony, which ran to several hundred pages in the official record, is only sampled in the following extract.

Major Vorin E. Whan, Jr., USA, Editor
A Soldier Speaks: Public Papers and Speeches of General of the Army Douglas MacArthur
© 1965, Frederick A. Praeger, Publishers, New York, NY

Senator Hickenlooper. Question No.5: Isn't your proposal for sea and air blockade of Red China the same strategy by which Americans achieved victory over the Japanese in the Pacific?

Gen. MacArthur. Yes, sir. In the Pacific we bypassed them. We closed in. You must understand that Japan had an enormous population of nearly 80 million people, crowded into 4 islands. It was about half a farm population. The other half was engaged in industry.

Potentially the labor pool in Japan, both in quantity and quality, is as good as anything that I have ever known. Some place down the line they have discovered what you might call the dignity of labor, that men are happier when they are working and constructing than when they are idling.

This enormous capacity for work meant that they had to

have something to work on. They built the factories, they had the labor, but they didn't have the basic materials.

There is practically nothing indigenous to Japan except the silkworm. They lack cotton, they lack wool, they lack petroleum products, they lack tin, they lack rubber, they lack a great many other things, all of which was in the Asiatic basin.

They feared that if those supplies were cut off, there would be 10 to 12 million people unoccupied in Japan. Their purpose, therefore, in going to war was largely dictated by security.

The raw materials - those countries which furnished raw materials for their manufacture - such countries as Malaya, Indonesia, the Philippines, and so on - they, with the advantage of preparedness and surprise, seized all those bases, and their general strategic concept was to hold those outlying bastions, the islands of the Pacific, so that we would bleed ourselves white in trying to reconquer them, and that the losses would be so tremendous that we would ultimately acquiesce in a treaty which would allow them to control the basic products of the places they had captured.

In meeting that, we evolved an entirely new strategy. They held certain bastion points, and what we did was to evade those points, and go around them.

We came in behind them, and we crept up and crept up, and crept up, always approaching the lanes of communication which led from those countries, conquered countries, to Japan.

By the time we had seized the Philippines, and Okinawa, we were enabled to lay down a sea and Navy blockade so that the supplies for the maintenance of the Japanese armed forces ceased to reach Japan.

The minute we applied that blockade, the defeat of Japan was a certainty.

The ultimate result was that when Japan surrendered, they had at least 3,000,000 of as fine ground troops as I have ever known, that laid down their arms because they didn't have the materials to fight with, and they didn't have the potential to gather them at the points of importance where we would attack. We hit them where they weren't; and, as a result, that magnificent army of theirs very wisely surrendered.

The ground forces that were available in the Pacific were probably at no time more than one-third of the ground forces that Japan had available; but, as I say, when we blockaded that way, when we disrupted their entire economic system, they could not supply the sinews to their troops that were necessary to keep them in active combat and, therefore, they surrendered.

Now, the problem with China is quite similar, only China has not got anything like the resource the Japanese Empire had.

It would be easier to blockade them. A blockade along their coasts would be a very simple problem if all the nations of the United Nations joined in.

The only other way in which China can get logistical support is from the Soviet. As I explained this morning, that railroad that runs from the great industrial centers of Russia, which are in European Russia, is already strained to the utmost to maintain the garrisons they have there now; to place them in a position - the increase of traffic that would be necessary to place them as a predatory expeditionary army would be too great.

There is a very definite limit to what they can give to Communist China. That, in my opinion, is why Communist China does not turn up with an adequate air force and an adequate navy. She can't build it herself, and the Soviet can't get it out to her.

It is for that reason that, in my own professional opinion, Communist China, its power to wage modern war, has been tremendously exaggerated; and I believe when we place the pressure, the blockade pressure, and the disruptive pressure of the air, on its distributive systems, that she would be forced to yield within a reasonable period of time.

You must understand that in China itself, they have the greatest difficulty in merely supplying their present civil population. I don't suppose there is a year in China that from 5 to 10 million people don't die either of starvation or of the results of malnutrition. It is an economy of poverty, and the minute you disrupt it, you will turn great segments of its population into disorder and discontent, and the internal strains would help to blow up her potential for war.....

Senator Morse. General, what explanation would you give to the fact, if it is a fact, that the South Korean Army was never trained to the high degree of efficiency and strength as was the North Korean Army?

Gen. MacArthur. I think that the explanation is quite clear, if you understand the basic conditions that existed in Korea.

There was an occupation by the Russians of North Korea, and an occupation by the Allies of South Korea.

The friction between the two sections grew, and in order to preserve the geographical limitations, both sides organized what might be called light troops. They were of the nature border patrols, a little stronger than the normal constabulary, but not comparable to troops of the line.

There had been, for over a year before the actual conflict a growing degree of irritation on that border. It had culminated in isolated small-unit attacks, patrol attacks, by both sides, sometimes of battalion size, in which those two forces had pretty carefully matched themselves, and in which both forces fundamentally realized that they were pretty safe from the other.

But back of that security force that the North Koreans had along the 38th Parallel, there was organized a new army. There was organized an army of a nucleus of veterans that had been fighting for years in Manchuria or Mongolia; there were many Koreans; there were men of other nationalities, mercenaries, mercenary types of men who made their living by combat.

That force was carefully organized; that force was carefully trained and drilled, quite possibly just north of the Yalu - certainly, in Manchuria. It was completely organized by the Soviets with supplies.

It was as smart, as efficient, and as able a force as I have ever seen in the field. That force could not have been launched on its combat mission without the full concurrence, not only of the North Korean Government but of Red China and of the Soviet Union.

When it struck, it struck like a cobra. It passed through their own security forces. As I recall, their security forces were organized into what they call four brigades. These brigades, in strength, were about the same as the North Korean division, but of a different type of organization. They passed through those people. The South Koreans were no match for them at all, and the disposition by the South Koreans of their logistic potential was extraordinarily poor.

They had put their supplies and equipment close to the

38th Parallel. They hadn't developed any positions in depth. Everything between the 38th Parallel and Seoul was their area of depot.

When they lost that immediate line, they lost their supplies. They were not able apparently to destroy them en masse; so that at one initial stroke this North Korean Army had a new supply base in the area between the 38th Parallel and Seoul, which enabled them to press south with the full strength of their base being immediately behind them; they no longer had to rely upon the long distance from the Yalu to get their supplies down.

When we intervened, the circumstances as far as I was concerned were these: I was summoned to a telecom conference from Washington. It was the first time I had ever in person been summoned to such a conference.

At that conference I received the orders initiating our entrance into Korea. I immediately flew over. We still had a field at Suwon and I pushed forward from Suwon to the Han, the outskirts of Seoul; and at that time it was quite apparent to me that the South Korean Army had been so hard hit that it was completely disintegrated and in full flight.

I felt that the line of the Han could not be maintained. I felt that it was entirely problematical whether we could save any remnants of the South Korean Army or establish any position in Korea.

My directives were to establish a beachhead in the neighbor-hood of Pusan and to take such steps as I felt I could within the means I possessed to support the Korean Government and help maintain the South Koreans.

I was reminded at the time that my resource for the time being was practically limited to what I had and that I must regard the security of Japan as a fundamental and basic policy.

I threw in troops from the Twenty-fourth Division by air in the hope of establishing a loci of resistance around which I could rally the fast-retreating South Korean forces.

I also hoped by that arrogant display of strength to fool the enemy into belief that I had a much greater resource at my disposal than I did.

I managed to throw in a part of two battalions of infantry, who put up a magnificent resistance before they were destroyed - a resistance which resulted, perhaps, in one of the most vital successes that we had.

The enemy undoubtedly could not understand that we would make an effort with such a small force.

Instead of rushing rapidly forward to Pusan, which he could have reached within a week without the slightest difficulty, he stopped to deploy his artillery across the Han River.

We had destroyed the bridges. It took him days to do that.

We gained 10 days by that process, before he had deployed in line of battle along the 150-mile front with Suwon as the pivotal point.

By that time, I had brought forward the rest of the Twenty-fourth Division, under General Dean. I gave him orders to delay the advance of the enemy until I could bring the First Cavalry Division and the Twenty-fifth Division over from Japan.

He fought a very desperate series of isolated combats in which both he and a large part of that division were destroyed.

By that time we had landed the Twenty-fifth Division at Pusan, and it was moving forward by rail. And we landed the First Cavalry Division on the east coast, and they moved over and formed a line of battle. I do not think that the history of the war will show a more magnificent effort against what should have been overwhelming odds as those two divisions displayed.

By that time the Eighth Army command had moved over under a very indomitable leader, General Walker. From that time on I never had the slightest doubt about our ability to hold a beachhead. And on July 19 in the first communique that I recall I issued, I predicted that we would not be driven into the sea.

We gradually built up. But the campaign you know, and I will not go into. But those were the initial features.

Ultimately we took out of Japan the three of the four divisions we had.

When I conceived the idea of the Inchon envelopment, in order to accumulate the necessary troops, I have explained how I reorganized the Seventh Division, which left Japan without any combat troops. The reaction of the Japanese was magnificent. They not only morally and spiritually supported everything that we did, but all of the incidental friction of democracy, such as labor struggles and everything, without any word from me, ceased at once. The entire nation spiritually placed itself behind the United Nations to do what it could under the restrictions of occupation and policy directives of the Far Eastern Commission.....

TEXAS LEGISLATURE
JUNE 13, 1951
AUSTIN, TEXAS

MacArthur recalls his early youth in Texas and the strong and dedicated fighting men from Texas who served in his command. He also honors General Walton H. Walker, a Texas son killed in Korea.

Edward T. Imparato, Editor

It is with a sense of high honor that I appear on this rostrum to address you - the elected representatives of the great State of Texas - a State which has contributed so abundantly to American progress and in which I feel so sincere a personal interest.

I have lived here in my younger days and observed at first hand the greatness of your people. It provides me the opportunity I have long wished, personally to pay tribute to that host of Texas sons who by valor and devotion on many battlefields have done so much to bring victory to American arms.

Their characteristic independence of spirit, invincibility of will, and unswerving fidelity have reflected the nobility of their Texas homes and built a tradition which all Americans now cherish as their own.

In the Korean struggle, led, until he gave his life at the front, by that intrepid military leader and distinguished son of Texas, Gen. Walton H. Walker, they have maintained this tradition in every way, and your pride in them may be very real and very great. I have not infrequently found in the forefront of the fight a small flag of Texas, planted by some Texas boy to dramatize his love and veneration for this land of his fathers.

As I appear before you a great debate over our political and military policy is stirring the Nation. The issue which has been raised is a simple one, but the potentiality of its consequences is momentous.

What is our policy for Korea? On this issue rests not only the lives of countless American boys and their allies committed to fight in that distant land, but, as well, the future security of our own country and the advance of our national leadership in the affairs of the world.

In the atmosphere of contention which has existed following my recall I have been peculiarly gratified by your invitation to address you as it has raised the issue to the nonpartisan level its character truly demands and reflects the high statesmanship which actuates your own consideration of the problem.

I have been amazed, and deeply concerned, since my return, to observe the extent to which the orientation of our national policy tends to depart from the traditional courage, vision, and forthrightness which has animated and guided our great leaders of the past, to be now largely influenced, if not indeed in some instance dictated, from abroad and dominated by fear of what others may think or others may do.

Never before in our history can precedent be found for such a sub-ordination of policy to the opinions of others with a minimum regard for the direction of our own national interest. Never before have we geared national policy to timidity and fear. The guide, instead, has invariably been one of high moral principle and the courage to decide great issues on the spiritual level of what is right and what is wrong.

Yet, in Korea today, we have reached that degree of moral trepidation that we pay tribute in the blood of our sons to the doubtful belief that the hand of a blustering potential enemy may in some way be thus stayed.

Munich, and many other historical examples, have taught us that, diplomatic appeasement but sows the seeds of future conflict. Yet, oblivious to these bloody lessons, we now practice a new and yet more dangerous form of appeasement - appeasement on the battlefield where under we soften our blows, withhold our power, and surrender military advantages, in apparent hope that in some nebulous way by so doing a potential enemy will be coerced to desist from attacking us.

In justification for this extraordinary action it is pleaded by those responsible for the condition of our national defense that we are not prepared to fight. I cannot accept such an estimate. I believe that, much as we abhor war and should do anything honorable to avoid it, our country has the inherent strength to face and defeat any who may attack.

I should be recreant, moreover, to my obligations of citizenship did I fail to warn that the policies of appeasement on which we are now embarked carry within themselves the very incitation to war against us. If the Soviet does strike it will be because of the weakness we now display rather than the strength we of right should display.

If, however, we be so weak, in fact, that we must cower before the verbal brandishments of others, the responsibility for such weakness should be a matter of the gravest public concern.

Who, we should ask, is responsible for the reduction of our military strength from the greatest on earth at war's end to that they now estimate is inadequate even to support our moral commitments?

Who plunged us into the Korean war and assumed other global commitments in the face of such alleged weakness without reckoning and being ready to meet their potential consequences? Who is responsible for so grave a past failure which has brought our Nation to so ignominious a pass that we must plead weakness before our fellow nations?

These are questions to which the Nation should address itself, if it would be in position to assess the policy judgments now in being and yet to be formulated. For it is elementary that if the defense of these policies is valid and we are indeed as weak as is pleaded, they who bear full responsibility for such weakness and they who formulate present policy are one and the same.

Can we, therefore, accept their present and future judgments in the light of past failures without the most serious misgivings as to our future fate as a free and sovereign Nation?

I am no seer to predict whether or not the Soviet aims at ultimately provoking and engaging in a global struggle. I give him infinitely more credit, however, than to believe he would embark upon so reckless and ill-conceived a course.

Up to now, there is no slightest doubt in my mind but that he has been engaging in the greatest bulldozing diplomacy history has ever recorded. Without committing a single soldier to battle he has assumed direct or indirect control over a large part of the population of the world. His intrigue has found its success, not so much in his own military strength nor indeed in any overt threat of intent to commit it to battle, but in the moral weakness of the free world.

It is a weakness which has caused many free nations to succumb to and embrace the false tenets of Communist propaganda. It is a weakness which has caused our own policymakers, after committing America's sons to battle, to leave them to continuous slaughter of an indecisive campaign by imposing arbitrary restraints upon the support we might otherwise provide them through maximum employment of our scientific superiority, which alone offers hope of early victory.

It is a weakness which now causes those in authority to strongly hint at a settlement of the Korean conflict under conditions short of the objectives our soldiers were led to believe were theirs to attain and for which so many yielded their lives.

In every war in which we have heretofore engaged, we have counter-balanced manpower with the doctrine of attack through our matchless scientific development. Yet, in Korea we are admittedly applying the doctrine of passive defense which in all history has never won a war - a doctrine which has been responsible for more military disaster than all other reasons combined. Does experience teach us nothing? Has shifting expediency replaced logical reasoning?

Of this we may be sure. The Soviet's moves, should it actually want war, will be dictated by its own assessment of the relativity of military force involved, actual and potential. It will not be so much influenced by the destruction it believes itself capable of inflicting upon us as by the punishment it knows it itself would have to accept should it embark upon so reckless an adventure. It will certainly not be influenced away from war by the blood tribute we are now paying in Korea to encourage it to preserve the peace.

This elementary logic, coupled with our own predominant superiority in many scientific facets of modern war, is ignored by those who seek support for our present unrealistic policies by the spread of a psychosis of fear throughout the land. They say that by meeting force with adequate counter force in Asia we would expand the war and threaten the involvement of Europe, while painting a grim picture of the consequent devastation of our great cities.

Nothing could be more unrealistic nor further from the truth. Our action would not be aimed at expanding but at ending the war and thus preventing its expansion. Our purpose would not be conquest but at neutralizing such of the enemy's offensive power as is already hurled against us. Europe's very survival is dependent upon our gaining a decisive victory in Asia where communism has already thrown down the gage of battle.

By confining their concern so assiduously to one area and ignoring the global nature of the Communist threat and the need to stop its predatory advance in other areas, they have become the isolationists of the present time. And it is a form of isolation which offers nothing but ultimate destruction. Our first line of defense for Western Europe is not the Elbe; it is not the Rhine - it is the Yalu. Lose there and you render useless the effort to implement the North Atlantic Pact or any other plan for regional defense.

What gullibility to think the free world would fight for freedom in Europe after refusing to do so in Asia. I am as intensely interested in saving Western Europe as any other threatened area, where the people show the will and the determination to mount their own full defensive power, but I believe the issue to be worldwide and not confined to any special privileged area.

I believe the free world has the strength to meet the enemy wherever he may threaten, be it on one front, two fronts, or many fronts. To hold the contrary - to say that freedom has not strength enough to meet communism wherever its predatory forces may attack - is an admission, even before the battle starts, of defeatism, without historical parallel.

Can anyone seriously believe that as we now build our own normal military strength, the Soviet will not do all in its power to match our increase with a corresponding one of its own? Time is not, as some would have us believe, invincibly on our side. As in the field of atomic development, where we now so predominantly lead, the gap between the Soviets aud ourselves may well decrease with each passing year.

The existing policy of appeasement is defended on the ground that if our military reaction be conventional and we carry the war to the enemy in a manner calculated to destroy his capability of killing our sons and those whose protection we have assumed, we would incur the wrath of the Soviet and provoke the start of a world at war. No argument could be more fallacious.

The surest way to insure World War III is to allow the Korean conflict to continue indecisively and indefinitely. The surest way, the only way, to prevent World War III is to end the Korean conflict rapidly aud decisively.

Like a cancer, the only cure is by major operation. Fail-ure to take such decisive action - as in cancer - is but to invite infection of the entire bloodstream. Yet the present plan of passive defense envisages the indefinite continuance of the indecisive stalemate with its compounding losses, in the vain hope that the enemy will ultimately tire and end his aggression. This, or that, at some indefinite future date, we will adopt the very policies of positive action designed to win the war and secure our stated objectives, which are now deprecated and decried.

Could anything be more naive, more unrealistic, more callous of our mounting dead?

Could there be any greater inconsistency than the argument pursued that we can defeat Red China in Korea without risk of Soviet intervention but our attack upon its sustaining bases across the Yalu would render intervention inevitable?

The defenders of the existing policy vacuum are the same who, suddenly and without slightest preparation or seeming consideration of the military and political potentialities, threw as into the conflict. These are the very men who, in the face of mounting peril, deliberately demobilized us at the peak of our military strength, and then at the lowest point of our disarmament with no slightest preparation or word of warning plunged us into a war which they now seem afraid to win.

No words can excuse or relieve the enormous disasters to the Korean people we are pledged to protect, inherent in a policy which arbitrarily confines the full impact of all our air and naval bombardment to the Korean Peninsula.

The protection we offer these unfortunate people, indeed, may well resolve itself into their complete obliteration. To what greater depths might morality possibly sink? Mighty efforts are underway to conceal these facts. But the march of events and the common sense of the American people cannot fail ultimately to reveal the full truth.

The very fate of the United Nations rests upon the outcome of the struggle to consummate its commitments to establish under its auspices and authority a "unified and democratic government in the sovereign State of Korea."

There can be no compromise with the moral principles which actuated the decisions underlying this United Nations objective. There can be no shortcut to its achievement and no turning back.

To hold now that anything less than its full accomplishment would satisfy our political and military requirements would be to repudiate the great sacrifices selflessly made and the host of those who died that such an objective might be realized. Anything short of that objective would destroy for all time the effectiveness of the United Nations as an instrumentality for international persuasion.

On September 2, 1945, after taking the surrender of Japan in Tokyo Bay, I warned of the need for a "spiritual recrudescence and improvement of human character that will synchronize with our almost matchless advances in science, art, literature, and material and cultural development."

Such an improvement is slow to come to pass. To the contrary, there is unmistakable evidence of a tendency toward moral deterioration throughout the free world. This moral deterioration does not occur through evolutionary change in human thought but rather from the relentless war being waged by a fifth column within the ranks of every free society.

This is a far greater threat to the free world than is the advance of predatory force. Its very purpose is to destroy faith in moral values, to introduce cynicism in human thought, and to transform tranquillity into confusion, disorder, and dismay.

Our own people harbor a strong spiritual urge in their hearts, but many leaders have become absorbed in the demands of political expediency, are not unwilling to compromise moral principle, and have lost the traditional American patriot's touch. Such a leadership offers no panacea for freedom's festering wounds.

My correspondence reflects a growing lack of faith by a large segment of our population in the responsibility and moral fiber of our own process of government. Truth has ceased to be keystone to the arch of our national conscience and propaganda has replaced it as the rallying media for public support. Corruption and rumors of corruption have shaken the people's trust in the integrity of those administering the civil power.

Government has assumed progressively the arrogant mantle of oligarchic power as the great moral and ethical principles upon which our Nation grew strong have been discarded or remolded to serve narrow political purposes. The cost of government has become so great and the consequent burden of taxation so heavy that the system of free enterprise which built our great material strength has become imperiled.

The rights of individuals and communities have rapidly been curtailed in the advance toward centralized power and the spiritual and material strength, amassed through our original concept of a federation - erected upon the local responsibility and autonomy of its several components - shows marked deterioration.

Possibly these adverse factors account for our inability to advance a vigorous and courageous leadership at a time when the world never more needed such a leadership. Whatever the cause, the facts are undeniable. Our prestige abroad has reached a tragically low ebb and our leadership is little wanted.

There are those who call piously for unity even while doing so much to prevent unity. Unity is indeed what all Americans earnestly desire - but unity of the American brand based upon considered judgment on what best serves the national interest and reflecting full freedom of thought and expression - not unity obtained through the whiplash of arbitrary power, with its devices for sowing fear and suppressing knowledge. Unity instead must come from the common effort to crystallize ideas and search for and publish the truth.

What arrogant prevarication by those who, joining with the voice of the Daily Worker and other Communist propaganda, claim I favor war or that I seek war's expansion. Every step I have taken, every word I have uttered, had the single purpose of bringing the war to its earliest end - to stop the terrific human slaughter now going on so endlessly in Korea. Before committees of the National Congress, in response to recent questioning, I had this, in effect, to say:

"No man in the world is more anxious to avoid the expansion of war than I. I am a 100% disbeliever in war. The enormous sacrifices that have been brought about by scientific methods of killing have rendered war a fantastic and impossible method for the solution of international difficulties. In war, as it is waged now, with the enormous losses on both sides, both will lose. It is a form of mutual suicide; and I believe that the entire effort of modern society should be concentrated on an endeavor to outlaw it.

"This would probably take decades before it could be actually accomplished; but you have to make a start. There is no halfway substitute. And the sooner we come to grips with the basic problem the sooner we will reach a solution - it is no more difficult to settle the fundamental issue than it is the various problems that are corollary to it.

"The world should have commonsense enough, when it surveys the last two wars, to understand that war has become incompatible with the survival of modern civilization. Time is running out on us. We have had our last chance, and I believe firmly that 99 percent of the people of the world agree.

"It is the establishment of the mechanics for its abolition that is so difficult. It is there our leaders fail us - they lag behind the hope and belief of the masses. I understand thoroughly that no one nation is going to put such a concept into effect until the others do so - at least until all the other great nations agree. They could, however, set the norm.

"If the four or five stronger countries should do so, it would be impossible for anyone else to violate the code. Pass such a legislative fiat making it conditional upon the others doing so and you will thus take the moral leadership of the world."

From those who so bitterly assail me there has been no word of response - only cynical silence - only the hypocrisy of pretense - only the constant flow of slanted propaganda. They are the real warmongers - they who refuse to end the Korean war - they who advocate "wait and see" while American blood - not dust as they would have it - settles in growing pools around the 38th parallel.

I am appearing before you without public responsibility, as a citizen of the Republic who, after long absence abroad, has returned from the scene of our Nation's spiritual as well as military campaigns in the Far East. Certain definite impressions have been made upon me - I am concerned for the security of our great Nation not so much because of any potential threat from without, but because of the insidious forces working from within which, opposed to all of our great traditions, have gravely weakened the structure and tone of our American way of life.

I am concerned over the moral degradation which will be ours in the aftermath of our failure fully and firmly to support the forces we have committed to battle in Korea, and to fulfill the obligation of protection we assumed when we accepted that unhappy nation's defense.

I am concerned over the position publicly taken by some of our leaders, for the first time in American history, that we are not prepared if necessary to defend ourselves. If we become actuated by fear, if we endeavor to obtain converts to policies resting upon fear through the spread of fear by propagandizing our own destruction, so long will we have that fear to contend with and to threaten us.

This great Nation of ours was never more powerful, never more prepared to extend a dynamic and courageous leadership to guide the world through the morass of artificially created timidity, complexity, and indecision - it never had less reason to fear. It was never more able to meet the exacting tests of leadership in peace or in war, spiritually, physically, or materially. As it is yet unconquered, so it is unconquerable. Its history still lies ahead. Our finest hours are yet to come.

Let us regain some of the courage and faith of the architects who charted the course to our past greatness. Let us look up as befits the most powerful nation on earth, both spiritually and physically. Let us tell all that, while firmly and invincibly dedicated to the course of peace, we will not shrink from defending ourselves if the alternative is slavery or some other form of moral degradation.

Let us proudly reassume our traditional role of readiness to meet and vanquish the forces of evil at any time and any place they are hurled against us. Let us make clear our eagerness to abolish the scourge of war from the face of the earth just as soon as others are willing to rise to so noble a stature with us. Let us renew our reverence for the blood of our sons and strike with all the power we can mount to support and protect those who now fight our battles in distant lands.

And above all else, let us regain our faith in ourselves and rededicate all that is within us to the repair and preservation of our own free institutions and the advance of our own free destiny.

FLAG DAY - RICE INSTITUTE STADIUM
JUNE 14, 1951
HOUSTON, TEXAS

MacArthur discusses and revisits the determination to take charge of the country. One cannot blame the Communist for all our ills, there is enough blame to go around to all of us unless we take charge by counterbalancing all the forces that tend to have us drift into apathy when a sound spiritual urge is capable of overcoming the inroads of Communism and our temptation to treat others to force the changes necessary to the infallible reminder that our greatest faith should rest upon two mighty symbols - the Cross and the Flag.

Edward T. Imparato, Editor

I am profoundly grateful for the opportunity you have given me to be with you in Houston and to see with my own eyes the magnitude of your civic progress since last I was in the Heart of Texas. You stand in the vanguard of the almost incredible material advance of our great Nation. I could wish that every American might capture the true picture as I see it of the immeasurable spiritual, physical and material strength inherent in our people. I was never more deeply inspired - never more confident that we have so relatively progressed that no nation nor combination of nations can offer a serious threat to our security. Yet, strangely, I find prevalent throughout the land a feeling of fear generated by the constant but false propaganda that we are weak - that we are not prepared to defend against any who may attack - that, against our every inclination and tradition, we must appease and compromise to encourage others to desist from attacking. There could be no greater illusion - no surer incitation to attack us - than the lack of confidence we thus show in ourselves. Why should we lose the courage and self-assurance with which we have met and overcome the threat of every past crisis in our history? Our Nation is young and virile and our future is still before us. Let no man tell you that we are old and decadent and tottering on the verge of national collapse. All that I have seen since my return is to the contrary. All that I have seen points to the fact that we were never so strong, either individually or collectively.

It is not from threat of external attack that we have reason for fear. It is from those insidious forces working from within. It is they that create the basis for fear by spreading false propaganda designed to destroy those moral precepts to which we have clung for direction since the immutable declaration of our independence became the great charter of our liberty.

This campaign to pervert the truth and shape or confuse the public mind with its consequent weakening of moral courage is not chargeable entirely to Communists engaged in a centrally controlled world-wide conspiracy to destroy all freedom. For they have many allies, here as elsewhere who, blind to reality, ardently support the general Communist aims while reacting violently to the mere suggestion that they do so. There are those who subvert morality as the means to gain or entrench power. There are those who, believing themselves liberals, chart a course which can but lead to destruction. There are those cynically inclined whose restless impulse is ever seeking change. There are those who are constantly trying to alter our basic concepts of freedom and human rights. There are those who seek to prevent men from fearlessly speaking their minds according to the dictates of their conscience. There are those who plan to limit our individual right to share in the sovereign power of the people. There are those who seek to subvert government from being the guardian of the people's rights, to make of it an instrument of despotic power. There are those who plan to alter the constitutional checks and balances established to preserve the integrity of our coordinate branches. There are those who seek to make the burden of taxation so great and the progressive increase so alarming that the spirit of adventure, tireless energy and masterful initiative which built the material strength of the Nation shall become stultified and inert. There are those who seek to make all men servants of the State. There are those who seek to change our system of free private enterprise which, whatever its faults, commands the maximum of energy from human resource and provides the maximum of benefits in human happiness and contentment. There are those who seek to convert us to a form of socialistic endeavor leading directly to the path of Communist slavery.

As a counter-balance to those forces is the deep spiritual urge in the hearts of our people - a spiritual urge capable of arousing and directing a decisive and impelling public opinion. This, indeed, is the great safeguard and resource of America. So long as it exists we are secure for it holds us to the path of reason. It is an infallible reminder that our greatest hope and faith rests upon two mighty symbols - the Cross and the Flag; the one based upon those immutable teachings which provide the spiritual strength to persevere along the course which is just and right - the other based upon the invincible will that human freedom shall not perish from the earth. These are the mighty bulwarks against the advance of those atheistic predatory forces which seek to destroy the spirituality of the human mind and to enslave the human body.

On this day annually set apart for all Americans to repledge their allegiance to the Flag and to the Republic for which it stands let us pray for the spiritual strength and innate wisdom to keep this Nation to the course of freedom charted by our fathers; to preserve it as the mighty instrument on earth to bring universal order out of existing chaos; to restore liberty where liberty has perished; and to reestablish human dignity where dignity has been suppressed.

Let me again thank this great metropolis for the warmth of its almost overwhelming reception of Mrs. MacArthur and myself. In this southland we both are indeed at home, but you have etched a new memory for us which we can never forget.

Cotton Bowl
June 15, 1951
Dallas, Texas

General MacArthur sees a general moral decline in the administration of affairs of state and encourages our people to force faster action to resolve its mounting problems. The people seem to see and fear a betrayal of our moral standards and the ethical principals which carried us to true greatness. Our government has failed us.

Edward T. Imparato, Editor

I am deeply grateful for the opportunity to participate today in this stirring demonstration by the citizens of Dallas. I should be unworthy indeed, however, did I take it unto myself as a personal tribute. I recognize it instead as an expression of an aroused American public opinion, merely incidentally timed upon an old soldier's return from campaigning abroad, to make emphatically clear the people's desire to regain the moral and ethical base upon which the nation was founded; to return to the deep spirituality which animated our fathers in the building of our national heritage; to recapture the simple courage and faith by which our country's course was safely charted through successive generations; and to refortify those of our institutions, political, economic and social, from which has emerged the pattern of American progress. It has indeed been a striking demonstration of the invincible strength of American character that our people thus assert their direct influence upon vital questions affecting the common weal. It serves warning to all men that Americans yet possess both the spiritual and material power - the fortitude and courage - to resist, and if need be aid others to resist, domination by sinister forces, whatever their form, wherever their origin. It cannot fail favorably to influence the course of future events.

In its relation to the Korean conflict it offers assurance that the people will not be misled by propaganda efforts to obscure the main issues through the injection for discussion of extraneous and relatively unimportant heretofore unquestioned incidents. It offers assurance that the people will not be misled by those who, while defending the existing policy vacuum as the best means to preserve peace decry, as the advocacy of a policy which leads to war, the military measures which have been urged to bring the war now in progress to a prompt and victorious end. How fantastically unrealistic it is for them to refuse to accept the factuality that we are already at war - a bitter, savage and costly war. If all other evidence were ignored, our mounting dead would alone stand as mute evidence that it is war in which we are now actually engaged. Yet, despite this, they seek to avoid the grave responsibility inherent in the fact of war - seek to divert public thought from the basic issue which war creates - how may victory be achieved with a minimum of human sacrifice. It is not a question of who wants war and who wants peace. All men of good conscience earnestly seek peace. The method alone is in issue. Some, with me, would achieve peace through a prompt and decisive victory at a saving of human life, others through appeasement and compromise of moral principle, with less regard for human life. The one course follows our great American tradition, the other can but lead to unending slaughter and our country's moral debasement.

I have no slightest doubt as to which viewpoint will ultimately prevail. The forceful expression of the people's will has made that quite clear. Indeed, there are increasing signs that our Korean policy is already progressively being reoriented toward a course of realism and relatively greater strength. It is becoming daily more apparent there is no other course which offers hope for the restoration of peace through an honorable ending of the war.

I am happily amazed at the material progress this city, and indeed all Texas, has made since I last visited this great State. It matches in every way our pattern of national progress and emphasizes the invincible will and resolute faith of your citizenry. It provides added evidence of the spiritual and material relativity of our Nation among all other nations of the world. Yet there is a constant flow of propaganda calculated to weaken our faith in ourselves aid to weaken the faith of others in us. We are told of the devastating destruction with which our great cities are under imminent threat and given such alarming estimates of our own weakness and the relative strength of our potential enemies that the wonder is any citizen retains the moral courage to question the omniscience of those who administer the power.

We should concern ourselves over this propaganda only insofar as it might be symptomatic of a general moral deterioration in administration - a lowering of the standards which traditionally have guided our conduct of public affairs. Its correction rests in our own hands. For no administration in a Republic can long defy the public opinion when adequately and vigorously expressed. Such is the case in our country today. The people, fearing a betrayal of those moral standards and ethical principles which carried our nation to true greatness, are now asserting their constitutional powers and responsibilities and making clear their determination in the future themselves to rule. I believe this is one of the healthiest signs since the birth of the Republic. It offers dynamic assurance that past in-roads into our liberties will be checked and that our future course will be guided more completely by the wisdom and faith of the masses.

If it be that my relief was the spark which ignited this great power of American public expression; which caused our people to rise above the level of narrow partisanship to unite in a common crusade to effect a spiritual renaissance in American life; which restored to the American people the full glory and dignity of self-rule under those same high principles and ideals which animated our fathers in charting the course of the Nation; which restored a lost faith in ourselves and our free institutions; which provided the symbol for rallying the mighty forces for good throughout the land - then I would be thankful, indeed, to a farseeing and merciful providence and could not ask for more.

Mrs. MacArthur and I shall ever hold close to our hearts the memory of your generous welcome and overflowing hospitality. We feel that we leave this delightful city blessed by a host of new and valued friends.

THE ALAMO
JUNE 15, 1951
SAN ANTONIO, TEXAS

MacArthur insists we, as a nation, may be abandoning the old spirit of sacrifice so evident at the Alamo. He insists we need to reignite the spiritual courage to adjudge issues upon the simple test of what seems right and what seems wrong. We should not abandon our basic principals to appease the savage instincts underlying ruthless aggression.
Edward T. Imparato, Editor

The Alamo! On this hallowed soil at a crucial moment in history, a small band of Texans stood and died rather than yield the precious concept of liberty. The sacrifice they here and then made has inspired the hearts and steeled the arms of all succeeding generations and has become a mighty and noble part of the American tradition. It has influenced the course of all battles we have since fought and has contributed effectively to all victories we have since won. It is in its spirit that our Nation has met and overcome the successive crises which have beset its progress. And it is in its spirit that we must meet the problems which now dominate human thought. The great issue of the day is whether we are departing from that spirit in the shaping of national policy to meet the challenge of the time. Are we failing it? Are we lacking the spiritual courage to adjudge issues upon the simple test of what seems right and what seems wrong? Are we content to compromise basic principle, to appease the savage instincts underlying ruthless aggression, to cower before the verbal whip-lash of an international bully? These are questions now agitating and disturbing the public conscience. Had your heroes who fought here and others who through the generations have matched their heroic example failed this simple but immutable spirit - had they been bound

by extraordinary limitations withholding the power essential to achieve victory - liberty would long ago have perished. Had they followed counsels of timidity and fear this great Nation might well have disappeared. Let us, therefore, beware of a dangerous tendency assiduously propagandized to under-rate our own strength and to overrate that of others. Let us have the courage and faith of the Alamo. I know of nothing more inspiring than to witness the clear demonstration I have seen since my return that the mass of the American people do not support false concepts; that they still cherish the fundamental ideals which built this great country, still harbor within themselves the self-reliance and invincible will which has been ours and our fathers since the independence of the Republic was proclaimed. They are aroused. The demand is voiced everywhere that our policies conform to our hallowed traditions and that the American way of life shall not deteriorate with the passage of time. What, I have been asked, is our greatest internal menace? If I were permitted but one sentence of reply, but one phrase of warning - it would be, "end invisible government based upon propaganda and restore truly representative government based upon truth." For propaganda is the primary instrument of totalitarian rule, whether Communist or Fascist, and, incredible as it may seem to those of my generation, it is practiced as though it were a legitimate art or science. Suppress the truth, curtail free expression and you destroy the basis of all the freedoms. We have indeed reached an astounding concept of morality when an official estimate such as that put out in December 1949 on Formosa, is now stated to be false and to have been intentionally publicized in order to mislead public opinion. Propaganda of this type closely parallels the Soviet system which we so bitterly condemn. Human liberty has never survived where such practice has flourished.

It is difficult to find words adequately to express my great happiness at again being in San Antonio and greeting so many of my old friends and former comrades-in-arms. In my boyhood I spent many happy years here. Indeed, I was one of the first graduates of the West Texas Military Academy, now the distinguished Texas Military Institute. I was not prepared, however, to see the astounding progress which has been made in this famous city since then. To me it is symbolical of our entire nation. If we all could but visualize the strength of this great land from my perspective, I am sure we would need fear no departure from the vision and courage of the past, no further need for propaganda as an artifice to conceal the truth. The more I see the more confident I become of the peace and security which lies ahead. If we contain the insidious forces working to destroy us from within, renew our faith in the moral and ethical standards of our fathers and look for guidance from the unfailing wisdom of the people as expressed in public opinion, we will be safe.

The reception this great city has given to Mrs. MacArthur and myself has been soul stirring. It has brought to both of us memories of other days spent in this hospitable atmosphere - of days of long ago when life was simpler and gentler. Yet, you have today scrolled in the warmth of our hearts something that will be with us always. We do not forget.

The General marvels at the great progress made in Texas in recent years and emphasizes the tremendous growth in free enterprise has produced great results yet he fears the insidious drift away from free enterprise may be threatening the initiative and incentive of the American people. To regain the high ground we must maintain the high principals and moral standards from which were evolved the great American tradition.

Edward T. Imparato, Editor

It has been a rare privilege for me to travel during the past four days through the heart of Texas and observe with my own eyes the almost miraculous progress which has been made in the development of your great State. I have found here a vast reservoir of spiritual and material strength which fills me with a sense of confidence in the future of our nation. It confirms my faith that with such resources none can excel us in peaceful progress nor safely challenge us to the tragedy of war. These facts should be thoroughly understood by every American citizen to offset efforts which are being made through propaganda to sow the seeds of fear and timidity in the American mind - to portray our nation as weak and our potential enemies as strong. There could be no greater disservice to our beloved country than is reflected in such a fantastic effort to lower our own self-assurance and enhance that of those unfriendly to us.

Texas, of which this great city is so vital a part, is a shining example of the power generated under conditions of human liberty. For in Texas men given freedom of opportunity have harnessed many of nature's vast stores and turned the resulting energy and material resource into the building of a mighty Nation dedicated to the advance of personal liberty and individual dignity. Nowhere are men found more devoted to the concepts of freedom and the preservation of the American system based upon truth and justice. None have contributed more to the advance of the traditional American ideal. None give more hope that an America conceived in liberty will survive in liberty. Yet, if this is to be so, every American must firmly share the responsibility attendant upon citizenship in a Republic. All must rally to the demand that administration of the civil power be on a level of morality which will command the public confidence and faith; that truth replace false and slanted propaganda in public information; that cynicism give way to confidence that our course of right will prevail; that fear and timidity be repudiated as having no place in shaping our destiny; and that national policy be determined with primary regard to the ultimate well-being of our own people.

We must clearly understand that despite our great reservoir of spiritual and material strength we must carefully guard the fundamental basis which produced them. For the drift away from our competitive system of free enterprise is threatening the initiative and incentive of our people and throttling the energies essential to maintain the level of our material progress. The drift away from the truth is leaving the people confused and bewildered. The drift away from these high principles and moral standards from which were evolved the American tradition is creating doubt and uncertainty and lowering the moral tone of the American way of life. The drift downward of the purchasing power of our currency which has progressively fallen as it has become increasingly influenced by the political fortunes of the moment continues unabated. The drift upward in the cost of bureaucracy and the expenditure of public funds in complete disregard of the tax burden has accelerated so alarmingly that the people are rapidly becoming the servants of the State. The drift toward Socialism through indirect internal pressures faces us with the inevitable collapse of individual incentive and full personal energy. This leaves the public safeguard in the direct hands of the American people in whom rests constitutionally the ultimate power to rule. Time and the course of events require thet every citizen do his full part in this essential undertaking.

My trip to Texas was not to receive but to pay an old Soldier's tribute to a great segment of the American people. It is a segment which has ever stood in the forefront of American patriots, invariably dedicated to the preservation of the American ideal and the building of the American nation. For all that you have done - for all that you yet stand ready to do - you fill me with inspiration and an intense pride that in my own youth I too was a Texas boy.

Mrs. MacArthur and I will carry with us always your greeting as we regretfully bid you goodby.

MacArthur was warned by many that an outspoken course, even if spoken in trust, would bring down upon his head ruthless retaliation. It has never been in MacArthur's forceful utterances to speak anything but the truth as he saw it. He then referred to Abraham Lincoln's striking code "To sin by silence when they should protest makes cowards of men." He continued, "I shall dedicate all my energies to restoring the immutable principals and ideals of our forebears. I shall raise my voice as loud and as often as I believe it to be in the interest of the American people."

Edward T. Imparato, Editor

In this historic forum I recall vividly and reverently the memory of those great architects and defenders of liberty who immortalized the Commonwealth of Massachusetts. To this section of the country men point as the cradle of our freedom.

For here was established more than three centuries ago a declaration of rights from which ultimately came the constitutional mandate guaranteeing our civil liberties. Here men arose militantly in protest against the tyranny of oppressive rule of burdensome taxation. Here men engaged in formal combat to sever the distasteful bonds of colonial rule.

Here men etched the patriot's pattern which all races who

harbored in their hearts a love for freedom have since sought to emulate. Here men, by their courage, vision, and faith, forged a new concept of modern civilization.

Before the descendants of these early American patriots I am honored, indeed, to address this legislative assembly in response to its thoughtful and kind invitation. I do so with neither partisan affiliation nor political purpose.

But I have been warned by many that an outspoken course, even if it be solely of truth, will bring down upon my head ruthless retaliation - that efforts will be made to destroy public faith in the integrity of my views - not by force of just argument but by the application of the false methods of propaganda. I am told in effect I must follow blindly the leader - keep silent - or take the bitter consequences.

I had thought Abraham Lincoln had pinned down for all time this ugly code when he declared: "To sin by silence when they should protest makes cowards of men."

I shall raise my voice as loud and as often as I believe it to be in the interest of the American people. I shall dedicate all of my energies to restoring to American life those immutable principles and ideals which your forebears and mine handed down to us in sacred trust. I shall assist in the regaining of that moral base for both public and private life which will restore the people's faith in the integrity of public institutions and the private faith of every man in the integrity of his neighbor.

I shall set my course to the end that no man need fear to speak the truth. I could not do less, for the opportunities for service my country has given me and the honors it has conferred upon me have imposed an obligation which is not discharged by the termination of public service.

Much that I have seen since my return to my native land after an absence of many years has filled me with immeasurable satisfaction and pride. Our material progress has been little short of phenomenal.

It has established an eminence in material strength so far in advance of any other nation or combination of nations that talk of imminent threat to our national security through the application of external force is pure nonsense.

It is not of any external threat that I concern myself but rather of insidious forces working from within which have already so drastically altered the character of our free institutions - those institutions which formerly we hailed as something beyond question or challenge - those institutions we proudly called the American way of life.

Foremost of these forces is that directly, or even more frequently indirectly, allied with the scourge of imperialistic Communism. It has infiltrated into positions of public trust and responsibility - into journalism, the press, the radio, and the schools.

It seeks through covert manipulation of the civil power and the media of public information and education to pervert the truth, impair respect for moral values, suppress human freedom and representative government, and, in the end, destroy our faith in our religious teachings.

This evil force, with neither spiritual base nor moral standard, rallies the abnormal and subnormal elements among our citizenry and applies internal pressure against all things we hold decent and all things that we hold right - the type of pressure which has caused many Christian nations abroad to fall and their own cherished freedoms to languish in the shackles of complete suppression.

As it has happened there it can happen here. Our need for patriotic fervor and religious devotion was never more impelling. There can be no compromise with atheistic Communism - no halfway in the preservation of freedom and religion. It must be all or nothing.

We must unite in the high purpose that the liberties etched upon the design of our life by our forefathers be unimpaired and that we maintain the moral courage and spiritual leadership to preserve inviolate that mighty bulwark of all freedom, our Christian faith.

It was the adventurous spirit of Americans which despite risks and hazards carved a great nation from an almost impenetrable wilderness; which established the pattern for modern industrialization and scientific development; which built our own almost unbelievable material progress and favorably influenced that of all others; which through the scientific advance of means of communication closed the international geographic gap to permit rapid and effective trade and commerce among the peoples of the world; which raised the living standard of the American people beyond that ever before known; and which elevated the laborer, the farmer, and the tradesman to their rightful station of dignity and relative prosperity.

This adventurous spirit is now threatened as it was in the days of the Boston Tea Party by an unconscionable burden of taxation. This is sapping the initiative and energies of the people and leaves little incentive for the assumption of those risks which are inherent and unescapable in the forging of progress under the system of free enterprise.

Worst of all, it is throwing its tentacles around the low income bracket sector of our society, from whom is now exacted the major share of the cost of government. This renders its paper income largely illusory

The so-called forgotten man of the early thirties now is indeed no longer forgotten as the Government levies upon his income as the main remaining source to defray reckless spendthrift policies.

More and more we work not for ourselves but for the State. In time, if permitted to continue, this trend cannot fail to be destructive. For no nation may survive in freedom once its people become the servants of the State, a condition to which we are now pointed with dreadful certainty. Labor, as always, will be the first to feel its frightful consequences.

It is quite true that some levy upon the people's earnings to pay the cost of government is unavoidable. But the costs of government, even discounting extraordinary military requirements, have risen at an accelerated, alarming, and reckless rate.

Nothing is heard from those in supreme executive authority concerning the possibility of a reduction or even limitation upon these mounting costs. No suggestion deals with the restoration of some semblance of a healthy balance. No plan is advanced for easing the crushing burden already resting upon the people.

To the contrary, all that we hear are the plans by which such costs progressively may be increased. New means are constantly being devised for greater call upon the taxable potential as though the resources available were inexhaustible. We compound irresponsibility by seeking to share what liquid wealth we have with others.

In so doing we recklessly speak of the billions we would set aside for the purpose, as though they were inconsequential. There can be no quarrel with altruism. Such has ever been a predominant quality making up the nobility of the American character. We should do all in our power to alleviate the suffering and hardship of other peoples, and to support their own maximum effort to preserve their freedom from the assaults of Communist imperialism.

But when this effort is carried beyond the ability to pay, or to the point that the attendant burden upon our own people becomes insufferable, or places our own way of life and freedom in jeopardy, then it ceases to be altruism and becomes reckless imprudence. I have yet to see evidence that such vast outlays were preceded by the slightest concern for the ultimate effect it will have upon our own liberties and standards of life.

This Nation's material wealth is built upon the vision and courage, the sweat and toil, hope and faith of our people. There has been no magic involved upon which we might again call to replenish our denuded coffers.

We can either advance upon the security of sound principles or we can plunge on to the precipice of disaster toward which we are now headed in the dangerous illusion that our wealth is inexhaustible and can therefore be limitlessly shared with others.

It is argued that we must give boundlessly if we are to be insured allies in an emergency.

I reject this reasoning as an unwarranted calumny against well-tested friends of long standing. The survival of the free world is infinitely more dependent upon the maintenance of a strong, vigorous, healthy, and independent America as a leavening influence than upon any financial aid which we might provide under our own existing stringencies.

The free world's one great hope for survival now rests upon the maintaining and preserving of our own strength. Continue to dissipate it and that one hope is dead. If the American people would pass on the standard of life and the heritage of opportunity they themselves have enjoyed to their children and their children's children they should ask their representatives in Government:

"What is the plan for the easing of the tax burden upon us? What is the plan for bringing to a halt this inflationary movement which is progressively and inexorably decreasing the purchasing power of our currency, nullifying the protection of our insurance provisions, and reducing those of fixed income to hardship and even despair?"

I fear these questions, if asked, would be met by stony silence. For just as in Korea there has been no plan. We have long drifted aimlessly with the sole safeguard against the ineptitude of our leaders resting upon American enterprise, American skill, and American courage. But once the incentive for the maximizing of these great attributes is lost the bulwark to support our failures is gone and the American way of life as we have known it will be gravely threatened.

Indivisible from this trend and probably contributory to it is a growing tendency to overlook certain forms of laxity in high quarters. Petty corruption in the public administration is a disease unfortunately common to all nations but I refer to an even more alarming situation.

Men of significant stature in national affairs appear to cower before the threat of reprisal if the truth be expressed in criticism of those in higher public authority.

For example, I find in existence a new and heretofore unknown and dangerous concept that the members of our Armed Forces owe primary allegiance and loyalty to those who temporarily exercise the authority of the executive branch of government, rather than to the country and its Constitution which they are sworn to defend.

No proposition could be more dangerous. None could cast greater doubt upon the integrity of the armed services.

For its application would at once convert them from their traditional and constitutional role as the instrument for the defense of the Republic into something partaking of the nature of a praetorian guard, owing sole allegiance to the political master of the hour.

While for the purpose of administration and command the armed services are within the executive branch of the Government, they are accountable as well to the Congress, charged with the policymaking responsibility, and to the people, ultimate repository of all national power.

Yet so inordinate has been the application of the Executive power that members of the armed services have been subjected to the most arbitrary and ruthless treatment for daring to speak the truth in accordance with conviction and conscience.

I hesitate to refer to my own relief from the Far Eastern commands as I have never questioned the legal authority underlying such action. But the three sole reasons publicly stated by the highest authority clearly demonstrate the arbitrary nature of the decision.

The first reason given was that, contrary to existing policy, I warned of the strategic relationship of Formosa to American security and the dangers inherent in this area's falling under Communist control. Yet this viewpoint has since been declared by the Secretary of State, under oath before congressional committees, to have been and to be the invincible and longstanding policy of the United States.

The second reason given was that I communicated my readiness to meet the enemy commander at any time to discuss acceptable terms of a cease fire arrangement. Yet, for this proposal, I was relieved of my command by the same authorities who since have received so enthusiastically the identical proposal when made by the Soviet Government.

The third and final reason advanced was my replying to a Congressman's request for information on a public subject then under open consideration by the Congress. Yet both Houses of Congress promptly passed a law confirming my action, which indeed had been entirely in accordance with a long existing and well recognized though unwritten policy.

This law states that no member of the Armed Forces shall be restricted or prevented from communicating directly or indirectly with any member or members of Congress concerning any subject unless such communication is in violation of law or the security and safety of the United States. And this formal enactment of basic public policy was approved without the slightest dissent by the President.

Is there wonder that men who seek an objective understanding of American policy thinking become completely frustrated and bewildered? Is there wonder that Soviet propaganda so completely dominates American foreign policy? And, indeed, what is our foreign policy?

We hear impassioned appeals that it be bipartisan - violent charges that sinister efforts are being made to obstruct and defeat it - but I defy you or any other man to tell me what it is. It has become a mass of confused misunderstandings and vacillations. It has meant one thing today - another tomorrow. It has almost blown with every wind, changed with every tide.

The sorry truth is we have no policy. Expediencies as variable and shifting as the exigencies of the moment seem to be the only guide. Yesterday, we disarmed; today we arm; and what of tomorrow? We have been told of the war in Korea, that it is the wrong war, with the wrong enemy, at the wrong time, and in the wrong place. Does this mean that they intend and indeed plan what they would call a right war, with a right enemy, at a right time and in a right place?

If successful in mounting the North Atlantic Pact in 1953 or 1954 or at one of the ever-changing dates fixed for its consummation, what comes then? Do we mean to throw down a gage of battle? Do we mean to continue the fantastic fiscal burden indefinitely to our inevitable exhaustion?

Is our only plan to spend and spend and spend? Do we intend to resist by force Red aggression in southeast Asia if it develops? Do we intend to take over commitments in the explosive Middle East? Do we intend to enter into a series of military alliances abroad? Do we intend to actually implement by force of arms the so-called Truman plan? These are questions that disturb us because there is no answer forthcoming. We do want and need unity and bipartisanship in our foreign policy - but when there is no policy we can but dangerously drift.

In Korea, despite the magnificent performance of our fighting forces, the result has been indecisive. The high moral purpose which so animated and inspired the world a year ago yielded to the timidity and fear of our leaders as after defeating our original enemy a new one entered the field which they dared not fight to a decision. Appeasement thereafter became the policy of war on the battlefield.

In the actual fighting with this new enemy we did not lose but neither did we win. Yet it can be accepted as a basic principle proven and reproven since the beginning of time that a great nation which enters upon war and fails to see it through to victory must accept the full moral consequences of defeat.

Now that the fighting has temporarily abated the outstanding impression which emerges from the scene is the utter uselessness of the enormous sacrifice in life and limb which has resulted. A million soldiers on both sides and unquestionably at least a like number of civilians are maimed or dead. A nation has been gutted and we stand today just where we stood before it all started.

The threat of aggression upon the weak by those callously inclined among the strong has not diminished. Indeed, nothing has been settled. No issue has been decided.

This experience again emphasizes the utter futility of modern war - its complete failure as an arbiter of international dissensions. Its threat must be abolished if the world is to go on-and if it does not go on it will go under.

We must finally come to realize that war is outmoded as an instrument of political policy, that it provides no solution for international problems; that it but threatens the participants with mutual national suicide. We must understand that in final analysis the mounting cost of preparation for war is in many ways as materially destructive as war itself. We must find the means to avoid this great sapping of human energy and resource.

This requires leadership of the highest order - a spiritual and moral leadership - a leadership which our country alone is capable of providing. While we must be prepared to meet the trial of war if war comes, we should gear our foreign and domestic policies toward the ultimate goal - the abolition of war from the face of the earth.

This is what practically all mankind - all the great masses which populate the world - long and pray for. Therein lies the road, the only road, to universal peace and prosperity. We must lead the world down that road however long and tortuous and illusory it may now appear.

Such is the role as I see it for which this great Nation of ours is now cast. In this we follow the Cross. If we meet the challenge we cannot fail. But no end may be achieved without first making a start - no success without a trial.

On this problem of greatest universal concern, unless we address ourselves to the fundamentals we shall get no farther than the preceding generations which have tried and failed. Convention after convention has been entered into designed to humanize war and bring it under the control of rules dictated by the highest human ideals. Yet each war becomes increasingly savage as the means for mass killing are further developed.

You cannot control war; you can only abolish it. Those who shrug this off as idealistic are the real enemies of peace - the real warmongers. Those who lack the enterprise, vision, and courage to try a new approach when none others have succeeded fail completely the simple test of leadership.

As I have traveled through the country since my return, I find a great transformation in American thought to be taking place. Our apathy is disappearing. American public opnion is beginning to exert its immense power. The American people are expressing themselves with dynamic force on foreign policy. This is exerting a profound influence upon the Soviet course of action.

Few events in the life of our Republic have been of more significant importance nor more heartening than this rallying of the collective will of the American people. They are putting pressure upon their own leaders and upon the leaders of those with whom we are directly or indirectly engaged. And just as it has cast its influence upon policy and events abroad it can be brought to bear with no less telling effect upon policy and events at home.

Therein lies our best hope in the battle to save America - the full weight of an aroused, informed, and militant public opinion. I stated in Texas:

"If it be that my relief was the spark which ignited this great power of American public expression; which caused our people to rise above the level of narrow partisanship to unite in a common crusade to effect a spiritual rebirth in

American life; which restored to the American people the full glory and dignity of self-rule under those same high principles and ideals which animated our fathers; which restored a lost faith in ourselves and our free institutions; which provided the symbol for rallying the mighty forces for good throughout the land - then I would be thankful, indeed, to a farseeing and merciful providence and could not ask for more."

We stand today at a critical moment in history - at a vital crossroad. In one direction is the path of courageous patriots seeking in humility but the opportunity to serve their country; the other that of those selfishly seeking to entrench autocratic power.

The one group stands for implacable resistance against Communism; the other for compromising with Communism. The one stands for our traditional system of government and freedom; the other for a Socialist state and slavery.

The one boldly speaks the truth; the other spreads propaganda, fear, and deception. The one denounces excessive taxation, bureaucratic government, and corruption; the other seeks more taxes, more bureaucratic power, and shields corruption.

The people, as the ultimate rulers, must choose the course our Nation shall follow. On their decision rests the future of our free civilization and the survival of our Christian faith. Not for a moment do I doubt that decision or that it will guide the Nation to a new and fuller greatness. Good night.

CITY HALL
JULY 26, 1951
BOSTON, MASSACHUSETTS

Mr. Mayor:

I thank you from the bottom of my heart for the signal honor this great city has conferred upon Mrs. MacArthur and myself. Its welcome and hospitality have been overwhelming and have etched a memory on our hearts we will never forget. Boston is rightly famous throughout the world for its courtesy and cordiality, but in our reception it has surely set a new and unsurpassable standard. We only wish that we might stay longer and have an opportunity to express more intimately and individually our great appreciation. It has been an inspiration to visit again this birthplace of American Freedom and you have given me a new and invincible feeling of hope and confidence. I feel this city, as always, will be in the vanguard to meet any crisis.

Again our warmest thanks.

RESPONSE TO RECEPTION
JULY 26, 1951
CHICOPEE FALLS, MASSACHUSETTS

I come to Chicopee Falls with a feeling of reverent respect. It was here that my father was born and it was here that my grandfather landed as an immigrant from Scotland. This visit today is therefore for me a pilgrimage of devotion and sentiment. Of all men I have ever known my father was the one I held in deepest respect and esteem. He seemed to epitomize those virtues for which this great state of Massachusetts is famous - courage, intelligence and morality. And I like to think that my coming in some way may re-emphasize my admiration for the greatness of its contributions of the past and my confidence in its future. From the bottom of my heart I thank you all for the sympathy and care you have taken of this old home. To see it has etched a memory I shall never forget.

For your kindness and hospitality today Mrs. MacArthur joins me in warmest appreciation. We only wish we could have stayed longer.

RESPONSE TO RECEPTION
JULY 26, 1951
SPRINGFIELD, MASSACHUSETTS

Mrs. MacArthur and I thank you from the bottom of our hearts for your cordial reception today. It has moved us both deeply and we only wish we could stay here longer to express to each of you personally our appreciation. Our trip to this great state has been an inspiring one for here was born the concept of American Liberty - and here we feel its survival is safe. We draw great hope from this thought at this critical moment when there are so many disbelievers. To me there is the added sentiment that nearby in Chicopee Falls is the birthplace of my father. It seems almost as though at last I were coming home. And it is in that spirit I will always think of and remember you.

Again our thanks and deepest appreciation.

WREATH LAYING
JULY 26, 1951
WALTHAM, MASSACHUSETTS

I place this wreath with great reverence. I do not know the dignity of the birth of these men but I do know the glory of their death. They died that our nation might live in freedom. Their memory should be held immortal and a merciful God will rest their souls.

GENERAL MACARTHUR'S CORRESONDENCE
TO THE PRIME MINISTER OF JAPAN
AUGUST 20, 1951

It was a splendid relationship that developed between MacArthur and the Japanese Emperor and his top advisors at the end of World War II. The response by Japan to MacArthur's administration of the occupation was an unexpected and favorable surprise. The demands from Washington - State Department and many members of the Congress sought the same firm and degrading ad-

ministration practiced with Germany - all attempts by Washington were rebuffed by MacArthur as he maintained his program of compassion and common sense during the occupation. The result has been a miracle of occupation philosophy never before experienced in the community of nations.

Edward T. Imparato, Editor

Dear Mr. Prime Minister:

I am delighted to have before me your thoughtful and generous note of July 13th.

I rejoice with you and the Japanese people that a fair and just treaty is projected for early consummation. It is indeed a source of immense personal satisfaction that the spiritual and moral values which throughout have guided the formulation of Occupation policy will find permanent reflection in the instrument designed formally to restore the peace. Thereby, Japan will reassume a position of dignity and equality within the family of nations and take a firm and invincible stand with the free world to repel those evil forces of international Communist tyranny which seek covertly or by force of arms to destroy freedom.

Upon the political, economic and social base established so largely under your distinguished leadership, Japan's history lies before it. Continue faithful adherence to the following sound political policies and principles of good government, and healthy national progress will be assured:

Public morality is the touchstone to the people's faith in the integrity of the governmental process.

Restraint and frugality in the use of the public purse produces economic stability, encourages individual thrift and minimizes the burden of taxation.

Avoidance of the excessive centralization of the political power safeguards against the danger of totalitarian rule with the suppression of personal liberty, advances the concept of local autonomy and develops an acute consciousness in the individual citizen of his political responsibility. Undue paternalism in government tends to sap the creative potential and impair initiative and energy in those who thereby come to regard governmental subsidy as an inalienable right.

The preservation, inviolate, of the economic system based upon free, private, competitive enterprise alone maximizes the initiative, the energy and in the end the productive capacity of the people.

The vigorous and faithful implementation of the existing land laws providing land ownership for agricultural workers and of the labor laws providing industrial workers a voice in the conditions of their employment is mandatory if these all-important segments of Japanese society are to enjoy their rightful dignity and opportunity, and social unrest based upon just grievance is to be avoided.

The Bill of Rights ordained by the Constitution must be vigilantly preserved if the government would be assured the people's full support. Public criticism should be encouraged rather than suppressed as providing a powerful check against the evils of maladministration of the political power. Freedom of speech as an inalienable right should never be challenged unless it directly violates the laws governing libel and slander.

The courts must function as the champion of human justice and the police power be exercised with primary regard to individual rights.

Without sacrifice of the principles of justice the devious advances of international Communism must be firmly repelled as a threat to internal peace and the national security. To such end, so long as existing international tensions exist in Asia, adequate security forces should be maintained to safeguard Japan's internal peace against any threatened external attack.

Indeed, a Japan erected firmly upon such a norm of political principle and policy as well as setting a sure course to its own free destiny, could not fail to exercise a profound and beneficial influence upon the course of events in Continental Asia. It would in addition contribute immeasurably to the spiritual and material advance of civilization.

I have faith that the Japanese people will hold invincibly to such a course.

Cordially yours,
Douglas MacArthur
"His Excellency Shigeru Yoshida, Prime Minister of Japan, Tokyo, Japan."

CITIZENS OF CLEVELAND, OHIO
SEPTEMBER 6, 1951
CLEVELAND, OHIO

Our military and political leaders have failed once again to capitalize on the gains of war to establish a stronger and more meaningful forward policy of strength and leadership for the world of nations. Instead our government proceeded to tear down our military, destroying our weapons and abandoning our true commitment to our Constitution to satisfy the liberal sector for political, not national, gain. The ever increasing centralization of government functions is bad policy and must be halted or we will see a trend of weakening the influence of States, Countries, cities and individual freedom and liberty.

Edward T. Imparato, Editor

It is gratifying indeed to have this opportunity to address the citizens of Cleveland and the State of Ohio - a State which has contributed so abundantly to America's leadership both past and contemporary. Indeed, indications multiply that this leadership may even increase in the not too distant future.

No section of our country symbolizes more forcefully the pattern of our national progress than does this great Midwest whose fertile fields and thriving industry combine to reflect the constructive energy of our people. You have molded a standard and pattern of life known to no other nation of the world, and I pray that we will have the vision and courage and statesmanship to keep it that way - that we will preserve an America which will provide increasing, not diminishing, opportunities for human advancement.

We have just passed another anniversary of the end of the war with Japan. Six years ago with a few strokes of the pen a calm descended upon the battlefields of the world and the guns grew silent. Military victory had been achieved for our cause and men turned their thoughts from the task of mass killing to the higher duty of international restoration, from destroying to rebuilding, from destruction to construction.

Everywhere in the free world they lifted up their heads and hearts in thanksgiving for the advent of a peace in which ethics and morality based upon truth and justice would thereafter fashion the universal code.

Then, more than ever in the history of the modern world, a materially strong and spiritually vibrant leadership was needed to consolidate the victory into a truly enduring peace for all of the human race. America at the very apex of her military power was the logical nation to which the world turned for such leadership. It was a crucial moment - one of the greatest opportunities ever known.

But our political and military leaders failed to comprehend it. Sensitive only to the expediencies of the hour, they dissipated with reckless haste that predominant military power which was the key to the situation.

Our forces were rapidly and completely demobilized and the great stores of war materiel which had been accumulated were disposed of with irresponsible waste and abandon.

The world was thus left exposed and vulnerable to an international communism whose long-published plan had been to await just such a favorable opportunity to establish dominion over the free nations. The stage had perhaps been unwittingly set in secret and most unfortunate war conferences. The events which followed will cast their shadow upon history for all time.

Peoples with long traditions of human freedom progressively fell victims to a type of international brigandage and blackmail, and the so-called "Iron Curtain" descended rapidly upon large parts of Europe and Asia.

As events have unfolded, the truth has become clear.

Our great military victory has been offset, largely because of military unpreparedness, by the political successes of the Kremlin. Our diplomatic blunders increased as our senseless disarmament became a reality.

And now the disastrous cycle is completed as those same leaders who lost to the world the one great chance it has had for enduring universal peace, frantically endeavor, by arousing a frenzy of fear throughout the land, to gear anew our energies and resources, to rebuild our dissipated strength, and to face again a future of total war.

Our need for adequate military defense, with world tensions as they were and are, is and should have been completely evident even before the end of the war. By what faith then can we find hope in those whose past judgments so grievously erred - who deliberately disarmed in the face of threatened Communism?

Can they now be blindly trusted as they so vehemently demand to set an unerring course to our future well-being and security? There are those of us who from neither partisan affiliation nor with political purpose think not.

At war's end the main agency for maintaining the peace became the United Nations. This organization was conceived in a common desire that the scourge of war should not again be visited upon the earth. It was dedicated to the principle that all mankind of inalienable right should live in justice and liberty and peace.

It represents perhaps the noblest effort man has yet made to evolve a universal code based upon the highest of moral precepts. It became the keystone to an arch of universal hope.

Yet in practice its efforts become increasingly doubtful of ultimate success. Its organization is inherently weak, legislatively, judicially, and executively. It lacks legislative strength because its members, not being elected but merely appointed, are not answerable directly to their people. It lacks judicial strength because there is no accepted international code of sufficient moral authority or purpose to mold and guide its decisions. It lacks executive strength because it controls no agencies of sufficient power to enforce its mandates.

It threatens to fail if the innate selfishness of its members does not yield to universal needs; if the mechanics of its operations are not corrected to prevent the will of one nation from counterbalancing the collective will of the others; if it does not obtain acceptance by member nations of its lawful decisions; if it does not stop obstructionist tactics, even by expulsion if necessary, of its own unruly members; if regional military alliances must be organized within its membership to undertake collective security measures against threat from other members; if it allows itself to be reduced to a mere forum for meaningless and acrimonious debate, and a springboard for propaganda.

Unless a strong and dynamic sense of responsibility emerges within its ranks capable of rallying the forces of good throughout the world; of establishing a higher moral tone to its deliberations and activities; of correcting its existing institutional and mechanical weaknesses, the United Nations may well go the way of its predecessor League and perish as a force to guide civilization.

But the great moral and spiritual purpose which animated its formation - the abolition of war from the face of the earth - will always live and a way must be found to achieve that purpose. This way cannot be found, however, if nations are so blind as not to see their own weaknesses - so weak as not to correct them.

In this postwar period of general failure to attain real peace one of the bright spots has been conquered Japan. That nation and its people long boasting of many centuries of unbroken military success - a self-sufficient warrior race with a history of almost complete isolation from the rest of the world - at war's end was reduced largely to rubble with its people impoverished and broken in mind, body, and spirit.

The sudden and general destruction of Japanese institutions brought about by complete defeat left a spiritual vacuum in Japanese life to be filled either by a philosophy of good, or a philosophy of evil. Fortunately for Japan and for the free world, the country was spared the dreadful consequences of a Soviet military occupation and was brought instead within the benign guidance of the American people.

Under this beneficent influence the Japanese gradually lifted themselves from the ashes of defeat and started to build a new nation - a nation dedicated to the pursuit of new concepts and new ideals, fashioned from a blend between the best of their own ancient culture and those high precepts of ethics and morals which have been the great pillars supporting America's origin and growth.

This oriental nation under the shadow of a continent plagued by the cruel misery of unending wars, pillage, and natural disasters, proved willing and adept under the guiding hand of an occupation not conceived in a spirit of vengeance or mastery, of victor over vanquished, but committed to the Christian purpose of helping a defeated, bewildered, and despairing people re-create in the East a nation largely designed in the image of the West.

New Japan was thus erected upon free institutions, somewhat similar to our own, which permitted the development of a moral base which cannot fail to favorably influence the course of events in Asia for generations to come. Discarded is the traditional intolerance of human rights, the restrictions upon human liberties, the callousness to human life and in their place have been accepted and fused into the Japanese heart many of the Christian virtues so predominantly embodied in the American character.

An enlightened constitution has become the great charter of Japanese liberty with enabling laws which give full effect to its immutable precepts.

The Government has become truly representative of the popular will, deriving its just powers from the consent of the governed. The principle of local autonomy has been established. This permits the balance of political power to rest with the citizen at the community level and thus serves as a constant check against the excesses of centralized authority.

The hated system of land tenure, so contributory to general unrest in Asia, has been abolished. Every farmer is now accorded the right and dignity of ownership of the land he long has tilled.

He thus reaps the full fruits which result from his toil and labors with the incentive of free enterprise to maximize his effort to achieve increasing production. Representing over a half of Japan's total population, the agriculture workers have become an invincible barrier against the advance of socialistic ideas which would relegate all to the indignity of state servitude.

Labor through the protection of modern laws has come into a new and heretofore unknown dignity and is making rapid strides along the course of a sound and healthy movement. The schools have been rid of the strictures upon academic freedom and public education is provided to all of the youth of the land.

Universal suffrage has been established and the women of Japan have assumed their rightful role in the political life of the nation. With dignity and resolution they have brought to bear upon public affairs the morality which centers in the home and are progressively asserting a strong and healthy influence upon the course of Japan's political destiny.

The courts are proceeding in their administrative and judicial roles with universally accepted principles of justice firmly implanted in the form of their procedure. The police have ceased to be masters and have become instead servants of the people with a decentralization in organization which permits exercise of their functions at the community, rather than national, level of government.

The economy of Japan has made rapid and effective advances toward the full restoration of stability and self-sufficiency and has achieved a sound basis for a frugal public administration. For the past three years, the national budget has been in complete balance with savings to permit substantial reductions in the tax load upon the people and corresponding raises in their living standard.

Japan's present course in the economy of public administration follows closely the pattern sagely advised by Thomas Jefferson when he warned in speaking of our own Government:

"I place economy among the first and most important virtues and public debt as the greatest of dangers to be feared. To preserve our independence, we must not let our leaders load us with perpetual debt. We must make our choice between economy and liberty, or profusion and servitude. The same prudence which in private life would forbid our paying our money for unexplained projects, forbids it in the disposition of public money. We are endeavoring to reduce the Government to the practice of rigid economy to avoid burdening the people and arming the magistrate with a patronage of money which might be used to corrupt the principle of government."

If Japan continues to heed this farsighted warning and our own leaders who pretend to be disciples of the Jeffersonian teachings continue to ignore it, the time may well come when the Japanese people will be firmly established within the protective folds of our own cherished liberties, while we ourselves shall have lost them because of the assumption of our leaders of that "patronage of money" with its consequent corruption of government against which Jefferson so clearly warned.

In such a tragic eventuality, we would be hard put to it indeed to answer the charge of our children and our children's children that we had recklessly squandered their rightful heritage of liberty, resource, and opportunity.

This is but a brief outline of the new Japan which is about to be restored to a position of international dignity and equality under a peace treaty which as presently proposed, while far from flawless, embodies much of human justice and enlightenment. It is a Japan which may now assume the burden of preparing its own ground defense against predatory attack and thus in short time release our own beloved divisions for return home.

With our air and naval support, Japan can with no great difficulty defend its own homeland, which forms so vital a sector of the inland defense system buttressing freedom and peace in the Pacific. It is a Japan in which we of the free world may find an alliance which shall merit our full faith. I realize well that there are nations who fought with us to victory while suffering grievous hurt from Japanese depredation who understandably disagree in whole or in part.

It is hard for them to accept the realistic but tragic fact that in modern war the victor is also the loser. He suffers materially with the vanquished - ofttimes more than does the vanquished. Indeed, our own country in the aftermath of victory pays with a burden of accumulated debt such as to place a mortgage upon the energy and resource of many future generations.

May we not hope that eventually through wise statesmanship and Christian tolerance the scars still left in war's wake may be finally healed and that victor and vanquished as befits the sacred cause of human freedom will be invincibly bound together in mutual preservation.

Since my return from service abroad I have enjoyed the privilege, the freedom, and the opportunities of private citizenship. I have seen many new and wonderful things but some which to me create a disturbing outlook for the future. Possibly one of the most pernicious is our steady drift toward totalitarian rule with the suppression of those personal liberties which have formed the foundation stones to our political, economic, and social advance to national greatness.

Our Government now differs substantially from the design of our forefathers as laid down in the Constitution. They envisaged a federation of sovereign States with only such limited power resting in the Federal authority as became necessary to serve the common interests of all.

But under the stress of national emergencies during the past two decades, there has been a persistent and progressive centralization of power in the Federal Government with only superficial restoration to the States and the people as emergencies subsided. This drift has resulted in an increasingly dangerous paternalistic relationship between Federal Government and private citizen, with the mushrooming of agency after agency designed to control the individual.

Authority specifically reserved to the States by constitutional mandate has been ignored in the ravenous effort to further centralize the political power. Within the Federal Government itself there has been a further and dangerous centralization.

For example, the Department of State, originally established for the sole purpose of the conduct of foreign diplomacy, has become in effect a general operating agency of Government, exercising authority and influence over many facets of executive administration formerly reserved to the President or the heads of other departments. The Department of State indeed is rapidly assuming the character of prime ministry notwithstanding that its Secretary is an appointed official, neither chosen by nor answerable directly to the people.

This drift toward totalitarian rule is reflected not only in this shift toward centralized power, but as well in the violent manner in which exception is taken to the citizens' voice when raised in criticism those who exercise the political power.

There seems to be a determination to suppress individual voice and opinion which can only be regarded as symptomatic of the beginning of a general trend toward mass thought control. Abusive language and arbitrary action, rather than calm, dispassionate, and just argument, ill becomes the leadership of a great nation conceived in liberty and dedicated to a course of morality and justice. It challenges the concept of free speech and is an attempt at direct suppression through intimidation of that most vital check against the abuse of politic power - public criticism.

If long countenanced by freemen, it can but lead to those controls upon conviction and conscience which traditionally have formed stepping stones to dictatorial power.

The issues which today confront the Nation are clearly defined and so fundamental as to directly involve the very survival of the Republic.

Are we going to preserve the religious base to our origin, our growth, and our progress, or yield to the devious assaults of atheistic or other antireligious forces?

Are we going to maintain our present course toward state socialism with Communism just beyond or reverse the present trend and regain our hold upon our heritage of liberty and freedom?

Are we going to squander our limited resources to the point of our own inevitable exhaustion or adopt common sense policies of frugality which will insure financial stability in our time and a worthwhile heritage in that of our progeny?

Are we going to continue to yield personal liberties and community autonomy to the steady and inexorable centralization of all political power or restore the Republic to constitutional direction, regain our personal liberties, and reassume the individual State's primary responsibility and authority in the conduct of local affairs?

Are we going to permit a continuing decline in public and private morality or reestablish high ethical standards as the means of regaining a diminishing faith in the integrity of our public and private institutions?

Are we going to continue to permit the pressure of alien doctrines to strongly influence the orientation of foreign and domestic policy or regain trust in our own traditions, experience, and free institutions, and the wisdom of our own people?

In short, is American life of the future to be characterized by freedom or by servitude, strength or weakness? The answer must be clear and unequivocal if we are to avoid the pitfalls toward which we are now heading with such certainty. In many respects it is not to be found in any dogma of political philosophy, but in those immutable precepts which underlie the Ten Commandments. During the five months since my return, I have been encouraged to believe that our citizens will not complacently tolerate further incursions against their cherished liberties and will move to correct this drift away from truly representative government.

I have found this encouragement in the rare opportunity to search the faces of millions of my fellow countrymen. Therein I have been given understanding of the meaning of Abraham Lincoln when he said:

"To the salvation of the Union there needs but one single thing - the hearts of a people like yours. When the people rise in a mass in behalf of the liberties of the country, truly it may be said that (nothing can) prevail against them."

I have seen in the faces of the American people that to which Mr. Lincoln prophetically referred. I have clearly seen that the soul of liberty is still living and vibrant in the American heart. It is neither Democratic nor Republican, but American. It will assert itself by constitutional process and with invincible force in the battle to save the Republic. The people will still rule.

ZION REFORMED CHURCH
"THE LIBERTY BELL CHURCH"
SEPTEMBER 21, 1951
ALLENTOWN, PENNSYLVANIA

The Liberty Bell - symbol of our liberty and justice, must never be forgotten.

Edward T. Imparato, Editor

One hundred seventy-four years ago on this hallowed spot your ancestors received into their solemn charge the liberty bell then sought by British Forces bent upon recasting that precious symbol of freedom into instruments to suppress freedom. Let us remember gratefully what they then did. Let us renew our devotion to the principles for which they then fought. And let us regain the faith they then had in an

America standing as a beacon of light to guide all mankind to the ways of truth and liberty and justice.

I pray today at this Shrine that we will have the wisdom, the resolution and the courage to preserve and pass on unimpaired the heritage of freedom drawn from their nobility and their sacrifice.

AMERICAN LEGION CONVENTION
OCTOBER 17, 1951
MIAMI, FLORIDA

MacArthur's allegiance to the fighting men of the military forces never wavered. He spoke out in their behalf and praised their performance, as they well deserved, all of his life. His greatest speeches were those directed to the enlisted ranks and on occasion to the officer corp as well. His praise of the foot soldier for their great defense of the Philippines in the first part of World War II - their valiant fight against superior Japanese forces - suffering under severe medical, physical and starving conditions. In the final stages of that struggle fighting for days and weeks on one-third rations, is a tribute to their determination to fight to the death.

Edward T. Imparato, Editor

I am deeply grateful for this opportunity to address those who brought victory to American arms in the past two great wars of world history. I do so as a member of this Legion holding no public office, advocating no partisan cause, and animated by the sole desire to help restore, preserve, and advance those great American principles and ideals of which we have been beneficiaries ourselves and are now trustees for future American generations.

No fraternity of men ever rested upon a more noble concept than does the American Legion. The indestructible bonds which unite its members were welded in a heat of battle by those who laid life and limb upon the altar of self-sacrifice.

From its very inception, it pledged itself to those high principles which form the preamble to its constitution. "For God and Country" it reads, and to these it has remained invincibly faithful. It has written a record of service to the Nation which commands the gratitude of every citizen.

To me, it is a source of added inspiration that the women's auxiliary has joined us here today. None will dispute the strength they have brought to the Legion in the fulfillment of its tasks. In these challenging times, they stand as a mighty spiritual force to inspire faith that we may maintain in American life the moral base upon which our true greatness has always depended.

Of all issues which today confront our people, possibly none is of more immediate concern to the Legion than is the direction of our military policy. That policy necessarily and traditionally has found its general orientation in the politi-

MacArthur at a West Point Cadet review. He stands in civilian clothes on the plain with Superintendent, MGEN Fred Irving, and cadets, September 29, 1951.

cal thinking which has guided our foreign affairs. But so closely interwoven have our military and foreign and even domestic policies become that it is impossible to ignore one when considering the others.

To understand the general direction of our military policy, we must therefore understand the animating impulses which guide our domestic and foreign affairs. Both, under the leadership now administering our Government, have departed sharply from tradition and constitutional mandate.

At the birth of the Nation, Washington counseled strongly against our entering upon entangling alliances abroad lest we find ourselves involved in Europe's wars. This was sound advice then, but has been necessarily outmoded by the progress of civilization.

For with the development of means of rapid communication, existing gaps between the several continental land masses have been narrowed and ocean barriers in themselves no longer set the stage for continental isolation nor offer an assured degree of protection for continental shores.

As a consequence, it is impossible to disassociate ourselves from the affairs of Europe and Asia. Major warfare in either has become our immediate military concern, lest they fall under the domination of those hostile to us and intent upon predatory incursions against our own land.

To counteract the potentiality of this danger, we have acted both in the East and in the West. In the Pacific we and our friends maintain an island defense chain off the coast of continental Asia which must be preserved inviolate at any cost.

Despite some public statements to the contrary, there is reason to fear that it is still the overriding purpose of some of our political leaders, under the influence of allies who maintain diplomatic ties with Communist China, to yield the island of Formosa at an opportune time to the Chinese henchmen of international Communism.

The effect of such action would be to breach our island defense chain, threaten peace on the Pacific, and ultimately endanger the security of our Pacific coastal area.

There is little doubt that the yielding of Formosa and the seating of Communist China in the United Nations was fully planned when I called upon the enemy commander in Korea on March 24 to meet me in the field to arrange armistice terms. This I did in view of the fundamental weakness of his military position due to the lack of an industrial base in China capable of supporting modern warfare.

The opposition I expressed to yielding Formosa and seating Red China, with the overwhelming support it received from the American people, unquestionably wrecked the secret plan to yield on these issues as the price for peace in Korea.

There followed the violent Washington reaction in personal retaliation against me for what was actually so normal a military move.

Across the Atlantic we have no similar island defense chain but, in view of the openly flaunted intention of international Communism to destroy throughout the world the concept of freedom and bring peoples everywhere under the subjugation and terror of police rule, it has become necessary to help the free nations of Western Europe prepare against the threat of predatory attack by Communist forces now occupying Eastern Europe.

And generally throughout the world, our policy has been enunciated to extend a helping hand to others whose freedom is threatened and who have the will but lack the entire resource essential to their own defense.

The soundness of this concept will depend upon the wisdom with which it is administered. Recklessly and abnormally applied, it could encompass our own destruction. This country obviously lacks the resource militarily to defend the world. It has the resource, however, reasonably to assist in that defense.

But such assistance must be contributory to, rather than in place of, maximum local national effort. It should be extended only upon condition -

That assistance to others be really for defense and that it should be so limited as not to deplete our own resources to the point of imperiling the survival of our own liberties; and that those we would assist be animated by the same love of freedom as we, and possess the will and determination to pledge their own lives and full resource to secure their own defense.

On the strict observance of these conditions rests our hope that present efforts to bolster Western Europe may justify the additional burden it places upon our own people. There are, however, many disturbing signs and reports to the contrary.

There are many of the leaders and people of Western Europe who mistakenly believe that we assist them solely to protect ourselves, or to assure an alliance with them, should our country be attacked. This is indeed fallacious thinking. Our potential in human and material resource, in alignment with the rest of the Americas, is adequate to defend this hemisphere against any threat from any power or any association of powers.

We do desire to retain our traditional friends and allies in Europe, but such an alliance must rest upon spiritual bonds fabricated from a mutuality of purpose and a common heritage of principle - not an alliance to be secured at a price.

There are other disturbing signs that some of the peoples we seek to bolster are showing a lack of will to muster their own full resource in their own defense.

There appear to be many among them who feel that their defense is, and should be, our sole responsibility and that beyond a token military collaboration they should confine their own energy and resource to the building of their civilian economy - some indeed who go so far as to advocate that money appropriated by our Congress for their military defense should be diverted to civilian purpose.

The startling thing is that such viewpoints are not lacking in support among our own leaders. Apparently, some of them, more in line with Marxian philosophy than animated by a desire to preserve freedom, would finance the defense of others as a means of sharing with them our wealth.

This wealth, accumulated by our own initiative and industry under the incentives of free enterprise, would then serve as the means of covering Socialist or Communist deficits abroad. The ultimate effect, whatever the intent, would be to reduce our own standard of life to a level of universal mediocrity.

We have committed ourselves to contribute six ground divisions to Western Europe. Notwithstanding that, only a small fraction of the great masses of its peoples have been called to the colors. Indeed, if the human resource and industrial potential of the Western European nations were effectively employed for defense, there would be minimum need for American ground forces or even great quantities of American munitions - air and naval power, yes, but little honest necessity for ground troops - unless it be solely for morale purposes.

Actually, if the European nations have the will to defend themselves, no question of morale would be involved. Our efforts to whip up enthusiasm among the Western European peoples for the defense of their own liberties find neither precedent nor support in common sense or logic.

One thing we must clearly understand is that the very course on which we are now embarked carries with itself grave risks to our own survival.

The exhaustive effort to build our own military power and supplement that of other free nations, however justified, is probably more or less in accord with Soviet planning. For just as we expend our resources to build military strength, inversely we progressively reduce ourselves to economic weakness, with a consequent growing vulnerability to the internal stresses and strains manipulated by Communists and their agents in our midst.

It may indeed prove that the preparation for a war which may never occur will exhaust us materially as completely as would such a war itself. Our leaders must throw off the complacent belief that the only threat to our survival is from without. All freedoms lost since war's end have been the result of internal pressures rather than external assault.

What action then do we propose to take against those Communist nations whose provocations have brought upon us so sad a state of affairs?

We now hear talk of force as bulwarking our foreign policy, but in Korea we restrain the use of the very force we possess where challenged on the battlefield.

And, while we hear such talk of force and our soldiers fight against our self-imposed odds, we and our allies continue to give the Soviet and its satellites the aid and comfort and immense satisfaction of full diplomatic relations and, with but limited exceptions, the rights, privileges, and opportunities of trade aud commerce normal to friendly international intercourse.

We negotiate and negotiate and negotiate, never seeming to learn that you cannot profitably negotiate with Communists any more than you can with any other type of malefactor in civilized society. The only persuasion that will move them is the resistance to their abusive pressure by adequate counter pressure.

Recent events point to a startling and dangerous shift in our basic military concept. After Communist China committed itself to war against our forces in Korea, our political and military leaders set aside our traditional military policy calling for the employment of all available power and means to achieve a prompt and decisive victory and adopted instead the doctrine of defense. Every distinguished military leader of the past and all military experience from the beginning of time warns this but invite failure.

Under this new conception, novel indeed to American military character, we are required in the midst of deadly war to soften our blows and send men into battle with neither promise nor hope of victory.

We have deprived them of supporting military power already on hand and available which would blunt the enemy's blows against them, save countless American lives, fulfill our commitmeut to the tragic people of Korea, and lead to the victorious end of a war which has already left so many thousands of American soldiers maimed or dead.

More than this, it could and would have removed the Chinese Communists as a threat to freedom in Asia and the peace of the world for generations to come.

The reason given for such a course has little validity. It has been argued in justification and seemingly to soothe the public concern that the application of conventional war measures against our enemy might provoke the Soviet into launching the third world war.

Yet, since the end of the Second World War, without committing a single soldier to battle, the Soviet, aided by our own political blunders, has gained a dominion over territory and peoples without parallel in all history - a dominion which it will take years for it to assimilate and administer. What then would be its purpose in provoking a war of most doubtful result to the Communist cause?

I have strong doubt that the start of a major war anywhere enters the Soviet plans at this stage. If and when it does, it will be at a time and place and under circumstances dictated with scarce regard to the incidents of Korea.

Could there be anything more discouraging and shocking to our soldiers on the line than the deprecating reference to their fierce and savage struggle as a "police action"? Could anything be more agonizing to the mothers of their dead than the belittling reference to it by the Joint Chiefs of Staff as the "Korean skirmish"?

What a lack of perspective! What a failure to place first things first! What a complete callousness to human feeling and soldier dignity!

Two great questions about Korea still remain unanswered. First, why did they start the war if they did not intend to win it? And second, what do they intend to do now? - go on piling up our dead indefinitely with no fixed purpose or end in sight?

Hardened old soldier though I am - my very soul revolts at this unnecessary slaughter of the flower of our youth.

I recall so vividly the American Legion's warning to the country at the close of the war some six years ago. Its resolution read as follows:

"...the only present guarantee of our Nation's safety and freedom and the best presently available assurance of world peace is to have in the hands of this great peace-loving Nation the mightiest armament in the world."

Sound and farsighted advice which considered the present and drew upon the lessons and experience of the past.

Had it been heeded by our political and military leaders, we would have been able to consolidate our great moral and military victory and lead the world to an enduring peace. We would not now be frantically endeavoring to restore our dissipated military strength. The Soviet would be but a negative influence upon world affairs, and the earth would be a much gentler place on which to live.

But our leaders failed to heed that advice. They failed to recognize the opportunity for leadership which victory had cast. They failed to see the enormity of the Communist threat to an impoverished postwar world.

And, failing this vision, they became animated solely by what appeared to be the political expediencies of the hour. They disarmed and demobilized our military power with reckless haste.

They disposed of our vast stores of military equipment with such irresponsible abandon that, when I sought to arm and equip a modest military reserve of 75,000 Japanese to help fill the power vacuum left in Japan when we moved our occupation divisions to the Korean front, I was informed that it would take 18 months, at a very minimum, before the requirements could be filled.

After reducing our military strength to possibly the lowest relative degree in American history, they suddenly reversed the process, to rearm with no less precipitate haste under the pressure of an artificially aroused fear psychosis throughout the land. It is quite natural that such sudden changes in basic policy have left our people confused and bewildered, and have lost us the faith of many other peoples.

The issue of war or peace is not based upon any sudden and unexpected change in the course of world events, or even direction of Soviet policy. Long before even the Second World War, the Soviet was known to plan suppression of the concept of freedom and the advance of Communism throughout the world as rapidly as conditions would permit.

We, ourselves, molded these conditions to the Soviet's plan by providing extraordinary facility for it to so deploy its military forces as to permit direct and decisive pressure upon many of the free nations of Europe and Asia.

This is now, of course, past history. The immediate problem calls for a dynamic political and military policy designed to secure the future and regain the lost faith of others in order that our moral influence may reassert itself to guide the world toward reason and right. And, in the formulation of such policies, it is well that we understand that battles are not won by arms alone.

There must exist above all else a spiritual impulse - a will to victory.

This can only be if the soldier feels his sacrifice is to preserve the highest of moral values.

The American Legion, composed of men who know and detest war for the scourge that it is, is peculiarly well fitted to stand guard over our heritage of American liberty. It must exercise unrelaxed vigilance. It must insure that neither political expediency nor foreign infatuation influences the expenditure of the vast sums now under contemplation for freedom's defense.

It must exercise its great influence to the end that:

We rearm, as rearm we must, in an atmosphere of confidence in our inherent strength, not under the hysteria of an artificially created fear;

That it is our implacable purpose to retain undisputed control of the seas, to secure undisputed control of the air, to vigorously implement our atomic program with a full commitment to the use as needed of the atomic weapon, and, while maintaining a well-balanced and highly developed ground force, to charge to our allies the main responsibility for ground operations in defense of their own spheres of territorial interest;

To curb the growing tendency of political and military leaders to publicize for political advantage classified data concerning scientific developments incident to our military effort, and thus to yield the all important element of surprise;

To do all, reasonably within our power, to help preserve freedom for those who have the will and determination to do all in their power to defend their own freedom;

To avoid being drawn into unreasonable and unnecessary expenditures for armament to create an artificial domestic prosperity for political ends;

To avoid contributing the fruits of our system of free enterprise to support Socialism or Communism abroad under the spurious pretense that it serves our own military security;

To avoid aligning ourselves with colonial policies in Asia and the Middle East, lest we invite the enmity of the traditionally friendly peoples of those vast areas of the world;

To give primary concern to our own security and the well-being of our own people;

To avoid distributing our wealth for the purpose of buying the loyalty of others, or of sharing with others the wealth and security which we hold in sacred trust for our progeny;

To apply all possible pressure, short of war, upon the Soviet or any associated power which by abuse and pressure upon us forces the expenditure of such vast outlays of our energy and resource as a measure of self-preservation;

To avoid a protracted and indecisive war in Korea with its endless slaughter - the Chief of Staff of the Army recently testified before a Congressional committee that it might last for 10 years;

To regain military faith in ourselves and the policies upon which our victories in the past have always rested;

To do all, reasonably within our power, to assist the Filipino and Japanese people to advance and fortify their liberties, and the Chinese people to regain theirs;

And, above all else, to preserve inviolate those great principles and ideals of moral authority upon which is based the American way of life, and the nobility of the cause for which our soldiers fight.

I do not associate myself with those who believe that World War III is imminent or inevitable, nor do I associate myself with those who hysterically talk of American cities being laid waste. I believe that this Nation has such potential strength, both spiritual and material, that no power or combination of powers would dare directly to attack it.

We must rebuild the military power, wantonly dissipated despite your warning and the clear portents of the situation in 1946, calmly and wisely and with sole regard to military requirements - not political expediency. We must not again permit our leaders to gamble with the national security to serve political ends.

We must rebuild our power, not so much as a measure of defense against any imminently threatened attack, but as a means to regain the faith of those peoples of the world - traditional friends of our country - who now languish in the chains of Communist slavery or whose wills are controlled by Communist threat, treachery, coercion, and brutality and to whom only the relativity of force no longer has practical meaning.

The complexity brought about by dislocations in the wake of two world wars has caught our beloved country in the vortex of a confused, distressed, and frightened world. It has been a time when the lack of a strong and positive and wise leadership - a leadership capable of rising above the level of petty politics with moral courage, self-effacing conviction, and resolute patriotism - has been most sorely felt.

I have faith that the wisdom and determination of the American people are not going to permit our country to continue down the road to national jeopardy. They will insist that American policy be reoriented to American tradition, American thinking, and American need - and will stop our headlong plunge toward Socialism and economic disaster.

Americans will not he fooled by the bombast of violent propaganda and vulgar language which inevitably meets every honest criticism directed at the Government. They were neither fooled nor their confidence impaired in the gallant Marines committed to battle in Korea when that fighting body of men of such illustrious tradition and fame was so grievously and unjustly assailed. They will not be ensnared by a sly Pied Piper technique which says one thing and does another.

The issues now confronting the Nation call for American solutions. They should interpret the national need and be responsive to vision and moral courage. The voice of the people must be heeded. Counsel such as yours must not again be disdained. The implacable guide must he faith in those immutable principles and ideals which give spiritual strength to our Constitution.

There must be reflected that degree of humility which recognizes the religious base upon which our Nation was founded, with an indomitable determination to preserve it. The threat to freedom in peace is no less sinister than in war. Our country's future must not go by default. The veteran must not fail the Nation's trust.

NATIONAL INSTITUTE OF SOCIAL SCIENCES UPON BEING AWARDED THE SOCIETY'S GOLD MEDAL
NOVEMBER 8, 1951
WALDORF-ASTORIA HOTEL, NEW YORK, NEW YORK

General MacArthur felt strongly that the outstanding success achieved in the occupation of Japan after World War II would influence all the nations of that region, at least, of the compassion and serious effort to rebuild a nation utterly devastated by war.

Edward T. Imparato, Editor

Mr. President:

The citation with which you have awarded this Medal moves me deeply. It so far exceeds my own individual accomplishment that I can accept it only as symbolical of that group of men who were associated with me in the great events which are memorialized and whose magnificent efforts yielded success.

I have been especially stirred by your reference to my role in the erection of New Japan upon the ashes left in the wake of war's destructive violence. Never in history has a nation and its people been more completely crushed than were the Japanese at the end of the struggle. They had suffered more than a military debacle, more than the destruction of their armed forces, more than the elimination of their industrial bases, more even than the occupation of their land by foreign bayonets. Their entire faith in the Japanese way of life, cherished as invincible for many centuries, perished in the agony of their total defeat. Into the ensuing spiritual vacuum flowed the American concept of honor and justice and compassion drawn from our Christian teachings. It was received with eagerness, and as understanding of its true meaning came to the Japanese mind, with growing reverence and devotion. Thus was born the new Japan.

The pages of history in recording America's twentieth century contributions to human progress may, perchance, pass over lightly the wars we have fought. But, I believe they will not fail to record the profound influence for good upon Asia which will inevitably follow the spiritual regeneration of Japan. And this is as it should be, for construction always serves memory long after the destruction it follows is forgotten.

If the historian of the future should deem my service worthy of some slight reference, it would be my hope that he mention me not as a Commander engaged in campaigns and battles, even though victorious to American arms, but rather as that one whose sacred duty it became, once the guns were silenced, to carry to the land of our vanquished foe the solace and hope and faith of Christian morals. Could I have but a line a century hence crediting a contribution to the advance of peace, I would gladly yield every honor which has been accorded by war.

Mr. President, I wish to express to you my thanks and deepest appreciation for the signal honor you have bestowed upon me. The field of Social Sciences which your distinguished Society represents embraces a symposium of art, culture, humanism and divinity which leads and guides both in peace and war. Its great traditions form the bulwark of modern civilization - the fruition of all man's hopes and dreams. I think you can therefore understand my pride in having my name scrolled on your tablets. You have etched for me a memory tonight I shall never forget.

OPENING - SEATTLE CENTENNIAL CELEBRATION
NOVEMBER 13, 1951
EDMONDSON PAVILION,
UNIVERSTIY OF WASHINGTON AT SEATTLE

Over 100 years ago the West Coast of the United States was the full extent of our nation for the protection of our country. For many years we felt secure in the knowledge that a well fortified West Coast of our country would protect us from any invader from the West. Travel was slower then and invaders from the West, though thousands of miles away, could be spotted early giving us time to assemble our forces to provide for our National security. Now, the situation has changed, "remember Pearl Harbor," and our security concern extends to Hawaii and the islands in the Western Pacific. Our concern now is the security of these far West islands extending our view and strategy to the new frontier, the islands of the Pacific and Formosa, the Philippines, Okinawa and Japan.

Edward T. Imparato, Editor

I am happy to be with you to share this milestone in human progress - happy to be able to pay personal tribute to your citizens, past and present, who have erected this great metropolis upon a century of American vision and, courage and faith. I have just crossed the continent in hours, where it took those who first pioneered the way as many long, tortuous and perilous months. Seattle proudly and majestically stands today at one hundred years of age full beneficiary of what the pioneering spirit has wrought upon this continent. It marks the fruition of the dream to bring the fruits of civilization to a vast and then uncharted wilderness. It has become a heritage which all Americans may share with pride and hope. The inspiration to be drawn from its one hundred years of the past builds faith in the next hundred years of the future.

But the courage and vision and determination of the pioneer by no means reflects the needs of a past era alone. Such qualities are just as essential now to the advance of civilization. Should the pioneering spirit cease to dominate the American character, our national progress would end. For a nation's life is never static. It must advance or it will recede. Only through the indomitable will characteristic of the early American can continued development be made in the arts and sciences, in industry and agriculture, in trade and commerce, and in all those things which raise the standard of human life. The pioneering spirit finds its incentives and guiding impulse in the freedoms Americans enjoy - of opportunity, of expression and of choice in what we do - freedoms bulwarked by a constitutional charter embodying the experience and wisdom of the ages in securing the liberty, the dignity and the general welfare of each individual citizen.

To the early pioneer the Pacific coast marked the end of his courageous westerly advance - to us it should mark but the beginning. To him it delimited our western frontier - to us that frontier has been moved beyond the Pacific horizon. For we find our western defense geared to an Island chain off the coast of continental Asia from which with air and sea supremacy we can dominate any predatory move threatening the Pacific Ocean area. Our economic frontier now embraces the trade potentialities of Asia itself; for, with gradual rotation of the epicenter of world trade back to the Far Fast whence it started many centuries ago, the next thousand years will find the main world problem the raising of the subnormal standard of life and its more than a billion Oriental peoples. The opportunities for international trade then, if pursued with the vision and courage of the early pioneer will be limitless. This city as a major gateway to that untapped wealth of opportunity would then indeed have a glittering future before it. The entire west coast well might then find its place on a parity with our eastern seaboard, each standing as a vital center of American industry with broad avenues of foreign trade and commerce immediately before it.

Such possibilities seem however beyond the comprehension of some high in our governmental circles who still feel that the Pacific coast marks the practical terminus of our advance and the westerly boundary of our immediate national interest - that any opportunity for the expansion of our foreign trade should be mainly in the area of Europe and the Middle East. Nothing could more surely, put a brake upon our growth as a strong and prosperous nation. Intentionally or not, it would yield to industrialized Europe the undisputed dominion over the trade and commerce of the Far East. More than this, it would in time surrender to European nations the moral, if not political, leadership of the Eastern Hemisphere. Nothing could more clearly attest a marked recession from that far-sighted vision which animated the pioneer of one hundred years ago.

It should be inconceivable that our leaders would close their eyes to any direction of opportunity - to concentrate upon any one avenue to the exclusion of any other. In the pioneering spirit, it should be our undeviating purpose to develop the maximum of global trade, ignoring only those unfriendly areas and peoples which our trade would assist in bringing abusive pressure against us.

Yet, the sad truth is that many in high authority show little interest in the western Pacific area. And this despite our engagement in Korea in one of the most savage wars of American history, our long partnership with the Filipino people, our traditional ties of friendship with Asia, our alliance with new Japan, and our western Pacific defense frontier. Having aided through blundering diplomacy the gaining of Communist control over China, the failure to enunciate a simple, forthright, and positive statement of policy understandable to the world as firm assurance against any future trafficking with the Communist movement in Asia arouses gravest doubts and fears.

There should be no rivalry between our East and our West - no pitting of Atlantic interests against those of the Pacific. The problem is global, not sectional. The living standard of the peoples of the oriental East must and will be raised to a closer relativity with that of the occidental West. Only the Communists and their blind disciples advocate the lowering of the one to achieve a raising of the other - the Karl Marx theory of an international division of wealth to achieve a universal level. To others, the course is clear. There must be such a development of opportunity that the requirements for a better life in the oriental East may be filled from the almost unlimited industrial potential of the occidental West. The human and material resources of the East would be used in compensation for the manufactures of the West.

Once this elementary logic is recognized, trade with the Far East may be expected rapidly to expand under the stimulus of American vision, American enterprise, and American pioneering spirit. The pioneer of the 20th century has in all respects as broad an avenue of advance as did the pioneer of the 19th century to whom we today do honor and offer thanks.

In the face of such future opportunities, any concept of "scuttling" in the Pacific would be a direct negation of the spirit of our pioneer forefathers who stopped at no river, at no mountain, at no natural barrier in their driving urge to open the West. It is indulged in only by those who lack the vision to comprehend and assess the full significance of global potentialities and who lack the moral courage to take maximum advantage of them.

Regardless of motive, those who thus belittle our interest in the Pacific in favor of concentrating attention on the Atlantic are just as isolationist in their thinking as would be those who belittle our interest in the Atlantic in favor of concentrating on the Pacific. Either reflects a dangerously unbalanced vision. Any concept which would neglect the Pacific would not only limit our further progress as a nation and render your shores wide open to predatory attack through neglected avenues of possible enemy advance, but would yield to others your great opportunity for economic progress. It would leave our foreign trade largely centered in those who hold every competitive advantage over you. Your economic future clearly lies to your west. Availing yourselves of its full potential, your opportunity for growth is boundless - failing to do so, your economic stature would be limited to the normal domestic possibilities in local growth. Trade with Asia has historically been largely a European monopoly, protected by colonial ties. This monopoly was broken with the demise of colonial rule at war's end and must never be restored.

If the national well-being is to be served, it is for us of this generation, as indeed for Americans of every generation, to assess the current strength of the pioneering spirit and appraise anew the incentives which alone can give it dynamic vitality. In so doing, it is well that we remember the composite of pioneering characteristics which have gone into the building of this great American city. Here strength overcame weakness, courage dominated fear, and the responsibility of life overshadowed the certainty of death. Here, men, through an exemplification of spirituality, fashioned character as a far more meaningful and valued heritage than the material results their labors brought forth. It is that heritage of character which must be preserved by our generation so that we could do now what they did then. The American heart still harbors that same love of liberty, indomitable will, and rugged determination which animated their early efforts. Yet, it would be folly compounded to ignore those internal pressures now at work to weaken that heritage of America's past.

These pressures have already caused us to depart sharply from the course so long held toward national strength and moral greatness. Our economic stature built under the incentives of free enterprise is imperiled by our drift through the back door of confiscatory taxation toward State Socialism. There has resulted an inevitable suppression of the incentive to maximize human energy, to encourage creative initiative, and to transform capital in one form to produce capital more needed in another. Our political stature, built upon wise and self-effacing statesmanship and sound domestic policy, has been sadly impaired by a succession of diplomatic blunders abroad and reckless spendthrift aims at home. Many peoples have lost faith in our leadership, and there is a growing anxiety in the American home as disclosures reveal graft and corruption over a broad front in our public service. Those charged with its stewardship seem either apathetic, indifferent, or in seeming condonation.

Freedom of speech and expression are no longer untrammeled. Slanted propaganda and abusive language are used to suppress criticism of the public administration and discourage dissemination of the truth. Suppression is now even sought through the spurious device of an information blackout with respect to public affairs - a so-called security measure, the like of which was never before attempted even during war. All this warns that an "iron curtain" may be threatening to descend upon our own land.

Expenditure upon expenditure, extravagance upon extravagance have so burdened our people with taxation and fed the forces of inflation that our traditionally high standard of life has become largely fictitious and illusory. Apart from the direct income tax impounded at source, every necessity of life gives constant warning of the diminishing value of both national currency and private income. As always, it is the great masses of the people, not the rich or the prosperous, but the farmer, the laborer, and the average office worker who suffer the most. This was aptly pointed out by Franklin D. Roosevelt when he said, "Taxes are paid in the sweat of every man who labors. If these taxes are excessive, they are reflected in idle factories and tax sold farms and in hordes of hungry people tramping the streets and seeking jobs in vain. Our workers may never see a tax bill but they pay it. They pay in deductions from wages, in increased cost of what they buy or in broad unemployment throughout the land." Some of these penalties are now obscured by the reckless extravagance of government spending which creates a false sense of security, but the day of reckoning is inevitable, and understanding and fear of this injects a tragic apprehension in the American mind. Yet our leaders offer neither plan nor hope for a return to frugality and reason. Our remaining tax potential has been so depleted that, if the reckless policies of government continue unchecked, the direct confiscation of capital to meet the ensuing obligations is almost inevitable. Therein lies the blueprint to a Socialist state. Therein lies the great issue now before our people - shall we preserve our freedom, or yield it to a centralized government under the concept of Socialism? There can be no compromise. It must be all or nothing. The traditional American way of life, or a totalitarian concept imported from abroad. All other issues are but secondary to this one which strikes at the very roots of our personal liberties and representative form of government. For Socialism, once a reality, destroys that moral fiber which is the creation of freedom. It breeds every device which produces totalitarian rule. It is true that our Constitution established checks and balances designed to safeguard against such dangers, but such safeguard is ignored by those who seek to entrench personal political power through preferential treatment for some at the general expense of all. This carnival of special privilege cannot fail to undermine our heritage of character. It discourages development of those moral forces which would preserve inviolate our representative form of government, answerable to the free will of the electorate.

The great bulwark of the Republic, individual and collective self-reliance, is under constant threat through a carefully designed and progressive paternalism which renders both community and individual increasingly dependent upon the support of the Federal Government. In all areas of private welfare, the Socialist planners seek to inject the Federal hand to produce a progressive weakening of the structure of individual character.

The area of possible resistance to this creeping sabotage of freedom is being constantly narrowed as the Federal Government arrogates to itself more and more of the remaining tax potential. There is an almost insatiate demand for money to finance policies seemingly designed but to spend and spend and spend. Should this trend continue, the

Federal Government may well become for all practical purposes the sole taxing power. Thereafter, the sovereignty of the States and autonomy of the communities, so pointedly recognized by the framers of the Constitution and nurtured through many generations of American life, will have been changed into a subservience to Federal direction in direct proportion to their dependence upon Federal grants for local support.

It has been truly said, "the power to tax is the power to destroy." It is, perhaps, the most sinister of all political powers. Administered despotically, it can and ofttimes has become an instrument of tyranny and oppression. As such, it has been possibly the greatest single cause of political revolt throughout the history of the human race. Indeed, the fundamental issue which precipitated our American Revolution was the arbitrary and oppressive tax levy by the British Crown.

Many pessimistic voices are being raised today throughout the land. But the times are full of hope if the vision and courage and faith of the early pioneer continue to animate the American people in the discharge of their sovereign responsibilities.

The people have it in their hands to restore morality, wisdom, and vision to the direction of our foreign and domestic affairs and regain the religious base which in times past assured general integrity in public and private life.

Despite failures in leadership, they have it in their power to rise to that stature which befits their material strength; to reject the Socialist policies covertly and by devious means being forced upon us; to stamp out Communist influence which has played so ill-famed a part in the past misdirection of our public administration; to reorganize our Government under a leadership invincibly obedient to our constitutional mandates; to reinforce existing safeguards to our economy of free enterprise; to reassert full protection for freedom of speech and expression and those other freedoms now threatened; to regain State and community autonomy; to renounce undue alien interference in the shaping of American public policy; to reestablish our governmental process upon a foundation of faith in our American institutions, American traditions, and the time-tested adequacy of American vision.

Our country will then reassume that spiritual and moral leadership recently lost in a quagmire of political ineptitude and economic incompetence. We will then regain the faith of our fathers and the strength to meet the issues which perplex us now with the same determination and wisdom with which they met the issues which perplexed them then. So invincible was their faith that they inscribed upon every coin of the United States down to and including even the penny their simple profession "In God we trust." Let our faith be no less.

The greatest hazard under which we now labor is the fear that the policy and propaganda of our present leadership may be setting the stage for a third world war. We are following the same path - the same historical record - the same political concept and leadership - which projected us into World War I, World War II, and the war in Korea. Since before the close of World War II, this leadership has contributed to the building of Soviet military strength by extravagant lend-lease aid quite beyond any common military need; by acquiescing in Soviet troop concentration and dispositions at highly strategic points in Europe and Asia; by abandoning our wartime allies to the pressure of Soviet conquest; and, at the same time, divesting ourselves of our own vast superior military strength, with reckless and precipitate haste.

Against this background, none will quarrel with the need to regain adequate security forces, not only that we may be prepared to meet any external threat, but that our diplomacy may be bulwarked with a power which will command universal respect. But we cannot be satisfied with a leadership which declaims a devotion to peace with constant platitudinous statements and phrases while taking steps which inexorably tend to lead toward war.

We fear a repetition of such precipitate action as projected us into the Korean war with neither the advice nor consent of the Congress and in complete disregard of the carefully developed war policies and plans of the United States. We deprecate a propaganda of fear among our people lest military levies and alliances be opposed by them. We question the hasty plunging into foreign quarrels, instead of holding the country on a high moral plane as an impartial and just arbiter of international dissensions.

We dislike bombastic and provocative statements which settle nothing and only increase existing world tensions. We resent the docile acceptance of abusive pressure against us without the application of adequate counter pressure available to us. We cannot reconcile a declared purpose to defeat Communism, while aiming our country with and supplying resources including arms to a Communist nation abroad and, at the same time, showing extraordinary reluctance to do the same for nations long recognized as uncompromising in their opposition to Communism. We condemn the effort to avoid possible public criticism by cloaking administrative functions behind a screen of secrecy under the doubtful pretext that the national security is directly involved.

We view with dismay the military advantage accorded the Soviet by permitting it long and protracted use of the Korean battle area as a training and proving ground for weapons and men with the protection of sanctuary beyond the Yalu.

We deplore the indefinite continuation of the Korean war when, ever since the entry of Communist China a year ago, we have had the means of bringing it to a prompt and victorious end and thus to save countless American lives and avoid the risk of its spreading into a global conflict inherent in its long continuance. And, in general, the pattern toward war is clearly defined.

I have faith that the American people will not be fooled - that they will demand that the national policy be charted to a course of international realism without regard to domestic political expediency - diplomacy rather than intrigue.

The potentiality of America's industrial strength in support of our expanding armament is guarantee against any willfully designed military action against us. But wars can come about through blundering statesmanship animated by a lust for political power.

Our course can and must be designed to promote the peace. This can only be if we regain our moral balance and follow a course of international justice for all peoples, without taking sides in issues which are not directly our concern. Friendship for those who would be our friends, and quiet but firm counter pressure against those who would not and bring abusive pressure upon us. Let the immortal words with which General Grant ended the bloody Civil War be our guide and beacon: "Let us have peace."

DEDICATION OF THE MEMORIAL TO HIS MOTHER, MARY PINKNEY HARDY
NOVEMBER 18, 1951
NORFOLK, VIRGINIA

MacArthur gives praise to his Mother for giving him insight into the gentle culture of the South. She taught him a devotion to God and love of country, and these two elements sustained him over periods of great strain and bitter moments of decision.

Edward T. Imparato, Editor

With a sense of deep humility and reverence, I join you today as the son of that gentle woman of Virginia whose memory you honor by this beautiful memorial at the hallowed site of her birth. I bring with me an inadequacy of words to describe the emotions which fill my heart.

In those troubled days when our country was engaged in civil strife, this lovely lady and her family were dedicated to the cause of the Confederacy. From this spot Hardys followed "Marse Robert's" flag on Virginia's bloody fields and a Hardy was at "Old Jack's" elbow that dark night when he fell on the sodden Plank Road near Chancellorsville. The rebel yell and the sound of "Dixie" have been in my ears since birth.

My Father was of the North - one of the most gallant soldiers who wore the Blue. Their marriage of deepest love and devotion came at the close of that mighty struggle between differing ideas but equally honest convictions. It seemed almost prophetic, as a prelude to the spiritual union which was later to unite again the North and South.

I am truly a mixture of the Blue and the Gray; a living symbol of that united America which largely resulted from the nobility and deep spirituality which mothers of both South and North brought to the welding of a new union between the States. Sons of both have been molded into an invincible comradeship through common hardships, common perils and common sacrifices in defense of a common heritage of freedom. Thus have been brought to fruition my Mother's and my Father's dreams and hopes sanctified at the altar of holy matrimony, even as the smoke and stench and anguish of the aftermath of battle still hung heavily over the hearts of men.

It was my sainted Mother who first taught me of the gentle culture of the South and of its long and noble traditions and who infused in me a deep and lasting veneration for them which is indelibly etched upon my heart. She taught me, too, a devotion to God and a love of country which have ever sustained me in my many lonely and bitter moments of decision in dis-

MacArthur dedicates a park to his mother on November 18, 1951.

tant and hostile lands. To her, at this shrine of memory, I can but yield anew a son's reverent thanks for her guidance to a path of duty as God gave me the light to see that duty.

I know how deeply stirred would "Pinky" Hardy be today could she look down upon this mark of honor and affection by her neighbors and her neighbor's children and children's children. And in her behalf and for all those of her blood, I offer you my heartfelt gratitude.

RECEIVING THE AWARD OF THE TOUCHDOWN CLUB AT THEIR ANNUAL DINNER
DECEMBER 6, 1951
ASTOR HOTEL, NEW YORK, NEW YORK

MacArthur's great love of sports of all kinds began in grammar school and continued into high school where he excelled in basketball, baseball, tennis and football. His great love was football and though too small in stature and weight to play on the West Point football team, he was the manager of the football squad and never lost touch with the coaches at the Point even with his assignments around the world.

Edward T. Imparato, Editor

I am deeply grateful for your citation of my service to the game of Football. But, in all frankness, I feel that you render me undue honor. I have been an avid follower of the gridiron for many years, but my contribution to the advance of this great sport has been no more than that of millions of others. With them I have recognized and enthusiastically supported it not only as a healthy character and body builder, but as a means toward furthering our traditional competitive spirit. And, perhaps, even more important and impressive is its unsurpassed ability to provide mental and physical relaxation for those who watch from the side lines. It certainly is Father and Mother to that delightful fellow - the Monday morning quarter-back.

From personal knowledge and intimate experience, I know how immeasurably football has contributed over the years to American leadership on the battle field. Just as in war, the very essence of success on the gridiron is a combination of physical prowess and skill, close coordination of men and maneuver and that indomitable courage which alone can produce the will to victory. I can repeat with the added conviction of time what I said many long years ago on the Plain at West Point:

"On the fields of friendly strife are sown the seeds that on other fields and other days will bring forth victory."

Possibly influenced by the times and circumstances in which we live, an over-balancing emphasis may in recent years have been given to the revenue-producing phase of modern college football. This has resulted perhaps in a consequent occasional compromise of the high standards of academic proficiency in the attendant competition to secure and hold the best available players. But I am proud to say no scandal of corruption, no hint of malfeasance of play, has compromised the integrity of the game itself. This is to the lasting credit of you who seek to hold the code squarely

upon the highest level of true sportsmanship. The fine character which has in general animated both the players and the leadership of participating schools and the unquestioned fairness of their devoted public following, have shared equally in the ceaseless responsibility of keeping clean the record of this great sport.

I have faith that any current excesses in the competition to secure players will be corrected within the sport itself. My only concern is that it does not fall within the eager clutches of rapidly expanding Federal controls. If I were to give you but one word of warning, it would be to keep Football and, for that matter, all other American sports free of governmental bureaucratic regulation. If it comes, it cannot fail to destroy the very essence of that sportsmanship which has contributed so fully to the molding of the American character. The game would no longer be a sport - it would be but another of our lost freedoms - a plaything for selfish politics - a pawn for greedy patronage - a helpless adjunct to a creeping centralization of power in government which would threaten athletic life, fortune and sacred honor.

I am of the football vintage of Walter Camp and Alonzo Stagg. I have thrilled to the blaze of Hinckey and Hefflefinger, of Haughton and Brickley, of Poe and Trenchard and Hare. I collaborated with Charlie Daly and Pot Graves and Bull Halsey, later to become our peerless fighting Admiral and my beloved comrade in arms of the Pacific, was then a midshipman back. I raised McEwan and Oliphant, Neyland and Blaik. I learned the hard way from Knute Rockne and Gipp and the Four Horsemen - and every year on every campus and every field throughout the land, I can see their counterparts. I can see their great ideals and performances being repeated over and over again - year on year - and, as each passes on, I find myself again and again with the same old catch in my throat, the same old pounding in my heart, the same old yell on my lips, "Well done, Mr. Football. Yours is the Touchdown."

RECEIVING SERVICE TO HUMANITY AWARD FROM THE SALVATION ARMY
DECEMBER 12, 1951
WALDORF-ASTORIA HOTEL, NEW YORK, NEW YORK

No honor I have ever received has moved me more deeply than does this citation for service to humanity by an organization which has given such noble and unstinting devotion to the cause of humanity.

The Salvation Army - truly a defender of the faith - stirs in me memories from early childhood of ministrations to raise the fallen, to save the distressed and to strengthen the weak. Accorded but sparing public recognition, its dedication to human welfare through the years has given living meaning to the name which it bears - Salvation. It has become a mighty moral force in the life of civilized communities.

In this day of gathering storms, as the moral deterioration of political power spreads its growing infection, it is essential that every spiritual force be mobilized to defend and preserve the religious base upon which this nation was founded. For it is that base which has been the motivating impulse to our moral and national growth. History fails to record a single precedent in which nations subject to moral decay have not passed into political and economic decline. There has been either a spiritual reawakening to overcome the moral lapse, or a progressive deterioration leading to ultimate national disaster.

In the modern world, the evil forces of Communism which seek to remove religion as the most formidable barrier to their advance have adopted the technique of infiltration. They strive to undermine public and private morals as a means of weakening and rendering indefensible areas of intended absorption. Their success serves to warn all free men of the depravity which has inevitably replaced spirituality where their dominion over peoples and races has become complete.

In many parts of the world, ancient religions have given way before the sweep of this concept of materialism which holds to the sanctity of no moral law and worships as its only god the power to suppress the Devine heritage of man. It first essays to make traitors among those of high degree and through them seeks to destroy nations and bend peoples to its malevolent will. Its plan is to abolish private property and free enterprise in order to secure that degree of power over material things necessary to render absolute its power to suppress the spiritual things. It first establishes collectivism as the idealistic refuge for those who lack the will and the courage and the capacity for self-expression. This is the half-way point on the direct and undeviating road to full Communism. Thereafter, all private control over means and sources of production is abolished, and then with the political power safely in hand, this concentration of material power becomes that fearful weapon whereby every vestige of spiritual value and human freedom may be suppressed at will. This is how it has happened before and it can happen again, unless the moral forces of a nation are sufficiently mobilized and alert to safeguard against so dreadful a threat to its cherished liberties.

Fortunately, the spiritual impulse is strong in many American hearts and constitutes a rugged bulwark in the defense of religious morality against any advance of atheistic immorality. There are those who would have us believe that Communism embraces but the philosophy of agnosticism, rather than atheism. But this shallow pretense is easily belied by the record of ruthless and complete disregard of moral law once Communism has seized power. Any complacent tolerance of this destructive force of evil should be replaced by an implacable and uncompromising determination to resist its every threat to basic and traditional ideals. Human freedom always find ostentatious vocal support from those most bent upon its suppression. It is essential, therefore, that there be assessed with cold and calculated realism the motivation of those who say much but do little. For there can be no compromise in the fight to preserve the sanctity of our religious base. We must condemn those who would corrupt the principles of individual liberty, freedom's mighty instrument of spiritual power. We must not view with indifference men of base or weak character, who do not fulfill their public stewardship. We must refuse to indulge those who are so blind they will not see the moral dangers now threatening the engulfment of our people. We must regain our

spiritual and intellectual balance that there may be restored a full faith in public integrity and a renewed devotion to private morality. We must face the gravity of the times honestly and fearlessly so that our beloved country may survive the man-made perils which now confront it.

This will not be easy. Moral decay and political irresponsibility have penetrated the roots of our cherished institutions. And powerful forces bent upon further entrenching political power at the expense of spiritual values resist public disclosures which question the moral integrity underlying public affairs. Our great strength rests in those high-minded and patriotic Americans whose faith in God and love of country transcends all selfish and self-serving instincts. We must command their maximum effort toward a restoration to public and private relationships of our age-old standards of morality and ethics - a return to the religious fervor which animated our leadership of former years to chart a course of humility and integrity as best to serve the public interest.

I have an abiding faith that this nation conceived in liberty under God will mount the moral force essential to preserve its free institutions against the assault of those bent upon their ultimate destruction. And that the Salvation Army will continue to contribute its own full measure of spiritual devotion, invincible dedicated to all that is generous and all that is good.

ARTILCE BY GENERAL MACARTHUR WHICH APPEARED IN THE JANUARY, 1952 ISSUE OF AMERICAN LEGION MAGAZINE

"THE CITIZEN SOLDIER AND HIS ROLE IN OUR NATIONAL MILITARY POLICY"

MacArthur gives major credit for fighting and winning our wars to the citizen soldier who rose by the thousands to enlist for the defense of our country and insure our obligation from the Constitution to protect and defend our country from all enemies.

Edward T. Imparato, Editor

One of the greatest contributions the American Legion has made to the nation has been in the strengthening of the potentialities of the citizen soldier. Since the Minute Men of 1776 formed the ranks of the Continental Army and brought victory to its arms in the American Revolution, the security of the United States has rested more than all else upon the competence, the indomitable will and the resolute patriotism of the citizen soldier. The professional has had his role - and it has been a major one - providing trained leadership, initial security against surprise attack and the nucleus to an expanding force under conditions of national emergency. But in all of our wars, from the Revolution to Korea, the citizen soldier has met the full shock of battle, has contributed all but a fraction of the dead and maimed and has accepted the responsibility for victory.

Yet, despite all of this, he has never received either from our political or military leadership full credit for his role in safeguarding the security of the nation, nor the support in peace which would better prepare him to carry his responsibilities in war.

The tendency has existed - as it still now exists - to regard him as an auxiliary rather than the main pillar supporting our national military strength. Only in rare instances have his views been sought or considered in the shaping of high policy governing the conduct of war or plans to secure the peace. Indeed, only in the most exceptional cases has he been called to share the authority of higher command or staff administration.

The need for a closer integration of the civilian defense components with the regular services was clearly understood by the American Legion following the close of World War I, and its efforts largely resulted in the reexamination of the then long-existing military policy of the United States. There followed enactment of the National Defense Act of June 4, 1920, providing for one army composed of the regulars, the National Guard and the organized reserves. This was a long step forward, but experience demonstrates that it has not resulted in providing for the country the added security both intended and needed. Its results have been largely indecisive. We still enter wars tragically unprepared, and theretofore have found ourselves entirely lacking in that degree of military strength essential to preserve the peace. At war's end we still demobilize in haste and divest ourselves of accumulated war materiel with reckless abandon. We still lack a realistic appraisal of future potentialities, and saddle our people with wholly uncalled for burdens to cover past errors by replacing anew the power we have squandered and dissipated in the afterglow of victory. There could be no more serious indictment of our political and military leadership than this failure to profit from the clear lessons of experience. It is a failure which following World War II, still vivid in the American mind, lost us the fruits of victory and brought to us a sense of insecurity hardly surpassed in midst of war itself.

Now our military policy again requires revision. Under Selective Service and other statutes, we have called up large increments of our citizen soldiery with which to prosecute the Korean War and to bolster our own defense and the defense of many other lands. We have adopted the principle of Universal Military Training, and the outlook is toward maintaining for many years -even in peace - an armed readiness for war.

All this, while intended and designed to strengthen freedom's defense, carries within itself the very germs to freedom's destruction. For it etches the pattern to a military state which, historically under the control of professional military thinking in constant search for means toward efficiency, has found in freedom possibly its greatest single impediment, to brush it aside as inimical to established military policy. To avoid this historic pitfall, it is essential that civilian control over the citizen army be extended and intensified. Particularly is this true in the administration of the program of Universal Military Training, if the youth of our land is to avoid being corrupted into a legion of subserviency to the so-called military mind.

This calls for a reassessment of the role of the citizen soldier now to become the major element of our military establishment during peace as well as during war. It calls for a realistic appreciation of the potential in professional competence which the citizen soldier can bring to the fulfillment of our military policy and aims. It calls for the elimination of arbitrary restrictions upon the advance of the citizen soldier in the ranks of military leadership, for which he may be trained or is already reasonably qualified. It calls for a much broadened opportunity for the professional preparation of the citizen soldier to permit his integration into the higher staff studies and planning designed to avert war if possible, to prosecute it to early victory if not.

This requires a basic change in attitudes. It requires recognition of the fact long understood but covertly denied that our Army, as befits a republic, is a citizen army. It requires that leadership from the top down be selected upon merit, carefully avoiding arbitrary class discrimination. It requires that the citizen soldier, if otherwise professionally qualified, have the opportunity to voice his views in the formulation of military and related political policy - a recognition that none have any monopoly upon the attributes to military leadership. It requires that we carefully avoid yielding to professional ambition at the expense of the primacy of the national interest.

Unless these principles are recognized and adhered to, we shall find that our citizen army lacks the esprit essential to the building of invincible force - that its officers lack the incentive to advance their professional competence - that the people lack faith in the integrity of their military arm.

This poses possibly the American Legion's greatest challenge. Its membership for the most part have been and are citizen soldiers of the Republic. They have learned, some from bitter experience, of the restrictions inherent in the long prevailing relationship between the Army's several components. They must insist upon that degree of efficiency and morale essential to maximize the strength of the new citizen army, which alone can come from close integration, with leadership and rank selected solely upon the basis of merit.

The American Legion is in best position to guide this normal development. It must alert itself against political efforts already noticeable to suppress the voice and opinion of the citizen soldier, whether active or inactive. It must insist that the role of the citizen army be to serve no special interests, but rather the common welfare and protection of all of the people.

Our country is facing one of the grave crises in American history - not so much from external threat, although the forces of evil which our own political and military blunders have helped so much to build, must by no means be ignored - but from internal pressures which threaten the very survival of our liberties. These pressures have already made sharp inroads into our free way of life and impaired much of the incentive which has encouraged development of those basic virtues and traits of character from which has emerged our traditional American initiative, American energy and that indomitable American will which in past has preserved our moral balance and produced our material strength.

It is essential that the traditional role of the Army in these distressing times be carefully preserved - that it be not used as an instrument of tyranny or oppression - a form of pretorian guard - by those seeking to strengthen and entrench personal political power - but that it be used instead as a force of free men dedicated to its sworn purpose of defending the "Constitution of the States against all enemies, foreign and domestic."

It is imperative that the citizen army now in the making be not corrupted by the sane influences which have tended to corrupt the principle of representative government - that it be sustained on that high moral plane which befits the noble purpose it is organized to serve. This can only be if the service of the citizen soldier is held to a level of dignity and opportunity which commands his fullest measure of devotion.

To this purpose, the American Legion should enlist its wisdom and undeviating interest. It should utilize its full influence to the end that our military policy be so oriented as to ensure a citizen army cast in the mold of our exalted traditions and dedicated to the primacy of the people's service.

RECEIVING THE "GOLD MEDAL OF ACHIEVEMENT" AWARD FROM THE POOR RICHARD CLUB OF PHILADELPHIA
JANUARY 15, 1952
WALDORF-ASTORIA HOTEL, NEW YORK, NEW YORK

I am profoundly grateful for the honor you do me - an honor whose deep significance rests upon its association with the anniversary of the birth of that peerless American patriot, Benjamin Franklin. Nothing which I might say would add luster to the exalted stature of this great man. For there is indelibly etched in detail upon the pages of history the record of his monumental works. His life exemplifies, possibly more than that of any other, the boundless opportunity with which Americans have been endowed since this continent became a sanctuary from tyranny and oppression.

Morality was easily the cardinal virtue which characterized his long years of public service, and he held justice to be "the surest foundation on which to erect and establish a new state." But, in his intensely practical mind, there were two virtues, industry and frugality, which he said "tend more to increase the wealth, power and grandeur of the community than all the others." He was essentially a man of peace, but when war came he knew there was no substitute for victory. Invincibly oriented to the course he charted, our country over many years grew prosperous and strong. We developed the spiritual resource to produce a culture and way of life based upon free individualism and rich in the essence of liberty and justice, for commercial and agricultural progress set a pattern which early commanded universal admiration; and, through evolutionary processes, we adjusted our human relationships to enhance both the fruits of industry and the dignity of labor.

In accordance with custom, your distinguished organization meets each year on the anniversary of his birth. It is fitting indeed that you do so. But, it would be even a greater tribute were we all to rededicate ourselves on such occasions to the great principles and ideals for which he stood - did we recheck our nation's course against our heritage of his great wisdom, so that the foundations supporting our free institutions which he did so much to erect remain impervious to the man-made stresses and strains which now so threaten our traditional way of life.

Again my thanks and deepest appreciation for the signal honor you have conferred upon me.

MISSISSIPPI LEGISLATURE
MARCH 22, 1952
JACKSON, MISSISSIPPI

With this speech MacArthur began to press in earnest his feeling that from a calm dedicated adherence to law and order and the precepts of the U. S. Constitution, our government began its inexorable slide from conservatism to Socialism begun by President Roosevelt. Since World War II the emphasis began to shift from conservatism to a more liberal emphasis to concentrate more and more to people policies and big government to insure a good life for all as only big government could provide it. The decimation of our Armed Forces after World War II began here and under democratic control of the Congress it has never ceased.

Edward T. Imparato, Editor

It is with a sense of high honor and distinction that I address the members of this legislative body and the citizens of the great State of Mississippi. Indeed, as I stand before you and recall the South's mighty contributions to our beloved country, my heart is filled with pride that I, too, by right of birth may claim its great and noble traditions as my traditions, its lofty heritage of honor as my heritage. For when the past decade is adjudged by the historian of the future, he will surely record that in the forefront of the fight to preserve constitutional Liberty to our country was the moral courage, the indomitable will, and the broad vision of most of the statesmen of the South. It is they who stood guard in our hour of gravest peril. It is they who departing from the tradition of politics rose to magnificent heights of patriotism to challenge those forces which sought to impose upon the States the autocracy of centralized government.

For many generations our country followed the constitutional pattern of a diffusion of political power. This was wisely designed to insure development of a social order deriving strength and direction from the moral character, the dignity, and the creative energy of the individual State, the individual community, and the individual citizen. Those chosen to exercise the Federal power accepted in spirit the political checks and balances designed to preserve inviolate the people's ultimate power of sovereignty.

During those many decades our country grew prosperous and strong. We developed the spiritual ideals to produce a culture and way of life rich in the essence of liberty and justice. Our commercial and agricultural progress set a pattern which commanded universal admiration; and through evolutionary processes, we adjusted our industrial relationships to enhance both the dignity of labor and the fruits of industry.

Our public affairs were conducted on such a plane of ethics as to command full faith in the integrity of the governmental process. Politics were but the means toward the selection of competent leaders.

The national administration gave unstintingly of its allegiance to the interests of the Nation as a whole. The President accepted as his primary obligation the discharge of his responsibilities to all of the people. And inversely the people supported him as their chosen leader without regard to the partisan politics which had elevated him into the office of Chief Magistrate.

Then, this constitutionally ordained balance in political affairs collapsed. The national administration came under a control characterized by narrow vision and overriding personal ambition. The power of government was used as a political leverage to obtain more and ever greater centralization of authority. Political greed became the dominant factor in government and the fortunes of the political party of the administration began to receive primary consideration over and above the public interest.

Laws and clearly defined precedents which obstructed this concentration of power were brushed aside and the democracy of representative government began to yield to the concept of governmental autocracy.

In the ensuing movement toward the ascendancy of men over laws, the meaning and intent of the Constitution became rapidly corrupted. Propaganda was the mighty weapon through which control was sought. The people were first brought to a state of bewilderment and confusion through the agitation among the masses of fear and misunderstanding. Then followed a mighty effort to inject upon the American scene a system of mass thought control - a plan which failed of success only because of the rugged individualism still characteristic of the American people. Time and again in their innate wisdom they have sensed the tragic errors inherent in our misguided public policy. They have demanded changes, not only in policy, but in responsible appointive officials. But such demands have gone unheeded and men who have lost the public confidence have arbitrarily been protected in their exercise of the power of government. Grievous, indeed, have been the blows at the very roots of the concept that government is "of the people, by the people, and for the people."

Our public opinion has not reflected partisan politics, but the far nobler sentiment known to us as Americanism. Indeed, as I have traveled through the country, I have found the sense of concern and outrage over the course of governmental leadership fully as deeply stirring the conscience of those adhering to the Democratic political faith as of those adhering to that of the opposition party. I have found the Democratic rank and file in the field fully as militant in the censure of the misdirection of public affairs as Republicans. And this is as it should be. For, coming from those who compose the governing political party it emphasizes the depth of the resentment for wrongs   done America by all who love America. It reflects a sense of patriotism which far transcends any fealty to individual, group, or political party. It is indeed a measure of the great spiritual strength of the American people.

Of possibly most immediate concern to the South has been the manner in which this Federal autocracy has sought by the unconstitutional assumption of authority and power of inordinate taxation to seize or suppress the sovereign powers expressly reserved to the States. Efforts to sequester their tideland resources or to regulate their purely local social problems are among the many recent incidents.

By the devious method of expenditure progressively beyond income and increasing taxation to keep pace with expenditure, these political leaders have been rapidly exhausting the remaining revenue producing potential of the citizenry. This has rendered the States and other communities increasingly dependent upon the Federal Government. It places the State in the position of a supplicant. This method of employing the power to tax is not only destroying the principle of State and community autonomy upon which is erected our constitutional system of representative government, but it is rapidly sapping the productive energies and the creative initiative of our people. If it continues, our economic system of free private enterprise, the great bulwark to political and economic freedom, must inevitably perish.

History records that human liberty has oft' times been destroyed by the sword, but never before by a disingenuous application of constitutional powers expressly designed to insure its preservation.

America now stands at a crossroads. Down one lies a return to those immutable principles and ideals upon which rested our country's past grandeur. Down the other lies the arbitrary rule of men leading to the ultimate loss of constitutional liberty. As Daniel Webster once said:

"Other misfortunes may be borne, or their effects overcome. If disastrous wars should sweep our commerce from the ocean, another generation may renew it; if it exhaust our treasury, future industry may replenish it; if it desolate and lay waste our fields, still under a new cultivation they will grow green again, and ripen to future harvests.

"It were but a trifle even if the walls of the Capitol were to crumble, if its lofty pillars should fall, and the gorgeous decorations be all covered by the dust of the valley. All these may be rebuilt.

"But who shall reconstruct the fabric of demolished government?

"Who shall rear again the well-proportioned columns of constitutional liberty?

"Who shall frame together the skillful architecture which unites national sovereignty with State rights, individual security, and public prosperity?

"No, if these columns fall, they will be raised not again. Like the Coliseum and the Parthenon, they will be destined to a mournful and melancholy immortality. Bitterer tears, however, will flow over them than were ever shed over the monuments of Rome or Grecian art; for they will be the monuments of a more glorious edifice than Greece or Rome ever saw, the edifice of constitutional American liberty."

Other issues which deeply stir the conscience of the American people are many and varied, but all stem from irresponsibility in leadership. Domestic policy is largely dictated by the political expediencies of the moment. Foreign policy is as shifting as the sands before the winds and tides. Spendthriftness and waste have lost us our heritage of stability; weakness and vacillation, the moral leadership of the world.

The domestic scene has witnessed the greatest orgy of spending in history - a fantastic phenomenon which defies all reason - which has induced a tax burden upon the people, largely upon the lower and middle income groups, which has already destroyed the opportunity to build for future security and is rapidly destroying the will to work. Yet, our leaders show not the slightest concern for the stark tragedy which will descend upon the Nation once the exhaustion of our resources brings this extravaganza of spending to an abrupt end. Then will our people face the reality that their energies and those of their children and children's children have been mortgaged for generations to come.

The corollary to this irresponsible handling of the national resource has been shocking disclosures of graft and corruption over a wide area of the public service. There has resulted a consequent deterioration in the traditional standards of American morals and ethics which heretofore had held us upon so high a spiritual plane. Yet, even such disclosures seemingly fail to stir the conscience of our leaders.

Indeed, the relationship which once existed between government and people when the open criticism of the conduct of public affairs was accepted as a safeguard against inefficient, irresponsible, or arbitrary administration is now all but lost. The people are told in effect that the administration of their Government is none of their affair. They are but to listen and to obey. The inner circles of government partake more and more of the nature of a pampered, exclusive club. Dangerous experiments with the public interest, creeping corruption in fiscal honesty, and reckless gambling with the public security have led us inexorably down the road toward moral decadence and political disintegration.

When voices are raised in alarmed protest over the reckless dissipation of our national resource, answer is made by the half-truth method of pointing to the rise in our national income in terms of the present dollar, with its debased and devalued relativity with the dollar which existed during the normalcy of sound public administration carefully concealed. Or, we are warned of the great peril to this country from Soviet attack, of the devastation of our great cities unless our military might is restored as rapidly as but a short time ago it was dissipated. And we are told it is unpatriotic to question expenditures no matter how fantastic.

All this propaganda gives point to Benjamin Franklin's sage warning that. "a half truth is often a great lie."

And as we continue these wastrel policies without promise or hope of regaining normalcy; as we repudiate the economic concepts which raised our standard of life beyond all comparison with others; as we conduct confiscatory levies upon incomes, gifts, and inheritances calculated to destroy the principle of private ownership of property; as we depart from American ideals and reverse the course which served us so long and benefitted us so well, it becomes increasingly clear that the pattern of American fiscal policy is being brought into consonance with the Karl Marx Communist theory that through a division of the existing wealth, mankind will be brought to a universal standard of life, a degree of mediocrity to which the Communists and their fellow travelers seek to reduce the people of this great Nation.

Whether it be by accident or design, such policy, formulated with reckless indifference to the preservation of constitutional liberty and our free-enterprise economy, coupled with the rapid centralization of power in the hands of a few, is leading us toward a Communist state with as dreadful certainty as though the leaders of the Kremlin themselves were charting our course. It implements the blueprints of Marx and Lenin with unerring accuracy and gives stark warning that unless the American people stem the present threatening tide, human liberty will inevitably perish from our land.

In the field of foreign policy, efforts are largely confined to the contribution of vast sums, which we do not have and must borrow, toward the rehabilitation of economies abroad, the rearming of other nations, and the relief of foreign underprivileged and distressed. As a good neighbor we do desire to help the rest of the world in every reasonable way, but certainly that is no excuse either for the wrecking of our economy at home, or for covert encouragement of the terrible psychosis of war.

The very character of our Nation is molded from those noblest of human virtues - faith, hope, and charity. But it is a well-tested good rule to let first things be first. Let us regain faith and hope in our ability to achieve our own free destiny and let charity begin at home. Let us concern ourselves first with our own underprivileged and distressed before we take further from the little they have. The will to be free either exists in the human heart or all the money in the world cannot put it there.

Thus, despite the billions we have poured abroad, I doubt that we have gained a single Communist convert to the cause of human freedom or inspired new or deeper friendships. And as, quite obviously, the people of Western Europe do not generally share with our own leaders the fear of Soviet military designs, despite these billions we seem to have made little progress in convincing them that they themselves should vigorously act to shore up their own defenses. We hear no clamor to pledge their own lives, their own fortunes, and their own sacred honor in defense of their own liberties.

We had the leadership of the world at war's end - the spiritual leadership supported by the greatest relative military power in all history. But we yielded that leadership. We dissipated our great spiritual influence through a succession of diplomatic moves by which we betrayed our wartime ally China into Communist control, gave the Soviet a strategic hold upon areas and nations on the continent of Europe, and otherwise built it into its dominant position in world affairs. And even as we did so, we reduced our own military strength with reckless haste to a position of acknowledged impotence. Yet, the same leaders who hear responsibility for this catastrophic reversal of the world balance of power now attempt to justify the further depletion of our national strength through vast sums they call upon us to send abroad under the guise of retaining world leadership.

Our world leadership may only be regained if we ourselves are strong - spiritually as well as physically - and have the moral courage and the vision to advance constructive ideas with the will ourselves to see them through. Ideas which will restore international business and credits to private hands; ideas which will free arbitrary restrictions upon the exchange of national currencies; ideas which will evolve sound methods for the advance of international trade and commerce among friendly nations; ideas which will chart a course toward the complete abolition of the scourge of war as an accepted instrument of international policy; and ideas which have for their purpose reestablishment of the integrity of national sovereignties, both of the weak and the strong, against external influences and pressures.

Indeed, it would be immediately helpful if we but purged our foreign policy of imperialistic tendencies - not imperialistic in the sense that we covet the territory of others - but imperialistic in the pressure we bring to bear upon the purely domestic affairs of others. For this is an era characterized by a universal sentiment of nationalism. This we must respect if we would gain the respect of others. The peoples of the world will only follow our leadership upon the basis of our moral integrity and spiritual as well as physical strength.

They will measure us not by the moneys we recklessly give them, but by the general attitudes with which we face the common problems of mankind.

Possibly in Asia, where the record is more fully developed and events themselves have more plainly written the judgment, has the irresponsibility of our national policy been most pronounced. There our betrayal of China will ever stand as a black mark upon our escutcheon. But the tragedy of Korea comes closer to the hearts of the American people. For there thousands of our beloved dead give mute evidence to the tragic failure of American leadership.

There, in the aftermath of victory in World War II, we first undertook the protection of the Korean people and the welding of their segments into a consolidated and free nation. Later, we repudiated that purpose and practically invited the aggression which ensued by withdrawing our forces, enunciating the policy that the defense and consolidation of Korea was no longer within our sphere of political and military interest, and simultaneously withholding the arms needed adequately to prepare the South Korean defense force. Yet, still later after its southern half had been brought under attack from the north, we reassumed its defense and consolidation.

We defeated the northern Korean armies. But in the wake of the commitment of Communist China against us, we again repudiated our purpose to weld all of Korea into a free nation and denied our own beleaguered forces the orthodox military means which offered promise of early victory. We had them fight to a stalemated position on the peninsula and left them there to die in a deadlocked struggle of position and attrition, while we entered into so-called "cease-fire negotiations" universally interpreted as our suing for peace.

These negotiations have been underway for eight months, the only noticeable result being that the enemy has gained time to bring up artillery, air and mechanical transport, and to perfect his anti- aircraft defenses and communications, all to gain strength where once his weakness was most pronounced. And the high and noble purpose which introduced us into the Korean conflict is now no nearer fruition than when our Nation was first committed to the task. At that time, it was our stated intent to punish the aggressor, but through our strange and unprecedented war policies, we have inflicted the punishment, not upon the aggressor, but upon our own forces and upon the Korean nation.

We have permitted the enemy with impunity to prepare his blows against us from behind arbitrary and unreasonable sanctuary. We have protected him by holding inviolate his own soil, his war making facilities, and his own nearby bases of attack.

We have protected him by preventing, with our own naval forces, any hostile movement against his flank by our faithful ally garrisoned on Formosa. And this despite the fact that such a movement would have relieved the pressure upon our own Army fighting in Korea and thereby saved countless American lives.

And, while we afforded him his measure of protection and the time and battle training to permit him to build and perfect his military strength to challenge our mastery of the air, we enforced upon the Korean people the dreadful tragedy involved in the exclusive use of their soil as the sole battleground. As a consequence, death has come to hundreds of thousands of defenseless Korean civilians and a nation brought under our sacred protection has been devastated and gutted.

As long as history is written the shame of this will be recorded, but its more immediate consequences will be found in the loss of the faith of Asia in our Nation's pledged word and the consequent undermining of the foundations to the future peace of the world. For our failure to sustain our solemn commitments in Korea will probably mean the ultimate loss of all of continental Asia to international Communism. It might well mean foreclosure upon the chances the Chinese may have had to throw off the chains of Red tyranny and oppression.

It perhaps will even mean the ultimate fulfillment of the Russian dream of centuries to secure warm-water outlets to the south as a means of gaining military posture of global omnipotence, with the hope of ultimate domination over the seaborne commerce of the world. Beyond Asia, Africa would then be exposed to Communist hordes dominating the Indian Ocean area, and Europe would come under a real threat of invasion.

I repeat here what I said many months ago - the first line of freedom's defense is not the Elbe, not the Rhine, but it is in Korea on the Yalu. Prejudiced and willful voices scoffed at this warning, but there is where the Communists elected to challenge our spiritual and military strength and there is where we have failed adequately to meet that challenge, even though we had the military resource and means at our command.

Our failure has been of the spirit, not of the arms - a bankruptcy of leadership in our American tradition. Yet this failure has furnished the Soviet the passkey to world conquest. Small wonder that such weakness and vacillation should cause us loss of faith and respect abroad. Not since the early days of the Republic has our Nation been so reduced in the universal esteem. Never have we as a people been held in such doubt by others.

This glaring failure in Korea is but symptomatic of a general bankruptcy of leadership over many fronts, both foreign and domestic. Indeed, we have yet to hear a comprehensive statement calculated to reassure the American people that the future holds prospects for peace and tranquillity and a return to the normalcy of happiness and progress in the great American tradition.

Despite the hypocrisy of many platitudinous statements, our leadership is fundamentally lacking in a capacity and spirit to chart a course which will bring true and lasting peace. Just as it plunged us unprepared into the Korean war, it is now preparing us for a war in Europe. As it tears down our structure of constitutional liberty, it rears the threat of converting us into a military state. It is and has been and will continue to be a leadership of war.

In this time of crisis when mounting taxes and prices point to the inevitability of ultimate human tragedy; when the constant threat of imminent world war keynotes Government propaganda designed to suppress criticism; when ever-mounting disclosures of scandal and corruption are seriously impairing popular faith in the integrity of the governmental process and making major inroads into preexisting standards of private morals; when appointive officials in whom the people have lost all confidence continue contemptuously to conduct the public affairs; when our citizens abroad are subjected with impunity to duress and physical violence by foreign governments with whom we are at peace; when we submit to blackmail and extortion and pursue a policy of fear in the prosecution of a war to which we have committed our beloved sons; when we witness our institutions being weakened by drawing upon the fruits of our free enterprise economy to underwrite the deficits of Socialist and Communist economies abroad; when the principle of State and community autonomy established by the Constitution as safeguard against the undue centralization of political power in the Federal Government is being corrupted; when our religious base is under constant pressure from Communists both at home and abroad - there is still that mightiest of resource which our Nation possesses - the love of individual liberty and the spiritual strength indelibly rooted in the American heart.

I have faith that that mighty bulwark of representative government - the civic conscience - will shortly assert itself under the processes established by the Constitution and that the people will thus rechart the Nation's course.

Let a leadership then emerge with the vision and moral courage to discard the dogma of political precedent which seeks to be all things to all people - a leadership firmly resolved to restore political morality; regain thrift and frugality as the cornerstone to national stability and progress; reestablish the diffusion of the political power; shore up the sagging beams of our free institutions; revitalize the battered remnants of our personal freedoms; reorient foreign policy to reality and reason; and renew a devotion to God and the religious base upon which our country was erected.

DEDICATION OF MACARTHUR PARK
MARCH 23, 1952
LITTLE ROCK, ARKANSAS

MacArthur's experience and emotional feeling toward his return to the place of his birth.

Edward T. Imparato, Editor

Words can but inadequately portray the deep sentiment which stirs my heart as I revisit this scene of my birth. I have just come from Christ Church where my beloved parents - a lovely lady of the South and a distinguished soldier of the North - first dedicated me through baptism to the service of God. My emotions are too deep for attempted utterance. I can but offer you the humble gratitude of a native son for the devoted care with which you have preserved this building. In my eyes it is hallowed for its memory of my sainted mother as she gave me the distinction of southern birth. I offer you, too, my thanks for the unfailing confidence and support you have given me throughout the years of my absence in the service of our country. I have drawn strength and inspiration from it during many lonely and difficult moments of doubt and decision.

I left Little Rock long, long years ago when life was simpler and gentler. The world has turned over many times since then and those days of old have vanished, tone and tint; they have gone glimmering through the dreams of things that were. To me their memory is a land of used to be, watered by tears and coaxed and caressed by the smiles of yesterday. It is filled with ghosts from far-off fields in khaki and olive drab, in navy blue and air corps gray. I can almost hear the faint, far whisper of their forgotten songs. Youth, strength, aspirations, struggles, triumphs, despairs, wide winds sweeping, beacons flashing across uncharted depths, faint bugles sounding reveille, far drums beating the long roll, the wail of sirens, the crash of guns, the thud of bombs, the rattle of musketry - the still white crosses!

And today I have come back from whence I started. For me the shadows are deepening, but I want to read you some lines which have helped me through the lengthening years. Perhaps they may help each of you as the future unrolls:

"Youth is not a time of life - it is a state of mind. It is not a matter or ripe cheeks, red lips and supple knees; it is a temper of the will, a quality of the imagination, a vigor of the emotions; it is a freshness of the deep springs of life.

"It means a temperamental predominance of courage over timidity, of the appetite for adventure over love of ease.

"Nobody grows old by merely living a number of years; people grow old by deserting their ideals. Years wrinkle the skin, but to give up enthusiasm wrinkles the soul. Worry, doubt, self-distrust, fear and despair - these are the long, long years that bow the head and turn the growing spirit back to dust.

"Whether seventy or sixteen, there is in every being's heart the love of wonder, the sweet amazement at the stars and the star-like things and thoughts, the undaunted challenge of events, the unfailing child-like appetite for what next, and the joy and the game of life.

"You are as young as your faith, as old as your doubt; as young as your self-confidence, as old as your fear; as young as your hope, as old as your despair.

"In the central place of your heart there is a wireless station; so long as it receives messages of beauty, hope, cheer, courage, grandeur and power, so long you are young.

"When the wires are all down and all the central place of your heart is covered with snows of pessimism and the ice of cynicism, then you are grown old indeed."

As I look around at this sea of glowing, youthful faces, I repeat I am glad to be back and glad to feel so young again.

Once more, not only for myself but for my best girl and my dear son, I give you my thanks and deepest appreciation for this welcome home. It is a memory that will be with me always.

MacArthur praises the people and industries of Michigan for the massive support given our Armed Forces through three wars. After World War II he sees the swift decline in government fiscal responsibility from the strong and solid base of productivity exampled by the people of Michigan to a tax and spend philosophy.

Edward T. Imparato, Editor

From this rostrum located at the very heart of our country's industrial strength, I cannot fail to pay tribute to the vision and courage, the imagination and will, the initiative and energy which have gone into the leadership this State has given our commercial growth as a Nation and our material progress as a people.

Few men have had so poignant an opportunity to see and evaluate our great resource of industrial power. In the violence of our last three wars abroad, when our country's very destiny hung in the balance, I have seen the sinews of battle pour from your factories in massive quantities to bring victory to American colors where otherwise defeat might well have been. This has not sprung so much from great advantage in raw resource, nor indeed, from any complete monopoly in wisdom and scientific knowledge, but more than all else, it has come from the character of this mighty blend of the universe known as the American people.

I have seen that character indelibly etched upon the faces of the millions I have met from north to south, from east to west; a spiritual character which seeks the supremacy of right over wrong; a determined character which will not yield the inalienable right of personal liberty; an aggressive character which has surmounted all obstacles in the forging upon this continent of a dynamic civilization which is at once the wonder, the inspiration, and the envy of the world.

The basic character of the American people is the energizing force behind America's past, the stabilizing influence to America's present, and the main hope of America's future.

Now it faces possibly its greatest modern test if our heritage of faith is to be preserved and our liberties survive. In this time of faltering leadership, it is the people themselves who must meet this challenge and rechart the Nation's course. For Lincoln's admonition has been proved and reproved through successive generations - that the people are wiser than their leaders.

Because of that which I have seen and heard since my return to this country more than a year ago, I have been impelled as a patriotic duty of simple citizenship and a disagreeable duty it has been - to expose for public consideration the failures and weaknesses, as I view them, which have brought our once righteous and invincible Nation to fiscal instability, political insecurity, and moral jeopardy at home and to universal doubt abroad.

Those voices which have been raised in opposition to what I have said, have avoided for the most part the merit of just argument. Instead, with narrow minded petulance, they either chide my right to wear the uniform in which I have served for over 53 years, or imply I must supinely submit myself to a prevarication of truth by defending rather than criticizing those who have guided the Nation into its present tragic circumstances.

They even contend that my advocacy of a return of this Nation to constitutional direction, of a restoration of those noble and well-tested principles and ideals which we were formerly so proud to call American tradition, of a revitalization of the moral fiber which once commanded full faith in our public institutions, is merely the pleading of partisan politics - that it renders mine the voice of a biased politician.

There is no politics in me, nor none intended in what I say. I plead nothing but Americanism.

We have strayed far indeed from the course of constitutional liberty if it be seriously contended that patriotism has become a partisan issue in contemporary American life. Yet, only recently, the indifference, if not the contempt, held by some in high authority for the Constitution and the wisdom of its architects, and the high principles and moral codes which in past have guided and insured our national progress, was graphically emphasized by reference to the advocacy of their restoration to American life as an antiquated and outmoded point of view - a dinosaur point of view was the actual sarcasm employed.

They loosely charge reaction to all who seek a rededication to the course of America's past greatness, and yet the course they seek to substitute follows meticulously the oppressive despotism from which our forefathers sought the sanctuary of political independence. They are thus the real reactionaries in this epoch of American history.

While none will dispute the need for a progressive and continuous reevaluation of our procedures to meet new conditions nor the absorption of sound and enlightened ideas designed to advance the general welfare, such a callous indifference to fundamental principles long and successfully standing as the bulwark of American progress finds support in neither statesmanship nor logic. Indeed, the masses of the people in their innate wisdom have sensed and resented the tragic mishandling of their public affairs and desperately sought a reorientation toward effective security, reasonable stability, and honest administration.

There is little need here to restate the tragic circumstances to which the country has been reduced by misdirection of public policy or to recount the errors through commission or omission which have brought about these circumstances. We cannot relive the past. All that we can do is from its lessons of failure redesign the present in order that we may provide needed safeguards for the future.

Nothing threatens us more acutely than our financial irresponsibility and reckless spendthrift policies which jeopardize all thrift and frugality. Our leaders seek to justify the high, unreasonable, and burdensome costs of Government on the grounds of its complexity under modern conditions. This is fallacious reasoning.

Government has indeed become complex, but it is largely a self-induced complexity. It springs from its increasingly arbitrary nature and the labyrinth of governmental agencies created in the endless effort toward centralization and the imposition of new and expanding Federal controls upon community and citizen.

A return to a diffusion of the political power so wisely ordained by the Constitution, leaving to the community the management of its local affairs and to the citizen the management of his personal life, would largely relieve this complexity.

We would at once revert to something of the directness of the past, when the primary test of sound administration lay in the simple determination of that which was right and that which was wrong. We would regain the Jeffersonian standard that the least government is easily the best government. Restore simplicity in public administration and you will at once not only drastically reduce the financial burden upon the people, but you will raise the standard of individual life and regain the level of community and personal dignity.

But, financially we must do much more than that. If the incentive to carry forward the dynamic progress this Nation has registered in past is to continue and insure accelerating progress in future, the entire burden of taxation must be further materially reduced. Indeed, a reasonable limit must be placed upon the very exercise of the power to tax, easily the most abused and, as history has shown, the most dangerous of all sovereign powers. This power must be applied only for the purpose of defraying the legitimate expense of a frugal Government, not with the ulterior motive of regulating and controlling our private lives and efforts.

It must be reoriented away from the Karl Marx Communist aim of redistributing the wealth and of sharing the fruits of private enterprise, not only internally, but externally.

We must avoid confiscating incomes and draining resources to the point that the private ownership of property will practically disappear from our economic system. We have so burdened our people with taxation that they are no longer able to build for old age and family security, and are rapidly losing the energizing incentive to work.

We are so heavily mortgaging the industry of our next generation that the heritage which we pass on will be but hollow mockery of that which we ourselves received. We have so inflated the cost of the necessities of life that those depending upon social security benefits, old-age pensions, and other fixed incomes are being reduced to desperate circumstances.

Indeed, it is part of the general pattern of misguided policy that our country is now geared to an arms economy which was bred in an artificially induced psychosis of war hysteria and nurtured upon the incessant propaganda of fear. While such an economy may produce a sense of seeming prosperity for the moment, it rests on an illusionary foundation of complete unreliability and renders among our political leaders almost a greater fear of peace than is their fear of war. A day of reckoning and adjustment is inevitably ahead when we find that the resources with which we might have cushioned the shock of readjustment and reconversion have been recklessly expended. Then, it will be crystal clear that the material cost and toll of so uneasy a peace has been almost as severe as that produced by war itself.

While we must rebuild the military strength irresponsibly dissipated at war's end, and honor our commitments to others who honor theirs to us, we must regain some degree of calmness, consistency, and common sense. We must reorient our economic policy toward reason and stability, or every man, woman, and child in America will share the bitter consequences. For on our present course, with neither forward planning nor sound and reasonable objectives, our economic structure could collapse with our great industrial centers becoming ghost towns almost overnight, and bitter, disillusioned, and resentful men forced to pound the streets in search of means by which to keep body and soul together.

Such an exhaustion of our economic health is what the leaders of the Kremlin most desire. It is what their disciples strive to achieve - these disciples who have infiltrated our press, radio, and television, our industrial plants, our banking institutions, our legal fraternity, our educational centers, our religious temples, and every facet of American life, including Government itself. It is our gravest danger and it is internal, not external. As Lincoln once said: "If this Nation is ever destroyed, it will be from within, not from without."

We must not underestimate the peril. It must not be brushed off lightly. It must not be scoffed at as our present leadership has been prone to do by hurling childish epithets, such as "red herring," "character assassin," "scandal monger," "witch hunt," "political gangster," and like vulgar terms designed to confuse or conceal the real issues and intimidate those who, recognizing the gravity of the danger, would expose it to the light of public scrutiny and understanding. For it is upon the shaking foundation stones of a complacent citizenry that minority pressures become controlling forces and liberty yields to tyranny.

Talk of imminent threat to our national security through the application of external force is pure nonsense. Our threat is from the insidious forces working from within which have already so drastically altered the character of our free institutions - those institutions which formerly we hailed as something beyond question or challenge - those institutions we proudly called the American way of life. They seek through covert manipulation of the civil power and the media of public information and education to pervert the truth, impair respect for moral values, suppress human freedom and representative government, and, in the end, destroy our faith in our religious teachings. They remember what Thomas Jefferson said, "The Bible is the cornerstone of liberty," and will have none of it. These evil forces, with neither spiritual base nor moral standard, rally the abnormal as well as the subnormal elements among our citizenry and apply internal pressure against all things we hold decent and all things we hold right - the type of pressure which has caused many Christian nations abroad to fall and their own cherished freedoms to languish in the shackles of complete suppression. As it has happened there, it can happen here.

Our need for patriotic fervor and religious devotion was never more impelling. There can be no compromise with atheistic communism - no halfway in the preservation of freedom and religion. It must be all or nothing. We must unite in the high purpose that the liberties etched upon the design of our life by our forefathers be unimpaired, and that we maintain the moral courage and spiritual leadership to preserve inviolate that mighty bulwark of all freedom, our Christian faith. For as Daniel Webster once said:

"If we abide by the principles taught in the Bible, our country will prosper and go on prospering; but, if we and our posterity neglect its instructions and authority, no man can tell how suddenly a catastrophe may overwhelm us, and bury all our glory in profound obscurity."

While many of our leaders seemingly have not as yet alerted themselves against this internal threat to our liberties, they do now acknowledge at long last that there is no immediate threat to our national security from the application of external force - that there is even no present danger to the units defending Western Europe from vastly superior Soviet and Soviet satellite forces to the East. This is not due to any material change in the military situation, as the relativity in air and ground forces in Europe is still so overwhelmingly to our disadvantage that no professional soldier would estimate our capability to even hold against determined attack with the force there in being.

But our leaders no longer issue alarming warnings that our great cities are about to be laid waste. They are coming perhaps to understand that the Communist technique is to reduce peoples by internal pressures, subversive infiltration, and psychological propaganda, rather than by the much more costly and hazardous application of direct military force. Once this is fully understood, the conclusion may not be avoided that with the inability for many years to mount sufficient force in Western Europe to match the superiority of Soviet force in Eastern Europe, peace and security in the West will rest, in final analysis, upon a spiritually and physically strong America.

We must preserve and conserve our industrial potential to counter any major threat against the general peace, with the invincible determination to meet any force hurled at us with adequate counter force. This requires that we husband our own resources and carefully avoid their dissipation in line with Soviet hopes - that those resources be so applied as to maintain a spiritual and temporal power adequate to cope with the responsibilities of leadership and insure not only the security of our own Nation, but encourage maintenance of the universal peace.

Through the increasing centralization of the political authority in the Federal Government and the long tenure of one group in public office, the disease of personal power has become deeply rooted. The effort to perpetuate that power through the patronage of money against which Thomas Jefferson so clearly warned has made undeniable progress in corrupting the body politic.

It is now even proposed that our two-party political system be abandoned for all practical purposes and that both parties unite under the leadership of the same individual. Could there be a more shocking proposal?

It would destroy representative government and, by completely silencing all opposition, reduce us to a despotism. We would be entirely dependent upon the paternalistic will of one man, and liberty as we have known it would disappear. The people would no longer be the master of their government but its servant. The hypocritical call for unity is always by those in power who seek by an appeal to the opposition's patriotism to silence all objection to that which they may have in mind to do.

Indeed, so open and menacing have the efforts become in our country to stifle opposition, suppress the issues, and enforce arbitrary and bipartisan acceptance of entrenched public policy that we now find some of the leaders of one party openly endorsing their own selection as the nominee of the opposition party. They encourage segments of their rank and file to infiltrate the opposition's ranks to influence the selection of its nominee for the Presidency.

We find many who traditionally have supported and identified themselves with one of the major political parties now throwing the full weight of their resources for persuasion and propaganda into the effort to influence and coerce the leaders and rank and file of the other in its nominee selection.

This is a practice heretofore unknown to American politics. It strikes at the very roots of our two-party system of government. It represents a political device, which, if successfully employed, would closely parallel the totalitarian practice of naming a single candidate for the public vote.

This form of political conniving is destructive to the very essence of true representative government and sets the stage for the emergence upon the American scene of the ugly threat of a military state.

The gravity of this danger cannot be overemphasized. The history of the world shows that republics and democracies have generally lost their liberties by way of passing from civilian to a quasi-military status. Nothing is more conducive to arbitrary rule than the military junta. It would be a tragic development indeed if this generation was forced to look to the rigidity of military dominance and discipline to redeem it from the tragic failure of a civilian administration. It might well destroy our historic and wise concept which holds to the supremacy of the civil power.

In foreign affairs our policies - or more truthfully our lack of policies - have been weak and vacillating and largely dictated from abroad. From the acknowledged leadership of the world six years ago, we have drifted into an equivocal position in which our main influence seems to be confined to that of paymaster.

Our leaders are unable to survey the world as a unit, but have become so infatuated with the one area of Western Europe that they have largely ignored the Communist assaults in many other sectors of the globe. However important Western Europe most assuredly is, this is a form of extreme isolationism - a term ironically enough with which they attempt to castigate all who oppose them. It is an isolationism which can only lead to confusion and bewilderment and blinds its disciples even to the impelling needs and interests of our own people.

Thus, we have but recently witnessed the stark reality of tragedy and distress brought to thousands of American homes over the area of eight States by the inundation of flood waters from the Missouri and Mississippi Rivers. Such tragedy could and should have been avoided.

I recall over 40 years ago working as an engineer officer on plans for the control of just such flood conditions. Such plans have long been perfected and engineers, both military and civilian, time and time again have appealed for the funds needed for the control measures indicated. But such funds were never forthcoming for so essential a protection of our own people, even though we remitted funds in far greater amounts to the peoples of Western Europe for purposes which included the consummation of similar protective projects. Nor is it a case involving merely existing American surplus or superabundance, as every dollar we send abroad must be extracted from the sweat and toil, sacrifice and venture, of all of the American people not only of this generation but of the generations yet to follow. This is but one of the many cases wherein policy has furthered the interests of others at the expense of our own.

In one sector of the world we oppose colonialism; in another we support it. In one sector we bristle; in another we appease. There is no continuity of purpose, no stability or determination of spirit. Our European preoccupation is so great we almost entirely ignore the enemy in other areas and even allow continental Asia to go by inertia and default - Asia which encompasses half of the population of the world and more than half of its raw resources. As it was so quaintly put, "Let us wait until the dust settles."

In Korea, where victory was in our grasp, we go from bad to worse. Our Armed Forces there, and the world has seen no braver, have been deprived of the soldier's greatest incentive - the will for victory. They have been forced to accept the defeatist attitude of mere defense. A mortal blow has thus been given to our military code and practice, the disastrous results of which in the future may be so far reaching in our defense forces as to be beyond all calculation.

No need to blame our enemy for this sad commentary, for he has but taken full advantage of our own deplorable indecision and of our own rejection of victory, our historic military goal. Rather than revile him we would do better to refortify the spirit which animates our fight, recrystallize that indomitable determination which evolved our great tradition, and regain faith in the invincibility of our cause.

Sooner or later a vital decision will have to be made. Will the United Nations, when no longer dealing merely with theory and propaganda, but actually facing fire and sword, finally sustain the integrity of the principle of collective security and thus justify the universal faith; or will they fail the dying gasps of those countless thousands who perished in that far-off land in their name?

This is a fundamental question, as the answer in Korea will have a major influence everywhere. Indeed, by what other standard may we measure the determination of our European alliance to support the principle of collective security there, if not by its record in Korea?

By what accomplishment may we justify the generous contribution we are making of our own material sustenance and the offer of the blood of our sons in support of the principle of collective security in Western Europe, if not by the record in Korea?

And, if an uneasy "cease-fire" eventually does come in Korea, what then? No answer has been forthcoming, but the dreadful fear is growing in many patriotic hearts that the decision will finally be "scuttle the Pacific" - a yielding to the Iron Curtain of all of our traditional friends and alliances and the raw resources of that half of the globe so vital in the balance of world power. Then would our Pacific coastal areas - California, Oregon, and Washington - be forced to assume the hazards of a defense frontier and curtail existing commercial advantages as major gateways to international trade.

Everywhere the long arm of foreign influence dominates and controls even against our own national interests. Our will, our courage, our initiative, seem almost paralyzed.

If I could voice but one solemn warning in the lengthening shadows of life, I would point to the jeopardy to our independence by the high-handed and reckless course of foreign-dominated national policy, and urge thoughtful reflection upon General Washington's stern and realistic order at another crisis in America's past: "Let none but Americans stand guard tonight."

CADILLAC SQUARE
MAY 16, 1952
DETROIT, MICHIGAN

MacArthur stresses the mighty workshops of Detroit through free enterprise and their brains and brawn and energy which created the mighty miracle of production.

Edward T. Imparato, Editor

Where can one find a source of higher inspiration and hope than comes from this great city of Detroit - this mighty workshop of America - built by the brain and brawn and energy which only an economy of free private enterprise can produce?

It has elevated the dignity of the working men and women of America and maximized the fruits of American industry to a point known to no other land. But the lessons to be drawn from Detroit's past are spiritual as well as material. For that past has taught that in the crucible of freedom and opportunity, peoples of differing races and tongues may harmoniously live together and work together and prosper together.

This harmony among individuals could apply with no less force among nations, if the leaders of the world would so permit. For the great masses of the human race are just as you and I. They want but to live their lives in peace and freedom and personal contentment and seek only the opportunity to contribute their mental and physical energies toward just such an end.

The gains which you have made here are responsive more than all else to the wisdom of that immutable charter of human liberty and equality - the Constitution of the United States. It must be preserved inviolate in spirit and in letter, if these gains, both to labor and to industry, are to be protected and further advanced. Both sides must adhere to a code which recognizes as arbiter and judge of all dispute - the public interest. This should follow naturally as the rank and file of industrial workers and the owners of industrial enterprise constitute a major segment of the public; and, as a consequence, the public interest is their own predominant interest.

Both in labor and in industry, this calls for a high level of statesmanship dedicated to the common purpose of advancing a liberal and unexploited labor movement and an industrial economy sufficiently free from government controls to maintain a reasonable profit potential.

Only thereby may our free enterprise economy develop its maximum dynamic force and have adequate safeguards against excesses by either government or labor or management. Only thus can the public interest be fully protected, the profit motive essential to healthy enterprise be secured and the gains of the working men and women of America be advanced in parallel with our industrial progress.

When we entered upon the occupation of Japan, I found a degree of labor exploitation there never known to this country. Under its feudalistic traditions, labor had been reduced almost to a form of economic serfdom difficult even to visualize here. But with the history of the American free labor movement as our guide and with the counsel and advice of officers of the major American labor organizations, patriotically furnished at my request, the workers of Japan were liberalized and oriented along the same lines as here.

But there, as here, the tendency may grow under the influence of political pressures to reverse the process and attempt the exploitation of industry by labor. Nothing could more thoroughly wreck labor's gains of the past century. For the exploitation of industry would in time destroy the very foundations upon which those gains have rested.

Such a tragedy can be avoided by a wise and sound labor leadership invincibly dedicated solely to the cause of labor's true welfare. Indeed, so delicate has become the balance that every worker in American industry, if he values his existing living standard, should concern himself with our general economic health; with the inroads into industry by governmental regulations, by tax levy and by political pressure; with the adequacy of protective measures against the destructive effects of any international trade policy which fails to provide for differentials in employment standards abroad or favors sweatshop conditions there.

It is essential not to thereby destroy the only means upon which he can rely to sustain his high economic position. He should above all concern himself with the public interest of which he is so major a part, to make certain that any immediate gain he may make by virtue of his employment is not more than canceled out by a corresponding loss to his share in that public interest. There is nothing to be gained by giving with the one hand and taking away with the other.

The working men and women of America, more perhaps than any other segment of American life, have both the responsibility of public duty and the responsibility of self-interest alike to insure that those mighty forces - spiritual, political and material - which gave them their present position of eminence in modern society and provided them with the world's best tools and technology and working conditions are nurtured and reserved in their maximum vitality.

They must resist experimentation by Government designed to replace our traditional freedom of competitive opportunity with collectivist theories and practices which have never successfully met the practical test of creating higher standards of human life.

They must resist the spendthrift policies of Government which may bring us to the brink of economic chaos and are forcing upon us an irresponsible economy apparently to

MacArthur speaks to a crowd in Detroit on May 16, 1952.

avoid the political impact of a return to the long-range protection of frugality and reason.

They must resist being betrayed into political indebtedness through the bestowal of special privilege unrelated to the general welfare by those exercising the political power of Government.

They must establish strong bulwarks against the pressures upon the free labor movement by Communism whose initial objective upon ascendency to political power has ever been the worker's enslavement. Collective bargaining and the right to organize and to strike are unknown under Communist tyranny. American industry, both workers and owners, must understand that the maintenance of a free and strong America and the full protection of their existing stake in such an America is dependent more than all else upon the wisdom, the vision and the courage with which they discharge their individual political responsibilities of citizenship.

They must insure that the course of Government be reoriented from the arbitrariness of autocratic rule which is leading inexorably toward the regimentation of a military state. We must return to those principles of American tradition upon which was erected our past greatness as a nation and our freedom and prosperity as a people.

They must insure that Government be reduced to the simplest and most economical form consistent with reasonable efficiency. This can he done through a diffusion of the political power as wisely ordained by the Constitution and the lifting of arbitrary and unreasonable controls now imposed upon community and individual citizen.

They must insure that Government be limited in its exercise of the taxing power to securing only the revenue needed to defray the legitimate expense of a frugal public administration and be deprived of the authority to advance the Communist concept of sharing the wealth and threatening the principal of private ownership of property through confiscatory levies upon capital, income and estates.

They must insure that Government be required to orient basic policy toward the preservation and strengthening of our economic system based upon free, private competitive enterprise. Government must avoid any action directed at undermining or reducing the incentive to maximized initiative and energy or to restrict the opportunities for our youth to build toward future security and family protection.

They must insure that Government be required to gear public policy toward a continuity of social progress, avoiding however the disease of paternalism which encourages those seeking to live by the sweat and toil, initiative and enterprise of others.

They must insure that Government be restored as the political instrumentality of all of the people by holding itself above political expediency, special privilege and the patronage of money - evils which rapidly corrupt the body politic.

They must insure that Government recapture the public faith in its stewardship of public affairs by regaining the concept that public service is a public trust. There must be a restoration of implacable honesty to the public administration and a return to that strong religious base upon which the Republic was founded.

They must insure that Government purge from the public service all communists, their sympathizers and others who do not firmly believe in the ideal of American freedom and are unable or unwilling to work diligently for its preservation and advancement.

They must insure that a Government act vigorously to shore up our defensive strength, recklessly dissipated in the aftermath of the Second World War, but avoid wasteful expenditure or expenditure aimed at the primary purpose of maintaining for political reason an artificial appearance of prosperity.

They must insure that Government reorient our foreign policy to a pattern of consistency and reason based upon global, rather than limited to sectional considerations, and having primary regard to our own overriding security and public welfare.

They must insure that public policy adhere to constitutional direction as the only means by which we may achieve our own free destiny as a government of law rather than men.

They must insure that Government, backed by the military strength adequate to secure our own political and territorial integrity, offer the world a leadership of constructive ideas designed to advance the goal of universal progress and enduring peace; to protect our law-abiding citizens abroad while yielding no further to international extortion or blackmail; to restore the will to victory as the cornerstone to our military policy once American arms have been committed to battle; and, while doing all reasonably within our power and means to encourage international good will and cooperation, to avoid the sending of American public resources abroad merely as a means of advancing the purposes of groups having overseas investments or other special interests.

These, as I see it, are the minimum conditions essential to the revitalization of American public and private life, if we would restore to ourselves and preserve to our posterity that degree of political and economic stability and freedom of opportunity which was our heritage from the past. Our tens of millions of industrial workers and fifteen million industrial owners share the political power to achieve these conditions.

From personal observation, I have seen reflected in their faces that fine basic character which is the hallmark of the American patriot, and I am confident they will take a firm and invincible stand in the coming constitutional battle to save America as we have known it.

REPUBLICAN NATIONAL CONVENTION
THIS ADDRESS IS SOMETIMES REFERRED TO AS
"THE 1952 REPUBLICAN KEYNOTE ADDRESS"
JULY 7, 1952
CHICAGO, ILLINOIS

Mr. Chairman, ladies and gentlemen, possibly never before has a soldier bean called to a rostrum such as this to participate in the deliberations of a great political party. I approach the task in a spirit of humility born of full understanding of my own marked limitations, but fortified by so solemn an obligation.

In this unusual assignment, I feel a deep consciousness of the nature and gravity of the crusade upon which we now embark - a crusade to which all sound and patriotic Americans, irrespective of party, may well dedicate their hearts and minds and fullest effort. Only thus can our beloved country restore its spiritual and temporal strength and regain once again the universal respect.

I speak with a sense of pride that all of my long life I have been a member of the Republican Party, as was before me my father, an ardent supporter of Abraham Lincoln. I have an abiding faith that this party, if it remains true to its great traditions, can provide the country with a leadership which, as in the days of Lincoln, will bring us back to peace and tranquillity.

Perhaps it is unnecessary here to indict the present administration for all of its tragic blunders. For that indictment has already found full expression in the resentments which have poured from the hearts of the American people from North to South, East to West, with no distinction of race, creed, color, or political affiliation.

I know. From the four corners of the land, I have seen; I have heard. It has been a spontaneous expression reflecting a deep sense of fear that our leaders in their insatiate demand for ever more personal power might destroy the Republic and erase from the earth those mighty principles of government which brought to this land a liberty, a dignity, and a prosperity never before known.

It has been an expression of faith in our ultimate destiny as a free people; an acknowledgment of individual responsibility in the achievement of that destiny; a vibrant testi-

monial that the love of liberty still burns unquenchable in the American heart.

Many of the people who thus register the depth of their resentments do not fully comprehend the nature and degree of the policy misdirection which has brought us to fiscal instability, political insecurity, and military weakness.

But they view with dismay the failures of our leaders in the short aftermath of victory which causes us, the once proud and mighty victor, unceasingly to call upon every American mother to yield her sons in a fight for national survival; which causes us to submit to extortion and blackmail for the release of our citizens unlawfully detained by nations with which we are at peace; which causes us to deprive our beloved divisions committed to battle in Korea of the power and the means and the will to achieve victory - our country's traditional military goal.

They view with dismay the alarming change in the balance of world power, arising from the tragic decisions taken by willful or guileless men representing us at Teheran, Yalta, Potsdam, and elsewhere. Those reckless men who, yielding to international intrigue, set the stage for Soviet ascendancy as a world power and our own relative decline.

They view with dismay the tragic weakness of our leaders reflected in their inability to rebuild our strength and restore our prestige, even after our commitment to war in Korea more than two long years ago dramatically emphasized the inadequacy of our security preparation; reflected

Republican National Convention Keynote Speech, July 7, 1952

in their inability to conserve our resources even while they warn of national peril; reflected in their tolerance of corruption or worse in the higher positions of the public service.

They view with dismay the rising burden of our fiscal commitments, the deprivation of the opportunity to accumulate resources for future security and family obligations, the growing tendency of Government to control personal life and suppress individual freedom.

Our people are desperate for a plan which will revive hope and restore faith as they feel the oppressive burden of the tax levy upon every source of revenue and upon every property transaction; as they see the astronomically rising public debt heavily mortgaging the industry, the well-being, and the opportunity of our children and our children's children; as they observe the rising costs of the necessities of life impairing the effectiveness of pensions, insurance, and other fixed incomes an reducing the aged and infirm to appalling circumstances.

They look to their leaders, but their protests are silenced by the grim warnings of the disaster of a possible total war. They see no sign of concern, hear no words of encouragement, find no basis for easing fear. Their every expression of hope for reduction in the tax burden is met by the angry rejoinder that taxes must go ever higher.

There is no plan to transform extravagance into frugality, no desire to regain economic and fiscal stability, no prospect of return to the rugged idealism and collective tranquillity of our fathers.

They yearn to regain the religious faith and spiritual rectitude of the past. They remember the counsel of General Washington when he said in his Farewell Address:

"Of all the dispositions and habits which lead to political prosperity, religion and morality are indispensable supports. In vain would that man claim the tribute of patriotism who should labor to subvert these great pillars of human happiness, these firmest props of the duties of men and citizens."

But the people detect no heed given this wise counsel. They witness instead only a ceaseless effort to spend and spend, to tax and tax, only a callous indifference to mounting disclosures of graft and corruption and waste in the public administration.

The religious devotion of the American people which has produced the universally reflected spirituality of the American home has been outraged by the materialism and selfishness which dominates the national administration.

Public policy no longer is geared to the simple determination of that which is right and that which is wrong.

The objective has been to build political strength even at the expense of the public interest.

This is incomprehensible to our people who understand fully the influence religion and morality have always exerted upon political stability. They know from the lessons of history that national strength and greatness inevitably find their true measure in existing moral and ethical standards.

But, one asks, how can it be that the party of Jefferson and Jackson, which once contributed so magnificently to the building of the Republic, would now sponsor and support so tragic a cleavage from our great traditions? How could it despoil those very concepts of humanity and government upon which rested our past spiritual and temporal strength?

The answer is as clear as it is distressing. That party of noble heritage has become captive to the schemers and planners who have infiltrated its ranks of leadership to set the national course unerringly toward the socialistic regimentation of a totalitarian state.

To such end they have sought to circumvent the safeguards to our liberties wisely written into the Constitution of the United States. At one stage there was even the attempt to subvert the independence of our Supreme Court by adding new members, pliable to the will of the Executive - at another, the claim of extraordinary "inherent" power without the slightest sanction in law.

They have too frequently regarded that immutable charter as an instrument of political expediency. In the hypocrisy of self-righteousness, they hail their course as true liberalism. Yet every move they make to circumvent the spirit of the Constitution, every move they make to centralize political power, every move they make to curtail and suppress individual liberty is reaction in its most extreme form.

For the framers of the Constitution were the most liberal thinkers of all the ages and the charter they produced out of the liberal revolution of their time has never been and is not now surpassed in liberal thought.

Our forefathers associated together into a sovereign state for the sole and only purpose of protecting their common liberties, not of yielding them again to a centralized Federal authority. Their concept held to the primacy of the individual's interest; that of our present leadership to the predominance of the state.

They who trample upon constitutional liberty by the undue centralization and imposition of political power are turning back the pages of history and gradually re-instituting those very excesses and abuses for which the British Crown was indicted in 1776 by our Declaration of Independence. They are the dangerous reactionaries in contemporary American politics.

They have trifled with that great American institution - free, private, competitive enterprise, keystone to the arch of our economic strength as a nation and prosperity as a people. By the imposition of oppressive and arbitrary controls upon business and production; by exhaustive taxation which withers initiative, reduces energy and, in the end, destroys the spirit of enterprise; by spendthrift policies which stagger the imagination; by discouraging adherence to the principle of private ownership of property, they have established the prerequisites to a socialistic or even, later, a communistic state. And, as they thus chart a course with such reckless abandon leading toward ultimate national bankruptcy, they endeavor to mislead and control the public mind by a patronage of money, by devices calculated to create an artificial appearance of prosperity, and by a continuous flow of irresponsible and deceptive propaganda.

But the people in their innate wisdom are not misled by such tactics of deception. Alert to reality, they know that the value of the dollar has diminished about 50 percent and is still going down. They find insufficient compensation in nominally higher income, however skillfully propagandized as a mark of prosperity.

They entertain a growing fear that the same policy misdirection which has thus debased the dollar will in time so impair our economy as to imperil the Nation's solvency and thus destroy our living standard. With the dollar down, prices up, and taxes increased, a higher wage buys less today than yesterday. Tomorrow may be even worse.

Let me read you this letter illustrating how millions of American wage earners are losing their living standard:

"In 1941, I was working as a railroad telegrapher, as I am today. My weekly wage was $35.58. Subtracting $1.17 for railroad retirement, I had $37.71 take home pay - no income tax. My weekly wage now is $71.32. But from that comes $4.46 retirement and $10.50 income tax. Net: $56.36. Also, the cost of living has gone up 189% in the meantime. My old take-home pay was equivalent to $71.27 today. But my take-home pay today actually is that $56.36. My loss in income is $14.91. In other words, after 11 years, and with no compensation for added experience or increased productivity due to technological developments, I have actually suffered a pay cut of about $15 per week."

And so it is with all of us.

In this march away from our traditional American standards, few of our former liberties have been left unimpaired. Rights and powers specifically reserved to State, community, and individual by constitutional mandate have been ruthlessly suppressed by a creeping Federal authority. Reckless abuse indeed has been made of that most dangerous of all sovereign powers - the power to tax. We find ourselves already past the point where higher taxes might be expected to produce higher revenue.

The propaganda of fear is replacing our once dynamic initiative, well-tested vision, and unparalleled energy in a frantic effort to whiplash the country into a maximum of production.

This misdirection of public policy, which so endangers survival of our traditional American way of life, finds its genesis in an alien and foreign philosophy, its application in American politics designed to further entrench a 20-year-old upon the political power.

It emphasizes with startling clarity the sage warning of a wise and farseeing Democratic leader of many years ago, Senator Benjamin Hill of the State of Georgia, who foresaw something of what has happened, but I daresay expected the responsibility would be chargeable to a Republican administration. He cautioned on the floor of the Senate of the United States:

"I have said I do not dread (industrial) corporations as instruments of power to destroy this country, because there are a thousand agencies which can regulate, restrain, and control them; but there is a corporation we may all well dread. That corporation is the Federal Government.

"From the aggressions of this corporation, there can be no safety if it is allowed to go beyond the well-defined limits of its power. I dread nothing so much as the exercise of ungranted and doubtful powers by this Government.

"It is, in my opinion, the danger of dangers to the future of this country. Let us be sure to keep it always within its limits. If this great, ambitious, ever-growing corporation become oppressive, who shall check it? If it become wayward, who shall control it? If it become unjust, who shall trust it?

"As sentinels on the country's watchtower, Senators, I beseech you - watch and guard with sleepless dread that corporation which can make all property and rights, all States and people, and all liberty and hope its playthings in an hour, and its victims forever."

How prophetic this warning. How far our institutions have been yielded to these very excesses of power which he so deeply feared - and this, ironically enough, under the stewardship of his own party. Let none say this is but a partisan conclusion. For North or South, East or West, men and women of whatever political faith recognize the tragic truth of this circumstance.

But our failures in domestic policy can be overcome, for government takes its tone, its character, even its general efficiency from its leadership.

Sound leadership can restore integrity to the public service; can economize in the public administration; can eliminate disloyal elements from public authority; can purge our educational system of subversive and immoral influence; can restore to youth its rightful heritage; can strengthen the fabric of our free economy; can raise the dollar to its true value; can reduce the tax burden on individual and industry; can regain the course of constitutional direction; can recapture personal liberties now impaired; can correct social inequities; can strengthen the position of both worker and owner in private industry, even while protecting the public interest; can fortify the initiative, energy, and enterprise of the farmer so as to insure the adequacy of the production of food in lean years and its distribution in those of plenty, without being crippled by the unwarranted interference and domination of government; and can rearm the Nation without undue burden upon the people.

The correction of domestic evils and lapses would not be too difficult provided the will to do so firmly exists.

Foreign policy has been as tragically in error as has domestic policy.

We practically invited Soviet dominance over the free peoples of Eastern Europe through strategic dispositions of Soviet force at the close of the European war; we deliberately withdrew our armies from thousands of square miles of hard-won territory, permitting the advance of Soviet forces to the West to plant the red flag of Communism on the ramparts of Berlin, Vienna, and Prague, capitals of Western civilization; we recklessly yielded effective control over areas of vast uranium deposits without which the Soviet might never have developed the threat of atomic power; we foolishly permitted the encirclement of Berlin by Soviet forces, rendering almost inevitable the tragically high cost we have had to pay to secure open lines of supply and communication between our zones of occupation there and in West Germany; we authorized, sponsored, or approved policies under which the German industrial plant was subjected to major postwar dismantling and destruction; we turned over to the Soviet for slave labor hundreds of thousands of German prisoners of war in violation of every humanitarian concept and tradition; we failed to protest the murder by the Soviet of the flower of the Polish nation; and even after victory had been achieved, we continued to supply the Soviet with quantities of war material, despite the clear and inescapable warnings of the Soviet threat to future peace.

In the East we gave over to Soviet control the industrial resources of Manchuria, the area of North Korea, and the

Kuriles pointed at the heart of the Japanese home islands. We condemned our faithful wartime ally, the Chinese people, to the subjugation of Communist tyranny. And in the course of these moves, we proceeded with precipitate haste to divest ourselves of our own military strength.

Despite the threat to our security then clearly apparent, our Executive flaunted and ignored the judgment and will of the Congress which appropriated funds for the expansion of our air arm which he arbitrarily refused to expend for such purpose.

Small wonder indeed that, from the combination of these tragic decisions and events, there occurred a reversal of the balance of world power such as history has never before recorded.

Then suddenly, with our military strength standing at possibly the lowest relativity in history, our divisions in Japan reduced from three to two regiments, our regiments from three to two battalions, our battalions from three to two companies; with our protection withdrawn from South Korea as a militarily indefensible peninsula, we there and then plunged our forces into war to defend it.

Few would take exception to the impulse, however idealistic, to support the preservation of freedom where we had done so much to implant the principles and spirit of freedom, but it is fatal to enter any war without the will to win it. I criticize not the morality of the decision, but its irresponsibility and recklessness.

We defeated the North Korean armies; but, when the Communist armies of China struck, our leaders lacked the courage to fight to a military decision, even though victory was then readily within our grasp - a victory which would not only have discharged our commitment to the Korean people, but which in the long run might well have saved continental Asia from Red domination.

And, after discarding victory as the military objective and thereby condemning our forces to a stalemated struggle of attrition and the Korean nation and people to progressive obliteration, we again yielded to Communist intrigue and entered into protracted armistice negotiations even though every lesson of experience had clearly shown such negotiations to be but the means whereby such an enemy gains time to reinforce his military capabilities.

While I have not been consulted with reference to Korea since my retirement from active assignment 15 months ago, I can unhesitatingly say that a leadership which by weakness and indecision has brought about such a military dilemma lacks the soundness of vision, the moral courage, and the resolute will to resolve it.

Yet, resolved it must be, for we cannot long carry so intolerable a burden. We must have a leadership capable of decision, as indecision in war is but the prelude to disaster.

No military problem is unsolvable. Korea stands today as the hallowed graveyard for countless American dead. We must not let it become as well a graveyard for American hope, American faith, and American honor.

In Europe, and indeed throughout the world, our foreign policy approach has been equally as vacillating and negative and, for the most part, sad indeed to relate, under the domination of others.

We have yielded to selfish pressures both at home and abroad and, doing, have unduly directed the distribution of our wealth into privileged channels; have taken sides in international disputes, which were fundamentally none of our affair; and have endeavored to impose our will on other nations' purely domestic problems in an imperialistic manner.

We have ignored traditional friends while showering our favors on others, and we have lost that sense of judicial fairness which formerly characterized our relations abroad. In our preoccupation with Europe, we have tended to discard from our concern those great people of Asia and the Middle East who historically have sought, not our wealth, but our friendship and understanding.

Our good-neighbor policy with respect to the peoples of Central America - of greater strategic concern than all others - has been largely subordinated. Through the paternalistic attitude which has dominated our material assistance abroad, we have promoted as much weakness as strength, as much resentment as friendship.

Animated by the doubtful belief that with money alone we could erect internal bulwarks against communism's growth, our leaders have expended much of our resource on the area of Western Europe.

Events have largely established the fallacy of this reasoning. Indeed, the history of mankind shows clearly that the love of liberty is a spiritual resource of the human heart which, if nonexistent, does not spring from money alone.

None will quarrel with the impulse to do all reasonably within our power to assist the best effort of the peoples of Western Europe to prepare their bastions for self-defense, but communism with its recently acquired strategic frontiers in Asia and Europe and its penetration elsewhere by internal minority influences, presents a worldwide problem, the solution of which involves consideration of every point of possible Communist pressure.

One would be foolhardy indeed to quench a fire in the kitchen while leaving another room aflame. The problem is global, not sectional. Nor would the free world be the gainer, if our own Nation which from its own conception in liberty has ever stood as a beacon of hope and inspiration should so exhaust itself of spiritual and material resource as to render its own survival subject to the will of others.

Such a tragedy would return civilization to the darkness of the Middle Ages and the ideal of human liberty might perish from the earth.

But the present administration ignores the lessons of history, however clear and unmistakable. It ignores the practical aspect that there is a limit even to our own vast resources.

It ignores the fact that our potential strength rests not so much upon any natural advantages which we have and others have not, but upon the initiative and vision, the enterprise and courage, the sweat and toil which alone spring from the incentive of freedom.

Destroy such incentive and our Nation can go the way of many others toward a universal level of mediocrity - a standard of life measured by the lowest common denominator which is communism's ultimate goal.

The administration is obsessed by the idea that we can spend ourselves into a position of leadership abroad, just as it believes we can spend ourselves into prosperity at home. Both are based upon illusory premises. Both challenge economic and social truths, deeply rooted in the experience of mankind.

World leadership can only rest upon world respect. Such respect is one of those spiritual deals which do not result from gifts, propaganda, salesmanship, or any artificial means.

It is not for barter to the highest bidder. It is not within the orbit of international trade.

It is influenced solely by the soundness of the ideas by which we better our own civilization, elevate to higher standards our own way of life, and strengthen the dignity of our own citizenry. Only through the exemplification of sound ideas which in the crucible of experience have produced for us a better and more serene life may we contribute in fullest measure to the well-being of others.

The higher our own standard and more stable we become, the greater our appeal to less fortunate peoples and the more they will look to us and our ways of guidance and leadership. This applies equally to those behind the Iron Curtain and those still blessed by the concept of human freedom. For the whole record of civilization proves that the tyranny has not as yet been devised which can long resist a sound idea.

Spiritually and physically we possess the resource, properly conserved and realistically applied, to lead toward a world freed from the exhausting wars which have so plagued the past. This is a practical purpose, not visionary. For the destructiveness of modern war has now in the atomic age become too frightful to contemplate by even a potential victor.

This then must be the direction of our foreign policy. We must, upon restoration of our military strength and spiritual balance recklessly dissipated in our headlong retreat from victory, chart from that strength a true and unequivocal course to peace and tranquillity - a peace and tranquillity which will be real, not fictitious; deep rooted, not superficial.

Our ideal must be eventually the abolition of war. Such is the longing hope of all of the masses of mankind of whatever race or tribe. Indeed, so well is this understood that even the despot, in order to assure a following, cloaks the threat or application of force with the hypocritical pretense that his purpose is to secure the peace.

But rarely has the present administration made a major move calculated to strengthen the fabric of world peace.

To the contrary, it has done much to advance the danger of global strife by its indecisive conduct of the campaign in Korea, with its shameful implication that we dare not strike back at those who strike at us, by its bellicose attitude toward all who oppose it in international diplomacy, and by its pattern of collective security agreements which, without as yet having mounted either the will or the physical power to successfully meet aggression, have divided the world into armed camps and rendered us dependent, not alone upon the wisdom of our own foreign policy to keep us out of war, but upon the foreign policies and diplomatic moves of other nations as well.

We must fully understand that, once we commit ourselves to the defense of others, the issue of war or peace is no longer in our exclusive hands, for we become but another pawn in the game of international power politics - a dangerous game - in which the present administration has demonstrated no peculiar adeptness.

It has talked and pledged peace while moving toward war.

Indeed, none can deny what history so clearly records - that the Democratic Party has well earned the doubtful distinction of being the war party of modern American politics. The dead of World War I, of World War II, and of the Korean war render mute testimony.

We must remain faithful to the commitments we have made to others, so long as they remain faithful to theirs made to us, but failure of the principle of collective security in Korea, where we have found ourselves holding responsibility without corresponding authority, plainly warns that too much must not be expected from collective security elsewhere.

Indeed, in Western Europe as in Korea, experience has shown a reluctance by many of the Allies to assume a fair and rightful share of the military burden, even though in the case of Western Europe the basic purpose would be the defense of its own soil.

This hesitancy does not spring from any insufficiency of manpower, nor the exhaustion of other needed resource, but rather from a seeming confident assurance that this Nation's blood and treasure will be committed to the fullest extent needed to accomplish the military objective.

The free peoples of Asia and the Middle East do not ask for American garrisons to defend their soil. All they seek is the necessary military equipment beyond their own capacity of production. They have both the will and adequate men, if properly equipped, themselves to conduct their defense and to turn the tide decisively against communism.

There is no logical reason why the same solution should not apply with respect to all others. In such circumstances, it should be our unalterable purpose to effect in due time withdrawal of our ground garrisons from service abroad.

By far our Nation's greatest resource is our youth. In 20 bitter campaigns I have witnessed its magnificence in the most trying experience of all, that of the battlefield. It has never failed our faith, never failed in invincible courage and a patriotism which subordinated life itself to duty.

Yet, as it now approaches the responsibility of civic leadership, it is confronted with a situation made almost desperate by the loss of such opportunity and resource as was our own heritage from the past. This is the greatest tragedy of all - that a national administration could have so yielded to the disease of power as to betray the youth of America.

Despite stresses and strains, the fine basic character of the American people remains unimpaired. It offers hope that under the inspiration of a strong, moral leadership the people - all the people - will hurl back insidious efforts to sow the seeds of suspicion, distrust, and hatred calculated not only to stir up racial or religious strife between the several segments of our society, but to destroy the unity and common understanding which has been the cornerstone to our growth as a nation.

The very survival of our liberties and, indeed, our civilization is dependent upon our citizenry of all races, creeds, and colors standing firmly and invincibly together with a singleness of purpose, a mutuality of faith, and a common prayer - God bless America.

It is this spiritual unity which offers assurance that the coming crusade to rechart the Nation's course toward peace and security and prosperity will find an aroused countryside ready and eager to march.

That crusade rests upon the humanitarian aspirations of mankind, its constitutional rights, and the moral necessity for human happiness. It demands a purification of the Nation's conscience and a refortification of its will and faith. Therein lies the Republican Party's challenge to leadership.

At the close of the Constitutional Convention, George Washington remarked to Benjamin Franklin that he believed the Constitution as finally evolved was a great and noble charter of liberty upon which the several States could rally, unite, and prosper. "Yes, General," Franklin responded, "if we can make it work."

We have made it work in the days of our great past. And come November, we will make it work again - so help us God.

57TH CONGRESS OF AMERICAN INDUSTRY, NATIONAL ASSOCIATION OF MANUFACTURERS
DECEMBER 5, 1952
NEW YORK, NEW YORK

Industry has provided the U. S. Military with arms and energy to win it's wars. Now that war is in abeyance, the assembly lines of industry have become a main line of our national defense. It also provides us with the psychological comfort of being a partner in our scheme for the defense of our country.

Edward T. Imparato, Editor

It is with a sense of rare distinction that I address this gathering of the Nation's industrial great. I do so as an old soldier who, in the march of events, finds service has shifted from the battle line to the assembly line. For modern war teaches that industry has become a main line of national defense. It has become the bulwark of human freedom.

It is an unassailable truth that the science of industry has become a major element in the science of war. The successful conduct of a military campaign now depends upon industrial supremacy. As a consequence, the armed forces of a nation and its industrial power have become one and inseparable.

The integration of the leadership of one into the leadership of the other is not only logical but inescapable. It has become indisputably clear that it is no longer the standing armies now in being, nor the naval and air forces which range freedom's vast frontiers, which stay the bloody specter of willful aggression, but rather a realistic appreciation of our massive potential of industrial power which is so capable of rapidly mounting the means to retaliate and to destroy.

Industry has thus become the leavening influence in a world where war and the threat and fear of war would otherwise completely distort the minds of men and violently react upon the peaceful progress of the human race.

In the mighty and almost limitless potential of American industry - the brilliance and rugged determination of its leaders; the skill, energy, and patriotism of its workers - there has been welded an almost impregnable defense against the evil designs of any who would threaten the security of the American Continent. It is indeed the most forceful and convincing argument yet evolved to restrain the irresponsibility of those who would recklessly bring down upon the good and peace-loving peoples of all the nations of the earth the disaster of total war.

I say the peace-loving peoples of all of the nations, for the masses behind the Iron Curtain just as do the masses of the free world long for real peace. It is political leaders who fail this great concept - whose talents have as yet been unable to solve the mechanics of a true solution. Indeed, until their spiritual and moral and literate stature has achieved the proportions which permit the unequivocal recognition of the futility of war as an arbiter of international discord, our industry will continue to be the best deterrent.

Its mighty potential, which not only imposes an almost impassable barrier before the tides of modern war, but also insures a continuity of human progress, must be preserved in full readiness. It must be left unimpaired as a dynamic promise to foster good and an inherent threat to repel evil.

But to preserve it, we must understand it. We must understand that it comprises not only a power in being, but a reserve power capable of being quickly mounted to meet and overcome any eventuality. We must understand that it represents a condition of readiness born of American enterprise and vision, nurtured upon American energy and incentive, and finding its ultimate strength in American will and determination.

It is the product of the capitalistic system. This system embraces every segment of our American society - the owners of industry, the workers in industry, and the public served by industry. It has been well said in describing it:

"This is America's age of triumph. The brain of man is abstracting from the universe its fundamental secrets. There are no limits any more to production. Historic deficits are transmuted into future surpluses. So fast is progress that today's wonder is tomorrow's obsolescence. More and more. Better and better.

"These things are the achievements of freemen. Freedom is not merely the right to worship God in one's own way, or to speak one's mind in public places, or to move about unmanacled. It is also, most importantly, the right to create, the right to work and the right to possess the fruits of that labor. Economic freedom is the basis of all other freedoms.

"It is this fundamental liberty that is the driving soul of Americanism. Degrade or abolish it and nothing is left but the shadow of hope.

"It is the age of triumph - in everything except the art of government. In that area barriers to progress are repeatedly erected. For, the world over, the politicians are engaged in a titanic struggle to seize control of the economies. Whether it be in the masquerade of Communism or Fascism or Socialism, their purpose is the same - to wipe out a primary element of freedom and usurp it for the state. They are the state. The threat is terrifying because it carries the certainty of disaster.

"It is imperative that we stand militantly for the most vital quality of Americanism - Economic Freedom."

Belabored by the Communists, their fellow travelers, and the Socialists, the capitalistic system has even been tacitly repudiated by some capitalists themselves. Succumbing to propaganda, they have wavered in their loyalty to a theory and a practice which has both served them well and built this Nation far beyond the wildest dreams of its architects. It has never failed to maximize the fruits of human energy and creative enterprise. It has never failed to provide the resource for an ever increasing standard for human life. It has never failed to provide the sinews for victory in war and has become now the one great hope in the struggle for peace.

Was there ever greater hypocrisy than that which flows from those who castigate private capitalism as an evil to be renounced by human society while avidly seeking to ensnare its benefits - those who regard American dollars as the panacea for all economic ills while denouncing and condemning the source of such wealth - those who seek American goods while scoffing at and deriding the very institutions by which those goods are produced?

The past 20 years have witnessed an incessant encroachment upon the capitalistic system through the direction of our own public policy. This has left our free economy badly bruised and sorely tried. The assault has taken various forms. For political expediency and even baser purposes, efforts have constantly been made by those in power or those seeking to be in power to provoke distrust and strife between industrial owners and industrial workers, between management and labor - to breach the community of purpose and effort which so logically must exist between these two great segments of our industrial economy. The effect of this has been to produce a sense of unrest and antagonism where a firm and confident alliance built upon a mutuality of faith and understanding and a community of purpose will not only serve the interests of both but further the well-being of that third great economic segment, the consuming public.

Another and yet more serious form of assault upon the capitalistic system has been the increasingly oppressive Government levies upon both capital and profit. The principle underlying such levies has not been to equalize the burden of meeting the legitimate costs of government by a just and uniform assessment, but has followed instead a conspiratorial design originally evolved by Karl Marx to first weaken and then destroy the capitalistic system. Thus, many of our tax laws amount in practical effect to a series of graduated penalties upon the efficiency and the thrift which produces profit and accumulates capital - penalties which strike at the very roots of the incentive to labor, to create, and to cheerfully accept the risks and hazards of enterprise in the traditional American pioneering spirit.

Karl Marx shunned the use of violence and sought the voluntary acceptance of the principle of communal ownership of the sources and means of production. The innate common sense of the human race, however, rejected this principle and the element of force was injected by the Bolshevik after the close of the First World War. Then was combined the theory of Karl Marx with the principle of Nihilism under which the control of public policy was sought through terrorism and assassination. This combination known as Communism was far more successful. The minority in many sectors of the globe was able to establish its rule over the majority. Only where the concept of human liberty was most deeply rooted and greatly advanced were such minority pressures decisively thrown back.

Such was the case in this Nation where our economy, built upon the principle of private capitalism, became recognized as the great barrier to the universal enforcement of the theories of modern Communism. There followed repeated and diversified efforts to reduce and destroy it. Resort was had to the control of private profit by the Marxism - inspired device of confiscatory taxation and the absorption of private wealth by inheritance, gift, and other direct levies upon privately accumulated resources. Most officials of our Government over the past years will deny, and justifiably, any intent to establish in this Nation the basis for the emergence of a Socialistic or even eventually a Communistic state, but the course of fiscal policy has done just that.

The fact is unmistakable and clear that if the capitalistic system - free enterprise - is to be preserved to the future generations of our people, the course of government must now be sharply reoriented and America's industrial leadership must assume an invincible and uncompromising defense of that system. Only thereby may there be fostered and preserved adequate incentive to encourage the thrift, the industry, and the adventure which brought our Nation to its present preeminence among all of the other nations of the earth and which alone can carry it forward in peace and security and progress.

In accordance with our constitutional precepts, we are now about to send a new administration to Washington to assume the reins of Government. It is an administration chosen by the American people in reliance upon the pledge that in domestic affairs it will root out corruption, waste, incompetence, and subversion in the public administration; that it will sharply reduce the costs of government and lighten the existing burdens of taxation; that it will abolish unnecessary control by government upon business and otherwise curb unjustifiable interference by government in private affairs; that it will stem the spiral of inflation and through sound fiscal policy gradually restore the lost purchasing value of the dollar; and that it will stop the advance of Socialism in this country and reestablish measures designed to encourage the development of our traditional free enterprise economy.

This pledge accepted by mandate of the electorate is deserving of the full faith of America's industrial leadership. For under our system of government and in the American tradition, it becomes our duty as citizens to rally in firm support of the new administration and give it every chance and assistance within individual and collective power to fulfill its pledge and restore to the country a prosperity based upon sound rather than illusory considerations.

We must not fear the return to this land of normalcy merely because of the possible temporary dislocation of our economy now so largely resting upon the production in massive quantifies of the sinews of war. We must not fear to end the reckless and exhausting extravagance of government merely because it may force upon us an increase of frugality. Better if need be we increase our own thrift than leave our children and children's children a heritage of want and despair.

All of these reforms cannot be accomplished overnight. It will take time to avoid a precipitate cure which might prove even more exhausting than the disease itself. But it is the responsibility of America's industrial leadership in the exercise of its great power and influence, not only to support the new administration in its efforts to eradicate existing economic evils, but to see to it that the administration does proceed with reasonable diligence to the task with which under our electoral process it has been charged and entrusted. This is a responsibility America's industrial leadership cannot abdicate and cannot avoid.

There is involved not alone a sharp revision of domestic policy, but of equal importance, the reorientation of foreign policy to conform to realism and the unmistakable lessons of history. We must recognize that the very survival of freedom as the concept best insuring the continuity of human progress, is now largely dependent upon a strong and vibrant American industrial economy, soundly rooted in a free and competitive system of private capitalism. We must by exemplification encourage other nations and peoples to build soundly for their own security and economic progress, and scrupulously avoid the underwriting at our own jeopardy of any ill-considered experiments with economic theories already tested and found wanting in the crucible of experience.

While helping to the extent reasonably possible, we must not assume purely from altruism the risks and burdens which rightfully belong to others. We must abolish the idea that world leadership and universal respect may be purchased for a price. We must not hypothecate beyond redemption our own liberties in the illusory belief that the pledge of our resources will alone suffice to secure the liberties of others. They must help themselves even as we help them.

We have only recently witnessed sharp debates on the question of isolationism. Few are so foolhardy as to wish to isolate this Nation from the community of nations drawn close by the advance of modern communications. But all, even the most advanced internationalists, wish in varying degrees to circumscribe the nature of our relations and commitments abroad. All see the danger to our national integrity from yielding too much of our sovereign individualism. Few realize, however, that the effect of our foreign policy over the past years has been to establish the very basis for isolation, whether we choose it or not. For we have not only lost many former friends abroad, but weakened many friendships which we still retain in varying degree.

This could have been avoided had our leaders but recognized the simple truism that a nation is but the collective expression of the individuals which comprise it, with all of the emotions which rule the individual mind. As a consequence, one finds in the experience drawn from the relationship between individuals a generally accurate guide as to the reactions to be expected in relationships between nations.

This should have taught us that nations are just as sensitive as are individuals; that nations recoil against arbitrary dictation by others just as do individuals; that nations lose their self-respect just as do individuals if the burdens they should bear themselves are borne by others; and that a nation's loss of self-respect more often than not is translated into antagonism against its benefactor just as it is that of the individual.

This, coupled with the loss of faith abroad due to the weakness and vacillation of our foreign policy, is forcing us into isolation just as surely as though we deliberately set out to sever our foreign contacts. It bespeaks the utter lack of realism underlying the approach to our foreign affairs and gives clear warning that we must get back to the fundamentals of history's

teachings if we would preserve a position of leadership and respect among the other nations of the world.

In Korea, the principle of collective security is now on trial. If it fails there - and thus far it shows few signs of succeeding - it will fail everywhere, and its failure will become one of the great contributing causes for nations to withdraw again toward isolation. For one is the very opposite of the other. This seems to be little recognized, for it is not the least of the strange anachronisms of these strange times that those who advocate most strongly the principle of collective security in the protection of Western Europe are either lukewarm or actually opposed to the successful application of the same principle in the protection of Korea and the Far East.

Indeed, if we would frankly face and review our own weaknesses, we need go no further than the great tragedy of Korea. While it is well known that my own views have not been sought in any way, yet I am confident there is a clear and definite solution to the Korean conflict. There has been a material change in conditions from those of 20 months ago when I left the scene of action, and the solution then available and capable of success is not now entirely applicable.

A present solution involves basic decisions which I recognize as improper for public disclosure or discussion, but which in my opinion can be executed without either an unduly heavy price in friendly casualties or any increased danger of provoking universal conflict.

On the other hand, our present course, with the mounting hatreds which it inspires, is inevitably leading toward a world war. No greater fallacy exists than by those who for varying reasons tell you otherwise.

Our respected President-elect has announced his intention to go there in search for an honorable end to so tragic a slaughter, and all Americans join in prayer that he may safely pass through the hazards involved and accomplish his self-appointed task with vision and wisdom. For until a solution is forthcoming, hundreds of thousands of the flower of American youth must continue their fight to hold barren wastes of unfriendly soil, with only an occasional uneasy rest before reentering the valley of the shadow of death.

So it has been these endless weeks and months which have now grown into years since Red China initiated war against us in Korea and the indecision of our leaders committed us to the terrible blood tribute exacted by this type of stalemated attrition. Never before has this Nation been engaged in mortal combat with a hostile power without military objective, without policy other than restrictions governing operations, or, indeed, without even formally recognizing a state of war. Wherever and whenever Americans foregather, this issue should be foremost in their deliberations, and the question must be asked and repeated time and time again of those in authority and responsibility, "What do you intend to do about Korea?" How else can we keep faith with those we ask to die in that distant land?

Today we stand on the threshold of a new life. What vast panoramas will open before us none can say. They are there, just beyond the horizon, just over there, and they are of a magnificence and a diversity far beyond the comprehension of anyone here today. Our progress up to now has been in direct ratio to the degree of human freedom afforded us. Our rate of progress in the future will be determined in identical fashion. With freedom assured, there can be no limit to the progress we can make. The new world that lies before us has no boundaries. It has no lost horizons. Its limits are as broad as the spirit and the imagination of man.

I have an abiding faith in the future of this Nation - a faith grounded in the invincible character of the American people. It has never failed to triumph in our hours of national adversity and peril, and, as it has in the past, it will again restore to our land the serenity of hope without fear. To such end, I am happy indeed to be among so distinguished a company as this, charged in the service of our beloved country with so primary a responsibility for the course of our destiny as a free, happy, and prosperous people.

Welcoming Address, on Behalf of the Association of Graduates, United States Military Academy, to Those Attending the Founder's Day Dinner March 14, 1953

Each year, on or about March 16, the graduates of the U.S. Military Academy, wherever they may be, gather to celebrate the founding of the Academy in 1802. From the largest of headquarters to the smallest of garrisons, the men of West Point participate in similar festivities. The Association of Graduates asked General MacArthur, as one of their most distinguished members, to prepare an address of welcome for the 1953 ceremony. As this address was read to his fellow graduates, the truce talks in Korea were slowly dragging to an end.

Major Vorin E. Whan, Jr., USA, Editor
A Soldier Speaks: Public Papers and Speeches of General of the Army Douglas MacArthur
© 1965, Frederick A. Praeger, Publishers, New York, NY

On behalf of the Association of Graduates, I welcome every-where all those attending the Founder's Day Dinner. This anniversary stirs many poignant memories in me - memories which in many respects are common to all graduates of the Military Academy. They take each one back to that ceremony on the Plain at West Point when he entered the military service and dedicated himself to "duty, honor, country." They carry through successive academic years toward mastery of the rudiments of military science and the art of war - toward absorption of one of the highest moral codes on any campus, to culminate in the assumption of the responsibilities and obligations of commissioned leadership. Thereafter, all paths diverge from that crucible of common experience, but all continue to rest upon a fundamental concept written in blood by our fighting men upon the battle-

MacArthur meets with President Eisenhower at the White House on March 18, 1954.

fields of all the world. It is that military strategy and tactics must produce victory.

Napoleon once said that military organization and tactics should be revised at least every ten years. He recognized that in the evolution of military science nothing would remain static and that new techniques would become indispensable to attain the changeless goal of victory. Down through the ages, the character of war, but not its purpose, is a constant record of change. From the elephant of Hannibal's day to the modern tank and airplane, the story is always the same - the tactics in one war are always deficient in the next, but the endless purpose remains immutable - victory.

I, myself, have witnessed this evolution over a span of more than fifty years. At the turn of the century, the target was one enemy casualty at the end of a rifle. Then came the machine gun designed to kill by the dozen. After that, the heavy artillery raining death upon the hundreds. Then the aerial bomb to strike by the thousands - followed by the atom explosion to reach the hundreds of thousands. Now electronics and other processes of science are being perfected to raise the destructive potential to encompass millions. But at each introduction of a new weapon or a new method, new tactics have been devised based upon the one unchanging fundamental purpose and ideal - victory. Always the aim has been the same - victory.

But, now, oblivious to the lessons of military history and the American tradition, a new concept has arisen from outside our ranks which tends to disavow victory as the combat objective and to advocate in its stead a new kind of tactic on which to base the battle. The result can be nothing but failure, nothing to repay the terrible human sacrifice of war. We of the military shall always do what we are told to do. But if this nation is to survive, we must trust the soldier once our statesmen fail to preserve the peace. We must regain our faith in those lessons and traditions which have always sustained our victorious march through the military perils which have beset our past. We must recapture the will and the determination to win come what may once American arms have been committed to battle. We must reject the counsels of fear which strange and alien doctrines are attempting to force upon us. We must proclaim again and again and again an invincible adherence to the proposition that in war there can be no substitute for victory. It is for this the "thin grey line" must stand.

Again my greetings and warmest welcome to you all.

ANNUAL WHOOPERS DINNER
APRIL 29, 1954
MANCHESTER, NEW HAMPSHIRE

Governor Gregg - and, with great pride, may I not now say - Fellow Citizens of New Hampshire:

It is indeed a great distinction to address you as an honorary citizen of this historic and beautiful state. It has contributed so much to American freedom, and culture, and progress. No one can ride over its network of modern highways without becoming enthusiastic about its picturesque scenery, its points of historic interest - its wooded hills, its blue lakes, its rustling streams, its deep glens, its tumbling waterfalls, make it beautiful indeed. From the granite highlands of its North with the Great Stone Face, to the lowlands of the sea coast harbor of Portsmouth in its South, through its maze of lakes and its measureless stretches of pine and spruce, its mixed stands of birch, maple, oak and elm, with the constant hint of the wild flowers of the field, the golden rod and purple asters of the roadside and the alpine growths of the high mountain slopes, there is etched an unforgettable picture. And always beating upon memory is the vital mark you and your forebears have placed upon the history of our nation. From the earliest settlement upon these shores down through all the grim crises which accompanied and followed the birth of our beloved Republic, New Hampshire has played its noble role.

Just south of Portsmouth stands the granite monument to the memory of those first settlers of 1623. Captain John Mason, from Hampshire County, England, with his colony at the mouth of the Piscataqua River, to trade in fish, furs and lumber can perhaps be called the Father of the State. Portsmouth, Dover, Exeter and Hampton were followed by Nashua, Manchester and Concord. Its village commons were the "muster fields" of the Minute Men of the Revolution. New Castle treasures its old fort, the scene of the war's first act of open rebellion. It took the lead of all the colonies in adopting a state Constitution. Down through the ages its great names are legion. Franklin Pierce, President of the United States; Horace Greeley that first and greatest of publishers; Mary Baker Eddy with her Christian philosophy; Thaxter, Proctor, French, MacDowell and an endless list. But to me, first and foremost of all stands the great name of Daniel Webster. He was the hero of my childhood's imagination as my Grandfather, a law associate of Rufus Choate, would regale me with stories of those two worthy adversaries of the bar. And always, it seemed that Webster with his outstanding oratory came out best in my Grandfather's eyes, despite his personal attachment to Choate. And as I grew older and my own studies of American History began to leave their impressions upon my mind, I realized that although Daniel Webster's life had not embraced those periods of mortal struggle - the first to achieve and the second to preserve the integrity of our Republic - during the interval between the two, he had contributed immeasurably toward the strengthening of our constitutional liberties and the preservation indivisible of our federal union. Thus, I have always felt, as an American citizen of New England ancestry, a peculiar obligation to pay my respects to the memory of this great man on the consecrated soil upon which he trod. I was glad, indeed, therefore, to receive the invitation of Governor Gregg to be with you here this evening. And I am doubly glad to meet here, on his native soil, my old and distinguished friend, Senator Styles Bridges. He represents both State and Nation brilliantly.

Possibly it is unnecessary for me to point out to you, that the struggle to preserve undefiled the edifice of national strength and unity which Daniel Webster and his contemporaries did so much to fabricate, still requires in these troublesome times the utmost of our devotion. In Webster's own words, "When the mariner has been tossed for many days in thick weather, and on an unknown sea, he naturally avails himself of the first pause in the storm, the earliest glance of the sun, to take his latitude, and ascertain how far the elements have driven him from his true course." For there have been, are now, and probably will continue to be, those abroad in the land, blind equally to the lessons history has taught and the facts of contemporary life, who, skeptical of our form of civilization and government, seek to change their underlying fundamentals. Just as did your forebears, we must ourselves, and instruct our children and children's children, to guard with increasing vigilance against adventurers in our midst who travel along with those whose evil purpose it is, covertly and cunningly, to subvert and tear down the structure of our free institutions. They hope by those means to ultimately destroy our sovereign independence and curb the constitutional rights and liberties we now enjoy as free men.

More than anything else, or at any time in our modern history, the nation needs leaders in the mould of New Hampshire's Daniel Webster. Leaders, who, with fearlessness and logic and unchallengeable integrity, will take an invincible stand against any compromise with those immutable principles upon which has always rested our strength as a free people. To such end we must constantly study and analyze, and restudy and reanalyze, our heritage of wisdom from the past, in order that, as our birth right, we may project its basic principles unerringly into the future. Progress and improvement and imaginative vision, yes. But we must reject any leadership which takes upon itself the arrogance arbitrarily to dismiss the lessons of the past as not applicable to the needs of the future. For just as those cardinal truisms of Daniel Webster's time came down from the ages, so will they live on through the ages yet to come. Just as individual life is but a fleeting second in the vast universe of time, so civilization will go on and on into eternity; and the sound ideas which were heeded by our forefathers then, we must ourselves heed now, and bequeath unsullied unto civilization a thousand years hence. For the only thing in the world that can go on forever is a sound idea. The only thing in this world you can't stop is a sound idea.

I recall Daniel Webster's words, uttered just two short years before his death, as he solemnly spoke of the life and works of those New Englanders who had preceded him, "Thanks to Almighty God" he reverently said, "who from that distressed, early condition of our fathers, has raised us to a height of prosperity and happiness, which they neither enjoyed, nor could have anticipated! We have learned much of them; they could have foreseen little of us. Would to God, my friends, would to God, that when we carry our affections and our recollections back to that period, we could arm ourselves with something of the stern virtues which supported them in that hour of peril, and exposure, and suffering. Would to God that we possessed that unconquerable resolution, stronger than bars of brass or iron, which nerved their hearts; that patience, 'sovereign o'er transmuted ill', and, above all that faith, that religious faith, which with eyes fast fixed upon heaven, tramples all things earthly beneath her triumphant feet!"

May we, in our day, maintain something of those "stern virtues" with which Webster and his contemporaries were endowed, just as he looked back upon his own forebears to maintain something of those which supported them. May

we supplant some of our wastefulness with their frugality, our timidity with their courage, our dependence with their self-reliance, our weakness under government with their strength over government. For only thus, may we preserve, unto ourselves and our posterity, that heritage which offers us the vision, and wisdom and strength to safely guide our beloved nation through the rocks and shoals which lie ahead. Let us perpetuate unto all time and all eyes these grand New Hampshire virtues.

Again, Governor Gregg, my thanks and appreciation for having made me a citizen of this great state.

RECEIVING AN AWARD OF THE PROTESTANT EPISCOPAL CHURCH JANUARY 26, 1955 LOS ANGELES, CALIFORNIA

MacArthur's assertion that he is a Christian and an Episcopalian. He maintains that all religions serve their people to their purpose in life and that they should practice their method of worship in their own way without undue interference or provide subsidy support from the government in order to gain some political advantage.

Edward T. Imparato, Editor

Your Honor, Your Grace, and all in reverent attendance at this convention, I cannot begin to express adequately my thanks and appreciation for the signal honor you have conferred upon me. It creates an unforgettable sense of distinction far in excess of any just merit, and arouses a feeling of gratitude that is indelible.

Much of my life has been dedicated to the profession of arms. Much of my experience has been in the practice of the art of war. For such a one it is a rare privilege indeed, when an occasion arises permitting construction rather than destruction; to build, not to destroy.

Such was the unusual and unique opportunity presenting itself in the field of religion when our victorious soldiers entered Japan. These were veteran troops; troops who had come from behind, soldiers constantly outnumbered, and consequently operating in the shadow of death. Now they had come through against all odds, and were duly thankful to a merciful God. They were spiritual to the highest degree. The most religious army of modern times. Men who prayed before they fought. Men who built their churches even before they built their hospitals.

Japan itself was in a state of utter collapse. It was completely exhausted. Its long war effort had reduced its industrial output to almost nothing. Its military defeat had destroyed not only its sense of self-reliance, but its sense of self-respect. The religious disintegration was even worse. It was universal and absolute.

In this vacuum - material, social, and spiritual - the occupation began. Three concepts of divinity existed in Japan prior to the war: Shintoism, bred to the native culture of the Japanese; Buddhism, introduced from the Asiatic mainland; and Christianity, an occidental importation, a poor third. The latter influence became negligible during the war.

The first two were practically taken over by the Government as a means of regimentation of the masses. The priesthood represented one of the most cultured, influential, and intellectual segments of society, but was dominated by the state. The temples were supported by national funds, and the priests themselves, to all intents and purposes, were but agents of those in political power.

Under Government tutelage, the people had been thoroughly indoctrinated with a belief in the invincible character of their armed forces. The propaganda was complete, and up to the very end no Japanese dreamed of anything but victory. The shock of sudden defeat was thus enormously increased, and left the populace doubtful and resentful, not only of their military and political leaders, but of their religions as well.

I am a Christian and an Episcopalian, but I believe in all religions. They may differ in form and ritual, but all recognize a divine Creator, a superior power, that transcends all that is mortal. I, therefore, felt that it became my duty as a soldier of God to attempt to restore and revive religion in Japan, to fill this moral vacuum, just as it was my duty as a soldier of the Republic to revitalize the material well-being of the country; that to fulfill my obligation it must be of the spiritual as well as of the flesh. But the problem was how.

Should I, with my full military power, arbitrarily decree the adoption of the Christian faith as a national religion? Like all men of human frailty in their hour of defeat and despairing agony, I knew they must turn to some higher spiritual power for moral comfort and support. Would not this be the moment to order them to abandon their own and turn to our God? Their utter helplessness, their dire necessity, born of complete disaster and dependence, would have perhaps forced an outward compliance, but it would have been only a fictitious and superficial sham, and would surely have defeated the very purpose I had in mind.

The solution I adopted I believe you would have approved. It was to befriend all religions; to permit complete freedom of religious worship as individuals might choose; to free all creeds - Shinto, Buddhist, and Christian - from any Government; to stop all proselyting of the church by national subsidy; to return to the temples their fundamental obligation of religious tutelage; to make the priest no longer an agent of political coercion or espionage activity. In short, to render unto God that which is His, and not unto Caesar which he would.

It worked like a charm. The priesthood responded to their relief from governmental dominance with a spiritual fervor that swept all before it. No slave passing to freedom ever exceeded their buoyant reaction. The religious vacuum disappeared, and because I was Christian, and had acted so, it aroused among the Shintoist and Buddhist a great curiosity of the religion which had dictated my decision.

Their own creeds, good in part as they were, were based to some extent on a quid pro quo concept that one should do good in this life, because he would profit from it in the life to come; that he would be repaid; that he would get back more than he put in as a reward in another world was a main incentive. The concept of faith, the concept of Christ that man should do what is right, even if it entailed personal sacrifice, that the urge of conscience was greater than any material reward, was something new and novel.

It seemed to me that the great opportunity was to guide Shintoism and Buddhism toward this basic concept of religious faith, rather than the impossible task of replacement by a conqueror's own creed. That if the lessons of the Scriptures of the Sermon on the Mount could be integrated and welded into their own religious cultures, if basic spirituality could be common to all, it would mean little whether a Japanese were a Buddhist, a Shintoist, or a Christian.

I called upon America for Bibles. An offer of 100,000 was raised by me to 10 million, with an ultimate figure of three times that number, and that is the story up to now.

I am not trained in ecclesiastical methods, nor am I skilled in theological lore, but I want you to know that with such frail personal equipment as was mine I did my best, and that no phase of the occupation, with its many attempted military, political, social, and economic reforms, has left me with a greater sense of personal satisfaction than my spiritual stewardship. Although I am of Caesar, I did try to render unto God that which is His. And I even dared to hope that through this resurgence of religion Japan will, in the struggle that lies ahead, be indissolubly confirmed against any whose doctrines embrace the deadly poison of atheism. It might prove more potent than bullets, or bayonets, or bombs, or even bread.

DEDICATION OF MACARTHUR PARK
JANUARY 26, 1955
LOS ANGELES, CALIFORNIA

I have listened with deep emotion to these solemn proceedings. My heart is too full for my lips to express adequately my thanks and appreciation for the extraordinary honor you do me. Even so, I understand full well that this memorial is intended to commemorate an epic rather than an individual; an armed force, rather than its commander; a nation, rather than its servant; an ideal, rather than a personality.

But this only increases my pride that my name has been one chosen as the symbol of an epic struggle in victory by millions of unnamed others.

It is their heroism, their sacrifice, their success, that you honor today in so unforgettable a manner. And this statue and this park are but the selected reminders of their grandeur.

Most of them were citizen soldiers, sailors, or airmen; men from the farm, from the city, from the schoolroom, from the college campus; men not dedicated to the profession of arms; men not primarily skilled in the art of war; men most amazingly like the men you see and meet and know each day of your life. But men inspired, animated, and ennobled by a sublime cause to the defense of their country, of their native land, of their very hearthstones.

The most divine of all human sentiments and impulses guided them, the spirit and the willingness to sacrifice.

He who dares to die, who lays his life on the altar of his nation's need, is beyond doubt the noblest development of mankind. In this he comes closest to the image of his Creator who died on the Cross that the human soul might live.

These men were my comrades in arms. With me they knew the call of the bugle at reveille, the distant roll of drums at nightfall, the endless tramp of marching feet, the incessant whine of sniper bullets, the ceaseless rattle of sputtering machine guns, the sinister wail of air sirens, the deafening blast and crash of bombs, the stealthy stroke of hidden torpedoes, the aimless lurch of perilous waves, the dark majesty of fighting ships, the mad din of battle lines, and all the stench and ghastly horror and savage destruction of a stricken area of war.

They suffered hunger and thirst, the broiling sun of relentless heat, the torrential rains of tropical storms, the loneliness and utter desolation of jungle trails, the bitterness of separation from those they loved and cherished. They went on and on and when everything within them seemed to stop and die. They grew old in youth; they burned out in searing minutes all that life owed them in tranquil years.

When I think of their patience under adversity, of their courage under fire, and of their modesty in victory, I am filled with an emotion I cannot express.

Many of them trod the tragic path of unknown fame that led to a stark, white cross on a lonely grave. And from their tortured, dying lips, with the dreadful gurgle of the death rattle in their throats, always came the same gasping prayer that we who were left would go on to victory.

I do not know the dignity of their birth, but I do know the glory of their death. And I am sure a merciful God has taken them unto Himself.

In these troublesome times of confused and bewildered international sophistication, let no man misunderstand why they did that which they did. These were patriots, pure and plain; these were men who fought and perchance died for one reason only - for their country, for America. No complex philosophy of world intrigue and conspiracy dominated their thoughts. No exploitation or extravagance of propaganda dimmed their sensibilities. Just the simple fact that their country called them, just the devoted doctrine of Stephen Decatur when he said: "My country, may she always be right. But, right or wrong, my country."

Be not deceived by strange voices heard across the land, decrying this old and proven concept of patriotism. From the very beginning it has been the main bulwark of our national strength and integrity.

Seductive murmurs are arising that it is now outmoded by some more comprehensive and all-embracing philosophy; that we are provincial and immature, or reactionary and stupid when we idealize our own country; that there is a higher destiny for us under another more general flag; that no longer when we send our sons and daughters to the battlefield must we see them through all the way to victory; that we can call upon them to fight and even to die in some halfhearted and indecisive effort.

That we can plunge them recklessly into war and then suddenly decide that it is a wrong war, or in the wrong place, or at a wrong time; or even that we call it not a war at all, but by some more euphemistic and generic name; that we can treat them as expendables, although they are our own flesh and blood. And even in times of peace, for some romantic reason, they must share - not as an act of generosity but as a bounden duty, their national blessings and goods

built from nothing to a height never before reached by man - with others because, whether for neglect or not, they have not fared so well.

That we, the strongest nation in the world, have suddenly become dependent upon others for our security and even our welfare. Listen not to these voices, be they from the one political party or from the other; be they from the high and the mighty, or the lowly and the forgotten. Heed them not. Visit upon them a righteous scorn born of the past sacrifices of your fighting sons and daughters.

Repudiate them in the marketplace, on the platform, in the pulpit. Those who are our friends will understand. Those who are not we can pass by. Be proud to be called patriots or nationalists or what you will, if it means that you love your country above all else, and will place your life if need be at the service of our flag.

I wish again to express to the citizens of this community my gratitude for their generosity in creating this memorial, and my thanks and appreciation to all those present here today.

You have etched for me in indelible memory, a patriotic friendship and sympathetic understanding. You have made me feel far greater than my just deserts and yet more humble than I care to admit.

LOS ANGELES COUNTY COUNCIL
OF THE AMERICAN LEGION
JANUARY 26, 1955
LOS ANGELES, CALIFORNIA

One of MacArthur's favorite comments "No one grows old by merely living a number of years. People grow old only by deserting their ideals - worry, doubt, self-distrust, fear, and despair - these are the long, long years that bow the head and turn the growing back to dust."
Edward T. Imparato, Editor

Your Excellency, Your Honor, Judge Pfaff, Commander Goshaw, and all those present tonight in this distinguished assemblage:

Seldom in history has living man been honored as this famous community of Los Angeles has honored me today. You have etched in my heart an unforgettable memory of patriotic fervor and national devotion. You have aroused an indelible emotion of gratitude that I am unable to express adequately in words. Yet, the reality of life enables me to apply an appraising perspective; to understand that your action springs not so much from a desire to memorialize a personality as to proclaim a people's adherence to ideals long ago fabricated into the warp and woof of what is called the American way of life. That you have chosen me to symbolize this rich heritage of principles is an honor which makes me feel far greater than any just merit; that my name should stand for the millions of unnamed others whose faith and courage built the immortal way from which was fashioned the true greatness of our country creates within me a feeling of humility far in excess of all possible pride. It makes me revere the stars in our flag far more than any stars on my shoulders.

I am so grateful to all who have wished me birthday greetings. I know such expressions of good will would have brightened the eyes of that gentle Virginia lady, my mother, on this, her day. Thank you - thank you in her name again and again - and, as "old soldiers never die," I promise to keep on living as though I expected to live forever. That famous barrack-room ballad apparently counts on us, those old soldiers who have escaped the carnage of the battlefield, to find the fountain of youth, and, indeed, we might if we only understood what the poet said, that "youth is not entirely a time of life - it is a state of mind. It is not wholly a matter of ripe cheeks, red lips, or supple knees. It is a temper of the will, a quality of the imagination, a vigor of the emotions, a freshness of the deep springs of life. It means a temperamental predominance of courage over timidity, of an appetite for adventure over love of ease. Nobody grows old by merely living a number of years. People grow old only by deserting their ideals. Years may wrinkle the skin, but to give up interest wrinkles the soul. Worry, doubt, self-distrust, fear, and despair - these are the long, long years that bow the head and turn the growing spirit back to dust. Whatever your years, there is in every being's heart the love of wonder, the undaunted challenge of events, the unfailing childlike appetite for what next, and the joy and the game of life. You are as young as your faith, as old as your doubt; as young as your self-confidence, as old as your fear; as young as your hope, as old as your despair. In the central place of every heart there is a recording chamber; so long as it receives messages of beauty, hope, cheer, and courage, so long are you young. When the wires are all down and your heart is covered with the snows of pessimism and the ice of cynicism, then, and then only, are you grown old" - and then, indeed, as the ballad says, you just fade away.

Many in this brilliant audience were my comrades-in-arms in the days of used-to-be. They have known war in all its horror and, as veterans, hope against its recurrence. How, we ask ourselves, did such an institution become so integrated with man's life and civilization? How has it grown to be the most vital factor in our existence? It started in a modest enough way as a sort of gladiatorial method of settling disputes between conflicting tribes. One of the oldest and most classical examples is the Biblical story of David and Goliath. Each of the two contesting groups selected its champion. They fought and, based upon the outcome, an agreement resulted. Then, as time went on, small professional groups known as armies replaced the individual champions. And these groups fought in some obscure corner of the world and victory or defeat was accepted as the basis of an ensuing peace. And from then on, down through the ages, the constant record is an increase in the character and strength of the forces with the rate of increase always accelerating. From a small percentage of the populace it finally engulfed all. It is now the nation in arms.

Within the span of my own life I have witnessed this evolution. At the turn of the century, when I entered the Army, the target was one enemy casualty at the end of a rifle or bayonet or sword. Then came the machine gun designed to kill by the dozen. After that, the heavy artillery raining death upon the hundreds. Then the aerial bomb to strike by the thousands - followed by the atom explosion to reach the hundreds of thousands. Now, electronics and other processes of science have raised the destructive potential to encompass millions. And with restless hands we work feverishly in dark laboratories to find the means to destroy all at one blow.

But, this very triumph of scientific annihilation - this very success of invention - has destroyed the possibility of war being a medium of practical settlement of international differences. The enormous destruction to both sides of closely matched opponents makes it impossible for the winner to translate it into anything but his own disaster.

The Second World War, even with its now antiquated armaments, clearly demonstrated that the victor had to bear in large part the very injuries inflicted on his foe. Our own country spent billions of dollars and untold energies to heal the wounds of Germany and Japan. War has become a Frankenstein to destroy both sides. No longer is it the weapon of adventure whereby a shortcut to international power and wealth - a place in the sun - can be gained. If you lose, you are annihilated. If you win, you stand only to lose. No longer does it possess the chance of the winner of a duel - it contains rather the germs of double suicide. Science has clearly outmoded it as a feasible arbiter. The great question is - does this mean that war can now be outlawed from the world? If so, it would mark the greatest advance in civilization since the Sermon on the Mount. It would lift at one stroke the darkest shadow which has engulfed mankind from the beginning. It would not only remove fear and bring security - it would not only create new moral and spiritual values - it would produce an economic wave of prosperity that would raise the world's standard of living beyond anything ever dreamed of by man. The hundreds of billions of dollars now spent in mutual preparedness could conceivably abolish poverty from the face of the globe. It would accomplish even more than this; it would at one stroke reduce the international tensions that seem so insurmountable now to matters of more probable solution. For instance, the complex problems of German rearmament, of preventive war, of satellite dominance by major powers, of universal military service, of unconscionable taxation, of nuclear development for industry, of freer exchange of goods and people, of foreign aid and, indeed, of all issues involving the application of armed force. It would have equally potent political effects. It would reduce immeasurably the power of leaders of government and thus render more precarious totalitarian or autocratic rule. The growing and dangerous control by an individual over the masses - the socialistic and paternal trends resulting therefrom - is largely by virtue of his influence to induce war or to maintain peace. Abolish this threat and the position of Chief Magistrate falls into a more proper civic perspective.

You will say at once that although the abolition of war has been the dream of man for centuries every proposition to that end has been promptly discarded as impossible and fantastic. Every cynic, every pessimist, every adventurer, every swashbuckler in the world has always disclaimed its feasibility. But that was before the science of the past decade made mass destruction a reality. The argument then was that human character has never reached a theological development which would permit the application of pure idealism. In the last 2,000 years its rate of change has been deplorably slow, compared to that of the arts and sciences. But now the tremendous and present evolution of nuclear and other potentials of destruction has suddenly taken the problem away from its primary consideration as a moral and spiritual question and brought it abreast of scientific realism. It is no longer an ethical equation to be pondered solely by learned philosophers and ecclesiastics but a hard-core one for the decision of the masses whose survival is the issue. This is as true of the Soviet side of the world as of the free side - as true behind the Iron Curtain as in front of it. The ordinary people of the world, whether free or slave, are all in agreement on this solution; and this perhaps is the only thing in the world they do agree upon. But it is the most vital and determinate of all. The leaders are the laggards. The disease of power seems to confuse and befuddle them. They have not even approached the basic problem, much less evolved a working formula to implement this public demand. They debate and turmoil over a hundred issues - they bring us to the verge of despair or raise our hopes to utopian heights over the corollary misunderstandings that stem from the threat of war - but never in the chancelleries of the world or the halls of the United Nations is the real problem raised. Never do they dare to state the bald truth, that the next great advance in the evolution of civilization cannot take place until war is abolished. It may take another cataclysm of destruction to prove to them this simple truth. But, strange as it may seem, it is known now by all common men. It is the one issue upon which both sides can agree, for it is the one issue upon which both sides will profit equally. It is the one issue - and the only decisive one - in which the interests of both are completely parallel. It is the one issue which, if settled, might settle all others.

Time has shown that agreements between modern nations are generally no longer honored as valid unless both profit therefrom. But both sides can be trusted when both do profit. It becomes then no longer a problem based upon relative integrity. It is now no longer convincing to argue, whether true or not, that we cannot trust the other side - that one maverick can destroy the herd. It would no longer be a matter depending upon trust - the self-interest of each nation outlawing war would keep it true to itself. And there is no influence so potent and powerful as self-interest. It would not necessarily require international inspection of relative armaments - the public opinion of every part of the world would be the great denominator which would insure the issue - each nation would so profit that it could not fail eventually to comply. This would not, of course, mean the abandonment of all armed forces, but it would reduce them to the simpler problems of internal order and international police. It would not mean utopia at one fell stroke, but it would mean that the great roadblock now existing to development of the human race would have been cleared.

The present tensions with their threat of national annihilation are kept alive by two great illusions. The one, a complete belief on the part of the Soviet world that the capitalist countries are preparing to attack them; that sooner or later we intend to strike. And the other, a complete belief on the part of the capitalistic countries that the Soviets are preparing to attack us; that sooner or later they intend to strike. Both are wrong. Each side, so far as the masses are concerned, is equally desirous of peace. For either side war with the other would mean nothing but disaster. Both equally dread it. But the constant acceleration of preparation may well, without specific intent, ultimately produce a spontaneous combustion.

I am sure that every pundit in the world, every cynic and hypocrite, every paid brain washer, every egotist, every troublemaker, and many others of entirely different mold, will tell you with mockery and ridicule that this can be only a dream - that it is but the vague imaginings of a visionary. But, as David Lloyd George once said in Commons at the crisis of the First World War, "We must go on or we will go under." And the great criticism we can make of the world's leaders is their lack of a plan which will enable us "to go on." All they propose merely gravitates around but dares not face the real problem. They increase preparedness by alliances, by distributing resources throughout the world, by feverish activity in developing new and deadlier weapons, by applying conscription in times of peace - all of which is instantly matched by the prospective opponent. We are told that this increases the chances of peace - which is doubtful - and increases the chances of victory if war comes - which would be incontestable if the other side did not increase in like proportion. Actually, the truth is that the relative strengths of the two change little with the years. Action by one is promptly matched by reaction from the other.

We are told we must go on indefinitely as at present - some say 50 years or more. With what at the end? None say - there is no definite objective. They but pass along to those that follow the search for a final solution. And, at the end, the problem will be exactly the same as that which we face now. Must we live for generations under the killing punishment of accelerating preparedness without an announced final purpose or, as an alternative, suicidal war; and trifle in the meanwhile with corollary and indeterminate theses - such as limitation of armament, restriction on the use of nuclear power, adoption of new legal standards as propounded at Nuremberg - all of which are but palliatives and all of which in varying form have been tried in the past with negligible results? Dangerous doctrines, too, appear - doctrines which might result in actual defeat; such doctrines as a limited war, of enemy sanctuary, of failure to protect our fighting men when captured, of national subversive and sabotage agencies, of a substitute for victory on the battlefield - all in the name of peace. Peace, indeed, can be obtained at least temporarily by any nation if it is prepared to yield its freedom principles. But peace at any price - peace with appeasement - peace which passes the dreadful finality to future generations - is a peace of sham and shame which can end only in war or slavery.

I recall so vividly this problem when it faced the Japanese in their new Constitution. They are realists; and they are the only ones that know by dread experience the fearful effect of mass annihilation. They realize in their limited geographical area, caught up as a sort of no man's land between two great ideologies, that to engage in another war, whether on the winning or the losing side, would spell the probable doom of their race. And their wise old Prime Minister, Shidehara, came to me and urged that to save themselves they should abolish war as an international instrument. When I agreed, he turned to me and said, "The world will laugh and mock us as impractical visionaries, but a hundred years from now we will be called prophets."

Sooner or later the world, if it is to survive, must reach this decision. The only question is, When? Must we fight again before we learn? When will some great figure in power have sufficient imagination and moral courage to translate this universal wish - which is rapidly becoming a universal necessity - into actuality? We are in a new era. The old methods and solutions no longer suffice. We must have new thoughts, new ideas, new concepts, just as did our venerated forefathers when they faced a new world. We must break out of the straitjacket of the past. There must always be one to lead, and we should be that one. We should now proclaim our readiness to abolish war in concert with the great powers of the world. The result would be magical.

This may sound somewhat academic in view of the acuteness of the situation in the Far East. Strategically, the problem there has developed along classical lines - the familiar case of a concentrated enemy in a central position deployed against scattered allies. Red China, inherently weak in industrial output for modern war but strong in manpower, engaged on three fronts - Korea, Indochina, and in civil war with Nationalist China. Fighting on all three simultaneously meant defeat, but individually the chances were excellent. The hope for victory depended on getting a cease-fire on some fronts so that the full potential of its limited military might could be thrown against the remaining one or ones. That is what has happened and is happening. First was the cessation of the civil war action by the isolation in the Formosa area, which practically immobilized Nationalist China, one of the allies. Red China then concentrated against Korea and Indochina. But even the double front was too much for its strained resources, so a cease-fire was obtained in Korea. This immobilized the so-called United Nations forces and the South Koreans and left Red China free to concentrate on the third front - Indochina and the French.

Successful there, the Reds now turn back to the old first front located in Formosa. As Napoleon Bonaparte once said: "Give me allies as an enemy so that I can defeat them one by one."

Militarily the situation demonstrates the inherent weakness of the theory of collective security - the chain is no stronger than its weakest link - and, what is even more vital, its full power can only be utilized when all links are brought simultaneously into action. The diverse interests of allies always tend toward separation rather than unity.

Whatever betides the ultimate fate of the Far East - and indeed of the world - will not be settled by force of arms. We may all be practically annihilated - but war can no longer be an arbiter of survival.

I cannot close without once more thanking this beautiful city of Los Angeles for its gracious hospitality. It has been an inspiration to be here, where missions once stood as lonely outposts in the advance of our Christian civilization, but where this great metropolis now stands as a monument to American industry and adventure - a symbolic reminder of Californian strength and fortitude. I hate to leave - but, as I once pledged under very different circumstances, I shall return.

REMARKS TO THE U.S. MILITARY ACADEMY FOOTBALL TEAM AT WEST POINT
SEPTEMBER 18, 1956

The fortunes of the Army football team are eagerly followed by sports fans all over the world. General MacArthur was one of the most ardent of these supporters. Each year he sent a message of encouragement to the team, with particular reference to victory over the Navy team in the final game of the season. In 1956, he visited the Academy during the early days of the season. After watching a practice session supervised by his old Army friend Coach Earl "Red" Blaik, he spoke to the cadet team in the dressing room of Michie Stadium.

Major Vorin E. Whan, Jr., USA, Editor
A Soldier Speaks: Public Papers and Speeches of General of the Army Douglas MacArthur
© 1965, Frederick A. Praeger, Publishers, New York, NY

This has been a real pleasure for me to have met personally the members of this season's football squad. Over the years I have known all of the great athletic figures of West Point's football Hall of Fame. Since our earliest gridiron victories, the story of their athletic prowess has been the talk and the boast of every campfire gathering - every barracks mess hall - every garrison assemblage of the American Army.

In my twenty campaigns, covering more than twenty-five years of foreign service, from the Rhine to the Yalu, from Vera Cruz to Tokyo, through the muddy sludges of Europe to the blistering jungle trails of Asia - in all that welter of breath-less struggle between life and death, always a central topic of discussion and of paramount interest was - will the Army team win this year? The gloom, the dreadful silence that would descend upon our armed men when you failed us was equaled only by the mortal thrust of the enemy. The pride - the unrestrained joy of your victories was the very tonic of our own battlefield successes. I repeat the words carved at the entrance to the gymnasium: "On the fields of friendly strife are sown the seeds that on other fields and other days will bring forth victory."

When the bells pealed out their triumphant tones on Armistice Day, long years before you were born, I seemed to hear the echo of the chimes of the Cadet Chapel. When we ground back into burning Manila, to liberate the Philippines, I seemed to see the reflection of the bonfire on the Plain welcoming home our winning team. When I received the solemn surrender of Japan, to close victoriously the Second World War, through the stuttering words I seemed to catch the roar of the long Corps yell. When we crushed the Reds at Inchon, the beat of my mind kept repeating the edict of our forefathers establishing the United States Military Academy at West Point. This great tradition - this great legend -

this great ideal - is now in your hands. We trust you. We have faith in you. You are our own of the long grey line.

Go out now and win for us!

EXCERPTS FROM AN ADDRESS
TO THE ANNUAL STOCKHOLDER'S MEETING
OF THE SPERRY RAND CORPORATION
JULY 30, 1957
NEW YORK, NEW YORK

As early as 1949, General MacArthur was approached with an offer of executive employment with the Remington Rand Corporation. Until 1952, he was not free to accept the offer. Following the end of his speaking tour of the United States after his return from the Far East, the way was finally clear. Later, following a merger with the Sperry Corporation, he became Chairman of the Board of the new Sperry Rand Corporation. It was in this capacity that he addressed the annual stockholders' meeting, discussing the impact of taxation on both the economy and the freedom of the American people.

Major Vorin E. Whan, Jr., USA, Editor
A Soldier Speaks: Public Papers and Speeches of General of the Army Douglas MacArthur
© 1965, Frederick A. Praeger, Publishers, New York, NY

… The world is entering an age of evolution greater than it has ever before known. Never in the two-billion-year history of human life, in the five billion years in which the earth has spun through the black vacuum of space from the sun, has man's faculty for learning assumed such immense new scope and power. We are acquiring an ever greater degree of control and mastery over the processes of nature. We are now exploiting, not only scientifically but practically, the cosmic energy. We are graduating from earthly to universal dimensions. This evolution has happened so quietly and naturally - without ceremony or undue emphasis, without great debate or acid controversy - that we hardly know the exact instant that the change occurred. The tick of the clock sometimes sounds so softly that we do not hear it; yet we now know the hour has struck. Vast panoramas will unfold before us, wave following wave, of a magnitude and diversity not as yet fully comprehended. Machines and mechanical devices will more and more operate other machines in an endless growing cycle, defined as automation of labor-saving and multiple production systems.

To believe that this will be an evil, threatening mass unemployment and a consequent social upheaval somewhat similar to the disorders individual labor temporarily sustained in the Industrial Revolution of the eighteenth and nineteenth centuries, would be illogical. Such an attitude would manifestly discount completely the relative slowness of the development and the corollary and beneficent improvements which always accompany progress. There will be changes in jobs requiring adaptation of the labor force, but nothing to cause a large volume of unemployment. Actually, the productivity of the national economy can be expected to grow at the rate of 3 to 4 per cent a year while the number of new workers, due to growth of population, will be only about 1.5 per cent.

Nuclear energy and electronic advances cannot fail to bring an age of relative plenty. For the first time there will be provided the tools which promise to mankind the satisfaction of his basic economic and material needs. Some of you may well live to see the day when we will be drawing energy not only from the sun but from the tides and the winds; will be creating unheard-of synthetic materials; will be purifying sea water; will be mining ocean floors for basic minerals; will be celebrating a life span of a hundred and more years; will be launching space ships to reach the moon; will see poverty for the first time faced with possible extinction. Living standards will be the highest, scientific advances will be the most revolutionary; world affairs will be the most exciting in all history....

If businessmen were to be allowed a wish, I am sure it would be unanimously for lower taxes. The tax burden now is so oppressive as to be almost confiscatory of venture capital. As Secretary of the Treasury Humphrey recently testified before a Congressional Committee, "The present heavy tax burden will seriously hamper necessary economic growth," adding that "Spending under existing government programs will rise as fast as the increase in revenues resulting from economic growth unless Congress and the Administration alter and reduce those programs."

Taxes for 1956 came to a staggering total of more than $100 billion. The Treasury received 70 billion and State and local governments the other 30 billion. This means that the cost of government consumes almost one-third of the national product, which is the sum of all goods and services by the entire population of the United States. The government's appetite for taxes has grown steadily and inordinately. In 1885 the per capita tax take was $1.98. In 1917 it was $7.92. During World War I it rose to $35.70. In 1932 there was a drop-off to $12.48. The high point of World War II was hit in 1945, at $312.86. Last year, the fiscal year of 1956, was the costliest of all, $446.86 per year for every one of us. Such jet-propelled figures are difficult to comprehend. Much is hidden from direct view in the form of unseen nibbles at the paycheck after payment of the direct income tax. You never know you are paying because they appear as part of the purchase price of the items you buy. For example, you pay in this indirect way: 20 per cent of the cost of your food; $800 on a $3,000 automobile; half the cost of a package of cigarettes; nearly nine-tenths of the price of a bottle of whiskey.

Taxes have grown so rapidly in recent years that now they are the largest single item in the cost of living. Americans will pay for government this year more than they will spend on food, clothing, medical care and religious activities combined.

Before you sit down to a meal, morning, noon or night, this is what happens:

The tax agent collects from the farmer who grew your food. He collects from the fertilizer companies and farm equipment manufacturers who supplied the farmer. He collects rail and truck transportation taxes, manufacturers' excise taxes, telephone taxes, property taxes, sales taxes, income taxes, social security taxes, gasoline taxes, license fees, inspection fees, permit fees; all these - and so many others that nobody even knows what they are. When you buy a dozen eggs you pay at least one hundred tiny taxes which do not appear on the bill. There are 151 taxes on a loaf of bread, at least as many and maybe more on a pound of beef-steak, a box of soap, a can of beans. Billions a year are drained off which should be invested in new or enlarged enterprises or spent on the products of these enterprises. I do not hesitate to predict that if government continues to wrest from the people the basis for future industries and businesses, our rapidly increasing population may eventually outgrow the number of jobs available and industrial labor will then face its greatest threat.

There seems to be no restraint in this lust for taxes. It began with the Federal Income Tax Law of 1914, which gave unlimited access to the people's wealth, and the power for the first time to levy taxes not for revenue only but for social purposes. Since then the sphere of government has increased with a kind of explosive force. Thomas Jefferson's wise aphorism, "That government is best which governs least" has been tossed into the wastebasket with ridicule and sarcasm. Whether we want it or not, we pay now for almost unlimited government; a government which limits our lives by dictating how we are fed and clothed and housed; how to provide for old age; how the national income, which is the product of our labor, shall be divided among us; how we shall buy and sell; how long and how hard and under what circumstances we shall work. There is only scorn for the one who dares to say, "The government should not be infinite."

Actually, the national budget now governs the economy. Unfortunately, it is becoming more and more abnormal. For years we have been spending far beyond our means. Our indebtedness is now estimated to be nearly $700 billion, a sum greater than the combined debt of all the other nations of the world. And it has been charged without challenge that our government this year proposes to spend as much as all other governments put together.

The Russian dictator Lenin, that implacable foe of the free enterprise system, predicted as early as 1920 that the United States would eventually spend itself into bankruptcy. How many of our leaders still hear the echo of Thomas Jefferson's voice when he warned with reference to the future of this country:

"I place economy among the most important virtues and public debt as the greatest of dangers to be feared. To preserve our independence, we must not let our leaders load us with perpetual debt. We must make our choice between economy with liberty, or profusion with servitude. The same prudence which in private life would forbid our paying our money, forbids it in the disposition of public money. We must endeavor to reduce the government to the practice of rigid economy to avoid burdening the people and arming the Magistrate with a patronage of money which might be used to corrupt the very principle of government.... The multiplication of public offices, increase of expense beyond income, growth of the public debt, are indications soliciting the employment of the pruning knife…. It is incumbent on every generation to pay its own debt as it goes."

How incomparably different in philosophy from Karl Marx, that patron saint of Communism, who fifty years later, while planning the destruction of all constitutional govern-

ment, said: "The surest way to overturn the social order is to debauch the currency."

He referred, of course, to the process of inflation, induced by extreme taxation; the process of "planned economy"; the process of controlling economic conditions and thereby controlling the lives of individuals - a control of fiscal, monetary and general economic forces which produces higher prices and a gradual devitalizing of the purchasing power of money. The continuing rise in the cost of living is due to our drift deeper and deeper into inflation until today our whole economic, social and political system is infected by an inflationary mentality which approaches a point where the very foundations of our structure are threatened. "Taxation, with its offspring, inflation," said Lenin in support of the basic thesis of Karl Marx, "is the vital weapon to displace the system of free enterprise" - the system on which our nation was founded - the system which has made us the most prosperous people of all history - the system which enabled us to produce over half of the world's goods with less than one-seventh of the world's area and population - the system which gave our people more liberty, privileges and opportunities than any other nation ever gave its people in the long history of the world. No wonder Herbert Hoover recently exclaimed in reviewing our situation, "The spirit of Karl Marx no doubt rejoices… . He recommended some such actions as the road to Socialism!" And by Socialism he meant the forcing of a centrally controlled economic life upon all persons in the nation, under an authoritarian monopoly that is politically managed.

Chief Justice John Marshall warned as early as 1819 that "the power to tax involves the power to destroy." And he might have added that the road to destruction is the road of Socialism. Its evidences which we see and talk about so much - the collectors and dispensers of socialistically used funds, the planning committees and enforcement bodies, the services they presume to render and the pyramids they build, the votes they coerce to maintain control - all these expressions of Socialism are but the offspring of excessive taxation. If we want economic liberty - want to be free to work most productively and to have what we produce - our concern must focus on the tax roots to shut off the revenue which nourishes the disease. To work at the other end and merely bemoan the detailed projects of Socialism or damn the persons who happen to be manning those projects at the moment, or even to change political personnel would be about as effective in stopping Socialism as changing undertakers would be to stop death.

Excessive taxation produces results somewhat resembling the evils of slavery and serfdom in days of old. To illustrate: the government takes in taxes over a third of the income of the average citizen each year. This means that he or she is required to work entirely for the government from January 1st until May 10th. This begins to resemble the Soviet forced labor system. It practically reduces the citizen for protracted periods to what amounts almost to involuntary servitude. It is indeed the modern although humanized counterpart in the twentieth century of the abandoned slavery and serfdom of the preceding centuries. We will be fortunate if it does not finally reduce individuals to the universal status of robots.

The present tax structure is even now probably adequate

eventually to socialize the United States. Our tax take is already greater than that of the admitted national socialistic countries, whether on this or the other side of the Iron Curtain. The effects may not yet be fully evident to the superficial eye, but the erosion of incentive, ingenuity and integrity that results will be as deadly as the hidden cancer is to life. It can in time change the basic character of this great nation as it has every other nation where it has become indelibly affixed.

In the last two decades our tax system has resulted in a creeping inflation which has devitalized the American dollar to 40 per cent of its previous purchasing power. If the present trend continues, the dollar may well sink to half its present value within another decade. Those who suffer most from such fiscal debasement are the men of small means - those living on fixed incomes, wages, annuities or pensions - especially the working man. But inflation does even more than debauch a nation's currency; it also debauches a nation's morals. It creates a false illusion of prosperity; it discourages thrift and honest effort; it encourages the kind of speculation that expects something for nothing. History shows how difficult it is for a nation to recover once it is in the sway of an irredeemably depreciating currency. The tendency is for prices to go higher and higher, the value of money to go lower and lower.

The inflationary forces which undermine the Western world of today are the same forces which were at work 1700 years ago during the decline of the Roman Empire. Just as in Rome, our civilization is living beyond its means. It is living more and more for the moment, trying to anticipate today the pleasures of tomorrow. Why save, asks the citizen, if savings are likely to be expropriated through taxes and inflation? Why wait for the day when we can afford a house, or a car, or a TV set, if we can buy these things today on credit? It is no longer enough that our economy grows annually faster than the increase in population; the call is for twice this growth. Wages must rise faster than productivity; the standard of living faster than income. This is the folly known as inflation; yet many prominent economists and innumerable others still preach the desirability of what they call "limited inflation." Few know that Lord Keynes, generally regarded as the modern apostle of inflation, because of his famous treatise on finance, is said to have remarked just before he died that he must write another book to warn the British people that "there is danger in inflation." Even ex-President Truman, a main protagonist of high taxation and free spending, recently wrote: "I do not wish to minimize the serious consequences of the type of inflation we are now experiencing. It has already brought hardships to a large segment of our population, in the cities as well as on the farm, and especially to those who have to live on pensions and fixed incomes." What a change is there, Oh, my countrymen! What a difference it would have made had it come at the zenith of his Presidential power rather than in the dismal aftermath of a paid newspaper column. But inflation is not a question of partisan politics. It can be controlled only if both political parties really wish to stop it; only if both patties are determined to limit spending so as to be within our means.

If financial output has to be increased in one segment it must be correspondingly decreased in another. If defense spending has to go up, other spending, whether for housing, roads, schools, farm aid, or social benefits, must be curtailed accordingly. This is only common sense. But, even though tax receipts have doubled during the post-war era, total public spending continues to exceed revenues. Promises continue to be made to expand all sectors of the economy at the same time. Some are 42 per cent larger than they were in 1953-54. Literally dozens of welfare projects little understood by the general public are hidden in the more than one thousand pages of the budget, which has grown so big that nobody has any clear idea how much waste it actually contains. Some almost incredible and fantastic falsities have been progressively foisted upon public opinion with reference to it. One is that it is a perfect example of scientific fact, that it is as true as two and two make four, that it is arithmetically a perfect equation which cannot be disputed, that its preparation is rooted in such learned hands as to be quite beyond the comprehension of the ordinary citizen. This is all complete bosh and nonsense. The national budget is but the guesswork of a small group of individuals, temporarily gathered in Washington by administrative assignment, whose previous training and experience has little to do with acquiring any specific knowledge of the nation's need. Each one, engrossed with the super-importance of his own function and power, estimates a maximum that he deems he can utilize, irrespective of extravagance. The sum of these, with some modification, becomes the budget unless someone at the top lowers the estimates to correspond with the actual resources expected to be available. The problem, a balanced budget, instead of being a mystic and untouchable phenomenon, is actually the commonest and most universal one in the world. It faces the head of every household every year of life. It is simply, how much can be spent safely on living expenses. The question is not what can be luxuriously used, not even what may be actually necessary, but what can be obtained with the money available without injudicious borrowing. If one's natural desires were followed they would always amount to much more than could be actually afforded. But the house-holder is forced to exercise prudent restraint and practice thrift or eventually he will face disaster. He must be able to say "no" to excess items when everything in him wants to say "yes."

It is exactly the same basic problem in government, with the vital difference that the money involved is not that of his own but that of others collected by taxation. But what a monumental difference this makes! Instead of being frugal, one becomes lavish. Instead of being careful, one becomes reckless. Instead of being conservative, one becomes radical. Temptation assails one from every angle. Ambition becomes very human, indeed, The pressure of political currents, the blandishments of powerful lobbies, the allurements of expanding horizons, the disease of power, all play their potent part. At best the result is but a guess, a speculative estimate with little or no controlling influence. How wrong it can be is testified to by the surpluses that have accumulated over the years. These surpluses, the over-estimates in the national budgets of actual needs, glut our warehouses from coast to coast. They are not limited to agricultural products but exist in practically every field and every commodity.

A member of the Hoover Commission which studied the

matter estimated to me that in the last decade perhaps $100 billion worth of surplus had accumulated. A large portion of this, he said, could probably never be gainfully used. This is but one facet depicting the frailty, the inaccuracy and the extravagance of the casual budget. I know from actual experience these frailties. For five years I made up the budget for the Army and Air Corps when I was the Chief of Staff, and for six years supervised the Japanese budget when Supreme Commander for the Allied Powers in the Far East. The estimates submitted to me were astronomical compared to the moneys available without borrowing; but it may interest you to know that the largest yearly budget I put in for the Army and Air Force, which were then combined, was approximately $400 million, and the highest for the entire Japanese nation of more than 80 million people was less than $2 billion. Yet, I can say confidently that the security of the United States was as relatively safe then as now, and that Japan's present prosperity, built on its post-war occupation budgets, has never been surpassed in modem times.

Only a month ago, Senator Byrd, the most potent financial voice in Congress, warned that he feared the country would "go over the precipice of financial disaster if the rise in government spending were not curtailed." He said the country faces a "great potential danger because the government has exhausted its power to tax and exhausted its power to borrow," that it has "no reserves."

Our swollen budgets constantly have been misrepresented to the public. Our government has kept us in a perpetual state of fear - kept us in a continuous stampede of patriotic fervor - with the cry of grave national emergency. Always there has been some terrible evil at home or some monstrous foreign power that was going to gobble us up if we did not blindly rally behind it by furnishing the exorbitant funds demanded. Yet, in retrospect, these disasters seem never to have happened, seem never to have been quite real.

Another of the great illusions is that the government gives tee people free much of what they get from its services. I am convinced that the average citizen has no idea who pays for big government and how much. The painful truth is this: the government produces nothing of itself. Whatever it spends for people it must previously take from the people in the form of taxes. Moreover, whenever the government gives a service to people, it must at the same time take away from the people the right to provide and decide for themselves. And the amount which government doles back to the people or spends to promote welfare is always only a fraction of what it takes away, because of the excessive cost of governmental administration. It is the little people that pay the largest part of the bill. Eighty-five per cent of all the billions of dollars paid in income taxes comes from the lowest rate - the 20 per cent paid by all persons with taxable income. Only 15 per cent is added by all the higher rates up to 91 per cent. Indeed, it has been suggested that one reason for the steep graduation of the income tax is to make the public think that people with high incomes pay most of the taxes. It is another illusion to think that excessive rates of a graduated income tax tend to redistribute the wealth. It merely prevents its accumulation and thereby blocks expansion of the nation's economic strength. The very source of new and better jobs thus disappears. This is economic folly based on the false proposition that growth can be maintained through continuous inflation.

But even greater issues are involved than any I have yet mentioned. Some years ago, the late President Woodrow Wilson made the following statement: "The history of liberty is the history of the limitation of governmental power, not the increase of it."

The contest for ages has been to rescue liberty from the constantly expanding grasp of governmental power. The great patriots of the American Revolution revolted not so much against the actual taxes imposed upon them by a British King but against the concept of government behind the taxes; the concept that government had unlimited power to do what government thought proper. They had a deep suspicion that government, if permitted, would waste the labors of the people and ultimately curtail the power of the people, always under the pretense of taking care of the people. That is why they tried to bind the government down with the modest restrictions of a Constitution, limiting the government's powers to the performance of carefully specified responsibilities.

Daniel Webster said on the floor of the United States Senate:

"All republics, all governments of law, must impose numerous limitations and qualifications of authority; they must be subject to rule and regulations. This is the very essence of free political institutions. The spirit of liberty is a sharp-sighted spirit; it is a cautious, sagacious, discriminating, far-seeing intelligence; it is jealous of encroachment, jealous of power, jealous of man. It demands checks, it seeks for guards, it insists on securities; it fortifies with all possible care against the assaults of ambition and passion. It does not trust the amiable weaknesses of human nature, and therefore it will not permit power to overstep its prescribed limits, though benevolence, good intent, and patriotic purpose come along with it. Neither does it satisfy itself with flashy and temporary resistance to authority. Far otherwise, it seeks for duration and permanence. It looks before and after; and, building on the experience of ages which are past, it labors diligently for the benefit of ages to come. This is the nature of constitutional liberty; and this is our liberty if we will rightly understand and preserve it. Our security is in our watchfulness of executive power. It was the constitution of this department, which was infinitely the most difficult part in the great work of creating our present government. To give to the executive department such power as should make it useful, and yet not such as should render it dangerous; to make it efficient, independent, and strong, and yet to prevent it from sweeping away everything by its union of military and civil authority, by the influence of patronage, and office, and favor; this indeed was difficult.

"I do not wish to impair the power of the President as it stands written down in the constitution. But ... I will not blindly confide, where all experience admonishes me to be jealous; I will not trust executive power, vested in the hands of a single magistrate, to keep the vigils of liberty."

He spoke those words one hundred and twenty-three years ago; but they could as well have been spoken but yesterday.

There are many who have lost faith in this early American ideal and believe in a form of socialistic, totalitarian rule, a sort of big-brother deity to run our lives for us. They no longer believe that free men can manage their own affairs. Their central thesis is to take your money away from you on the presumption that a handful of men, centered in government, largely bureaucratic not elected, can spend the proceeds of your toil and labor to greater advantage than you who create the money. Nowhere in the history of the human race is there justification for this reckless faith in political power. It is the oldest, most reactionary of all forms of social organization. It was tried out in ancient Babylon, in ancient Greece and ancient Rome; in Mussolini's Italy, in Hitler's Germany, and all Communist countries. Wherever and whenever it has been attempted, it has failed utterly to provide economic security, and has generally ended in national disaster. It embraces an essential idiocy, that individuals who, as private citizens, are not to manage the disposition of their own earnings, become in public office supermen who can manage the affairs of the world.

The Soviets have tried to legislate the perfect society; and today the average Soviet citizen has little more freedom and less comfort than the inmates of American jails. The old American philosophy of government more effectively promoted the ideal of human freedom, with greater material abundance for more people, than any social system ever propounded: freedom to live under the minimum of restraint - freedom to make your own mistakes if you will. The fundamental and ultimate issue at stake therefore is not merely our money, it is liberty, itself; the excessive taxation of an over-grown government versus personal freedom; a least common denominator of mediocrity against the proven progress of pioneering individualism; the free enterprise system or the cult of blind conformity; the robot or the free man.

On September 12, 1952, Senator Robert Taft conferred at Morningside Heights with his successful convention rival for the nomination for the Presidency of the United States, General Eisenhower. They later issued a manifesto containing the following statement:

"There is and has been one great fundamental issue.... It is the issue of liberty against the creeping socialization in every domestic field. Liberty was the foundation of our government, the reason for our growth, the basis of our happiness and the hope of our future. The greatest threat to liberty today is internal, from the constant growth of big government through the constantly increasing power and spending of the federal government.... The essential thing is to keep our expenditures... at a percentage of our total income which will not destroy our free economy at home and further innate our debt and our currency."

How I wish that instead of my feeble voice I could sound those words as though they were written in blazing rainbow colors on the very arch of the sky.

ADDRESS AT THE ANNUAL FOOTBALL
HALL OF FAME DINNER
DECEMBER 1, 1959
NEW YORK, NEW YORK

General MacArthur's interest in athletics was not restricted to the game of baseball. A football fan from the early days of the game, he was also the cadet manager of the West Point eleven. His long connection with the sport, both as participant and spectator, was the basis on which he was honored at the second annual awards dinner of the National Football Foundation. The General, usually reserved and serious in public, on this occasion allowed his sense of humor to show through.

Major Vorin E. Whan, Jr., USA, Editor
A Soldier Speaks: Public Papers and Speeches of General of the Army Douglas MacArthur
© 1965, Frederick A. Praeger, Publishers, New York, NY

No honor I have ever received moves me as deeply as this award. Perhaps this is because no honor I have ever received is less deserved by me. Many among you more richly deserve it, but none could more deeply appreciate it. I can accept it only as symbolical of the nameless thousands who admire and support football. Unhappily, I possess neither that eloquence of diction, that poetry of imagination, that brilliance of metaphor, to say what I feel. I can only express my gratitude with a simple but heartfelt "thank you."

I am of the football vintage of Walter Camp and Alonzo Stagg. I have thrilled to the blaze of Hinkey and Hefflefinger, of Brickly and Houghton, of Poe and Trenchard and Truxton Hare. I collaborated with Charley Daly and Pot Graves and that fine midshipman back, Bull Halsey, who was destined to become our fighting Admiral and my beloved comrade-in-arms of the Pacific war. I raised McEwan and Oliphant, Neyland and Biff Jones, Blaik and Ed Garbisch. I listened with thirsty ear to the witching voice of Grantland Rice. I learned the hard way from Knute Rockne and George Gipp and the Four Horsemen. And every year on every campus and every field throughout this broad land of ours I can see and hear their counterparts. I can see their ideals and dazzling performances being repeated over and over again, year on year, and as each passes on, I find myself again and again with the same old catch at my throat, the same old pounding in my heart, the same old yell on my lips, "Well done, Mr. Football. Yours is the touchdown."

The game has become a symbol of our country's best qualities - courage, stamina, coordinated efficiency. Many even believe in these cynical days of doubt and indecision that through this sport we can best keep alive the spirit of virility and enterprise which has made us great.

In all my own long national service, both in war and peace, it is in the football men I have found my greatest reliance. I recall so vividly the group from West Point which joined me in Korea for what turned out to be my last campaign.

Two names I shall never forget. One was the captain of the unbeaten 1949 eleven - Jim Trent. He was one of the Army's finest defensive ends. He was assigned to the command of a platoon on the extreme end of our line. The enemy launched an enveloping movement to turn that flank, but failed largely due to the determined resistance of Trent's unit. He was mortally wounded and, as he lay dying on the ground, his commanding officer bent over him to catch his final words. And through those bloody lips came that last gasping whisper, "Stupid thinking they could turn my end."

And the other was from the same undefeated team, its quarterback, noted for his long ball-passing ability, Arnold

Galiffa. He was given command of a key platoon in one of our attacks. But the enemy held in spite of all our firepower to dislodge him. Our whole line shivered to a halt, some thirty yards short of its objective, when suddenly Galiffa rose up, seized a package of hand grenades and began rapidly lobbing them into the enemy's machine-gun nests, barking in his staccato, signal-calling voice, "Colonel Blaik always told me when we were held in the line to go through the air." A breach was blasted, his platoon went through the hole, the goal was reached, and victory won. Thus, just as on the gridiron, the very essence of success in war depends on the same combination of strength and speed and skill, the same close coordination of men with maneuver, the same indomitable courage which alone can produce the will for victory. I can repeat with the added conviction of time what I said many long years ago on the Plain at West Point: "On the fields of friendly strife are sown the seeds that on other fields and other days will bring forth victory."

No more glittering accolade could be given to this game than to recall its personal impact on many of the contemporary chief magistrates of our great nation. President Eisenhower at last year's dinner in earnest words tendered his own moving tribute. I remember the remark of President Theodore Roosevelt made to me more than fifty years ago when I was serving as his aide-de-camp, on the day of the Harvard-Yale game: "Douglas," he said, "I would rather be in the Harvard backfield today than be in the White Howe." And President Woodrow Wilson, when I called to thank him at the end of the First World War for giving me the command at West Point: "General, I want the football game between West Point and Annapolis renewed. If we could only extend and expand this sport throughout the world, perhaps we would not need a League of Nations." And President Warren Harding visiting West Point with his first question to me as Superintendent, "How goes my favorite group of cadets - the football team?" And President Calvin Coolidge when I took him to an Army-Notre Dame game at the old Polo Grounds here in New York and told him of my enthusiastic support of football as a builder, not only of body but of basic character, and as a cardinal means toward furthering our traditional competitive spirit, with his dry comment: "I'm glad the players are not all Democrats." And President Herbert Hoover inquiring my views as Chief of Staff whether he could muster sufficient public support to ban war-time bombing from the air, and when I replied in the negative, his whimsical comment, "If it were a football problem, I could arouse popular sentiment quickly enough." And President Franklin Roosevelt, when I was about to complete (my) tour as Chief of Staff and enter upon that long, lonesome, desperate seventeen years of unbroken service in the Far East, asking my recommendation of a successor, and when I named the possibilities, his prompt query, "Which

MacArthur with "Red Bliak" during the Army vs. Syracruse football game. September, 1957.

is a football man?" And that was the one chosen - Malin Craig, an old Army back of the 1897 team. And President Truman surely showed some of the characteristics of a fullback when he kicked me out of the Far East.

And can I ever forget a talk with my old friend, John McGraw, the immortal manager of the New York Giants in our great companion game of baseball. I asked him who in his opinion was the best fielding pitcher he had ever known. I already knew he regarded Christy Mathewson as the greatest throwing pitcher, so was not surprised when he said Mathewson. I then remarked I had seen him at West Point play the greatest single football game at fullback I had ever known, telling of his booting two field goals, each of more than fifty yards. He looked a little puzzled, John was no wizard at football, and then said rather quizzically, "I do remember his booting a bunt down the third base line but it was only for a couple of feet."

Since that never-to-be-forgotten first scrimmage on the field at Rutgers, the world has turned over many, many times. The thrust into outer space of the satellite spheres and missiles marked the beginning of a new epoch in the long story of man-kind, the chapter of the Space Age. In the five or more billions of years the scientists tell us it has taken to form the earth, in the three or more billion years of development of the human race, there has never been a greater or more abrupt evolution. We deal now, not with things of this earth only, but with the inimitable distances and as yet unfathomed mysteries of the universe. We have found the "lost horizon," we have discovered a new and boundless frontier.

We Speak now in strange new terms, of harnessing the cosmic energy, of making the tides and winds work for us, of purifying sea water for our drink, of creating new and unheard of synthetic materials to supplement or even replace our old standard basics, of mining ocean floors for new fields of wealth and food, of disease preventatives to expand life into the hundreds of years, of controlling weather for our equitable adjustment of heat and cold, of rain and shine, of space ships to the moon; of the prime target in war no longer the armed forces of an enemy but instead his civil populations, of ultimate conflict between a united human race and the sinister force of another planetary galaxy, of such dreams and fantasies as to make life the most exciting of all time.

And through all this welter of change and development, It cannot fail to be a source of inspiration to all football enthusiasts and supporters to see how steadily and invincibly their great tradition has continued to command the absorbing interest of our people.

For youth as it steps across the threshold of manhood, it has become a rallying point to build courage when courage seemed to die, to restore faith where there seemed to be little cause for faith, to create hope as hope became forlorn. And this mantle of good embraces not only our Foundation, but the schools that feed the college campus and the postgraduates who form the backbone of the professional ranks

MacArthur with President Harry S. Truman, October 15, 1950.

with their unsurpassed ability to provide mental and physical relaxation for the millions who watch from the sidelines. Many connected with the professional game have proffered their assistance in building our College Hall of Fame, but, grateful as we are, we do not believe, as yet anyway, that such an integration would be wise. I am reminded of a pertinent anecdote recently told me of an old darkey who visited the dining room of this hotel. He seated himself at a table in that ornate pavilion and when the waiter came for his order said, "Ah'll have me some turnip greens boiled with pork slivers." And when the waiter, astonished, gasped that nothing like that was on the menu, he said, "Then ah'll have me some black-eyed susan beans with baked corn pones." And when the now speechless waiter merely shook his head, he sighed and said, "Then, ah'll have me some hominy grits fried in molasses, black molasses." And when he realized that this too was unknown to our imported French chef, the old man rose with majestic dignity to take his leave, saying: "Ah sees, suh, that this yere Waldorf-Astoria Hotel ain't as yet ready for integration." I was born in Little Rock. Thank you for coming tonight and for your generous support, and good night

---

Order of Lafayette Luncheon
May 19, 1961
Plaza Hotel, New York, New York

President General, this award moves me deeply, coming from a group I admire so greatly and in a cause I fought so strongly, it fills me with an emotion I cannot express. I possess neither that brilliance of diction, that power of imagination, nor that command of speech to say adequately what is in my heart.

This audience is composed largely of Veterans. Since they fought in France, the world has turned over many times. The thrust into outer space, of satellites and missiles, mark the beginning of a new epoch in the long story of mankind - the chapter of the space age. In the five or more billions of years the scientists tell us it has taken to form the earth, in the three or more billions of years in the development of the human race, there has never been a grater or more abrupt evolution. We deal now not with things of this world only, but with the illimitable distances and, as yet unfathomed mysteries of the universe. We have found the "lost horizon." We have discovered a new and boundless frontier.

We speak now in strange new terms of "harnessing the cosmic energy," of "making the winds and tides work for us," of purifying sea water for our drink; of creating new and unknown synthetic articles to supplement or even replace our old standard basics; of mining ocean floors for new fields of wealth and food, of disease preventatives to expand life into the hundreds of years, of controlling the weather for a more equitable distribution of heat and cold, of rain and shine; and of spaceships to the moon. The primary target in war no longer is the armed forces of an enemy, but instead is civil populations; of ultimate struggle between a united human race and a sinister force of some other planetary galaxy; of such dreams and fantasies as to make life the most exciting of all times, and of all changes, none is more drastic than that dealing with war.

Strategy is, of course, a science and its application, therefore, is immutable, but techniques are completely flexible and vary directly with the weapons available. Never has there been a greater change than in the last decade. Electronics and other processes of science have raised the destructive potential to encompass mass annihilation. But this very triumph of intellect, this very success of ingenuity has destroyed the possibility of global war being the medium of practical settlement of international differences. It can no longer be regarded as the ultimate weapon of statecraft, as the apotheosis of diplomacy. It is no longer the shortcut to national power and wealth of closely matched opponents which makes it impossible for even the winner to translate it into anything but disaster. The last World War, with its even now antiquated arms, clearly illustrates that the victor must bear, in large part, the very injuries inflicted by it. Our country expended billions of dollars and untold effort in healing the wounds of Germany and Japan.

Civilian population will not solve the problem of factories, nor the relative strength of the two great exponents will vary little with the years.

What then are the basic lessons to be drawn from the situation? Each of you will probably draw your own conclusions; mine I give you for what you think they are worth.

First, the chance of calculated and deliberate global war has become most remote. The people of both sides desire peace - both dread war. It is the one issue upon which both sides can agree, or it is the one issue on which both sides will profit equally. It is the one issue in which the interests of both are parallel. It is possibly the only issue in the world on which they can agree.

The main flaw in this deduction is that the constant acceleration of preparedness may ultimately precipitate, without specific intent, a kind of spontaneous combustion. And, second, if global war does come, the main objectives of the enemy will be no longer our armed forces, but instead, our civil populations. Global war now means the nation in arms has man, woman and child involved. The most vulnerable targets are the great industrial cities with their huge populations - paralyze them and you immobilize the whole. The citizenry then may force the government to yield.

I remember well a prediction made by the German Field Marshall, Von Hindenburg, shortly after the Armistice of the first World War. My division, the Old Rainbow, may its tribe increase, was stationed on the Rhine, just below Cologne and just above Coblentz. The Field Marshall was talking to a group of American officers. He said, "I predict that ultimately victory in war will depend largely upon the ability of civil populations to withstand and absorb attack." it will be a question of nerves. That nation will lose whose nerves snap first. Let's hope it will not be ours. Let's hope that this nation will continue to be a rallying point to bring courage when courage seems to fail, to restore faith when their seems to be little cause for faith, to create hope when hope becomes forlorn. May we sustain our two mighty symbols - the cross and the flag. The one based on those immutable teachings which provide the spiritual strength to sustain the cause of justice; the other based on an interminable will that human freedom shall not perish from the earth.

I thank you all again for the honor you have conferred upon me. It etches a memory which will be with me always.

101ST COMMENCEMENT, MICHIGAN STATE UNIVERSITY JUNE 11, 1961 LANSING, MICHIGAN

MacArthur's strong emphasis on character is revisited here from his days as a West Point Cadet. He considered character one of the strongest elements in a military man's psyche - to MacArthur a man without strong character traits can never be a true soldier.

Edward T. Imparato, Editor

President Hannah and distinguished members and friends of this great university, graduation day reflects one of the great moments of life. In later years, when you have grown old, its memory will be watered by tears and coaxed and caressed by the smiles of yesterday. It marks the great dividing line between hope and destiny - between the dreams of fancy-free fantasy and the realization of the grim realities of adult responsibility. It marks the fulfillment of the first great task of life, the surmounting of the first great hurdle on the road to success. For youth as it crosses the threshold of manhood, it has become a rallying point to build courage when courage seems to die, to restore faith when there seems little cause for faith, to create hope when hope becomes forlorn. Unhappily, I possess neither that eloquence of diction, that poetry of imagination, nor that brilliance of metaphor to tell you members of the graduation class of 1961 all that it means. But I can tell you some of the things your professors hope that your course of instruction has produced in addition to the acquired knowledge and accumulation of facts that it necessarily accomplished.

They hope above all else that it has been a builder of basic character; that it has molded you for your future roles as the custodians of the Republic; that it has taught you to be strong enough to know when you are weak, and brave enough to face yourself when you are afraid; that it has taught you to be proud and unbending in honest failure but humble and gentle in success, not to substitute wishes for actions, not to seek the path of comfort but to face the stress and spur of difficulty and challenge, to learn to stand up in the storm but to feel compassion for those who fall, to have a heart that is clear, a goal that is high, to master yourself before you seek to master others, to learn to laugh yet never forget how to weep, to reach into the future yet never neglect the past, to be serious yet never to take yourself too seriously, to be humble so that you may always remember the simplicity of true greatness, the open mind of true wisdom, the meekness of true strength; that it has given you a temper of the will, a quality of the imagination, a vigor of the emotions, a freshness of the deep springs of life, a temperamental predominance of courage over timidity, of an appetite for adventure over love of ease; that it has created

in your heart the sense of wonder, the undaunted challenge of events, the unfailing hope for what next, and the joy and inspiration of life; that it has taught you in this way to be an American.

And what, you might well ask, is this world which you now face? Since you were born it has turned over many, many times. The thrust into outer space of the satellite spheres and missiles marked the beginning of a new epoch in the long story of mankind - the chapter of the space age. In the five or more billions of years the scientists tell us it has taken to form the earth, in the three or more billion years of development of the human race, there has never been a greater, a more staggering or abrupt evolution. We deal now not with things of this world only but with the illimitable distances and, as yet, unfathomed mysteries of the universe. We have found the "lost horizon." We have discovered a new and boundless frontier. We speak now in strange new terms: of harnessing the cosmic energy; of making the winds and the tides work for us; of purifying sea water for our drink; of creating new and unheard of synthetic materials to supplement or even replace our old standard basics; of mining ocean floors for new fields of wealth and food; of disease preventives to expand life into the hundreds of years; of controlling weather for a more equitable adjustment of heat and cold, of rain and shine; of spaceships to the moon; of the prime target in war no longer the armed forces of an enemy but instead his civil populations; of ultimate conflict between a united human race and the sinister force of some other planetary galaxy; of such dreams and fantasies as to make life the most exciting of all time.

And how goes this life in this our own beloved country? Two schools of thought exist - the one almost utopian in outlook, the other warning of dangers.

The optimist, Allen Drury, says:

"This land, by the grace of God and the unceasing efforts of its people, is free. The first object of a free people should be the preservation of their liberty. This takes courage as it at times tends toward governmental inefficiency. Some peoples have it, some peoples do not. The 20th century, most violent crucible yet provided for the human race, is rapidly finding out which is which. In that testing, our country, the great Republic of the West, still stands supreme, battered though she is by the vicious and incessant onslaughts of her enemies and the occasional confusions and wearings of will by her own citizens. Her freedom is not perfect - but it is better than that of most of her contemporaries. Her liberties are not everywhere as thorough and complete as they should be - but compared to the grimly laughable mockeries of liberty that go on elsewhere, they shine like a tenfold beacon in the night. Our errors are those of the good-hearted; our ineptitudes those of a contender who cannot yet quite conceive of the utter evil arrayed against us. We are awkward at times. Shortsighted at times. At times hesitant and uncertain and almost willfully stupid. We are, now and again, an object of ridicule to a carping world and, upon occasion, an object of scorn. But we are free. There is nothing simple or easy in this freedom, which so many peoples shout about and so few really understand. It is only in a few favored lands that it has ever been achieved. Ours is one."

Yet, in deep warning we hear the voice of one of our greatest statesmen, Senator Byrd:

"Continuing centralization of government is destroying our freedom and strength. We have already gone too far. With excessive centralization comes excessive central edict, regulation, and taxation limiting and drastically curtailing personal freedom. The requirements of free government are simple - honesty and individual initiative, self-reliance and willing work, constructive production and free competition, progressive development with sound financing. Without these there will be neither solid progress nor security. We are being challenged from abroad and undermined at home. We are showing signs of weakness just when we should be strongest. Our strength is being sapped by deficit financing indulged in too long; Federal paternalism grown too big; courts grown too mighty; power groups grown too arrogant. These are subverting our system, changing our attitudes and hobbling our will for freedom. For 15 years the United States has been the world's banker, the world's policeman, the world's Santa Claus. We are showing the strain. We are in a dangerous storm."

And President Kennedy declared in his first address to Congress:

"Before my term has ended, we shall have to test anew whether a nation organized and governed such as ours can endure. The outcome is by no means certain."

And all this now becomes your problem. Our two great political parties will divide over you - over what you are - over what you ought to be - over what you can be. The one will preach citizen individuality, the other group collectivism; the one based on the individual, the other on the mass.

If I were permitted but one word of advice to you young men and women now standing on the threshold of these challenging opportunities and responsibilities, it would be to hold inviolate the immutable principles upon which has rested our hallowed traditions of liberty and freedom. I realize well that it is in the very nature of things that the restless spirit of youth seeks change. But change should not be sought for the sake of change alone. It should be sought only to adapt those time-tested principles to the new requirements of an expanding society. For just as in war strategy is immutable while tactics must change to meet new field conditions, so in peace basic principles which have been proved in the crucible of human experience should remain immutable while the administration for their application changes to meet the requirements of an ever-advancing civilization. The problem for ages has been to rescue liberty from the grasp of despotic power.

"The spirit of liberty," said one of our greatest past Senators, Daniel Webster, "should be bold and fearless, but it should also be cautious, sagacious, discriminating, farsighted. It should be jealous of encroachment, jealous of power, jealous of man. It should demand checks; it should seek for guards; it should insist on securities. It should fortify itself with all possible care against the assaults of ambition and passion. It should not trust the amiable weaknesses of human nature and thereby permit power to overstep its prescribed limits, even though benevolence, good intent, and patriotic purpose come along with it. It should look before and after and, building on the experience of ages which are past, should labor diligently for the benefit of ages to come."

And overshadowing all other problems you will face, intruding upon every thought and action, encompassing all that you hold most dear, dictating not only the past but your very future, is the master problem of global war. How, you can well ask, did such an institution as war become so integrated with man's life and civilization? How has it grown to be the most vital factor in our existence?

It started in a modest enough way as a sort of gladiatorial method of settling disputes between conflicting tribes. One of the oldest and most classical examples is the Biblical story of David and Goliath. Each of the two contesting groups selected its champion. They fought and, based upon the outcome, an agreement resulted. Then, as time went on, small professional groups known as armies replaced the individual champions. And these groups fought in some obscure corner of the world and victory or defeat was accepted as the basis of an ensuing peace. And from then on, down through the ages, the constant record is an increase in the character and strength of the forces with the rate of increase always accelerating. From a small percentage of the population it finally engulfed all. It is now the nation in arms. Within the span of my own life I have witnessed much of this evolution. At the turn of the century, when I joined the Army, the target was one enemy casualty at the end of a rifle, a pistol, a bayonet, a sword. Then came the machine gun designed to kill by the dozens. After that the heavy artillery raining death upon the hundreds. Then the aerial bomb to strike by the thousands - followed by the atom explosion to reach the hundreds of thousands. Now electronics and other processes of science have raised the destructive potential to encompass millions. And with restless hands we work feverishly in dark laboratories to find the means to destroy all at one blow.

But this very triumph of scientific annihilation - this very success of invention - has destroyed the possibility of war being a medium for the practical settlement of international differences. The enormous destruction to both sides of closely matched opponents makes it impossible for even the winner to translate it into anything but his own disaster.

The late war, even with its now antiquated armaments, clearly demonstrated that the victor had to bear in large part the very injuries inflicted on his foe. We expended billions of dollars and untold energies to heal the wounds of Germany and Japan.

Global war has become a Frankenstein to destroy both sides. No longer can it be a successful weapon of international adventure. If you lose, you are annihilated. If you win, you stand only to lose. No longer does it possess even the chance of the winner of a duel - it contains now only the germs of double suicide.

Time was when victory in war represented a shortcut to power, a place in the sun, economic wealth, and accelerated prosperity. It was the final weapon of statecraft; the apotheosis of political diplomacy. Its application, however, was regulated, controlled, and limited by the basic principle that a great nation that entered upon war and did not see it through to victory would ultimately suffer all the consequences of defeat. That is what happened to us in Korea. With victory within our grasp, and without the use of the atom bomb which we needed no more then than against Japan, we failed to see it through. Had we done so we would have destroyed Red China's capability of waging modern war for generations to come. Our failure to win that war was a major disaster to the free world. Its fatal consequences are now increasingly being felt in the military rise of Red China into a mighty colossus which threatens all of continental Asia and bids fair to emerge as the balance of military power in the world. This would jeopardize freedom on all continents.

But the conditions that prevailed in the Korean war exist no longer and will come no more. Then we were the sole possessors of nuclear power - we stood alone in military might. Now all this is changed. Others possess this weapon. Relative strengths from now on will probably change little with the years. Action by one will promptly be matched by reaction from the other.

The great question is, can global war now be outlawed from the world?

If so, it would mark the greatest advance in civilization since the Sermon on the Mount. It would lift at one stroke the darkest shadow which has engulfed mankind from the beginning. It would not only remove fear and bring security - it would not only create new moral and spiritual values - it would produce an economic wave of prosperity that would raise the world's standard of living beyond anything ever dreamed of by man. The hundreds of billions of dollars now spent in mutual preparedness could conceivably abolish poverty from the face of the earth. It would accomplish even more than this; it would at one stroke reduce the international tensions that seem to be insurmountable now to matters of probable solution. This would not, of course, mean the abandonment of all armed forces, but it would reduce them to the simpler problems of internal order and international police. It would not mean utopia at one fell stroke, but it would mean that the great roadblock now existing to the development of the human race would have been cleared.

You will say at once that although the abolition of war has been the dream of man for centuries every proposition to that end has been promptly discarded as impossible and fantastic. But that was before the science of the past decade made mass destruction a reality. The argument then was along spiritual and moral lines, and lost. But now the tremendous evolution of nuclear and other potentials of destruction has suddenly taken the problem away from its primary consideration as a moral and spiritual question and brought it abreast of scientific realism. It is no longer an ethical equation to be pondered solely by learned philosophers and ecclesiastics but a hard-core one for the decision of the masses whose survival is the issue. This is as true of the Soviet side of the world as of the free side - as true behind the Iron Curtain as in front of it. The ordinary people of the world, such as you and I, whether free or slave, are all in agreement on this solution; and this, perhaps, is the only thing in the world they do agree upon, but it is the most vital and decisive of all. We are told that we must go on indefinitely as at present - with what at the end none say - there is no definite objective. The search for a final solution is but passed along to those who follow and, at the end, the problem will be exactly that which we face now.

It may take another cataclysm of destruction to prove the bald truth that the further evolution of civilization cannot take place until global war is abolished. This is the one issue upon which both sides can agree for it is the one issue upon which both sides will profit equally. It is the one issue in which the interests of both are completely parallel. It is the one issue which, if settled, might settle all others.

The present tensions with their threat of national annihilation are fostered by two great illusions. The one a complete belief on the part of the Soviet world that the capitalistic countries are preparing to eventually attack them; that sooner or later we intend to strike. And the other, a complete belief on the part of the capitalistic countries that the Soviets are preparing to attack us; that sooner or later they intend to strike. Both are wrong. Each side, so far as the masses are concerned, is desirous of peace. Both dread war. But the constant acceleration of preparation may, without specific intent, ultimately precipitate a kind of spontaneous combustion.

Many will tell you, with mockery and ridicule, that the abolition of war can be only a dream - that it is but the vague imaginings of a visionary. But we must go on or we will go under. And criticism is that the world has no plan which will enable us to go on. We have suffered the blood and the sweat and the tears. Now we seek the way and the truth and the light. We are in a new era. The old methods and solutions for this vital problem no longer suffice. We must have new thoughts, new ideas, new concepts. We must break out of the straitjacket of the past. We must have sufficient imagination and moral courage to translate this universal wish - which is rapidly becoming a universal necessity - into actuality. And until then we must be fully prepared, whatever the cost or sacrifice, lest we perish.

President Hannah, no award I have ever received moves me more deeply than to have my name scrolled upon the honorary tablets of this great university. Perhaps this is because I am informed that no institution of learning is more devotedly dedicating its full strength to the preservation of those fundamental principles upon which this Nation was conceived and nurtured to greatness. None more ardently is resisting compromise with that free way of life we reverently call Americanism. None espouses more energetically that bulwark of national freedom - rugged individual thought and action. Please extend to all concerned my deepest thanks and appreciation.

To you, of '61, goes my hope that all good things may come to each and every one of you, and my prayer that a merciful God will protect and preserve you always.

Goodby.

ARRIVAL MANILA AIRPORT, THE PHILIPPINES
JULY 3, 1961

Mr. President, your excellencies, my dear friends, I have returned. I am once again in this land that I have known so long; and amongst this people that I have loved so well. Unfortunately I possess neither that eloquence of diction, that poetry of imagination, nor that brilliance of metaphor to say adequately what is in my heart. When your distinguished President invited me to come once again to these friendly shores, I felt as though I were at last really coming home; for it was here I lived my greatest moments and it is of here I have my greatest memories. President Garcia my dear old comrade-in-arms of the liberation, I report to you my presence as an honorary citizen of the Philippines. I say to you Sir, that in spite of my long absence you have in all your broad land no more loyal and devoted a Filipino. I thank you from the bottom of a full heart for this opportunity to renew old ties and old friendships and I anticipate the next few days as amongst the happiest of my life. I bring with me one of your country's staunchest admirers, my beloved wife, Jean. She joins me, Mr. President, in a pledge of allegiance.

Mabuhay![19]

INDEPENDENCE DAY CEREMONIES
JULY 4, 1961
MANILA, PHILIPPINE ISLANDS

MacArthur addresses the issues of the great strides the Philippines have made in agriculture, manufacturing and education since becoming an independent nation.

Edward T. Imparato, Editor

Mr. President, my good friends, just 15 years ago today I stood on this same Luneta, proud witness to the birth of your new Republic. It was the culmination of your hopes and aspirations of 48 years under my country's beneficent guidance. It was the final act in a drama, initiated by the American Revolution, which had brought to the world's stage the political philosophy that a people should have of right the opportunity for independence and freedom from outside rule.

It was the redemption of my country's pledge and constant reaffirmation that, after a period of reasonable preparation, the political bonds which united us would voluntarily be severed. It brought into sharp focus with dramatic clarity the irreconcilable difference between the totalitarian system which seeks mastery over others and the free system which seeks equality with others.

On that day, July 4, 1946, I said to you gathered here just as you are today:

"Let history record this event in the sweep of democracy through the earth as foretelling the end of mastery over peoples by power of force alone - the end of empire as the political chain which binds the unwilling weak to the unyielding strong. Let it be recorded as one of the great turning points in the agelong struggle of man for liberty, for dignity, and for human betterment."

Despite this historic triumph of liberty and justice, the scene that day was one of desolation and destruction inevitable in the wake of war. There was sorrow and bereavement in countless Philippine homes. Fire and sword had taken a toll of personal tragedy searing the hearts and souls of every Philippine citizen.

Yet in all that multitude I saw not a tear, heard not a sob. All before me - men and women, boys and girls - reflected not the gloom of the recent past but only a firm faith in a destiny yet to be unfolded. The spiritual strength in those eager upturned faces, with eyes looking forward, not backward, confirmed my own complete faith in the future of your Republic.

That faith has been fully justified. You have taken your place in the counsels of the nations of the world with dignity and universal respect. Your cities have been restored, your economy revived.

You have turned your farm shortages into surpluses. Your mines have produced increasing wealth. Your commerce has expanded. Your products now reach the markets of the world. Your industry has engendered abroad a new confidence and faith.

But only a seer might forecast just what the future has in store for you and I would consider myself brash indeed, were I to attempt to do so. There will be many perils ahead to test the wisdom and courage and statesmanship of your leaders.

For since I left you 15 years ago, the world has turned over many, many times. The thrust into outer space of the satellite spheres and missiles marked the beginning of a new epoch in the long story of mankind - the chapter of the space age.

In the five or more billions of years the scientists tell us it has taken to form the earth - in the three or more billion years of development of the human race - there has never been a greater or more abrupt evolution.

We deal now not with things of this world only, but with the illimitable distances and as yet unfathomed mysteries of the universe. We have found the "lost horizon." We have discovered a new and boundless frontier.

We speak now in strange new terms of harnessing the cosmic energy; of making the winds and the tides work for us; of purifying sea water for our drink; of creating new and unheard of synthetic materials to supplement or even replace our old standard basics; of mining ocean floors for new fields of wealth and food; of disease preventatives to expand life into the hundred of years; of controlling weather for a more equitable disposition of heat and cold, of rain and shine; of spaceships to the moon; of the prime target in war, no longer the armed forces of an enemy, but instead his civil populations; of ultimate conflict between a united human race and the sinister force of some other planetary galaxy.

Of such dreams and fantasies as to make life the most exciting of all time. And amidst all this welter of change and development it is my hope and prayer that this land will continue to be a rallying point to build courage when courage seems to fail, to restore faith when there seems to be little cause for faith, to create hope when hope becomes forlorn.

In this great assemblage I see many of my former comrades in arms of the war. To them I wish to express once again my admiration for that enduring fortitude, that patriotic self-abnegation, and that unsurpassed courage which has made the name of the Philippine soldier stand forth in such luster.

The memorials of character wrought by you will never be forgotten. You have stamped yourself in blazing flames upon the souls of your countrymen. You have carved your statue in the hearts of your people. You have built your monuments in the memory of your compatriots.

---

[19] Philippine expression regarding "long life.

And you may be sure, that if you fight again, Americans will be at your side, shoulder to shoulder, once again, just as before, comrades in arms. And you may be sure that as your old commander in chief I shall do all in my limited power to see that you receive full reward for your past service.

The tide of world affairs ebbs and flows in and out. Old empires die, new nations are born, alliances arise and vanish. But through all this vast confusion the mutual friendship of our two countries shines like a tenfold beacon in the night.

Together we suffered the blood and the sweat and the tears. Together we seek the way and the truth and the light. In this long twilight era that is neither war nor peace we stand together just as firmly as before.

In the effort to build a world of economic growth and solidarity, in the effort to build an atmosphere of hope and freedom, in the effort to build a community of strength and unity of purpose, in the effort to build a lasting peace of justice, the Philippines and the United States of America have become indivisible.

And now, even as I hail you, I must say farewell. For that is the nature of my visit: To greet once again those with whom I have stood, as with their fathers before them, in building and defending on these shores a citadel of freedom and liberty, and then to bid you an affectionate goodby. For I must admit, with a sense of sadness, that the deepening shadows of life cast doubt upon my ability to pledge again, "I shall return."

So, my dear friends, I close with a fervent prayer that a merciful God will protect and preserve each and every one of you and will bring to this beloved land peace and tranquillity always.

Good-bye.

Joint Session of the Congress
of the Republic of the Philippines
July 5, 1961
Manila, Philippine Islands

MacArthur makes a broad-brush review of major advances by the Philippines since the end of World War II. Now is the time to look at business and politics and government advancement for we have entered a new world of geopolitics.

Edward T. Imparato, Editor

The last time I spoke before this August body, the war still raged outside. The crash of guns rattled windows, the sputter of musketry drowned voices, the acrid smell of smoke filled our nostrils, the stench of death was everywhere. And now, 16 years later, although those incidents have become but a dark memory, the possibility of war still hangs like a cloud before our eyes. It overshadows all other problems, intruding upon every thought and action, encompassing all that we hold most dear, dictating not only the present but our very future.

Many in this brilliant audience were my former comrades in arms. They have known war in all its horror and, as veterans, hope against its recurrence. How, they well may ask, did such an institution as war become so integrated with man's life and civilization? How has it become the most vital factor in our existence?

It started in a modest enough way as a sort of gladiatorial method of settling disputes between conflicting tribes. One of the oldest and most classical examples is the Biblical story of David and Goliath. Each of the two contesting groups selected its champion. They fought and, based upon the outcome, an agreement resulted. Then, as time went on, small professional groups known as armies fought in some obscure corner of the globe, and victory or defeat was accepted as the basis of an ensuring peace.

And from then on, down through the ages, the constant record is an increase in the character and strength of the forces, with the rate of increase always accelerating. From a small percentage of the population it finally engulfed all. It is now the nation in arms.

Within the span of my own life, I have witnessed much of this evolution. At the turn of the century, when I joined the Army, the target was one enemy casualty at the end of a rifle, a pistol, a bayonet, a sword. Then came the machine gun, designed to kill by the dozens. After that, the heavy artillery - raining death upon the hundreds. Then the aerial bombs to strike by the thousands - followed by the atom explosion to reach the hundreds of thousands.

Now, electronics and other processes of science have raised the destructive potential to encompass millions. And with restless hands we work feverishly in dark laboratories to find the means to destroy all at one blow.

But this very triumph of scientific annihilation - this very success of invention - has destroyed the possibility of war being a medium for the practical settlement of international differences. The enormous destruction to both sides of closely matched forces makes it impossible for even the winner to translate it into anything but his own disaster.

The late war, even with its now antiquated armaments, clearly demonstrated that the victor had to pay in large part the very injuries inflicted on his foe. My country expended billions of dollars in healing the wounds of Germany and Japan.

Global war has become a Frankenstein to destroy both sides. No longer is it a weapon of adventure - a shortcut to international power. If you lose, you are annihilated. If you win, you stand only to lose. No longer does it possess even the chance of the winner of a duel. It contains now only the germs of double suicide.

Time was when victory in war represented economic wealth, accelerated prosperity, a place in the international sun. It was the final weapon of statecraft, the apotheosis of diplomacy. Its application, however, was regulated, controlled, and limited by the basic principle that a great nation that entered upon war and did not see it through to victory must ultimately suffer all the consequences of defeat. That is what happened to us in Korea. With victory within our grasp, and without the use of the atom bomb which we needed no more then than in Japan, we failed to see it through.

Had we done so, we would have destroyed Red China's capability of waging modern war for generations to come. Our failure to win that war was a major disaster for the free world. Its fatal consequences are now increasingly being felt in the military rise of Red China into a mighty colossus which threatens all of Asia and bids fair to emerge as the balance of military power in the world. This would jeopardize freedom on all continents.

But the conditions that prevailed in the Korean war exist no longer and will come no more. Then we were the sole possessors of nuclear power - we stood alone in military might. Now all is changed. Others possess this weapon. Relative strengths from now on will probably change little with the years. Action by one will be promptly be matched by reaction from the other.

The great question is: Can global war now be outlawed from the world? If so, it would mark the greatest advance in civilization since the Sermon on the Mount. It would lift at one stroke the darkest shadow which has engulfed mankind from the beginning. It would not only remove fear and bring security - it would not only create new moral and spiritual values - it would produce an economic wave of prosperity that would raise the world's standard of living beyond anything ever dreamed of by man.

The hundreds of billions of dollars now spent in mutual preparedness could conceivably abolish poverty from the face of the earth. It would accomplish even more than this; it would at one stroke reduce the international tensions that seem to be insurmountable now, to matters of more probable solution. This would not, of course, mean the abandonment of all armed forces, but it would reduce them to the simpler problems of internal order and international police. It would not mean utopia at one fell stroke, but it would mean that the great roadblock now existing to the development of civilization would have been cleared.

You will say at once, that although the abolition of war has been the dream of man for centuries, every proposition to that end has been promptly discarded as impossible and fantastic. But that was before the science of the past decade made mass destruction a reality. The argument then was along spiritual and moral lines, and lost. But now the tremendous evolution of nuclear and other potentials of destruction has suddenly taken the problem away from its primary consideration as a moral and spiritual question and brought it abreast of scientific realism. It is no longer an ethical equation to be pondered solely by learned philosophers and ecclesiastics, but a hard-core one for the decision of the masses whose survival is the issue.

This is as true of the Soviet side of the world as of the free side - as true behind the Iron Curtain as in front of it. The ordinary people of the world, whether free or slave, are all in agreement on this solution; and this perhaps is the only thing in the world they do agree upon, but it is the most important and decisive of all. We are told we must go on indefinitely as at present - with what at the end, no one says - there is no definite objective. They but pass along to those that follow the search for a final solution. And at the end, the problem will be exactly that which we face now.

It may take another cataclysm of destruction to prove the bald truth that the further evolution of civilization cannot take place until global war is abolished. But this is the one issue upon which both sides can agree, for it is the one issue upon which both sides will profit equally. It is the one issue in which the interests of both are completely parallel. It is the one issue which if settled, might settle all others.

The present tensions with their threat of national annihilation are fostered by two great illusions. The one, a complete belief on the part of the Soviet world that the capitalistic countries are preparing to attack them; that sooner or later we intend to strike. And the other, a complete belief on the part of capitalistic countries that the Soviets are preparing to attack us; that sooner or later they intend to strike.

Both are wrong. Each side, so far as the masses are concerned, is desirous of peace. Both dread war. But the constant acceleration of preparation may, without any specific intent, precipitate a kind of spontaneous combustion.

Many will tell you with mockery and ridicule that the abolition of war can be only a dream - that it is but the vague imagining of a visionary. But we must go on or we will go under. And the great criticism that can be made is that the world lacks a plan that will enable us to go on.

We are in a new era. The old methods and solutions for these problems no longer suffice. We must have new thoughts, new ideas, new concepts. We must break out of the straitjacket of the past. We must have sufficient imagination and courage to translate this universal wish for peace - which is rapidly becoming a universal necessity - into actuality. And, until then, at whatever cost or sacrifice, we must be fully prepared - lest we perish.

And what you may well ask is my opinion as to the present state of the Philippine defense. As your former military advisor I give it for what you may think its worth.

Your most powerful safeguard again predatory attack is the broad expanse of sea water which separates you from your neighbors. There is no hostile fleet challenging naval control of that vital area. No enemy flotilla capable of conducting an amphibious movement of troops to your soils. You are safe from such occupational assault as long as the United States maintains sea and air supremacy in the Pacific Ocean. You may be hurt but you cannot be taken. Militarily you enjoy a position of relative security. You are a bastion of strength.

The other tactics of Communism in its aggression upon areas of freedom, are infiltration and internal subversion. The former, infiltration, is difficult for you to defend against because of your long and broken shoreline. But internal movement of any major alien groups should be readily detected by an alert security force aided by your thoroughly loyal and war tested citizenry. The latter, internal subversion, the tactic most success, offers only a minor threat to the Philippines. The magnificent spiritual resistence of your people to the oppressors of the Japanese occupation coupled with your cultural strength and long history in defense of your liberties, offers safe guarantees against this type of inroad. Indeed I would say that of all the countries of the free world none is more proof against being brought under alien subversion than is the Philippines.

To sum up, I believe that you have little to fear from the Communist conspiracy as long as you have an alert and mobile security force capable of maintaining internal order and intercepting any group which might infiltrate your beaches with hostile intent. The military policy developed prior to World War II and so efficiently carried out since then, may safely be continued as the guideline to your defensive posture. In the far east the focal center of hostile pressures now lies in Southeast Asia where it is possible that the alliance of which you are a member may intervene directly or indirectly in order to shore up local defenses. I would not presume even to suggest what course military or otherwise this alliance could take but I would unhesitatingly observe that with the lessons of the Korea in the so recent past, no nation or no alliance of nations should be so reckless to commit troops to fight on the mainland of Asia without considering the potentiality of the reaction of the enemy being supported by his Communist allies, and above all without being prepared with both the will and the means to destroy the centers and lines of supply of larger ground forces enjoying marked logistical advantages. Nor should defeatist military doctrines be permitted as was done in Korea under the rhetorical disguise of such misleading phrases as passive offense, aggressive defense, privilege sanctuary, police action. Such nonsense has no place in the lexicon or conduct of war. War by its very nature necessitates the bringing of maximum violence to bear upon the enemy. There can be no half way measures, no soft blows, no enemy sanctuaries. The only limitation is the degree of violence essential to insure success, for in war, as is attested by the history of the world, there is no substitute for victory.

Military defense must have as its natural corollary a strong and viable economy. This you are far along the road toward achieving. Despite your population growth you have transformed long existing farm shortages into surpluses. You have changed an unfavorable balance of international trade into one of reciprocal equity. And you have introduced a moderate program of industrialization to broaden the scope of employment and to lessen your dependence upon foreign manufacture. By these process you are not only enhancing the contentment and happiness of your people by raising their standards of life but at the same time you are building an ever stronger bulwark behind your defense establishment and military policy.

It is with great satisfaction and pride I have observed this progress. Satisfaction as one whose life has been interwoven with yours for nearly 60 years and pride of honorary citizenship, a distinction which you conferred upon me many years ago. As I pass from the Philippine scene it is with a heart full of gratitude for the recent honors you have added to those of the past. They have etched a new memory for me which will be with me always.

God grant this nation and people a long era of peace and prosperity and bring our two peoples, Filipino and American, ever closer together in understanding, affection, and common cause.

DEDICATION OF THE MACARTHUR HIGHWAY
JULY 6, 1961
PHILIPPINES

MacArthur is pleased and humble over the naming of the MacArthur Highway.

Edward T. Imparato, Editor

No human being could fail to be deeply moved by such a tribute. Coming from a people I admire so greatly and located in a land I served so long, it fills me with an emotion I can not express. But this memorial is not primarily to commemorate a personality; it is the symbol of a great moral right - the right to national freedom of a race of oldest culture and most ancient descent. That is the animation of this project. For all eyes and for all times it is a Proclamation of Liberty.

That the Philippines should have immutably integrated my name with so noble an ideal fills me with a sense of pride - and yet of humility - that will be with me always.

The story which this highway commemorates is known to all of you. It needs no profuse panegyrics. It is the story of the Philippine soldier supported by his American comrades. My estimate of him was formed on the battlefield many years ago and has never changed. I regarded him then, as I regard him now, as one of the world's noblest figures - not only as one of its finest military characters but also as one of its most stainless. His name and fame are the birthright of every Filipino citizen In his youth and strength, his love and loyalty, he gave all that mortality can give. He needs no eulogy from me or any other man - he has written his own history and written it in red on his enemy's breast - but when I think of his patience under adversity, of his courage under fire, and of his modesty in victory I am filled with an emotion I can not express. He belongs to history as furnishing one of the greatest examples of successful patriotism; he belongs to posterity as the instructor of future generations in the principles of liberty and freedom; he belongs to the present - to us - by his virtues and by his achievements.

The code which he perpetuates embraces the highest moral laws. It will stand the test of any ethics or philosophies ever promulgated for the uplift of mankind. Its requirements are for the things that are right, and its restraints are from the things that are wrong. The soldier, above all other men is required to perform the highest act of religious teaching - sacrifice. In battle and in the face of danger and death he discloses those divine attributes which his Maker gave when He created man in His own image. No physical courage and no brute instincts can take the place of the spiritual uplift which will alone sustain him. However horrible the incidents of war may be, the soldier who is called upon to offer and to give his life for his country is the noblest development of mankind.

On such an occasion as this my thoughts go back to those men who went with me to their last battle. Never again for them those broiling suns of relentless heat, those torrential rains of devastating storm, the desolation and utter loneliness of jungle trails, the bitterness of separation from those they loved and cherished, the deadly pestilence of tropical disease, the ghastly horror of stricken areas of war. Never again the wind and rain of murky foxholes, the stench of ghostly trenches, the grime of dripping dugouts. Never again faint bugles sounding reveille, far drums beating the long roll, the crash of guns, the rattle of muskets. They are gone beyond the mists that blind us here. Under white crosses in chambered temples of silence the dust of their dauntless valor sleeps, waiting in the chancery of Heaven the final reckoning of Judgment Day.

Never will I forget.

COMMEMORATION OF LANDING
JULY 8, 1961
TACLOBAN, LEYTE, PHILIPPINES

I cannot tell you the emotion I feel at standing once again on this beach. It was here the tide of war turned against the enemy - it was here I redeemed my sacred pledge - "I shall return."

It was nigh unto seventeen years ago that your renowned Colonel Kangleon joined me with his splendid guerrilla force to mark the beginning of the Liberation. It was through the surf lapping this shore that your dauntless president waded ashore with me. Two are with me today who stood at my shoulder as we traversed the fire of the invaders - your distinguished Ambassador, Carlos Romulo, and my old friend, Courtney Whitney. Two of my finest soldiers.

The scene that day was one of desolation and destruction. Fire and sword had ravaged many a Filipino home. Starvation and disease had taken their heavy toll. The despotic grasp of the conqueror was at your throat. But the soldier of the Philippines there showed himself at his best. Swift and sure in attack, resourceful and determined in defense, he wrote his own history in red on his enemy's breast. When I think of his patience under adversity, of his courage under fire and of his modesty in victory, I am filled with an emotion of admiration I cannot express. He belongs to history as furnishing one of the greatest examples of successful patriotism; he belongs to posterity as the instructor of future generations in the principles of liberty and freedom; he belongs to the present - to us - by his virtues and by his achievements. His name and fame have become the birthright of every Philippine citizen.

To those of them who are left, I want you to know that if you fight again Americans will be at your side, shoulder to shoulder, just as before, comrades-in-arms. And you may be sure, my veteran soldier, that I will do all in my power to help you obtain the full reward for your past war service.

And once again I cannot fail to commend with deepest admiration the invincible resistance by all Philippine citizens, men, women and children, to the Japanese invaders. This indomitable attitude of the civilian population was a vital factor in the Liberation. No more dominant figure stood forth in this great patriotic movement than the Senator from Bohol, now President of the Philippine Republic, my old friend now standing by my side, Carlos Garcia.

As I travel again through this land I have known so long and meet again a people I have loved so well, I feel a sense of greatest pleasure and satisfaction at the rehabilitation that has taken place since the war. Your cities have been restored. Your economy revived. Your schools reopened. You have turned your farm shortages into surpluses. Your mines have produced increasing wealth. Your commerce has expanded. Your products now reach the markets of the world. You have taken your place in the counsels of the nations of the world with dignity and universal respect. Everywhere I see light and laughter and a growing prosperity. And this is as it should be.

I wish to thank you for the warmth of your greeting today. It moves me more deeply than I can say. And now as I bid you farewell I do so with a prayer in my heart that a merciful God will continue to protect and preserve each and every one of you always.

Mabuhay!

REUNION WITH FORMER PRESIDENT OSMENA
JULY 9, 1961
CEBU, CEBU, PHILIPPINES

I thank you from the bottom of my heart for the warmth of your welcome. It moves me more deeply than I can say. Coming from a people I have known so long and a land I have loved so well, it etches for me a new memory which I shall never forget.

It is an especial pleasure to meet again my friend of more than half a century, Sergio Osmena. All Americans know and honor him as one of the foremost architects of the Philippine Republic. He was a leader in that great political philosophy that a people should have of right the opportunity for independence and freedom; that there should be an end of mastery by power of force alone - the end of empire which binds the unwilling weak to the unyielding strong.

When last I was here, sixteen years ago, the scene was one of desolation and destruction incident to the war. There was sorrow and bereavement in your homes where fire and sword had taken a fearful toll of personal tragedy. But now your city has been restored. Your commerce revived. Your schools reopened. All is light and laughter. And as I see the happiness in your faces, the prosperity of your community, a great gladness fills my heart. I feel again a profound gratitude to the Filipino soldier for the magnificent part he played in the Liberation. When I think of his patience under adversity, of his courage under fire and of his modesty in victory, I am filled with an emotion I cannot express. He belongs to history as furnishing one of the greatest examples of successful patriotism; he belongs to posterity as the instructor of future generations in the principles of liberty and freedom; he belongs to the present - to us - by his virtues and by his achievements.

To those of them who are left, I want you to know that if you fight again Americans will be at your side, shoulder to shoulder, just as before, comrades-in-arms. And you may be sure, my veteran soldiers, that I will do all in my power to help you obtain the full reward for your past war service.

And once again I cannot fail to commend with deepest admiration the invincible resistance by all Philippine citizens, men, women and children, to the Japanese invaders. This indomitable attitude of the civilian population was a vital factor in the Liberation. No more dominant figure stood forth in this great patriotic movement than the Senator from Bohol, now President of the Philippine Republic, my old friend now standing by my side, Carlos Garcia.

And now I must say farewell. It has been a great inspiration to renew old ties and old friendships, and to join hands once again with those with whom for more than a century I helped build here a citadel of liberty and freedom. I bid you an affectionate goodbye with the prayer that a merciful God will protect and preserve each and every one of you always.

Mabuhay!

REMARKS TO THOSE ASSEMBLED
JULY 10, 1961
ILOILO CITY, PANAY, PHILIPPINES

I thank you from the bottom of my heart for the warmth of your greeting. It moves me more deeply than I can say. Coming from a people I have known so long and a land I have loved so well, it etches for me a new memory which I shall never forget.

It is a great pleasure to be again in Iloilo as it was here I had my first assignment, nearly sixty years ago. As an officer of Engineers I was directed to build a pier and dock on the island of Guimaras just across the way. And I remember it even more vividly as being a leading community in that great political philosophy that a people should have of right the opportunity for independence and freedom; that there should be an end of mastery by force alone - the end of empire which binds the unwilling weak to the unyielding strong.

When last I was here, sixteen years ago, the scene was one of desolation and destruction incident to the war. There was sorrow and bereavement in your homes where fire and sword had taken a fearful toll of personal tragedy. But now your city has been restored. Your commerce revived. Your schools reopened. All is light and laughter. And as I see the happiness in your faces, and the prosperity of your community, a great gladness fills my heart and I feel again a profound gratitude to the Filipino soldier for the magnificent part he played in the Liberation. When I think of his patience under adversity, of his courage under fire, and of his modesty in victory, I am filled with an emotion I cannot express. He belongs to history as furnishing one of the greatest examples of successful patriotism; he belongs to posterity as the instructor of future generations in the principle of liberty and freedom; he belongs to the present - to us - by his virtues and by his achievements.

To those of them who are left, I want you to know that if you fight again Americans will be at your side, shoulder to shoulder, just as before, comrades-in-arms. And you may be sure, my veteran soldiers, that I will do all in my power to help you obtain the full reward for your past war service.

And once again I cannot fail to commend with deepest admiration the invincible resistance by all Philippine citizens, men, women and children, to the Japanese invaders. This indomitable attitude of the civilian population was a vital factor in the Liberation. No more dominant figure stood forth in this great patriotic movement than the Senator from Bohol, now president of the Philippine Republic, my old friend now standing by my side, Carlos Garcia.

And now I must say farewell. It has been a great inspiration to renew old ties and old friendships and to join hands once again with those with whom for more than half a century I helped build here a citadel of liberty and freedom. I

---

bid you an affectionate goodbye with the prayer that a merciful God will protect and preserve each and every one of you always.

Mabuhay!

CIVIC ORGANIZATIONS,
ACCEPTANCE OF HONORARY DEGREE OF DOCTOR
OF LAWS FROM THE LYCEUM OF THE PHILIPPINES
JULY 11, 1961
FIESTA PAVILION, MANILA HOTEL

My dear friends. I just ordered a truck to take home all the presents you presented me but I was afraid for a moment that you were going to take my girl away from me.

I thank you from the bottom of a full heart for these awards and above all the naming of the MacArthur Highway which was done at your insistence. No human being could fail to be moved by such a tribute coming from a people I admire so greatly and located in a land I served so long. It fills me with an emotion I cannot express.

But this memorial, the naming of this road, was not primarily intended to commemorate a personality. It was the statement of a great moral right. The right of a free people to national freedom. That was the real motivation of this concept. For all eyes and for all time, it was to be a proclamation of liberty. That the people of the Philippines should so immutably integrate my name with so noble an ideal, fills me with a sense of pride and yet of humility which will be with me always.

The story which the MacArthur Highway is intended to commemorate is known to all of you. It requires no profuse panegyrics. It is the story of the Philippine soldier supported by his American comrades. My estimate of him was formed on the battle field many years ago and has never changed. I regarded him then, as I regard him now, as one of the world's noblest figures, not only as one of the finest military characters, but also as one of the most stainless. His name and fame have become the birthright of every Philippine citizen.

In his youth and strength, his love and loyalty, he gave all that mortality can give. He needs no eulogy from me or from any other man. He has written his own history and written it in red on his enemy's breast. When I think of his patience under adversity, of his courage under fire, and of his modesty in victory, I am filled with an emotion of admiration I cannot put into words. He belongs to history as furnishing one of the finest examples of successful patriotism He belongs to posterity as the instructor of future generations in the principals of liberty and freedom. He belongs to the present to us, by his virtues and achievements.

The code which he perpetuates embraces the highest moral laws and will stand the test of any ethics or philosophies ever promulgated for the uplift of mankind. Its requirements are for the things that are right and its restraints are from the things that are wrong. The soldier above all other men, is required to practice the highest law of religion - sacrifice. In battle and in the face of danger and death, he discloses those divine attributes which his maker gave when he created man in his own image. No physical courage and no brute instincts can take the place of the spiritual uplift which alone can sustain him.

On such an occasion as this, my thoughts go back to those men who went with us to their last campaign. I do not know the dignity of their birth but I do know the glory of their death. They died unquestioning, uncomplaining, with faith in their hearts, and on their lips the hope that we would go on to victory. Never again to them those broiling suns of relentless heat, those torrential rains of devastating storm the loneliness and utter desolation of jungle trails, the bitterness of long separation from those they loved and cherished. The deadly pestilence of tropical disease, the ghastly horror of stricken areas of war. Never again the slime of murky fox holes, the stench of ghostly trenches, the mire of dripping dugouts. Never again faint bugles blowing reveille, hard drums beating the long row, the crash of guns, the rattle of musketry. They have gone beyond the mist that blinds us here. Their flags will wave again only in the evening of our memories. Under white crosses and chambered temples of silence, the dust of their dauntless valor rests waiting, waiting, in the chancery of heaven the final reckoning of judgment day. Never will I forget and always will I do all within my limited power to see that they and you receive the full reward for your past glorious services.

Departure Manila International Airport
July 12, 1961

Mr. President, my dear friends, my sentimental journey has carried me through this fair land from one end almost to the other. Everywhere I have found a growing prosperity, a growing populace, a growing destiny; everywhere, friendship and affection. You are now a nation of gladness and goodwill. A bright light shining in a cloudy troubled world. A merciful providence cannot fail to protect and preserve this gem of the Far East. Thank you for a wonderful reception to an old soldier and his sweetheart wife. We bid you good bye and again, Mabuhay!

U.S. Military Academy
This Address is often Popularly Referred to as "Duty, Honor and Country."
May 12, 1962
West Point, New York

MacArthur's great Duty, Honor, Country speech. One of his best speeches said to have been made extemporaneously.
Edward T. Imparato, Editor

No human being could fail to be deeply moved by such a tribute as this [Thayer Award]. Coming from a profession I have served so long and a people I have loved so well, it fills me with an emotion I cannot express. But this award is not intended primarily to honor a personality, but to symbolize a great moral code - the code of conduct and chivalry of those who guard this beloved land of culture and ancient descent. That is the meaning of this medallion. For all eyes and for all time, it is an expression of the ethics of the American soldier. That I should be integrated in this way with so noble an ideal arouses a sense of pride, and yet of humility, which will be with me always.

Duty - Honor - Country. Those three hallowed words reverently dictate what you ought to be, what you can be, what you will be. They are your rallying point to build courage when courage seems to fail, to regain faith when there seems to be little cause for faith, to create hope when hope becomes forlorn.

Unhappily, I possess neither that eloquence of diction, that poetry of imagination, nor that brilliance of metaphor to tell you all that they mean.

The unbelievers will say they are but words, but a slogan, but a flamboyant phrase. Every pedant, every demagog, every cynic, every hypocrite, every troublemaker, and, I am sorry to say, some others of an entirely different character, will try to downgrade them even to the extent of mockery and ridicule.

But these are some of the things they do. They build your basic character. They mold you for your future roles as the custodians of the Nation's defense. They make you strong enough to know when you are weak, and brave enough to face yourself when you are afraid.

They teach you to be proud and unbending in honest failure, but humble and gentle in success; not to substitute words for actions, not to seek the path of comfort, but to face the stress and spur of difficulty and challenge; to learn to stand up in the storm, but to have compassion on those who fall; to master yourself before you seek to master others; to have a heart that is clean, a goal that is high; to learn to laugh, yet never forget how to weep; to reach into the future, yet never neglect the past; to be serious, yet never to take yourself too seriously; to be modest so that you will remember the simplicity of true greatness, the open mind of true wisdom, the meekness of true strength.

They give you a temper of the will, a quality of the imagination, a vigor of the emotions, a freshness of the deep springs of life, a temperamental predominance of courage over timidity, of an appetite for adventure over love of ease.

They create in your heart the sense of wonder, the unfailing hope of what next, and the joy and inspiration of life. They teach you in this way to be an officer and a gentleman.

And what sort of soldiers are those you are to lead? Are they reliable? Are they brave? Are they capable of victory?

Their story is known to all of you. It is the story of the American man-at-arms. My estimate of him was formed on the battlefield many, many years ago, and has never changed. I regarded him then, as I regard him now, as one of the world's noblest figures; not only as one of the finest military characters, but also as one of the most stainless.

His name and fame are the birthright of every American citizen. In his youth and strength, his love and loyalty, he gave all that mortality can give. He needs no eulogy from me, or from any other man. He has written his own history and written it in red on his enemy's breast.

But when I think of his patience under adversity, of his courage under fire, and of his modesty in victory, I am filled with an emotion of admiration I cannot put into words. He

MacArthur and JFK at the Football Hall of Fame Dinner, December 1961.

MacArthur receives the Alfred Thayor Award with General Groves on May 12, 1962.

belongs to history as furnishing one of the greatest examples of successful patriotism. He belongs to posterity as the instructor of future generations in the principles of liberty and freedom. He belongs to the present, to us, by his virtues and by his achievements.

In twenty campaigns, on a hundred battlefields, around a thousand camp-fires, I have witnessed that enduring fortitude, that patriotic self-abnegation, and that invincible determination which have carved his statue in the hearts of his people.

From one end of the world to the other, he has drained deep the chalice of courage. As I listened to those songs of the glee club, in memory's eye I could see those staggering columns of the First World War, bending under soggy packs on many a weary march, from dripping dusk to drizzling dawn, slogging ankle deep through the mire of shell-shocked roads; to form grimly for the attack, blue lipped, covered with sludge and mud, chilled by the wind and rain, driving home to their objective, and, for many, to the judgment seat of God.

I do not know the dignity of their birth, but I do know the glory of their death. They died, unquestioning, uncomplaining, with faith in their hearts, and on their lips the hope that we would go on to victory.

Always for them: Duty - Honor - Country. Always their blood, and sweat, and tears, as we sought the way and the light and the truth. And twenty years after, on the other side of the globe, again the filth of murky foxholes, the stench of ghostly trenches, the slime of dripping dugouts, those broiling suns of relentless heat, those torrential rains of devastating storms, the loneliness and utter desolation of jungle trails, the bitterness of long separation from those they loved and cherished, the deadly pestilence of tropical disease, the horror of stricken areas of war.

Their resolute and determined defense, their swift and sure attack, their indomitable purpose, their complete and decisive victory, always victory, always through the bloody haze of their last reverberating shot, the vision of gaunt, ghastly men, reverently following your password of "Duty - Honor - Country."

The code which those words perpetuate embraces the highest moral laws and will stand the test of any ethics or philosophies ever promulgated for the uplift of mankind. Its requirements are for the things that are right and its restraints are from the things that are wrong. The soldier, above all other men, is required to practice the greatest act of religious training -sacrifice. In battle, and in the face of danger and death, he discloses those divine attributes which his Maker gave when He created man in His own image. No physical courage and no brute instinct can take the place of the Divine help which alone can sustain him. However hard the incidents of war may be, the soldier who is called upon to offer and to give his life for his country is the noblest development of mankind.

You now face a new world, a world of change. The thrust into outer space of the satellite, spheres, and missiles marks a beginning of another epoch in the long story of mankind. In the five or more billions of years the scientists tell us it has taken to form the earth, in the three or more billion years of development of the human race, there has never been a more abrupt or staggering evolution.

We deal now, not with things of this world alone, but with the illimitable distances and as yet unfathomed mysteries of the universe. We are reaching out for a new and boundless frontier. We speak in strange terms of harnessing the cosmic energy, of making winds and tides work for us, of creating unheard of synthetic materials to supplement or even replace our old standard basics; to purify sea water for our drink; of mining ocean floors for new fields of wealth and food; of disease preventatives to expand life into the hundreds of years; of controlling the weather for a more equitable distribution of heat and cold, of rain and shine; of spaceships to the moon; of the primary target in war, no longer limited to the armed forces of an enemy, but instead to include his civil populations; of ultimate conflict between a united human race and the sinister forces of some other planetary galaxy; of such dreams and fantasies as to make life the most exciting of all times.

And through all this welter of change and development your mission remains fixed, determined, inviolable. It is to win our wars. Everything else in your professional career is but corollary to this vital dedication. All other public purposes, all other public projects, all other public needs, great or small, will find others for their accomplishment; but you are the ones who are trained to fight.

Yours is the profession of arms, the will to win, the sure knowledge that in war there is no substitute for victory; that if you lose, the Nation will be destroyed; that the very obsession of your public service must be Duty - Honor - Country.

Others will debate the controversial issues, national and international, which divide men's minds. But serene, calm, aloof, you stand as the Nation's war guardian, as its lifeguard from the raging tides of international conflict, as its gladiator in the arena of battle. For a century and a half you have defended, guarded, and protected its hallowed traditions of liberty and freedom, of right and justice.

Let civilian voices argue the merits or demerits of our processes of government: Whether our strength is being sapped by deficit financing indulged in too long, by Federal paternalism grown too mighty, by power groups grown too arrogant, by politics grown too corrupt, by crime grown too rampant, by morals grown too low, by taxes grown too high, by extremists grown too violent; whether our personal liberties are as thorough and complete as they should be.

These great national problems are not for your professional participation or military solution. Your guidepost stands out like a tenfold beacon in the night: Duty - Honor - Country.

You are the leaven which binds together the entire fabric of our national system of defense. From your ranks come the great captains who hold the Nation's destiny in their hands the moment the war tocsin sounds.

The long gray line has never failed us. Were you to do so, a million ghosts in olive drab, in brown khaki, in blue and gray, would rise from their white crosses, thundering those magic words: Duty - Honor - Country.

This does not mean that you are warmongers. On the contrary, the soldier above all other people prays for peace, for he must suffer and bear the deepest wounds and scars of war. But always in our ears ring the ominous words of Plato, that wisest of all philosophers: "Only the dead have seen the end of war."

The shadows are lengthening for me. The twilight is here.

My days of old have vanished - tone and tint. They have gone glimmering through the dreams of things that were. Their memory is one of wondrous beauty, watered by tears and coaxed and caressed by the smiles of yesterday. I listen vainly, but with thirsty ear, for the witching melody of faint bugles blowing reveille, of far drums beating the long roll.

In my dreams I hear again the crash of guns, the rattle of musketry, the strange, mournful mutter of the battlefield. But in the evening of my memory always I come back to West Point. Always there echoes and reechoes: Duty - Honor - Country

Today marks my final roll call with you. But I want you to know that when I cross the river, my last conscious thoughts will be of The Corps, and The Corps, and The Corps.

I bid you farewell.

REMARKS ON ACCEPTANCE OF A CONGRESSIONAL RESOLUTION THANKING MACARTHUR FOR HIS SERVICE AS A MILITARY LEADER
AUGUST 16, 1962
WASHINGTON, D.C.

In 1962, the U.S. Congress unanimously adopted a reso-lution thanking General MacArthur for his many services to the nation. At eighty-two, he was still a commanding fig-ure. Although slowed down by age, his voice was firm as he accepted the resolution of the Congress from House Speaker John W. McCormack on the steps of the Capitol. As was customary with the General, he shared his latest honor with the men who had made it possible.

Major Vorin E. Whan, Jr., USA, Editor
A Soldier Speaks: Public Papers and Speeches of General of the Army Douglas MacArthur
© 1965, Frederick A. Praeger, Publishers, New York, NY

Mr. Vice-President, Secretary McNamara, Mr. Speaker, and Members of the Congress. I cannot tell you how greatly embarrassed I am at the compliments that have been showered upon me today. I am sorry to say I won't live to be a hundred years old, as Mr. Rivers said, but as long as I do live I shall remember and treasure this day.

I am grateful to receive this highest award conferred by the American Government on one of its citizens. I am grateful to the American Congress, that body famous as the most forward-looking law-makers of the world, after a lapse of sufficient time to be swayed neither by sentiment nor emotion, has rendered an opinion of my services that I feel does me too much honor.

MacArthur receives the thanks of Congress award on August 16, 1962.

248

I am grateful to the American men-at-arms who were my comrades in the vital exploits involved. A general is just as good or just as bad as the troops under his command make him. Mine were great! Something of the luster of this citation glows on each one's shoulders.

I am grateful to the citizens of this powerful republic who accorded me opportunities challenging memorable results. They sent me to West Point. They gave me a chance to battle for my country. They placed me in command positions where the nation's destiny to some extent was in my hands.

I am grateful to each member of the Congress who voted for this resolution, and thereby joined in its general purpose. This body wields the power of the nation they speak the voice of the people. Accordingly my thanks are deeper than any words can convey.

I am grateful, above all, to Almighty God, who has so often guided me through the shadows of the valley of death and who nerved me in my hours of lonely vigil and deadly decision.

Mr. Speaker, again my grateful appreciation to you all.

Address at a Luncheon Marking the Announcement by Columbia College of the Establishment of a Chair in International History in MacArthur's Honor
April 19, 1963

General MacArthur was impressed at an early period in his career with the utility of history for the professional soldier. A number of times in his reports and other writings, he referred to the historical background of current events, and he showed a thorough understanding of the evolution of military history. It was quite fitting therefore, that a chair of history should be established in his honor at Columbia College. His address on this occasion shows a different facet of MacArthur's character, particularly his well-developed sense of history.

Major Vorin E. Whan, Jr., USA, Editor
A Soldier Speaks: Public Papers and Speeches of General of the Army Douglas MacArthur
© 1965, Frederick A. Praeger, Publishers, New York, NY

Words can but inadequately describe the depth of my gratitude for the honor you do me. The over-generous introduction by the distinguished Governor of this great state - the presence here of so eminent an assemblage of leaders whose resourceful wisdom and penetrating vision contribute so much to the strength of the nation - and the action of Columbia College in authorizing a chair in international history to bear my name - all leave me with a sense of the most profound appreciation. I thank you from the bottom of an old soldier's heart.

If there is one thing I have learned during my long years of experience it is that if we would correctly solve the problems of the present and chart a safe course into the future we must study and weigh and understand the manifold lessons of which history is the great - indeed the only competent teacher. For as Cicero put it eighty years before the birth of Christ, "Not to know what happened before one was born is always to be a child."

What then is history? That is the subject of as many different and conflicting views as there are philosophers, statesmen, soldiers and authors. Thus Plutarch complained, "So difficult a matter is it to determine the truth of anything by history." Yet Cicero said, "History indeed is the witness of the times - the light of truth." General George Meade of Civil War fame - after victory by the Union - observed cynically, "I don't believe the truth will ever be known and I therefore have great contempt for history." But General Robert E. Lee - after defeat - took a more philosophical view. "The march of providence is so slow," he said, "and our desires so impatient - the work of progress is so immense and our means of aiding it so feeble - the life of humanity is so long - that of the individual so brief - that we often see only the ebb of the advancing ways - and are thus discouraged. It is history that teaches us to hope." Napoleon took a particularly cynical view that history "is but a fable agreed upon. Historians are like sheep - they copy that which their predecessors have written . . without troubling themselves to enquire into reasons or even probabilities." Similarly cynical was Thomas Jefferson. "A morsel of genuine history," he lamented, "is a thing so rare as to be always valuable."

Ralph Waldo Emerson expostulated, "I am ashamed to see what a shallow village tale our so-called history is. There is less intention in history than we ascribe to it. We impute deep-laid far-sighted plans to Caesar and Napoleon - but the best of their power was in nature - not in them." While to the contrary, Thomas Carlyle held that "Universal history - the history of what man has accomplished in this world - is at bottom the history of the great men who have walked here." The Duke of Wellington - long after Waterloo - complained, "I should like much to tell the truth - but if I did I should be torn to pieces - here and abroad!" And years later - after the surrender at Appomattox - General Lee observed in similar vein, "The time is not come for impartial history. If the truth were told just now it would not be credited."

This cynicism toward history finds reflection in the views of countless others. Thomas Carlyle: "Happy the people whose annals are blank in history books." Robert Walpole: "Anything but history - for history must be false." Voltaire: "The history of the great events of this world is hardly more than the history of crimes. How much charlatanry has been put into history - either by astonishing the reader with prodigies - or by titillating human malignity with satire - or by flattering the families of tyrants with infamous praise." Edward Gibbon said, "History is little more than the register of crimes - follies and misfortunes of mankind." And John Quincy Adams once cryptically observed, "The public history of all countries - and all ages - is but a sort of mask - richly colored. The interior working of the machinery must be foul." "Historians," Benjamin Franklin complained, "relate - not so much what is done - as what they would have believed."

Few philosophers or writers or leaders in the arts and sciences speak kindly of history. For the historians who seek to chronicle contemporary events - with few exceptions - are animated by those most human of emotions, bias and prejudice. Few - if any - can meet the test laid down by

Cicero: "The first law is that the historian shall never dare to set down what is false - the second - that he shall never dare to conceal the truth - the third - that there shall be no suspicion of either favoritism or prejudice." Edmund Burke drew a distinction between the historian who writes of the present and he who writes of the past. "We are very incorrupt and tolerably enlightened judges of the transactions of past ages," he said, "where no passions deceive and where the whole train of circumstances - from the trifling cause to the tragical event - is set in an orderly series before us. Few are the partisans of departed tyranny."

Samuel Johnson - in his *Life of Boswell* - gave this profile of an historian: "Great abilities are not requisite for an historian - for in historical composition all of the greatest powers of the human mind are quiescent. He has facts ready to hand - so there is no exercise of invention. Imagination is not required to any high degree - only about as much as is used in the lower kinds of poetry." But Macaulay summed up the rarity of competent historians by pointing out that "To be a really good historian is perhaps the rarest of intellectual distinctions." And Francis Bacon said, "It is the true office of history to represent the events - themselves - and to leave the observation and conclusions thereupon to the liberty and faculty of every man's judgment."

Despite his cynical estimate of historians, Napoleon did not underestimate the value of a knowledge and understanding of history in the development of the human mind. "History wants no illusions," he said. "It should illuminate and instruct - not merely give descriptions and narratives which impress us. Tacitus did not sufficiently study the mystery of facts and thoughts - did not sufficiently investigate and scrutinize their connection - to give posterity a just and impartial opinion. History should know how to catch men and peoples as they would appear in the midst of their epoch. It should take account of external circumstances which would necessarily exercise an important influence on their actions - clearly see within what limits that influence wrought.... The patrimony of history should be nothing but the truth. It is by that quality that it is rendered respectable and worthy to serve as a perpetual instruction to man."

Contemporary historians - biographers and other chroniclers of historic events - are probably no better nor worse than have been their predecessors through the ages. Not many possess that high degree of self-discipline which will permit them to rise above emotion. For bias and prejudice color many historical writings to confuse and mislead the student. His task must be to winnow out fact from fiction. It is my earnest hope that he who occupies this chair will diligently guide those under his tutelage through the man-made labyrinth of confusion and uncertainty with which the facts of history are so often enshrouded - that he will inculcate into their hearts and minds the knowledge that history is a sacred trust - that no written record is worth more than the integrity of the writer - that he include in his curriculum ample and accurate accounts of the life and works of the men and women of action who have developed our industries - who have forged our great nation from a wilderness - and who have advanced our liberty and freedom. His will

partly be the responsibility that the fires of patriotism and sacrifice burn brightly in the soul of this and future generations. For in such history lies the fountainhead of those human forces which alone can preserve us as a free nation.

REMARKS TO A DELEGATION OF CADETS FROM THE U.S. MILITARY ACADEMY ON THE OCCASION OF MACARTHUR'S 84TH BIRTHDAY CELEBRATION JANUARY 26, 1964

After his retirement from active service, General MacArthur lived in the Waldorf-Astoria Hotel in New York City. His proximity to West Point permitted the Corps of Cadets of the Academy to deliver personally their birthday greetings each year. This annual custom was continued through the General's last birthday, in 1964. Following the formal presentation of the greeting from the Corps, General MacArthur made an informal talk to the delegation of cadets present. In what was to be his last personal message to the men of West Point, he summed up the important lessons he had learned from his education at the Academy. At the age of eighty-four, the General had sent his last message to the long grey line. After this, only silence . . .

Major Vorin E. Whan, Jr., USA, Editor
A Soldier Speaks: Public Papers and Speeches of General of the Army Douglas MacArthur
© 1965, Frederick A. Praeger, Publishers, New York, NY

What can I say that has not already been said by me so many times before? High honors have come my way, but I shall always believe that my greatest honor was being a West Point graduate.

The Military Academy taught me many things some of them not within the covers of books or written by any man. The first of these is tolerance: not to debase nor deprive those from whom one may differ by character or custom, by race or color or distinction.

The second is balance: a sense of proportion and ability to put first things first. A realization that there is a time and place for everything, but a recognition of the old maxim "nothing too much" - what the ancients meant by the "golden mean."

The third is intelligence, rather than sentiment or emotion. Sentimentalism has muddled many problems, has settled none. Intellect is a man's only hope for improvement over his present state.

And last, but by no means least, is courage: moral courage - the courage of one's convictions - the courage to see a thing through. This is not easy. The world is in constant conspiracy against the brave. It is the age-old struggle of the roar of the crowd on one side and the voice of your conscience on the other.

Tolerance, balance, intelligence, courage. These should be the hallmarks of every graduate of the Military Academy at West Point.

Your visit today has moved me deeply, and to you and to every other member of the Corps of Cadets go my warmest and most affectionate greetings.

BIBLIOGRAPHY

John M. Pratt, Editor
Revitalizing a Nation: A Statement of Beliefs, Opinions & Policies Embodied in the Public Pronouncements of General of the Army Douglas MacArthur
©1952, Chicago: The Heritage Foundation, Inc., Heritage Press

Major Vorin E. Whan, Jr., USA, Editor
A Soldier Speaks: Public Papers and Speeches of General of the Army Douglas MacArthur
©1965 Frederick A. Praeger, Publishers, New York, NY

Frank C. Waldrop, Editor
MacArthur On War
Duell, Sloan and Pearce, New York
©1942 by Frank C. Waldrop

U.S. Senate, 88th Congress, 2nd Session, Document No. 95
Compiled by the Legislative Reference Service, Library of Congress
Representative Speeches of General of the Army Douglas MacArthur
April 29, 1964 - Ordered to be printed
U.S. Government Printing Office, Washington: 1964

Audio Tape
World War II - Six speeches delivered during World War II
Produced by: General Douglas MacArthur Foundation

Audio Tape
Sentimental Journey - Five speeches delivered during return to the Philippines, July 3-12, 1961
Produced by: General Douglas MacArthur Foundation

Armel Dyer
The Oratory of Douglas MacArthur
Dissertation, University of Oregon, Ph.D., 1968
©1968 by Armel Dyer

General George C. Kenney
The MacArthur I Know
Duell, Sloan and Pearce, New York, ©1951

General of the Army Douglas MacArthur
Reminiscences
McGraw-Hill Book Company, New York, 1964

Major General Courtney Whitney
MacArthur: His Rendezvous With History
Alfred A. Knopf, New York, 1956

James W. Zobel
Archivist, General Douglas MacArthur Foundation
Norfolk, Virginia

Historian
United States Military Academy
West Point, New York

General MacArthur, General Southerland, General Irving and Major Langhortel.

The American Flag flying free over Astugi and the Japanese Empire. The sign of the conquer, August 28, 1945.

General Sir Thomas Blaney, Major General Whitehead, and General MacArthur.

MacArthur arriving in his C-54 at Atsugi, Japan on schedule at 2PM, August 30, 1945.

MacArthur in his usual pose with his ever-present corn cob pipe surrounded by his staff and military admirers, August 30, 1945.

Printed in the USA
CPSIA information can be obtained
at www.ICGtesting.com
JSHW050524160524
63198JS00014B/613